YELLOW BOOK

of:

Super Fast
Spoken English

VOCABULARY

Published By:

Invincible Publication Pvt. Ltd.

Published by
Invincible Publication Pvt. Ltd.
201A, SAS Tower, Sector 38, Gurugram – 122003
www.invinciblepublishers.com

Invincible Publication Pvt. Ltd.
Sales Office: -4760-61/23, Basement, Pratap Street, Ansari Road,
Daryaganj, New Delhi - 110002
Email: invinciblepublishers@gmail.com

ISBN: 978-93-88333-96-2
Book Name: Yellow Book of Super Fast Spoken English Vocabulary

Third Edition
2023 VOLUME - 2

The DSL®
AN ISO 9001:2008 CERTIFIED

The School of English Studies and Personality Development

यह ***Super Fast Spoken English Vocabulary*** की

पुस्तक आपके हाथ में है। इसका मतलब आप अंग्रेजी बोलने का पहला कदम बढ़ा चुके हैं। इस पुस्तक को मात्र किताब न समझें ।

बल्कि इसका प्रयोग ***Day to Day*** करके अपने आपको औरों से बेहतर बनायें ।

तो आइये आगे चलते हैं...

सभी छात्रों को मेरी ओर से ढ़ेर सारी

शुभकामनायें

धर्मेन्द्र सर

PREFACE

हर व्यक्ति अपना पूरा जीवन तीन काल में जीता है। अक्सर भूतकाल को लेकर खुश या नाखुश रहता है या फिर भविष्य की योजना बनाकर खुश रहता है। वर्तमान में बहुत कम लोग अपना जीवन जीते हैं। परंतु अंग्रेजी सीखने के लिए हमें वर्तमान, भूत और भविष्य तीनों कालों का ज्ञान होना अति आवश्यक है। यहीं से जन्म होता है - **Spoken English** का ।

जिस प्रकार हम हिन्दी बोलकर एक-दूसरे को समझाने का प्रयास करते हैं उसी प्रकार अंग्रेजी बोलकर एक-दूसरे को समझाना चाहते हैं।

आज भी हम भारतीय सिर्फ एक ही चीज से डरते हैं और वह है- धाराप्रवाह अंग्रेजी बोलना । इस पुस्तक के माध्यम से अब, आप धाराप्रवाह अंग्रेजी बोलने से नहीं डरेगें। यह पुस्तक आपके जीवन में एक चमत्कार की तरह साबित होगी क्योंकि आपके आस-पास दैनिक जीवन में उपयोग होने वाली वस्तुएँ एवं अन्य क्षेत्रों में प्रयोग किये जाने वाले अंग्रेजी के शब्दों को इस पुस्तक में शामिल किया गया है। जो इस पुस्तक को बाजार में उपलब्ध अन्य सभी पुस्तकों से आपने आपको अलग एवं श्रेष्ठ सात्रित करता है।

Yellow Book of Super Fast Spoken English Vocabulary के साथ - साथ आपके पास धर्मेन्द्र सर की **Basic English Book** और **Spoken English Book** का होना भी जरूरी है। ये दो पुस्तकें अंग्रेजी के क्षेत्र में और आपके जीवन में क्रांतिकारी साबित होगीं ।

धर्मेन्द्र सर

यहाँ से शुरू करें पढ़ना
और
चमत्कार देखें

यह

English Spoken Book

आपके लिए वरदान साबित होगी।
यह आप पर निर्भर करता है
कि आप इसका उपयोग कैसे करते हैं।

CONTENTS

CHAPTER 1

- Use of words for spoken
- Important vocabulary for spoken
- Interrogative words for spoken
- Stationery words for spoken
- Miscellaneous words for spoken

Best Of Luck

Use of words for spoken

ऐसे महत्वपूर्ण शब्द जिनका ज्ञान होना बहुत ही आवश्यक है।

Words	हिन्दी
I	मैं/मैने
I also	मैं/भी
Myself	मैं स्वंय
Only me / I	मैं ही
You	तुम
You all	तुम सब / आप सब
Yourself/Yourselves	तुम स्वंय / आप लोग स्वंय
Only you	तुम ही
Now	अब
From now	अब से
Just now	अभी / तुरन्त
Then	तब
From then	तब से
Just then	तभी
That time	तब की बार / उस समय
That matter	तब की बात
Then when	फिर कब
When	कब/कब-कब
From when	कब से
Whenever	जब कभी
Never	कभी भी नहीं
He	वह
He also	वह भी
Himself	वह स्वयं
That was a period	वह भी एक जमाना था
They	वे
They also	वे भी
They all	वे सब

Words	हिन्दी
Those people	वे लोग
Themselves	वे स्वंय
Only they	वे ही / केवल वे
We	हम
We also	हम भी
We all	हम सब
We people	हम लोग
Ourselves	हम स्वयं
Ours/Us	हमारे / हमे
Companion	हमसफर
Name sake	हमनाम
Duplicate	हम शक्ल
Ours	हमारे / हमारा
Our country	हमारा देश
Own	अपना / खुद का
Only owns	खुद का भी
Our people	हमारे लोग
Closeness	अपनापन
For ourselves	अपनी खातिर
By self	खुद /अपने आप / अकेले
Adopt	अपनाना / गोद लेना
For whom	जिनके/जिनके लिए
From whom	जिनसे
On which	जिस पर
Because of	जिस कारण / के कारण
By which	किससे
Whose	जिसका / जिसकी / जिसके

Words	हिन्दी
Whom	जिन्हें
It/this	यह/इस
On this/On it	इस पर
So/therefore	इस लिए
On this matter	इस बात पर
When	जब/कब
As soon as	जैसे ही .... तैसे ही
	ज्यों ही .... त्यों ही
From any where	कहीं से भी
From nowhere	कहीं से भी नहीं
At some place	कहीं पे
For what reason	किस कारण से
Anytime	किसी भी समय
His/her	उसका/उसकी
He	वह पु.लिंग
she	वह स्त्रीलिंग
Him/her	उसे / उसको
Those days	उन दिनों
Then	तब
As possible	यथा संभव/जैसे संभव हो
But	लेकिन
Once upon a time	किसी समय
Among them	उनमें भी
Her action	उनकी अदा
Him	उसे/उसको
Their	उनका/उनकी
On that matter	उस बात पर
Them	उन्हें
How	कैसे
at any cost	किसी भी कीमत पर

Words	हिन्दी
How not/How it will not	कैसे नहीं
For what purpose	किस उद्देश्य
How is it done?	कैसे किया?
How did you go?	कैसे गये?
How are you?	कैसे हो?
How were you?	कैसे थे?
How is it?	यह कैसा है?
How it happened?	कैसे हुआ
However	कैसे भी
Anyhow	कैसे भी
On which matter	किस बात पर
For which purpose	किस काम से
On which time	किस समय
It's a matter	एक बात है
It is same	एक ही बात है
Similar	एक ही समान
Once	एक बार
One time	एक समय
Similar nature	एक ही थाली के चट्टे-बट्टे
No one	कोई नही
Only one	केवल एक
In that period	उस जमाने में
Together	साथ-साथ
One mind	एक मन
One heart	एक ही जान
Equal	एक समान
There was a time	एक जमाना था
For each other	एक-दूसरे के लिए
Till today	आज तक

Till tomorrow	कल तक
Till day after tomorrow	परसों तक
Till evening	शाम तक
Till an hour	एक घंटे तक
Till work	कार्य तक
Suppose	मानो / मानों कि
Suppose that	मान लो कि
If you can consider	अगर आप/तुम जान सको तो
Respect	मान-सम्मान/आदर करना
Let us assume that	माना की
Such	ऐसा
Such type	ऐसा
Not this way	ऐसे नहीं
It is so	ऐसा ही है
Not that in way	उस तरह से नहीं
Why?	क्यों?
Because	क्योंकि
Why did it happen?	क्यों हुआ?
Why not?	क्यों नहीं?
That time the matter was different	जब की बात ही कुछ और थी
It is matter of those days	उन दिनों की बात है
How will it not be possible?	कैसे नहीं होगा

Important vocabulary for spoken

ऐसे कुछ महत्वपूर्ण शब्द जो संबंध दर्शाते हैं।

Words	हिन्दी
How long	- कहां तक
Upto	- तक (अधिकतम)
Do you know?	- क्या आप जानते हैं?
Above	- से ऊपर, के ऊपर, से अधिक
About	- पास, लगभग, बाबत, एवज पर
Across	- के आर-पार
After	- बाद में, के बाद, पीछे
Against	- से, पर, जबाव में, विरूद्ध हेतु
At	- पर, ऊपर, साथ
Along	- के साथ-साथ
Amidst	- के मध्य, के बीच
Around	- के चारों ओर, के आस-पास
By	- द्वारा, मार्फत
But	- किंतु, परंतु, अलावा, के सिवाय
Before	- के सामने, से पहले / के पहले
Below	- नीचे, से नीचे
Behind	- के बाद, के पीछे
Beyond	- से बाहर, से आगे, दूसरी ओर
Beneath	- नीचे, तले के या नीचे
Down	- नीचे
For	- के लिए, के कारण
Of	- का, के, की
On	- पर, ऊपर
Over	- पर, के ऊपर, पर से
Since	- से (निश्चित वास्ते)
Only for you	- सिर्फ तुम्हारे लिये
Is	- है
Are	- हैं
Was	- था

Words	हिन्दी
Were	- थे
Whether	- चाहे/या
Till	- तक/जब तक
Until	- तब तक नहीं
Unless	- जब तक............तब तक नहीं
No sooner	- ज्यों ही................जैसे ही
Scarcely	- मुश्किल से
Otherwise	- अन्यथा
While	- जब/के क्षण/के पल
Though	- यद्यपि
Yet	- फिर भी
Hardly	- मुश्किल से
After	- बाद में
As soon as	- ज्योही...........त्यों ही
As long as	- जब तक .... तब तक
Although	- येद्यपि
As far as	- जहां तक
Rather than	- अपेक्षा
So that	- ताकि
Too	- बेहद
So	- इसलिए
Not only	- केवल ही नहीं/ न केवल
Should be	- होना चाहिए
Would be	- होगा
Would not be	- नहीं होगा
As	- जैसा
Because	- क्योंकि

Words	हिन्दी
Since	- जब से ....तब से / से / चुंकि
Since then	- तब से
At least	- कम से कम
If	- यदि
Much	- ज्यादा + UCN
Many	- बहुत + PCN
Little	- बहुत कम/थोड़ा सा + UCN
Few	- बहुत कम/थोड़ा + PCN
Can	- सकना
Could	- सका
Wish	- इच्छा करना
hot	- गर्म
Instead of	- के बजाय
Besides	- के अतिरिक्त
Do	- करना
Did	- किया
No one	- कोई नहीं
Either	- या तो / दो में से कोई एक
Neither	- ना तो/ दो में से कोई नहीं
Nor	- नहीं
With someone	- किसी के साथ
Or	- या
And	- और
Ever	- कभी
Never	- कभी नहीं
During	- के दौरान
In	- में (बड़े स्थान के लिए)
At	- पर (छोटे स्थान के लिए)
Between	- के बीच में (दो के)
Beside	- निकट/बगल में
There	- वहां

Words	हिन्दी
Perhaps	- शायद
None of these	- इसमें से कोई नहीं
Any of you	- तुममें से कोई
Tit for Tat	- जैसे को तैसा
Loudly	- जोर-जोर से
About	- के बारे में/लगभग
Bent on	- तुले
Based on	- तथ्यों पर आधारित
From	- से
By	- के द्वारा / से / तक
With	- साथ/सहित
Of	- का / की / के
For	- के लिए
Today	- आज
Tomorrow	- आने वाला कल
Sudden	- अचानक
Sometimes	- कभी-कभी
Even	- अभी भी/यहां तक की
Now	- अब
Till now	- अब तक
From here	- इधर से
Also	- भी
These	- ये
Towards	- के तरफ, की ओर, के लिए
Up	- के ऊपर, ऊपर उठते हुए
Without	- बिना, के बिना, बगैर
Within	- के अंदर
Near	- पास, पास में, के पास
Till	- तक
So far as	- जहां तक

Lest	– कहीं ऐसा न हो
No less than	– से कम
Too much	– बहुत अधिक
Yet	– अभी तक
Any	– कोई
No	– नहीं
One of these	– इनमें से कोई
Some of us	– इनमें से कुछ
Any of you	– तुममें से कोई
None of them	– उनमें से कोई नहीं
Many	– कई / बहुत
Small	– छोटा / थोड़ा
Much	– ज्यादा / अधिक
Much of	– अधिकांश
Less	– कम
Both	– दोनों
Indeed	– वस्तुत:
Of course	– वास्तव में, निसंदेह
Every	– प्रत्येक
Somewhere	– कहीं
Something	– कुछ/ कुछ चीज
Anything	– कोई चीज
Nothing	– कुछ भी नहीं
Someone	– कोई
Somebody	– कोई
Whole	– सम्पूर्ण/सारा/पूरा
No one	– कोई नहीं
Everything	– प्रत्येक वस्तु
Everyone	– प्रत्येक
All the time	– हर समय
In all respects	– सभी मामले में
How Long	– कब तक
All around	– चारों तरफ

Interrogative words for spoken

ये सभी शब्द प्रश्नवाचक हैं, इनकी सहायता से प्रश्न पूछा जाता है।

Words	हिन्दी
When?	– कब?
Where?	– कहाँ?
Who?	– कौन?
What?	– क्या?
How?	– कैसे?
Why?	– क्यों?
For what?	– किस लिए?
From where?	– किधर से? / कहाँ से
Till when?	– कब तक?
Why not?	– क्यों नही?
What happened?	– क्या हुआ?
Anything else	– और कुछ
Which?	– कौन सा/कौन सी?
Then when?	– तो फिर कब?
What is up there?	– वहाँ क्या हो रहा है?
What now?	– अब क्या है?
How are you?	– आप कैसे हो?
How long?	– कितने दिनों तक?
For whom?	– किसके लिए?
For how much time?	– कितने समय में?
How many?	– कितने?
What is happened?	– क्या हुआ?
What will happen?	– क्या होगा?
Who is?	– कौन है?
What is?	– क्या है?

Words	हिन्दी
How are?	– कैसे हो?
How were?	– कैसे थे?
May I come?	– मैं आऊँ?
May I go?	– मैं जाऊँ?
Let us start	– शुरु करें
Where are you going?	– तुम किधर जा रहे हो?
When did you come?	– तुम कब आये?
Is anyone there?	– वहां कोई है?
Don't you know?	– क्या तुम्हें मालूम नहीं?
What is?	– क्या हैं?
Why are?	– क्यों हैं?
Why was?	– क्यों था?
When did?	– कब किया?
Who Was?	– कौन था?
Where is?	– कहाँ है?
Which one?	– कौन सी?
To whom?	– किसको?
Whose?	– किसकी / किसका?
How?	– कैसा / कैसी?
How far is it?	– कितनी दूर है?
How Much + UCN?	– कितना/कितनी + UCN?
How long?	– कितना लम्बा/कितना समय?

Stationery words for spoken

अध्ययन में काम आने वाली वस्तुएँ

Words	हिन्दी
Black ink	- काली स्याही
Dictionary	- शब्दकोश
Crayon	- खड़िया पेंसिल
Register	- रजिस्टर
Gum	- चिपकाना
Clip	- चिमटी
Bench	- चौकी
Punching machine	- छेद करने का यंत्र
Bodkin	- छेद करने का सूआ
Punch	- छेदनी
Nib	- जीभी (नोक)
Pocket book	- जेबी किताब
Postage stamp	- टिकट (डाक)
Revenue stamp	- टिकट (रसीदी)
Table	- टेबल
Tag	- डोरी (कीलदार)
Drawing-pin	- ड्रांइग पिन
Carbon Paper	- नकल करने का कागज
Copying pencil	- नकल करने की पेंसिल
Map	- नक्शा
Invitation card	- निमंत्रण पत्र
Blue black ink	- नीली-काली स्याही
Blue ink	- नीली स्याही
Divider	- परकार
Quill pen	- पर की कलम
Call bell	- पुकारने की घंटी
Pencil	- पेंसिल
Post card	- पोस्टकार्ड
Tracing paper	- अक्स कागज
Newspaper	- अखबार

Words	हिन्दी
Almirah	- अलमारी
Counterfoil	- आधी रसीद
Easy chair	- आराम कुर्सी
Pin	- आलपिन
Pin Cushion	- आलपिन लगाने की गद्दी
Pen	- कलम
Paper	- कागज
Paper cutter	- कागज तराश
Paper weight	- कागज दाब
Card	- कार्ड
Tape	- फीता
Visiting card	- भेंट कार्ड
Seal	- मोहर
Tracing cloth	- मोमी कपड़ा
Eraser	- रबर
Rubber stamp	- रबर की मोहर
Waste paper basket	- रद्दी की टोकरी
Receipt book	- रसीद बही
Ruler	- पैमाना
Ink	- रोशनाई
Ink pad	- रोशनाई का गद्दा
Packing paper	- लपेटने का कागज
Sealing wax	- मुहर बन्द लगाने की
Writing pad	- लिखने की पट्टी
Envelope	- लिफाफा
Glue	- गोंद
Blank paper	- सादा कागज
Wire	- तार
Stool	- तिपाई
Inkpot	- दवात

Miscellaneous words for spoken

कुछ महत्वपूर्ण मिश्रित शब्द

Words	हिन्दी	Words	हिन्दी
Metal	– धातु	Glass	– गिलास
Patriot	– देशभक्त	Room	– कमरा
Stan	– शैतान	Spoon	– चम्मच
Volcano	– ज्वालामुखी	Beard	– दाढ़ी
Advantage	– फायदा	Principle	– सिद्धांत
Glory	– गौरव	Talent	– प्रतिभा
Joy	– हर्ष	Wing	– पंख
Mischief	– शरारत	Nomad	– बंजारा
Pity	– दया	Oasis	– मरूदेश में हरियाली भूमि
Poison	– जहर	Obloquy	– गाली, निंदा
Suspicion	– शक	Onlooker	– तमाशा देखनेवाला
Colour	– रंग	Opaque	– अस्पष्ट
Mercy	– दया	Orthodox	– परम्परागत
Sin	– पाप	Outwit	– बुद्धि या चतुराई से बढ़ जाना
Character	– चरित्र	Pander	– नीच काम में सहायता करना
Odour	– गंध	Paradox	– असभ्याभास
Juice	– रस	Parlous	– संकटपूर्ण
Limit	– सीमा	Peculiar	– विचित्र
Luck	– भाग्य	Peevish	– झगड़ालू, चिड़चिड़ा
Life	– जीवन	Penitence	– पछतावा
Motion	– गति	Peril	– संकट
Seed	– बीज	Picaroon	– समुद्री लुटेरा
Sleeve	– अस्तीन	Piffle	– बकवास
Bag	– थैला	Placid	– शांत
Basket	– टोकरी	Porous	– छिद्रपूर्ण, झरझर
Bucket	– बाल्टी	Prattle	– बकबक करना
Bottle	– बोतल	Precedent	– पहले का निर्णय, मिसाल
Box	– संदूक	Prejudice	– अविचारपूर्वक निर्णय, पक्षपात
Cup	– कप	Procession	– जुलूस, शोभायात्रा, बारात

Words	हिन्दी
Punitive	– दंड देनेवाली
Quaint	– पुराने ढंग का
Rapacious	– लुटेरा, लालची
Rapture	– अत्यंत हर्ष, आनंद
Ravish	– अपहरण करना
Redress	– ठीक कर देना, सुधारना
Reliance	– विश्वास, श्रद्धा, भरोसा
Remorse	– पश्चाताप, पछतावा
Resort	– गमन करना, जाना
Revolution	– क्रांति
Riddle	– पहेली
Rift	– दरार
Rubble	– मलबा, रोड़ी
Rummage	– खोज करना
Ruth	– दया, दूसरों के कष्ट पर तरस
Sabotage	– हड़तालियों का जानबूझकर यंत्र इत्यादि तोड़ना
Samson	– अति बलवान मनुष्य
Sanity	– समझदारी
Saviour	– रक्षक
Scandal	– घोटाला
Sceptic	– संदेहवादी
Sedulous	– उद्योगी, परिश्रमी
Shrewd	– चतुर
Shrug	– बेबसी
Simulate	– भेष बदलना
Slam	– तेज आवाज के साथ बंद करना
Slaughter	– हत्या
Slender	– दुबला-पतला
Smite	– मारना, हराना
Solitude	– अकेलापन
Sonority	– सुरीलापन
Specious	– दिखावा
Spouse	– पति या पत्नी
Stab	– छुरी मारना
Strife	– विवाद, झगड़ा
Stroll	– घूमना
Successor	– वारिस
Suffuse	– फैलाना, रंग भरना
Swell	– फैलना, बढ़ना
Taboo	– अवरोध, रूकावट
Tantalize	– तरसाना
Tattered	– चीर, चिथड़ा
Tendency	– स्वभाव
Tremendous	– जबर्दस्त
Throb	– धड़कन
Ridicule	– उपहास
Rigidity	– कठोरता
Ruckus	– अशांति
Rumpus	– कोलाहल
Sanctum	– पवित्र स्थान एकांत कमरा
Sapience	– बुद्धिमानी
Savour	– स्वाद, रस. गंध
Scapegoat	– बलि का बकरा
Scoff	– तिरस्कार
Sentience	– चेतना
Shriek	– जोर से चिल्लाना
Siege	– अवशेध या घेरा
Skimpy	– अपर्याप्त
Slander	– कलंक लगाना
Sleek	– चिकना
Slouch	– शरीर ढीला करके बैठना

Words	हिन्दी
Sneak	– चोर की तरह भाग जाना
Sombre	– काला, अंधेरा
Soothe	– शांत करना, प्रसन्न करना
Spinster	– अधिक आयु की कुंवारी स्त्री
Squeak	– हल्की चीख
Statutory	– वैधानिक
Stringency	– कठोरता
Subvert	– पलटना, ढहाना
Sue	– अभियोग या मुकदमा चलाना
Supper	– रात्रि का भोजन
Swot	– हथेली से मारना या कुचलना
Taciturn	– कम बोलनेवाला
Tardy	– मंदा / सुस्त, धीमा, विलंबी
Tedious	– थकाने वाला
Terra-cotta	– पकी हुई मिट्‌टी की मूर्ति
Thick	– घना, मोटा
Tidy	– शुद्ध, स्वच्छ, सुथरा
Timorous	– डरपोक
Topsy-turvy	– उल्टा-पुल्टा
Trifle	– हल्की बात
Triumph	– विजय, जीत
Turbid	– गाढ़ा
Tyranny	– क्रूर शासन, कठोरता
Uncouth	– गंवार
Unwind	– खोलना
Utensils	– रसोई का पात्र, बर्तन
Valorous	– वीर, साहसी
Violate	– तोड़ना, उल्लंघन करना
Waif	– लावारिस, बेघर
Web	– मकड़ी का जाल

Words	हिन्दी
Wheedle	- चापलूसी करना
Whippy	- पतला तथा लचीला
Wit	- बुद्धिमत्ता
Woe	- दुःख (शोक)
Yearn	- इच्छा करना
Zest	- मजा, उत्साह
Alumni	- पुराने विद्यार्थी
Acquaintance	- जान-पहचान
Scholar	- बुद्धिमान
Home-town	- गृह नगर
Inhabitant	- निवासी
Giddy	- चक्कर
Feverish	- बुखार से त्रस्त
Adamant	- हठी
Scarcity	- कमी
Dubitable	- संदिग्ध
Indomitable	- दूसरों से न दबने वाला
Brackish	- खारा
Aqua	- पानी
Porch	- बाहरी छाया
Titular	- केवल नाममात्र का
Treacherous	- कपटी, अधर्मी
Tripod	- तिपाई
Tug	- प्रयत्न से खींचना
Twaddle	- बकवास करना
Unbidden	- बिना बुलाये
Undermine	- कमजोर बनाना
Upbeat	- प्रसन्न
Usurp	- हड़पना
Vacillate	- संदेह

Words	हिन्दी
Vindictive	- बदला लेनेवाला
Void	- शून्य, रिक्त
Weary	- थका
Weed	- घास फूस
Whim	- मन की लहर
Winsome	- मनोहर, प्रसन्न
Wobble	- इधर-उधर घूमना
Woo	- प्रेम दिखलाना
Yummy	- स्वादिष्ट
Turban	- पगड़ी
Lumpish	- भोंदू
Aromatic	- खुशबूदार
Astray	- आवारा
Auction	- निलामी
Awe	- डर
Bog	- दलदल
Penury	- गरीबी
Dagger	- खंजर/कटार
Callous	- पत्थर दिल
Carnage	- नरसंहार
Pygmy	- बौना
Denizen	- निवासी
Riots	- दंगा-फसाद
Salon	- संगोष्ठी
Scrimpy	- कंजूस
Vicinity	- पड़ोस
Manure	- खाद्य
Crony	- यनिष्ठ भित्र
Fate	- किस्मत
Foe	- दुश्मन

Words	हिन्दी
Folks	- घर वाले
Inmates	- कैदियो
Outmates	- बाहर वाले
Inlaws	- ससुराल
Outlaws	- मायका
Adore	- पूजा करना
Affray	- दंगा-फसाद
Agenda	- कार्यक्रम
Aghast	- भयानक
Ailment	- बीमारी
Akin	- रिश्तेदार
Amuck	- पागल
Saga	- वीरगाथा
Monk	- साधु/फकीर
Monition	- मौत की घंटी
Myrtle	- मेहंदी
Ninny	- घनचक्कर
Leisure	- फुर्सत
Tipsy	- नशेड़ी
Gypsy	- आवारा, बंजारा
Urchin	- छोंकरा
Vanity	- घमंड
Vicious	- अत्याचारी
Voracious	- भूक्कड़
Ware-house	- गोदाम
Coy	- शर्मिला
Bare-faced	- बेशर्म
Sot	- दारू-बाज
Sluggish	- लीचड़ इंसान
Cad	- कमीना

Words	हिन्दी
Slime	– कीचड़
Slur	– कलंक
Spunk	– साहस
Zeal	– जोश
Hard-ship	– कष्ट
Hatred	– नफरत
Foot-loose	– गैर-जिम्मेदार
Foppish	– छिछोरा
Fop	– छैला
Dog-day	– बहुत बुरा दिन
Gala-day	– बहुत खुशी का दिन
Gamy	– शादी
Sucrose	– चीनी
Suds	– साबुन का पानी
Jaunty	– मस्तमौला
Haze	– धुंध
Hail-stone	– ओले
Jaggery	– गुड़, शक्कर
Jubilant	– खुशी
Demerits	– खामियाँ
Slur	– कलंक
Weather	– मौसम
Peace	– शांति
Pleasant	– प्रसन्नता
Society	– समाज
Citizen	– नागरिक
Lazy	– सुस्त
Farmer	– किसान
Healthy	– स्वस्थ
Wise	– बुद्धिमान

Words	हिन्दी
Honest	– ईमानदार
Enough	– पर्याप्त
All	– सब
People	– लोग
Gentle	– नेक इंसान
Useless	– बेकार
Helpless	– बेसहारा
Complaint	– शिकायत
Naughty	– शरारती
Dirty	– गंदा
Noise	– शोर
Patient	– मरीज
Great	– महान
Habit	– आदत
Difficult	– कठिन
Problem	– समस्या
Mystery	– राज, रहस्य
Round	– गोल
Pocket	– जेब
Some	– कुछ
Enemy	– दुश्मन
Pal	– मित्र
Satisfaction	– संतुष्टि
Sun	– धूप
Dark	– अंधेरा
Subjects	– प्रजा
Coal	– कोयला
Flame	– आग की लपटें
Fearful	– डरावना
Sweet	– मीठा

Words	हिन्दी
Moral	– नैतिक
Simple	– साधारण
Flower	– फूल
Tree	– पेड़
Medicine	– दवा
Clever	– चालाक
Laborious	– मेहनती
Fat	– मोटा
Thin	– पतला
Pygmy	– बौना
Hungry	– भूखा
Timid	– डरपोक
Poet	– कवि
Singer	- गायक
Doctor	- डॉक्टर
Postman	- डाकिया
Writer	- लेखक
Artist	- कलाकार
Ready	- तैयार
Rich	- अमीर
Poor	- गरीब
Thief	- चोर
Cop	- पुलिस
Ugly	- बदसूरत
Wrong	– गलत
Innocent	– निर्दोष
Lucky	– भाग्यशाली
Kind	– दयालु
Present	– उपस्थित
Saint	– साधु

Words	हिन्दी
Faithful	– वफादार
Seller	– विक्रेता
Buyer	– खरीदार
Silent	– चुप
Proud	– घमंड
Tired	– थका हुआ
Always	– हमेशा
Egg	– अण्डा
Ink-pot	– दवात
Umbrella	– छाता
Dangerous	– खतरनाक
Sky	– आकाश
Star	– तारा
Music	– संगीत
Bad	– बुरा
Right	– सही
Strong	– मजबूत
Old	– पुराना
New	– नया
Weak	– कमजोर
Educated	– शिक्षित
Beggar	– भिखारी
Foolish	– मूर्ख
Player	– खिलाड़ी
Lawyer	– वकील
Robber	– डाकू
Guilty	– दोषी
Fair	– गोरी
Busy	– व्यस्त
Engineer	– इंजीनियर

Words	हिन्दी
King	– राजा
Queen	– रानी
Maid	– नौकरानी
Actor	– अभिनेता
Actress	– अभिनेत्री
Unripe	– कच्चा
Tasty	– स्वादिष्ट
Thirsty	– प्यासा
Villager	– गांव वाले
Lovely	– प्यारा
Policy	– नीति
True	– सच
False	– झूठ
Gem	– रत्न
Rare	– दुर्लभ
Axe	– कुल्हाड़ी
Owl	– उल्लू
Ant	– चींटी
Water	– पानी
Oil	– तेल
Tea	– चाय
Student	– विद्यार्थी
Ideal	– आदर्श
Famous	– प्रसिद्ध
Dishonest	– बेईमान
Rotten	– बासी / सड़ा हुआ
Timber	– लकड़ी
Inn	– सराय
Hotel	– होटल
Salt	– नमक

Words	हिन्दी
Costly	– महंगा
Cheap	– सस्ता
River	– नदी
Lake	– झील
Pond	– तालाब
Long	– लंबा
Short	– छोटा
Small	– छोटा
Bay	– खाड़ी
Young	– जवान
Blind	– अंधा
Deaf	– बहरा
Dum	– गूंगा
Able	– समर्थ
Feeble	– दुर्बल
Large	– बड़ा
Rich	– धनी
Simple	– सरल
Intense	– तीव्र
Town	– शहर
Winter	– सर्दी
Summer	– गर्मी
Rain	– बरसात
Painful	– दुखदायी
Disease	– बीमारी
Clear	– साफ
Peak	– चोटी
Popular	– लोकप्रिय
Dear	– महंगा
Important	– महत्वपूर्ण

Words	हिन्दी
Mankind	– मानव जाति
Dry	– सूखा
Wet	– गीला
Moment	– क्षण
Bright	– तेजस्वी
Broad	– चौड़ा
Deep	– गहरा
Flat	– चपटा
Fresh	– ताजा
Hard	– कठिन
Less	– कम
Loose	– ढीला
Red	– लाल
Ripe	– पका हुआ
Sad	– दुखी, उदास
Straight	– सीधा
Tight	– कसा हुआ
Weak	– कमजोर
Aware	– अवगत
Like	– समान
Ugly	– कुरूप
Pure	– शुद्ध
Central	– केन्द्रीय
Modern	– आधुनिक
Popular	– लोकप्रिय
Final	– अंतिम
Glad	– खुश
Wide	– चौड़ा
Length	– लंबाई
Strength	– ताकत

Words	हिन्दी
Threat	– धमकी
Beauty	– सुंदरता
Danger	– खतरा
Slave	– गुलाम
Throne	– सिंहासन
Tomb	– कब्र, मकबरा
Jeopardy	– संकट
Scrutiny	– छानबीन
Arrive	– आगमन
Remove	– निकालना
Break	– तोड़ना
Marry	– विवाह
Waste	– अपव्यय
Ample	– पर्याप्त
Dry	– सूखा
Barren	– अनुपजाऊ/बांझ
ill	– बीमार
Lawful	– वैध
Aimless	– लक्ष्यहीन
Safe	– सुरक्षित
Cruel	– क्रूर
Certain	– निश्चित
Frigid	– ठंडा
Elastic	– लचीला
Inferior	– घटिया
Actual	– वास्तविक
Brutal	– निर्दयी
Formal	– औपचारिक
Mental	– मानसिक
National	– राष्ट्रीय

Words	हिन्दी
Real	– वास्तविक
Regular	– नियमित
Spiritual	– आध्यात्मिक
Chaste	– पवित्र
Futile	– व्यर्थ
Fertile	– उपजाऊ
Insane	– पागल
Obscene	– अश्लील
Serene	– शांत
Agile	– फुर्तीला
Sincere	– ईमानदार
Scarce	– दुर्लभ
Sensitive	– संवेदनशील
Available	– उपलब्ध
Capable	– समर्थ
Practicable	– वाहनीय
Credible	– विश्वसनीय
Eligible	– योग्य
Flexible	– लचीला
Possible	– संभव
Responsible	– जिम्मेदार
Stable	– स्थिर
Frail	– दुर्बल
Loyal	– वफादार
Greed	– लालच
History	– इतिहास
Audacious	– ढीठ
Ferocious	– क्रूर
Anxious	– व्याकुल
Anonymous	– गुमनाम

Words	हिन्दी
Curious	– जिज्ञासु
Humble	– विनम्र
Profound	– गहरा
Honest	– ईमानदार
Modest	– शर्म
Fault	– दोष
Broad	– चौड़ा
Brief	– संक्षिप्त
Coward	– कायर
Gallant	– वीर
Supreme	– सर्वोच्च
Warm	– गर्म
Diligence	– परिश्रम
Radiance	– चमक
Ancestor	– पूर्वज
Beast	– पशु
Sensation	– सनसनी
Compassion	– दयाभाव
Caution	– सावधानी
Stone	– पत्थर
Bush	– झाड़ी
Butter	– मक्खन
Angel	– देवदूत
Peril	– खतरा
Spring	– बंसत ऋतु
Emphasis	– जोर
Department	– विभाग
Anger	– क्रोध
Use	– उपयोग
Wonder	– आश्चर्य

Words	हिन्दी
Intention	– इरादा
Miracle	– चमत्कार
Nation	– राष्ट्र
Nature	– प्रकृति
Silence	– शांति
Surprise	– आश्चर्य
Violence	– हिंसा
Emotion	– भावना
Culture	- संस्कृति
Foetus	- गर्भ
Influence	– प्रभाव
Tribe	– जनजाति
Fog	– धुंध कोहरा
Knot	– गांठ
Bone	– हड्डी
Cloud	– बादल
Dew	– ओस
Fat	– चर्बी
Flour	– आटा
Thrift	– किफायत
Atom	– परमाणु
Ghost	– भूत
Aroma	– सुगंध
Brain	– मस्तिष्क
Custom	– रिवाज
Diet	– आहार
Discipline	- अनुशासन
Gas	– वाष्प
Picture	– चित्र
Gaga	– पागल

Words	हिन्दी
Scorching hot day	– झुलसाने वाला गर्म दिन
Provoke	– भड़काना
Rebuke	– फटकार लगाना
Mess	– खराब करना
Haggle	– मोलभाव करना
Authentic	– पक्की
Rumble	– गड़गड़ाहट
Privilege	– सुविधा
Ferocious	– खूँखार
Shrug	– कंधे उचकाना
Peevish	– चिड़चिड़ा
Vivid	– साफ-सुथरा
Vivacious	– जिंदादिल
Hilarious	– हँसमुख
Scoff	– मजाक करना
Sniff	– छींकना
Illicit	– नाजायज
Crinkle	– हाथ मोड़ना
Appetite	– भूख
Inclination	– रूझान/रूचि
Rebellion	– खून-खराबा
Bother	– तंग करना
Flock	– झुंड
Bluff	– धोखा देना
Biography	– जीवनी
Boggle	– बौखलाना
Big-gun	– अफलातून
Bounce	– उछालना
Commotion	– शोरगुल
Sagacious	– समझदार

Words	हिन्दी
Make a fuss	– बात का बतंगड़ बनाना
Wag	– बातें बनाना
On the wane	– पतन शील
Fidget	– हिलना-डुलना
Paragon	– आदर्श
Toilsome	– कमर तोड़
Foster	– मुंह बोला
Infuriate	– अचानक से क्रोध आना
Drizzle	– बूँदा-बाँदी
Mizzle	– ओस पड़ना
Blizzard	– बर्फीला तूफान
Humidity	– उमस
Shuffle	– टालमटोल
Gabble	– बकवास
Nitpick	– बुराई करना
ill eyes	– नजर लगाना
Timid look	– डरी हुई निगाहें
Coy look	– शर्मीली निगाहें
Saucy look	– गुस्ताखी भरी निगाहें
Down look	– गिरी हुई नजरें
Eyesore	– दुख का कारण
Adulate	– झूठी तारीफ करना
Vex	– परेशान करना
Hard-up	– कड़की
Biff	– घूसा
Foxy	– मक्कार
Lissom	– लचकदार
Penance	– तपस्या
Pebble	– कंकड़
Sanitation	– सफाई

Words	हिन्दी
Decline	– इंकार करना
Rankle	– सताना
Tickle	– गुद्‌गुदी करना
Destination	– मंजिल
Talkative	– बातूनी
Time-killer	– चिपकू
Abase	– नीचा करना, मान घटाना
Affable	– सुशील, मिलनसार
Anarchy	– अराजकता, अव्यवस्था
Augment	– वृद्धि करना, बढ़ाना
Belle	– रूपवती स्त्री. सुंदरी
Blaze	· धधकना
Brute	– पशु, मूर्ख, निर्दयी
Bystander	– दर्शक
Catalogue	– सूचीपत्र वर्णक्रमानुसार
Closet	– गुप्त कोठरी
Contemplation	– ध्यान, चिंतन
Daft	– पागल, झक्की
Debility	– शक्तिहीनता
Deceit	– कपट, छल, वंचना
Diminution	– कमी, अवनति
Dungeon	– काल कोठरी
Epitome	– सारांश, निचोड़
Fable	– कल्पित कथा मनगढ़ंत कहानी
Ferocious	– भयंकर, निर्दयी
Hearth	– अग्निकुंड, अंगीठी
Insatiable	– लोभी/लालची
Invoke	– प्रार्थना करना, माँगना
Jingle	– टनटनाहट
Litigate	– मुकदमा करना

Words	हिन्दी
Meagre	– दुर्बल, क्षीण, अपूर्ण
Metamorphose	– रूप बदलना
Nap	– झपकी
Nefarious	– पापी, अधर्मी
Nettle	– चिढ़ाना, उद्विग्न करना
Repel	– खदेड़ना
Riddle	– पहेली
Dignity	– मर्यादा
Culprits	– अपराधी
Grateful	– नमक हराम
Lickerish	– चटोरा
Adolescence	– यौवन, युवावस्था
Affront	– अपमानित करना
Apathy	– जड़ता, अनुभव-शून्यता
Binary	– दोहरा (द्विगुण), जोड़ा
Blench	– चौंक उठना
Burglar	– सेंधमारने वाला, चोर
Castigate	– आलोचना, दंड देना
Catastrophe	– बड़ी आपत्ति, दुर्गति
Coarse	– सामान्य, घटिया
Coronation	– राज्याभिषेक, राजतिलक
Damn	– शाप देना, निंदा करना
Debris	– टूटे हुए टुकड़े, मलबा
Decline	– अवनत होना, अस्वीकार करना
Dogma	– सिद्धांत, धर्ममत, नीति, प्रमाण
Evoke	– पुकारना, बुलाना
Fanatic	– हठधर्मी
Frenzy	– उन्माद, आवेश
Hereditary	– परंपरा द्वारा प्राप्त, पैतृक
Insipid	– बेस्वाद, निर्जीव

Words	हिन्दी
Jiggle	– धीमे-धीमे झटका देना या हिलाना
Linger	– देर तक ठहरना
Lunacy	– उन्माद, पागलपन
Meek	– विनीत, नम्र
Mirth	– आनंद, प्रमोद (हँसी)
Nausea	– जी मिचलाना
Neoteric	– नवीन (आधुनिक)
Niggard	– कृपण मनुष्य, कंजूस
Nimble	– फुर्तीला
Nuptial	– वैवाहिक, विवाह संबंधी
Obesity	– स्थूलता, मोटापा
Occultist	– जादूगर, तांत्रिक
Omen	– घटना, शगुन
Onslaught	– मारकाट, भयंकर
Opulence	– धन, वैभव, ऐश्वर्य
Otiose	– निरर्थक, सुस्त
Ovation	– जयध्वनि, जयजयकार
Pantheon	– सब देवताओं का मंदिर
Parch	– भुनना, झुलसाना
Pasture	– चारागाह
Pedestrian	– पैदल चलनेवाला
Perfuse	– जल छिड़कना
Perverse	– बिगाड़ने वाला
Picky	– नकचढ़ा
Pioneer	– मार्ग प्रदर्शक
Pragmatic	– व्यावहारिक
Precarious	– खतरनाक
Precis	– सार, संक्षेप
Prevention	– रूकावट, रोकथाम

Words	हिन्दी
Proficient	– प्रवीण, कुशल
Purgatory	– शोधक, पाप नाश करने का स्थान
Pyre	– चिता
Quagmire	– दलदल
Radiance	– प्रकाश, चमक
Rapport	– संबंध, नातेदारी, संपर्क
Rattler	– फेंकू
Recreation	– विश्राम, मनोरंजन
Relegate	– बहिष्कार करना, देश से निकालना
Relish	– आनंद लेना
Renounce	– त्यागना, छोड़ना
Revert	– पलटना, फिर आना

❑❑❑

CHAPTER 2

- Most important daily used phrase for spoken
- Daily routine used sentence for spoken
- Three forms of verbs for spoken
- Words in daily used for spoken
- Words of personality for spoken
- Mathematical words for spoken
- Astrology words for spoken
- Short words and sign for spoken
- Official words for Govt. Department

Most important daily used phrase for spoken

दिनचर्या में बात करने के लिए ऐसे अंग्रेजी के वाक्यों का प्रयोग करें।

Words	हिन्दी
Dribs and drabs	– छोटी सी गुजारिश
Period of test	– परीक्षा की घड़ी
Early Life	– प्रारंभिक जीवन
Humour	– हंसी छुटवाना
Partner of joy and sorrow	– सुख-दु:ख का साथी
After education	– शिक्षा के पश्चात्
Ruin	– सत्यानाश, बेड़ा गर्क
Have a fancy	– कल्पना करना
Friendly	– मिलनसार
Most	– सबसे अधिक
By the dint of	– के बल पर, बलबूते पर
Hypocrite	– पाखंडी
Before all	– सबके सामने
In the company of	– साथ में/संगत में
Somewhat	– कुछ-कुछ, थोड़ा सा
All alone	– बिल्कुल अकेला
Not only this	– इतना ही नहीं
Stand on his own legs	– अपने पैरों पर खड़ा होना
In the hour of need	– आवश्यकता के समय में
No questions appears	– कोई सवाल ही पैदा नहीं होता
As time passed on	– जैसे जैसे समय बीतता गया
Put up the question	– प्रश्न पूछना / प्रश्न रखना
In this way	– इस प्रकार
Simple food, Coarse-food	– रूखा-सूखा भोजन
Tears burst out of	– आंसू निकल आना
Childish question	– बच्चों वाले प्रश्न
In every possible way	– हर संभव तरीके से

Words	हिन्दी
Nothing is known	– कुछ ज्ञात नहीं
Have attachment for	– लगाव हो जाना / प्रेम हो जाना
After my departure	– मेरे जाने के बाद
Soon after this	– इसके थोड़ी देर बाद ही
Appear	– प्रतीत होना / लगना
On his own	– अपने बलबूते पर
Later	– बाद में
Self interested	– मतलबी / स्वार्थी
Tired and spent	– हारे-थके/थके-हारे
Proverb	– कहावत
Lay emphasis	– जोर डालना
Anyhow	– किसी न किसी तरह
For half value	– आधे दामों में
Outward show	– बाहरी दिखावा
Describe in detail/Narrate in Detail	– विस्तार से बताना
Belong to	– संबंधित होना
Most important	– सबसे जरूरी
Think of	– विषय में सोचना / ध्यान करना
With the passes of time	– समय के बीतने के साथ
On one hand	– एक तरफ
On the other hand	– दूसरी तरफ
Ray of hope	– आशा की किरण
For the first time	– पहली बार
Hyperbole	– अतिश्योक्ति
Have nothing to do with	– कोई सरोकार न होना
Higher category	– उच्च श्रेणी
Last long	– अधिक चलना (कोई वस्तु)
The very next moment	– अगले ही क्षण
Duck diamond	– प्रेमिका
Fair sex	– नारी जाति

Words	हिन्दी
Hen pecked husband	– जोरू का गुलाम
Saga	– विस्तृत कथा
Small fry	– तुच्छ आदमी
Dick and Harry	– ऐरा गैरा आदमी / ऐरा गैरा नत्थूखैरा
A slow coach	– सुस्त व बेवकूफ आदमी
Amuck	– पागल
Powerful	– प्रतापी / शक्तिशाली
Moody person	– मन मौजी आदमी
Sweet words	– मीठी-मीठी बातें
Fast colour	– पक्का रंग
Light food	– हल्का भोजन
Courtship	– विवाह से पूर्व प्रेमाचार
Irony of fate	– भाग्य की विडम्बना
Mixture	– मिश्रण
Choice	– पसंद
Rise before eyes	– आँखों के सामने आ जाना
Stand for	– तात्पर्य है
Day end	– दिन का अंत
Bear the fruits	– फल लगना (पेड़ पर)
Couplet	– दोहा
Riddle	– पहेली
Silly fellow	– मूर्ख साथी
Quite dull	– नदिस
Back biter	– चुगलखोर
Joke	– चुटकुल्ला
Pregnant	– गर्भवती
Hot tempered	– गर्म मिजाज
Roguery	– गुंडागर्दी
Out of fear	– डर के मारे
Displeased	– खफा

Words	हिन्दी
Come to like	- पसंद आ जाना
Move one's heart deeply	- दिल दहला देना
Put the cart before the horse	- उल्टा काम करना
Cut one of the quick	- किसी के दिल को चोट पहुंचाना
Call a spade a spade	- खूब खरी खोटी सुनाना
Beat black and blue	- कचूमर निकाल देना
Make much of oneself	- अपने आप में बहुत बनना
Make a fun of	- किसी का मजाक उड़ाना
Have no speaking terms with	- बोलचाल न होना (किसी से)
Meet a watery grave	- डूबकर मर जाना
Beat about the bush	- इधर-उधर की हाँकना
Throw dust into one's eyes	- आँखों में धूल झोंकना
Move heaven and earth	- आकाश पाताल एक करना
Poison one's ears	- कान भरना
Spin a yarn	- गप्प हाँकना
Take a sigh of relief	- जान में जान आना
Be surprised	- दांतों तले उंगली दबा लेना
Mint money	- चांदी काटना
Teach a lesson	- मजा चखाना
Poke one's nose	- टांग अड़ाना
Miss a chance	- अवसर गँवा (खो) देना
A world of difference	- जमीन-आसमान का अंतर
Have one's own way	- अपनी मनमानी करना
Make a match for	- टक्कर लेना
Lose one's wits	- होश उड़ जाना
Hold out a threat	- धमकी देना
Bring back to life	- जिंदा कर देना
Invite the trouble	- आफत/झगड़ा मोल ले लेना
Feel the pulse	- दिल की बात जानना / टोह लेना
Take an oath of	- कसम खाना

Words	हिन्दी
Give a slip	- चकमा देना
Feel pity for	- तरस आना (रोना आना)
Open one's heart	- अपने दिल की बात कह देना (डालना)
Get fever	- बुखार आना
Take bold step	- ठोस कदम उठाना
Be overjoyed	- फूला न समाना
Fall in love with	- किसी के प्यार में लट्टू हो जाना
Hit upon a plan	- उपाय सोचना
Try one's best	- अपनी पूरी कोशिश करना
Feel no shame	- बिल्कुल भी शर्म न करना
Shoot one dead	- गोली मारकर हत्या कर देना
Face hardships	- यातनाएं सहन करना
Burn oneself to death	- जलकर मर जाना
Plunge into grief	- शोक में डूब जाना
Faint voice	- पतली आवाज
Positive proof	- पक्का सबूत
Face value	- अंकित मूल्य/छपा हुआ मूल्य
Border	- पल्ला (साड़ी का)/सीमा
Indolent	- कामचोर/निकम्मा
Iron will	- पक्का इरादा/विचार
Black sheep	- नीच आदमी
Queer fish	- सनकी आदमी
Handsome salary	- अच्छी तनख्वाह
Statement	- बयान/कथन
Early education	- प्रारंभिक शिक्षा
Administration	- शासन-व्यवस्था
Metal road	- पक्की सड़क
What's to follow ?	- इसके आगे क्या होगा?
Pie	- समौसा/कचौड़ी
How is corn ?	- मक्का कैसा है?

Words	हिन्दी
How long/Upto what time	– कब तब / किस समय तक
Why is this so	– ऐसा क्यों हैं?
Sea of	– खून खराबा
Seal up	– बंद कर देना
That is to say	– अर्थात्
In the other words	– दूसरे शब्दों में
See	– समझना
Oh, I see	– ओह समझ गया
See the light	– जन्म लेना / पैदा होना
Well done !	– शबास !
What's the necessity ?	– क्या जरुरत या पड़ी
This is exactly so	– और क्या?
Occur in mind	– मन में आना
Feel happy	– जी हरा होना / खुश होना
Be satisfied	– मन भर जाना
Set heart on	– मन लगाना / लगना
Set fire on	– आग लगा देना
Set the watch	– घड़ी मिलाना
Set the watch back	– घड़ी पीछे करना
Slap	– थप्पड़ / तमाचा
Give a slap to	– थप्पड़ मारना / थप्पड़ खींच देना
Impotent	– नामर्द / हिजड़ा
Ungrateful	– नमक हराम
Hatred	– नफरत
Hell	– नरक
Non-stop	– धारा प्रवाह / लगातार
Influence	– रौब/प्रभाव डालना
Moneyed person	– धन्नासेठ / पैसे वाले लोग
Hunger	– भूख
Feel hungry	– भूख लगना

Words	हिन्दी
Make off	– चंपत हो जाना / भाग जाना
Burn on self to death	– जलकर मर जाना
In olden time	– प्राचीन काल में
Suffer hardships	– तकलीफ उठाना
Highly educated	– सुशिक्षित
On the sly	– चुपके से / छिपे तौर पर
Have a cold	– जुकाम हो जाना
With these words	– इन शब्दों के साथ
Take for	– समझ बैठना (गलती से)
Be out of money	– हाथ तंग होना / खाली हाथ होना
Be out of wits	– होश उड़ जाना
Sit idle	– हाथ पर हाथ रखकर बैठ जाना
Have a mind	– दिल करना
Sum and substance is that	– सौ बातों की एक बात है
Perform one's duty	– हक अदा करना
Feel like	– जी करना / मन करना
Fall for	– आकर्षित हो जाना
Get up	– उठ जाना
High and mighty	– घमंडी
Give ear	– सुनना
Fly out	– अपशब्द कहना
Great and small	– हर तरह के लोग
Early and late	– हर समय
Fall behind	– पीछे रह जाना
Fall asleep	– नींद आ जाना
Hang upon	– ध्यान से सुनना
Chop off the head	– सिर कलम कर देना
Make merry	– मौज करना / उड़ाना
Run out	– खत्म हो जाना
Draw a long bow	– लंबी-चौड़ी हांकना

Words	हिन्दी
Try on	- पहन कर देखना
Spoil all pleasure	- मजा किर-किरा कर देना
Sit up	- उठ बैठना (लेटे हुए)
Feather one's own nest	- अपना मतलब गांठना
By and by	- आहिस्ता-आहिस्ता
Speak up	- जोर से बोलना
At dead of night	- आधी रात को (में)
Few and far between	- बहुत कम
Put to death	- मौत के घाट उतार देना
Fellow feelings	- अपनापन / भाईचारा
Develop close intimacy	- पेट में घुसना
Give a slip	- चकमा देना
Once in a while	- कभी-कभार, एकाध बार
go off one's head	- बुद्धि भ्रष्ट हो जाना
Be out of favour with	- खफा होना
Be out of mind	- पागल हो जाना
Put one to shame	- लज्जित करना
Hard to hearing	- कुछ कम सुनने वाला व्यक्ति
Speak one's mind	- साफ-साफ बता देना
Stand one's ground	- अपनी बात पर अड़े रहना
What not	- अगैरा-वगैरा इत्यादि
Die for	तीव्र इच्छा रखना
Cry up	- प्रशंसा करना
Cry down	- निंदा करना
Clear up	- स्पष्ट करना
Without fail	- निश्चित रूप से
Wise as an owl	- महामूर्ख
Upto the mark	- उचित स्तर का
Be all ears	- ध्यान से सुनना
At sea	- परेशान

Words	हिन्दी
Chicken heated	डरपोक व्यक्ति
Time and tide	समय और अवसर
Talk big	शेखी मारना / बघारना
Dry up	- सूख जाना
Then and there	उसी समय
Ring up	- फोन करना
Run away with	- लेकर भाग जाना
Haves and have nots	- अमीर और गरीब
Hush up	- चुप हो जाना
Under the sun	- किसी भी स्थान पर / सब जगह
Dog in the manger	- स्वार्थी व्यक्ति
Unfaithful	- नमक हराम
Tie of blood	- खून का रिश्ता
Shyless lady	- बेशर्म औरत
Stands on one's own leg	- अपने पैरों पर खड़े होना
Smell a rat	- संदेह होना
Put up a questions	- प्रश्न पूछना
Once again	- एक बार फिर
Make a mountain of mole hill	- बात का बतंगड़ बनाना
Sign of wonder	- चमत्कार
Pin pricks	- छोटी-मोटी परेशानी
Of late	- हाल ही में
Nig nog	- बेवकूफ
Lord it over	- धौंस जमाना (किसी पर)
Sharp practice	- धोखा धड़ी
Lend one ear	- सुनना
Seal of love	- प्यार की निशानी
In merry pin	- मजाक में
See the light	- जन्म लेना
After a fashion	- एक सीमा तक

Words	हिन्दी
A.B.C.	– प्रारंभिक ज्ञान
Lock up	– ताला लगाना
Heart rending news	– हृदय विदारक समाचार
Be on the run all time	– भागा-भागा फिरना
Speak ill of others	– दूसरों की बुराई करना
Drive away	– भगा देना
Raise smoke	– धुंआ करना
Was deeply pained	– बड़ा दुख हुआ
It's likely	– हो सकता है
Sleep soundly	– गहरी नींद सोना (लेना)
Take interest in	– मन लगाना (किसी काम में)
Moreover	– ओर तो ओर
Do not remember	– ध्यान न रहना

Daily routine used sentences for spoken

ऐसे महत्वपूर्ण वाक्य जिनका प्रयोग दिनचर्या में बोलने के लिए किया जाता है।

हिन्दी	Sentences
ये बात अलग है।	It's a different matter
तुम बहुत गिरे हुए इंसान हो।	You are a vile man
बात तो कोई भी बना सकता है।	Anyone can make talk
मैंने तेरे साथ कौन-सा बुरा कर दिया?	What wrong have I done to you?
मैंने तो उसी दिन से कान पकड़ लिया।	I took a vow since that day
कुछ बातें ऐसी भी होती है?	Somethings are like this
यह सड़क कहाँ को जाती है?	Where does this road lead to?
यह पक्की सड़क हमारे गाँव को जाती है।	This metaled road leads to our village
यहाँ अब मेरा मन नहीं लगता।	I don't feel at home here
कृपया रास्ता छोड़ दो।	Please leave the way.
तुम किसकी बात कर रही हो?	Who are you talking of?
तुम किससे बात कर रहे हो?	To whom are you talking ?
आप अपने काम में ध्यान दो।	Attend your work / business
सफाई देने की कोई जरूरत नहीं है।	No need of explanation
जिसे जरूरत होगी वह खुद आयेगा।	Needy person will come himself
वह तो बड़ी नखरे बाज है।	She is very coquettish
वैसे तो तुम भी पागलों से कोई कम थोड़े ही हो।	You are not less than a fool
मैंने इस बात का कोई ठेका थोड़े ही ले रखा है।	I am not responsible for it
पैसा ही सब कुछ नहीं होता।	Money is not everything
भाग्य भी कोई चीज होती है।	Fate is also something
इसमें बुरा मानने की क्या बात है?	What's there to mind
बहम की तो कोई दवा नहीं है।	No solution for doubt
इससे तुम पर क्या फर्क पड़ता है?	What does it make difference to you
इससे मेरे पर कौन-सा फर्क पड़ता है?	It doesn't matter to me
भगवान आपकी जरूर सुनेगा?	God will grant your prayer
तुम्हें डर किस बात का है?	What makes your terrified
हाथ पर हाथ रखकर मत बैठो।	Don't sit idle

हिन्दी	Sentences
सुनो सबकी, करो अपने मन की।	Listen to everyone, but do as you like.
ऐसी भूल कभी मत कर देना।	Never commit such mistake.
तुम हर वक्त मजाक मत किया करो।	Don't cut jokes every time.
इस कमीज को पहन कर देख लो।	Try to put on this shirt.
तुम बेकार की बात मत करो।	Don't talk nonsense .
तुम दिल छोटा मत करो।	Don't lose your heart.
ज्यादा देर मत लगाना।	Don't be long.
जो होना है वो तो होगा ही	What will be, will be.
सच बात तो यह है।	To tell you the truth.
साफ बात है।	To be frank.
भगवान ना करे।	God forbid.
बाकी सब ठीक है।	Rest is fine.
क्यों क्या हुआ?	Why what happened?
हद से हद क्या होगा?	If the worst comes to the worst.
ज्यादा से ज्यादा इतना ही तो हो सकता है कि	It may be the worst that.
तेरी जान की कसम, यार	By your life, yar.
तुम्हें मेरी कसम।	By me to you.
मेरी बात को मजाक में मत टालो।	Don't take my matter in joke.
कुदरत का कमाल तो देखिए।	See the miracle of nature.
उसके सामने तो तुम्हारी बोलती बंद हो जाएगी।	You will be tongue tied before him.
कहीं भांडा न फूट जाए।	Secrecy should not be out.
तुम्हारा तो दिमाग खराब हो गया है।	You have run amuck.
वह कुछ पागल है।	He is somewhat mad.
मेरे सिर की कसम खाओ।	Take oath of my head.
भगवान सब देखता है।	God looks at everything.
अपना दिमाग लगाओ।	Employ your mind.
चाहे इसमें मेरी जान ही क्यों न निकल जाए।	No matter it may cost my life.
वह तुम्हारा बाल भी बांका नहीं कर सकता।	He won't be able to touch your body.
आपको रोक कौन रहा है?	Who holds you?

हिन्दी	Sentences
पकड़ किसने रखा है तुझे?	Who is holding you?
सब कुछ खत्म हो गया?	All is lost Or All is finished
यदि उसे कुछ हो गया ना।	If any wrong happened to he'
आपको ऐसा करना शोभा नहीं देता।	It won't be modest for you to do so
मुझे कोई जल्दी नहीं हैं।	I have no hurry
ये तो बड़े सौभाग्य की बात है।	It is very fortunate
यहाँ क्या हो रहा है?	What's going here?
तुम्हें इस पर विश्वास/यकीन नहीं आयेगा।	You won't believe it
अब तुम खुद ही देख लो।	Now see yourself
सब पैसे का खेल है।	All depends on money
एक बात तो है **या** एक बात तो जरूर है।	One thing is sure
अब तो तुम कुछ भी समझ लो **या** अब तुम कुछ भी अर्थ लगा लो।	Now, put any meaning upon it
ये कब की बात है?	When did it happen?
बात कुछ जमी नहीं।	It doesn't hold good
कुछ न कुछ बात तो जरूर है?	Something or the other is sure
तुम क्या कर लोगो मेरा?	What wrong can you do with me?
मुझसे फालतू मत बोलो	Don't speak in advance with me
चल-चल ज्यादा भाषण मत झाड़।	Go, don't deliver speech
तुझे कहने का क्या अधिकार है?	What right do you have to day.
इसमें बुरा मानने की क्या बात है?	What's there to mind?
नीचता की भी एक हद होती है।	Rascality has a limit
तुम जैसे सैकड़ों मेरी जेब में रहते हैं **या** तुम जैसे सैकड़ों मेरे पीछे फिरते हैं।	Many like of you run after me
किसी के माथे पर थोड़े ही लिखा होता है।	It's not inscribed on the face of anyone
वह मेरा कुछ नहीं है।	He is nothing to me
तुम रईस होंगे अपने घर के होंगे।	You may be aristocrat in your house
तुम किस बात पर हंसी?	What made you laugh?
तुझे बहुत घमंड है।	You have much ego

एक दिन में तो कुछ नहीं होता।	Nothing is done in one day.
आपने गलत सुना।	You got wrong information.
सब यही धरा का धरा रह जायेगा।	Everything will remain here.
अरे, तो अकड़ क्यों रहे हो?	Hey, why are you flaunting.
यह बात मेरे दिमाग से निकल गयी।	It slipped from my memory.
अच्छा तो यह ऐसा है।	So, it is like this.
हम भी कोई ऐसे वैसे नहीं है।	We are not riff-raff.
कुल मिलाकर बात यह है।	Sum and substance is that.
तुम तो बेपैंदी का लोटे हो।	You are a rolling stone.
तुम्हारा कोई भरोसा नहीं।	You are not reliable.
इसमें मेरा क्या कसूर है।	What's my fault in it.
वह तो बड़ा लीचड़ आदमी है।	He is very sluggish.

❑❑❑

Three forms of verbs for spoken

क्रिया के तीनों रूपों का अच्छी अंग्रेजी बोलने के लिए अध्ययन करें।

	V^1	V^2	V^3
लक्ष्य साधना	aim	aimed	aimed
अनुमति देना	allow	allowed	allowed
साथ जाना	accompany	accompanied	accompanied
गाली देना	abuse	abused	abused
जोड़ना	add	added	added
कार्य करना	act	acted	acted
सलाह देना	advise	advised	advised
मन बहलाना	amuse	amused	amused
प्रशंसा करना	admire	admired	admired
स्वीकार करना	accept	accepted	accepted
भर्ती करना, मनाना	admit	admitted	admitted
रहना	abide	abode	abode
घोषणा करना	announce	announced	announced
उत्तर देना	answer	answered	answered
क्षमा मांगना	apologize	apologized	apologized
सच्ची प्रार्थना करना	appeal	appealed	appealed
दिखाई पड़ना	appear	appeared	appeared
सहमत होना	agree	agreed	agreed
बदलना	alter	altered	altered
खण्ड करना	analyse	analysed	analysed
आवेदन पत्र देना	apply	applied	applied
उठना	arise	arose	arisen
प्रबंध करना	arrange	arranged	arranged
बंदी बनाना	arrest	arrested	arrested
आ जाना, पहुंचना	arrive	arrived	arrived
पूछना	ask	asked	asked
विश्वास दिलाना	assure	assured	assured

	V^1	V^2	V^3
आक्रमण करना	attack	attacked	attacked
प्रयत्न करना चेष्टा करना	attempt	attempted	attempted
ध्यान लगाना	attend	attended	attended
आकर्षित करना	attract	attracted	attracted
जागना	awake	awoke	awoken
आरंभ करना	begin	began	begun
देखना	behold	beheld	beheld, behold
विश्वास करना	believe	believed	believed
झुकना, झुकाना	bend	bent	bent
वंचित करना	bereave	bereft	bereft
मिन्नत करना	beseek	besought	besought
आज्ञा देना, बोली देना	bid	bade, bid	bidden, bid
बांधना	bind	bound	bound
काटना (दांतों से)	bite	bit	bitten
पकाना	bake	baked	baked
रोक लगाना	ban	banned	banned
होना	be (is, am, are)	was, were	been
जन्म देना	bear	bore	born
सहन करना	bear	bore	borne
मारना, पीटना	beat	beat	beaten
हो जाना	become	became	become
भीख मांगना	beg	begged	begged
पैदा करना	beget	begot	begotten, begot
खून बहाना	bleed	bled	bled
पालना	breed	bred	bred
लाना	bring	brought	brought
प्रसारण करना	broad cast	broad cast	broad cast
बनाना (मकान आदि)	build	built	built
जलाना, जलना	burn	brunt	brunt

	V[1]	V[2]	V[3]
फट पड़ना	burst	burst	burst
खरीदना	buy	bought	bought
आशीर्वाद	bless	blessed	blessed
फूंक मारना, हवा का चलना	blow	blew	blown
उबालना, उबलना	boil	boiled	boiled
तोड़ना	break	broke	broken
सांस लेना	breathe	breathed	breathed
बेंत से मारना	cane	caned	caned
जीत कर, पकड़ लेना	capture	captured	captured
परवाह करना	care	cared	cared
धोखा देना	cheat	cheated	cheated
चबाना	chew	chewed	chewed
झिड़कना	chide	chided	chided
चुनना	choose	chose	chosen
साफ करना	clean	cleaned	cleaned
स्पष्ट करना	clear	cleared	cleared
चीरना	cleave	cleaved	cleaved
पुकारना	call	called	called
रद्द करना	cancel	cancelled	cancelled
उठाकर ले जाना	carry	carried	carried
फेंकना	cast	casted	casted
पकड़ना	catch	caught	caught
रस्म मनाना	celebrate	celebrated	celebrated
बदलना	change	changed	changed
चढ़ना	climb	climbed	climbed
चिमटना	cling	clung	clung
बंद करना	close	closed	closed
कपड़े पहनाना	clothe	clothed	clothed
इकट्ठा करना	collect	collected	collected

	V^1	V^2	V^3
कंघी करना	comb	combed	combed
आना	come	came	come
तुलना करना	compare	compared	compared
विवश करना	compel	compelled	compelled
गिनना	count	counted	counted
ठीक करना	correct	corrected	corrected
पत्र व्यवहार करना	correspond	corresponded	corresponded
मूल्य होना	cost	cost	cost
परामर्श देना	counsel	counseled	counseled
रेंगना	creep	crept	crept
पार करना	cross	crossed	crossed
मुर्गे का बोलना	crow	crowed	crowed
चिल्लाना	cry	cried	cried
पूर्ण करना	complete	completed	completed
छिपाना	conceal	concealed	concealed
घबरा देना	confuse	confused	confused
विजयी होना	conquer	conquered	conquered
दिलासा देना	console	consoled	consoled
परामर्श करना	consult	consulted	consulted
काबू में रखना	control	controlled	controlled
पकाना	cook	cooked	cooked
नकल करना	copy	copied	copied
इलाज कराना	cure	cured	cured
श्राप देना	curse	cursed	cursed
काटना	cut	cut	cut
क्षति पहुंचाना	damage	damaged	damaged
नाचना	dance	danced	danced
हिम्मत करना	dare	dared	dared
व्यापार करना	deal	dealt	dealt

	V¹	V²	V³
इरादा करना	determine	determined	determined
हजम करना	digest	digested	digested
अपमान करना	disgrace	disgraced	disgraced
निराश करना	disappoint	disappointed	disappointed
तलाक देना	divorce	divorced	divorced
घोलना	dissolve	dissolved	dissolved
अप्रसन्न करना	displease	displeased	displeased
चीरना (शरीर)	dissect	dissected	dissected
भेष बदलना	disguise	disguised	disguised
अंतर करना	distinguish	distinguished	distinguished
खोदना	dig	dig	dig
बांटना, अलगाना	divide	divided	divided
निर्णय करना	decide	decided	decided
सजाना	decorate	decorated	decorated
छलना, ठगना	deceive	deceived	deceived
घटना	decrease	decreased	decreased
हराना	defeat	defeated	defeated
अलग होना	depart	departed	departed
वंचित रखना	deprive	deprived	deprived
राजसिंहासन छुड़ाना	dethrone	dethroned	dethroned
मरना	die	died	died
इंकार करना	deny	denied	denied
घसीटना	drag	dragged	dragged
टपकाना	drop	dropped	dropped
सुखाना	dry	dried	dried
रहना	dwell	dwelt	dwelt
करना	do	did	done
संदेह करना	doubt	doubted	doubted
खींचना	draw	drew	drawn

	V[1]	V[2]	V[3]
स्वप्न देखना	dream	dreamt	dreamt
पीना	drink	drank	drunk
चलाना	drive	drove	driven
रंगना	dye	dyed	dyed
खाना	eat	ate	eaten
कमाना	earn	earned	earned
पत्र संपादन करना	edit	edited	edited
शिक्षित करना	educate	educated	educated
निर्वाचन करना, चुनना	elect	elected	elected
नियुक्त करना	employ	employed	employed
साहस बढ़ाना	encourage	encouraged	encouraged
आनंद लेना	enjoy	enjoyed	enjoyed
धनी बनाना	enrich	enriched	enriched
सजाना, संवारना	equip	equipped	equipped
भूल करना	err	erred	erred
बच निकलना	escape	escaped	escaped
हटाना, बचाना	evade	evaded	evaded
परीक्षा करना	examine	examined	examined
गिरना	fall	fell	fallen
असफल होना	fail	failed	failed
महसूस करना	feel	felt	felt
खिलाना	feed	fed	fed
गिराना	fell	felled	felled
लड़ना	fight	fought	fought
पाना	find	found	found
समाप्त करना	finish	finished	finished
भाग जाना	flee	fled	fled
फेंकना	fling	flung	flung
बहना	flow	flowed	flowed

	V^1	V^2	V^3
उड़ना	fly	flew	flown
मना करना	forbid	forbade	forbidden
भूलना	forget	forgot	forgotten
क्षमा करना	forgive	forgave	forgiven
छाड़ना	forsake	forsoak	forsaken
जम जाना	freeze	froze	frozen
भूनना	fry	fried	fried
लेना, प्राप्त करना	get	got	gotten
देना	give	gave	given
जाना	go	went	gone
पैदा करना, बढ़ना	grow	grew	grown
पीसना	grind	ground	ground
पकड़ना	grip	gripped	gripped
जुआ खेलना	gamble	gambled	gambled
कराहना	groan	groaned	groaned
बुड़बुड़ करना	grumble	grumbled	grumbled
चरना	graze	grazed	grazed
रखना	has/have	had	had
लटकाना	hang	hung	hung
फांसी पर लटकाना	hang	hanged	hanged
घृणा करना	hate	hated	hated
सुनना	hear	heard	heard
सहायता करना	help	helped	helped
काटना	hew	hewed	hewed
चोट मारना	hit	hit	hit
छिपाना	hide	hid	hidden
पकड़ना	hold	held	held
उपेक्षा करना	ignore	ignored	ignored
सूचित करना	ınform	informed	informed

	V[1]	V[2]	V[3]
आक्रमण करना	invade	invaded	invaded
निमंत्रण देना	invite	invited	invited
सम्मिलित होना	join	joined	joined
न्याय करना	judge	judged	judged
कूदना	jump	jumped	jumped
रखना	keep	kept	kept
ठोकर मारना	kick	kicked	kicked
झुकना	kneel	knelt	knelt
जानना	know	knew	known
बुनना	knit	knitted	knitted
खटखटाना	knock	knocked	knocked
मारना (जान से)	kill	killed	killed
रखना	lay	laid	laid
नेतृत्व करना	lead	led	led
झुकना	lean	leaned	leaned
कूदना	leap	leapt	leapt
याद करना	learn	learnt	learnt
छोड़ना	leave	left	left
खोना	Lose	lost	lost
प्यार करना	Love	Loved	Loved
देखना	Look	looked	looked
लादना	Load	loaded	loaded
लेटना	lie	lay	laid
झूठ बोलना	lie	lied	lied
प्रकाश	Light	Lighted	Lighted
उधार देना	Lend	lent	lent
किराये पर देना	Let	let	let
ताला लगाना	Lock	locked	locked
पसंद करना	Like	liked	liked

	V^1	V^2	V^3
उठाना	Lift	lifted	lifted
रहना	Live	lived	lived
हंसना	Laugh	laughed	laughed
बनाना	Make	made	made
शादी करना	Marry	married	married
मिलना	Meet	met	met
पिघलना	Melt	melted	melted
सुधारना	Mend	mended	mended
मतलब रखना	Mean	meant	meant
जिक्र करना	Mention	mentioned	mentioned
सकना	May	might	might
चूकना	Miss	missed	missed
हिलना	Move	Moved	Moved
मातम मनाना	Mourn	mourned	mourned
कत्ल करना	Murder	murdered	murdered
नापना, मापना	Measure	measured	measured
दूध दुहना	Milk	milked	milked
नाम रखना	Name	named	named
जरूरत होना	Need	needed	needed
देखना	Notice	noticed	noticed
आज्ञा मानना	Obey	obeyed	obeyed
आपत्ति करना	Object	objected	objected
खोलना	Open	opened	opened
विरोध करना	Oppose	opposed	opposed
जीतना	Overcome	overcame	overcome
छिपकर सुनना	Overhear	overheard	overheard
आज्ञा देना, बोली देना	Order	ordered	ordered
घेर लेना	Occupy	occupied	occupied
कृतज्ञ होना, देना	Owe	owed	owed

	V^1	V^2	V^3
दे देना	Pay	paid	paid
क्षमा करना	Pardon	Pardoned	Pardoned
भाग लेना	Partake	partook	partaken
छीलना (सेब)	Pare	pared	pared
छीलना (संतरा)	Peel	peeled	peeled
झांकना	Peep	peeped	peeped
मनाना	Persuade	persuaded	persuaded
खेलना	Play	played	played
हल चलाना	Plough	ploughed	ploughed
लूटमार करना	Plunder	plundered	plundered
रखना	Place	placed	placed
प्रसन्न करना	Please	pleased	pleased
तोड़ना (फूल)	Pluck	plucked	plucked
रोकना	Prevent	prevented	prevented
उपस्थित करना	Present	presented	presented
तैयार करना	Prepare	prepared	prepared
अधिक पसंद करना	Prefer	preferred	preferred
प्रार्थना करना	Pray	prayed	prayed
उपदेश देना	Preach	preached	preached
बचाना	Protect	protected	protected
उन्नति करना	Progress	progressed	progressed
पौधा लगाना	Plant	planted	planted
जहर देना	Poison	poisoned	poisoned
स्थगित करना	Postpone	postponed	postponed
अपवित्र करना	Pollute	polluted	polluted
डालना (पानी आदि)	Pour	poured	poured
प्रशंसा करना	Praise	praised	praised
तरक्की करना	Promote	promoted	promoted
वादा करना	Promise	promised	promised

	V^1	V^2	V^3
भविष्यवाणी करना	Predict	predicted	predicted
बहाना करना	Pretend	pretended	pretended
दंड देना	Punish	punished	punished
प्रकाशित करना	Publish	published	published
अनुमति करना	Permit	permitted	permitted
सिद्ध करना	Prove	proved	proved
खींचना	Pull	pulled	pulled
दया करना	Pity	pitied	pitied
रखना	Put	put	put
झगड़ा करना	Quarrel	quarreled	quarreled
प्रश्न करना	Question	questioned	questioned
छोड़ना	Quit	quitted	quitted
वर्षा होना	Rain	rained	rained
उठाना	Raise	raised	raised
निवेदन करना	Request	requested	requested
प्राप्त करना	Receive	received	received
झिड़कना	Rebuke	rebuked	rebuked
इंकार करना	Refuse	refused	refused
त्याग पत्र देना	Resign	resigned	resigned
विद्रोह करना	Rebel	rebelled	rebelled
सवार होना	Ride	rode	ridden
बजना बजाना	Ring	rang	rung
आराम करना	Rest	rested	rested
जवाब देना	Reply	replied	replied
वापस आना	Return	returned	returned
पढ़ना	Read	read	read
पहुंचना	Reach	reached	reached
मरम्मत करना	Repair	repaired	repaired
उठना, चढ़ना	Rise	rose	risen

	V1	V2	V3
गलना सडना	Rot	rotted	rotted
दौड़ना	Run	ran	run
नाश करना	Ruin	ruined	ruined
खुशी मनाना	Rejoice	rejoiced	rejoiced
पछताना	Repent	repented	repented
दोहराना	Revise	revised	revised
दोहराना	Repeat	repeated	repeated
ठीक/राजी होना	Recover	recovered	recovered
सूचित करना	Report	reported	reported
हटा देना	Repeal	repealed	repealed
आदर करना	Respect	respected	respected
याद करना	Remember	remembered	remembered
कहना	Say	said	said
बचाना	Save	Saved	Saved
प्रणाम करना	Salute	salute	salute
आरे से चीरना	Saw	sawed	sawed
हिलाना	Shake	shook	shaken
दिखाना	Show	shoed	shown
बंद करना	Shut	shut	shut
गोली मारना	Shoot	shot	shot
[illegible]ना	Shine	shone	shone
[illegible] सर्दी से)	Shiver	shivered	shivered
	Sing	sang	sung
बेठना	Sit	sat	sat
तलाश करना	Search	searched	searched
बेचना	Sell	sold	sold
भेजना	Send	sent	sent
सेवा करना, परोसना	Serve	served	served
देखना	See	saw	seen

	V^1	V^2	V^3
चुनना	Select	selected	selected
सीलना	Sew	sewed	sewed
डूबना	Sink	sank	sunk
हस्ताक्षर करना	Sign	signed	signed
सोना	Sleep	slept	slept
कत्ल करना	Slay	slew	slain
फिसलना	Slip	slipped	slipped
चुपके से चले जाना	Slink	slunk	slunk
सिकुड़ना	Shrink	shrank	shrunk
हजामत करना	Shave	shaved	shaved
खुशबू देना	Smell	smelt	smelt
मुस्कुराना	Smile	smiled	smiled
हल करना	Solve	solved	solved
बीज बोना	Sow	sowed	sowed
खर्राटे लेना	Snore	snored	snored
खड़ा होना	Stand	stood	stood
शुरू करना	Start	started	started
भूखा मरना	Starve	starved	starved
अध्ययन करना	Study	studied	studied
रूकना	Stop	stopped	stopped
ठहरना	Stay	stayed	stayed
चुराना	Steal	stole	stolen
चिपके रहना	Stick	stuck	stuck
बोलना	Speak	spoke	spoken
खर्च करना	Spend	spent	spent
कातना	Spin	spun	spun
बिखेर देना	Spill	spilt	spilt
थूकना	Spit	spat	spat
खराब करना	Spoil	spoiled	spoiled

	V^1	V^2	V^3
फैलाना	Spread	Spread	Spread
डंक मारना	Sting	stung	stung
हड़ताल करना	Strike	struck	struck
छुरा घोंपना	Stab	stabbed	stabbed
पीड़ा होना	Suffer	suffered	suffered
सफल होना	Succeed	succeeded	succeeded
तैरना	Swim	swam	swum
झाड़ू देना	Sweep	swept	swept
कसम खाना	Swear	swore	sworn
झूलना	Swing	swung	swung
सूजना	Swell	swelled	swelled
लेना	Take	took	taken
पढ़ाना	Teach	taught	taught
फाड़ना	Tear	tore	torn
बताना	Tell	told	told
सोचना	Think	thought	thought
थकना	Tire	tired	tired
छूना	Touch	touched	touched
विश्वास करना	Trust	trusted	trusted
यात्रा करना	Travel	travelled	travelled
व्यवहार करना	Treat	treated	treated
कुचलना	Tread	treaded	treaded
प्रयत्न करना	Try	tried	tried
फेंकना	Throw	threw	thrown
धन्यवाद देना	Thank	tanked	tanked
धमकी देना	Threat	threatened	threatened
खुशहाल होना	Thrive	throve	thriven
घुसेडना	Thrust	thrust	thrust
बाधना	Tie	tied	tied

	V^1	V^2	V^3
कष्ट देना	Trouble	troubled	troubled
मिलाना	Unite	united	united
जोर देना	Urge	urged	urged
प्रयोग करना	Use	used	used
कद्र करना	Value	valued	valued
जागना	Wake	woke	woken
चलना	Walk	walked	walked
घूमना	Wander	wandered	wandered
धोना	Wash	washed	washed
प्रतीक्षा करना	Wait	waited	waited
चाहना	Want	wanted	wanted
व्यर्थ गंवाना	Waste	wasted	wasted
चेतावनी देना	Warn	warned	warned
शादी करना	Wed	wed	wed
पहनना	Wear	wore	wore
बुनना	Weave	wove	wove
रोना	Weep	wept	wept
सफेदी करना	Whitewash	whitewashed	whitewashed
सीटी मारना	Whistle	whistled	whistled
इच्छा करना	Wish	wished	wished
देखना, निगरानी रखना	Watch	watched	watched
घायल करना	Wound	wounded	wounded
गीला करना	Wet	wet	wet
जीतना	Win	won	won
हट जाना	Withdraw	withdrew	withdrawn
रोक लेना	Withhold	withheld	withheld
सामना करना	Withstand	withstood	withstood
निचोड़ना	Wring	wrung	wrung
लिखना	Write	wrote	written

Words in daily used for spoken

प्रतिदिन बात करने के लिए उपयोग में आने वाले महत्वपूर्ण शब्द

Words	हिन्दी
In the first place	– पहली बात तो यह है
Secondly	– दूसरी बात तो यह है
After all	– आखिरकार
In response to	– के जवाब में
As a result	– परिणामस्वरूप
On behalf of	– की ओर से
Ever since	– कभी पहले
More over	– और फिर
The way	– जिस प्रकार से
Since long back	– बहुत पहले से
In terms of	– के रूप में
At a stretch	– एक ही बार में
Readily/Soon	– जल्दी ही
As and when	– जब जब
Otherwise also	– वैसे ही
At least	– कम से कम
To start with	– शुरू-शुरू में
So far	– अभी तक
In a short span of time	– बहुत थोड़े समय में
Then and there	– वहीं के वहीं
Now and here	– यहा-वहाँ
Anyway	– खैर
In place of	– के स्थान पर
Before	– सामने
Because of which	– जिससे, जिसके कारण
Come what May	– चाहे जो हो जाए
Then	– तब
Being	– होने के नाते, के नाते
It is, for this reason	– इसी कारण
While	– जबकि
By the by	– बात बात में
Even today	– आज भी
At the most	– अधिक से अधिक
For a short while	– थोड़ी देर के लिए
Even Then/Yet	– फिर भी
In the mean time	– इसी बीच
Broad day light	– दिन-दहाड़े
Day in and Day out	– आये दिन
By fits and starts	– रूक-रूक कर
By the first instance	– पहली बार में
Slowly	– धीरे-धीरे
Every now and then	– बीच-बीच में
In the blink of an eye	– पलक झपकते ही
As like	– की तरह
By this reason	– इसी कारण से
By which	– जिसकी वजह से
That is why	– इसलिए
From	– से
Also	– भी
Far and wide	– दूर-दराज से
Cat & Dogs	– मूसलाधार
Otherwise	– अन्यथा / वरना
Often	– अक्सर / प्राय:
Hot cake	– चर्चा का विषय
Keep in view	– ध्यान में रखना
Turn the table	– पासा पलटना
Cast a spell	– जादू सा कर देना
Lion share	– बड़ा हिस्सा
Other way	– दूसरे रास्ते से

Words of personality for spoken

ऐसे शब्दों का प्रयोग व्यक्तित्व को दर्शाने के लिए किया जाता है।

Words	हिन्दी
Diffident	– शर्मीला व्यक्ति
Realistic	– वास्तविक जीवन जीने वाला व्यक्ति
Patriotic	– देश प्रेम करने वाला व्यक्ति
Sadistic	– दूसरों को सता कर खुश होने वाला व्यक्ति
Dogmatic	– कर्म और वचन से सर्वश्रेष्ठ रहने वाला व्यक्ति
Optimistic	– आशावादी व्यक्ति
Dominant	– सर्वोपरी व्यक्ति
Truculent	– स्वभाव से रूखा एवं जंगली व्यक्ति
Quixotic	– कल्पना में तल्लीन होने वाला व्यक्ति
Blase	– सांसारिक मामलों में रूचि न रखने वाला व्यक्ति
Inhibited	– अपनी बात समाज और भीड़ के सामने न कहने वाला व्यक्ति
Dominant	– सर्वोपरी व्यक्ति
Extrovert	बाहरी मामले और चीजों में रूचि रखने वाला व्यक्ति
Introvert	– केवल अपने में ही सीमित रहने वाला व्यक्ति
Pessimistic	– निराशावादी व्यक्ति
Gregarious	– हमेशा दूसरों की संगत में रहने की इच्छा करने वाला व्यक्ति

❑❑❑

Mathematical words for spoken

गणित के कुछ ऐसे शब्द जो अंग्रेजी में बोले जाते हैं।

Words		हिन्दी
Plus/Addition		जोड़
Minus/Subtraction		घटाव
Multiplication, Multiplied by		गुणा
Division, Divided by		भाग
Square root	-	वर्गमूल
Rectangle	-	आयात
Square / Circle		वर्ग/वृत
Number / Count		संख्या / (गिनती)
Vertical	-	लंबवत् (खड़ा)
Equal	–	बराबर, समान
Angle	–	कोण
Circumference	–	परिधि
Difference	–	अंतर
Less than	–	लघुत्तर
Greater than	–	अधिकतर
Foot/ Inch	–	फुट/इंच
Infinity	–	अनंत
Ratio	–	अनुपात
Parallel	–	समानांतर
Right angle	–	समकोण
Equation	-	समीकरण
Average	-	औसत/औसतन
Horizontal	-	क्षितिज
Cube root	–	घनमूल
Perpendicular	–	लंबवत्

Astrology words for spoken

ज्योतिष से संबंधित महत्वपूर्ण वाक्य

Words		हिन्दी
Aries	-	मेष राशि
Taurus	-	वृष राशि
Gemini	-	मिथुन राशि
Cancer	-	कर्क राशि
Leo	-	सिंह राशि
Virgo	-	कन्या राशि
Libra	-	तुला राशि
Scorpio	-	वृश्चिक राशि
Sagittarius	-	धनु राशि
Capricorn	-	मकर राशि
Aquarius	-	कुंभ राशि
Pisces		मीन राशि
Sun	-	सूर्य
Moon	-	चंद्र
Mars	-	मंगल
Mercury	-	बुध
Jupiter	-	बृहस्पति
Venus	-	शुक्र
Saturn	-	शनि
Uranus	-	अरुण
Neptune	-	वरुण

Short words and sign for spoken

Short Forms	Words	हिन्दी
C/o	Care of	द्वारा, मार्फत
S/o	Son of	की पुत्र, वल्द
D/o	Daughter of	की पुत्री
W/o	Wife of	की पत्नी
H/o	Husband of	की पति
B/o	Brother of	का भाई
S/o	Sister of	की बहन
&	and	और
A/c	Account of	लेखा
@	At the rate of	कीमत पर, की दर से
%	Percentage	प्रतिशत
W.E.F.	With effect from	से लागू, से प्रमाणित
V/s	Versus	बनाम

Official words for Govt. Department

आधिकारिक तौर पर शब्दों का प्रयोग

Words		हिन्दी
Education Department	–	शिक्षा विभाग
Finance Department	–	वित्त विभाग
Defence Department	–	सुरक्षा मंत्रालय
Human Resources Department	–	मानव संसाधन विभाग
Home Ministry	–	गृह मंत्रालय
Agricultural Department	–	कृषि विभाग
Industry Department	–	उद्योग विभाग
Information and Broadcasting Department	–	सूचना एवं प्रसारण विभाग
Irrigation Department	–	सिंचाई विभाग
Food Resources Department	–	खाद्य संसाधन विभाग
External Affair Department	–	विदेश विभाग
Labour and Welfare Ministry	–	श्रम एवं कल्याण मंत्रालय
Law & Justice Ministry	–	विधि एवं न्याय मंत्रालय

CHAPTER 3

- Description about industry words for spoken
- Industrial & factory words for spoken
- Judiciary vocabulary for spoken
- Name of worship words
- Name of week
- Name of months
- Name of directions
- Name of colours

Description about industry words for spoken

औद्योगिक क्षेत्र में बोले जाने वाले महत्वपूर्ण शब्द

Words		हिन्दी
Laundry	–	धुलाई
Book binding	–	जिल्दसाजी
Cold Storage	–	शीत गृह
Commercial Establishment	–	वाणिज्य अधिष्ठान
Film Industry	–	फिल्म उद्योग
Printing press	–	मुद्राणालय
Leather Industry	–	चमड़ा उद्योग
Fruit Jams	–	फलों के मुरब्बे
Vegetable sauce	–	सब्जियों की चटनी
Graded ferrous & non-ferrous casting	–	लौह एवं अलौहनीय ढ़लाई
Dying and printing null	–	रंगाई एवं छपाई मिल
Tobacco Industry	–	तंबाकू उद्योग
Steel Industry	–	इस्पात उद्योग
Sugar mill	–	चीनी मिल
Paper mill	–	कागज मिल
Oil Refinery	–	तेल शोधक कारखाना
Fertilizer Industry	–	उर्वरक उद्योग
Textile Mill	–	सूत मिल
Coal & Mines industry	–	कोयला एवं खनिज उद्योग
Ice and Ice-cream	–	बर्फ एवं आइसक्रीम
Chemical Industry		रसायन उद्योग
Foundry works		ढलाई कारखाना
Aerated Drinks		वातित पेय
Plywood		परतदार लकड़ी
Jute mill		पटसन मिल
Readymade Garments		सिले सिलाये कपड़े

Words		हिन्दी
Tin plating and printing		टिन प्लेटिंग और प्रिंटिंग
Engineering Industry		अभियंत्रण उद्योग
Irrigation work	-	सिंचाई कार्य
Digging of yell and tanks		कुंए एवं तालाब की खुदाई
Rice and flour mill		चावल एव आटा मिल
Pulse-and oil mill		दाल एव तेल मिल
Public motor transport	-	लोक मोटर परिवहन
Engineering motor transport work depot	-	यांत्रिक परिवहन कार्यशाला
Automobile	-	मोटर गाड़ी
Chicken's work	-	चिकन के कार्य
Matches Industry	-	दियासलाई उद्योग
Bakery and Biscuit	-	बेकरी और बिस्कुट
Asbestos cement	-	ऐस्बेस्टस सीमेंट
Geysers	-	गीजर्स
Synthetic Knitwears	-	कृत्रिम बुनाई
Denim Garments	-	सिलेसिलाये मोटे रंगीन कपड़े
Knitted Cotton Hosiery	-	निटेड कॉटन हॉजरी

Industrial & factory words for spoken

कारखानों और कार्यालयों में बोले जाने वाले महत्वपूर्ण शब्द

Words		हिन्दी
Safety Committee	-	सुरक्षा समिति
Government Inspection		सरकारी निरीक्षण
Attendance		हाजरी
Flagging		झण्डा फहराना
Maintenance		मरम्मत
Renewal		नवीनीकरण
License		लाईसैंस
Manpower		जनशक्ति
Purchase Department		क्रय विभाग
Steno Typist		आशुलिपिक
Commercial Manager		व्यावसायिक प्रबंधक
Plant Manager		प्लांट मैनेजर
Marketing Manager		मार्किटिंग मैनेजर
Store Manager	-	गोदाम / भंडार प्रबंधक
Assistant	–	सहायक
Clerk	–	लिपिक
Worker	–	कामगार
Union	–	संगठन
Suspend	–	निलंबित करना, हटाना
Leader	-	नेता
Strike	-	हड़ताल
Go slow	–	धीरे होना
Occupier	–	मालिक/दखलकार
Partner	–	हिस्सेदार
Managing Director (M.D.)	–	प्रबंध निदेशक
Chair man	–	अध्यक्ष
Vice President (V.P-)	–	उपाध्यक्ष

Words		हिन्दी
Dy. General Manager (D.G.M.)		उप महाप्रबधक
Personnel Manager	-	कार्मिक प्रबंधक
Factory Manager	-	कारखाना प्रबंधक
Administration		प्रशासन
Disciplinary action		अनुशासनात्मक कार्यवाही
Sales Department	-	विक्रय विभाग
Closure	-	बंदी
Retrenchment	-	छंटनी
Excise		उत्पादकता शुल्क
Production		उत्पादन
Supervisor		पर्यवेक्षक
Helper		मददगा·
Operator		मशीन चलान वाला
Labour		मजदूर
Domestic Enquiry		घरेलू जांच
Enquiry officer		जाच अधिकारी
Charge sheet	-	आरोप पत्र
Warning		चेतावनी
Dismissal	-	बर्खास्त

□□□

Judiciary vocabulary for spoken

न्यायालयों में बोले जाने वाले शब्द

Words	हिन्दी
Bond Documents	दस्तावेज़
Bail	जमानत
Case	मुकदमा
Claim	दावा
Civil court	दीवानी कचहरी
Crime	अपराध, जुल्म
Criminal	अपराधी
Client	मुवक्किल
Degree	उपाधि
Chief justice	मुख्य न्यायाधीश
Advocate	वकील
Application	पार्थना-पत्र
Applicant	प्रार्थी (प्राथना करने वाला)
Appeal	प्रार्थना करना
Attorney	न्यायवादी
Acquittal	रिहाइ
Accused	दोषी
Act Law	कानून
Decision	फैसला
Defendant	प्रतिवादी
Evidence	सबूत, साक्ष्य
Explanation	बयान स्पष्टीकरण
Fine	जुर्माना
Forgery	जालसाजी
Fitter	बेड़ी
Prisoner	कैदी

Name of worship words

धर्म से संबंधित महत्वपूर्ण शब्द

Words		हिन्दी
Goddess	–	देवी
Devotee		भक्त
Devotion	–	श्रद्धा
Religious	–	धार्मिक
Temple	–	मंदिर
Mosque	–	मस्जिद
Gurudwara	–	गुरूद्वारा
Church	–	गिरजाघर
God	–	भगवान
Ashram	–	आश्रम
Inn	–	सराय
Flower		फूल
Garland	–	फूलमाला
Priest	–	पुजारी
Statue / Idol	–	मूर्ति

Name of week

साप्ताहिक दिनों के नाम

Words		हिन्दी
Sunday	–	रविवार
Monday		सोमवार
Tuesday	–	मंगलवार
Wednesday	–	बुद्धवार
Thursday		गुरूवार
Friday	–	शुक्रवार
Saturday	-	शनिवार

Name of months

महीनों के नाम

Words		हिन्दी
January	–	जनवरी
February	–	फरवरी
March	–	मार्च
April	–	अप्रैल
May	–	मई
June	–	जून
July	–	जुलाई
August	–	अगस्त
September		सितंबर
October	–	अक्टूबर
November	–	नवंबर
December	–	दिसंबर
Leap year	–	लीप वर्ष

Name of colours

रंगों के नाम

Words		हिन्दी
Brown	–	भूरा रंग
Black	–	काला रंग
Blue	–	नीला रंग
Crimson	–	खूनी रंग
Gray	–	सलेटी रंग
Green	–	हरा रंग
Maroon	–	मेहरूम रंग
Orange	–	संतरी रंग
Purple	–	गहरा लाल रंग
Red	–	लाल रंग
Rosy	–	गुलाबी रंग
Scarlet	–	गहरा लाल रंग
Violet	–	बैंगनी रंग
White	-	सफेद रंग
Yellow		पीला रंग

Name of directions

दिशाओं के नाम

Words	हिन्दी
East	पूरब
West	पश्चिम
North	उत्तर
South	दक्षिण

CHAPTER 4

- Name of games & sports
- Name of season & weather
- Name of sounds
- Cries of birds, animals & insects
- Types of sounds
- Young ones of Animals
- Men & Animals and their homes
- Name of Places

Name of games & sports

खेल जगत में बोले जाने वाले महत्वपूर्ण शब्द

Words		हिन्दी
Ludo		लूडो
Volley Ball	-	वॉलीबॉल
Cricket	–	क्रिकेट
Kabbadi	–	कबड्डी
Gulli danda	–	गुल्ली डंडा
Hockey	–	हॉकी
Kho Kho	–	खो–खो
Base Ball		बेस बॉल
Carom board		कैरम बोर्ड
Snooker		स्नूकर
Billiards		विलियार्डस
Polo	–	पोलो
Wrestling	–	कुश्ती
Shotput	–	गोला–फेंक
Boxing	-	मुक्केबाजी
Hammer throw	-	गोला फेंक
Disc throw	-	चक्का फेंक
Swimming	–	तैराकी
Run	-	दौड
Jump	-	कूद
Judo Karate	-	जूडो कराटे
Kite show	–	पतंगबाजी
Gymnastic		जिम्नास्टिक
Gliding	–	ग्लाइडिंग
Cycle race	-	साइकिल दौड़
Horse racing	-	घुड़ दौड़

Gambling		जुआ
Casino		कैशिनो
Shooting		निशाने बाजी
Badminton		बैडमिंटन
Tennis		टेनिस
Basket Ball	–	बॉसकेट बॉल
Hand ball	–	हाथ गेंद
Taikando	–	ताइकान्डो
Kunu fu	–	कुंगफू
Football		फुटबाल
Play Card	–	ताश
Game of chess		शतरंज का खेल
Riding	–	घुड़सवारी
Are you Interested in sports?	–	क्या तुम खेलकूट में रूचि रखते हो?
Which game do you like?	–	तुम्हें कौन-कौन सा खेल पसंद है?
He is a good sportsman	–	वह खेलो में अच्छा है?
The game has started		खेल शुरू हो गया है।
Flying a kite		पतंग उड़ाना
They do drill once in a week	-	वे सप्ताह में एक बार ड्रिल करते हैं
Can I play with you?	-	क्या मैं तुम्हारे साथ खेल सकता हूँ
Who won the game?	-	खेल में कौन जीता
Who defeated in the game?	–	खेल कौन हारा
He is a fast racer	–	वह तेज धावक है
Which games do you prefer to play?	–	तुम कौन-सा खेल प्रसन्द
Boating	–	नाव चलाना
Wielding	–	लाठी चलाना
Football is the ancient game of India	–	भारत का प्राचीन खेल फुटबाल है।

Name of season & weather

ऋतुओं और मौसमों के नाम

Words	हिन्दी
Winter season	शरद ऋतु
Summer season	ग्रीष्म ऋतु
Rainy season	बरसात ऋतु
Autumn Season	बसंत ऋतु
Shivering cold	कंपकपाती ठंड
Shivering Lip	थरथराते होंठ
Strong wind	तेज हवा
Nip in the air	हवा में ठंडक
Cold wind	हल्की ठंड
Blowing	हवा बहना
Flowing	पानी बहना
Shivering	ठिठुरना, थरथराना
Spray	बौछार
Biting cold	कड़ाके की सर्द
Drizzling	थोड़ी-थोड़ी वर्षा
Raining heavily	जोरों की वर्षा
Heavy downpour	मूसलाधार बारिश
Thunder Storm	बिजली कड़कना
Heavy rain fall	अधिक वर्षा
To get drenched	भींगना
Perspiring	पसीना बहना

Name of sounds

वातावरण और वस्तुओं से उत्पन्न होने वाली ध्वनियों के नाम

Words		हिन्दी
Tinkling Sound		टन-टन
Croaking Sound		टर-टर
Banging Sound		धडाम-धडाम
Thudding Sound		धड-धड- धडाक धडाक
Sharp Sound		पटाक-पटाक
Cracking Sound		कडाम-कडाम
Crackling Sound		चटाक-चटाक
Cracking Sound		कड-कड
Splashing Sound		छप-छप/छपाका
Gnashing Sound		किट-किट
Warbling sound		झुन-झुन
Burning Sound		चट चट चट
Palpitation Sound	-	धक-धक
Ringing Sound	-	छन-छन
Jingling Sound	-	झुन-झुन
Rumbling Sound	-	गुड-गुड
Rattling Sound	-	घडघडाना
Tinkling Sound	-	घनघनाहट
Drizzling / Dripping Sound	-	टप-टप/टिप-टिप
Jingling Sound		झन-झन
Jingling Sound		झमाझम
Thudding/ Thumping Sound		धमक
Mumbling Sound	-	बुदबुदाहट
Repeated Sound	-	सड़ासड़
Joyous Screeching Sound	-	किलकारी
Harsh Tone	–	कर्कस आवाज
Rustling Sound	–	पत्तियों की खर-खर

Cries of birds, animals & insects

पक्षियों जानवरों और कीट-पतंगों के आवाजों के नाम

Animals	हिन्दी	Sound
Apes	लंगूर	Gibber
Asses	गधे	Bray
Bears	भालू	Growl
Bees	मधुमक्खियाँ	hum
Birds	पक्षी	chirp
Bulls	सांड	bellow
Camels	ऊँट	Grunt
Cats	बिल्लियाँ	mew
Cattle	पशु	low
Jackals	गीदड़	howl
Kittens	बिलौटे	mew
Lambs	मेमन	bleat
Larks	लवा पक्षी	Sing
Lions	सिंह	Roar
Mice	चूहे	Squeak
Monkeys	बंदर	Gibber
Nightingales	बुलबुल	Warble
Cocks	मुर्गे	Crow
Crows	कौए	Caw
Ducks	बत्तखे	Quack
Foxes	लोमड़ियाँ	Yelp
Geese	हंस	Cackle
Goats	बकरियाँ	bleat
Hens	मुर्गियाँ	Cackle
Horses	घोड़े	Neigh
Owls	उल्लू	hoot

Animals	हिन्दी	Sound
Oxen	बैल	low
Parrots	तोते	talk
Pigeons	कबूतर	coo
Serpents	साँप	hiss
Snakes	साँप	hiss
Sparrows	चिड़िया	chirp
Puppies	[illegible]	yelp
Wolves	भेड़िये	howl
Vultures	गिद्ध	scream
Tiger	शेर	roar
Swans	बत्तख	cry
Squirrels	गिलहरियाँ	squeak
Sheep	भेड़	bleat
Pig	सुअर	grunt
Peacock	मोर	scream
Cows	गायें	low
Flies	मक्खियाँ	buzz/ hum
Frogs	मेढ़क	croak

Types of sounds

Words		हिन्दी	Words		हिन्दी
Creaking of shoes	–	जूतों का चरमराहट	Knocking of door	–	दरवाजे की खटखटाहट
Clanking of chairs	–	कुर्सियों की चरमराहट	Rustling of leaves	–	पत्तियों की सरसराहट
Chattering of teeth	–	दांतों की चटचटाहट	Thundering of light	–	बिजली की गड़गड़ाहट
Clattering of hoofs	–	खुरों की खटखटाहट	Tinkling of bells	–	घंटी की टनटनाहट
Flapping of wings	–	**पंखों की फड़फड़ाहट**	Jingling of coins	–	सिक्कों की खनखनाहट
Whistling of wind	–	हवा की सरसराहट	Ringing of bells	–	घंटियों की झनकार
Hissing of steam		भाप का बहना	Splash of water	–	पानी की छपछपाहट

Young ones of Animals

जानवर और उनके बच्चों के नाम

Animal	Child	Animal	Child
Ass	Foal	Cat	kitten
Deer	Fawn	Duck	Duckling
Goat	Kid	Goose	Gosling
Horse	Colt	Stag	Fawn
Lion	Cub	Tiger	cub
Bear	cub	Cow	calf/Heifer
Dog	Puppy	Frog	Tadpole
Fox	cub	Hen	Chicken
Sheep	Lamb	Hare	Leveret
Swan	Cygnet	Wolf	cub

Men & Animals and their homes

पेशा और उनके रहने के स्थान

पेशा	हिन्दी	स्थान
Convict	अपराधी	Prison
King	राजा	Palace
Lunatic	पागल	Asylum
Knight	बहादुर	Mansion
Monk	भिक्षु	Monastery
Officer	अफसर	Bungalow
Dog	कुत्ता	Kennel
Horse	घोड़ा	Stable
Mouse	चूहा	Hole
Spider	मकड़ी	Web
Pig	सुअर	Sty
Nun	भिक्षुणी	Convent
Parson	पादरी	Parsonage
Peasant	किसान	Cottage
Person	व्यक्ति	House
Prisoner	कैदी	Cell
Soldier	सिपाही	Camp

पेशा	हिन्दी	स्थान
Fox	लोमड़ी	Earth
Lion	बब्बर शेर	Den
Owl	उल्लू	Tree
Sheep	भेड़	Pen, fold
Tiger	शेर	Lair

Name of Places

खेल एवं उनके स्थान

Games	
Badminton	Court
Cricket	Pitch
Gymnastic	Gymnasium
Racing	Track
Wrestling	Arena
Boxing	Ring
Football	Ground
Hockey	Ground
Tennis	Court
Horse-race	Race course

वस्तुएँ एवं उनके रखने का स्थान

Things	Where stored
Aeroplanes	Aerodrome
Fruit trees	Orchard
Grapes	Vineyard
Motor cars	Garage
Clothes	Wardrobe
Grain	Granary
Curious	Museum
Luggage at Railway station	Clock-room

प्राणी एवं उनके रहने के स्थान

Creatures	Where kept
Birds	Cage
Birds & Animals	Zoo
Caged wild animals	Menagerie

CHAPTER 5

- Name of worms & insects
- Name of birds
- Name of minerals
- Name of musical instrument
- Conditions of the body & disease
- Name of trees, germs and their parts
- Name of building and their parts
- Name of relatives
- Name of foods & Spices

Name of worms & insects

कीट-पतंगों के नाम

Words	हिन्दी	Words	हिन्दी
Boa	अजगर	Hood	फन
Earthworm	केंचुआ	Fly	मक्खी
Bug	खटमल	Web	मकड़ी का जाला
Beetle	झींगुर	Mosquito	मच्छर
Body lice	चीलर	Honey bee	मधुमक्खी
Poison	जहर	Lobster	महाचिंगट (झींगा मछली)
Glowworm	जुगनू	Frog	मेढक
Leech	जोंक	Cocoon	रेशम का कीड़ा
Grass hopper	टिड्डा	Nit	लीख
Wasp	ततैया भिड	Shark	शार्क
Hippopotamus	दरियाई घोड़ा	Oyster	सीप (कस्तूरा मछली)
Turtle	कछुआ, कच्छप	Flea	पिस्सू
Crab	केकड़ा	Scorpion	बिच्छू
Adder	गेहुवन साँप	Spider	मकड़ी
Snail	घोंघा	Crocodile	मगरमच्छ
Lizard	छिपकली	Fish	मछली
Fangs	जहर के दाँत	Bee	मधुमक्खी (मादा)
Lice	जूँ	Rat flea	मूषक पिस्सू
Cricket	झींगुर	Tadpole	मेढक का बच्चा
Locust	टिड्डी	Silk-worm	रेशम
Butter fly	तितली	Eel	सर्प मीन
Termite	दीमक	Snake	साँप
Cobra	नाग		

Name of birds

पक्षियों के नाम

Words		हिन्दी	Words		हिन्दी
Swallow	–	अबाबील	Chicken	–	चूजा
Woodpecker	–	कठफोड़वा	Parrot	–	तोता
Raven	–	काला कौवा	Wing	–	पर (परिंदो का)
Cuckoo	–	कोयल	Dove	–	फाख्ता
Drake	–	बत्तख (नर)	Hen	–	मुर्गी
Duck	–	बत्तखी	Peacock	–	मोर
Weaver bird	–	बया	Lark	–	लवा
Hawk	–	बाज	Swan	–	हंस (राजहंस)
Eagle	–	गरूण	Owl	–	उल्लू
Sparrow	–	गौरेया	Pigeon	–	कबूतर (कपोल)
Kite	–	चील	Duckling	–	बत्तख का बच्चा
Partridge	–	तीतर	Nightingale	–	बुलबुल
Magpie	–	नीलकंठ	Quail	–	बटेर
Feather	–	पंख	Cock	–	मुर्गा
Crow	–	कौवा	Chicken	–	मुर्गी का बच्चा
Vulture	–	गिद्ध	Peahen	–	मोरनी
Bat	–	चमगादड़	Crane	–	सारस

Name of minerals

धातु एवं खनिज पदार्थों के नाम

Words		हिन्दी	Words		हिन्दी
Cornelian	–	हकीक या स्फटिक	Copper	–	ताँबा
Mica	–	अभ्रक	Steel	–	पक्का लोहा
Bronze	–	कसकुट	Mercury	–	पारा
Bell-metal	–	काँसा	Brass	–	पीतल
Coal	–	कोयला (पत्थर का)	Tin	–	राँगा
Chalk	–	खड़िया	Antimony	–	सुरमा
Mine	–	खान	Cinnabar	–	हिंगुल, सिंदूर
Sulphur	–	गंधक	Lead	–	सीसा
Ochre	–	गेरू	White lead	–	सफेदा
Flint	–	चकमक पत्थर	Vermilion	–	सिंदूरी रंग
Silver	–	चाँदी	Marble	–	संगमरमर
Zinc	–	जस्ता	Iron	–	लोहा

Name of musical instrument

संगीत वाद्ययंत्रों के नाम

Words		हिन्दी	Words		हिन्दी
Bell	–	घंटी	Drum tom	–	ढोलक
Cymbal	–	झाँझ	Piano	–	पियानो
Flute	–	बाँसुरी	Jew's Harp	–	मुरचंग
Violin	–	बेला/सारंगी	Clarion	–	शहनाई
Bagpipe	–	मसक बाजा	Guitar	–	सितार
Tambourine	–	डफ	Whistle	–	सीटी
Drum	–	ढ़ोल/नगाड़ा	Harmonium	–	हारमोनियम

Conditions of the body & disease

शरीर के रोगों के नाम

Words		हिन्दी	Words		हिन्दी
Hydrocele	–	अंडवृद्धि	Vomit	–	उल्टी करना
Blind	–	अंधा	Jaundice	–	पीलिया
Shortsight	–	अल्पदृष्टि	Typhoid	–	काला ज्वर
Acidity	–	खट्टापन	Bronchitis	–	श्वासनली का रोग
Diarrhoea	–	अतिसार /दस्त	One eyed	–	काना
Syphilis	–	गरमी/उपदेश	Hunchbacked	–	कुबड़ा
Conjunctivitis	–	आँख आना	Leprosy	–	कुष्ठ या कोढ़
Hernia	–	आँत उतरना	Constipation	–	कब्ज
Tears	–	आँसू	Worms	–	कीड़े
Yawn	–	उबासी	Eczema	–	खुजली
Nausea	–	ओकाई	Tumour	–	रसौली
Squint-eyed	–	भेंगा	Dumb	–	गूँगा
Bubo	–	गांठ	Bald	–	गंजा
Goitre	–	कंठमाला	Wound	–	घाव
Stature	–	कद	Giddiness	–	चक्कर
Phlegm	–	कफ/बलगम	Botch	–	मुंहासा या फुंसी

Words	हिन्दी
Obesity	मोटापा
Hurt	चोट
Short	छोटा
Dropsy	जलोदर
Carbuncle	बड़ा फोड़ा
Coryza	जुकाम
Ague	शीत ज्वर
Fever	ज्वर
Chill	ठंड
Belch	डकार
Pimple	फुंसी या दाना
Asthma	दमा
Headache	सिर दर्द
Cough	खाँसी
Anaemia	खून की कमी
Haemorrhage	नकसीर
Rheumatism	गठिया
Abortion	गर्भपात
Whitlow	ऊंगली पर सूजन
Hoarseness	गला बैठना
Insomnia	अनिंद्रा
Stone	पथरी
Sweat	पसीना
Mad	पागल
Insanity	पागलपन
Bile	पित्त
Pus	मवाद
Dysentery	पेचिश
Leucorrhoea	प्रदर रोग

Words	हिन्दी
Thirst	प्यास
Piles	बवासीर
Diabetes	मधुमेह
Chiblain	सर्दी का लगना
Dwarf	बौना
Fistula	नासूर
Dyspepsia	पेट में जलन
Griping	मरोड़
Mole	मस्सा/तिल
Pestilence	महामारी
Epilepsy	मिरगी
Lock Jaw	दाँत बैठना
Ringworm	दाद
Lean	दुबला-पतला
Long sight	दूरदृष्टि
Sprain	मोच आना
Sinus	शिरानाल
Urine	मूत्र
Fat	मोटा
Cataract	मोतियाबिंद
Influenza	मोतीझरा
Acne	मुँहासे
Paralysis	लकवा
Saliva	लार
Lame	लंगड़ा
Dengue	लंगड़ा बुखार
Sunstroke	लू लगना
Small pox	शीतला
Leucoderma	श्वेत कुष्ठ

Words		हिन्दी	Sprue	–	संग्रहणी
Breath	–	साँस	Voice	–	स्वर
Swelling	–	सूजन	Hiccough	–	हिचकी
Albino	–	रंगहीनता	Cholera	–	हैजा
Gonorrhoea	–	सुजाक	Consumption	–	क्षय
Words		हिन्दी			

Name of trees and their parts

वृक्ष और उनसे संबंधित वस्तुओं के नाम

Words		हिन्दी	Words		हिन्दी
Guava	–	अमरूद	Divider	–	परकाल
Marking gauge	–	खतकस	Soap	–	साबुन
Mango	–	आम	Plough	–	पलाऊ
Trying Angle	–	गुनियाँ	Casket	–	सिंगारदान
Tamarind	–	इमली	Clamp	–	पाहू
Gauge	–	गोलची	Pitcher, Jug	–	सुराही
Graft	–	कलम	Syringe	–	पिचकारी
Gum	–	गोंद	Bud	–	कली
Awl	–	टेकुवा	Rasp	–	चोसा
Pine	–	चीड़	Wood	–	काठ
Oar		पतवार (नाव के लिए)	Thorn	–	कांटा
Bark	–	छाल	Loom	–	करघा
Nut	–	ढिबरी	Colter	–	खुरपा
Skin, Rind	–	छिलका	Trowel	–	करनी
Balance	–	तराजू	Blowpipe	–	फुंकनी
Coir	–	जटा (नारियल)	Compass	–	कुतुबनुमा
Lancet	–	नश्तर	Auger	–	बरमा
Root	–	जड़	Axe	–	कुल्हाड़ी
Stamen	–	जीरा	Drill	–	बरमी
Rudder	–	पतवार			

Words		हिन्दी
Scissors	–	कैंची
Adze	–	बसूली
Oil Mill	–	कोल्हू (तेली)
Fishing Angle	–	बंसी
Sugar Mill	–	कोल्हू (ईख पेरने)
Stock and dies	–	बादिया
Vice	–	बाँक
Mallet	–	मुंगरी
Jack plane	–	रन्दा
Bellows	–	भाठी
File	–	रेती
Lever	–	रंभा
Anchor	–	लंगर

Words		हिन्दी
Needle	–	सूई
Bolt	–	पेंच
Pincers	–	सड़सी
Screw Driver	–	पेंचकस
Hubble bubble	–	हुक्का
Cleat	–	कील
Tools	–	औजार
Spade	–	फरसा
Saw	–	आरी
Hone	–	सिल्ली
Plumbline	–	साहुल
Spanner	–	हथकल
Hammer	–	हथौड़ी
Plough	–	हल
Plough share	–	हल का फार
Hand Vice	–	हाथ बांक

Name of building and their parts

इमारत और उनके भागों के नाम

Words		हिन्दी
Attic	–	अटारी
Orphanage	–	अनाथालय
Niche	–	आला
Fireplace	–	अंगीठी
Hospital	–	अस्पताल
Courtyard	–	आंगन
Eaves	–	ओरी
Building	–	इमारत
Brick	–	ईट
Room	–	कमरा
Abattoir	–	कसाईखाना
Factory	–	कारखाना
Fort	–	किला
Bracket	–	कोनियाँ
Tile	–	खपरैल
Granary	–	खलिहान
Window	–	खिड़की
Storey	–	खंड

Words		हिन्दी
Cupola	–	गुम्बज
Platform	–	चबूतरा
Cesspool	–	चहबच्चा
Aviary	–	चिड़ियाखाना
Lime	–	चूना
Door Frame	–	चौखट
Bar	–	छड़
Roof	–	छत
Shed	–	छप्पर
Lattice	–	जाली (पत्थर की)
Chain	–	जंजीर
Cottage	–	झरोखा
Railing	–	डंडहरा
Step	–	डंडा (सीढ़ी का)
Cell	–	तहखाना
Door	–	दरवाजा
Peg	–	खूंटी
Church	–	गिरजाघर

Name of relatives

रिश्तेदारों के नाम

Words		हिन्दी
Guest	–	अतिथि, यजमान
Adopted Daughter	–	दत्तक कन्या
Teacher	–	अध्यापक
Mother	–	अम्मा, माता
Tenant	–	किराएदार

Words		हिन्दी
Mistress	–	उप-पत्नी
Preceptor	–	गुरु
Customer	–	ग्राहक
Uncle	–	चाचा
Aunt	–	चाची

Words		हिन्दी	Words		हिन्दी
Landlord	–	जमींदार	Friend	–	दोस्त, मित्र
Sister in law	–	ननद, जेठानी, देवरानी	Maternal-Grandfather	–	नाना
Father	–	पिता	Maternal-Grandmother	–	नानी
Son	–	पुत्र	Husband	–	पति
Daughter	–	पुत्री	Wife	–	पत्नी
Love affection	–	प्रेम	Daughter-in-law	–	पतोहू
Lover	–	प्रेमी	Mistress	–	रखैल
Sister	–	बहन	Patient	–	रोगी
Brother-in-law	–	बहनोई	Heir	–	वारिस
Nephew	–	भतीजा, भांजा	Pupil	–	शिष्य
Niece	–	भतीजी, भांजी	Own	–	सगा
Brother	–	भाई	Father-in-law	–	ससुर
Maternal Uncle	–	मामा	Mother-in-law	–	सास
Maternal Aunt	–	मामी	Relation	–	संबंध
Client	–	मुवक्किल	Relative	–	संबंधी
Mother's sister	–	मौसी	Step daughter	–	सौतेली पुत्री
Adopted son	–	दत्तक पुत्र	Step son	–	सौतेला पुत्र
Grandfather	–	दादा	Step father	–	सौतेला बाप
Grandmother	–	दादी	Step sister	–	सौतेली बहन
Son-in-law	–	दामाद	Step brother	–	सौतेला भाई

Name of foods & Spices

खाद्य पदार्थ एवं उनके मसालों के नाम

Words		हिन्दी	Words		हिन्दी
Milk	–	दूध	Gum acacia	–	बबूल का गोंद
Paddy	–	धान	Ice	–	बरफ
Tomato sauce	–	टमाटर की चटनी	Pearl millet	–	बाजरा
Cheese	–	पनीर	Biscuit	–	बिस्कुट
Loaf	–	पाव रोटी	Corn-ear	–	भुट्टा
Poppy	–	पोस्ट	Feast	–	भोज, दावत

Words		हिन्दी
Food	–	भोजन
Pickle	–	अचार
Grain	–	अनाज, धान्य, कर्ण, दाना
Pigeon Pea	-	अरहर
Arrowroot	–	अरारोट
Flour	–	आटा
Comfit	–	इलायची दाना
Phaseolies Mungo	-	उड़द
Curry	–	कढ़ी, रसा, शोरबा
Tea	–	चाय
Beaten Paddy	–	चिड़वा
Sugar	–	चीनी
Bran	–	चोकर
Cheese	–	छैना, पनीर
Millet	–	ज्वार, बाजरा, मोटा अनाज
Snacks	–	जलपान
Oat	–	जई
Coffee	–	कहवा
Mince meat	–	कीमा
Ice-cream	–	कुल्फी
Cluster bean	–	ग्वार
Wheat	–	गेहूँ
Clarified butter	–	शुद्ध घी
Field pea	–	गोल मटर
Sauce	–	चटनी
Gram	–	चना
Chapati	–	चपाती
Rice	–	चावल
Lunch	–	दिन का भोजन

Words		हिन्दी
Maize		पकई
Butter	-	मक्खन
Pea	-	मटर
Whey	–	मट्ठा
Cream	–	मलाई
Lentil	–	मसूर
Meat	–	मांस
Beef	–	मांस (गाय का)
Oat-meal	–	जई का आटा
Barley	–	जौ
Great millet	–	जुवार, चोलम
Broth	–	जूस, यूष, शोरबा
Vegetable	–	तरकारी, सब्जी
Sesame	–	तिल
Oil	–	तेल
Gruel	–	दलिया
Curd	–	दही
Pulse	–	दाल
Mutton	–	मांस (बकरे का)
Pork	–	मांस (सूअर का)
Sweetmeat	–	मिठाई
Sugar candy	–	मिश्री
Murabba	-	मुरब्बा
Puffed rice	–	मुरमुरा
Kidney-bean	–	मूंग
Maida	–	मैदा
Buck-wheat	–	मोथी
Mustard	–	राई, सरसों
Dinner	–	रात का भोजन

Words		हिन्दी
Castor seed	–	रेंडी
Bread	–	रोटी, डबलरोटी
Loaf sugar	–	पाव चीनी
Syrup	–	शर्बत
Treacle	–	शीरा, राब, चाश्नी
Wine	–	शराब
Honey	–	शहद
Mustard	–	सरसों
Vinegar	–	सिरका
Semolina	–	सूजी
White Mustard	–	सफेद सरसों
Caraway	–	अजवाइन
Linseed	–	अलसी का बीज
Phyllanthus emblica	–	आंवला
Cardamom	–	इलायची
Catechu	–	कत्था, खैर
Camphor	–	कपूर
Nitre	–	कलमी शोरा
Mace	–	जावित्री
Cumin	–	जीरा
Niger	–	तिली, रामतिल
Basil	–	तुलसी
Cassia	–	तेजपात
Cinnamon	–	दालचीनी
Coriander seed	–	धनिया
Salt	–	नमक
Menthol	–	पोदिने का सत
Indian madder	–	मजीठा
Gallnut	–	माजूफल
Red pepper, Chilli	–	लाल मिर्च
Liquorice	–	मुलेठी
Clove	–	लौंग
Musk	–	कस्तूरी
Black pepper	–	काली मिर्च
Saffron	–	केसर
Cocaine	–	कोकन
Yeast	–	खमीर
Poppy seed	–	खसखस
Sandal	–	चंदन
Chirata	–	चिरायता
Nutmeg	–	जायफल
Meadow saffron	–	शरद केसर
Origanum	–	शिकाकाई
Saltpetre	–	शोरा
Pistil	–	स्त्री केसर
Betel-nut	–	सुपारी
Dry ginger	–	सौंठ
Sago	–	साबूदाना
Turmeric	–	हल्दी
Myrobalan	–	हड
Asafoetida	–	हींग

CHAPTER 6

- Name of flowers, fruits, dry fruits & vegetables
- Name of professions & occupations
- Animals english names
- Special verbs for spoken
- Antonyms

Name of flowers, fruits, dry fruits & vegetables

फल, फूल, मेवा और सब्जियों के नाम

Words		हिन्दी
Chestnut		अखरोट
Ginger		अदरक
Pineapple		अनानास
Pomegranate		अनार
Guava		अमरूद
Lily	–	कमलिनी कुमुदिनी
Bitter gourd	-	करेला
Cashewnut		काजू
Red pumpkin gourd		काशीफल
Currant		रसभरी
Mushroom		कुकुरमुत्ता
Fig		अजीर
Mango	–	आम, अम्ब
Peach	–	आड़ू
Potato	–	आलू
Bokhara plum	-	आलू बुखारा
Tamarind	–	इमली
Sugarcane	–	ईख
Cucumber	–	ककड़ी ख़ीरा
Jack Fruit	–	कटहल
Pumpkin	-	कद्दू
Carambola	–	कमरख
Oleander	–	कनेर
Lotus	–	कमल
Daisy	–	गुलबहार
Rose	–	गुलाब
Balln flower	–	गूलर का फूल
Marigold	–	गेंदा
Grass	–	घास
Luffa	–	छिया, तुरई
Colocasia antiquorum	–	अरबी
Snake gourd	–	चिचिंडा
Jasmine	–	चमेली

Words		हिन्दी
Luffa gourd	–	चिकनी तोरी
Sapodilla	-	चीकू
Sugar beet		चुकदर
Amorphophallus	–	जमीकंद
Pandanus	–	केतकी, केवड़ा
Banana	–	केला
Cucurbit gourd	–	कोहड़ा, फूट
Date	–	खजूर
Musk Melon	–	खरबूजा
Lime	–	खट्टा नींबू
Sour cherry	-	खट्टी चेरी
Apricot	-	खुबानी
Citron		गलगल, चकोतरा
Carrot	–	गाजर
Cabbage		बंद गोभी
Touch-me-not	-	हुई मुई
Crab apple		जंगली सेब
Prickly amaranth	–	कटीली चौलाई
Plum	–	आलू बुखारा
Black berry	–	जामुन
Olive	–	जैतून
Tobacco	–	तंबाकू
Water melon	–	तरबूज
Currant	–	दाख
Belladonna	–	धतूरा
Coriander	–	धनिया
Narcissus	–	नरगिस
Prickly pear	–	नागफनी
Coconut	–	नारियल
Amaranthus	–	चौलाई

Name of professions & occupations

पेशा एवं व्यवसायों के नाम

Words		हिन्दी	Words		हिन्दी
Newspaper vendor	–	अखबार वाला	Oilman	–	तेली
Teacher	–	अध्यापक	Tailor	–	दर्जी
Engineer	–	अभियंता	Broker	–	दलाल
Milkman	–	अहीर, ग्वाल	Druggist, Chemist	–	दवा विक्रेता
Turner	–	खरादने वाला	Midwife	–	दाई
Retailer		खुदरा विक्रेता	Dentist		दंत चिकित्सक
Prose-writer	–	गद्य लेखक	Shopkeeper	–	दुकानदार
Perfumer	–	इत्र	Messenger	–	दूत
Milkmaid	–	अहीरन, ग्वालन	Nurse	-	धाय
Compounder	–	औषधि बनाने वाला	Carder	–	धुनिया
Novelist	–	उपन्यासकार	Washerman	-	धोबी
Poet	–	कवि	Washerwoman	–	धोबिन
Butcher	–	कसाई	Draftsman	–	नक्शानवीस
Artist	–	कलाकार	Dancer	–	नाचने वाला
Artisan	–	कारीगर	Coachman	–	गाड़ीवान
Chauffeur	–	कार-चालाक	Peon	-	चपरासी
Farmer	–	किसान	Author	–	ग्रंथकार
Potter	–	कुम्हार	Artist, Painter	–	चित्रकार
Green vendor	–	कुंजड़ा	Vaccinator	–	चेचक के टीके लगाने वाला
Coolie	–	कुली	Watchman	–	चौकीदार
Coachman	–	कोचवान	Surgeon	–	सर्जन – शल्य चिकित्सक
Treasurer	–	खजांची	Landlord	–	जमींदार
Brasier	–	ठठेरा	Magician	–	जादूगर
Contractor	–	ठेकेदार	Book-binder	–	जिल्दसाज
Doctor	–	डॉक्टर	Weaver	–	जुलाहा
Postman	–	डाकिया	Shoemaker	–	जूता बनाने वाला
Tabla player	–	तबलची	Jeweller	–	जौहरी
Betel-seller	–	तमोली, पनवाड़ी	Compositor	–	टाइप करने वाला

Words		हिन्दी
Operator	–	मशीन चलाने वाला
Cleaner	–	मशीन साफ करने वाला
Boatman	–	मल्लाह
Water carrier	–	महरा
Sailor	–	मांझी (जहाजी)
Carrier	–	माल ढोने वाला
Proprietor	–	मालिक
Gardener	–	माली
Enameller	–	मीनाकार
Mechanic	–	मिस्त्री
Agent	–	मुनीम
Printer	–	मुद्रक
Clerk	–	मुंशी, लिपिक
Sweeper	–	मेहतर (भंगी)
Cobbler	–	मोची
Chemist	–	रसायनशास्त्री
Cook	–	रसोइया
Mason	–	राजमिस्त्री
Politician	–	राजनीतिज्ञ
Cashier	–	रोकड़िया (खजांची)
Dramatist	–	नाटककार
Baker	–	नानबाई
Inspector	–	निरीक्षक
Auctioneer	–	नीलाम करने वाला
Examiner	–	परीक्षक
Priest	–	पुरोहित
Constable	–	पुलिस का सिपाही
Publisher	–	प्रकाशक
Manager	–	प्रबंधकर्ता

Words		हिन्दी
Hawker	–	फेरीवाला
Photographer	–	फोटो खींचने वाला
Carpenter	–	बढ़ई
Draper	–	बजाज
Conductor	–	बस का टिकट देने वाला
Seedsman	–	बीज विक्रेता
Butler	–	भंडारी
Fisherman	–	मछुवारा
Sculptor	–	मूर्तिकार
Editor	–	संपादक
Barber	–	हज्जाम, नाई
Train Ticket Examiner	–	टिकट पर्यवेक्षक
Ink man	–	रोशनाई वाला
Painter	–	रंगसाज
Dyer	–	रंगरेज
Writer	–	लेखक
Blacksmith	–	लौहार
Advocate	–	वकील
Physician	–	वैद्य
Artisan	–	शिल्पकार
Teacher	–	शिक्षक
Glazier	–	शीशा लगाने वाला
Musician	–	संगीतकार
Sanitary, Inspector	–	सफाई
Goldsmith	–	सुनार
Merchant	–	सौदागर
Confectioner	–	हलवाई
Waiter	–	होटल में खाना खिलाने वाला

Animals english names

जानवरो के नाम

Words	हिन्दी
Camel	ऊँट
Kangaroo	कंगारू
Bitch	कुतिया
Rabbit	खरगोश
Musk-deer	कस्तूरी मृग
Dog	कुत्ता
Mule	खच्चर
Hare	खरगोश
Hoof	खुर, शफ
Cow	गाय
Rhinoceros	गैंडा
Porcupine	साही
Lion	सिंह
Deer	हिरन
Elephant	हाथी
Ass	गधा
Squirrel	गिलहरी
Zebra	गोरखर (जैब्रा)
Mare	घोड़ी
Panther	चीता
Mouse	चूहा
Boar	जंगली सूअर
Horse	घोड़ा
Colt	घोड़ का बच्चा
Ant eater	चींटीखोर
Mole	छछूदर
Giraffe	जिराफ
Pony	टट्टू
Mongoose	नवला
Beast	पशु
Sire	नरपशु
He-goat	बकरा

Words	हिन्दी
She-calf	बछिया
Kitten	बिल्ली का बच्चा
Chimpanzee	वनमानुष
Hind	बारहसिंगा मादा
Bear	भालू
Sheep	भेड़
Lamb	भेड़ का बच्चा
Ram	भेड़
Rat	मूसा, चूहा
Hyena	लकड़बग्घा
Hound	शिकारी कुत्ता
Spaniel	झबरा कुत्ता
Leopard	तेंदुआ
Tail	दुम
Claw	पंजा
Puppy	पिल्ला
She-goat	बकरी
Calf	बछड़ा
Cat	बिल्ली
Monkey	[illegible]
Tiger	[illegible]
Ox	[illegible]
Wolf	[illegible]
Ewe	[illegible]
Buffalo	[illegible]
Kid	मेमना
Fox	लोमड़ी
Ape	लंगूर
Bull	साँड
Jackal	सियार, गीदड़
Pig Swine	सूअर
Fawn	हिरण का बच्चा

Special verbs for spoken

कुछ महत्वपूर्ण मिश्रित शब्द

1. Bestow – प्रदान करना
2. Bet – शर्त लगाना
3. Betray – विश्वासघात करना
4. Beware – सावधान होना
5. Bewilder – मरमाना
6. Bewitch – मोहित करना
7. Bid – आज्ञा देना
8. Bid – नीलामी में बोली देना
9. Billow – लहराना
10. Blacken – काला करना
11. Blame – इल्जाम लगाना
12. Blend – मिलना, मिलाना
13. Blood – खून
14. Bless – आशीर्वाद देना
15. Blindfold – आँख पर पट्टी बांधना
16. Blink – आंख मारना
17. Bloat – फूलना. सूजना
18. Blow – हवा का चलना, फूंक मारना
19. Bloom – वहना/फूंक मारना
20. Bluff – धोखा देना
21. Blunder – भारी भूल करना
22. Board – चढ़ना, सवार होना
23. Boast – शेखी मारना
24. Boil – उबालना
25. Boost – मजबूत बनाना
26. Borrow – उधार लेना
27. Bother – परेशान करना
28. Bow – सिर झुकाना
29. Bowl – गेंद फेंकना
30. Breath – सांस लेना
31. Breastfeed – दूध पिलाना
32. Breed – पालना
33. Brim – भरना
34. Bring – लाना
35. Broadcast – प्रसारित करना
36. Brood – सोचना, ध्यान करना
37. Browbeat – धमकाना
38. Budge – हिलना
39. Build – बनाना
40. Bulge – फूल जाना
41. Burn – जलना, जलाना
42. Burst – फटना
43. Bust – गिरफ्तार करना
44. Buzz – भिनभिनाना
45. Cal – पुकारना
46. Cancel – रद्द करना
47. Cane – बेत से पीटना
48. Canvass – पक्ष प्रचार करना
49. Capsize – उलटना
50. Carve – तराशना
51. Approve – मंजूरी देना
52. Arise – उठना
53. Arouse – जगाना
54. Arrange – इंतजाम करना
55. Arrive – आगमन होना
56. Ascend – चढ़ना

57. Aspire – तीव्र इच्छा होना
58. Assassinate – कत्ल करना
59. Assault – आक्रमण करना
60. Assemble – इकट्ठे होना
61. Assess – आँकना
62. Assist – सहायता करना
63. Associate – संयुक्त करना, मिलाना
64. Assure – विश्वास दिलाना
65. Astonish – चकित करना
66. Atone – प्रायश्चित करना
67. Attach – लगाना, जोड़ना
68. Attach – कुर्की करना
69. Attempt – प्रसन्न होना
70. Attract – आकर्षित करना
71. Avail – फायदा उठाना
72. Await – प्रतीक्षा करना
73. Awake – जागना
74. Barter – आदान–प्रदान करना
75. Base – आधारित होना
76. Batter – पीटना
77. Be – होना
78. Bear – जन्म देना, सहन करना
79. Beckon – हाथ से संकेत करना
80. Become – बनना
81. Befall – मुसीबत आ पड़ना
82. Befool – मूर्ख बनना
83. Boa – मिमियाना
84. Bake – सेंकना
85. Ban – रोक लगाना
86. Bar – रोकना
87. Bandage – पट्टी बांधना
88. Banish – देश से निकालना
89. Bargain – सौदेबाजी/मोलभाव करना
90. Beg – भीख मांगना
91. Begin – आरंभ करना, शुरू करना
92. Behold – देखना
93. Belittle – बेइज्जती करना
94. Belong – संबंध रखना
95. Bend – मोड़ना, झुकना
96. Benefit – फायदा होना
97. Bereave – वियोग, वंचित करना
98. Be seech – विनती करना
99. Beset – घेर लेना
100. Be set – व्याकुल करना
101. Abandon – त्यागना
102. Abduct – अपहरण करना
103. Abide – रहना
104. Abhor – घृणा करना
105. Abolish – समाप्त करना
106. Absolve – छोड़ना (मुक्त करना)
107. Absurb – सीखना
108. Abstain – परहेज करना
109. Accompany – साथ देना
110. Accumulate – इकट्ठा करना
111. Accuse – इल्जाम लगाना
112. Achieve – प्राप्त करना
113. Aquire – प्राप्त करना
114. Acuit – इल्जाम से मुक्त करना /बरी करना
115. Act – काम करना
116. Adapt – इस्तेमाल के लिए ठीक करना

117. Addict - लत पड़ना / आदी होना
118. Address - संबोधित करना
119. Adjourn - स्थगित करना
120. Administer - प्रबंध करना
121. Admire - प्रशंसा करना
122. Admit - मानना, स्वीकार करना
123. Adopt - गोद लेना
124. Adore - पूजना
125. Advise - सलाह देना
126. Advocate - वकालत करना
127. Affix - चिपकाना
128. Afford - खर्च कर पाना
129. Agitate - क्रोधित करना
130. Argue - बहस करना
131. Agree - सहमत होना
132. Aid - मदद करना
133. Aim - लक्ष्य साधना
134. Alert - सावधान रहना
135. Alight - उतारना
136. Allure - प्रलोभित करना
137. Ally - मैत्री करना संबंध करना, ज़ोड़ना
138. Amass - इकट्ठा करना
139. Amaze - आश्चर्यचकित होना
140. Amuse - मन बहलाना
141. Analyze - विश्लेषण करना
142. Annihilate - नष्ट करना
143. Annoy - चिढ़ाना
144. Annul - रद्द करना,
145. Anticipate - प्रत्याक्षित करना
146. Apologize - क्षमा मांगना
147. Appeal - प्रार्थना करना
148. Appear - प्रकट होना
149 Appease - शान्त करना
150. Apply - लगाना, मलना
151. Cast - ढालना
152. Cause - कारण होना
153. Celebrate - उत्सव मनाना
154. Cease - बन्द करना
155. Chain - जकड़ना
156. Challenge - ललकारना
157. Chase - पीछा करना
158. Chat - बातचीत करना
159. Chatter - बकवास करना
160. Cheat - धोखा देना
161. Chew - चबाना
162. Chide. - डाटना
163. Chirp - चहकाना
164. Choke - दम घोटना
165. Chop - काटना
166. Charm - मोहित करना
167. Clamber - चढना
168. Cleave - चीरना
169. Climb - चढ़ना
170. Coax - बहकाना
171. Collapse - ढहना गिरना
172. Collect - इकट्ठा करना
173. Collide - टक्कर मारना
174. Compel - मजबूर करना
175. Complain - शिकायत करना
176. Communicate- वार्तालाप करना

177. Comply - नियम मानना
178. Conceal - छिपना छिपाना
179. Conceive - गर्भधारण करना
180. Concentrate - ध्यान लगाना
181. Conclude - निष्कर्ष निकालना
182. Confess - गलती स्वीकार करना
183. Confirm - प्रमाणित करना
184. Confuse - व्याकुल करना
185. Conserve - सुरक्षित करना
186. Console - सांत्वना देना
187. Construct - निर्माण करना
188. Contaminate - प्रदूषित करना
189. Conquer - जीतना
190. Consume - उपभोग करना
191. Contemplate - विचार करना
192. Converge - एक जगह इकट्ठा
193. Cough - खांसना
194. Corrupt - भ्रष्ट करना
195. Co-operate - सहयोग करना
196. Correct - ठीक करना
197. Correspond - पत्र व्यवहार
198. Cram - रटना
199. Crash - धड़ाके से टकराना
200. Crawl - रेंगना
201. Creep - रेंगना
202. Cremate - दाह संस्कार करना
203. Cross-quest - जिरह के सवाल
204. Crouch - झुककर बैठना
205. Crumble - धीरे-धीरे टूटकर गिरना
206. Crush - कुचलना
207. Cry - चिल्लाना
208. Cultivate - फसल उगाना
209. Curb - रोकना
210. Curve - मोड़ना झुकना
211. Damage - हानि करना
212. Dare - हिम्मत / साहस
213. Darn - रफू करना
214. Dawn - सुबह होना
215. Doze - घबराना, चौंधियाना
216. Dazzle - चकाचौंध करना
217. Deal - व्यापार करना
218. Debar - रोकना
219. Decamp. - एक-एक भाग जाना
220. Decant - निथारना
221. Decay - गलना, सड़ना
222. Decipher - समझना
223. Decide - निश्चय करना
224. Decrease - कम करना
225. Dedicate - समर्पित करना
226. Defeat - हराना
227. Defecate - मल त्यागना
228. Defend - रक्षा करना
229. Deter - टालना
230. Define - परिभाषा देना
231. Defy - उल्लंघन करना
232. Deliver - बाँटना
233. Demand - मांग करना
234. Demarcate - सीमा स्थिर करना
235. Dement - पागल करना
236. Demolish - ढाहना, ध्वस्त करना

237. Demonstrate - प्रदर्शन करना
238. Demote - पदावनत करना
239. Denote - सूचित करना
240. Deny - मना करना
242. Depend - निर्भर होना
243. Deploy - तैनात करना
244. Depress - उदास करना
245. Deprive - वंचित करना
246. Deposit - जमा करना
247. Depict - वर्णन करना
248. Derail - पटरी से उतरना
249. Descend - उतरना
250. Desert - त्यागना, छोड़ना
251. Deserve - योग्य होना
252. Desire - इच्छा करना
253. Design - रचना करना
254. Despoil - खसोटना
255. Detach - अलग करना, पृथक करना
256. Detain - रोकना
257. Deter - रूकावट डालना
258. Determine - दृढ़ निश्चय करना
259. Deteriorate - बिगड़ना
260. Detonate - फटना
261. Dethrone - राजगद्दी से उतारना
262. Devastate - नाश करना / उजाड़ना
263. Devour - लालच से खाना
264. Devote - समर्पित करना
265. Die - मरना
266. Differ - भिन्न करना
267. Dig - खोदना
268. Digest - पचाना, पचना
269. Direct - निर्देश देना
270. Disagree - सहमत न होना
271. Disappoint - निराश करना
272. Disburse - चुकाना
273. Disclose - प्रकट करना
274. Disconnect - काटना
275. Discover - खोजना
276. Discriminate - भेदभाव करना
277. Disgorge - उगलना
278. Disgrace - कलंकित करना
279. Disguise - भेष बदलना
280. Dislike - ना पसंद करना
281. Disgust - अरूचि उत्पन्न करना
282. Disperse - तितर-बितर करना
283. Display - प्रदर्शित करना
284. Dismantle - आवरण हटाना
285. Dismay - निराश करना
286. Dismiss - नौकरी से निकालना
287. Disrupt - अस्त-व्यस्त करना
288. Dissect - चीड़-फाड़ करना
289. Dissolve - घुलना, घोलना
290. Distribute - बांटना
291. Distinguish - भेद करना
292. Divide - भागों में बांटना
293. Divorce - तलाक देना
294. Dive - गोता लगाना
295. Divulge - भेद खोलना
296. Dodge - दूर भागना
297. Dominate - प्रभुत्व जमाना

298. Doubt – शक करना
299. Drag – खींचना
300. Dress – कपड़े पहनना
301. Drink – पीना
302. Draw – खींचना
303. Drizzle – बूंदा-बांदी होना
304. Dive – गोता लगाना
305: Drop – छोड़ना
306. Droop – झुकना / सूखना
307. Dry – सूखना, सुखाना
308. Dupe – धोखा देना
309. Dust – धूल
310. Dye – रंगना
311. Earn – कमाना
312. Ease – शांत करना
313. Edit – पत्र का संपादन करना
314. Educate – शिक्षित करना
315. Eject – बाहर निकालना
316. Elect – चुनना
317. Eliminate – हटाना, निकालना
318. Elevate – उठाना, उखाड़ना
319. Elope – घर से भागना
320. Elucidate – प्रकाश डालना
321. Embarrass – लज्जित करना
322. Embed – गाड़ना, दबाना
323. Embroider – कढ़ाई करना
324. Emit – छोड़ना, निकालना
325. Enamour – मोह लेना
326. Enclose – बंद करना, घेरना
327. Enact – लागू करना
328. Emphasize – जोर देना
329. Enable – योग्य बनाना
330. Encounter – मुठभेड़ करना
331. End – अंत होना
332. Endure – सहन करना
333. Enforce – लागू करना
334. Engage – नौकरी पर रखना
335. Engrave – नक्काशी करना
336. Engulf – पूरी तरह से निगलना
337. Enlarge – बड़ा करना
338. Enrage – क्रोधित करना
339. Enrich – धनी बनाना
340. Enslave – दास बनाना
341. Ensure – निश्चित करना
342. Entertain – मनोरंजन करना
344. Equip – सजाना, संवारना
345. Eradicate – खत्म करना
346. Error – गलती करना
347. Erupt – फटना
348. Escape – बचकर भागना
349. Escort – रक्षा के लिए साथ जाना
350. Establish – स्थापित करना
351. Estimate – मूल्य लगाना
352. Evacuate – बाहर निकालना
353. Exaggerate – बढ़ा-चढ़ाकर कहना
354. Examine – जांचना
355. Exasperate – क्रोधित करना
356. Exceed – बढ़ना
357. Excel – विशिष्ट होना
358. Excite – उत्तेजित होना

359. Exclaim - चिल्लाना

360. Exclude अलग करना

361. Execute - फांसी देना

362. Exhale - सांस लेना निकालना

363. Exhaust - खाली करना. छोड़ना / थकाना

364. Exhibit बढाना

365. Exonerate मुक्त करना हक बहाल करना

366. Expand बढान

367. Expel - निकाल देना

368. Expect आशा करना

369. Experience अनुभव करना

370. Expiate प्रार्याश्चित करना

371. Explode फटना

372. Exploit शाषण करना

373. Explore खोजना

374. Export निर्यात करना

375. Express व्यक्त करना

376. Extinguish बुझाना

377. Fabricate - निर्माण करना

378. Fade - फीका करना

379. Fascinate - मोह लेना

382. Fetch - लाना

383. Finalize - अंतिम रूप देना

384. Flatter चापलूसी करना

385. Flee - भाग जाना

386. Fling - फेंकना. छानना

387. Flicker - झिलमिलाना

388. Flirt - छल करना. किसी चीज के प्रति गंभीर होने का दिखावा करना

389. Float - तैरना

390. Flourish - समृद्धशाली होना

391. Flutter - फड़फड़ाना

392. Fold - मोड़ना, झुकना

393. Fondle - लाड करना

394. Forbear - धैर्य रखना

395. Forbid - मना करना

396. Forecast पूर्वानुमान लगाना

397. Foresee पहले से जान लेना

398. Forgo छोड़ना त्यागना

399. Form बनाना

400. Forsake छोड़ना

401. Forswear झूठी कसम खाना

402. Found स्थापित करना

403. Fracture [illegible]

404. Freeze जमाना, जमना

405. Frighten - डराना

406. Frown - मुँह बनाना

407. Fry - तलना

408. Fumble - टटोलना

409. Gag - मुँह मे कपड़ा ठूसना

410. Gain - लाभ प्राप्त करना

411. Gainsay - अस्वीकार करना

412. Garland माला पहनना

413. Gamble जुआ खेलना

414. Gargle गरार करना

415. Gasp - हाफना

416. Gaze - टक-टकी लगाकर देखना

417. Generate - उत्पन्न करना

418. Germinate - पैदा करना

419. Get - प्राप्त करना

420. Gift - तोहफा देना
421. Glare - चमकना
422. Gleam - जगमगाना
423. Glint - चमकना
424. Glower - तिरछी निगाह से देखना
425. Glue - चिपकना
426. Gnash - क्रोध में दांत पीसना
427. Gossip - गप्प मारना
428. Govern - शासन करना
429. Grant - प्रदान करना
430. Grasp - पकड़ना, समझना
431. Graze - चरना, चराना
432. Greet - अभिवादन करना
433. Grieve - दुख महसूस करना
434. Grin - दांत दिखाते हुए हँसना
435 Grind - पीसना
436. Grip - मजबूती स पकड़ना
437. Groan - कराहना
438. Grope - अंधेरे में टटोलना
439. Grow - उगना, उगाना
440. Gulp - जल्दी से निगलना
441. Gut - नष्ट करना
442. Halt - ठहरना
443. Handcuff - हथकड़ी
444. Hang - टांगना, लटकाना
445. Harass - पीड़ा देना, क्लेश करना
446. Hasten - जल्दी करना
447. Hate - घृणा करना
448. Haul - खींचना
449. Head - मार्ग दर्शन करना
450. Heal - घाव भरना
451. Hear - सुनना
452. Heave - आहें भरना
453. Heed - ध्यान देना
454. Hesitate - संकोच करना
455. Hew - काटना
456. Hoist - ऊपर उठाना, फहराना
457. Hop - कूदना, फुदकना
458. Horrify - डराना
459. Hover - मंडराना
460. Hug - गले लगाना
461. Hum - भिनभिनाना
462. Hush - चुप होना
463. Hypnotize - सम्मोहित करना
464. Identify - पहचानना
465. Illuminate - प्रकाशित करना
466. Imagine - कल्पना करना
467. Impersonate - भेष बदलना
468. Implicate - फंसाना
469. Implore - प्रार्थना करना
470. Import - आयात करना
471. Impose - लादना
472. Imprison - कैद करना
473. Inaugurate - उद्घाटन करना
474. Indicate - संकेत करना
475. Indulge - मौजमस्ती
476. Inrect - सही होना
477. Inflict - दण्ड देना
479. Infuriate - क्रोधित करना
480. Inhale - सांस लेना

481. Inlay – सड़ना
482. Inspire – प्रेरणा देना
483. Install – लगाना
484. Instruction – निर्देश देना
485. Intend – इरादा
487. Intercept – रोकना
488. Interrogate – प्रश्न पूछना
489. Intervene – हस्तक्षेप करना
490. Interweave – गूंथना, बटना
491. Interview – साक्षात्कार करना
492. Intoxicate – नशे में चूर होना
493. Intrigue – साजिस करना
494. Intrude – बिना अधिकार प्रवेश करना
495. Invent – अविष्कार करना
496. Involve – मिलना, मिलाना
497. Irritate – चिढ़ाना
498. Jab – घुसाना
499. Jeer – हंसी उड़ाना
500. Jeopardize – आपत्ति में डालना
501. Judge – निर्णय करना
502. Justify – उचित कारण बताना
503. Kid – ढकोसला करना
504. Kindle – प्रज्वलित करना
505. Knead – गूंधना
506. Kneel – घुटनों के बल बैढना
507. Knit – बुनना
508. Knock – खटखटाना
509. Lament – दुख प्रकट करना
510. Laminate – परत चढ़ाना
511. Lay – अण्डा देना
512. Lead – नेतृत्व करना
513. Lean – झुक जाना / झुकना
514. Leap – कूदना
515. Leave – छोड़ना
516. Lend – उधार देना
517. Let – अनुमति देना
518. Levy – कर लगाना
519. Liberate – मुक्त करना
520. Lick – चाटना
521. Lie – लेटना, झूठ बोलना
522. Lighten – हल्का करना
523. Limit – सीमा के भीतर बंद करना
524. Listen – सुनना
525. Lit – जलाना
526. Loiter – आवारा गर्दी करना
527. Lounge – आलस्य में पड़े रहना
528. Malign – नुकसान पहुचाना
529. Manifest – प्रकट होना
530. Masquerade – बहाना करना, स्वांग करना
531. Melt – पिघलना
532. Meditate – ध्यान लगाना
533. Mend – मरम्मत करना
534. Mention – वर्णन करना
535. Mishear – सुनने में भूल करना
536. Mislay – गलत जगह रखना
537. Moan – कराहना
538. Mortgage – गिरवी रखना
539. Motivate – उत्तेजित करना
540. Mount – चढ़ाना,
541. Mourn – शोक करना

542. Mow - घास काटना
543. Munch - चबाना
544. Multiply - गुणा करना
545. Murmur - बड़बड़ाना
546. Muster - इकट्ठा करना
547. Mutter - बड़बड़ाना
548. Narrate - वर्णन करना
549. Neglect - उपेक्षा करना
550. Negotiate - समझोता करना
551. Nibble - कुतरना
552. Nick - काटकर निशान लगाना
553. Nip - चुटकी लेना
554. Nod - सिर हिलाना
555. Nudge - कोहनी मारना
556. Nurse - बिमारी में देखभाल करना
557. Nurture - पालना, ध्यान रखना
558. Obscure - छिपाना
559. Observe - ध्यान देना
560. Obtain - प्राप्त करना
561. Occupy - पद ग्रहण करना। / छेकना
562. Occur - घटित होना
563. Omit - त्यागना
564. Operate - कार्य करना
565. Oppose - विरोध करना
566. Outbit - अधिक मूल्य लगाना
567. Outdo - आगे बढ़ना
568. Overdraw - जमा शशि ले अधिक निकालना
569. Over-see - निरीक्षण करना
570. Over-take - आगे निकल जाना
571. Own - मालिक होना
572. Pacify - शांत करना
573. Pamper - पूर्ण संतुष्ट करना
574. Pardon - क्षमा करना
575. Pare - कुतरना
576. Partake - भाग लेना
577. Participate - भाग लेना
578. Pat - थपथपाना
579. Patrol - गश्त लगाना
580. Patronize - संरक्षण करना
581. Pawn - गिरवी रखना
582. Peel - छिलका छिलना
583. Peep/Peer - झांकना
584. Penetrate - घुसाना
585. Perceive - ध्यान देना
586. Pick - इकट्ठा करना
587. Pierce - छेदना, भेदना
588. Pity - दया करना
589. Plant - भूमि में गाड़ना
590. Plead - प्रार्थना करना
591. Poke - फोड़ना
592. Poison - जहरीला बनाना
593. Plunder - लूटना
594. Poach - शिकार करना
595. Plunge - डूबना, डुबाना
596. Possess - अधिकार करना
597. Postpone - स्थगित करना
598. Pounce - झपटना
599. Practise - अभ्यास करना
600. Praise - प्रशंसा करना
601. Preach - उपदेश देना

602. Predict - भविष्य बताना
603. Prefer - अधिक पसंद करना
604. Preserve - रक्षा करना
605. Prescribe - निर्धारित करना
606. Preside - अध्यक्षता करना
607. Pretend - बहाना बनाना
608. Prick - चुभना, चुभाना
609. Proceed - आगे बढ़ना
610. Produce - उत्पन्न करना
611. Propagate - उत्पन्न करना
612. Propel - ढकेलना
613. Propose - प्रस्ताव रखना
614. Prosper - समृद्ध होना
615. Protest - विरोध करना
616. Protect - रक्षा करना
617. Pull - खींचना
618. Pursue - पीछा करना
619. Push - धक्का देना
620. Puzzle - व्याकुल होना
621. Quarrel - झगड़ा करना
622. Quaver - कांपना
623. Quench - प्यास बुझाना
624. Quiver - कांपना
625. Rage - क्रोध करना
626. Ram - टक्कर मारना
627. Ransack - लूटना
628. Ravage - नाश करना
629. Reach - पहुंचना
630. Realize - महसूस करना
631. Rear - पालना-पोषण करना
632. Rebel - विद्रोह करना
633. Rebuke - डांटना
634. Recite - कविता पढना
635. Recommend - सिफारिश
636. Rectify - ठीक करना
637. Reel - लड़खड़ाना
638. Refer - निर्देश देना
639. Regard - आदर करना
640. Regret - दुखी होना
641. Reign - शासन काल
642. Reinforce - मजबूत करना
643. Rejoice - आनंदित करना
644. Rejuvenate - फिर से युवा करना
645. Relieve - राहत देना
646. Rely - विश्वास करना
647. Remain - रहना
648. Repay - वापस चुकाना
649. Sacrifice - बलिदान देना
650. Salvage - नुकसान होने से बचाना
651. Satiate - संतुष्ट करना
652. Saw - आरी से चीरना
653. Scald - झुसलाना
654. Scale - तोलना
655. Scare - डराना
656. Scatter - बिखेरना
657. Scent - सुगंधित करना
658. Scold - डांटना
659. Scorch - झुलसाना
660. Scour - मांजना
661. Scream - चीखना

662. Scribble - घसीटना मारना
663. Scrub - रगड़ना
664. Seek - ढूँढ़ना
665. Scrutinize - सूक्ष्म जांच करना
666. Seem - लगना
667. Sense - आभास होना
668. Separate - जुदा होना
669. Serve - सेवा करना
670. Sew - सिलना
671. Shed - बहाना, बिखरना
672. Sharpen - पैना करना
673. Shirk - काम से जी चुराना
674. Shiver - ठंड से कांपना
675. Shoot - गोली मारना
676. Shout - चिल्लाना
677. Shower - बरसाना
678. Shrink - सिकुड़ना
679. Shrivel - सिकुड़ना, झुर्री पड़ना
680. Shudder - कांपना
681. Scuffle - नाश फेंकना
682. Shut - बंद करना
683. Sigh - आह भरना
684. Simmer - धीरे टपकना
685. Sink - डूबना
686. Situate - सचेत होना
687. Sleep - सोना
688. Slap - चाटा मारना
689. Slay - वध करना
690. Slink - धीरे-धीरे निकल भागना
691. Slobber - लार टपकना
692. Smear - पोतना
693. Smooch - आलिंग करके चुम्मा लेना
694. Smother - गला घोंटना
695. Snap - तोड़ना
696. Snatch - छीनना
697. Snigger - हसी उड़ाना
698. Snore - खर्राटे लेना
699. Snuff - सूंघना
700. Soak - भिगाना
701. Soar - ऊंचा उड़ान भरना
702. Sob - सुबकना, सिसकना
703. Soothe - शांत करना
704. Sort - छांटना
705. Sow - बीज बोना
706. Spare - रक्षा करना
707. Spatter - छितराना
708. Specialize - विशेष बनाना
709. Spell - बोलना
710. Spill - छलकना, छलकाना
711. Spin - सूत कातना
712. Spit - थूकना
713. Sponge - स्पन्ज से साफ करना
714. Sprain - मोच आना
715. Sprinkle - छिड़कना
716. Sprout - अंकुरित होना / करना
717. Sputter - बकना
718. Spy - जासूस
719. Squander - बहुत खर्च करना
720. Squeeze - निचोड़ना
721. Stab - पेट में चाकू मारना

722. Stagger - लड़खड़ाना
723. Stammer - हकलाना
724. Startle - डराना
725. Starve - भूखा मरना
726. State - वर्णन करना
727. Steer - रास्ते पर लाना
728. Stick - चिपकना
729. Sting - डंक मारना
730. Stir - हिलना, हिलाना
731. Stitch - सिलना
732. Stoop - झुकना
733. Strain - प्रयत्न करना
734. Strangle - गला घोंटना
735. Strangulate - गला घोंटकर मारना
736. Strengthen - शक्ति शाली बनना
737. Stress - जोर देना
738. Stretch - फैलाना
739. Strike - टकराना
740. Strip - खाल उतारना
741. Stub - बुझाना
742. Struggle - संघर्ष करना
743. Stuff - भरना
744. Stumble - ठोकर मारना
745. Stutter - हकलाना
746. Suck - चूसना
747. Submerge - डूबना
748. Suffer - पीड़ित होना
749. Suffocate - दम घोंटना
750. Suggest - सुझांव देना
751. Summon - बुलवाना
752. Supply - पूर्ति करना
753. Suppress - दमन करना
754. Survey - जांचना
755. Suspect - शक करना
756. Suspend - निलंबित करना
757. Swell - सूजना
758. Sustain - जारी रखना
759. Swagger - अकड़कर चलना
760. Swallow - निगलना
761. Swat - हाथ से मारना / कुचल देना
762. Swindle - ठगना
763. Swing - झूलना
764. Swoon - बेहोश होना
765. Swoop - झूलकर उतरना
766. Symbolize - प्रतीक होना
767. Symphathize - सहानुभूति जताना
768. Tally - मिलाना
769. Tame - पालना
770. Tear - फाड़ना
771. Telecast - प्रसारित करना
772. Tempt - प्रलोभन देना
773. Tend - देखभाल करना
774. Terminate - अंत करना
775. Terrify - डराना
776. Testify - प्रमाणित करना
777. Thaw - पिघलना
778. Threaten - धमकी देना
779. Thrill - रोमांचित करना
780. Thrive - समृद्ध होना
781. Throng - लगना

782. Thrust - धकेल देना
783. Thump - थपथपाना
784. Thunder - गरजना
785. Tie - बांधना
786. Tighten - मजबूत बनाना
787. Till - जोतना
788. Tolerate - सहन करना
789. Torment - दुख देना
790. Topple - लुढ़ककर गिरना
791. Trail - घसीटना
792. Trap - फँसना, फँसाना
793. Trample - कुचलना
794. Translate - अनुवाद करना
795. Transmit - प्रसारित करना/ देना
796. Tread - कदम रखना
797. Treat - व्यवहार करना
798. Tremble - कांपना
799. Trumpet - चिघांड़ना
800. Twist - ऐंठना, मोड़ना
801. Trust - भरोसा करना
802. Trim - काट-छांट करना
803. Unbend - सीधा करना
804. Undergo - गुजरना
805. Underlie - नीचे पड़े रहना
806. Undertake - आरम्भ करना
807. Undo - नाश करना
808. Untie - खोलना
809. Uphold - सहारा देना
810. Uplist - ऊँचा उठाना
811. Uproot - जड़ से उखाड़ना
812. Upset - परेशान करना
813. Urge - अनुरोध करना
814. Utter - उच्चारण करना
815. Value - कीमत लगाना
816. Vandalize - तोड़-फोड़ मचाना
817. Vanish - गायब होना
818. Vary - बदलना
819. Violate - उल्लंघन करना
820. Vomit - उल्टी करना
821. Wade - पानी में कठिनाई से पार जाना
822. Wail - विलाप
823. Wake - जागना
824. Walk - टहलना
826. Wander - भटकना
827. Warn - चेतावनी देना
828. Way-Lay - घात लगाना
829. Weave - बुनना
830. Whip - कोड़ा मारना
831. White - शुद्ध करना
832. Whisper - कानाफूसी करना
833. Widen - चौड़ा करना
834. Wield - फिराना
835. Wind - चाबी भरना
836. Wish - इच्छा होना
837. Withdraw - निकालना
838. Withhold - थामना
839. Wither - मुर्झाना
840. Withstand - रोकना, अड़ाना
841. Wobble - थर्राना, लड़बड़ाना

842. Wrestle - कुश्ती लड़ना
843. Wrap - ओढ़ना, लपेटना
844. Wriggle - तड़पना.
845. Wring - निचोडना
846. Yawn - जम्हाई लेना
847. Yell - चिल्लाना
848. Yex - हिचकी लेना
849. Yoke - नाथना
850. Yammer शिकायज करना
851. Yield - उत्पन्न करना
852. Younger जवान आदमी
853. Yokel - गंवार आदमी
854. Yore पुराना जमाना
855. Yule बड़ दिन का त्यौहार
856. Zany - मसखरा
857. Zebu - कूबडदार बैल
858. Zeal जाश

Antonyms

विपरीतार्थक शब्द

Words		Antonyms	
1. Truth	– सत्य	False	– असत्य
2. Unity	– एकता	Diversity	– भिन्नता
3. Verbal	– मौखिक	Written	– लिखित
4. Victory	– विजय	Defeat	– हार
5. Virtue	– गुण	Vice	– बुराई
6. Wisdom	– बुद्धिमानी	Folly	– मूर्खता
7. Wide	– चौड़ा	Narrow	– संक्रीण
8. Wild	– जंगली	Tame	– पालतू
9. Zeal	– उत्साह	Indifference	– उदासीनता
10. Allow	– स्वीकृति देना	Disallow	– अस्वीकृत करना
11. Advantage	– लाभ	Disadvantage	– हानि
12. Agree	– सहमत होना	Disagree	– असहमत होना
13. Appear	– प्रकट होना	Disappear	– अदृश्य होना
14. Approve	– स्वीकृत करना	Disapprove	– अस्वीकृत करना
15. Arm	– हथियारों से लैसे होना	Disarm	– बिना हथियारों के
16. Honest	– ईमानदार	Dishonest	– बेईमान
17. Honour	– सम्मान	Dishonour	– अपमान
18. Inclined	– झुका हुआ	Disinclined	– न झुका हुआ
19. Like	– पसन्द करना	Dislike	– न प्रसन्न करना
20. Order	– क्रम	Disorder	– क्रमहीन
21. Obey	– अज्ञा मानना	Disobey	– अज्ञा न मानना
22. Please	– प्रसन्न करना	Displease	– अप्रसन्न करना
23. Quality	– योग्य होना	Disqualify	– अयोग्य होना
24. Respect	– सम्मान	Disrespect	– असम्मान
25. Mount	– चढ़ना	Dismount	– उतरना
26. Ability	– योग्यता	Inability	– अयोग्यता
27. Arrest	– गिरफ्तार करना	Release	– मुक्ति करना

Words		Antonyms	
28. Armament	– शस्त्रीकरण	Disarmament	– निशस्त्रीकरण
29. Absurd	– असंगत	Reasonable	– तर्कसंगत
30. Acquit	– निर्दोष ठहराना	Convict	– दोषी ठहराना
31. Barren	– बंजर	Fertile	– उपजाऊ
32. Blessing	– आशीर्वाद	Curse	– अभिशाप
33. Boon	– वरदान	Bane	– विनाश
34. Bravery	– बहादुरी	Cowardice	– कायरता
35. Busy	– व्यस्त	Idle	– सुस्त
36. Brave	– बहादुर	Coward	– कायर / डरपोक
37. Broad	– चौड़ा	Narrow	– तंग, संकरा
38. Beautiful	– सुंदर	Ugly	– बदसूरत
39. Big	– बड़ा	Small	– छोटा
40. Beneficial	– लाभकारी	Harmful	– हानिकारक
41. Barbarous	– जंगली, असभ्य	Civilized	– सभ्य
42. Bold	– बहादुर	Timid	– कायर
43. Bright	– चमकीला	Dull	– धुंधला
44. Base	– नीच	Noble	– सज्जन
45. Beauty	– सुंदरता	Ugliness	– बदसूरती
46. Beginning	– शुरुवात	End	– अंत
47. Blunt	– बिना धार का	Sharp	– तेज, नुकीला
48. Belief	– विश्वास	Doubt	– संदेह
49. Benefit	– लाभ	Loss	– हानि
50. Blame	– दोष लगाना	Praise	– प्रशंसा करना
51. Care	– देखभाल करना	Neglect	– उपेक्षा करना
52. Cheerful	– प्रसन्न	Cheerless	– दु:खी
53. Clever	– चालाक	Stupid, dull	– मूर्ख
54. Clear	– साफ	Cloudy	– बादलों से ढका हुआ
55. Clean	– साफ	Dirty	– गंदा
56. Courageous	– साहसी	Discourageous	– हतोत्साहित

Words		Antonyms	
57. Complicated	– जटिल	Simple	– साधारण
58. Compliance	– पालन	Refusal	– अस्वीकृति
59. Condemn.	– न मानना, निंदा	Approve	– अनुमोदन करना
60. Confess	– स्वीकार करना	Deny	– अस्वीकार करना
61. Credit	– जमा करना	Debit	– त्रणांकन करना
62. Certain	– निश्चित	Doubtful	– संदेहजनक
63. Cheap	– सस्ता	Dear	– महंगा
64. Coarse	– मोटा	Fine	– पतला
65. cold	– ठंडा	Hot	– गर्म
66. cool	– ठंडा	Warm	– गर्म
67. Conceal	– छिपाना	Reveal	– प्रकट करना
68. Construct	– निर्माण करना	Destroy	– नष्ट करना
69. Construction	– निर्माण	Demolition	– ढ़हाव
70. Common	– साधारण	Rare	– अपूर्व, अनूठा
71. Casual	– आकस्मिक	formal	– यथादीति
72. Conquer	– जीतना	Yield	– झुकना
		Surrender	– हार मानना
73. Cruel	– निष्ठुर	Kind, Merciful	– दयावान
74. Close	– बंद करना	Disclose	– खोलना
75. Conclude	– निष्कर्ष निकालना	Begin	– आरंभ करना
76. Confidence	– आत्मविश्वास	Distrust	– अविश्वास
77. Continue	– जारी रखना	Discontinue	– जारी न रखना
78. Civilized	– सभ्य	Savage	– असभ्य
79. Compare	– तुलना करना	Contrast	– अंतर बताना
80. Consent.	– सहमति	Dissent	– असहमति
81. Concord	– संयोग	Discord	– विरोध
82. Coverage	– एक केन्द्र में मिलना	Diverge	– केन्द्र से विस्तृत होना
83. Caution	– सावधान	Negligent	– असावधान
84. Day	– दिन	Night	– रात

Words		Antonyms	
85. Dark	– अंधेरा	Light	– प्रकाश
86. Danger	– खतरा	Safety	– सुरक्षा
87. Dead	– मृत	Alive	– जीवित
88. Defeat	– हार	Victory	– जीत
89. Desolate	– निर्जर, उजाड़	Inhabited	– बसा हुआ
90. Docile	– विनम्र	Stubborn	– जिद्दी
91. Domestic	– पालतू	Wild	– जंगली
92. Distress	– परेशानी	Comfort	– आराम
93. Deficit	– घाटा	Surplus	– फालतू/अतिरिक्त
94. Demand	– मांग	Supply	– पूर्ति
95. Dwarf	– बौना	Giant	– विशालकाय
96. Dynamic	– गतिशील	Static	– स्थिर
97. Deposit	– जमा करना	Withdraw	– निकालना
98. Delay	– देर	Haste	– जल्दी
99. Disclose	– प्रकट करना	Conceal	– छिपाना
100. Defensive	– रक्षक	Offensive	– घातक
101. Deep	– गहरा	Shallow	– उथला / छिछला
102. Difficult	– कठिन	Easy	– आसान
103. Deficient	– न्यून, कम	Sufficient	– पर्याप्त
104. Diligent	– परिश्रमी	Idle	– सुस्त
105. Disease	– बीमारी	Health	– स्वास्थ्य
106. Diminish	– कम करना	Increase	– बढ़ाना
107. Dull	– कमजोर	Bright	– होशियार
108. Death	– मृत्यु	Birth	– जन्म
109. Despair	– निराशा	Hope	– आशा
110. Earn	– कमाना	Spend	– खर्च करना
111. Early	– जल्दी, सवेरे	Late	– देर से
112. Economical Frugal	– मितव्ययी	Extravagent	– फिजूलखर्ची

Words		Antonyms	
113. Empty	– खाली	Full	– भरा हुआ
114. Enjoy	– आनंद उठाना	Suffer	– कष्ट उठाना
115. Encourage	– उत्साहित करना	Discourage	– हतोत्साहित करना
116. Entrance	– प्रवेश	Exit	– बहि–द्वार
117. Enthusiasm	– उत्साह	Indifference	– उदासीनता
118. Exterior	– बाहरी	Interior	– अंदर का
119. Expressed	– प्रकट किया हुआ	Understood	– छिपा हुआ
120. Expedite	– शीघ्र भेजना	Delay	– देर करना
121. Ebb	– छीड़ हो जाना	intensify	– तीव्र होना
122. Easy	– आसान	Difficult	– कठिन
123. Friendly	– मित्रता	Hostile	– शत्रुता
124. Freedom	– स्वतंत्रता	Slavery	– दासता
125. False	– झूठ	True	– सत्य
126. Fat	– मोटा	Thin	– पतला
127. Fame	– यश	Defame	– अपयश
128. Failure	– असफलता	Success	– सफलता
129. Fact	– वास्तविकता	Fictitious	– काल्पनिका/झूठा
130. Fast	– तेज	Slow	– धीमा
131. Fair	– साफ, सुंदर	Rough	– खुरदरा
132. Famous	– प्रसिद्ध	Notorious	– बदनाम
133. Fickle	– चंचल	Constant	– स्थिर
134. Final	– अंतिम	Initial	प्रारंभिक
135. Finite	– निश्चित	Infinite	– अनंत
136. Frank	– स्पष्टवादी	Reserve	– संकोची
137. Fresh	– ताजा	Stale	– बासी
138. Friend	– मित्र	Foe, enemy	– शत्रु
139. Fertile	– उपजाऊ	Barren	– बंजर
140. Fortune	– सौभाग्य	Misfortune	– दुर्भाग्य
141. Firm	– दृढ़	Weak	– कमजोर

Words		Antonyms	
142. First	– पहला	Last	– अंतिम
143. Foul	– अशुद्ध	Fair	– शुद्ध
144. Facility	– सुविधा	Difficulty	– कठिनाई
146. Foolish	– मूर्ख	Wise	– बुद्धिमान
147. Full	– भरा हुआ	Empty	– खाली
148. Fine	– बारीक	Coarse	– मोटा
149. Flexible	– लचीला	Rigid	– कठोर
150. Frown	– त्योरियाँ चढ़ाना	Smile	– मुस्कराना
151. Front	– सामने	Back	– पीछे
152. Foreign	– विदशी	Native	– स्वदेशी/देशवासी
153. Gain	– लाभ	Loss	– हानि
154. Glory	– यश	Shame	– शर्म
155. Genuine	– असली	Duplicate	– नकली
156. Giant	– विशालकाय	Dwarf	– बौना
157. Grant	– स्वीकार करना	Refuse	– अस्वीकार करना
158. Gather	– इकट्ठा करना	Scatter	– फैलाना
159. Glad	– प्रसन्न	Sad	– दुःखी
160. Grave	– गंभीर	Cheerful	– प्रसन्न
161. General	– सामान्य	Particular	– विशेष
162. Guilty	– अपराधी	Innocent	– निर्दोष
163. Gentle	– सभ्य	Rude	– असभ्य
164. Grand	– शानदार	Ordinary	– साधारण
165. Great	– महान	little	– तुच्छ
166. Guest	– मेहमान	Host	– मेजबान
167. Handsome	– सुंदर	Ugly	– कुरूप
168. Harsh	– कठोर, तीखा	Gentle	– सभ्य
169. Humble	– विनम्र	Proud	– अभिमानी / घमण्डी
170. Happiness	– प्रसन्नता	Misery	– दुःख, कष्ट
171. Hard	– सख्त, कठिन	Soft, Easy	– मुलायम, आसान

172. Haste	– जल्दी	Delay	– देरी
173. Hate	– घृणा करना	Love	– प्यार करना
174. Heavy	– भारी	Light	– हल्का
175. Heaven	– स्वर्ग	Hell	– नर्क
176. High	– ऊँचा	Low	– नीचा
177. Hope	– आशा	Despair	– निराशा
178. Honest	– ईमानदार	Dishonest	– बेईमान
179. Honour	– सम्मान	Dishonour	– अपमान
180. Heredity	– आनुवंशिकता	Environment	– पास-पड़ोस
181. Hopeful	– आशापूर्ण	Hopeless	– निराशापूर्ण
182. Import	– आयात	Export	– निर्यात
183. Increase	– बढ़ाना	Decrease	– घटाना
184. Ignorance	– अज्ञानता	Knowledge	– ज्ञान
185. Intentional	– इच्छानुरूप	Accidental	– अचानक
186. Illiterate	– अनपढ़	Literate	– पढ़ा लिखा
187. Include	– शामिल करना	Exclude	– निकालना
188. ill	– बीमार	Well	– भला चंगा
189. Innocent	– निर्दोष	Guilty	– अपराधी
190. Initial	– प्रारंभिक	Final	– अंतिम
191. Joy	– आनंद	Sorrow	– दुःख
192. Junior	– कनिष्ठ	Senior	– वरिष्ठ
193. Kind	– दयावान, दयालु	Unkind, cruel	– निर्दयी
194. Keen	– उत्सुक	Dull	– उदासीन
195. Lenient	– उदार	Strict	– कठोर
197. Love	– प्यार	Hatred	– घृणा
198. Laborious	– परिश्रमी	Lazy	– आलसी
199. Lie	– झूठ	Truth	– सत्य
200. Loose	– ढीला	Tight	– तंग
201. Limited	– सीमित	Unlimited	– असीमित
202. Lad	– लड़का	Lass	– लड़की, कुमारी

Words		Antonyms	
203. Lack	– कमी	Abundance	– पर्याप्त
204. Like	– पसंद करना	Dislike	– नापसंद करना
205. Logical	– तर्क संगत	illogical	– तर्कहीन
206. Little	– थोड़ा	Much	– बहुत
207. Light	– हल्का	Heavy	– भारी
208. Merit	– योग्यता	Demerit	– अयोग्यता
209. Miser	– कंजूस	Spendthrift	– अतिव्ययी
210. Mortal	– नश्वर	Immortal	– अमर
211. Mourn	– शोक मनाना	Rejoice	– खुशी मनाना
212. Mount	– चढ़ना	Dismount	– उतरना
213. Make	– बनाना	Mar	– बिगाड़ना
214. Master	– स्वामी	Servant	– नौकर
215. Maximum	– अधिकतम	Minimum	– न्यूनतम
216. Mad	– पागल	Sane	– स्वथ्य / समझदार
217. Material	– भौतिक	Spiritual	– पारलौकिक
218. Majority	– बहुमत	Minority	– अल्पमत
219. Minor	– अल्पव्यस्क	Major	– व्यस्क
220. Miserable	– दु:खी	Happy	– प्रसन्न
221. Minimise	– कम करना	Maximise	– अधिक करना
222. Neat	– साफ	Dirty	– गंदा
223. Noise	– शोर	Silence	– खामोशी
224. Negative	– नकारात्मक	Positive	– सकारात्मक
225. New	– नया	Old	– पुराना
226. Noble	– सज्जन	Ignoble	– दुर्जन
227. Natural	– प्राकृतिक	Artificial, Unnatural	– बनावटी
228. oral	– मौखिक	Written	– लिखित
229. Optimist	– आशावादी	Pessimist	– निराशावादी
231. Praise	– प्रशंसा करना	Blame	– दोष लगाना
232. Polite	– विनम्र	Impolite	– अशिष्ट
233. Poverty	– गरीबी	Affluence	– समृद्धि

Word	Meaning	Antonym	Meaning
234. Pious	– पवित्र	Impious	– अपवित्र
235. Prefix	– उपसर्ग	Suffix	– प्रत्यय
236. Prohibit	– मना करना, रोकना	Permit	– स्वीकृति देना
237. Precious	– कीमती	Worthless	– मूल्यहीन
238. Positive	– सकारात्मक	Negative	– नकारात्मक
239. Poetry	– कविता	Prose	– गद्य
240. Profit	– लाभ	Loss	– हानि
241. Pride	– अभिमान, घमंड	Humility	– विनम्रता
242. Punish	– दंड देना	Reward	– इनाम देना
243. Pure	– शुद्ध	Impure	– अशुद्ध
244. Peace	– शांति	Struggle	– संघर्ष, अशाक्ति
245. Permanent	– स्थायी	Temporary	– अस्थायी
246. Plenty	– बहुतायत	Scarcity	– न्यूनता-कमी
247. Prosperity	– समृद्धि	Adversity	– संकट, मुसीबत
248. Persuade	– राजी करना	Dissuade	– हतोत्साहित करना
249. Quick	– तेज	Slow	– मंदा
250. Quit	– छोड़ना	Occupy	– घेरना
251. Quiet	– शांत	Noisy	– शोरगुल पूर्ण
252. Question	– प्रश्न	Answer	– उत्तर
253. Real	– वास्तविक	Fictitious	– बनावटी
254. Rigorous	– कठोर	Simple	– सादा, साधारण
255. Recognise	– पहचानना	Ignore	– उपेक्षा करना
256. Reject	– अस्वीकार करना	Grant	– स्वीकार करना
257. Religious	– धार्मिक	Irreligious, secular	– अधार्मिक
258. Remember	– याद रखना	Forget	– भूल जाना
259. Reap	– काटना	Sow	– बोना
260. Retreat	– पीछे हटना	Advance	– आगे बढ़ना
261. Recover	– प्राप्त करना, ठीक होना	Loss	– खोना
262. Reduce	– कम करना	Increase	– बढ़ाना
263. Relief	– आराम	Trouble	– परेशानी
264. Rough	– खुरदरा	Smooth	– चिकना

Words		Antonyms	
265. Renowned	– प्रसिद्धि	Disgrace	– अपमान
266. Revel	– प्रकट करना	Conceal	– छिपाना
267. Rich	– अमीर	Poor	– गरीब
268. Rude	– अशिष्ट	Gentle	– शिष्ट
269. Rational	– विचारयुक्त	Emotional	– भावुक
270. Regular	– नियमित	Irregular	– अनियमित
271. Safe	– सुरक्षित	Unsafe	– असुरक्षित
272. Savage	– असभ्य	Civilised	– सभ्य
273. Sea	– समुद्र	Land	– धरती
274. Sensible	– समझदार	Senseless	– नासमझ
275. Simple	– साधारण	Complex	– जटिल
276. Strange	– अपरिचित	Femiliar	– परिचित
277. Strong	– मजबूत	Weak	– कमजोर
278. Sweet	– मीठा	Sour	– खट्टा
279. Superior	– श्रेष्ठ	Inferior	– तुच्छ
280. Strict	– कठोर	Lax	– शिथिल
281. Sickness	– बीमारी	Health	– स्वास्थ्य
282. Sympathy	– सहानुभूति	Antipathy	– घृणा
283. Stern	– कठोर	Mild	– कोमल
284. Sacred	– पवित्र	Profane	– अपवित्र
285. Steadfast	– दृढ़	Fickle	– अस्थिर
286. Solid	– ठोस	Liquid	– द्रव
287. Tighten	– कसा हुआ	Lossen	– ढीला
288. Thick	– मोटा	Thin	– पतला
289. Tame	– पालतू	Wild	– जंगली
290. Take	– लेना	Give	– देना
291. Timid	– कायर	Bold	– साहसी
292. Top	– चोटी	Bottom	– पेंदी
293. Tragedy	– दुखांत नाटक	Comedy	– सुखांत नाटक
294. Transparent	– पारदर्शक	Opaque	– अपारदर्शी
295. Tie	– बांधना	Untie	– खोलना

Words		Antonyms	
296. Above	– ऊपर	Below	– नीचे
297. Active	– सक्रिय	Passive	– निष्क्रिय
298. Accept	– स्वीकार करना	Refuse	– अस्वीकार करना
299. Acceptance	– स्वीकृति	Refusal	– अस्वीकृति
300. Alone	– अकेला	Together	– साथ-साथ
301. Acknowledge	– स्वीकार करना	Deny	– मना करना
302. Acute	– नोकीला, तीव्र	Obtuse	– मंद
303. Adversity	– विपत्ति, कष्ट	Prosperity	– सम्पन्नता
304. Affirm	– निश्चयपूर्वक कहना	Deny	– मना करना
305. Asleep	– सोया हुआ	Awake	– जागा हुआ
306. Analysis	– विश्लेषण	Synthesis	– संश्लेषण
307. Angel	– देवदूत	Devil	– शैतान
308. Ancient	– प्राचीन	Modern	– आधुनिक
309. Arrival	– आगमन	Departure	– गमन
310. Ascend	– चढ़ना	Discend	– उतरना
311. Assent	– स्वीकार करना	Dessent	– मतभेद करना
312. Attack	– आक्रमण करना	Defend	– रक्षा करना
313. Absent	– अनुपस्थित	Present	– उपस्थित
314. Attract	– आकर्षित करना	Repel	– पीछे हटाना, टालना
315. Admit	– स्वीकार करना	Deny, Refuse	– मना करना
316. Ample	– काफी	Meagre	– कम
317. Aware	– जागरुक	Unaware	– अनभिज्ञ
318. Adequate	– पर्याप्त	Inadequate	– अपर्याप्त
319. Advance	– आगे बढ़ना	Retreat	– पीछे हटना
320. Active	– क्रियाशील	Inactive	– निष्क्रिय
321. Accurate	– ठीक	Inacurate	– गलत
322. Correct	– शुद्ध	Incorrect	– अपूर्ण
323. Complete	– पूर्ण	Incomplete	– अपूर्ण
324. Definite	– निश्चित	Indefinite	– अनिश्चित
325. Direct	– प्रत्यक्ष	Indirect	– अप्रत्यक्ष
326. Efficient	– निपुण	Inefficient	– अनिपुण
327. Excusable	– क्षमा के योग्य	Inexcusable	– क्षमा के अयोग्य
328. Eligible	– उपयुक्त	Ineligible	– अनुपयुक्त

Words		Antonyms	
329. Effective	– प्रभावकारी	Ineffective	– प्रभावहीन
330. Sensible	– समझदार	Insensible	– नासमझ
331. Sincere	– सच्चा	Insincere	– बेईमान
332. Sufficient	– काफी	Insufficient	– कम
333. Able	– योग्य	Unable	– अयोग्य
334. Comparable	– तुलना के योग्य	Incomparable	– अतुल्य
335. Certain	– निश्चित	Uncertain	– अनिश्चित
336. Equal	– समान	Unequal	– असमान
337. Familiar	– परिचित	Unfamiliar	– अपरिचित
338. Fortunate	– भाग्यशाली	Unfortunate	– अभागा
339. Faithful	– वफादार	Unfaithfull	– विश्वासघाती
340. Fit	– योग्य	Unfit	– अयोग्य
341. Grateful	– कृतज्ञ	Ungrateful	– कृतघ्न
342. Happy	– प्रसन्न	Unhappy	– अप्रसन्न
343. Impressive	– प्रभावशाली	Uninpressive	– अप्रभावशाली
344. Important	– आवश्यक	Unimportant	– अनावश्यक
345. Just	– न्यायसंगत	Unjust	– अनुचित
346. Kind	– दयालु	Unkind	– निर्दयी
347. Lock	– ताला लगाना	Unlock	– ताला खोलना
348. Pardonable	– क्षमा के योग्य	Unpardonable	– क्षमा के अयोग्य
349. Prepared	– तैयार	Unprepared	– बेतैयार/कच्चा
350. Profitable	– लाभकारी	Unprofitable	– अलाभकारी
351. Pleasant	– प्रसन्न	Unpleasant	– अप्रसन्न
352. Real	– वास्तविक	Unreal	– अवास्तविक
353. Reliable	– विश्वसनीय	Unr	– अविश्वसनीय
354. Ripe	– पका हुआ	Unripe	– कच्चा
355. Sound	– स्वस्थ	Unsound	– अस्वस्थ
356. Steady	– स्थिर	Unsteady	– अस्थिर
357. Successful	– सफल	Unsuccessful	– असफल
358. Suitable	– योग्य	Unsuitable	– अयोग्य
359. Tie	– बांधना	Untie	– खोलना
360. True	– सत्य	Untrue	– असत्य
361. Usual	– साधारण	Unusual	– असाधारण

362. Wise	– बुद्धिमान	Unwise	– बुद्धिहीन
363. Movable	– अस्थिर	Immovable	– स्थिर
364. Moral	– नैतिक	Immoral	– अनैतिक
365. Probable	– संभावित	Improbable	– असंभाव
366. Pure	– शुद्ध	Impure	– अशुद्ध
367. Proper	– उचित	Improper	– अनुचित
368. Perfect	– पूर्ण	Imperfect	– अपूर्ण
369. Guide	– मार्गदर्शन करना	Disguide	– पथभ्रष्ट करना
370. Legal	– कानूनी	Illegal	– गैर-कानूनी
371. Legible	– पढ़ने योग्य	Illegible	– जो न पढ़ा जा सके
372. Noble	– सज्जन	Ignoble	– दुर्जन
373. Normal	– सामान्य	Abnormal	– असामान्य

CHAPTER 7

- Synonyms
- Homophones
- One words substitution
- Idioms and phrases
- Root words for spoken

Synonyms

समानार्थक शब्द

	Words	Synonyms	अर्थ
1.	Victory	conquest, success, triumph	(विजय)
2.	Vigilant	alert, watchful, cautions	(सावधानी)
3.	Vanish	disappear, depart, dissolve	(अदृश्य होना)
4.	Vice	sin, guilt, crime, evil	(बुराई, दोष)
5.	Vines	creepers	(बेल)
6.	Vendor	seller	(बेचने वाला)
7.	Vivid	glaring, Palpable	(स्पष्ट)
8.	Ways	manners	(ढंग)
9.	Wicked	evil, bad, cruel, sinful, wrong	(बुरा)
10.	Wisdom	prudence, sagacity, foresight	(बुद्धिमानी)
11.	Wealth	money, riches, property, assets	(धन)
12.	Wretched	unfortunate, mean, miserable	(अभागा, दुःखी)
13.	Wretch	rascal, brute	(नीच)
14.	Wedlock	marriage	(विवाह)
15.	Wise	sagacious, discerning, intelligent	(बुद्धिमान)
16.	Work	task, toil, labour, performance	(कार्य)
17.	Worry(V)	bother, stress, chafe	(चिन्ता करना)
18.	Worth	value, estimate, price, virtue	(कीमत)
19.	Wrong(N)	Amirs, false	(गलत)
20.	Wrong(Adj.)	awry, bad	(अशुद्ध)
21.	Withhold	unclean, imhure, incorrect resist, detain desidevate,	(रोकना)
22.	Yearn	pine, long, hanker, crave	(इच्छा होना)
23.	Yield	produce, give, bestow, surrender	(देना, समर्पण करना)
24.	Zeal	passion, eagerness, enthusiasm	(उत्साह)
25.	Zealous	fervent, eager, earnest, ardent	(उत्साहपूर्ण)
26.	Zenith	summit, top, apex, climax	(चोटी)
27.	Zigzag	crooked, oblique, rambling, devious	(टेढ़ा-मेढ़ा)

	Words	Synonyms	अर्थ
28.	Beautiful	handsome, charming	(सुन्दर)
29.	Build	construct, make, erect, raise, frame	(बनाना)
30.	Brief	concise, short, terse, compact	(संक्षिप्त)
31.	Bravery	valour, boldness	(बहादुरी)
32.	Battle	war, fight, encounter, combat	(युद्ध)
33.	Begin	start, Commence, induct	(आरम्भ करना)
34.	Big	vast, huge, immense, bulky	(बड़ा)
35.	Bane	curse, harm, injury	(शाप, हानि)
36.	Banish	expel, dismiss, oust, exile, debar	(निर्वासित करना, निकालना)
37.	Bear	tolerate, endure, suffer, sustain	(सहन करना)
38.	Benefit	gain, profit, good, advantage	(लाभ)
39.	Belief	faith, confidence, trust, credence	(विश्वास)
40.	Busy	occupied, engaged employed, unjust	(व्यस्त)
41.	Cruel	merciless, tyrant, unkind, unjust	(अत्याचारी क्रूर)
42.	Confess	admit, accept, own, acknowledge	(स्वीकार करना)
43.	Candid	frank, blunt, outspoken	(निष्कपट)
44.	Capture	seize, apprehend, arrest, trap, grasp	(पकड़ना)
45.	Chaste	clean, pure, virtuous, undefiled	(पवित्र)
46.	Champion	supporter, defender, victor, protector	(समर्थक)
47.	Commend	admire, praise, applaud, approve	(प्रशंसा' करना)
48.	Conceal	hide, veil, disguise, cover, shroud	(छिपाना)
49.	Concern	anxiety, worry, import, eagerness	(चिन्ता, सम्बन्ध)
50.	Conquer	win, vanquish, triumph, overcome	(जीतना)
51.	Contain	hold, consist, comprise, include, receive	(रोकना)
52.	Convict	captive, criminal, prisoner, felon	(अपराधी)
53.	Copious	ample, plentiful, adequate, enough, abundant	(पर्याप्त, बहुत)
54.	Corrupt	pervert, debased, dishonest, demoralised	(भ्रष्ट, पतित)
55.	Cunning	crafty, witty, shrewd, sly, clever	(चालाक)
56.	Courage	boldness, audacity, valour, gallantry	(साहस)
57.	Considerate	kind, humane, sympathetic, thoughtful	(हमदर्द)

	Words	Synonyms	अर्थ
58.	Contribute	subscribe, give, help, assist, share, supply	(देना)
59.	Confess	admit, accept	(स्वीकार करना)
60.	Consolation	solace, comfort	(धैर्य)
61.	Clever	skillful	(कुशल चतुर)
62.	Cultivate	grow, develop, produce, foster	(उत्पन्न करना)
63.	Conflict	strife, clash, fight, combat	(सघर्ष)
64.	Crime	vice, sin	(अपराध)
65.	Curtail	shorten, diminish, reduce, lessen	(कम करना)
66.	Delightful	pleasing, enjoyable, charming	(आनन्दपूर्ण)
67.	Dispute	quarrel, strife, fight, contention, controversy	(झगड़ा)
68.	Discover	find, reveal, discern, invent	(पता लगाना)
69.	Deny	refuse, reject, oppose, contradict	(इन्कार करना)
70.	Doubt	suspect, distrust, disbelief, hesitate	(सन्देह करना)
71.	Determination	resolution, will, decision	(निश्चय)
72.	Deliberate	cautious, thoughtful, intentional, careful	(विचारपूर्ण)
73.	Desolate	barren, lonely, forlorn, dreary	(निर्जन)
74.	Dead	lifeless, obsolete, extinct, deceased	(मृतक)
75.	Deed	work, action, act, exploit	(कार्य)
76.	Defeat	conquer, subdue, foil, frustrate	(हराना)
77.	Defer	postpone, suspend, delay, stay	(टालना)
78.	Dejection	sorrow, grief, despondency	(निराशा, दुःख)
79.	Delay	postpone, put off, defer, prolong	(देर करना)
80.	Deliver	give, handover, free, liberate	(देना)
81.	Demolish	destroy, wreck, ruin, raze	(नष्ट करना)
82.	Denounce	curse, accuse, decry, condemn	(निन्दा करना)
83.	Depict	portray, describe, show, exhibit	(वर्णन करना)
84.	Destination	goal, end, target, objective, aim	(लक्ष्य, मंजिल)
85.	Devastate	destroy, ruin, ravage, wipe out	(नष्ट करना)
86.	Develop	grow, cultivate, evolve, produce	(बढ़ाना)
87.	Destroy	ruin, raze, demolish, devastate	(नष्ट करना)

	Words	Synonyms	अर्थ
88.	Diminish	reduce, dwindle, lessen, waive	(कम करना)
89.	Discard	reject, abandon, oust, eliminate	(त्यागना
90.	Discord	strife, contention, clash, disagreement	(झगड़ा)
91.	Disaster	misfortune, calamity, tragedy, mishappening	(संकट)
92.	Devotee	votary, worshipper, disciple, enthusiast	(भक्त)
93.	Derogatory	defamatory, humiliation, disparaging	(अपमानजनक)
94.	Dexterous	clever, adept, deft, skillful, artful	(चुतर)
95.	Disgrace	insult, shame, dishonour, humiliation	(अपमान, अपयश)
96.	Display	show, manifest, exhibit, spread	(प्रदर्शित करना)
97.	Distribute	divide, classify, scatter, dispose	(बाँटना)
98.	Distress	trouble, grief, anxiety, discomfort	(संकट)
99.	Diversity	variety, variation, difference, dissimilarity	(विभिन्नता)
100.	Divine	holy, celestial, godlike, heavenly	(ईश्वरीय)
101.	Docile	gentle, humble, submissive, meek	(नम्र)
102.	Dreadful	fearful, horrible, awful, panicky	(भयंकर)
103.	Dull	boring, uninteresting, stupid	(नीरस, भद्दा)
104.	Dynamic	vigorous, forceful	(गतिशील)
105.	Earnest	serious, solemn, determined, intense	(गम्भीर, महत्वपूर्ण)
106.	Enemy	foe, opponent, adversary, antagonist	(शत्रु)
107.	Envy	jealousy	(ईर्ष्या)
108.	Effort	attempt, venture, endeavour	(प्रयत्न, प्रयास)
109.	Enough	sufficient, ample, plenty, adequate	(पर्याप्त)
110.	Error	mistake, fault, blunder, appear, delusion	(भूल)
111.	Emerge	arise, appear, issue	(निकालना)
112.	Encourage	cheer, incite, inspire, urge	(साहस बढ़ाना)
113.	Endure	bear, suffer, tolerate, undergo, sustain	(सहन करना)
114.	Endeavour	attempt, try, strive	(प्रयत्न करना)
115.	Enormous	huge, vast, immense, gigantic	(विशाल)
116.	Enthusiasm	Zeal, fervor, spirit, force, passion	(उत्साह)
117.	Entreat	request, implore, solicit, plead	(प्रार्थना करना)

	Words	Synonyms	अर्थ
118.	Eradicate	uproot, abolish, destroy, root out	(नष्ट करना, उखाड़ना)
119.	Erect	Build, construct, raise, set-up	(निर्माण करना)
120.	Esteem	honour, regard, respect, reverence	(सम्मान)
121.	Eternal	permanent, everlasting, endless, perpetual	(शाश्वत)
122.	Estimate	calculation, assessment	(गणना)
123.	Excuse	forgive, pardon	(क्षमा)
124.	Famous	popular, well known, renowned, eminent	(प्रसिद्ध)
125.	Fabricate	make up, invent, construct, build	(बनाना)
126.	Fame	repute, renown, eminence	(प्रसिद्धि)
127.	Fade	vanish, languish, dim, wither, pale	(मुर्झाना)
128.	Fatal	deadly, mortal, fateful	(घातक)
129.	Fierce	fearful, ferocious, violent	(भयंकर)
130.	Flaw	defect, mistake, error, fault	(दोष)
131.	Forbid	ban, prohibit, debar, restrain	(निषेध करना)
132.	Fraud	deceit, duplicity, deception, guile	(धोखा)
133.	Frenzy	fury, rage, madness, agitation	(उन्माद)
134.	Fortitude	courage, patience, endurance	(धैर्य)
135.	Freedom	liberty, self-reliance, independence	(स्वतन्त्रता)
136.	Faith	belief	(विश्वास)
137.	Force	power, strength, compel	(शक्ति, विवश करना)
138.	Gift	present, donation, contribution bounty	(उपहार)
139.	Gloom	darkness, shadow, dejection, sadness	(उदासी)
140.	Grief	sorrow, sadness, distress, misery	(दुःख)
141.	Grateful	thankful	(कृतज्ञ)
142.	Gentle	kind, placid, mild, docile, calm	(सज्जन)
143.	Grant	accept	(स्वीकार करना)
144.	Guess	suppose	(अनुमान लगाना)
145.	Hardship	difficulty, adversity, calamity	(कठिनाई)
146.	Hard	difficult	(कठिन)
147.	Homage	tribute	(श्रद्धांजलि)

	Words	Synonyms	अर्थ
148.	Humane	kind, merciful, sympathetic	(दयालु, मानवीय)
149.	Humble	meek, submissive, modest, lowly	(विनम्र)
150.	Hardly	scarcely	(मुश्किल से)
151.	Haughty	proud, arrogant, overbearing	(घमंडी)
152.	Holy	sacred, pious, saintly, godly	(पवित्र)
153.	Horror	fear, terror, dread, aversion	(भय)
154.	infinite	endless, limitless, boundless	(अनंत)
155.	Incredible	unbelievable	(अविश्वसनीय)
156.	Idle	inactive, lazy, unoccupied	(आलसी)
157.	Ideal	model, paragon, perfect, example	(आदर्श)
158.	Ignoble	low, mean, base, shameful	(अधर्म)
159.	Illustrious	famous, eminent, renowned	(प्रसिद्ध)
160.	Immense	great, huge, vast, tremendous	(बड़ा, विशाल)
161.	Immortal	perpetual, eternal, deathless, everlasting	(अमर)
162.	Impediment	obstacle, hindrance, obstruction	(बाधा)
163.	Incessant	continual, unceasing, unending	(निरन्तर)
164.	Independence	freedom, liberty, self-reliance	(स्वतंत्रता)
165.	Incite	stir, instigate, provoke, excite	(उत्तेजित)
166.	Industrious	active, hardworking, diligent	(परिश्रमी)
167.	Illegal	unlawful	(अवैधानिक)
168.	Indifference	apathy, unconcern	(अरुचि)
169.	Impression	effect	(प्रभाव)
170.	Joy	pleasure, delight, happiness	(प्रसन्नता)
171.	Junk	rubbish, refuse	(कबाड़)
172.	Knave	scoundrel, villain, rascal, rogue	(दुष्ट)
173.	Legal	legitimate, lawful	(कानूनी)
174.	Lack	shortage, need, want, deficiency	(कमी)
175.	Languish	decline, weaken, fade, droop	(कमजोर होना)
176.	Lazy	idle, indolent, sluggish	(सुस्त, आलसी)
177.	Liberty	freedom, independence, emancipation	(मुक्ति, आजादी)

	Words	Synonyms	अर्थ
178.	Lieutenant	deputy	(डिप्टी)
179.	Mad	insane	(पागल)
180.	Massacre	carnage, slaughter, butchery	(हत्याकांड)
181.	Magnificent	grand, splendid, noble, majestic	(शानदार)
182.	Mourn	grieve, lament, bewail, bemoan	(विलाप करना)
183.	Mysterious	secret, baffling, obscure, hidden	(रहस्यपूर्ण)
184.	Mutiny	rebellion, revolt	(विद्रोह)
185.	Manifest	show, display, disclose	(स्पष्ट करना)
186.	Melancholy	sad, dejected, depressed	(दु:खी)
187.	Marvel	a wonderful thing	(आश्चर्यजनक वस्तु)
188.	Mistake	error	(भूल, गलती)
189.	Misery	misfortune	(दुर्भाग्य)
190.	Naughty	troublesome, mischievous, wayward	(नटखट)
191.	Nefarious	evil, wicked, unlawful	(शर्मनाक)
192.	Obligatory	necessary, imperative, compulsory	(आवश्यक)
193.	Obsolete	extinct, outworn, discarded	(अप्रचलित)
194.	Obstacle	hindrance, barrier, obstruction	(बाधा)
195.	Obtain	get, attain, acquire, procure, gain	(प्राप्त करना)
196.	Obvious	clear, evident, plain, manifest, distinct	(स्पष्ट)
197.	Offence	attack, wrong, misdeed, insult	(अपराध)
198.	Oppressive	tyrannical, cruel, grinding	(अत्याचारी)
199.	Overcome	conquer, overthrow, defeat, subdue	(विजय प्राप्त करना)
200.	Oust	remove, dislodge, depose	(हटाना)
201.	Outstanding	remarkable, eminent, prominent	(प्रमुख)
202.	Obscene	indecent, filthy	(अश्लील)
203.	Oral	verbal	(मौखिक)
204.	Occupation	Profession	(पेशा)
205.	Opportunities	Chances	(अवसर)
206.	Opposite	reverse	(उल्टा)
207.	Obedient	dutiful	(आज्ञाकारी)

	Words	Synonyms	अर्थ
208.	Pledge	promise, vow, oath	(प्रतिज्ञा)
209.	Pact	treaty, agreement, bargain, accord	(समझौता)
210.	Pardon	excuse, forgive, overlook, tolerate	(क्षमा करना)
211.	Peril	danger, risk, hazard, snare	(खतरा)
212.	Peak	top, summit, zenith, climax, apex	(चोटी)
213.	Pensive	thoughtful, sad, dejected, reflective	(उदास)
214.	Perpetual	ceaseless, everlasting, eternal	(नित्य)
215.	Prey	victim	(शिकार)
216.	Pace	progress	(उन्नति)
217.	Power	strength, force	(शक्ति)
218.	Pain	sorrow	(दुःख)
219.	Pay(N)	salary	(वेतन)
220.	Possible	probable	(सम्भव)
221.	Praise(N)	applause, admiration, approval, tribute	(प्रशंसा)
222.	Prohibit	forbid	(मना करना)
223.	Pierce	penetrate, puncture	(चुभना)
224.	Plead	urge	(प्रार्थना करना)
225.	Polite	courteous, civil, refined, polished	(विनम्र)
226.	Ponder	think, reflect, muse, deliberate	(सोचना)
227.	Postpone	defer, delay, put off, adjourn	(स्थगित करना)
228.	Pray	beg, request, entreat, implore	(प्रार्थना)
229.	Precious	costly, invaluable, priceless	(बहुमूल्य)
230.	Prevent	check, stop, hinder, restrain, interrupt	(रोकना)
231.	Prize	trophy, medal, award,	(इनाम)
232.	Proceed	Progress, advance, move, continue	(आगे बढ़ाना)
233.	Prominent	eminent, distinguished	(प्रसिद्ध)
234.	Protect	guard, save, defend, shield	(रक्षा करना)
235.	Quarrel	dispute, controversy	(झगड़ा)
236.	Queer	strange, odd, peculiar, unusual	(विचित्र)
237.	Quiet	peaceful, silent, serene, still, placid	(शान्त)

	Words	Synonyms	अर्थ
238.	Quit	leave, abandon, forsake, relinquish	(छोड़ना)
239.	Recover	regain, redeem, obtain, restore	(प्राप्त करना)
240.	Release	free, liberate, relinquish, discharge	(मुक्त करना)
241.	Reliable	responsible, trustworthy, dependable	(विश्वास योग्य)
242.	Rescue	save, liberate, free	(बचाना)
243.	Rage	anger, wrath, fury, resentment	(क्रोध)
244.	Raise	lift, increase, incite, elevate	(उठाना)
245.	Rapid	quick, swift, speedy, fast, agile	(तेज, शीघ्र)
246.	Raze	destroy, demolish, level, join	(नष्ट करना)
247.	Reach	arrive, attain, gain, land, join	(पहुंचना)
248.	Rival	opponent, contender, competitor	(विरोधी, प्रतिद्वंद्वी)
249.	Ruin	destruction, week, downfall	(विनाश)
250.	Rude	uncivil, insolent, discourteous	(असभ्य, अशिष्ट)
251.	Rigid	strict, inflexible	(कठोर)
252.	Regular	steady	(नियमित)
253.	Revolt	rebellion	(राजद्रोह)
255.	Savage	wild, rude, barbarous, uncivilized	(जंगली)
256.	Scorn	contempt, disdain, hate, dislike	(घृणा करना)
257.	Scrupulous	exact, careful	(सचेत, सावधान)
258.	Seize	grasp, arrest, capture, confiscate	(पकड़ना)
260.	Strange	queer, odd, unusual	(विचित्र)
263.	Summit	top, apex, peak, zenith	(चोटी)
264.	Spurious	false, counterfeit, deceptive, sham	(नकली)
265.	Stable	lasting, steady, firm, unchanging	(स्थिर)
266.	Stain	blot, spot, mark, speck	(धब्बा)
267.	Stately	grand, majestic, dignified, lofty	(शानदार)
268.	Steady	firm, stable, lasting, enduring	(दृढ़)
269.	Steal	rob, bluff, plunder, thieve	(चुराना)
270.	Stern	severe, austere, rigorous, harsh	(कठोर)
271.	Still	silent, calm, noiseless, motionless	(शान्त)

Words	Synonyms	अर्थ
272. Stop	halt, cease, hinder, block, impede	(रोकना)
273. Story	tale, fable, anecdote, fiction, myth	(कहानी)
274. Storm	tempest, agitation, commotion	(तूफान)
275. Straight	direct, right, erect, regular	(सीधा)
277. Strong	mighty, sturdy, robust, powerful	(शक्तिशाली)
279. Stupid	dull, foolish, obtuse	(मूर्ख)
280. Target	aim, mark, goal, object	(लक्ष्य)
281. Tedious	boring, wearisome, dull, monotonous	(थकाने वाला)
282. Timid	shy, cowardly, afraid, fearful, diffident	(डरपोक)
283. Timber	tone	(ध्वनि)
284. True	correct	(सत्य, ठीक)
285. Trust	belief, faith, reliance, confidence, hope	(विश्वास)
286. Tremendous	huge, enormous, vast, immense	(विशाल)
287. Triumph	victory, conquest, achievement	(विजय, सफलता)
288. Traits	qualities, characteristics	(गुण)
289. Teach	coach	(पढ़ाना)
290. Transient	momentary, not lasting	(अस्थिर)
291. Thick	not fine	(मोटा)
292. Unique	matchless, rare, uncommon	(अद्वितीय)
293. Ugly	homely, plain, repulsive, hideous	(कुरुप)
294. Uphold	support, maintain, approve, champion	(समर्थन करना)
295. Uproar	tumult, confusion, hubbub	(कोलाहल)
296. Urge	lead, exhort, solicit	(आग्रहपूर्वक निवेदन करना)
297. Urgent	pressing, compelling, immediate	(आवश्यक)
298. Unite	join, connect	(जोड़)
299. Vague	indistinct, obscure, indefinite	(अस्पष्ट)
300. Venture	dare, risk, undertake, hazard	(साहस करना)
301. Absurd	Funny, stupid, senseless	(भद्दा)
302. Aid	help, support, assistance, relief	(सहायता)
303. Allow	Permit, assent, accord	(स्वीकृति देना)

304.	Abstain	Refrain	(बचे रहना)
305.	Admit	Confess	(स्वीकार करना)
306.	Anger	resentment, wrath, fury rage	(क्रोध)
307.	Adept	Skillful, expert, dexterous, apt	(कुशल)
308.	Ascent	Rise, lift, elevation, upswing	(चढ़ाव)
309.	Assent	Consent	(सहमत होना, स्वीकृति देना)
310.	Attack	assault, invasion, aggression	(आक्रमण)
311.	Attain	win, gain, achieve	(प्राप्त करना)
312.	Ability	capacity	(योग्यता)
313.	Abandon	give up, forsake, relinquish, quit	(छोड़ना)
314.	Abhor	hate, detest, dislike, despise	(घृणा करना)
315.	Abide	dwell, wait, live, stay	(रहना, प्रतीक्षा करना)
316.	Alter	change, vary, transform, modify	(बदलना)
317.	Antipathy	dislike	(घृणा)
318.	Ask	inquire, enquire, demand, beg, entreat	(पूछना, मागना)
319.	Aim	purpose	(उद्देश्य)
320.	Accept	grant. agree, assent, concur, receive	(स्वीकार करना)
321.	Alarm	danger, fright, fear, dread, panic, terror	(खतरा)
322.	Advantage	profit, gain, benefit, utility, help	(लाभ)
323.	Aggression	Attack, invasion, assault, onslaught	(आक्रमण)
324.	Abolish	Finish	(समाप्त करना)
325.	Achieve	accomplish	(प्राप्त करना)
326.	Apology	pardon, excuse, regret	(क्षमा)
327.	Arrogance	pride, insolence	(अभिमान)

Homophones

कुछ ऐसे शब्द जिनके उच्चारण भ्रमित करते हैं।

1.	Accept	स्वीकार करना	I gladly accept your gift.
	Except	अतिरिक्त, सिवाय	Except Ram all came to see me.
2.	Accede	सहमत होना	The principal acceded to my request
	Exceed	अधिक होना	My expenses exceed my income.
3.	Affect	प्रभाव डालना	His speech affected everyone.
	Effect	प्रभाव	My warning has no effect on you
4.	Assent	अनुमति	She has given her assent to me
	Ascent	चढ़ना	The ascent of Mt. Everest was a heroic event.
5.	Advice	शिक्षा सलाह	He gave me much advice.
	Advise	शिक्षा देना	The Doctor advised him to have bed-rest.
6.	Access	पहुँच	I have no access to the manager.
	Excess	अधिकता	Excess of everything is bad.
7.	Ant	चींटी	An Ant is a very small creature.
	aunt	मौसी	My Aunt is an M.B.B.S. Doctor.
8.	Allusion	सूचना, संकेत	I can give you several allusions to prove your point.
	Illusion	छल, इन्द्रजाल	We are living in a world of illusion.
9.	Altar	पूजा की बेदी	People still make animal sacrifice at the altar of gods and goddess.
	Alter	बदलना	We cannot alter the original plan.
10.	Apposite	योग्य, यर्थात्	Your remarks were quite apposite
	Opposite	विरुद्ध	There is a cinema opposite my house.
11.	All ready	सभी तैयार	My friends are all ready to help me.
	Already	पहले से	I have already seen the picture.
12.	All together	सभी साथ	The members walked out all together
	Altogether	पूर्णरूप से	Your ideas are altogether different from mine
13.	Aught	कोई वस्तु, बात	Have you taken any aught
	Ought	चाहिये	You ought to serve your old parents.
14.	Adopt	गोद लेना, विचार अपनाना	1. I have adopted the son of my brother or other. 2. Do not adopt western culture.
	Adapt	अनुकूल बनाना	My parents cannot adapt themselves to present atmosphere.
	Adept	चतुर	I am an adept in making friends.

	Word	Meaning	Sentence
15.	Bail	जमानत	The accused was released on bail.
	Bale	गाँठ	I have received four bales of cotton.
16.	Berth	सोने का स्थान	I got a berth reserved in Malwa express.
	Birth	जन्म	People are delighted at the birth of a son.
17.	Bridal	वैवाहिक	She brought many bridal presents to her husband's house.
	Bridle	लगाम	It is very difficult to bridle the horse.
18.	Beside	निकट	He was sitting beside me in the hall
	Besides	अतिरिक्त	He gave me books besides helping me with money.
19.	Born	पैदा होना	Mahatma Gandhi was born in 1869.
	Borne	सहन किया गया	He has borne his difficulties.
20.	Brake	गति अवरोधक यंत्र	The brakes of my cycle are not in order.
	Break	तोड़ना	You cannot break this stick.
21.	Blue	नीला	The sky is blue.
	Blew	हवा में उड़ना/बजाया	1. Some important papers blew away into the wind. 2. The hunter blew his horn.
22.	Berry	एक फल	I do not like to have a berry.
	Bury	दफनाना	Hindus do not bury the dead body.
23.	Beer	एक प्रकार की शराब	Do you like to have cold beer.
	Bier	शव के जाने की टिकठी	His dead body is being carried on a bier.
24.	Cast	फेकना, चलचित्र के अभिनेता	1. Fishermen cast the wire net in the river. 2. Mother India is picture with and all star cast.
	Caste	जाति	My friend is a brahmin by caste.
25.	Cannon	तोप	The roar of cannons startled the soldiers.
	Canon	सिद्धान्त	His conduct is against the canon of good manners.
26.	Conmplement	पूरक	His daughter's salary is a complement to the income of the family.
	Compliment	सम्मान	Pay my best compliments to your brotl er.
27.	Coarse	मोटा	Mahatma Gandhi wore coarse cloth.
	Course	मार्ग, पाठ्यक्रम	This river changes his course every year.
28.	Canvas	किरमिच	My shoes are made of canvas.
	Canvass	प्रचार करना	During election days people are seen busy

canvassing for their candidate.

	Word	Meaning	Example
29.	Cite	उदाहरण देना	He cited many examples from history to prove his argument.
	Site	स्थिति	Our college building has a good site.
30.	Check	रोकना, जांचना	1. Now I can't check him from drinking. 2. The teacher has not checked the answer-books yet.
	Cheque	बैंक का चैक	He gave me a cheque of Rs. 200.
31.	Cattle	पशु	The cattle are grazing in the field.
	kettle	केतली	Kettle is used for boiling water.
32.	Cession	छूट	I cannot make a cession of my land at this stage.
	Session	मीटिंग, अधिवोन	Half of this session is over.
33.	Ceiling	छत या अन्दरूनी भाग	I bought a ceiling fan yesterday.
	Sealing	सील लगाना	The servant is sealing the bundle.
34.	Calendar	कलैन्डर, पंचांग	This is a beautiful calendar
	Calender	स्त्री करना	Please calender my shirt.
35.	Currant	किशमिश	I like to take currants in the morning.
	Current	धारा	It is hard to swim against the current of this river.
36.	Corps	सेना की एक तकनीकी शाख	He belongs to the medical corps.
	Corpse	मृत शरीर	The corpse to the thief was lying by the roadside.
37.	Council	सभा	He is a member of the legislative council of U.P.
	Counsel	वकील	1. He did not listen to my counsel. 2. Mr. Mishra is a senior counsel of High Court.
38.	Chord	तांत	His violin has fine chords.
	Cord	डोरी	He tied the four legs of the horse with strong cord.
39.	Casual	रस्सी	1. He took all his casual leaves. 2. He is very casual about his duties.
	Causal	कारण अनौपचारिक बताने वाला	There is causal relationship between our deeds and our fortune.
40.	Confidant	विश्वासपात्र	He is my confidant in this matter.
	Confident	आत्मविश्वास	My son has a confident of getting a first division in the examination.

41.	Cell	कोठरी	The old woman died in her cell.
	Sell	बेचना	He sells the mangoes for six rupees a kilo.
42.	Credible	विश्वास के योग्य	The gatekeeper's statement is not credible.
	Creditable	प्रशंसा के योग्य	His performance is creditable.
43.	Considerable	काफी	The Principal has considerable experience of dealing with students.
	Considerate	विचारशील	He is very considerate to all.
44.	Decease	मृत्यु	The decease of Rajiv Gandhi is a great loss to the country.
	Disease	बीमारी	Cancer is a fatal disease.
45.	Dye	रंगना	I dye my hair every month.
	Die	मृत्यु	He died last night.
46.	Dear	प्यारा	My dear friend died last night.
	Deer	हिरन	Deer runs very fast.
47.	Dose	खुराक	I have taken two doses of this medicine.
	Doze	हल्की नींद	Some boys doze in the class.
48.	Dual	दोहरा	I hate those who follow dual policy.
	Duel	मल्ल या द्वंद्व युद्ध	Gama was never defeated in the duel.
49.	Defer	टालना	The President deferred his visit to kashmir.
	Differ	भिन्न होना	Hobbies differ with the people as their tastes differ.
50.	Dew	ओस	Dew drops can be seen on the grass in the morning.
	Due	उचित, निश्चित	I have got my due share.
51.	Desert	रेगिस्तान, छोडना	The Sahara is the largest desert.
			My friends deserted me in adversity.
	Dessert	भोजन उपरांत फल या मिठाई	We enjoyed dessert after dinner.
52.	Draught	घूँट	The patient wants only a draught of water.
	Drought	सूखा	India was affected by a severe drought last year.
53.	Deference	सम्मान	All have high deference for the principal
	Difference	मतभेद	Difference of opinion on this point is natural.
54.	Dairy	दुग्धशाला	I buy milk from a dairy.
	Diary	डायरी	I have a beautiful diary.
55.	Dissent	असहमत होना	There was a murmur of dissent among the members

	Word	Meaning	Example
			of parliament
	Decent	अच्छा	He maintains a decent standard of living.
56.	Eligible	चुने जाने के उपयुक्त	You are not eligible for the post.
	Illegible	जो पढ़ा न जा सके	This letter is illegible.
57.	Eminent	प्रसिद्ध	My brother is an eminent Doctor.
	Imminent	निकट	He is in imminent danger of losing his job.
58.	Empire	साम्राज्य	Have you read about Mughal Empire.
	Umpire	निर्णायक, विचारक	Defeated players often criticize the Umpires.
59.	Expend	खर्च करना	He expends a lot of money for a decent standard of living.
	Expand	विकसित करना	Iron expands when it is heated.
60.	Ensure	सुनिश्चित करना	Self-confidence ensures success in life.
	Insure	बीमा करना	My car is insured.
61.	Essay	निबन्ध	Write an essay on dowry system.
	Assay	परखना	He has assayed this piece of gold.
62.	Ear	कान	Please listen to me with your ear.
	Year	वर्ष	There are twelve months in a year.
63.	Eight	आठ	Eight hundred rupees is not a big sum.
	Ate	खाया	He ate two apples and six mangoes.
64.	Flour	आटा	Breads are made of wheat-flour.
	Floor	फर्श	It is easy to sweep a cemented floor
65.	Fourth	चौथा	We shall meet in the fourth period.
	Forth	आगे	He moved forth to welcome the chief guest.
66.	Foul	गंदा, अनुचित	He has earned money by foul means.
	Fowl	पक्षी	Fowl is a kind of a bird.
67.	Fair	सुन्दर, अच्छा	I am pleased with his fair work.
	Fare	किराया	Railway fare will increase this year.
68.	Feet	पैर	Every human being has two feet.
	Feat	दांव पेच कार्य	A juggler entertains the people with his feats.
69.	Flea	खटमल	Fleas are very troublesome.
	Flee	भाग जाना	Why do you not flee to save yourself.
70.	Gait	चाल	She has a fine gait.

	Word	Meaning	Sentence
	Gate	फाटक	The stranger was stopped at the gate
71.	Goal	उद्देश्य	What is the goal of your mission.
	Gaol	जेल	The terrorist was sent to gaol.
72.	Hoard	जमा करना	The goldsmith hoarded a lot of gold.
	Horde	जत्था, कबीला	A horde of hill-men attacked the fort.
73.	Hair	बाल	His hair has turned grey.
	Hare	खरगोश	I saw a hare in the bush.
	Heir	वारिस	He is our heir.
74.	Heal	जख्म का भरना	The wound is healing up.
	Heel	एड़ी	Short-statured girls wear sandals with high heels.
75.	Hale	स्वस्थ	I found him hale and hearty.
	Hail	दूर से अभिवादन करना	1. He does the hail of us 2. The hail storm destroyed the crops
76.	Human	मानव	To err is human.
	Humane	दयालु	Be humane to the weak and helpless.
77.	Hole	बिल	I saw a rat entering its hole.
	Whole	संपूर्ण	The stranger ate up the whole watermelon.
78.	Hart	नर हिरन	He has a beautiful pair of harts.
	Heart	हृदय	His song appealed to my heart.
79.	Idle	सुस्त	Do not be idle, be up doings.
	Idol	मूर्ति	We should not hate idol worship
80.	In	अन्दर	My father is in the room.
	Inn	सराय	We slept in an inn last night.
81.	Incite	उत्तेजित करना	Who has incited you against me.
	Insight	सूक्ष्म दृष्टि	Dr. Radha krishnan was a man of insight.
82.	Industrious	परिश्रमी	This boy is very industrious.
	Industrial	औद्योगिक	Modi Nagar is an industrial town.
83.	Judicial	न्यायिक	There should be a judicial enquiry into this case.
	Judicious	चतुर	Our Principal is very Judicious.
85.	Yolk	अण्डे का पीला भाग	Only the yolk of an egg is conductive to health.
	Yoke	जुआ, बंधन	India became free from the yoke of British rule in 1947.

86.	Later	बाद में	Sooner or later, people will long for peace in the world.
	Latter	बाद वाला	Of the lion and tiger, the latter is more fearful.
	Letter	पत्र	I wrote a letter yesterday.
87.	Lose	खोना	I often lose my umbrella.
	Loose	ढीला	I like to wear loose dress.
88.	Lion	शेर	Lion is the king of forest.
	Loin	कमर	He is in the habit of wearing loin cloth.
89.	Loan	उधार, ऋण	Banks give loans to the poor people.
	Lone	अकेला	He was a lone figure in the jungle.
90.	Mail	डाक	He received a fat mail from abroad.
	Male	पुरुष, पुल्लिंग	Males are stronger than females.
91.	Minor	नाबालिग, छोटा साधारण	1. Ravi cannot vote because he is minor 2. Do not bother about these minor things.
	Miner	खनिक	The life of a miner is very hard.
92.	Metal	धातु	Gold is a precious metal.
	Mettle	साहस	He showed his mettle by fighting against his enemies?
93.	Meet(V)	मिलना	When shall we meet again?
	Meat	मांस	My friend does not eat meat.
94.	Main	मुख्य	Tell me the main point of his speech.
	Mane	पशुओं की गर्दन के लम्बे बाल	Some horses have long mane on the neck.
95.	Medal	तमगा, पदक	He got a gold medal last year
	Meddle	हस्तक्षेप करना	It is not proper to meddle with other people's affairs.
96.	Merry	प्रसन्न	She gave a merry smile to child.
	Marry	विवाह	He is too old to marry.
97.	Meter	मीटर (यंत्र)	The meter gives correct reading.
	Metre	मापने का फीता	Cloth is sold by the meter.
98.	Moral	नैतिक	What is the moral of this story.
	Morale	मनोवल/मानसिक या नैतिक	The morales of our soldiers is always high.

		अवस्था	
99.	Naughty	शैतान	He is a very naughty boy.
	Knotty	कठिन	This is not a knotty problem
100.	Not	नहीं	He will not help you.
	Knot	गांठ	The knot of your neck-tie is loose.
101.	Naught	कुछ भी नहीं, व्यर्थ	All his plans come to naught.
	Nought	शून्य	There are fine nought helped me.
102.	None	कोई नहीं	None of my friends helped me
	Nun	भिक्षुणी	Nuns are very sincere teachers.
103.	Need	आवश्यकता	I need money.
	Knead	आटा गूंथना	My mother is kneading the flour.
104.	Nay	नहीं	Nay, you cannot sing like Rafi.
	Neigh	हिन-हिनाना	The horse is neighing.
105.	Oar	नाव चलाने वाला चप्पू	You cannot row a boat without an oar.
	Ore	कच्ची धातु	There is a huge stock of iron ore in India
106.	One	एक	1. This is a one-man institution. 2. One of my friends was badly hurt.
	Won	जीता	He won many medals in the Olympic games.
107.	Pair	जोड़ा	I want a pair of shoes.
	Pare	काटना	Pare this apple, please.
108.	Pain	दर्द	He has pain in his foot.
	Pane	शीशा	Who has broken this window pane?
109.	Plain	स्पष्ट, साधारण	His style of living is plain and simple.
	Plane	समतल, रंदा	1. These lines are in the some plane. 2. Plane this piece of wood.
110.	Pail	बाल्टी	She brought water in a pail.
	Pale	पीला	He went pale with fear.
111.	Practice	अभ्यास	Practice makes a man prefect.
	Practise	अभ्यास करना	The lawyer practises at Delhi.
112.	Precede	आगे होना	The police man will precede the main culprit.
	Proceed	आगे बढ़ना	They were proceeding towards the police station.

113.	Principal	प्रधानाचार्य	Mr. D.C. Sharma is the principal of our college.
	Principle	सिद्धान्त	Mahatma Gandhi followed the principle of truth and non-violence.
114.	Pour	टपकना, उड़ेलना	pour some milk into this cup.
	Pore	त्वचा के छिद्र	1. Dirt is thrown out through the pores in the body.
115.	Peace	शन्ति	He has lost his peace of mind
	Piece	टुकड़ा	I want a piece of paper.
116.	Peer	सामत	Do your know the peer of this locality.
	Pier	खम्भा	An old woman was sitting near a pier of the ridge.
117.	Pray	प्रार्थना करना	I pray to God daily for your success.
	Prey	शिकार	The deer fell a prey of the lion.
118.	President	अध्यक्ष, सभापति	Dr. Rajendra Prasad was elected the first President of the republic of India.
	Precedent	उदाहरण/नज़ीर	He quoted many precedents in the support of his arguments.
119.	Petrol	पेट्रोल	My car has run short of petrol
	Patrol	गश्त लगाना	The police was patrolling the streets of the city.
120.	Quite	बिल्कुल	She is now quite well.
	Quiet	शान्त	Keep quiet, please.
121.	Root	जड़	Poverty is the root cause of all evils.
	Route	रास्ता	Which is the shortest route of the Red Fort.
122.	Rain	बारिश	Heavy rains expected this year.
	Reign	राज्यकाल	The people were very happy during the reign of Ashok?
	Rein	लगाम	Hold the reins of the horse tightly.
123.	Reck	ध्यान, चिंता, या परवाह करना	The patient began to get well in the reck of the nurse.
	Wreck	टूट जाना	The ship wrecked in the terrible storm. The terrible storm left the ship ashore in total wreck.
124.	Ring	बजना, बजाना, अंगूठी	1. The bell is ringing. 2. She has lost her ring.
	Wring	निचोड़ना, ऐंठना	It is no use wringing your hands in sorrow.
125.	Raise	उठाना	They could not ra ise the heavy log.

	Word	Meaning	Example
	Rays	किरणें	The rays of the Sun are very piercing in May and June.
	Raze	नष्ट करना	The house was razed to the ground.
126.	Respectful	सम्मान करने वाला	Ravi is a very respectful boy.
	Respectable	सम्मानित	She comes of a respectable family.
127.	Right	सही, सीधा, अधिकार	1. Show me your right hand. 2. You have no right to talk like this
	Rite	उत्सव	The funeral rites were duty performed.
	Wright	बनाने वाला	Shakespeare was a great play wright.
128.	Sail	चलाना	He sailed the boat out of the storm.
	Sale	बिक्री	This furniture is on sale.
129.	Stair	सीढ़ी	Unfortunately he fell down the stairs.
	Stare	घूरना	It is bad manner to stare at ladies.
130.	Soar	उड़ना	The skylark soars higher and higher.
	Sore	कष्ट में	His eyes are sore.
131.	Sole	अकेला	This child is the sole survivor of the tragedy.
	Soul	आत्मा	The soul never dies.
132.	Straight	सीधी	Draw a straight line on the paper.
	Strait	तंग, दशा	She is in a sore strait.
133.	Suit	सूट, उपयुक्त	1. Any time will suit me. 2. The climate of Calcutta does not suit him.
	Soot	कालिख	The soot of the chimney was removed by means of a brush.
	Suite	कमरों का सैट	He has rented a suite of rooms in the Ashoka Hotel.
134.	Stationary	स्थिर	The sun is stationary.
	Stationery	कागज, पेंसिल	My brother deals in stationery.
135.	Seem	प्रतीत होना	He seems to be a good man.
	Seam	बखियां या सिलाई	The seam of my shirts one good.
136.	Some	कुछ	Please, give me some money.
	Sum	रकम, प्रश्न	1. He gave me a sum of four hundred rupees. 2. I cannot do this sum.
137.	Steal	चुराना	We must not steal anything.

	Word	Meaning	Example
	Steel	स्पात	I do not use steel utensils.
138.	Story	कहानी	I told him an interesting story.
	Storey	मंजिल	I have my office is the third storey of his building.
139.	Style	विधि या शैली	1. His hair style is very simple. 2. His style of writing is very impressive.
	Stile	सीढ़ी	You can go up the wall with the help of a stile.
140.	Tale	कहानी	He narrated a fairy tale in the class.
	Tail	पूँछ	The peacock has a beautiful tail.
141.	Team	टोली	Our cricket team won the match.
	Teem	भरपूर होना	This pond teems with fish.
142.	Tear	आँसू	The tears toy are slopping in her eyes.
	Tear	फाड़ना	Why did you tear the important paper?
	Tier	पंक्ति	It is comfortable to travel in two tier compartment.
143.	Temper	मानसिक दशा	He is a man of sweet temper.
	Tamper	दखल देना	Some one has tampered with this document.
144.	Toe	पांव का अंगुली	Do not tread upon the toe of others.
	Tow	रस्सी से खींचना	The boatman towed his boat ashore.
145.	Vain	निष्फल, घमण्ड	1. He tried to reform his son, but in vain. 2. She is very vain about her good looks.
	Vein	नाड़ी	Veins carry the back to the heart.
	Vane	वायु दिशा दर्शक यंत्र	There is a vane on the top of the church.
146.	Vale	घाटी	Kashmir is a beautiful vale.
	Veil	घूँघट	She covered her face with veil.
	Wail	दुखी होना	Do not wail for those things which you do not possess.
147.	Vine	लता	There is a beautiful vine in my courtyard.
	Wine	शराब	Wine is injurious to health.
148.	Waste	नष्ट करना	He wastes his time in idle gossip.
	Waist	कमर	The tailor is measuring his waist.
149.	Wave	लहर	The waves of the sea broke the ship into two pieces.
	Waive	त्यागना	He waived his right to the property.

150.	Wear	पहनना	She is wearing a blue sari.
	Ware	सामान	The peddler was carrying his wares.
151.	Wait	प्रतीक्षा करना	Please wait till I come.
	Weight	भार	My weight is 65 kg.
152.	Week	सप्ताह	He may come next week.
	Weak	कमजोर	Your son is weak in English.
153.	Weather	मौसम	The weather is very fine today.
	Whether	यदि	Please let me know whether you will be able to accompany me.
154.	Wet	भीगा होना	Her clothes were wet.
	Whet	तेज करना	The barber whets his razor every now and then.
155.	Weigh	तोलना	The luggage was weighed.
	Way	रास्ता	There seems to be no way out.
	Whey	मट्ठा	He is allowed to take only whey and no other food.

❑❑❑

One words substitution

किसी शब्द समूह के पूर्ण भाव को प्रकट करने के लिए सार्थक लिखना

जैसे–

1. Which cannot be read- **Illegible** (जो पढ़ा न जा सके)
2. Which cannot be changed or cancelled- **Irrevocable** (अपरिवर्तनीय)
3. Which cannot be believed- **Incredible** (अविश्वसनीय)
4. Which cannot be interpreted in any way- **Ambiguous** (अस्पष्ट)
5. That cannot be avoided- **Inevitable** (अवश्यंभावी)
6. That cannot be explained - **Inexplicable** (अकथनीय)
7. That cannot be overcome or taken by force - **Impregnable** (अभेद्य)/ अखंडनीय
8. Too good or clever to be imitated- **Inimitable** (अनोखी)
9. Incapable of being understood- **Unintelligible** (समझ के बाहर)
10. Incapable of being reached- **Inaccessible** (पहुंच के बाहर)
11. Which causes death- **Fatal** (घातक)
12. No longer in use- **Obsolete** (अप्रचलित)
13. Easily made angry- **Irritable** (जल्दी नाराज होने वाला)
14. Work or post for which no salary is paid- **Honorary** (अवैतनिक)
15. Which is fit to eat or consume- **Edible** (खाने योग्य)
16. Which cannot be reversed or revoked- **Irreversible** (अपरिवर्तनीय)
17. Which cannot be understood or known- **Inscrutable** (रहस्यमय)
18. Which cannot be wounded or hurt- **Invulnerable** (अभेद्य)
19. Preparation used for killing insects- **Insecticide** (कीटनाशक)
20. Travelling from place to place- **Itinerant** (सैलानी)
21. Done without intention - **Involuntary** (अनैच्छिक)
22. Combining excessive patriotism with contempt for other countries- **Jingoism** (आक्रामक देशभक्ति)
23. Person who travels to a sacred place as an act of religious devotion- **Pilgrim** (तीर्थयात्री)
24. Which can be carried about- **Portable** (सुवाहन)
25. Which is fit to drink- **Potable** (पेय)
26. Speaking and writing several languages- **Polyglot** (बहुभाषी)
27. A person who lives alone and avoids other people - **Recluse** (संयासी)
28. Someone who spends too much and spends wastefully- **Spendthrift** (अपव्ययी)

29. Of a town or city- Urban (शहरी)

30. Characteristic of, suitable for, the country side- Rural (देहाती)

31. Use of physical force so as to damage or injure- Violence (हिंसा)

32. Person who makes tiresome and unnecessary display of learning- Pedant (पांडित्य प्रदर्शन करने वाला)

33. Property inherited from one's father or ancestors- Patrimony (विरासत)

34. Substance used to destroy pests, especially. insects- Pesticide (कीटनाशक)

35. A thing that kills germs - Germicide (जीवाणुनाशक)

36. Hard to please - Fastidious (नाजुक मिजाज)

37. Hard but easily broken - Brittle (आसानी से टूटने वाला)

38. One who gives up his religion - Apostate (स्वधर्म त्यागने वाला)

39. A special van carrying the wounds and sick- Ambulance (रोगी वाहन)

40. A long journey in a ship- voyage (समुद्री यात्रा)

41. A long narrative poem about a national hero or heroes- Epic (महाकाव्य)

42. beginning of a new period in history - Era (युग)

43. That which cannot be tamed - Wild (जंगली)

44. A general pardon of political offenders - Amnesty (सार्वजनिक क्षमा)

45. One who is against all government, law and order- Anarchist (अराजकतावादी)

46. Nations engaged in war- Belligerents (युद्धकारी)

47. One who lacks courage -Coward (कायर)

48. A person who relies on experiment and observation - Empiric (अनुभववादी)

49. Something contrary to law- Illegal (अवैधानिक)

50. That which causes injury- Injurious (हानिकारक)

51. A person who is womanish in his habits-Effeminate (जनानी आदतों वाला)

52. A man who a devoted to the welfare of women- Feminist (स्त्री जाति के कल्याण का प्रेमी)

53. A person who is not married or who has taken the first degree of a university- Bachelor (कुँआरा)

54. A person whose wife is dead- Widower (विधुर)

55. A person who can read and write- Literate (पढ़ा-लिखा)

56. A person who cannot read and write- Illiterate (अनपढ़)

57. A person who takes pride in magnifying his doing - Egoist (अहंकारी)

58. A person who travels on foot- Pedestrian (पैदल यात्री)

59. A person who is indifferent to pleasure and pain - Stoic (आत्मसंयमी)

60. A person who depends on others - **Parasite** (परजीवी)

61. A person who assumes a character or title not his own for the purpose of deceiving others- **Imposter** (पाखण्डी)

62. A person who holds strongly to an opinion or belief in defiance of reason of argument - **Bigot** (धर्मान्ध)

63. A person works only for money or reward- **Mercenary** (केवल धन के लिये काम करने वाला)

64. A person who undergoes penalty of death or suffering for any great cause- **Martyr** (शहीद)

65. A person widely known for evil deeds- **Notorious** (कुख्यात)

66. A person who totally abstains from alcoholic liquor- **Teetotaler** (नशा न करने वाला)

67. A person holding conventional beliefs specially in matters of religion- **Orthodox** (रुढ़िवादी)

68. A person who introduces new things- **Innovator** (नई रीति चलाने वाला)

69. A person or an artist that draws comic pictures-**Cartoonist** (कार्टूनिस्ट)

70. A person who lends money at a very high rate of interest - **Usurer** (सूदखोर)

71. A person who helps others by giving them monetary help and encouragement-**Patron** (संरक्षक)

72. A person with long experience -**Veteran** (अनुभवी)

73. A person who is opposed to changes - **Conservative** (रुढ़िवादी)

74. A person who is advocate of the doctrine of equality among men-**Equalitarian** (समानतावादी)

75. A woman whose husband is dead- **Widow** (विधवा)

76. A child whose parents are dead- **Orphan** (अनाथ)

77. A child born after the death of father- **Posthumous** (मरणोत्तर)

78. A child brought up by persons who are not his parents - **Foster child-** (धाय पालित संतान)

79. A student who runs always from his class without permission- **Truant** (भगोड़ा विद्यार्थी)

80. One who knows everything- **Omniscient** (सर्वज्ञाता)

81. One who is all powerful - **Omnipotent** (सर्वशक्तिमान)

82. One who is present everywhere at the same time- **Omnipresent** (सर्वव्यापी)

83. A period of seven day- **Week** (सप्ताह)

84. A period of fifteen days- **Fortnight** (पखवाड़ा)

85. A period of ten years- **Decade** (दशक)

86. A period of hundred years- **Century** (शताब्दी)

87. That which happens once in one year- **Annual** (वार्षिक)

88. That which happens one in two years- **Biennial** (द्विवार्षिक)

89. That which happens one in three years- **Triennial** (त्रैवार्षिक)

90. A diplomatic messenger of the highest order sent by one sovereign power to another-**Ambassador**

(राजदूत)

91. People assembled to see an incident of scene - **Spectators** (दर्शक)
92. People living at the same time- **Contemporary** (समकालीन)
93. Assembly of listeners - **Audience** (श्रोता)
94. A man who is quarrelsome. noisy and nagging-**Shrewd** (धूर्त)
95. A traveler in space - **Astronaut** (अंतरिक्ष यात्री)
96. Which can be seen through - **Transparent** (पारदर्शी)
97. Which cannot be seen through- **Opaque** (अपारदर्शी)
98. A sound which can be heard- **Audible** (जो सुनी जा सके)
99. A sound which cannot be heard- **Inaudible** (सुनाई न देने वाला)
100. A large number of people- **Majority** (बहुमत)
101. A fewer number of people- **Minority** (अल्पमत)
102. Eclipse of the Sun- **Solar Eclipse** (सूर्यग्रहण)
103. Eclipse of the Moon- **Lunar Eclipse** (चन्द्रग्रहण)
104. Morning prayer in the church- **Matin** (गिरजाघर की प्रातःकालीन प्रार्थना)
105. Evening prayer in the church- **Vesper** (गिरजाघर की सायंकालीन प्रार्थना)
106. Government by the people, of the people and for the people - **Democracy** (प्रजातंत्र)
107. Government by one person only- **Autocracy** (निरंकुश शासन)
108. Government by officials - **Bureaucracy** (नौकरशाही)
109. Government by a monarch- **Monarchy** (साम्राज्यवाद, राजतंत्र)
110. Government by the nobles- **Aristocracy** (कुलीन तंत्र)
111. Government by the gods- **Theocracy, Thearchy** (ईश्वरीय गुण सम्पन्न लोगों की राजसत्ता)
112. Government by all- **Pantisocracy** (सर्वतंत्र)
113. Government by the rich- **Plutocracy** (धनिक तंत्र)
114. Government by few - **Oligarchy** (अल्पजन तन्त्र)
115. Government by mob- **Mobocracy** (भीड़ तन्त्र)
116. The state of being married - **Matrimony** (विवाह संस्कार)
117. The state of being unmarried- **Bachelorhood** (कुँआरापन)
118. Murder of mother- **Matricide** (माता की हत्या)
119. Murder of father - **Patricide** (पिता की हत्या)
120. Murder of king -**Regicide** (राजा की हत्या)

121. Murder of infant- Infanticide (शिशु हत्या)
122. Murder of brother - Fratricide (भाई की हत्या)
123. Murder of oneself - Suicide (आत्महत्या)
124. Murder of one man by another- Homicide (मानव हत्या)
125. Animals which give milk-Mammals (स्तनधारियों)
126. Animals which live in flocks - Gregarious (झुण्ड में रहने वाले)
127. Animals which live on others - Parasites (परजीवी)
128. Animals which live in water- Aquatics (जल में रहने वाले जन्तु)
129. Animals which live both on land and in sea - Amphibia (स्थल और जल श्रेणी के जन्तु)
130. An animal's living on flesh of other animals - Carnivorous (माँस भक्षी पशु)
131. Practice of having two husbands or wives at a time- Bigamy (द्वि-विवाह प्रथा)
132. Practice of having more than one wife at a time- Polygamy (बहु-विवाह)
133. Practice of having more than one husband at a time- Polyandry (एक से अधिक पति रखन की प्रथा)
134. Practice of marrying one at a time- Monogamy (एक बार विवाह करने की प्रथा)
135. Medical examination of the dead body - Postmortem (शवपरीक्षा)
136. Surgical performance of the body- Operation (शल्य चिकित्सा)
137. Things which contain elements of the same nature- Homogeneous (सजातीय)
138. Things which contain elements of opposite nature- Heterogeneous (विजातीय)
139. A medicine which counteracts poison - Antidote (विषनाशक)
140. The act of speaking aloud one's thoughts which alone- Soliloquy (आत्मभाषण)
141. A place where experiments are carried- Laboratory (प्रयोगशाला)
142. The passes of soul after death from one body to another- Transmigration (पुनर्जन्म)
143. Tendency to fight or quarrel- Pugnacity (कलह की इच्छा)
144. Words which are inscribed on the grave or tomb in the memory of the buried- Epitaph (समाधि-लेख पर लिखा स्मरण लेख)
145. A fellow worker- Colleague (साथी)
146. The study of the nature of beauty- Aesthetics (सौन्द्रर्य शास्त्र)
147. A remedy for all troubles, diseases etc - Panacea (रामबाण)
148. The art practiced by statesmen and politicians - Diplomacy (कूटनीति)
149. Use of more words than necessary - Verbosity (शब्दों का वृक्षा प्रयोग)
150. Speaking disrespectfully about sacred things - Blasphemy (ईश्वर निन्दा)
151. School for children too young to begin formal education- Kinder garden (बाल-विहार)

152. To carry away a person by force -Kidnap (अपहरण)

153. A document written by hand -Manuscript (हस्तलिपि)

154. A list of books- Catalogue (पक्ष)

155. A life history of an man written by himself- Autobiography (आत्मकथा)

156. A life history of a man written by someone else- Biography (जीवन कथा)

157. The first speech delivered by a person- Maiden (प्रथम भाषण)

158. (Spoken or done) without previous preparation-Extempore (तात्कालिक)

159. A short sentence often quoted- Proverb (कहावत)

160. A medicine that induces sleep- Narcotic (निन्द्राकारी)

161. One who tells the future from the stars- Astrologer (ज्योतिषी)

162. A disease which spreads by contact- Infectious (संक्रामक)

163. A disease which spreads over a huge area- Epidemic (व्यापक रोग)

164. Goods received by one country from the other- Import (आयात)

165. Goods sent from one country to another-Export (निर्यात)

166. Belief in many gods- Polytheism (अनेक देवताओं में विश्वास)

167. A place for keeping weather plants, animals, fish etc. - Aquarium (जल कुष्ठ / मछली घर)

168. A place for keeping various animals- Zoo (चिड़ियाघर)

169. A place for keeping birds- Aviary (पक्षीशाला)

170. A building used for storing and exhibiting curiosities and antiquities- Museum (अजायबघर)

171. A place for cremating (burning to ashes) corpses-Crematorium (शमशान)

172. A place for burials other than a churchyard - Cemetery (कब्रिस्तान)

173. A Festival of the hundredth anniversary- Centenary (शतवार्शिकी)

174. A place where clothes are placed- Wardrobe (कपड़े रखने की अलमारी)

175. A person who speaks too much of himself- Egotist (अहंकारी)

176. Statement accepted as true without proof or argument -Axiom (स्वयंसिद्धि)

177. A person who is unable to pay his debts- Bankrupt (दिवालिया)

178. A person who kills, cuts up and sells animals for food- Butcher (कसाई)

179. Public room or building for gambling and other amusements - Casino (नृत्यशाला, जुआघर)

180. (Of disease) spreading by contact- Contagious (संक्रामक)

181. Which can be believed- Credible (विश्वसनीय)

182. A person who travels in space in a space vehicle- Cosmonaut (अंतरिक्ष यात्री)

183. Sleeping-room with several or many beds, in a school or institution Dormitory -Dormitory (शयनागार, छात्रावास)

184. A Person sent to deliver a message (Often of an unpleasant and secret kind) - Emissary (दूत)

185. A large retail store- Emporium (वाणिज्य केन्द्र)

186. Something which shows, on a small scale, the characteristics of somethings much larger-Epitome (सार)

187. A person running away from justice, danger, etc- Fugitive (भगोड़ा)

188. A shopkeeper selling vegetables and fruit- Greengrocer (सब्जीवाला)

189. A building in which planes are housed -Hanger (विमानशाला)

190. A person who goes from house to sell goods- Hawker (फेरीवाला)

191. A woman who entertains guests-Hostess (परिचारिका)

192. Not qualified for the post- Ineligible (अयोग्य)

193. A thing that catches fire easily- Inflammable (ज्वलनशील)

194. (Of a person) that cannot be corrected- Incorrigible (अशोध्य)

195. That cannot be dispensed with- Indispensable (अपरिहार्य)

196. Of one mind or opinion- Unanimous (एकमत)

197. Which cannot be conquered- Invincible (अजेय)

198. Which cannot be seen- Invisible (अदृश्य)

199. Which cannot be repaired or remedied- Irreparable (जो सुधारा न जा सके)

200. Which cannot be divided- Indivisible (अविभाज्य)

201. A person residing in a country of which he is not a citizen-A theist (विदेशी)

202. A person who pursues an art, games or sport for pleasure, not for money - Amateur (किसी शिल्प या वद्या का अवैतनिक अनुयायी)

203. A person who does not believe in the existence of God - Atheist (नास्तिक)

204. A person who believes in the existence of God - Theist (आस्तिक)

205. A person who looks at the bright side of things - Optimist (आशावादी)

206. A person who looks to the dark side of things - Pessimist (निराशावादी)

207. A person who depends on and believes in fate - Fatalist (भाग्यवादी)

208. A person who renounces the world and devotes himself to a strictly devout life, starving the body for the good of the soul - Ascetic (संन्यासी)

209. A person who is filled with excessive and mistaken enthusiasm in religious matter - Fanatic (हठधर्मी)

210. A peson who is well-versed in any subject-connoisseur. (पारखी)

211. A person with whom money or gain is the most important consideration- Materialistic (भौतिकवादी)

212. A person who is proficient in many languages - Linguist (अनेक भाषाएं जानने वाला)

213. A person who studies structure of earth, rocks, etc - Geologist (भूगर्भ शास्त्री)

214. A person who studies ancient buildings and monuments - Archaeologist (पुरातत्ववेत्ता)

215. A person who is hater of reasoning of knowledge - Misologist (तर्क व विद्या से घृणा करने वाला)

216. A person who is lover and collector of books - Bibliophile (पुस्तकों का प्रेमी एवं सग्रहकर्त्ता)

217. A person who does not care for art and literature - Philistine (कला तथा साहित्य के प्रति चिन्ता रहित)

218. A person who studies plants - Botanist (वनस्पति शास्त्र का पंडित)

219. A person who studies animals - Zoologist (जन्तु विज्ञान शास्त्री)

220. A person who studies the origin and growth of languages - Philologist (शब्द शास्त्रज्ञ)

221. A person who collects stamps - Philatelist (डाक टिकट संग्रहकर्त्ता)

222. A person who regards the whole world as his country - Cosmopolitan (विश्वामित्र)

223. One who studies the Moon, the Sun, the planets and the stars - Astronomer (खगोलशास्त्री)

224. A person who studies the development of man from primitive times - Anthropologist (नरतत्वीय विज्ञानवेत्ता)

225. A person who believes easily -(सहज विश्वासी)

226. A person who is easily be fooled- Gullible (सहज में मूर्ख बनाया जाने वाला)

227. A person who is free from all mistakes and failures - Infallible (भूल न करने वाला)

228. A person who believes in total abolition of war- Pacifist (युद्ध की समाप्ति में विश्वास करने)

229. A person who is frank and open- Ingenuous (निष्कपट)

230. A person who is fond of fighting - Bellicose (लड़ाका)

231. A person who is very careful about his health- Hygienist (आरोग्ज्ञशास्त्री)

232. A person who amuses himself by love making- Philanderer (प्रेमालापी)

233. A person who eats everything - Omnivorous (सर्वभक्षी)

234. A person who eats herbaceous plant-Herbivorous (शाकाहारी)

235. A person who lives on vegetables-Vegeterian (शाकाहारी)

236. A person who eats meat also- Non-vegeterian (माँसाहारी)

237. A person who eats human flesh- Cannibal (नरभक्षी)

238. A person who comes to an country from another to settle there- Immigrant (दूसरे देश से बसने वाला)

239. A person who leaves his own country to live in another- Emigrant (परदेश में बसने वाला)

240. A person who loves his own country- Patriot (देशभक्त)

241. A person who takes arms against the government of his own country-Rebel (राजद्रोही)

242. A person who excels at many things - Versatile (दक्ष)

243. A person can easily be approached - Accessible (उपलब्ध)

244. A person who is unable to pay his debts- Insolvent (दिवालिया)

245. A person who is wasteful in expenditure-(1995) - Extravagant (लुटाऊ)

246. A person who is lover of mankind of humanity in general- Philanthropist (मानव का हितैषी)

247. A person who hate mankind-Misanthropist (मानव से घृणा करने वाला)

248. A person who is hater of womankind-Misogynist (स्त्री जाति से घृणा करने वाला)

249. A person who hates the institution of marriage- Misogamist (विवाह से घृणा करने वाला)

250. A person who is lover of women- Philogynist (स्त्रियों का प्रेमी)

251. That which can not be removed -Indelibel (अमिट)

252. Worship of idols- Idolatry (मूर्ति पूजा)

253. A person to whom a matter is referred for settlement - Referee (पंच)

254. A small canvas or leather bag for carrying papers, books or clothes- Satchel (तनीवाला थैला)

255. A rope or chain for tying up an animal- Tether (जानवर बांधने की रस्सी)

256. Take possession of by force or without right- Usurp (बलपूर्वक अधिकार करना)

257. One who pretends to be what he is not- Hypocrite (पाखंडी)

258. Building or part of a building in which an audience site- Auditorium (सभागार

259. List of books and writings of one author or about one subject-Bibliography (ग्रथ सूची)

260. The study of crime and criminal technology - Criminology (अपराध विज्ञान)

261. Liable to error - Fallible (त्रुटि करने योग्य अपूर्ण)

262. Person having great and exceptional capacity of the mind or imagination -Genius (प्रतिभाशाली)

263. A man who receives and entertains his guests- Hospitable (सत्कारशील)

264. Person who works for the welfare of all human beings by reducing suffering - Humanitarian (मानवतावादी)

265. Which cannot be cured - Incurable (असाध्य)

266. (Of substance) which cannot be dissolved - Insoluble (अघुलनशील)

267. A person who ignores religion, art, music etc. Materialist (भौतिकवादी)

268. Person sent to preach his religion, esp. among people who are ignorant of it - Missionary (धर्मप्रचारक)

269. A shop at a school, selling eatables, esp. sweets- Tuckshop (मिठाई की दुकान)

270. General knowledge test - Quiz (प्रश्नोत्तरी)

Idioms and phrases

इनका प्रयोग प्रभावित तरीके से बोलने के लिए किया जाता है।

(A)

Act for - किसी के स्थान पर कार्य करना

The senior clerk was asked to act for head clerk when he went on leave.

Act upon- 1. प्रभावित करना

Heat acts upon bodies and causes them to expand.

2. भरोसा रखना, भरोसा रखकर कार्यवाही करना

Acting upon a witness evidence the police caught the thief.

Ask for - मांग करना

You can ask for anything you need.

Aghast at - हक्का-बक्का होना

As she entered the hospital she looked aghast at the bed of the wounded.

All of a sudden - अचानक

All of the sudden the walls of the room started shaking.

At daggers drawn - दुश्मनी होना

Once upon a time they were friends, but now they are at draggers drawn over the issue of money.

At once - तुरन्त

The boss was furious over secretary's mistake and asked him to come to his room at once.

At the eleventh hour - अंतिम क्षण पर, ऐन मौके पर

The mob was getting out of control but at the eleventh hour the police arrived and averted riots.

(B)

Back out- दिए हुए वचन से मुकर जाना

He had promised me two hundred rupees but later he backed out from his words.

Bring to book- दण्ड देना

They never bring me to book.

Bank on - भरोसा रखना

We should not bank on foes.

Blow out - बुझाना

On her birthday she blew out fifteen candles on her cake.

Break down- 1. (यंत्र का) खराबी के कारण बंद पड़ना, रुकना

Our car broke down on the way to Agra.

2. भावना के उद्वेग से रो पड़ना

She broke down at his departure.

3. विश्लेषण करना, अलग-अलग सूची बनाना

If you break down the figures you will find out your mistake.

Break into - चोरी से अथवा जबरदस्ती अंदर घुसना

you break into the bank and stole the money from its lockers.

Bring out - बाहर निकालना

War bring out the worst in people.

Bring up - लालन-पालन करना

Anil was brought up by his uncle.

Be all ears - बहुत ध्यान से सुनना

The children were being all ears as I began to tell the story of Alibaba.

Be in the way - रास्ता रोकना

Is this chair in your way?

Be no more - मर जाना

Since her husband is no more she fell quite lost.

Be well -off - धनवान होना

They own a house and a car , so they certainly are well-off.

Bed of rose - सुख चैन की व्यवस्था

Life is no bed of rose.

Better half - पत्नी

His better half takes good care of him.

Black sheep - बदनाम आदमी

Ramesh is the black sheep of the family.

Blind alley - एक तरफ से बंद गली

They had to turn back as they had entered a blind alley.

Bring to light - राज खोलना

The C.I.D. brought to light a hideous conspiracy to assassinate the police chief.

Bring to hammer - नीलाम करना

As he went bankrupt, all his goods were brought to the hammer.

Broad daylight - दिन दहाड़े

Yesterday the bank near our house was robbed in broad daylight.

By and By - आहिस्ता-आहिस्ता

by and by people began to come into the lecture hall.

By the way - बात-बात में यूँ ही

By the way, are you married?

(C)

Call off - रद्द करना

I had called off the party because of my wife's illness.

Carry on - 1. चालू रखना, कार्य करते रहना

Despite the accident they carried on with the show.

Come of - नतीजा निकालना

Nothing came of his proposal.

Come round- धीरे-धीरे स्वास्थ्य सुधरना

My friend was seriously ill for some days, but he is coming round more.

Come through - सफल होना

As I' ve studied hard for the examination I am quite confident that I'll come through.

Count on - भरोसा रखना

You can always count on my help.

Call a spade a spade - साफ-साफ कह देना

I'am not rude but at the same time I don't hesitate to call a spade a spade.

Capital Crime - मौत की सजा जैसा गुनाह

Murder is a capital crime.

Capital Punishment - मौत की सजा

The murderer was awarded capital punishment.

Chicken-hearted fellow - डरपोक आदमी

A chicken-hearted man like. you will never make a soldier.

Close- fisted man - कंजूस

Although having a lot of money, he is a close-fisted man.

Close shave - बाल-बाल बचना

My car was just about to dash against the lamp post. It was quite a close shave.

Cock and bull story - मनगढ़ंत कहानी

Who would believe such a cock and bull story?

Cold feet - डर जाना

At the sight of his appointment he got cold feet.

(D)

Dispose of - बेच देना

He disposed of all his property and became sadhu

Dwell on - किसी बात पर अधिक देर तक बोलना

In his speech he dwelt on the importance of prompt action.

Day in, day out - रोज-रोज

He worked, day in, day out in pass his C.A. Examination.

Dead against - बिल्कुल खिलाफ

Her mother is dead against her acting in the films.

Dead loss - कतई पूरा न होने वाला नुकसान

He invested quite a lot of money in paper business but it proved to be a dead loss.

Dead of night - आधी रात को

The thief entered the house at dead of night.

Dog-eared book - पुस्तक के रुप में बिगाड़ देना।

The dog-eared book suggests that you have read it carefully and marked the important pages.

Dutch courage - शराब पीकर आने वाली झूठी वीरता

He showed a lot of Dutch courage, but got lightened as the drink wore off.

(F)

Fly at- अचानक क्रोध करना

I asked him to lend me five rupees and all once he flew at me.

Fool around- सुस्ती समय गवाना

Stop foiling around and get to work.

Fool away- व्यर्थ गंवा देना

Don't fool away your time like this.

Fed up with - तंग आ जाना

I am fed up with this daily drudgery.

For good- हमेशा के लिए

He propossed leave India for good.

For the time being - कुछ समय के लिए

For the time being I am staying at a hotel, but I propose to rent a flat shortly.

Fair Sex - नारी जाति

She was the only representative of the fair sex at the meeting.

(G)

Get along - घुल मिलकर रहना, दोस्ती रखना।

She is highly sociable and can get along with everybody.

Get off - बस से या मोटर गाड़ी से उतरना

We have to get off the bus at the next stop.

Get on - 1. बस या मोटर गाड़ी पर सवार होना

I saw him get on to the bus at the last stop.

2. प्रगति करना – Get on

Ashok is quite industrious and sure to get on in the world.

Give away- 1. बांटना

The chief guest gave away the prizes.

2. रहस्य खोलना

He gave away Ram's name as he had drawn teacher's cartoon.

Go back - मुकर जाना

He promised to give me his history notes but now he has gone back on his words.

Go for - हमला करना

The boys went for, the poor dog with stone.

Give ill eyes- नजर लगाना

She gives me ill eyes daily.

Grow upon- आदत लगना

The habit of taking drugs is growing upon college boys.

Gain ground - धीरे-धीरे प्रगति करना

India lost the first two matches, but began to gain ground gradually.

Get into a soup - झंझट में पड़ना

You will get into a soup if you neglect your studies like this.

Get on one's nerves - नाक में दम करना

She talks so much that she gets on my nerves.

Get rid of - छुटकारा पाना

Don't ask what all I had to go to get rid of a bore like Vinay.

Get the sack - नौकरी से हटाया जाना

He is thoroughly incompetent and I know that one day he will get the sack.

Get wind of- रहस्य का पता लगाना

There was a well-guarded conspiracy, but somehow the government got wind of it.

Give a ring- टेलीफोन करना

I'll give a ring as soon as I get there.

Give the slip- चकमा देकर भाग जाना

As the thief saw the policeman he gave him the slip by getting into a hereby lane

Good deal- बहुत मात्रा में

The sofa set has cost me a good deal of money.

(H)

Hue & cry- हल्ला गुल्ला

There is not but hue & cry in the class.

Hand over - सौंपना

The retiring sales engineer handed over the charge to the new engineer.

Hunt for - ढूँढना

What were you paper.

Hammer and tongs - जार-जार से

The opposition went for the government's policies hammer and tongs.

Hard up - रुपयों की तंगी होना

Ever since he has left his job he has been quite hard up.

Haul over the coals - कोसना, भर्त्सना करना

The boss hauled him over the coals for his insubordination.

Have a mind - राजी होना, दिल करना

He can be very funny if he has a mind.

Hit it off- घुल मिल जाना

she and her husband do not seem to hit it off.

Hush money - रिश्वत

A lot of hush money passed between the minister and his favourite business house.

(I)

In a fix - दुविधा में पड़ना

I could not decide whether to 'leave or stay- I was in a fix.

In a mess - संकट में पड़ना

Do your work properly, else you'll get into a mess.

In all - सब मिलकर

In all there were thirty students in all the class.

(K)

Keep an eye on - निगरानी रखना

Please keep an eye on my suit case while I buy my ticket.

(L)

Let down- निराश करना, धोखा देना

I was counting on your help, but you let me down.

Let out- किराये पर देना

As I am hard up nowadays I had to let out a portion of my house

Look after - संभालना, ध्यान देना

Will you please look after the house in my absense.

Looked into - जांच करना

Have the police looked into the matter relating to theft at your house

Laid up with- बीमार होकर बिस्तर पर पड़े रहना

He was out in the rain yesterday and now is laid up with cold and fever.

Laugh in one's sleeve - मन में हंसना

He was wearing a funny dress at the party. And everyone was laughing in his sleeve.

Lay bare - राज खोलना

I can't rest until I've laid bare this conspiracy.

Lay down the law- हुक्म चलाना

In his house his wife lays down the law.

Lend a hand - सहायता करना

Let us all lend him a hand in carrying these books to the basement.

Let the cat out of the bag - भेद खोलना

Ramesh let the cat out of the bag when he said Renu was just pretending to be ill because she did not to go to school.

Lion's share - बहुत बड़ा हिस्सा लेना

The lion's share of his profit was appropriated by his financier.

Little by little - धीरे-धीरे

His health is improving, but little by little.

Live from hand to mouth - मुफलिसी में गुजारा करना

Majority of Indian population lived from hand to mouth.

Live it up - ऐश आराम की जिंदगी बिताना

The richman's son went to America and lived it up.

Lord it over - शासन करना

Try to be independent. Don't let others lord over you.

Lose ground- पिछड़ जाना

To begin with he was ahead of others in the race, but later he lost ground.

(M)

Make marry - मौज मनाना

As we have now an unexpected holiday, so let us make marry.

Mix up - गड़बड़ घोटाला करना

As they were introduced to me in a hurry I mixed up their names and called him by the wrong name.

Make a hash - गड़बड़ घोटाला कर देना

Don't meddle in my cooking. You will make a hash of everything.

Make off with - चोरी से लेकर भाग जाना

The thief made off with a thousand rupees.

Make up to - खुशामद करना

Ram krishan has been making up to the manager in the hope of a promotion.

Man of straw- जिसमें कुछ दम नहीं, ऐसा व्यक्ति

Gulzar is a man of straw. You cannot possibly rely on him.

Meet one half way- समझौता करना

I cannot accept, but I am prepared to meet you half way.

Miss the boat - अवसर खोना

It was a golden opportunity for him to make a profit, but choosy as he is he missed the boat.

Moot point - विवाद का विषय

Whether school children should be given sex education or not is a moot point.

(N)

Narrow escape - बाल-बाल बचना

No sooner did we run out of the burning house than it collapsed. It was indeed a narrow escape.

Null and void- व्यर्थ

This offer is open for six months, after which it will become null and void.

(O)

Of late - आजकल

Of late many girls have started dressing like boys.

Off an and on - कभी-कभी, अनियमित रूप से

He drops in off and on for a chat with me.

Oily tongue - खुशामद की भाषा

I have seen many people failing prey to his oily tongue.

On purpose - जानबूझकर

I suspect he made the mistake on purpose.

Out and out - पूरी तरह से

He is out an out a docile character.

Out at elbow - गरीब. निर्धन

He had suffered heavy losses in business and is now out at elbow.

Out of favour - खफा करना

India lost the first two matches, but began to out of favour gradually.

Over and over - बार-बार

He is such a dull boy that I have to explain to him the same thing over and over.

Over head and ears - दिलो जान से (प्यार करना)

He is over head and ears in love with her.

(P)

Palm off - ठगना

He tried to palm off a forged hundred rupees note on me.

Pass away - मरना

Kumar's father passed away yesterday.

Pay off - हिसाब चुकता कर छुट्टी देना

He was not happy with his servant so he paid him off.

Play off- एक को दूसरे से भिड़ाना

The crooked man played off the two friends against each other for his own benefit.

Play with - छेड़खानी करना

It is dangerous to play with fire.

Put off - स्थगित करना

The match had to be put off because of bad weather.

Put on - 1. कपड़े पहनना

She put on her best dress for the party.

2. दिखाना

Don't put on as if you don't know anything.

Put out - 1. बुझाना

He put out the light and went to sleep.

Put up - रहना, निवास करना

Where should put up in Bombay?

Pick a lock - कुंजी के बिना ताला खोलना

The burglar picked the lock and broke into the house.

Pick holes - त्रुटियाँ निकालना

Scientists fried to pick holes in his theory.

Pick Pocket - पाकिट मारना

A young boy was arrested by the police for picking a man's pocket.

Piping hot- बहुत गर्म/ताजा

I always prefer to have my tea piping hot.

Play the game - नियमानुसार करना

Whatever you do, always play the game.

Play truant - भाग जाना

Playing truant is a bad practice among school children which should be checked at a proper stage.

Play up to - खुशामद करना

Ravi plays up to every girl he meets.

Point blank - तत्काल

When I asked him to loan me 200 rupees, he refused point blank.

Put down in black and white- लिखकर रखना

I am not lying, The evidence is here in black and white.

Put the screw - जबरदस्ती रोकना

Unless you put the screw on your extravagant expenditure you'll be in debt soon.

Put up to - उकसाना

Who put you up to this mischief ?

(R)

Rail at - शिकायत करना

He has always railed at his parents for not understanding him.

Rake up - पुराना झगड़ा फिर से शुरु करना

Please do not rake up old quarrels at this critical juncture.

Reckon on - भरोसा रखना

I was reckoning on her presence at the function.

Run after- पीछे दौड़ना

Running after money does not speak well of you.

Run for - चुनाव लड़ना

He ran for presidentship in the college election.

Run over - गाड़ी के नीचे आना

The unlucky dog was run over by a car.

(S)

Send for - बुला भेजना

She was falled unconscious. Please send for a doctor immediately.

Serve up - परोसना

she served up a tasty meal.

Search me - मुझे पता नहीं

"Why did she get so angry suddenly ?" search me

Seasoned food- मसालेदार भोजन

Seasoned food is tasty, but not good for digestion.

Sink or swim - करो या मरो

Whatever be the situation I will never leave you. We shall sink or swim together.

Small fry - तुच्छ प्राणी

I have a factory of my own, but as compared to a big industrialist like you I am only a small fry.

Snake in the grass - आस्तीन का सांप

Don't ever trust Mohan. He is a snake in the grass.

Spin a yarn - कहानी कहना

Are you telling the truth or just spinning a yarn.

Split hairs - बहुत बारीक फर्क निकालना

He should not split hairs, but take a broad view of the mat r.

Stand one's ground - अपनी बात पर डटे रहना

He put forth many objections to my proposal but I stooo ny ground.

Sworn enemies - कट्टर दुश्मन

Nothing can bring these too sworn enemies together.

(T)

Take down- लिख लेना

Take down carefully whatever I say.

Take off - समझ बैठना

I took him for a doctor.

Take place - घटित होना

Where did the meeting take place?

Take up - पढाई आरंभ करना

After completing school he took up mechanical eng eering.

Talk shop - अपने काम के बारे में बातचीत करना

The two lawyeres always talk shop.

Tide over - निभा लेना

Will this amount enable you to tide over your financial difficulties.

Take a fancy - बहुत पसंद आना

Although there is nothing outstanding about this bed sheet, yet I have taken a fancy to it.

Take it easy- अधिक फिक्र न करना

The test is still quite far. So take it easy.

Take it ill- बुरा मानना

I hope you will take it ill if I tell you the truth.

Take time off - छुट्टी लेना

Since I was not feeling well I took two day ff last week.

Task to task - कोसना भर्त्सना करना

Mother took Naresh to task for his idlene s.

Through and through - पूर्णतः

I was caught in the rain yesterday and by the time I reached home I was wet through and through.

Throw away money - अधाधुध खर्च करना

If you throw away money like this you will soon be on the streets.

Time after time - बार-बार

He applied for a professor's job time after time but could not succeed.

To a man - सब के सब

They rose to a man and left the room agitatedly.

To and fro - आगे-पीछे

Preoccupied with his emotional problems he walked to and fro about the room in a pensive mood.

(W)

Wear off - धुंधला करना

This colour will wear off soon.

Wink at - अनदेखी करना

I can wink at this faults no longer.

What not - इत्यादि

She went to the market on a shopping spree and bought shirts, socks ties and what not.

What's what - किसी परिस्थिति में क्या उचित है

He is an intelligent person and knows what's what.

Within an ace - करीब-करीब

He was within an ace of being killed by the tiger.

Chew the fat - गप्पे लड़ाना

We shouldn't Chew the fat in the class room.

Forbid the banns - किसी की शादी पर आपत्ति करना

You need for forbid the banns to my cronies.

What will be will be - जो होगा देखा जायेगा

Just bid him what will be will be.

Bring to book - दण्ड देना

I used to bring my pals to book.

Call names - गाली देना

He is accustomed to calling me names.

Black &White - लिखकर देना

You will be given all the evidence in black & white.

Grain Ground - पैर जमा लेना

Outsiders are graining ground in our Delhi.

Cut a sorry figure - लज्जित करना

Your folks cut me a sorry figure in that gamy.

❑❑❑

Root words for spoken

1. WORTHY (लायक, योग्य)

Blameworthy – निंदा के योग्य

Praiseworthy – प्रशंसनीय

Newsworthy – समाचार का विषय बनने योग्य

Trustworthy – विश्वसनीय

Respect-worthy – आदर के योग्य

2. WIDE (व्यापी)

City-wide – शहरीव्यापी

Country-wide – देशव्यापी

Nation-wide – राष्ट्रव्यापी

State-wide – राज्यव्यापी

World-wide – विश्वव्यापी

3. WARE (बर्तन)

Silverware – चाँदी के बर्तन

Earthenware – मिट्टी के बर्तन

Glassware – काँच के बर्तन

Chinaware – चीनी मिट्टी के बर्तन

Cookware – खाना बनाने के बर्तन

4. WARD/WARDS (की ओर)

Downward – नीचे की ओर जाने वाला

Downwards – नीचे की ओर

Homeward – घर की ओर जाने वाला

Homewards – घर की ओर

Backwards – पीछे की ओर

Outwards – बाहर की ओर

Upward – ऊपर की ओर जाने वाला

Upwards – ऊपर की ओर

Westward – पश्चिम की ओर जानेवाला

Westwards – पश्चिम की ओर

5. VORE/ VOROUS (भक्षी)

Herbivore – घास खानेवाला जानवर

Insectivore – कीड़ों को खाकर जीवित रहने वाला जानवार

Insectivorous – कीटभक्षी

Omnivore · सर्वभक्षी

Carnivore – माँसभक्षी जानवर

Carnivorous – म म्भक्षी जानवर

6. VICE (उप)

Vice-captain – उप कप्तान

Vice-president – उपाध्यक्ष

Vice-principal – उप प्राचार्य

7. UNI (एक)

Unicycle एक पहिए की साईकल

Unify - ५ रू होना/करना

Uniform – एक समान

Uniformity – एकरूपता

Unite – एक करना या होना

Unity – एकता

8. UNDER (अधीन)

Undercooked कम पका हुआ

Underdeveloped कम विकसित

Undermentioned ा लिखा हुआ

Undernourished अल्पपाषित ,कुपोषित

Undersigned - नीचे हस्ताक्षर करने वाला

Undersized – साधारण के कम कद का

9. An (अकेला)

Canadian कनाडा का

Russian शेया का

American रीका का

African मा वासी

Asian – एशिया का

Australian – अस्ट्रेलिया का

European – युरोप का

Italian – इटली का

Indian – भारत का

Korean – कोरिया का

10. ULTRA (अति)

Ultra-modern – अत्याधुनिक

Ultra-fashionable – अत्यंत फैशनेबल

Ultra-rich – अति धनवान

Ultra-fast – अत्यंत तेज

Ultra-clean – अत्यंत स्वच्छ

Ultra-powerful – अंत्यत शक्तिशाली

11. TRI (तीन)

Trilateral - त्रिपक्षीय

Triangle – त्रिकोण

Triangular त्रिभुजाकार

Tricolor तिरगा

Tricycle - तीन पहियों वाली साईकिल

Tripod तिपाई

12. THERMO (उष्मा)

Thermal – उष्मा से संबंधित

Thermometer – तापमान यंत्र

Thermostat – तापस्थायी

13. TELE (दूर)

Telephone – दूरभाष

Telescope – दूरबीन

Teleprinter – दूर मुद्रक

Teleprinting – दूर मुद्रण

Television – दूरदर्शन

14. TECHN (तकनीकी)

Technical - तकनीकी

Technician - तकनीशियन

Technology - प्रौद्योगिक

15. SUPER (उत्तम)

Super-modern - अत्याधुनिक

Super-rich - अतिसंपन्न

Super-computer - उत्कृष्ट कम्प्यूटर

Super-fine - बहुत अच्छा

Super-power - महाशक्ति

16. SUB (उप)

Sub-Zero - शून्य से कम

sub-rub - उप नगर

sub-editor - उप संपादक

sub-center - उप केन्द्र

sub-branch - उप शाखा

sub-division - उप विभाग

17. STRICKEN (ग्रस्त)

Grief-stricken - दुख से पीड़ित

Famine-stricken - अकाल ग्रस्त

Fear-stricken - भयग्रस्त

Poverty-stricken - गरीबी से पीड़ित

18. STEP (सौतेला)

Stepson - सौतेला बेटा

Stepdaughter - सौतेली बेटी

Stepfather - सौतेला पिता

Stepmother - सौतेली माता

19. SEMI (अर्ध)

Semi-circle - अर्धवृत्त

Semi-final - उपांत्य

Semi-liquid - थोड़ा पतला

Semi-naked – अर्ध नग्न

Semi-automatic – अर्ध स्वचालित

20. SELF (आत्म)

Self-centred – आत्मक्रेन्दीय

Self-confidence – आत्मविश्वास

Self-confident – आत्मविश्वासी

Self-defence – आत्मरक्षा

Self-appointed – आत्मघोषित

Self assurance – आत्मअश्वासन

Self-control – आत्मनियत्रंण

Self-declared – आत्मघोषित

Self-dependence – आत्मनिर्भर

Self-destructive – आत्मघाती

21. SEISM (भूंकप)

Seismic - भूंकप का

Seismograph – भूंकप की तीव्रता दर्ज करने वाला यंत्र

Seismology – भूंकप विज्ञान

Seismologist – भूंकप वैज्ञानिक

22. RIDDEN (ग्रस्त)

Debt-ridden – कर्ज ग्रस्त

Fear-ridden – भय ग्रस्त

Flood-ridden – बाढ़ ग्रस्त

Superstition-ridden – अंधविश्वास से ग्रस्त

23. QUADRI (चार)

Quadruped - चार पैरों वाला जानवर

Quadruple - चार गुना करना

Quadruplet - एक महिला से चार बच्चों का एक साथ जन्म लेना

24. Re (पुनः)

Repay – वापस देना

Rebirth – पुनर्जन्म

Rebuild – फिर से निर्माण करना

Recapture – फिर से पकड़ना
Reconsider – पुनः विचार करना
Re-enter – पुनः प्रवेश करना
Refill – फिर से भरना
Renew – फिर से नया करना
Reopen – फिर से खोलना/खुलना
Repay – वापस देना
Reprint – पुनः मुद्रित करना
Reread – फिर से पढना
Restart – फिर से आंरभ करना
Rethink – फिर से सोचना
Reunite – फिर से एकत्रित करना

25. BIO (जीव)

Biography – जीवन चरित्र
Biology – जीवविज्ञान
Biographer – जीवन चरित्र लेखक

26. PROOF (रोधक)

Fireproof – अग्निरोधक
Bullet-proof – बंदुक की गोली का रोधक
Soundproof – ध्वनिरोधक
Rust-proof – जंग रोधक
Rain-proof – बारिश से सुरक्षित

27. PRO (समर्थक)

Pro democracy – लोकतंत्र समर्थक
Pro Government – सरकार समर्थक

28. PRE (पूर्व)

Pre election – मतदान पूर्व
Preplanned – पूर्व नियोजित
Premarital – विवाह पूर्व
Pre-war – युद्धपूर्व

29. POST (बाद का)

Post election – मतदान के बाद का

Post date – उत्तर दिनाकिंत करना

Post graduate – स्नातकोत्तर

Post war – युद्धोत्तर

Post natal – जन्मोत्तर

30. POLY (बहु)

Polytheism – अनेक ईश्वरों पर विश्वास

Polygon – बहुभुज आकृति

Polytechnic – बहु, तकनीकी (महा-विद्यालय)

31. PATER/PATRI (पैतृक)

Paternity – पैतृक

Patriarch – कुल अथवा परिवार प्रमुख

Patriarchal – पुरूष प्रधान

Patricide – पितृहत्या

Patriarchy – पुरूष प्रधान समाज

Paternal – पिता का, पैतृक

32. PAN (सारा)

Pan-indian – अखिल भारतीय

Pan-national – अखिल राष्ट्रीय

33. OVER (अधिक)

Overconfidence – अति आत्मविश्वास

Overburden – अत्यधिक बोझ, भार

Overcrowded – अत्यधिक भीड़वाला

Overweight – ज्यादा वजन

Overspend – बहुत ज्यादा खर्च करना

Overuse – बहुत अधिक उपयोग

34. OUT (ज्यादा)

Outlast – ज्यादा देर टिकना

Out live – ज्यादा समय तक जीना

Outnumber – संख्या से अधिक होना

35. OMNI (सर्व)

Omnipotent - सर्वशक्तिमान

Omniscient - सर्वज्ञानी

omnipresent - सर्वव्यापी

Omnivorous - सर्वभक्षी

36. LOGY (शास्त्र)

Biology - जीव विज्ञान

Zoology - प्रॉणि विज्ञान

37. NON (नहीं)

Non-violence - अहिंसा

Non-violent - अंहिसक

Non-resident - अनिवासी

Non-existent - जो अस्तित्व में ना हो

Non-living - निर्जीव

Non-smoker - धूम्रपान न करने वाला

38. MONO (एक)

Monolingual - एक भाषा

Monocle - एक आँख का चश्मा

Monotheism - एक ही ईश्वर में विश्वास

39. MIS (गलत)

Misbehave - दुर्व्यवहार करना

Misbehaviour - दुर्व्यवहार

Misconduct - बुरा आचरण

Misdeed - गुनाह

Mishear - गलत सुनना

Misinform - गलत जानकरी देना

Misinformation - गलत जानकरी

Mislead - गलत मार्ग दिखाना

Misprint - छपाई की गलती

40. MINI (लघु)

Mini bus – छोटी बस

Mini library – लघु पुस्तकायल

Mini camera – छोटा कैमरा

Mini market – छोटा बाजार

41. MILLI (एक हजारवाँ हिस्सा)

Milligram – ग्राम का एक हजारवाँ हिस्सा

Millilitre – लीटर का एक हजारवाँ हिस्सा

Millimetre – मीटर का एक हजारवाँ हिस्सा

Millisecond – सेकंड का एक हजारवाँ हिस्सा

42. MICRO (सूक्ष्म)

Microbiology – सूक्ष्मजीव विज्ञान

Microscope – सूक्ष्मदर्शी यंत्र

Micro-organism – अति सूक्ष्मजीव

Microgram - ग्राम का दस लाखवाँ हिस्सा

Microsecond - सेकंड का दस लाखवाँ हिस्सा

Micrometre – मीटर का दस लाखवाँ हिस्सा

43. METER (मापक)

Speedometer - गतिमापक यंत्र

Thermometer – तापमापक यंत्र

Barometer - वायुदाबमापक यंत्र

Chronometer - काल/मापक यंत्र

44. MATER/MATRI (मातृ)

Maternity – मातृत्व

Matricide – मातृहत्या

Matriarch - स्त्रीप्रधान समाज की कुटुंब प्रमुख स्त्री

Matriarchy – स्त्रीप्रधान समाज रचना

Maternal – माँ से संबधित

45. MATE (साथी)

Room-mate – एक ही कमरे में रहने वाला साथी

Team-mate – सघंमित्र

Class-mate – सहपाठी

School-mate – स्कूल मित्र, सहपाठी

46. LONG (लंबी अवधि)

Life-long – उम्रभर

Hour-long – घंटाभर

Night-long – रातभर

Week-long – हप्ताभर

Year -long – साल भर

47. KiLO (किलो)

Kilolitre – 1000 लीटर

Kilogram – 1000 ग्राम

Kilometre – 1000 मीटर

Kilowatt – 1000 वाट्

48. ITIS (सूजन)

Bronchitis – श्वास नली की सूजन

Dermatitis – त्वचा की सूजन

Appendicitis – अन्त्रापुच्छ की सूजन

Hepatitis – यकृत की सूजन

Tonsillitis – गले की गांठों की सूजन

Nephritis – गुर्दे/ मूत्रपिंड की सूजन

49. IST (विशेषज्ञ)

Botanist – वनस्पति शास्त्री

Dentist – दाँत रोग विशेषज्ञ

Dramatist – नाटककार

Novelist – उपन्यासकार

Physicist – भौतिकशास्त्री

50. ISH (का/सा)

Spainish – स्पेन का
British – ब्रिटेन का
English – इंग्लैड का
Turkish – तुर्की का
Reddish – लाल सा/ थोड़ा लाल
Yellowish – पीला सा/थोड़ा पीला
Whitish – सफेद सा
Greenish – हरा सा
Bluish – नीला सा
Fattish – मोटा सा
Childish – बच्चों जैसा
Womanish – औरतों जैसा
Foolish – मूर्खो जैसा
Girlish – लड़कियों जैसा
Owlish – उल्लू जैसा
Slavish – गुलाम जैसा

51. INTRA (अंतर्गत)

Intra-party – पक्षांर्गत
Intra-family – पारिवारिक
Intra-city – शहर के अंदर चलने वाला

52. INTER (अंदर/अधीन)

Inter city – अंतर शहरीय
Interstate – अंतर्राज्यीय
Inter-racial – अंतरवंशीय
Intercaste – अंतरजातीय
Inter-continental – अंतरमहाद्विपीय
Interpersonal – परस्पर
International – अतंराष्ट्रीय
Intercollegiate – विभिन्न कालेजों के बीच
Inter-dependent – अंतर निर्भर

53. ICS (शास्त्र)

Economics – अर्थशास्त्र
Linguistics – भाषाशास्त्र

54. IAN/ICIAN (विशेषज्ञ , कार)

Musician – संगीतकार

Historian – इतिहासकार

Grammarian – व्याकरणकार

Magician – जादूगर

Paediatrician – बाल रोग विशेषज्ञ

Mathematician – गणित विशेषज्ञ

55. HYPER (अत्यधिक बहुत)

Hyper-sensitive – अति संवेदनशील

Hypertension – उच्च रक्त दाव

Hyper-critical – अत्यधिक आलोचनात्मक

56. GREAT (से एक पीढ़ी दूर)

Great-Grandfather – परदादा, परनाना

Great-Grandmother – परदादी, परनानी

Great-grandson – परपोता

Great-Granddaughter – परपोती

Great Great grandfather – दादा के दादा

Great-uncle – माता अथवा पिता के मामा/चाचा

57. GON (कोण)

Octagonal – अष्टकोणी

Octagon – अष्टकोण

Pentagon – पंचकोण

Hexagon – षट्कोण

Heptagon – सप्तकोण

58. GASTRO (पेट)

Gastrologist – पेट विकार विशेषज्ञ

Gastric – पेट का

59. GEO (भू)

Geology – भूविज्ञान

Geography – भूगोल

Geometry – रेखागणित

60. Free (स्वतंत्र)

Carefree – चिंता मुक्त

Interest-free – ब्याजमुक्त

Germ-free – जीवाणु मुक्त

Debt-free – कर्जमुक्त

Dust-free – धूलरहित

Pollution-free – प्रदूषण मुक्त

61. Extra (अतिक्ति)

Extra-curricular – पाठ्यक्रम के अतिरिक्त

Extra-marital – अतिरिक्त वैवाहिक

Extra-ordinary – असामान्य

Extra-terrestrial – पृथ्वी के बाहर का

62. Ex (पूर्व-भूतपूर्व)

Ex-wife – पूर्व पत्नी

Ex-president – पूर्व राष्ट्रपति

Ex-soldier – पूर्व सैनिक

63. Ever (निरंतर, हमेशा)

Ever-increasing – निरंतर बढ़ने वाला

Ever-available – हमेशा उपलब्ध

Ever-changing – हमेशा बदलने वाला

Ever-growing – निरंतर बढ़ने वाला

Ever-willing – तैयार

64. Equi (सम)

Equiangular – समकोण

Equidistant – समान दूरी पर स्थित

Equilateral – समभुज

65. ER/OR (करने वाला)

Buy – खरीदना

Buyer – खरीदने वाला

Collect – संग्रह करना

Collector – संग्रह करने वाला

Compile – संकलन करना

Compiler - संकलन करने वाला

Conquer - जीतना

Conqueror - जीतनेवाला

Control - नियंत्रण करना

Controller - नियंत्रक

Create - निर्माण करना

Creator - निर्माता

Lose - हार जाना

Loser - हारने वाला

Oversee - निरीक्षण करना

Overseer - निरीक्षक

Talk - बोलना

Talker - बोलने वाला

Think - सोचना

Thinker - सोचने वाला

Interview - साक्षात्कार लेना

Interviewer - साक्षात्कार लेने वाला

66. Deci (दसवाँ हिस्सा)

Decimetre - मीटर का दसवाँ हिस्सा

Decilitre - लीटर का दसवाँ हिस्सा

Decigram - ग्राम का दसवाँ हिस्सा

67. DE (बाहर निकालना)

Decentralize - विकेन्द्रीकरण करना

Depressurize - हवा का दबाव कम करना

Dehydrate - पानी निकाल देना

Decolourize - रंग निकाल देना

Deforest - जंगल काटना

Defrost - जमा हुआ बर्फ निकाल देना

De-ice - जमा हुआ बर्फ हटाना

Demilitarize - फौज निकालना

Defog/demist - कोहरा हटाना

68. Bound (की ओर)

Northbound – उत्तर की ओर

Eastbound – पूर्व की ओर

Southbound – दक्षिण की ओर

Westbound – पश्चिम की ओर

Outbound – (किसी जगह से) बाहर की ओर

Snowbound – हिमपात की ओर

Weatherbound – मौसम सम्बन्धी

Housebound – घर की ओर

69. Co (सह/सहायक)

Co author – सह लेखक

Co editor – सह संपादक

Co driver – सह चालक

Co worker – सह कर्मी

Co founder – सह स्थापक

Co education – सह शिक्षा

Co operate – सहकार्य करना

Co pilot – सह विमान चालक

Co writer – सह लेखक

Co producer – सह निर्माता

70. Cide (हत्या)

Fratricide – भ्रातृहत्या

Homicide – मानवहत्या

Genocide – वंशहत्या

Infanticide – शिशुहत्या

Patricide – पितृहत्या

Regicide – राजहत्या

Suicide – आत्महत्या

Germicide – जीवाणु नाशक

Insecticide – कीटनाशक

Pesticide – जीवाणु नाशक

SPOKEN VOCABULARY
Set - 1

1. **A** ए-अंग्रेजी वर्णमाला का पहला अक्षर, सर्वोच्च, बहुत अच्छा

He is an A class artist.

I got an A grade in my English test.

2. **A/An** अ/ऐन-एक, प्रत्येक, कोई

1. Do you have a book of short stories?

I drink milk twice a day.

2. (Indefinite articles) A & An as indefinite articles are used before a single countable noun. A is used before a con sonant sound and An before a vowel sound:

Seema is a teacher.

Rahul is an engineer.

3. **Abandon (v.)** अबैन्डन-त्यागना, जाने देना

Why did you abandon your studies?

4. **Cab (n.)** कैब-घोड़ागाड़ी टैक्सी

I hired a cab to go to the railway station.

5. **Cabbage (n.)** कैबिज-बंदगोभी

Cabbag is my favourite vegetable.

6. **Cabin (n.)** केबिन-1. कमरा, कोठरी

Which is the General Manager's cabin?

2. कुटी, कुटीर

The poor family lived in cabin on the edge of the town.

7. **Cabinet (n.)** कैबिनट-1. आलमारी,पेटिका

Uma arranged the new crockery on the shelves of the cabinet.

2. मंत्रिमंडल

Mostly decisions are taken unanimously by the cabinet.

8. **Ugly (adj.)** अँग्लि-बदसूरत, कुरुप

Cinderella had two ugly sisters. They were unkind to her.

9. **Ulterior (adj.)** अँल्टिअरिअर्-गुप्त, छिपाकर रखा गया

The servant agreed to work for us at a very low price. There must be some ulterior motive behind it.

10. **Ultimate** अँल्टिमट-सर्वोत्तम

(adj.) Serving our clients with honesty is the ultimate aim of this organisation.

(n.) The movie was the ultimate in cinemotography.

(adv.) An unbalanced diet will ultimately lead to poor health.

11. **Ultimatum (n.)** अल्टिमटम-अंतिम चेतावनी

She issued an ultimatum-either he finds a job or they will get divorced.

12. **Baby (n.)** बेबी-बच्चा, शिशु

She took her baby into the lap.

13. **Bachelor (n.)** बैचलर्-अविवाहित, कुमार

Bhishma Pitamah remained a bechelor all his life.

14. **Back (n.)** बैक - 1. पीठ, पृष्ठ

There is a mole on my back.

2. पिछवाड़ा, पृष्ठभाग

The little boy had blotches of ink at the back of his hand.

He ran to the back of the house.

(v.) पीछे हटना/करना

I backed my car before taking the turn.

(adj.) पिछला

The thief entered the house through the back door.

3. (adv.) वापस

Please come back quickly.

15. Backward (adj.) बैकवर्ड-पिछड़ा हुआ

Many of the Indian villages are still backward with no electricity.

16. Fable (n.) फ़ेबल-कहानी, नीतिकथा

Give your child Aesop's Fables to read.

17. Fabric (n.) फ़ैब्रिक-कपड़ा, वस्त्र

Cotton fabric is good for the skin.

18. Fabulous (adj.) फ़ैब्यलस-उत्कृष्ट

I had a fabulous dream in which I become a millionaire.

19. Face (n.) फ़ेस-1. चेहरा, मुख

Go and wash your face.

2. (v.) सामना करना, विरोध करना

Rohit faced strong opposition from his parents in his inter-caste marriage.

20. Yacht (n.) याच-छोकी नौका

We cruised around the river in a small yatch.

21. I (pron.) आइ-मैं

I want to go home.

22. Ice (n.) आइस-बर्फ़, हिम

Please get me some ice from the fridge.

23. Gadget (n.) गैजिट-छोटा उपकरण

He has a good knowledge of the latest gadgets.

24. Gain (v.) गेन-1. पाना, प्राप्त करना

You will gain many friends if you have a helpful nature.

(n.) There is no gain without pain.

2. लाभ, नफ़ा (होना)

Gain and loss are part of any business.

25. Gait (n.) गेट-चाल

Broken shoe affected her gait.

26. Galaxy (n.) गैलक्सि-आकाशगंगा

There are numerous stars in the galaxy.

27. Label लेबल-लेबल, परचा, लेबल लगाना

(n.) I put a label on the bottle to show that it contained a poisonous chemical.

(v.) Have you labelled all the packets?

28. Laboratory (n.) लबॉरट्रि-प्रयोगशाला

Does your school have a well-equipped science laboratory?

29. Labour लेबर्-1. परिश्रम, मेहनत (करना)

(n.) Gandhiji taught us the dignity of labour.

(v.) The farmer labours in the fields to feed the country men.

2. (n.) श्रमिक (वर्ग), मजदूर

I heard you had some labour trouble in your factory.

30. Lace (n.) लेस्

1. जालीदार कपड़ा

She stitched lace in her dress.

2. फ़ीता

Tie your shoelaces.

3. फ़ीता कसना

(v.) Lace up your shoes.

31. Habit (n.) हैबिट-आदत, अभ्यास, मिज़ाज़

You must leave bad habits and cultivate good ones.

32. Haggard (adj.) हैगर्ड-दुबला, पतला, मरियल

The haggard looking servant was quick in doing tasks efficiently.

33. Hail (n.) हेल-1. ओला

Last night it rained hailstones.

2. (v.) स्वागत करना, पुकारना

I saw my friend at a distance and hailed him.

34. Hair (n.) हेअर्-बाल, केश

Some people dye hair to hide their premature grey ng.

35. Jab (v.) जैब-चुभाना, कोंचना

I grimaced in pain when the doctor jabbed a needle into my arm.

(n.) I have to go for my cholera jab tomorrow.

36. Jackal (n.) जैकल-गीदड़

The jackal in the story fell into a tank of paint.

37. Jacket (n.) जैक्ट- जाकैट, मिरजई, आवरण

Please iron my jacket.

38. Jackfruit (n.) जैकफ्रूट-कटहल

Mother bought jackfruit from the market.

39. Pace पेस-क़दम, पग, टहलना, क़दम-क़दम जाना

(n.) Please walk quickly and try to keep pace with me.

(v.) I paced up and down the room.

40. Pacify (v.) पैसिफ़ाई-किसी नाराज़ व्यक्ति को शांत करना

The little girl was pacified only when we of fered her a bar of chocolate.

41. Pack (v.) पैसिफ़ाई-किसी नाराज़ व्यक्ति को शांत करना

Have you packed all your thirgs?

2. Have you packed all your things?

How much tea does his pack contain?

42. Pad (n.) पैड-लि व के लिए एक-से कटे क़ागजों का संग्रह

I want to buy a letter pad.

43. Keen (adj.) कीन-1. उत्सुक, उत्साह तेज़

I am very keen to spend my vacations in Goa.

2. तीक्ष्ण, पैना, तेज़

Do you have a knife with a keen edge?

44. Keep (v.) कीप-1. रखना, पास रखना

You may keep this pencil if you need it.

2. ध्यान रखना

Keep an eye on the child.

3. चलाना, चलना

Keep to the left of the road.

4. पूरा करना, निबाहना

Once you make a promise, you must keep it up.

5. देख-रेख करना

Who keeps the house for you?

6. ठीक रहना, नहीं बिगड़ना

Can we keep these bananas for a couple of days?

7. जारी रखना, निरंतर करते रहना

Keep smiling.

8. (n.) भोजन और आवास का संरक्षण

How much do you pay for your keep?

45. Kerb (n.) कर्ब-सड़क का किनारा

Don't drive too near the kerb.

46. Kernel (n.) कर्नल-गिरी

Almond kernels are good both for the brain and the eyes.

47. Machine (n.) मशीन-यन्त्र, मशीन

Is this a printing machine?

Have you insured the machinery in your factory?

My brother-in-law is a mechanic in Delhi Cloth Mills.

48. Mad (adj.) मैड-1. पागल, लिक्षिप्त

Has she gone mad?

2. उत्तेजित, क्रुद्ध

She felt mad when her servant burnt her favourite saree while ironing.

3. मूर्खतापूर्ण

The idea of leaving your house for ever is really mad.

49. Maestro (n.) माइस्ट्रो-संगीताचार्य

Jagit Singh is a great ghazal maestro.

50. Magic (n.) मैजिक-जादू

Many people still believe in magic.

Yesterday I took my children to a magic show.

51. Sachet (n.) सैशे-प्लास्टिक या काग़ज का छोटा पैकेट

Get a sachet of coffee from the nearby shop.

52. Sack सैक्

1. (n.) बोरा

She filled up the sack with potatoes.

2. (v.) नौकरी से बर्खास्त करना

He was sacked from the job because of bad behaviour.

53. Sacred (adj.) सेक्रिड-पवित्र, पावन, धार्मिक

Gita is a sacred book of Hindus.

54. Sacrifice (v.) सेक्रिफाइस-त्याग करना, हानि उठाना

Those who sacrifice their personal interests for a great cause never fail.

(n.) His sacrifices for the country will always be remembered.

55. Nag (v.) नैग-सिर खाना, तंग करना

Don't nag your servant so much.

56. Nail नेल-1. कील, मेख, कील ठोंकना, कील से जड़ना

(v.) Nail a new board on the wall.

(n.) Hang this picture on that nail.

2. नाखून, नख

Always keep your nails clean.

Never bite your nails.

57. Naive (adj.) नाइव-भोला-भाला

(adj.) Don't be so naive to work for free.

(n.) They laughed at her for her naivety.

58. Naked (adj.) नेकिड-1. नंगा, निर्वस्त्र

I pitied the naked child in the arms of the beggar.

2. खुला, अनावृत

Was fire caused by the naked electric wires?

59. Table (n.) टेबल-1. मेज़

Put the teapot on the table.

2. तालिका

Before we buy a book, we always look at the table of contents.

60. Tablet (n.) टैबलेट-टिकिया, दवा की गोली

The doctor told me to take the tablet every four hours.

61. Taboo (n.) टबू-वर्जित शब्द या कर्म

Divorce is still considered a taboo in many Indian societies.

62. Tack (v.) टैक-1. टाँकना

If you tack the dress, I shall be able to try it on.

2. हवा के विरुद्ध जहाज़ को चलाना

We had to tack to reach the harbour.

3. पतली कीलें जड़ना

I tack the picture to the frame.

63. Oar (n.) ऑर्-चप्पू

I rowed the boat with a pair of oars.

64. Oath (v.) ओथ-शपथ, सौगन्ध

The President is administered the oath of office by the Chief Justice of India.

65. Obses (adj.) ओबीस्-स्थूलकाय

She was an obese child.

66. Obey (v.) ॲबे-आज्ञा मानना

My children obey my instructions.

(adj.) They are obedient children.

(n.) We shall act in obedience to our manager's orders.

67. Xmas (n.) क्रिमसम-बड़ा दिन, ईसा का जन्म दिवस, 25 दिसम्बर

Sometimes we spell Christmas as Xmas.

Xmas is an important festival of Christians.

68. Quack (n.) क्वैक-1. नीम हकीम

Do not ever visit that doctor. He is a quack and does not hold a medical degree.

2. (v.) काँ-काँ करना

The ducks quaked until they were fed.

69. Quadruped (n.) क्वाड्रुपेड-चौपाया

A cow is a quadruped.

70. Quail (v.) क्वेल-काँपना

The convict quailed when he was s entenced.

71. Quaint (adj.) क्वेंट-निराला, अजीब

The old man's house was old and quaint.

I saw a quaint old lady.

72. Each (adj.) ईच-प्रत्येक, हर एक, एक-एक परस्पर

The two neighbours were abusing each other.

The teacher checked each and every student's homework.

73. Eager (adj.) ईगर्-उत्सुक, इच्छुक

You look eager to go home early.

74. Eagle (n.) ईग्ल-गरुड़

Can any other bird fly as high as the eagle?

75. Ear (n.) इअर- 1. कान, कर्ण

My father bought a hearing-aid for his left ear.

2. वाली, भुट्टा

Look at those ears of corn heaped in the field.

76. Zeal (n.) ज़ील-उत्साह, जोश, सरगर्मी

He has a great zeal for work.

Zeal without knowlege is like an expendition in the dark.

77. Wacky (adj.) वैकि-मसखरा, मज़ाकिया

She is full of such wacky ideas.

78. Waddle (v.) वॉडल-(बत्तख की तरह) चलना, बत्तख की चाल

Very fat people often waddle as they walk along. Ducks waddle.

79. Wade (v.) वेड-पानी में चलना, पार करना

I like to wade in the river. You are not wading but having a swim.

80. Wafer (n.) वेफ़र्-पतला बिस्कुट

Usually we take a wafer with an ice cream.

81. Dagger (n.) डैगर्-छुरा, कटार

A collection of daggers was on display in the museum.

82. Daily (adv.) डेलि-1. प्रतिदिन

The doctor advised the heart patient to take a walk daily in the morning.

2. (n.) दैनिक अखबार

Reena is employed as a reporter in a local daily.

(adj.) Exercise is an essential part of daily routine of a healthy person.

83. Dainty (adj.) डेन्टि-सुकुमार, रुचिर

We were all charmed by the dancer's dainty performance.

84. Rabbit (n.) रैबिट-खरगोश, खरहा

The rabbit is a small and furry animal that digs holes in the earth to live in.

85. Race (n.) रेस-1. जाति, वंश

We all belong to the human race.

2. दौड़

Suresh came first in the 3 kilometre race.

3. (v.) दौड़ लगाना/लगवाना

Let us race to the next door.

Hamid races his pigeons every day.

86. Rack (n.) रैक-1. सामान रखने की जगह

Put these books in the rack.

2. (v.) दुखना

After working in the field the whole day, his body racked with pain.

3. लगाना

Try to rack your brain to solve the problem.

87. Racket (n.) रैकिट-1. शोर, कोलाहल, गुलगपाड़ा

What a racket the children are making!

2. रैकिट

We use a racket while playing badminton.

88. Vacant (adj.) वेकन्ट-खाली, रिक्त

The shop will be vacant on Monday and we can them move in.

(n.) There is no vacancy in office.

89. Vacation (n.) वकेशन-अवकाश, (लंबी) छुट्टी

We have two months' vacation each year.

90. Vaccinate (v.) वैक्सिनेट-टीका लगाना

The children are being vaccinated.

(n.) Vaccination against contagious diseases is essential.

The vaccinators should take care of cleanliness.

91. Vacuum (n.) वैक्युअम-शून्य, खाली जगह, रिक्त स्थान

Tinned food is mostly vaccum packed.

It is put into a tin and all the air is forced out of the tin-pot before it is sealed.

92. Paddy (n.) पैडि-धान

Our train travelled through paddy fields.

93. Page (n.) पेज-पृष्ठ

How many pages of this book have you read?

94. Pail (n.) पेल-बाल्टी, डोल

I filled the pail with water from the tap.

95. Pain (n.) पेन-क्लेश, तकलीफ़, व्यथा, पीड़ा देना

The doctor gave me a tablet to relieve the pain in my stomach.

(v.) You misbehaviour pained me greatly.

96. Backwards (Adv.) बैकवर्ड्ज़-पीछे की ओर

On seeing the lion in the forest, everyone ran backwards.

97. Bad (Adj.) बैड - 1. बुरा, खराब

Do not keep company with bad boys.

2. न खाने लायक

We cannot eat this fish, as it has gone bad.

3. (adv.) बुरी तरह से, अत्यधिक

The driver was badly injured.

98. Badge (n.) बैज्-बिल्ला

Every student is required to wear the school badge.

99. Baffle (v.) बैफ़ल-चकरा देना, निष्फल कर देना

Students were baffled by the difficult question paper.

100. Abbreviation (n.) अब्रीविएशन-संक्षेप, संक्षिप्त रुप

U.N.O is the abbreviation of United Nations Organisation.

SPOKEN VOCABULARY
Set - 2

1. **Abide (v.)** अबाइड-कानून आदि का पालन करना
   We should abide by the laws of the country.
2. **Ablaze (adj.)** अब्लेज़्-जलता हुआ
   Fireman rushed to the house, which was ablaze.
3. **Able (adj).** एबुल-योग्य, समर्थ
   Anil was not able to play football as he had broken his leg in an accident.
4. **Cable (n.)** केबल-1. रस्सा, समुद्री तार
   The workmen dug the ground to repair the telephone cables.
   2. तार भेजना
   My brother cabled from London that he was coming to India.
5. **Cafe (n.)** कैफे़-कॉफी हाउस, कहवा
   A South Indian cafe usually serves a nice cup of filter coffee.
6. **Cage** केज-पिंजरा, कटघरा, पिंजरे में बंद करना
   (n.) The little girl brought a cage for her pet parrot.
   (v.) Rahul caged his pet rabbits before going out.
7. **Cajole (v.)** कजोल-खुशामद से अपनी बात मनवाना
   We can't cajole him into being a part of our team.
8. **Umbrella (n.)** अम्ब्रेला-छाता, छतरी
   An umbrella protects us from the rain or the sun.
9. **Umpire (n.)** अम्पाइअर्-निर्णायक, रेफरी, अम्पायर
   The umpire declared that the batsman had been run out.
10. **Umpteen (adj.)** अम्प्टीन-बहुत बार
   I can watch that movie umpteen number of times.
11. **Un (pre.)** अन-रहित के अर्थ में,
12. **Dacoit (n.)** डैकोइट-डकैत
   There used to be dacoits in the Chambal Valley many years ago.
13. **Facet (n.)** फै़सिट-पहलू
   We must consider all the facets of this project before taking it up.
14. **Facillity (n.)** फ़सिलटि-सुविधा
   The school provides excellent sports facilities.
15. **Fact (n.)** फैक्ट-सत्य, सच्चाई
   The police recorded all the facts of the murder case.
16. **Factor (n.)** फै़क्टर-1. गुणक, गुणन खंड
   Find out the factors of this number.
   2. कारण, निमित
   Corruption was the main factor behind the fall of the government.
17. **Yacht (n.)** याच-छोकी नौका
   We cruised around the river in a small yatch.
18. **Yam (n.)** यैम-रतालू, अरबी
   Yam is used in spicy preparation on vegetables.
   Yam is a favourite vegetable of African people.
19. **Icon (n.)** आइकॉन
   1. कम्प्यूटर के स्क्रीन पर प्रोग्राम के लद्युचित्र
   Suddenly the icons vanished from my computer.
   2. किसी वस्तु का प्रतीक
   She is the style icon of the college.
20. **Idea (n.)** आइ 'डिआ-भावना, धारणा, मत विचार
   What a good idea!
   How do you like the idea of going on a trip

to Agra this Sunday?

21. Ideal (adj.) आइ 'डिअल्-आदर्श, आदर्श (स्वरुप) काल्पनिक

Sohna is an ideal place for a picnic.

22. Identical (adj.) आइडेन्टिकल-बिल्कुल समान

This problem is identical to the one we faced last year.

23. Gale (n.) गेल-झंझा, आँधी, हवा का झोंका

A gallant young man saved the two drwoning girls.

(n.) The policeman was rewarded for his gallantry

24. Gallery (n.) गैलरि-1 कलाभवन

In which gallery are you exhibiting your picture?

2. वीथी, गैलरी

The patient's relatives were sitting in the gallery in front of the operation theatre.

25. Gallop (v.) गैलप-1 सरपट दौड़ना या दौड़ाना

The horse had to gallop to keep pace with the motor-car

2. (n.) टाप

The gallop of Rehman's horse could be heard from a distance.

26. Gamble गैम्बल-1 जुआ खेलना, जुआबाजी

(n.) David's parents did not know that he had taken to gambling.

2. दाँव पर लगाना

Starting a business is a gamble.

(v.) He gambled the entire night and lost everything he had.

27. Lack लैक-कमी/अभाव (होना)

(n.) We always suffer from a lack of water in summer.

(v.) The dish lacked salt.

28. Lad (n.) लैड-लड़का, युवक

Your son has grown into a fine young lad.

29. Ladder (n.) लैड(र्)-सीढ़ी

Use the ladder to climb up to the roof,

30. Lady (n.) लेडि-महिला

Your daughter has grown into a polished young lady.

31. Half (adj.) हाफ़-आधा

The time is half past six.

32. Hall (adj.) हॉल-1. बड़ा कमरा, हॉल

The school's annual function was held in a spacious hall.

2. सभा भवन

Did you attend the meeting at the Town Hall?

33. Hallucination (n.) हैल्यूसिनेशन्-मतिभ्रम

You saw your dead grandfather last night! It must be a hallucination.

34. Halt हॉल्ट-विराम, रुकाव, पड़ाव, रुकना, रोकना

(v.) I did not halt till I reached the station.

(n.) A fire accident in our office brought all works to a halt.

35. Hamlet (n.) हैम्लट-खेड़ा, बहुत छोटा गाँव

My native place is a hamlet of a few houses.

36. Hammer हैमर्-1. हथौड़ा (मारना), ठोकना

(n.) Where is your hammer?

(v.) Have you hammered the nail properly?

37. Hammock (n.) हैमक-झूला

I have fixed a hammock in my garden.

38. Hamper (v.) हैम्पर्-1. रोड़ा अटकाना, विघ्न डालना

The strikers tried to hamper the traffic movement.

2. डलिया

All the boys had brought hampers on the trip.

39. Jagged (adj.) जैगिड-1. काँटेदार, दाँतेदार

Be careful; this saw has ajaggededge.

2. नुकीला और खुरदरा

We can see jagged rocks on the sea coast.

40. Jail (n.) जेल-कैदखाना, कारागृह

How far is the local jail from here?

(v.) You can be jailed for rash driving.

41. Jam (n.) जैम-1. मुरब्बा

I want to buy a jar of apple jam.

2. भीड़

Ram somehow managed to reach the station in time despite facing a major traffic-jam.

42. Jar (n.) जार्-1. मर्तबान

Please give me a jar of face cream.

2. (v.) धक्का लगाना

I was badly jarred when my bicycle struck the fence.

3. (adj.) कानों को बुरी लगने वाली

You should oil this door to stop its jarring sound.

43. Kerosene (n.) केरसीन-मिट्टी का तेल

Do you cook on a kerosene stove?

44. Ketchup (n.) टमाटर की चटनी

Can I have some tomato ketchup?

45. Kettle (n.) केटल-केतली, देगची

I use an electic kettle for making tea.

46. Key (n.) की-कुंजी, चाबी

Where have you kept the key of the safe?

47. Magistrate (n.) मैजिस्ट्रे'ट-दण्डनायक, दण्डाधिकारी

I was summoned to the magistrate's court to give evidence.

48. Magnet (n.) मैग्नट्

1. चुंबक

(n.) Her eyes are attractive as a magnet.

2. चुंबकीय, व्यक्तित्व

(adj.) He has a magnetic personality.

49. Magnificent (adj.) मैग्निफिसन्ट-शानदार

You can get a magnificent view of the sea from the terrace of our building.

50. Magnify (v.) मैग्निफ़ाइ-आवर्धन करना, बढ़ाना

This lens magnifies the object fifty times.

Look at this small insect through a magnifying glass.

50. Sad (adj.) सैड-उदास

Why are you so sad today?

(n.) दु:ख

I cannot understand the reason of your sadness.

51. Saddle (n. & v.) सैडल-ज़ीन, काठी

(n.) The rider put the saddle on his horse's back.

(v.) We saddled our horses and got ready to march.

52. Safe सेफ़

1. (adj.) सुरक्षित

Is it safe driving in this area?

2. (n.) अलमारी या तिजोरी

Keep the money in the safe.

53. Safeguard (v.) सेफ़गार्ड-संभावित खतरों से सुरक्षा देने वाली वस्तु

He promised to safeguard our interests in the deal.

54. Name नेम-1. नाम (रखना)

(v.) Whatever you want, just name it.

2. ख्याति, नाम

(n.) What is your name?

I am sure your son will make a name for himself.

55. Nap (n.) नैप-झपकी

Do you take a nap after lunch?

56. Naphthalene (n.) नैफ़्थलीन-फ़िनाइल की गोलियां

I put some napthalene balls in the wollens to protect them from insects.

57. Napkin (n.) नैप्किन-नैपकिन

Please keep some napkins on the dinner table.

58. Tackle (v.) टैकल-1. हाथ में लेना, में जुट जाना

Aunt says she must tackle a lot of sewing today.

2. (n.) मछली पकड़ने का काँटा

You can buy a fishing tackle at this shop.

3. फुटबॉल मैच में प्रतिपक्षी को रोकने की क्रिया

That was a fine tackle!

59. Tact (n.) टैक्ट-कला, व्यवहार-कौशल

You have the tact of persuading the men to go back to work.

60. Tadpole (n.) टैड्पोल-मेंढक का बच्चा

We caught a tadpole in the garden.

61. Tag (n.) टैग-लुप्पी, लेबल, लटकन

Every article in the shop should bear a tag showing its price.

62. Object (n.) ऑब्जे'क्ट-1. उद्देश्य, लक्ष्य

What is the object of your foreign tour?

2. पदार्थ, चीज़

What is that object floating in the lake?

3. (v.) आपत्ति/विरोध करना

I object to your rude remarks.

(n.) I have an objection to them.

(adj.) Your habit of coming late to every important meeting is objectionable.

63. Oblige (v.) अब्लाइज-1. आभारी बनाना, उपकृत करना

Dinesh obliged his friends with dinner party.

2. बाध्य/विवश करना

Do not oblige me to accompay you.

My duties oblige me to work late.

64. Oblivious (adj.) अब्लिवियस-बेखबर

He was sleeping on his desk oblivious of the people around him.

65. Obnoxious (adj.) अब्नॉक्शस-घिनौना

The worms inside the garden were obnoxious.

66. Quake (v.) क्वेक-काँपना

You are quaking with cold.

67. Qualify (v.) क्वॉलिफ़ाइ-1. योग्य होना

You do not qualify for this post.

2. (adj.) प्रमाण-पत्र प्राप्त करना

Are you qualified for this post.

3. योग्यता

What are your qualifications?

68. Quality (n.) क्वॉलटी-1. किस्म, कोटि

This tea is not of good quality.

2. गुण

Honesty is one of the qualities of an ideal businessman.

69. Qualm (n.) क्वाम-परेशानी

I have no qualms about going to his place again and again.

70. Early अर्लि

1. (adv.) शीघ्र, पहले

I went to the show early because I wanted a good seat.

2. (adj.) प्रातःकाल, प्रातःकालीन

I have my breakfast early in the day.

71. Earn (v.) अर्न्-कमाना, प्राप्त करना

How much do your earn every month?

72. Earnest (adj.) अर्नेस्ट्-उत्साही, जोशीला, गंभीर

If you want to succeed in life, you must be earnest about your work.

73. Earth (n.) अर्थ- 1. पृथ्वी, धरती

What is the shape of the earth?

2. मिट्टी, ज़मीन

Labourers were digging the earth to lay telephone cables.

74. Zebra (n.) ज़ेब्रा-अफ्रीका का एक प्रकार का घोड़ा जिसके शरीर पर काली व सफ़ेद धारियां होती हैं

A zebra has white and black stripes on its body.

75. Wag वैग

1. (n.) ठट्ठेबाज़, दिल्लगीबाज़

Uncle Arora is quite a wag.

2. (v.) हिलाना

The puppy wags its tail when it is happy.

76. Wage (n.) वेज-वेतन, मज़दूरी

Harish's wages as a mason is 90 rupees a day.

Give the labourer his wage before his perspiration be dry.

77. Waggon, Wagon (n.) वैगन-छकड़ा

Usually every farmer has a wagon on his farms. He carries hay in the wagon.

78. Waif (n.) वेफ़-दुबला-पतला, लावारिस

No one knows the sufferings of a waif.

He was sad because he was waif.

79. **Dairy (n.)** डेअरि-डेरी, दुग्धशाला

From which dairy do you get your milk supply?

80. **Dam (n.)** डैमू-बाँध

Have you seen the Bhakhra Dam?

81. **Damage** डैमिज्-नुकसान, नुकसान पहुँचाना

(v.) You will damage the apples if you let them fall on the ground.

(n.) The storm caused a lot of damge to the garden.

82. **Damage** डैमिजिज्-हरजाना, क्षतिपूर्ति

The principal asked the students to pay damages for the window panes they had broken while playing in the classroom.

83. **Radish** रैडिश-1. मूली

We can buy a bunch of radishes at the green-grocer's

84. **Radium (n.)** रेडियम-1 एक बहुमूल्य धातु

Radium is used in the treatment of many diseases.

85. **Radius (n.)** रेडिअस्

1 व्यासार्ध

The teacher asked the students to draw a circle with a radius of our expertise.

2 घेरा

This job is not within the radius of our expertise

86. **Rag (n.)** रैग-1 चीथड़ा, लत्ता

The beggar's clothes were in rags.

2. (v.) डांटना, सताना, चिढ़ाना

The senior students of the medical college ragged the first year students.

87. **Vagabond (n.)** वैगबॉन्ड-आवारागर्द, आवारा, घुमक्कड़

We don't know about his whereabouts; he is a vagabond

88. **Vague (adj.)** वेग-अस्पष्ट, धुंधला, अनिश्चित

When I asked my son where he had been, he gave me vague answer

89 **Vain (adj.)** वेन-व्यर्थ, बेकार

Hari made a vain search for his pen.

He couldn't find it anywhere.

(adv.) He shouted in vain for help.

90. **Valiant (adj.)** वैलिअन्ट-शूर-वीर, साहसी

Abhimanyu was a valiant warrior.

(Adv) The soldiers fought for their country valiantly

91. **Paint (v.)** पेन्ट-1 चित्र बनाना रंगना

Do you know how to paint?

2 (n.) रंगलेप

What paint would you like for the walls of your room?

92. **Pair (n.)** पेअर्-जोड़ा

I want to buy a new pair of shoes

93. **Palace (n.)** पैलस-राजभवन, प्रासाद, महल

The Queen of England lives in Buckingham Palace.

94. **Pale (adj.)** पेल-विवर्ण, फीका, निस्तेज

Your face looks so pale.

95. **Cake (n.)** केक-केक, मीठा पकवान पेस्ट्री जैसा

My father bought a big cake for my birthday

96. **Calamity (n.)** कलैमटि-कठोर विपत्ति

It is always difficult to deal with a natural clamity.

97. **Calculate (v.)** कैल्क्युलेट-हिसाब लगाना, गणना करना

Harish known well how to calculate.

99. **Calender (n.)** कैलिन्ड (र्)-पंचांग, जंत्री, सूची, कालदर्श

Companies use calendars for their publicity.

100. **Abnormal (adj.)** ऐब्नॉमल- अपसामान्य

It is quite abnormal to have rain along with the sunshine.

SPOKEN VOCABULARY
Set - 3

1. **Aboard (adj.)** अबॉर्ड-जहाज, हवाई जहाज या रेलगाड़ी में सवार

   We had great fun aboard the plane on our way to the U.S.A

2. **Abolish (v.)** अबॉलिश-समाप्त करना, हटा देना

   Some people think we should abolish the death sentence

3. **About (prep.)** अबाउट-1. (के) विषय में.

   I am reading a book about birds.

   2. चारों ओर, यहां-वहां

   The children walked about the zoo.

   3. निकट, समीप

   He came here at about ten O'clock.

   4. करीब उतना ही

   Sudha is about as tall as Meena.

4. **Unable (adj.)** ॲनेबल्-अयोग्य, असमर्थ

   I shall be unable to attend the meeting tomorrow.

5. **Unaffected (adj.)** ॲनूअफे़क्टिड-अप्रभावित

   Has was totally unaffected by the loss.

6. **Unanimous (adj.)** युनैनिमस-एकमत

   The farmers were unanimous in their opposition to selling their fields to the industrialist

7. **Uncle (n.)** अकल-ताया चाचा मामा फू़फा मौसा

   Father's brother is Uncle Gopal.

   Mother's brother is Uncle Lal

   Minakshi is fond of both her uncles.

8. **Bag (n.)** बैग - 1. थैला, झोला, बोरा

   He put all the books in his school bag.

   2 (v.) हस्तगत करना, जीतना

   Dinesh bagged the first prize in the eassy competition

9. **Baggage (n.)** बैगिज-सामान

   I put all my baggage in the brake van

10. **Bail (n.)** बेल-जमानत

    The accused was released on bail ब

11. **Bait (n. & v.)** बेट-प्रलोभन (देना), सताना

    (n.) He put a piece of cheese in the mouse-trap as a bait.

    (v.) Rahul baited his hook to catch the fish

12. **Factory (n.)** फै़क्टरि-कारखाना

    What articles do you manufacture in your factory?

13. **Faculty (n.)** फै़क्ल्टि-विश्वविद्यालय या कॉलेज का शिक्षक वर्ग

    Contact the faculty members to get your doubts cleared.

14. **Fade (v.)** फे़ड-फीका हो जाना, मन्द पड़ना

    The colour of quality cloth doesn't fade easily.

15. **Fail (v.)** फे़ल-1. असफल होना

    Did he pass or fail in the examination?

    2. काम करना बन्द कर देना

    While we were having dinner, the power suddenly failed.

16. **Yard (n.)** यार्ड-1. गज

    Three feet make one yard.

    2. अहाता, बाड़ा

    There is a fence round the yard.

17. **Yardstick (n.)** यार्डस्टिक-मानदंड

What would be the yardstick to judge the performance by?

18. Yarn (n.) यार्न-1. सूत, धागा

There was a shortage of yarn, so the weavers had to face unemployment.

2. कहानी

The old sailor told his children an interesting yarn.

19. Yawn यॉन-उबासी

(v.) She yawned and put down the book she was reading.

(n.) "I'm feeling sleepy," she said with yawn.

20. Identification (n.) आइडेन्टिफ़िकेशन-पहचान, शिनाख़्त

The bodies of the dead were beyond identification.

21. Identity (n.) आइडेन्टटि-किसी वस्तु या व्यक्ति की पहचान

This place has lost its artistic identity.

22. Ideology (n.) आइडिऑलजि-विचारधारा

Hinduism proclaims many ideologies; it depends on the followers which one to choose.

23. Idiom (n.) इडियम-मुहावरा

Can you tell me the meaning of the idiom' apple of the eye'?

24. Game (n.) गेम-1. खेल, क्रीड़ा

What games do you play?

2. शिकार

I hear you are big game hunter.

3. खेलों का सामान

All kinds of game are sold in this shop.

25. Gang (n.) गैन्ग-टोली, गिरोह

The police made intensive efforts to trace the gang of car thieves.

26. Gangway (n.) गैन्ग्वे-मार्ग, सीढ़ी

I walked down the gangway of the theatre to reach my seat in the front row.

27. Gap (n.) गैप-1. छेद, दरार

The thieves made a gap in the garden wall to enter the house.

2. रिक्त, खाली जगह, अन्तराल, कमी

The police found many gaps in the bank manager's account of the bank robbery.

28. Lag (v.) लैग-पिछड़ना, पीछे रह जाना

Suresh lagged behind other athletes in the race because of a pain in his leg.

29. Lake (n.) लेक-झील, सरोवर

We went for a swim in the lake.

30. Lamb (n.) लैम-मेमना

My child was delighted to see the frisky young lamb jump around.

31. Lame (adj.) लेम-लंगड़ा, पंगु

It was so kind of you to help the lame man cross the busy street.

32. Hand (n.) हैन्ड-1. हाथ

Have you hurt your hand?

2. सूई

The hands of my watch are broken.

3. (v.) देना, सौंपना

Please hand me over that book.

33. Handcuffs हैंडकफ़्स-हथकड़ी

(n.) The handcuffs were dangling from the peg in the police station.

(v.) The police handcuffed the thief.

34. Handicap हैन्डिकैप-अड़चन, बाधा, असुविधा

(n.) Not knowing English is a handicap on a trip abroad.

(v.) Excess luggage handicaps one while traveling.

35. Handicraft (n.) हैन्डिक्राफ़्ट-हस्तशिल्प, दस्तकारी

At the handicrafts emporium, one can buy genuine items.

36. Jerk (n.) जर्क-झटका, झटकना, झटका देना

When I heard a sound near my bed, I got up with a jerk.

(v.) Don't jerk the steering wheel.

37. Jest जे'स्ट-मज़ाक, हँसी (करना)

(v.) Don't jest on Rakesh's accident as he hurt himself badly.

(n.) Please don't mind what I said in jest.

38. Jigsaw (n.) जिग्सॉ-चित्रखंड प्रहेलिका

There were forty pieces in the jigsaw puzzle.

39. Jingle जिंगल-छनक, छनकना, छनकाना

(n.) We heard the jingle of bells.

(adj.) The jingling sound in the stret made the children run out of their home.

(v.) The young boy jingled the coins in his pocket.

40. Keyboard (n.) कीबॉर्ड-कम्प्यूटर का कुंजीपटल

Some of the keys in my keyboard are not working.

41. Keyword (n.) कीवर्ड-कम्प्यूटर निर्देशक शब्द

Try some other keyword to get the information you are searching for.

42. Kick किक-लात/ठोकर (मारना)

(v.) Please be careful. this horse kicks.

(n.) The goalie dived to his left to clear an angular kick.

43. Kid (n.) किड-1. मेमना, बच्चा

The young of a goat is called a kid.

Tell the kids not to play in street.

2. (v.) मज़ाक करना, चिढ़ाना

Are you kidding?

44. Maid (n.) मेड-नौकरानी, कुमारी

Our house-maid is honest and industrious.

45. Mail (n.) मेल-डाक

Has the postman delivered today's mail?

46. Mailbox (n.) मेलबॉक्स-ई-मेल का मेलबॉक्स

My mailbox was full of his mails.

47. Main (adj.) मेन-मुख्य, प्रमुख

The chief guest was the main speaker at the school function.

Does this lane join the main road?

48. Saffron (adj.) सैफ़्रन्-केसरी

She was wearing a saffron-coloured saree.

49. Sag (v.) सैग-लटक जाना

The skin on her arms was sagging.

50. Sage (n.) सेज-पंडित, विवेकी

(n.) A true sage is he who has the deepest love for mankind.

(adj.) His sage advice saved my life.

51. Sail (n. & v.) सेल-पाल, जलयात्रा (करना)

(n.) Jack put up the sail of the ship.

(v.) He will not sail until all dangers are over.

52. Narrate (v.) नरेट-कथा का वर्णन करना

Please narrate the whole incident to me.

53. Narrow (adj.) नैरो-तंग, संकीर्ण

Can our car pass through a narrow lane?

54. Nasal (adj.) नेज़ल-नाक का

I have a cold, please give me some nasal drops.

55. Nasty (adj.) नास्टि-1. गन्दा, अप्रिय

This chemical has a nasty smell.

(adv.) Don't behave so nastily.

2. खतरनाक

There is a nasty bend in the road.

56. Tail (n.) टेल-1. पूँछ

Most animals and birds have tails.

The monkey uses its tail when climbing tress.

2. दुम से मिलती-जुलती वस्तु-पुछल्ला

I fastened a tail to my kite.

57. Tailor (n.) टेलर्-दरज़ी, कपड़े सीने वाला

Is your cousin not a tailor?

My tailor is expert in stitching woollen suits.

58. Take (v.) टेक-1. ले जाना

Father is going to take Hamid and Majid to sea for fishing.

2. पकड़ना

My father takes the 9 a.m. bus to go to his office

3. लगना

It will take half an hour to reach there.

4. ले जाकर देना

Please take this bag to your mother.

5. किराये पर लेना

We have taken this room for a month

6. विजय प्राप्त करना

After heavy fighting, the army took control of the city.

7. लेना

Do you take any interest in drawing?

Balwant Singh will take off his turban.

59. Tale (n.) टेल-1. कहानी, कथा, किस्सा

The mother told the child a fairy tale before making her sleep.

2. विवरण, वृत्तांत

The reporters told different tales about the accident.

60. Obscene (adj.) अबसीन-अश्लील

The scenes that the director claimed to be a sethetic were considered obscene by the censor board.

61. Obscure (v.) अब्स्क्युअर्-1. ढक जाना, दिखाई न देना

Everything was obscured by the mist.

2. (adj.) अस्पष्ट, दुर्बोध

Your motive in writing such a letter is ob scure to me.

3. अज्ञात

This poem was composed by an obscure poet.

62. Observe (v.) अब्ज़र्व्-1. देखना, अवलोकन करना

Observe how a pair of sparrows makes its nest.

2. नियमों और निर्देशों का पालन करना

All good players observe rules of fair play.

3. अपनी राय देना

My friend observed that I should not attend the club meeting.

(n.) The rising level of river water was under observation of the flood control department.

63. Obsess (v.) अब्सेस-किसी बात से मन का पूर्णतया ग्रस्त हो जाना

She seems to be obsessed with cleanliness.

64. Quantity (n.) क्वॉन्टटि-मात्रा, परिमाण

Pearls are found in large quantities in this part of the sea.

Just add a small quantity of water to the medicine.

65. Quarantine (n.) क्वॉरन्टीन-संग उठने-बैठने के लिए मनाही करना, सक्रामक रोगियो को दूसरों से मिलने-जुलने पर रोक देना

We may not see Umesh because he is in quarantine.

66. Quarrel क्वॉरल-झगड़ा (करना), कलह (करना)

(v.) The children are quarrelling about who should have the red pen.

(n.) We don't know the cause of their quarrel.

67. Quarry क्वॉरि-1. खुली खान, खदान खोदना

(v.) Large quantities of slate are quarried in Wales.

2. (n.) शिकार

The hunter followed his quarry for several hours.

68. Earthquake (n.) अर्थक्वेक-भूकंप

The earthquake destroyed the whole village.

69. Earthworm (n.) अर्थवर्म-केंचुआ

There were a number of earthworms in the garden.

70. East (n.) ईस्ट-पूर्व, पूरब

In the morning, I pray facing the east.

71. Easy ईज़ि-आसान, सरल

(adj.) Some Maths problems are very easy to solve.

(v.) If you taken an Aspro tablet, it will ease your headache.

72. Zebra (n.) ज़ेब्रा-अफ्रीका का एक प्रकार का घोड़ा जिसके शरीर पर काली व सफ़ेद धारियां होती हैं

Vehicles must stop at the zebra crossing to allow the pedestrians to cross the road safely

73. Wail वेल-बिलखना. रोना-चिल्लाना विलाप (करना)

(v.) Don't wail over your lost money, for I am sure you will soon find it

(n.) The wails of the aricrash victims' relatives could be heard in the hospital

74. Waist (n.) वेस्ट-कमर. कटि. मध्यभाग. कमरबद

Do you wear a belt round your waist?

I like to wear a waist band.

75. Wait वेट-प्रतीक्षा (करना), बाट (जोहना)

(v.) Wait here until I come back.

(n.) I had a long wait for the train.

True waiting means waiting with eagerness.

76. Wake (n.) वेक-जगाना, जागना

Please wake me up whenever you want.

I usually wake up at six o'clock in the morning.

(adj.) Were you awake the whole night?

77. Damp (adv.) डैम्प-गीला, आर्द्र

We shall catch a cold if we wear damp clothes.

78. Dance (n. & V.) डाउन्स-नाच, नाच करना

(n.) Radha became famous after her first dance performance.

(v.) At the farewell party, the teachers and students danced together.

79. Danger (n.) डेंजर्-खतरा, संकट

Roma was seriously ill last week, but now she is out of danger.

80. Dangle (v.) डैंग्ल-झूलना, झुलाना, लटकना, लटकाना

The boy saw a kite dangling from the tree.

81. Rage रेज-क्रोध या रोष (करना), क्रोधोन्माद (होना), प्रचंड होना

(n.) Sultana could not control her rage when Rashid broke her toy

(v) His father raged about the room as if he were mad

A storm was raged all night long.

82. Raid रेड-छापा (मारना) धावा (बोलना). छापामारी

(v.) The police raided an illicit liquor distillery

(n.) Many areas were destroyed in the air raids.

The enemy raiders attacked the radio station.

83. Rail (n.) रेल-1. छड़, पटरी, बाड़ा, घेरा, जंगला

When you come down the stairs, keep your hand on tha rail.

2. रेलवे

These parcels should be sent by rail.

My cousin works in the railways.

84. Rain रेन-वर्षा (होना), बरसात, बौछार (होना)

(n.) Don't go out in the rain.

Rajasthan has had a low rainfall this year.

(v.) It is raining. You should put on your raincoat.

(adj.) Lay by something for a rainy day.

85. Vagabond (n.) वैगबॉन्ड-आवारागर्द, आवारा, घुमक्कड़

We don't know about his whereabouts; he is a vagabond.

86. Vague (adj.) वेग-अस्पष्ट, धुंधला, अनिश्चित

When I asked my son where he had been, he gave me vague answer.

87. Vain (adj.) वेन-व्यर्थ, बेकार

Hari made a vain search for his pen.

He couldn't find it anywhere.

(adv.) He shouted in vain for help.

88. Valiant (adj.) वैलिअन्ट-शूर-वीर, साहसी

Abhimanyu was a valiant warrior.

(Adv.) The soldiers fought for their country valiantly.

89. Palm (n.) पाम-1. हथेली, करतल

Can you read a palm?

2. ताड़, ताल वृक्ष

Kerala is a land of palm trees.

90. Palpitate (v.) पैल्पिटेट्-जोर-जोर से दिल धड़कना

My heart was palpitating with fear.

91. Paltry (adj.) पॉल्ट्रि-तुच्छ

I was offered a paltry amount of money to do that work.

92. Pamper (v.) पैम्पर्-बहुत लाड़-प्यार करना

If you pamper the child, you will spoil it.

93. Dare (v.) डेअ(र्)-1. साहस करना

How dare he say such a nasty thing about you!

2. अनुमान लगाना, विश्वास करना

I dare say I shall be able to come.

94. Dark डार्क्-1. अंधेरा, अंधकारपूर्ण

(adj.) Are you not afraid to go out in a dark night?

2. गहरा

Some people dye their hair to make them dark black.

(n.) Don't go out in the dark.

95. Darling डालिंग-प्रेमपात्र, परम प्रिय

(adj,) I want my darling daughter to be a famous singer.

(n.) A new prime minister is usually the darling of the media when he assumes charge.

96. Dart (v.) डार्ट-झपटना, चौंककर भाग जाना

The squirrel was darting from branch to branch in the garden.

97. Above (prep.) अबव-ऊपर

The plane flies above the clouds.

98. Abreast (adj.) अब्रेस्ट-एक कतार में

The soldiers marched forward abreast.

99. Abridge (v.) अब्रिज-किसी कथन (प्राय : पुस्तक) को संक्षिप्त करना

(v.) We cannot abridge this book; it is copyrighted.

(adj.) This is the abridged version of Jane Austen's Pride and Prejudice.

100. Abroad (adj.) अब्रॉड-विदेश में

I spent four years abroad.

SPOKEN VOCABULARY
Set - 4

1. **Calf (n.)** काफ़्-1. बछड़ा (गाय का बच्चा)

The calf walked behind the cow.

2. पिण्डली, पिण्डिका

The doctor dressed the wound on the labourer's calf.

2. **Calibre (n.)** कैलिबर्-योग्यता

She has the calibre of translating the book into German without any mistake.

3. **Call (v.)** कॉल-1. बुलाना, पुकारना

I called out loudly when I saw Ram.

2. कहना, नाम रखना

A heart specialist is called the cardiologist.

3. मिलने जाना

The Prime Minister called on the President.

4. (n.) टेलीफोन कॉल

I have a phone call to make.

5. (n.) भेंट करने वाला

Sunil had many callers yesterday.

4. **Callous (adj.)** कैलस-निष्ठुर

The master was callous enough to make his ill servant work.

5. **Under (prep.)** ॲन्डर्-नीचे, (के) अधीन, (से) कम

The dog jumps over the fence. The pig crawls under it.

I was sitting under a tree.

I am working under the supervisor.

(adj.) Are you under-age?

6. **Undergo (v.)** ॲन्डरगो-सहना, झेलना

The doctor says Asha will have to undergo an operation.

7. **Underground (adj.)** अंडर्ग्राउन्ड-भूमिगत

We found an underground passage leading from the temple to the palace.

8. **Undermine (v.)** ॲन्डर्माइन-क्षति पहुँचाना, नष्ट करना

By smoking too much, he has undermined his health.

Don't undermine your health by getting up very late every day.

9. **Bake (v.)** बेक-पकाना, सेंकना

She baked bread for her family.

Balance (v.) बैलन्स-1. संतुलित होना, करना या रखना

The acrobat balanced himself on the high rope.

2. तराजू, कांटा, तुला

An honest shopkeeper keeps an accurate balance.

3. रोकड़ बाकी

I want to know the balance in my bank account.

10. **Bald (Adj.)** बॉल्ड-गंजा, अपावृत, अनलंकृत, नीरस

Bald men have formed an organisation called Baldies International.

11. **Bale (n.)** बेल-गट्ठा, गठरी

Bales of cotton were lying in the compound of the textile mill.

12. **Faint** फ़ेन्ट-1. मन्द, हलका/हलकी

(adj.) I heard faint noises of someone crying.

2. (v.) बेहोश होना

When you faint, you look as if you are in a deep sleep.

13. **Fair (adj.)** फ़ेअर्-1. गोरा, गौर, सुंदर, निर्मल

Your daughter has a fair complexion.

2. उचित, निष्पक्ष, न्यायसंगत

I believe in fair play.

3. मामूली, साधारण

Sheela's performance in the examination was just fair.

4. (n.) मेला

People came in large numbers to see the trade fair.

14. Faith (n.) फ़ेथ-1. विश्वास, भरोसा

I have full faith in Indu, so I believe that she is not telling lies.

2. (adj.) वफ़ादार, सही, वास्तविक

Our servant is very faithful.

Give me a faithful account of what you did.

15. Fake फ़ेक-फ़र्जी

(n.) All these currency notes are a fake.

(adj.) These are fake currency notes.

(v.) He faked the documents.

16. Year (n.) यिअर्-1. वर्ष, साल

A year has twelve months and fifty-two weeks.

2. आयु

You look young for your years.

A leap year comes once in four years.

(adv.) Companies give bonus to their employees from yearly profits.

17. Yearn (v.) यर्न-ललकना, लालायित होना

Abha is yearning for a bicycle.

The mother yearns to see her lost son.

18. Yeast (n.) यीस्ट-ख़मीर

Yeast is added to flour and water to make bread

19. Yell ये'ल-चीखना, चिल्लाना, किलकारना, अट्टहास, किलकारी

(n.) The speaker was greeted with yells of challenge

(v.) I saw the dog yelling with pain

20. Idiot (n.) इडिअट-मूर्ख, जड़बुद्धि

Don't behave like an idiot.

21. Idle (adj.) आइडल-बेकार, निकम्मा, आलसी, सुस्त

An idle minds is devil's workshop.

Why do you waste you time in idleness?

22. Idol (n.) आइडल-मूर्ति, बुत

Who made the Idol in this temple?

23. If (conj.) इफ़्-1. अगर, यदि

If you ask him politely, he will tell you the truth.

2. कि, क्या

Can you tell me the details, if you are taking a leave tomorrow?

24. Garage (n.) गैरिज-गराज

Our house has a garage.

25. Garbage (n.) गार्बिज-कूड़ा-कचरा

She threw all the useless pieces of furniture in the garbage.

26. Garden (n.) गार्डन-बाग़, बगीचा

We have a small garden at the back of our house.

27. Garland गार्लेन्ड-फूलों का हार

(n.) We welcomed the chief guest with garlands.

(v.) The priest garlanded the deity.

28. Lament लमेंट-विलाप/शोक (करना)

(v.) We cannot but lament the passing away of our dear ones.

(n.) The dead accident victim's relatives' lament was heartrending.

29. Lamp (n.) लैम्प-बत्ती, चिराग

As the electricity failed. I lit a lamp.

30. Land (n.) लैण्ड-1 भूमि जमीन

I have bought a piece of land to build a house

2 देश प्रदेश

I like to read books about faraway lands

3 (v.) पहुँचना (जमीन पर) उतरना

When will your plane land in Mumbai?

31. Landlord (n.) लैन्ड्लॉर्ड-मकान-मालिक

The landlord demanded the rent of three months in advance.

32. Handkerchief (n.) हैन्कर्चिफ़्-रुमाल

Always carry a handkerchief in your pocket.

33. Handle (v.) हैन्डल-1. छूना, संभालना, चलाना

Can you handle this job?

2. (n.) मूठ, दस्ता

The handle of my umbrella is broken

34. Hang (v.) हैन्ग-1. घटना, घटित होना

Hang the picture on the wall.

2. फाँसी देना

The murderer was hanged to death.

35. Handsome (adj.) हैन्सम

1. आकर्षण (पुरुष)

He is a handsome young man

2 बड़ी (धनराशि)

We made a handsome profit in our business

36. Jinx जिक्स-अशुभ व्यक्ति या वस्तु

(n.) He broke the jinx of not starting a new work on Saturday

(adj.) When the family lost their third child, they thought the house was jinxed.

37. Job (n.) जॉब-नौकरी, काम, कार्य

Did you get the job for which you had applied?

38. Jog जॉग्-धीरे-धीरे दौड़ना

(n.) I go for a jog every morning.

(v.) Jogging for half an hour every morning is a healthy exercise.

39. Join (v.) जॉइन-1. शामिल होना, भाग लेना

Would you like to join our party?

2. मिल जाना, मुड़ जाना

Does this lane join the main road?

3. जोड़ना, मिलाना, एकत्र/संबद्ध करना

Please join the two ends of the string.

40. Ram (n.) रैम-1. भेढ़ा

A male sheep is called ram.

2. ठूंसना

I hastily rammed my papers into my bag.

3. टक्कर मारना

The steamer rammed our boat in the dark night.

41. Random रैंडम-निरुद्देश्य, बिना किसी निश्चित उद्देश्य के

(n.) The enemy fired at random.

(adj.) You should not mind his random remarks

42. Range (n.) रेंज़-1. चूल्हा

Dinner was cooked on the kitchen range.

2. फैलाव, क्षेत्र

This gun has a range of twenty-five miles.

3. (v.) विचरना

Elephants range in the thick forest

43. Rank (n.) रैंक-1 पंक्ति

Dinner was cooked on the kitchen range

2 फैलाव क्षेत्र

This gun has range of twenty-five miles

3 (v.) विचरना

Elephants range in the thick forest

44. Kidnap (v.) किडनैप-अपहरण करना

The child was kidnapped for money.

45. Kidney (n.) किड्नी-अपहरण करना

My doctor is treating me for some kidney trouble.

46. Kill (v.) किल मार डालना या हत्या करना

Don't you have anything to do except killing flies?

2. नष्ट करना, बंद करना

The cold winter has killed the flowers in my garden.

47. Kind (n.) काइन्ड-1. वर्ग, जाति

I saw all kinds of people at the function.

2. किस्म, प्रकार

What kind of fabric is this?

3. (adj.) कृपालु

It was very kind of you to help me.

48. Maintain (v.) मेन्टेन-1. भरण-पोषण करना

These days it's difficult to maintain a big family.

2. दावा करना

Do you still maintain that you were right?

3. (मरम्मत करके) ठीक-ठीक बनाए रखना

The old house costs a great deal to maintain.

49. Majestic (adj.) मेजेस्टिक-शानदार

(adj.) The Himalayas are regal and majestic mountains.

(n.) The majesty of Himalayas is unparalleled.

50. Major (adj.) मेजर्-1.मुख्य, बड़ा

The soldier spent major portion of his life in guarding the country's frontiers.

2. (n.) वयस्क, बालिग़

Is your brother a major now?

51. Make मेक-1. बनाना, निर्माण करना

(v.) Please make me a cup of tea.

My shirt is made of cotton.

2. ज़बरदस्ती करना

Please don't make me go there.

3. करना, देना

I have to make a speech tomorrow.

(n.) At the showroom, television sets of different makes were exhibited.

52. Saint (n.) सेंट-धर्मात्मा, संत

Many people claim to be saints, but very few of them are true.

53. Sake (n.) सेक-कारण, हेतु

She will help for our mother's sake.

You should go for a walk for the sake of your health.

Please do come home for the sake of your dear mother.

54. Salad (n.) सैलड-सलाद

She preferred to have salad over a heavy meal.

55. Salary (n.) सैलॅरि-वेतन

I receive a good salary as a manager in the firm.

56. Nation (n.) नेशन-1. राष्ट्र, कौम, जाति

For the progress of mankind, friendly ties between all nations are essential.

2. राष्ट्रीयता

What is your nationality?

(adj.) I think you are acting in an anti-national manner.

57. Native (n.) नेटिव-मूल निवासी

I am a native of India.

(adj.) Hindi is the native language of northern India.

58. Nature (n.) नेचर्-1. निसर्ग, प्रकृति, स्वरुप

Have you seen the beauty of nature in the hills?

59. Natural (adj.) नैचरल-स्वाभाविक, नैसर्गिक

It is natural for the parents to feel concerned when their child is ill.

60. Talent (n.) टैलन्ट-प्रतिभा, योग्यता, क्षमता

She showed her talent for painting at a very early age.

61. Talk टॉक-बोलना, बातचीत करना, वार्तालाप

(v.) The baby cannot talk yet; as she grows up, she will learn to talk.

Vagish often talks to his parents about his college.

Please stop talking and listen to me.

(n.) We had a long talk about going to Mumbai.

62. Tall (adj.) टॉल-लंबा, ऊँचा

Sony is a tall girl.

Rita is taller than Sony.

She is the tallest in our family.

There are some very tall buildings in Mumbai.

How tall are you?

63. Tame टेम-पालतू, पालतू बनाना

(adj.) A cat is a tame animal. It is not wild.

There are tame elephants in the zoo on whose backs children can have rides.

(v.) Coaches tame animals in circus.

64. Obsolete (adj.) ऑब्सलीट्-अप्रचलित

Making students learn the text has become an obsolete teaching technique now.

65. Obstacle (n.) ऑब्स्टकल-बाधा, अड़चन

Is there any obstacle in your taking a holiday tomorrow?

66. Obstinate (adj.) ऑब्स्टिनट-ज़िद्दी, दुराग्रही

Raju is an obstinate child.

(n.) Sometimes he shows great obstinacy.

67. Obstruct (v.) ऑब्स्ट्रक्ट-बाधा डालना

The path was obstructed by the farmer's cart.

(n.) Illiteracy is a great obstruction in the path of progress.

68. Quart (n.) क्वॉर्ट-1.14 लीटर

There are two pints in a quart.

Do you need three quarts of milk?

69. Quarter (n.) क्वॉर्टर्-1. चौथाई भाग

It is quarter to four.

Would you like to have a quarter of bread?

2. दिशा

We went to all the quarters of Rohtak district.

(adv.) You may pay your instalments quarterly.

70. Quartz (n.) क्वॉर्ट्स्-काँच, माजि या स्फटिक नामक सख्त पत्थर की चट्टान

71. Queen (n.) क्वीन-1. राजा की पत्नी-रानी

King Dashratha had three queens.

2. शासक, रानी

Queen Elizabeth was very successful ruler.

(adj.) She has queenly manners.

72. Eat (v.) ईट-खाना

Would you like something to eat?

73. Eccentric (adj.) इक्सेन्ट्रिक-सनकी

He is an eccentric old man.

74. Echo (n. & v.) एको-प्रतिध्वनि, गूंज

(n.) If you speak loudly in a big and empty hall, you can hear the echo of your voice.

(v.) His voice echoed in the empty hall.

75. Eclipse (n.) इक्लिप्स- 1. ग्रहण, तेजहीन

Do you observe a fast during an eclipse of the sun or the moon?

2. (v.) निस्तेज कर देना

One defect in character can eclipse many good qualities.

76. Zest (n.) ज़ेस्ट-उत्साह की भावना

He has zest for knowledge.

77. Zero (n.) ज़िअरो-सिफर, शून्यांक

In winter, in most western countries, the temperature falls below zero and the ponds freeze.

He got zero marks in Mathematics.

78. Zigzag ज़िगज़ैग-टेढ़ा-मेढ़ा (बढ़ना)

(adj.) Draw a zigzag line to represent rivers.

(v.) The boat had to zigzag to avoid being struck by big rocks.

79. Zinc (n.) ज़िंक-जस्ता

Zinc is a hard white metal.

80. Walk वॉक-1. भ्रमण (करना), चाल, टहलना

(v.) I walk to the office every day.

(n.) Let us go for a morning walk.

2. रास्ता

We use the walk along the top of the cliff to get to our village.

81. Wall (n.) वॉल-भित्ति, दीवार

We raised the wall of our house.

Wall-paper is used for decorating the walls.

82. Wallet (n.) वॉलिट-मुड़ने वाला चपटा जेबी बटुआ

Always keep your all-route bus pass in your wallet.

83. Walnut (n.) वॉल्नट-अखरोट

The wood of the walnut tree is used for making fine furniture.

84. Dash (v.) डैश- 1. झपटना, तेज दौड़ना

Suresh dashed into my room to give me

the news of his selection in the school cricket team.

2. हौसला गिराना, अनुत्साहित करना

Rakesh's hopes of playing for the school were dashed when he was not selected in the hockey team.

3. (n.) जोश, तेज़ दौड़

The waiting passengers made a dash for the bus.

85. Data (n.) डेटा-सूचना संग्रह

The data stored in the computer has corrupted.

86. Database (n.) डेटबेस-सूचना सामग्री

Prepare a database of all our customers.

87. Date (n.) डेट-तारीख, दिनांक

What will be the date next Monday?

(v.) तारीख डालना

Always date the official letters and job applications.

88. Radar (n.) रेडार्-यात्रा में दिशा ज्ञात करने के लिए प्रयोग किया जाने वाला रेडियो-यंत्र, रडार

Aeroplanes use radar to find their direction.

89. Radiant (adj.) रेडिअंट-1. प्रसन्नमुख, प्रफुल्लित

Asha was radiant when she learnt that she had stood first in the class.

2. चमकता हुआ

The morning sun was radiant. It made everything look bright.

90. Radiate (v.) रेडिएट-1. प्रसारित करना, केन्द्र से किरणें या गर्मी आदि बाहर फेंकना

The electric heater radiates heat to all parts of the room.

(n.) प्रसारक

The room is heated by electric radiators.

91. Radio (n.) रेडियो-1. आकाशवाणी, प्रसार केन्द्र

My father works in All India Radio, New Delhi.

2. रेडियो (सेट)

We bought a new radio set

3. (v.) बेतार-यंत्र द्वारा सूचना देना

Ships in danger radio for help.

92. Valid (adj.) वैलिड-वैधानिक रुप से मान्य

Give me a valid reason for coming late every day.

93. Valley (n.) वैलि-घाटी

A valley is a place between two hills.

94. Value (n. & v.) वैल्यू-मूल्य (लगाना), मूल्य (निर्धारित करना)

(n.) The chief value of my motorcyle is that it lets me get about so quickly.

Physical expercises are of great value for strengthening your muscles.

(v.) The automobile dealer had valued my old scooter at five thousands rupees.

I value the advice my elders give me.

(adj.) I find his advice valuable in many ways.

95. Valve (n.) वैल्व-वाल्व

A valve prevents the air from leaking out of tyre.

96. Pamphlet (n.) पैम्फ्लिट-पुस्तिका, चौपन्ना

Our party has brought out a pamphlet on its aims and objectives.

97. Pan (n.) पैन्-हत्थेदार छिछला बर्तन

Make an omelette in the pan.

98. Pane (n.) पेन-शीशा

Who broke this window pan?

99. Panel (n.) पैनल

1. खिड़की का शीशा

The child broke the glass panel.

2. मंडल

The panel of judges declared them the clear winners.

100. Daughter (n.) डॉटर-बेटी, पुत्री

How old is your daughter?

SPOKEN VOCABULARY
Set - 5

1. **Dawn (n.)** डॉन-प्रभात, मोर, उषाकाल
   The villagers usually get up at dawn.
2. **Day (n.)** डे-दिन, दिवस
   I have to go to Mumbai for a couple of days.
3. **Daze (n.)** डेज़्-चकित या भौंचक्का करना, सुन्न कर देना
   I was so dazed by the accident that I did not know what to do.
4. **Abrupt (adj.)** अब्रप्ट-अचानक, आकस्मिक
   The music competition came to an abrupt end when the lights went out.
5. **Abscess (n.)** ऐब्सेस-व्रण, शरीर के किसी भाग में मवाद भर जाना
   The doctor removed the abscess from Dinesh's foot.
6. **Absent (adj.)** ऐब्सन्ट-अनुपस्थित
   Four boys were absent from school today.
   (n.) अनुपस्थिति
   My absence from office was due to my illness.
7. **Absent-minded (adj.)** ऐब्सन्ट्-माइन्डिड - भुलक्कड़
   (adj.) He is always absent-minded in the class.
   (adv.) The student replied to the teacher absent-mindedly.
8. **Calm (adj.)** काम - शांत
   One should always be calm and composed.
9. **Camel (n.)** कैमूल-ऊँट
   Camel is called the ship of the desert.
10. **Camera (n.)** कैमरा-कैमरा
    A professional photographer requires a good camera.
11. **Camp** कैम्प-शिविर, पड़ाव, पड़ाव डालना
    (n.) The boy-scout's summer camp was a great success.
    (v.) The soldiers camped by the side of the river.
12. **Undersigned (n.)** अॅन्डरसाइन्ड-अधोहस्ताक्षरी
    The undersigned is directed to infrom you that your services are no longer required for the trust.
13. **Understand (v.)** अॅन्डरस्टैन्ड-समझना, जानना, ज्ञान होना
    Mother seems to understand every word the baby says.
    I understand how radio and television work.
14. **Undertake (n.)** अॅन्डर्टेक-उत्तरदायित्व लेना (का) भार लेना
    Prof. Raman has undertaken to deliver a lecture once a week.
15. **Underwear (n.)** अॅन्डर्वेयर-अंदर पहनने का कपड़ा, कच्छा, बनियान, जांघिया
    Have you washed your underwear?
16. **Ball (n.)** बॉल-1.गेंद
    The children were playing with a ball.
    2. नाच
    We were invited to a ball.
17. **Balloon (n.)** बलून-गुब्बारा
    Children like to play with balloons.
18. **Ballot (n. & adj.)** बैलट-मतपत्र, मतदान
    (adj.) The election officer sealed the ballot papers after the voting was over.
    (n.) The new chairman was chosen through a ballot.
19. **Balm (n.)** बाम्-मरहम
    She applied balm on her forehead to get

rid of headache.

20. Fall फ़ॉल-गिरना, पतन

(v.) Take care lest you fall down.

(n.) 'Pride hath a fall'.

21. False (adj.) फ़ॉल्स-1. ग़लत, असत्य

We should never make a false statement.

2. कपटी, निष्ठाहीन

Never be a false friend.

3. दिखावटी, कृत्रिम

Do you wear false teeth?

22. Fame (n.) फ़ेम-ख्याति

His fame increased by the success of his new book.

23. Familiar (adj.) फ़ॅमिलिअर्-सुपरिचित

Your face looks familiar, but I don't remember your name.

Ram was familiar with Rohit's entire family.

(n.) Too much familiarity breeds contempt.

24. Yellow (adj.) ये'लो-पीला

A fully ripe banana is yellow.

Children mostly like yellow colour.

25. Yes (inter.) ये'स-हां, अवश्य, सचमुच

If you can do something, you must say - Yes, I can.

I want a straight yes or no from you.

26. Ignite (v.) इग्-नाइट-सुलगाना या सुलगना

Strike a match and ignite the fire.

A little spark can ignite a stack of dry hay cause a serious fire.

27. Ignore (v.) इग्नॉर्-उपेक्षा करना, अवज्ञा करना

You should not ignore your parents.

Why do you ignore the poor?

Never ignore the signals while driving.

28. Ignorant (adj.) इग्नरन्ट-अशिक्षित, अनजान

How can I employ such an ignorant person?

29. Ill (adj.) इल-बीमार, अस्वस्थ

She was seriously ill last week.

30. Handy (adj.) हैन्डि-उपयोगी, सुविधाजनक

A basket is handy when we go for shoping.

31. Hangar (n.) हैंगर्-विमानों को रखने की इमारत

The planes were kept in the hangar.

32. Hanger (n.) हैंगर्-अलमारी में कपड़े टांगने वाला हैंगर

I hanged my shirt in a hanger.

33. Hanker (v.) हैंक्र-किसी वस्तु को बहुत अधिाक चाहना

He is always hankering after money.

34. Joke जोक-दिल्लगी, मज़ाक (करना)

(n.) If you tell good jokes, you will be popular at parties.

(v.) Please stop joking and be serious for a while.

35. Jolly (adj.) जॉलि-प्रसन्न, मिलनसार

Arun was liked by all because of his jolly nature.

36. Jolt जोल्ट-धक्का, झटका लगना

Passengers got a severe jolt when the bus stopped suddenly.

(v.) The news of the my friend's accident jolted me badly.

37. Kindergarten (n.) किंडगार्टन-के.जी. स्कूल

Her daughter is studying in kindergarten now.

38. Kindle (v.) किन्डल

1. सुलगाना

Kindle the fire; it's so cold.

2. भावनाएं या रुचि उत्पन्न करना

She kindled my interest in photography.

39. King (n.) किंग-राजा

The child wished to play the role of the king.

40. Malaria (n.) मलेरिआ-मलेरिआ, शीतज्वर

I was down with malaria last month.

41. Male (n.) मेल-नर, पुरुष

A male is supposed to support his family.

(adj.) How many male children do you have?

42. Malice (n.) मैलिस-दुर्भावना

She intends no malice to anyone, but her language is bad.

43. Mammoth (adj.) मैमथ-विशाल

Yesterday I attended a mammoth public meeting.

44. Man (n.) मैन-1. मानव, इंसान

All men are mortal.

2. नर, पुरुष, श्रमिक

Do you know that man?

Has the milkman not come yet?

45. Sale (n.) सेल-1. बिक्री, विक्रय

He made a good profit on the sale of his car.

2. नीलाम, बोली देकर बेचना

Furniture is put up for sale at this shop every Sunday.

3. सस्ते में बेचना

I purchased my shoes at a reduction sale.

46. Salient (adj.) सेलिअन्ट-प्रमुख

What are the salient features of this book?

47. Salon (n.) सैलॉन-सैलून

She went to a beauty salon to get her hair cut.

48. Salt (n.) साल्ट-नमक

We add salt to make our food tasty.

There is salt is the sea water.

(adj) The sea water is salty.

49. Salute (v. & b.) सैल्यूट-सलामी (देना), अभिवादन (करना)

(v.) An English man salutes a lady by raising his hat.

(n.) Soldiers must greet their officers with a salute.

50. Salvation (n.) सैल्वेशन-मुक्ति

Buddha showed the path of salvation to man.

51. Naughty (adj.) नॉटि-नटखट, शरारती

My younger son is very naughty.

52. Near (adj.) नियर्-निकट, पास

Who was the man sitting near you at the party?

My school is near Birla Mandir.

53. Nearly (adv.) निर्अलि-प्रायः, लगभग

My job is nearly finished.

54. Neat (adv.) नीट-साफ़-सुथरा, सुव्यवस्थित

You are very neatly dressed.

(adj.) His room is very neat.

55. Necessary (adj.) नेससरि-आवश्यक, ज़रुरी

If you want to score good marks, it is necessary for you to study hard.

56. Neck (n.) नेक-गरदन

She has a beautiful long neck.

57. Tan टैन्-धूप में देर तक बैठने से पड़ा त्वचा का ताँबे जैसा रंग

(n.) Prolonged exposure to sun gave her skin a dusky tan.

(v.) Prolonged exposure to sun tanned her skin.

58. Tangible (adj.) टैन्जिबल-स्पष्ट

The tension between them was quite tan gible.

59. Tangle टैन्गल-गुच्छा (उलझा हुआ), उलझना

(n.) Her hari is in a tangle.

(v.) The kitten played with knitting wool and tangled it up.

60. Tank (n.) टैंक-1. तालाब, टंकी

We have a tank for rainwater at our backdoor.

2. मिलिट्री टैंक

Tanks are used in war. They are able to cross rough land.

3. टंकी, तेल ढोने वाला जहाज

A ship specially made to carry oil is called a tanker.

61. Obtain (v.) अब्टेन-पाना, प्राप्त करना

Have you obtained visa for your proposed visit to America?

62. Obvious (adj.) ऑब्विअस-सुस्पष्ट, प्रत्यक्ष

It is obvious that you are preparing for a journey.

Uma's angry looks made it obvious that she was displeased with Rekha.

63. Occasion (n.) अकेशन-अवसर, सुयोग, घटना

We gave a party on the occasion of our son's first birthday.

That party was a happy occasion.

64. Occupation (n.) ऑक्युपेशन-व्यवसाय

What is your father's occupation?

65. Xerox जिअ़रॉक्स-छायाप्रति

(n.) This is a xerox of the original document.

(v.) Get this document xeroxed.

66. Queer (adj.) क्विअर्-1. विचित्र, अनोखा

Ahmad is a queer man. He talks to nobody.

2. अस्वस्थ

Rishi felt a little queer after taking rice.

3. संदिग्ध, संदेहशील

We should not trust the queer characters.

67. Quell (v.) क्वे'ल-रोकना

The fighting was quelled by the police.

68. Eco-friendly (adj.) ईको-फ्रेंड्लि-पर्यावरण के अनुकूल

Paper bags look good and are eco-friendly.

69. Ecstasy (n.) एक्स्टसि-आनंद की भावना

His ecstasy about the examination results knew no bounds.

(adj.) He was ecstatic about his examination results.

70. Edge (n.) एज- 1. धार

Be careful, that knife has sharp edge.

2. कोर, किनारा

Don't go near the edge of the cliff.

71. Edible (adj.) एडिब्ल-खाने योग्य

Which is the edible part of a potato?

72. Zip ज़िप-ज़िप

(n) Undo the zip of the bag.

(v.) Zip the bag properly.

73. Walrus (n.) वॉल्रस-'सील' की तरह की समुद्रीजीव

A walrus is a large sea animal which looks like a seal.

74. Waltz वॉल्स-नाच, नाचना, इस नाच के साथ बजने वाला संगीत

(n.) Two persons played on old-time waltz.

(v.) He waltzed you round and round.

75. Wan (adj.) वॉन-पीला, विवर्ण, फीका, हल्का, मंद

He was ill for many days so his face was pale and wan.

76. Wand (n.) वॉन्ड-छड़ी

In a fairy tale, the fairy always waves her magic wand to make dreams come true.

77. Raise (v.) रेज़्-1. उठाना, खड़ा करना, उत्तेजित करना

She raised her arms above her head.

2. बढ़ाना, वेतन वृद्धि (करना)

The manager agreed to raise her wages from the next month.

3. इकट्ठा करना

We should raise enough funds to buy a new TV set for our school.

4. ऊँचा बोलना

Please raise your voice so that we may be able to hear you.

78. Raisin (n.) रेज़न-किशमिश, द्राक्ष, सुखाये हुए अंगूर

Raisins are put in cakes and puddings.

79. Rake रेक-1. एकत्र करना

(v.) The farmers were raking up the hay.

(n.) I need a rake to gather the hay.

2. छानबीन करना

We raked among the heap but could not find the bracelet.

80. Rally (n.) रैलि-1. जमघट

The leader addressed a youth rally.

2. (v.) (आदेश पालन करने के लिए) इकट्ठा होना

The young students rallied around their leader.

81. Van (n.) वैन-गाड़ी, बंद माल डिब्बा

A van is a car that is used for carrying load.

We put trunks in the luggage van.

82. Vanish (v.) वैनिश-लुप्त होना, गायब होना

When the sun rose, the mist vanished.

83. Vapour (n.) वेपर्-वाष्प, भाप

Vapour rises from boiling water.

84. Varnish वार्निश-रोगन (करना), चमकाना

(n.) The windows have been given a new coat of varnish.

(v.) He painted the door and then varnished it.

85. Pang (n.) पैंग-कसक

On seeing her winning the race, she was taken over by a sudden pange of jealousy.

86. Panic पैनिक-आंतक, भगदड़, तहलका, संत्रस्त

(n.) Panic spread in the crowd when it saw a man waving a pistol.

(v.) Please don't panic.

87. Pant (v.) पैन्ट-हाँफ़ना

Sunil ran so fast that he began to pant.

88. Pants (n.) पैन्ट्स-पैंट

I bought a new pair of pants yesterday.

89. Editor (n.) एडिटर्-संपादक

The editor of a newspaper is responsible for whaterver it publishes.

90. Educate (v.) एजुकेट-पढ़ाना-लिखाना, शिक्षा देना

Good art can educate as well as amuse us.

(n.) Education contributes a lot in building a person's career.

91. Effect (n.) इफ़ेक्ट-नतीजा, परिणाम, प्रभाव

Doctor was not sure whether the rashes on the patient;s body were the side-effect of the medicine he had taken.

92. Egg (n.) एग-अंडा

I like boiled eggs for breakfast.

93. Absolutely (adv.) ऐब्सल्यूट्लि-सर्वथा, बिल्कुल

Your hands must be absoulutely clean before you have your meal.

94. Absorb (v.) अब्सॉर्ब-सोखना या चूसना

Blotting paper absorbs ink.

(To be) absorbed in लीन होना

The children were so absorbed in the story that they did not hear the bell ring.

95. Absurd (adj.) अब्सर्ड-मूर्खतापूर्ण, निरर्थक, हासयास्पद

Ramesh's absurd talk showed his foolishness.

96. Abundant (adj.) अबन्डन्ट-प्रचुर, अधिक

This library has an abundant stock of books.

Rice is abundant in Kerala.

(n.) अधिकता

The fruits are in abundance in Himachal Pradesh.

97. Campaign (n.) कैम्पेन-अभियान, युद्ध, मुहिम

The government launched a campaign against smugglers.

(v.) He spent his life campaigning for the rights of the poor.

98. Campus (n.) कैम्पस-परिसर

I've lost my purse in the school campus itself.

99. Can (n.) कैन-1. पात्र, डिब्बा

I bought a can of apple jam.

2. (v.) सकना, समर्थ होना

Can you drive a car?

100. Canal (n.) कनैल-नहर, नाली

Punjab is a land of canals.

SPOKEN VOCABULARY
Set - 6

1. **Undesirable (adj.)** अन्डिज़ाइअरबल-अवांछनीय, जिसकी आवश्यकता न हो

Your presence is undersirable here. Rogues are undesirable persons, people do not want to be friendly with them.

2. **Undo (v.)** अॅन्डू-1. नष्ट करना, बिगाड़ना

When the new manager is appointed, he usually undoes most of the work done previously.

2. खोलना (गाँठ या बटन)

We must undo all our buttons before taking off our shirt.

3. **Undoubtedly (adv.)** अॅन्डाउटिडली-निस्सन्देह, निश्चयपूर्वक

We shall undoubtedly reach Mumbai by next week.

4. **Undue (adj.)** अॅनड्यू-परेशान

You should not take undue advantage of your friends.

5. **Ban** बैन्-प्रतिबंध

(n.) The government put a banon sale of liquor in the city.

(v). The screening of the movie was banned in Gurjarat.

6. **Banana (n.)** बनाना-केला

Eating bananas with milk is a nutritious breakfast.

7. **Band (n.)** 1. बैंड

We had a big band at my sister's wedding

2. दल, समूह

A band of devoted workers helps in popularising a poltical party.

3. फ़ीता

The clerk put a rubber band round the file.

8. **Bandage (n.)** बैन्डिज-पट्टी, पट्टी बांधना

The doctor put a bandage round a wound on Deepak's foot.

9. **Family (n.)** फ़ैमली-परिवार, घराना

Have you sent away your family to Mumbai?

10. **Famine (n.)** फ़ैमिन-अकाल

The famine killed many people in Orissa.

11. **Famous (adj.)** फ़ेमस-अत्यंत विख्यात

A Nobel prize winner becomes famous worldwide.

12. **Fan (n.)** फ़ैन-पंखा

I would like to buy a table fan.

13. **Yesterday (n. & adv.)** ये'स्टर्डे-बीता हुआ कल

Yesterday is the day before today.

Have you got yesterday's newspaper?

14. **Ill-feeling (n.)** इल-फीलिंग-दुर्भावना

I do hope you have no ill-feeling for me.

15. **Ill-treat (v.)** इलट्रीट-दुर्व्यवहार करना

If you ill-treat your servant, he will leave you soon.

16. **Illegal (adj.)** इलीगल-गैरकानूनी, अवैध

If is illegal to possess a revolver without a licence.

You will have to face the consequences of your illegal actions.

17. **Illegible (adj.)** इलेजबल-अपाठ्य

The print on the old newspaper was quite

illegible.

18. Garlic (n.) गार्लिक-लहसुन

Do you use garlic in your cooking?

19. Garment (n.) गार्मन्ट-कपड़ा, वस्त्र

Some businessmen have made good money in garment export.

20. Garnish (v.) गार्निश-भोजन को सजाना

The cook garnished the dish with fresh coriander leaves.

21. Gas (n.) गैस-गैस, पैट्रोल

How much does a cylinder of cooking gas cost?

22. Landmark (n.) लैन्डमार्क

1. पहचान-चिह्न

Tell me some landmark so that I find the way to your place easily.

2. कोई महत्त्वपूर्ण घटना

The Revolt of 1857 was a landmark in Indian history.

23. Lane (n.) लेन-गली, पथ

Does this lane join the main road?

24. Language (n.) लैङ्ग्विज-भाषा

How many languages can you speak?

25. Lantern (n.) लैन्टर्न-लालटेन

Don't go out into the dark of night without a lantern.

26. Haphazard (adj.) हैपहैज़र्ड-बेतरतीब

Your article is written in a haphazard way.

27. Happen (adj.) हैपन-1. घटना, घटित होना

Did an accident happen here?

2. संयोग होना

Do you happen to know Sudhir?

28. Happy (adj.) हैपि-खुशी, खुश, प्रसन्न

The parents were happy to learn about their son's getting a good job.

Many happy returns of the day!

29. Happy-go-lucky (adj.) हैप्पी - गो- लकी - बेपरवाह

He is a happy-go-lucky person.

30. Jot (v.) जॉट-1. (संक्षेप में) लिख देना

Have you jotted down the points of the speech you are going to make?

2. (n.) तनिक भी

We don't care a jot for what you say.

31. Journal (n.) जर्नल-पत्र, अखबार, पत्रिका

Many reputed companies publish their monthly house journals.

32. Journey (n. & v.) जर्नि-यात्रा/सफ़र (करना)

(n.) How much time will your journey to Chennai take?

(v.) The pilgrims journeyed on foot from Delhi to Haridwar.

33. Jovial (adj.) जोविअल-प्रसन्न

He was in a jovial mood yesterday.

34. Kiosk (n.) कीऑस्क-खोका

Get a newspaper from the nearby kiosk.

35. Kiss किस-चुम्बन करना

(v.) The mother kissed her weeping child.

(n.) The mother gave the child a toffee and a kiss.

36. Kit (n.) किट-किट, सामान, औज़ार

Has the fisherman taken his kit for fishing?

37. Kitchen (n.) किचिन-रसोईघर

Normally I have my meal in the kitchen.

38. Manage (v.) मैनिज-1. देखरेख करना, संभालना

Who manages your business?

2. सफल होना, युक्ति निकालना

Can you manage to come early?

3. वश में रखना

Would you be able to manage such naughty children?

39. **Mandatory (adj.)** मैन्डेटरि-अनिवार्य

The college authorities made it mandatory to submit the original documents at the time of admission.

40. **Mane (n.)** मेन-अयाल, घोड़े या शेर के लंबे बाल

The lion's mane was shining in the sun.

41. **Manhole (n.)** मैनहोल-मैनहोल

The people called the Municipal committee to clean the manhole.

42. **Same (adj.)** सेम-1. वही (उसी)

Luv and Kush were born on the same day

2. समान (एक से रुप आकार वाला)

Her twin daughters look the same in height and appearance.

Whether you come to me or I come to you, is all the same to me.

43. **Sample (n.)** सैम्पल-1. नमूना

By a small sample we may judge the whole piece.

2. (v.) चखना, स्वाद या किस्म जानने के लिए खाना

Mother allowed us to sample the Diwali sweets while she was making them.

44. **Sanction (v.)** सैंक्शन-स्वीकृति देना

The officer refused to sanction my leave.

45. **Sanctuary (n.)** सैङ्क्चुअरि-अभयारण्य

There is a bird sanctuary in Bharatpur.

46. **Necklace** ने'कलस-हार

This necklace will look more beautiful on a long neck.

47. **Nectar (n.)** ने'क्टर-पराग

The honeybees collect nectar from flowers.

48. **Need** नीड्-आवश्यकता/अनिवार्यता (होना)

(n.) There was a great need of field workers in the new political party.

(v.) I need somebody's help in this matter.

Need I go to the market immediately?

(adj.) The needy should apply for help.

49. **Needle (n.)** नीडल-सूई

Bring a needle and thread to stitch this button.

The needle of this meter is not working.

50. **Tantrum (n.)** टैनट्रम-चिड़चिड़ेपन का दौरा

Tantrums that this child throws are difficult to handle.

51. **Tap (n.)** टैप-1. नलका, टूटी

See that all the water-taps are turned off before you leave the house.

Who left the tap running?

2. हल्की चपल

She felt a tap on her shoulder.

52. **Tape (n.)** टेप-1. फीता, माप-पट्टी

The dress-maker uses a tape when he measures a man for a new dress.

2. आवाज़ रिकार्ड करना, रिकार्ड की गई आवाज़

(v.) Did you tape Lata's new song?

(n.) Have you heard Lata's latest tape?

53. **Tar (n.)** टार्-तारकोल

Tar was applied to the roof of the house to make it waterproof.

54. **Occupy (v.)** ऑक्सुपाइ-1. रहना, निवास करना

Which room are you occupying in this hotel?

2. कब्ज़ा करना

The landlord was fighting a oase in the court against the tenants who had occupied his house.

3. व्यस्त रखना

How do you occupy yourself during the holidays?

55. Occur (v.) ऑकर्-1. घटित होना

A serious accident occurred near our house last evening.

The total solar eclipse is a rare occurrence.

2. मन में आना, सूझना

Has it occurred to you that you are taking a risk?

56. Ocean (n.) ओशन-सागर

The ocean was gurgling with life.

57. Odd (adj.) ऑड-1. विलक्षण, असाधारण

How odd that you should find me at home in the morning!

2. विषम संख्या (1, 3, 5, आदि)

I asked the students to write down some odd numbers.

3. बीच-बीच का (काम), फुटकर (स्थायी नहीं)

They need a person to odd jobs in the factory.

58. Quench (v.) क्वेंच-आग बुझाना

The flames were quenched with gallons of water.

59. Zodiac (n.) ज़ोडिऐक-राशि चिह्

My zodiac sign is Cancer.

60. Wander (v.) वॉन्डर्-भटकना

He was wandering around the whole city.

61. Wane वेन-कम होना, घटना, ह्रास

(v.) As time passed, my hopes of getting money waned.

(n.) From today, the moon will be on the wane.

62. Want (n. & v.) वॉन्ट-(का) अभाव होना, आवश्यकता होना, चाहना

(n.) Poor people are in want of food.

(v.) Father's shoes want mending.

Do you want more money?

63. War (n.) वॉर्-युद्ध, संग्राम, लड़ाई, शत्रुता

Soldiers win wars and generals get the credit.

64. Dazzle डैज़ूल-चकाचौध (करना या होना)

(v.) The sun will dazzle you if you look at it.

(n.) The dazzle of money attracts everybody.

65. Dead (adj.) डेड-मृत, मरा हुआ

The dead woman left her property to a distant poor relative.

66. Deadline (n.) डेडलाइन-किसी कार्य को पूरा करने के लिए निर्धारित अंतिम तिथि

The boss was very happy with our team when we met the unrealistic deadline.

67. Deadlock (n.) डेडलॉक-गतिरोध

I tried to make them reconcile with each other, but their talks had reached a deadlock.

68. Rank (n.) रैंक-1. पंक्ति

The boys stood in a rank.

2. (v.) गिनना, श्रेणीबद्ध करना

Do you not rank me among your intimate friends?

3. (n.) स्तर, रुतबा, कोटि

Is he an artist of a high rank?

4. (v.) पदवी, पद, दरजा (रखना)

An admiral ranks higher than a captain.

69. Ransack (v.) रैन्सैक-1. लूटना

The burglars ransacked the house and took away some valuables.

2. छान मारना, खोजबीन करना

My wife ransacked the suitcase but she could not find her wrist watch.

70. Ransom (v.) रैन्सम-1. माँगाा हुआ मूल्य चुकाना

The ruler was ransomed by the capitalists

(n.) किसी का अपहरण करके माँगी गयी राशि

The kidnappers demanded a large ransom for the child they had kidnapped.

71. Rap रैप-खटखट (करना), ठकठक (करना)

(n.) Give a rap on the door.

(v.) I rapped on the door but nobody opened it.

72. Vary (v.) वेअरि-बदल जाना, बदल देना, रुपान्तरित करना

The weather varies from day to day.

The size of the books varied. Some were large, others were small.

(adj.) The police tried various ways to make the thief confess.

73. Vase (n.) वाज़्-फूलदान, गुलदान

We put flowers in a vase. It is called a flower-vase.

74. Vast (adj.) वास्ट-सुविस्तृत, विशाल, बड़ा

This printing machine has cost a vast sum of money.

75. Vault (n.) वॉल्ट-तहखाना, सुरक्षित स्थान

Valuables are stored in a vault at the bank.

76. Paper (n.) पेपर्- 1. कागज़

Give me a piece of paper.

2. अख़बार

Where is today's paper?

3. प्रश्न-पत्र

Yesterday's question paper was very difficult to answer.

4. निबंध

The professor read out a paper on atomic energy.

5. कागज़ात, प्रमाण

This building is mine, I have the papers to prove it.

77. Par (n.) पार-गुणवत्ता का स्तर

She is a writer par excellence.

78. Parable (n.) पैरबल-नीतिकथा

The parables of Panchantantra are still as fresh as they were ages ago.

79. Parachute (n.) पैरशूट-पैराशूट

The man jumped from the helicopter with a parachute

80. Fancy फैन्सि-1. कल्पना (करना)

(v.) I fancy I heard noises in the night.

2. चाहना, पसंद करना

I do not fancy gaudy clothes.

3. (adj.) रंग-बिरंगा, भड़कीला

Youngsters like fancy clothes.

4. (n.) विचार, कल्पना

A fancy passed through my mind,

81. Fantastic (adj.) फैन्टैस्टिक-उत्कृष्ट

This is a fantastic book; you must read it.

82. Far फ़ार्-1. दूर

(adj.) Ram's office was not too far from his home.

He went far and wide in search of his lost brother.

2. (adj.) कहीं अधिक

This nut is far harder to crack than I had imagined.

83. Fare (n.) फ़ेअर्-1. भाड़ा, किराया

It's illegal to travel in the bus without paying the fare.

2. (v.) सफल या विफल होना

Dolly fared well in the examination.

84. Abuse (v.) अब्यूज़्-1. गाली देना, दुर्वचन कहना

Children should be taught never to abuse anybody.

2. दुरुपयोग करना

Kundan was clever but he abused his cleverness when he cheated the poor man.

3. (n.) अनुचित उपयोग

Overstaying in the host's house will be an abuse of his hospitality.

85. Academy (n.) अकैडमि-1. पाठशाला, विद्योपार्जन का स्थान

He teaches singing in an academy of music.

2. विद्वत् परिषद्, ज्ञान समाज

The Sahitya Academy published books on literature.

86. Accent (n.) ऐक्सन्ट-बोलने की या उच्चारण की पद्धति

Raman speaks English with a South Indian accent.

87. Accept (V.) अक्सेप्ट-1. लेना, स्वीकार करना

The beggar accepted alms from the rich man.

2. विश्वास करना

I am sorry I cannot accept what you say.

88. Cancel (n.) कैन्स्ल-रद्द करना, हटा देना

He cancelled all his appointments as he was not feeling well.

89. Candid (adj.) केन्डिड-स्पष्टवादी

She gave a candid reply when asked why she was still single

90. Candidate (n.) कैन्डिडेट-उम्मीदवार, प्रत्याशी, परीक्षार्थी

My elder brother was a candidate in the last municipal election.

91. Candle (n.) कैन्ड्ल्-मोमबत्ती

She bought a box of candles for Diwali.

92. Uneasy (adj.) ॲन्ईज़ि-परेशान

Uneasy lies the head that wears a crown.

Mother becomes uneasy if you come late.

93. Uneducated (n.) ॲनएजुकेटिड-अशिक्षित, निरक्षर

I spend my spare time in teaching the uneducated.

94. Unemployed (adj.) ॲनिइम्प्लॉइड-बेकार होना

Are you still unemployed?

(n.) Unemployment is a great curse.

95. Unequal (adj.) ॲन्ईक्वल-1. (के) अयोग्य

The manager is unequal to his task.

2. असमान, कभी अच्छा कभी बुरा

Your quality of work is very unequal, sometimes it is fair, sometimes not.

96. Bandit (n.) बैन्डिट-डाकू

Bandits live in forest.

97. Bang बैंग

1. किसी पर ज़ोर से प्रहार करना

(v.) He angrily banged the table.

2. धूम-धड़ाका

(n.) The Indian hockey team is back with a bang.

98. Bangle (n.) बैंगल-चूड़ी

The bride was wearing bangles made of gold.

99. Banish (n.) बैनिश-निर्वासित करना, देश निकाला देना, निकाल देना

The king banished his rebellious son from the kingdom.

100. Farewell (n.) फ़ेअवेल-विदाई

I gave a farewell party to my friend who was going abroad.

SPOKEN VOCABULARY
Set - 7

1. **Farm (n.)** फ़ार्म-खेत

   I have built a small cottage in my farm.

2. **Fashion (n.)** फ़ैशन-1. फ़ैशन, भूषाचार

   Narrow trousers are not in fashion these days.

   2. (v.) बनाना, निर्माण करना

   He fashioned the sword and spear with great skill.

3. **Fast** फ़ास्ट-1. तेज़

   (adj.) Life in Delhi is very fast.

   Walk fast, it is too late.

   2. (adj.) पक्का, स्थिर

   I held fast to my umbrella in the gale.

   3. उपवास, रोज़ा, अनशन, उपवास करना

   (n.) My grandmother observes a fast every Monday.

   (v.) My father fasted for three days.

4. **Yet** ये'ट-अभी तक

   (adv.) Has the manager not come yet?

   Sorry, he is not here yet.

   2. (conj.) तो भी

   The work is very hard, yet it is worth trying.

   She wasn't well, yet she managed to appear for the examination.

5. **Illiterate (adj.)** इलिटरट्-अनपढ़

   (adj.) Special classes are held in the nearby school for adult illiterates.

   (n.) Illiteracy is a major cause of backwardness in the village.

6. **Illogical (adj.)** इलॉजिकल-तर्कहीन

   Visiting Ladakh in the winters appeared an illogical idea to me.

7. **Illuminate (v.)** इलूमिनेट-प्रदीप्त करना, प्रकाश डालना, समझाना

   The main bazaars and streets are illuminated on Diwali.

   (n.) Let us go to see the illuminations at the Rashtrapati Bhawan.

8. **Illusion (n.)** इलूशन-भ्रम, धोखा

   This line looks longer than the other but it is an optical illusion.

   Don't be under the illusion that have not seen through your trick.

9. **Gasp (v.)** गास्प्-1. हाँफना

   Running so fast made Rahul gasp for breath,

   2. (n.) हँफनी

   Why did you give a gasp of surprise when you saw me?

10. **Gate (n.)** गेट-फाटक, द्वार

    Our garden will has an iron gate.

11. **Gather (v.)** गैदर्-1. एकत्र करना/होना

    Please gather your books and put them in

young bag.

Many people gathered at the meeting.

Really there was a great gathering.

2. जमा करना, चुनना

The reporter gathered enough information before writing a feature on kidnaping.

12. Gauge गेज-माप, नाप, पैमाना

(n.) If you fix a gauge on your cooking gas cylinder you will know the amount of gas inside.

(v.) How do you gauge the amount of water in this barrel?

13. Lap (n.) लैप-1. गोद, अंचल

My cat is fond of sitting in my lap.

2. (v.) चाटना, लप-लप पीना

I put some milk in saucer for my cat to lap up.

14. Lapse लैप्स-भूल, गलती, अवनति, बीत जाना, समाप्त होना

(n.) I am sorry for his lapse on my part.

(v.) How much time has lapsed since we met last?

15. Large (adj.) लार्ज-बड़ा, प्रचुर, विस्तृत

I went a large tube of tooth-paste.

Some trains are very large.

16. Lash लैश-1. कोड़ा, कोड़े की मार कोड़े लगाना

(v.) The tonga-driver was lashing his horse cruelly.

2. बाँधना

People usually lash their dogs at their house' entrance.

3. घुमाना

My cat lashed its tail in excitement when I threw up the ball.

(v.) The thief was sentenced fifty lashes on his back.

4. बरौनी

Sheela has long eye-lashes.

17. Harbour (n.) हार्बर्-बन्दरगाह

When we went to Mumbai, we saw many ships anchored at the harbour.

18. Hard (adj.) हार्ड-1. कड़ा, सख्त

I cannot sleep on a hard bed.

2. कठिन, दुर्भेद्य

Do you find Physics a hard subject?

(adv.) If you work hard, you can score good marks in the examination.

19. Hardly (adv.) हार्ड्लि-मुश्किल से

After the night duty, a press worker was so exhausted that he ciould hardly keep his eyes open.

20. Harass (v.) हैरस-सताना

He harassed his wife long after their divorce.

21. Joy (n.) जॉय-आनंद, हर्ष

The children while watching the magic show were full of joy.

(adj.) Amit returned from the picnic in a joyful mood.

22. Jubliation (n.) जुबिलेशन-हर्षोल्लास

Christmas was celebrated with great joy and jubilation.

23. **Jubilee (n.)** जुबिली-जयंती महोत्सव

They invited all their friends for the silver jubilee party of their marriage.

24. **Judge (n. & v.)** जॅज-न्यायाधीश, पारखी, न्याय करना, आँकना

My uncle is a judge in the High Court.

Never judge a man by his clothes.

25. **Kite (n.)** काइट-चील, पतंग

Do you know how to fly a kite?

I saw a kite high up in the sky.

26. **Kitten (n.)** किटिन-बिलौटा

Our cat has given birth to four kittens.

27. **Kitty (n.)** किटि-जमा पूंजी

She has some good projects in her kitty.

28. **Knack (n.)** नैक्-योग्यता

She has a knack for writing poetry.

29. **Mania (n.)** मेनिआ-उन्माद

The IPL mania came to an end with Rajasthan Royals taking away the trophy.

30. **Manifest (v.)** मैनिफ़ेस्ट-किसी वस्तु को स्पष्टतया प्रकट करना

God always manifests Himself in human forms.

31. **Manifold (adj.)** मैनिफोल्ड-कई गुना

The texture paint complementing the decor increased the beauty of the room manifold.

32. **Manipulate (v.)** मैनिप्युलेट-किसी को अपने पक्ष में प्रभावित कर लेना

He is a shrewd politician. He can manipu late any situation in his favour.

33. **Sand (n.)** सैंड-1. रेत

They took the children to play on the sands.

2. (अर्थात्) कच्चा आधार

You cannot build up a house on sand.

34. **Sandal (n.)** सैंडल-सैंडिल, खड़ाऊँ

The child put on his sandals a before going to market.

35. **Sandalwood (n.)** सैंडलवुड-चंदन

The perfume had the fragrance of sandalwood.

36 **Sandcastle (n.)** सैंडकासल्-रेत का घरौंदा

The kids made a sancastle at the beach.

37. **Negative (adj.)** नेगटिव-1. नकारात्मक

I have received a negative reply to my proposal.

2. (n.) निगेटिव, प्रतिचित्र

Can you develop this negative?

38. **Neglect (v.)** निग्लेक्ट-उपेक्षा करना, ध्यान नहीं रखना

You must not neglect your homework.

(n.) You will be dismissed for your negligence.

39. **Negotiable (adj.)** निगोशिअबल-मोल-भाव करना, किसी मुद्दे पर विचार करना

(adj.) The prices of all the items in the shop are negotiable.

(v.) She negotiated the price of the jewellery.

(n.) The demands of the workers are still under negotiation.

40. **Neighbour (n.)** नेबर्-पड़ोसी

Our neighbour is a very friendly person.

41. Tardy (adj.) टार्डि-सुस्त, मंदगति

I was tardy in replying to her letter.

42. Target (n.) टार्गिट-लक्ष्य

Their target was to collect five thousands rupees for the poor.

43. Tariff (n.) टैरिफ़-शुल्कदार

The tariff at our hotel was hundred ru pees for lunch and dinner.

44. Tarnish (v.) टार्निश-बदरंग हो जाना

Your silver glasses will be tarnished unless you polish them often.

Your bad behaviour will tarnish your name.

45. Odour (n.) ओडर्-गन्ध, बू

The odour of frying garlics is very strong.

Many chemicals have a bad odour.

46. Offend (v.) अफ़ेन्ड-नाराज़ करना, अपमान करना

I hope I have not offended you by my plain speaking.

(n.) Is it not an offence in America to drive on the left hand side of the road?

47. Offer (n.) ऑफ़र्-1. प्रस्ताव

I regret to inform you that your offer is not acceptable to me.

2. (v.) प्रस्ताव करना/रखना, सामने रखना

I offer to pay your railway fare if you want to visit Agra.

48. Office (n.) ऑफ़िस

1. दफ़्तर

I have my office tomorrow.

2. आधिकारिक पद

He is holding the office of foreign affairs.

49. Query क्वे'रि-1. प्रश्न, संदेह

(n.) Please solve my queries marked in this book.

2. (v.) संदेह करना

I would like to query these facts.

50. Quest (n.) क्वे'स्ट-खोज

The herd of elephants wandered in the jungle in quest of water.

51. Question (n.) क्वे'स्चन-1. प्रश्न, सवाल

I request you to answer my questions.

2. विचारणीय बात

The question is, how to beat the competitors.

3. संदेह, संशय

Please accept my proposal without any question.

4. (v.) सवाल करना

I would like to question you.

52. Queue (n.) क्यू-1. पंक्ति, लाइन

Please stand in a queue.

Please take your place in the queue.

2. (v.) लाइन लगाना

People queue at the bus-stop.

53. Zone (n.) ज़ोन-क्षेत्र, मंडल

During the floods, people were evacuated from the danger zone.

54. Ward वॉर्ड-आश्रित, वार्ड, रोगी कक्ष, रक्षा करना

(n.) Since his parents died he has been the ward of his grandfather.

She was in the children's ward.

(v.) A warden wards his area and look after his patients.

55. Wards (suffix.) वॉर्ड्स-(के) प्रति, (की) ओर

Is the Chinese language written downwards?

56. Warden (n.) वॉर्डन-रक्षक, अध्यक्ष

The warden in our boarding school was very kind.

Were you not a traffic warden at the time of your retirement?

57. Warder (n.) वॉर्डर्-जेलर, वार्डर, जेलखाने का इंचार्ज

The warder of our jail was a very cruel man.

58. Deaf (adj.) डेफ़-बहरा, बधिर

The accident had made him deaf in one ear.

59. Deal (v.) डील-1. संबंध रखना

Ram's job is to deal with routine correspondence in his office.

2. लेन-देन करना, व्यापार करना

We deal with M/s. Pustak Mahal and we have no complaint.

3. (n.) मात्रा, परिमाण

Rats destroy a great deal of foodgrain.

60. Dean (n.) डीन-प्रमुख अधिकारी

You need to take the permission from the dean for it.

61. Dear (adj.) डिअर्-प्रिय, प्यारा

Ramesh is a dear friend of mine.

62. Rapid (adj.) रैपिड-तेज़, शीघ्रगामी

We should make a rapid journey by Frontier Mail.

63. Rapport (n.) रैपॉ-सौहार्द

I share a good rapport with most my colleagues.

64. Rapture (n.) रैन्चर्-हर्षोन्माद

She was into raptures to stand first in the whole university.

65. Rare (adj.) रे'अर्-1. दुर्लभ

I have got some rare stamps in my collection.

2. कभी-कभी

Ganesh lives far away from his parents, so he pays rare visits to them.

(adj.) We rarely see a chariot these days. They are out of fashion.

66. Zoo (n.) जू-चिड़ियाघर

Many wild animals and birds are kept in the zoo.

What did you like best at the Delhi zoo?

67. Wardrobe (n.) वार्डरोब-अल्मारी, कपड़े रखने की जगह

Is your wardrobe not our of fashion?

Bring my suit from the wardrobe.

68. Ware (n.) वेअर्-माल, सौदा

Wares of all kinds are stored in warehouses.

69. Warm वॉर्म-गर्म, गुनगुना, उत्साही, गर्म करना

(adj.) It is warm day.

In western countries, people use warm water for bathing.

(v.) Please warm some water for me.

Warm your palms on the heater.

70. Warn (v.) वॉर्न-चेतावनी देना, सचेत करना

The manager warned the clerk about his repeated negligence.

I warned him not to skate on thin ice.

(n.) Your failure in the monthly tests is a kind of warning to you.

71. Dearth (n.) डर्थ-अपर्याप्तता

There is a dearth of talented professionals in this industry.

72. Death (n.) डे'थ-मृत्यु, मौत

Death of all living beings is ain.

73. Debate डिबेट-विवाद

(n.) I won the debtate competition held in the school last week.

(v.) Rather than wasting time in debating, it's better we work on the solution to this problem.

74. Debit (v.) डेबिट-बैंक के खाते से पैसे की निकासी करना

The instalment of the loan was debited di rectly from my bank account.

75. Debris (n.) डेब्री-मलबा

A lot many people are feared to be buried beneath the earthquake debris.

76. Debt (n.) डे'ट-कर्ज़ ऋण

Ram paid penalty to the bank because he could not clear his debt in time.

77. Raring (adj.) रेअरिंग-कुछ करने के लिए आतुर

They were raring to bid for the new project.

78. Rascal (n.) रास्कल-1. धूर्त, दुर्जन

He is a rascal, don't trust him.

2. शैतान लड़का

The little rascal has finished the whole packet of biscuits.

80. Rash (adj.) रैश-1. उतावला

Don't be rash in taking a decision.

2. (n.) त्वचा पर निकली लाल-लाल फुंसियाँ

When we saw the rash, we came to know that the young boy had chicken-pox.

81. Raspberry (n.) राज़बरि-रसभरी

I like raspberries very much.

82. Rat (n.) रैट-बड़ा चूहा, मूषक

That cat caught a rat.

83. Vegetable (n.) वेजटबल-शाक भाजी, सब्जी, तरकारी, वनस्पति

Potatoes, pumpkins, carrots, onions, turnips and beans are all vegetables.

A farmer grow gegetables in the field.

84. Vehicle (n.) वीअकल-गाड़ी, सवारी, वाहन

Motor cars, buses, trucks and carts are all vehicles.

Language is a good vehicle for expressing our feelings.

85. Veil (v. & n.) वेल-(पर) पर्दा (डालना), घूंघट (करना)

(v.) Muslim women are always veiled when they go out of their homes.

Could you veil your digust at his conduct?

(n.) The bride wore a colourful veil.

86. **Vein (n.)** वेन-धारी, नस, रग, मनोवृत्ति

He is so skinny that one can clearly see his veins on his hands.

87. **Parade** परेड-क़वायद, जलूस, परेड करना

(n.) The parade will take place on the parade ground.

Thousands of people watch the Republic Day Parade.

(v.) The army will parade at dawn.

88. **Paradox (n.)** पैरडॉक्स-विडंबना

It is really a paradox that despite being an introvert, he likes to chat with strangers.

89. **Paragraph (n.)** पैराग्राफ-पैरा, अनुच्छेद

Write an eassay of three paragraphs on Diwali.

90. **Parallel** पैरलेल

1. (adv.) समानांतर

This lane runs parallel to main road.

2. (n.) सादृश्य

His quality of work is without parallel

91. **Paralyse (v.)** पैरलाइज़्-लकवा मार जाना, हिलने-डुलने में असमर्थ हो जाना

I was paralysed with fear to see two armed men in the house.

92. **Gay (adj.)** गे-1. प्रफुल्ल, प्रसन्नचित्त, विनोदी

Your gay laughter cheers me up.

2. चमकीला, भड़कीला

Youngsters favour gay colours in their clothes.

93. **Gaze (v.)** गेज़्-ताकना, टकटकी लगाकर देखना टकटकी, ताक

I gazed at the beautiful painting for a ling time.

I stood at the seashore and gazed at the sea.

(n.) He fixed his gaze at the object moving outside the window.

94. **Gem (n.)** जेम

1. रत्न

Diamond is a precious gem.

2. उत्कृष्ट व्यक्ति

She is gem of a person.

95. **Gender (n.)** जेन्डर-लिंग

In the olden times, gender was a major cause of bias.

96. **Access** ऐक्सेस-किसी वस्तु को प्रयोग में लाने का अवसर

(n.) I do not have access to Internet.

(v.) You need to contact your service provider if you cannot access the internet.

97. **Accident (n.)** ऐक्सिडन्ट - 1. दुर्घटना, आकस्मिक घटना

Gopal met with a car accident yesterday.

98. **Acclaim** अक्लेम-प्रशंसा

(n.) In spite of an average business, the movie won critical acclaim.

(v.) The shadow Lines was acclaimed by the readers.

99. **Accommodation (n.)** अकॉमडेशन-रहने की जगह अथवा सुविधा

She is looking for accommodation these days.

100. **Cane (n.)** केन-1 गन्ना, ईख, बेंत

Sugar is made from cane.

2. (v.) बेंत बुनना, बेंत-प्रहार करना

The unruly mob was caned by the police.

SPOKEN VOCABULARY
Set - 8

1. **Cannibal (n.)** कैनिब्‌ल-नरभक्षी

   Power-hungry politicians have really turned into a race of annibals.

2. **Cannon** कैनन-तोप, गोलाबारी करना टकराना

   (n.) The fort was protected by cannons mounted on its turrets

   (v.) The fort was cannoned by the enemy

3. **Cantonment (n.)** कैन्टांनमन्ट-सैन्य छावनी

   No outsiders were allowed in the cantonment area

4. **Unexpected (adj.)** अँनिइक्स्पेक्टिड्-अप्रत्याशित, जिसकी अपेक्षा न हो

   Amar's visit to us was quite unexpected, as we thought he was still out of station.

5. **Unfair (adj.)** अँनफ़ेअर्-अन्यायपूर्ण

   It was so unfair to demote him from a senior post.

6. **Unfit** अँनफिट-अयोग्य, अस्वस्थ

   You were unfit to play hockey because you had hurt your knees.

7. **Bank (n.)** बैंक-1. बैंक

   It is safe to keep money in the bank.

   2. किनारा, तीर, तट

   I walked along the bank of the river

   3. (n.) भरोसा रखना

   Can I bank upon you help?

8. **Bankrupt** बैंकरप्ट-दिवालिया

   (n.) His increasing losses and growing debts eventually made him bankrupt.

   (v.) The increasing losses bankrupted him.

9. **Banner (n.)** बैनर्-झंडा, ध्वजा

   During elections, banners of various political parties are seen everywhere.

10. **Banquet (n.)** बैन्क्विट-दावत, भोज

    The visiting head of state was given a grand banquet.

11. **Bar (n.)** बार्-1. डण्डा, छड़, सलाख

    The wooden bars erected in a row divided the courtyard into two parts.

    2. मधुशाला, पानागार

    Among the Indian middle class people, going to the bar daily is not considered good.

    3. (v.) रोकना, रोक लगाना, अर्गल लगाना

    The policeman barred the entry of traffic into the procession route.

12. **Fasten (v.)** फ़ासन-बांधना

    Fasten your seatbelts, the plane is about to take off

13. **Fat (adj.)** फ़ैट-1. मोटा, मांसल

    If you eat too much, you will become fat.

    2 (n.) चरबी, मेद

    Do you cook in fat or oil?

14. **Fatal (adj.)** फ़ेटल-विनाशक, दुर्भाग्यपूर्ण

    I heard your neighbour met with a fatal accident.

15. **Fate (n.)** फ़ेट-किस्मत, भाग्य

    If you eat too much, you will become fat.

    2. (n.) चरबी, मेद

Do you cook in fat or oil?

16. Yield (v.) यील्ड-1. उत्पन्न करना, पैदा करना

Your efforts will definitely yield success.

2. पराजय स्वीकार करना, घुटने टेकना

Though the warrior was defeated, he refused to yield the post.

3. (n.) उपज

We have an excellent yield of mangoes this year.

17. Illustrate (v. & adj.) इलस्ट्रेट-सचित्र करना (उदाहरण देकर) स्पष्ट करना

Books for children should be illustrated extensively.

(adj.) I want to buy an illustrated storybook for my child.

18. Image (n.) इमिज-1. चित्र, मूर्ति

Have you seen the huge image of Kubera at the Reserve Bank entrance?

2. प्रतिबिंब

One can see one's image in the clear water of a lake.

3. प्रतिरुप, प्रतिकृति

You are the very image of your father.

4. धारणा, कल्पना

When we go abroad, we should always try to project a good image of India.

19. Imagine (v.) इमैजिन-समझना, कल्पना करना, मान लेना

She imagines that she is a wonderful singer.

Criminals do not want to imagine the serious consequences of their action.

(n.) If you want to be a poet, you must have a good imagination.

(adj.) Kalidasa was one of India's most imaginative poets.

20. Knead (v.) नीड-गूँथना, सानना

If you want soft bread, you must knead the flour well.

21. Mankind (n.) मैन्काइन्ड-मानव-जाति

Pollution is harmful to the whole mankind.

22. Manner (n.) मैनर्-ढंग, रीति प्रकार

Your polished manners ensure a welcome for you everywhere.

23. Manor (n.) मैनर्-सामंत-भवन

We have a huge manor in our native village.

24. Manpower (n.) मैन्पाउअर्-श्रमशक्ति

The strength of our company is the skilled manpower.

25. Sandstorm (n.) सैंडस्टॉर्म-आंधी

The sandstorm blinded our vision.

26. Sandwich (n.) सैन्विज्-डबल रोटी के दो टुकड़ों के बीच में सब्ज़ी आदि का भराव

Do you like jam sandwiches?

27. Sane (adj.) सेन-स्वस्थ चित्त, समझदार

You should take a decision in a sane state of mind.

(adj.) We must behave sanely in times of stress and strain.

28. Sapphire (n.) सैफ़ाइअर्-नीलम

The astrologer advised her to wear a sapphire.

29. Neither (adv.) नाइदर्-1. दोनों में से कोई नहीं

I neither saw nor heard you coming.

2. नहीं

You do not play hockey and neither do I.

30. Nephew (n.) नेफ्यू-भतीजा, भानजा

I have one nephew and two nieces.

31. Nerve (n.) नर्व-स्नायु, धैर्य

You are a man of strong nerves.

32. Nervous (adj.) नर्वस-1. व्यग्र, उत्तेजित

Don't be so nervous, father will not punish you.

2. स्नायु-संबंधी

The patient was suffering from a nervous breakdown.

33. Tarpaulin (n.) टार्पॉलिन्-तिरपाल

The luggage was packed on a lorry and covered with a large tarpaulin.

34. Tart (adj.) टार्ट-चरपरा, तीखा़

Some fruits are very tart.

This mango is very tart. It can't be eaten.

35. Task (n.) टास्क-1. काम, कर्त्तव्य

One of my tasks is to teach my niece.

2. (v.) काम का अतिरिक्त बोझ (लेना)

Never task your strength by carrying heavy loads.

36. Taste टेस्ट-स्वाद, जायक़ा, स्वाद लेना, चखना

(n.) Lemons have a sour taste.

(v.) The brave never taste defeat.

(adj.) Water is tasteless.

(adj.) Aunt made a tasty cake for us.

2. गुण एवं दोष का ज्ञान, रुचि

My sister has a good taste in makeup.

37. Often (adv.) ऑफ़न-अक्सर, प्राय:

I offen play chess with my neighbour.

38. Ointment (n.) ऑइन्टमेन्ट-मरहम

Can you give me some ointement for boils?

39. Old (adj.) ओल्ड-1. उमर का

How old is your father?

2. बूढ़ा, वृद्ध

My father is a very old man.

3. लंबे समय से

Anil and I are old friends.

4. पुराना (फटने को तैयार)

My shoes are getting old.

40. Omen (n.) ओमन-शकुन

Throbbing of the right arm of men is considered a good omen.

41. Quiet क्वाइअट-चुप, मौन, शांत

(adj.) Be quiet, please.

Some people like a quiet life.

(n.) I love the sweet quiet of the countryside.

(v.) Try to quieten the child.

(adv.) Please move quietly.

42. Ego (n.) ईगो-अहंकार

Self-pride is good, but ego is dangerous.

43. Either आइदर्- 1. दोनों में कोई एक/प्रत्येक

(pron.) I have two pens, you can use either of them.

(conj.) Please have either an apple or an orange.

I will either write or read.

2. (adj.) दोनों

Put a flower pot on either side of the gate.

44. Elaborate (v.) इलैबरेट- 1. विस्तार देना, सविस्तार प्रतिपादित करना

Will you please elaborate on this point?

2. (adj.) विस्तृत, अलंकृत

The bride wore an elaborate dress.

45. Elastic (adj.) इलैस्टिक-लचीला

This rubber is not elastic enough.

46. Warrant (n.) वॉरन्ट-(गिरफ़्तारी) वारंट, आज्ञा-पत्र

A policeman will not search your house

unless he has a warrant from a magistrate.

Can you pay my bill until you get a warrant from the treasurer?

47. Wary (adj.) वेअरि-सावधान, चौकस, चौकन्ना, सतर्क

Be wary of the dog. for it is very fierce.

(adj.) Please walk warily lest you should fall.

48. Wash वॉश-धोना, स्नान करना, स्नान, प्रक्षालन

(n.) Daily wash is essential for good health

(v.) We should wash ourselves regularly to remain clean.

49. Wasp (n.) वॉस्प-ततैया, भिड़, बर्र

(v.) We must not waste food.

Don't waste your money in buying things you don't need.

(n.) Haste makes waste.

50. Decay (v.) डिके-सडना बिगड़ना, नष्ट होना, क्षय

Fruits decay fast if not kept in the refrigerator.

(n.) Eating chocolates causes tooth decay.

55. Decade (n.) डेकेड-दशक

Hindi cinema has undergone a dramatic change over the past one decade.

56. Deceive (v.) डिसीव्-ठगना, धोखा देना

The cheat could not deceive the wise trader.

57. Decent (adj.) डीसन्ट-शालीन, उचित, मर्यादित

Your friend is a decent fellow.

58. Rate रेट-1. दर, भाव (निर्धारित करना)

(n.) Please tell us your rates.

2 अनुपात, स्तर

This is a first-rate TV set.

3 (v.) मानना, समझना

Don't rate your chances of success highly.

4. सम्मान करना, स्थान निर्धारित करना

Indians rate kalidasa as one of the greatest poets of the world.

5. (n.) गति

The cycle was moving at the rate of ten miles an hour

6. दर

The rate of interest for home loans has risen.

59. Rather (adv.) रादर्-1. थोड़ा-सा

My mother is feeling rather ill today.

2. बल्कि (अथवा अधिक ठीक कहें तो)

The rising sun is golden, rather red.

3. कुछ हद तक

Your brother's behaviour is rather foolish.

60. Ratio (n.) रेशिओं-अनुपात

The sex ratio of men to women is falling in our country.

61. Ration रैशन-वस्तु के कम होने पर सीमित मात्रा में वितरण (करना)

(n.) There was shortage of grain in the country, so each family received a ration every week.

(v.) Grain was rationed.

62. Velvet (n.) वे'लविट-मखमल, रोयेंदार, मुलायम कपड़ा

Velvet is a soft cloth. It is smooth to touch.

63. Vengeance (n.) वे'न्जन्स-प्रतिशोध

Nothing is more poisonous than vengeance.

In fact, vengeance has no foresight.

64. Venom (n.) वे'नम-विष, जहर

The venom of a cobra is highly powerful and causes death quickly.

(adj.) The word venomous is often used to mean very unkind or spiteful.

65. **Ventilation (n.)** वे'न्टिलेशन-वायु संचार

The room needed ventilation after remaining closed for two days.

(v.) Father opened the window to ventilate the room.

66. **Parameter (n.)** पैरमीटर-मापदंड

Flawless language cannot be the only parameter to a good story.

67. **Paranoid (adj.)** पैरनॉइड-इस मिथ्या संदेह से ग्रस्त कि कुछ अशुभ होगा या अन्य लोग कोई हानि पहुंचाएंगे

Stop being a paranoid about going out in the evening.

68. **Parboil (v.)** पा(र्) बॉईल-थोड़ा पकने तक उबालना

Mother paraboiled the rice

69. **Parcel (n.)** पार्सल-पारसल, पार्सल बनाना

Please wrap up this parcel for me.

70. **Pardon** पार्डन-क्षमा (करना)

(n.) I beg your pardon.

The thief asked the judge for pardon.

(v.) Many prisoners were pardoned on the eve of the king's birthay.

71. **Hardship (n.)** हार्डशिप-तंगहाली

She has faced a lot of hardship in bringing up her children

72. **Hardware (n.)** हार्डवेअर्-कम्प्यूटर की मशीनरी

Buy a new monitor from the computer hardware shop

73. **Hard-working (adj.)** हार्ड वर्किंग मेहनती

He is one of the most hard-working people in his company.

74. **Hare (n.)** हेअर्-खरगोश

Can you run as fast as a hare?

75. **Judiciary (n.)** जूडिशरि-न्यायतंत्र

She lost faith in judiciary when the court released her son's killer.

76. **Knee (n.)** नी-घुटना

My left knee was injured in fall.

77. **Mansion (n.)** मैन्शन-हवेली, कोठी, प्रासाद

We live in an old mansion built by our grandfather.

78. **Manual** मैनुअल्

1. (adj.) हस्त-चरित

Manual labour is very expensive abroad.

2. (n.) परिचालन-निर्देशपुस्तिका

This manual will teach you different recipes of cheese.

79. **Manufacture (v.)** मैन्युफैक्चर्-उत्पादन करना, बनाना

What articles do you manufacture in your factory?

80. **Manure (n.)** मेन्युअर्-खाद

The farmer added manure to the soil to make it more fertile

81. **Sarcams (n.)** साकैज़्म-कटाक्ष

(n.) Sarcams was dissolved in his words.

(adj.) He made a sarcastic comment on her looks

(adv.) She laughed sarcastically at her.

82. **Sash (n.)** सैश-दुपट्टा, कमरबंद, पेटी

Village-girls put on coloured and decorated sashes.

83. **Satellite (n.)** सैटलाइट-उपग्रह

The moon is a satellite of the earth.

84. **Satire (n.)** सैटाइअर्-उपग्रह

That author is good at writing satire.

85. Nest ने'स्ट-घोंसला, बसेरा

(v.) Don't disturb the sparrows when they are nesting.

(n.) The tree in our garden is full of nests.

86. Net (n.) ने'ट-जाल

Do you use a hair-net?

87. Network (n.) नेटवर्क-अनेक अंगों को जोड़ कर बनाया गया समूह

India has the largest network of railways.

88. Tattered (adj.) टैटर्ड्-फटा-पुराना

The beggar covered himself with a tattered blanket on the cold winter night.

89. Tattoo टैटू-शरीर पर गोदा गया चित्र

(n.) I got a ta'too painted on my ankle.

(v.) I got my ankle tattooed.

90. Taut (adj.) टॉट्-कसा हुआ

In youth, the skin is taut. But in the old age, it begisn to sag.

91. Tax (v. & n.) टैक्स-कर, टैक्स (लगाना)

(v.) The new law did not tax the people heavily.

(n.) Have you paid the income tax?

Taxes are levied on property, income, profits and many other items.

92. Taxi (n.) टैक्सी-किराये की गाड़ी (टैक्सी)

Taxis go about the streets for people to hire them. They are driven by taxi-drivers.

Bring me a taxi for New Delhi railway-station.

93. Ominous (adj.) ऑमिनस-अपशकुनी

The black cat is considered ominous by many.

94. Omit (v.) ओमिट-छोड़ देना, नहीं करना

Do not omit Amitabh's name from the list of invitees.

We read the play omitting the last two scenes.

95. Once (adv.) वन्स-1. एक बार

I have visited America only once.

2. किसी समय, कभी

Once upon a time, there lived a great king.

96. Only ओन्लि-1. केवल, सिर्फ

(adv.) She only did it for a joke.

I cam to the party only because you were coming.

2. (adj.) अकेला, एकमात्र

Sunil is the only boy who can solve this problem.

This bus is for ladies only.

97. Quick (adj.) क्विक-तेज़, शीघ्रगामी, तत्काल

We should take quick decisions.

Rishi Raj has a very quick mind.

Be quick please. We don't have much time.

"Quick march", said the drill-master.

(adv.) Please don't walk quickly.

98. Elbow एल्बो-कोहनी, मोड़ कोहनी मारना

(n.) Don't put yout elbows on the table.

(v.) He elbowed his way through the crowd.

99. Elder (adj.) एल्डर्-आयु में बड़ा

My eleder sister is a journalist.

(n.) वयोवृद्ध लोग

We should respect our elders.

100. Elect (v.) इलेक्ट-चुनना, निर्वाचित करना

The members of the company met to elect a new chairman.

(n.) Congratulations on your election as the chairman of the company.

When are the general elections going to be held?

SPOKEN VOCABULARY
Set - 9

1. **Electricity (n.)** इलेक्ट्रिसटि-बिजली, विद्युत

   Electricity is one of the greatest inventions of science.

   (n.) Have you taken your diploma as an electrician?

   I would like to buy an electric iron.

2. **Watch (n.)** वॉच-1. जेब या हाथ की घड़ी

   Father had a pocket watch.

   Mother wore a watch round her wrist.

   2. (v.) देखना, रखवाली करना

   We watched for our friend coming home at night.

   A watchman is a man who watches the building during the night.

3. **Water** वॉटर्-पानी (देना), जल (से सींचना), छिड़कना

   (n.) We drink water when we are thirsty.

   The pond is full of muddy water. The sea is full of salty water.

   (v.) You should water the lawn every day in dry weather.

   Every morning, I water my potted plants.

4. **Watt (n.)** वॉट-वाट

   This is a 100-watt bulb.

5. **Wave** वेव-1. लहराना, फहराना, हिलाना

   (v.) Wave you hand to us as you leave.

   When the guard waved his green flag, the train steamed off.

   2. (n.) लहर, तरंग, हिलोर

   A wave turned their boat over.

   How long is this cold wave going to last?

6. **Deception (n.)** डिसेप्शन-धोखा

   (n.) This is a deliberate deception by the management to conceal the future plans.

   (adj.) Looks are often deceptive.

7. **Decide (v.)** डिसाइड-निर्णय करना

   I couldn't decide whether to go to Shimla or Mumbai for my holidays.

   The prime minister's decision to step down surprised both the politicians and the journalists.

8. **Decipher (v.)** डिसाइफ़र्-कूटवाचन करना

   Can you decipher which medicine the doctor has prescribed?

9. **Decisive (adj.)** डिसाइसिव-निर्णायक

   The First Battle of Panipat was a decisive battle that established the Mughal rule in India.

10. **Rational (adj.)** रैशनल्-तर्कसंगत

    Her argument was rational and logical.

11. **Rationale (n.)** रैशनल्-तर्क

    The sales representative explained the rationale behind the new product.

12. **Rattle (v.)** रैटल-1. खड़खड़ाना

    The storm makes windows and doors rattle noisily.

    2. खनखनाना, बजाना

    The child rattled the coins in the tin box.

13. **Rave (v.)** रेव-1. बड़बड़ाना

    She raved in her sleep when she had a nightmare.

    2. मूर्खता-भरी बातें करना

    The young lady raved about the film stars.

14. **Venture (v. & n.)** वे'नचर्-जोखिम (में डालना)

(v.) Do not venture int the woods on such a dark night.

(n.) It is a risky venture to start a college in the village.

15. Venue (n.) वेन्यू-कार्यक्रम स्थल

I will reach the venue in an hour.

16. Veranda (n.) वरैन्डा-बरांडा, बरामदा

I like to sit in veranda in the evening and talk to the neighbours.

17. Verb (v.) वर्ब-क्रिया

There are two kinds of verb-transitive and intransitive.

18. Parents (n.) पे'अरन्ट्स-माँ बाप

Where are your parents, little boy?

Karma Singh has a royal parentage.

19. Park (n.) पार्क-1. उपवन, उद्यान

We go to the park every evening.

2. पार्क करना, खड़ा करना

Parking is not allowed here.

(v.) May I park my motor cycle here while I visit the market?

20. Parliament (n.) पार्लमन्ट-संसद, लोकसभा

There was a chaos in the Parliament.

21. Part (n.) पार्ट-1. भाग, हिस्सा

This book is divided into three parts.

2. भूमिका

I have a major part in the play to be put up by our club.

3. (v.) अलग करना/होना

The two friends were sad when they parted to go in different directions.

4. पक्षपात, पक्ष पोषण

We thank you for taking our part.

22. Partial (adj.) पार्शल-1. आंशिक, अपूर्ण

I am only in partial agreement with what you say.

2. पक्षपाती

Parents are naturally partial to their children.

23. Imitate (v.) इमिटेट-अनुकरण/नकल करना

If you keep imitating other people's paintings, your will never become an original painter.

(n.) The lady was wearing a necklace of imitation pearls.

24. Immaculate (adj.) इमैक्यलट-त्रुटिहीन

His eassay was immaculate.

25. Immaterial (adj.) इमटिअरिअल-महत्त्वहीन

When yo die, it is immaterial what happens to your body.

26. Immature (adj.) इम्मैच्युअर्-अपरिपक्व

His behaviour was too immature.

27. Accompany (v.) अकम्पनि - 1. साथ देना या चलना

Sudhir was accompanied by his wife to the musical concert.

2. साथ गाना या बजाना

The musician played the Sitar and his young son accompanied him on the table.

28. Accomplish (v.) अकम्प्लिश-पूर्ण करना, सिद्ध करना

Congratulations on accomplishing such a difficult task!

29. According to (prep.) ऑकर्डिंग टू-के अनुसार

(prep.) We must act according to our strategy.

Adv:- Whenever you are in trouble follow your mind and act accordingly

30. Account (n.) अकाउंट - 1. वर्णन, कथन

His account of the event was very interesting

2. गणना आय-व्यय का लेखा

I do not know how to keep accounts.

3. (v.) कारण बतलाना

How did kamal account for being late today?

31. Accountable (adj.) अकाउंटेबल-जवाबदेह

I am not accountable for what happened yesterday.

32. Canoe (n.) कनू-डोंगी, बनहटी

The adventurous young man crossed the sea in a canoe.

33. Canvas (n.) कैन्वस-किरमिच, कैन्वस

Sportsmen wear shoes of canvas.

34. Cap (v.) कैप-1. टोपी

The cap provides protection from the sun.

2. (v.) मात कर देना, से बढ़कर होना

The batsman capped his brilliant century with a sixer.

35. Capable (adj.) केपब्ल्-1. प्रतिभाशाली

A capable execitive always rises in his organisation.

2. योग्य, समर्थ, क्षम

Are you capable of handling office correspondence independently?

36. Unfold (v.) ॲन्फोल्ड-खोलना, प्रकट होना

Unfold the letters and read it.

A wonderful view of nature unfolded before us.

37. Uniform (adj.) यूनिफ़ॉर्म-एकरुप, सब प्रकार से एक समान

All the benches in our school are uniform.

The legs of a chair are of uniform length.

2. (n.) वर्दी

Soldiers, policemen and firemen always wear their uniforms.

38. Union (n.) यूनिअन, यूनयॅन-संगठन

Union is strength.

A trade union is a group of workers in the same trade who join together to get fair wages and good conditions of work.

39. Barbarous (Adj.) बार्बरस-क्रूर, असभ्य

In ancient times, barbarous customs like human sacrifice prevailed in our country.

40. Barber (n.) बार्बर्-नाई, हज्जाम

I went to the barber's shop to have a haircut.

41. Bare (adj.) बेअर्-नंगा, गंजा, अरक्षित, खाली

The poor man walked bare foot in the hot sun.

42. Barely (adv.) बेअर्लि-कठिनाई से

I could barely hear her voice from there.

43. Bargain बार्गेन-सौदा या समझौता करना

(n.) For fifty rupees, this chair is a good bargain.

(v.) The customer bargained hard with the shopkeeper.

44. Fatal (adj.) फ़ेटल-विनाशक, दुर्भाग्यपूर्ण

I heard your neighbour met with a fatal accident.

45. Fate (n.) फ़ेट-किस्मत, भाग्य

We can never know what our fate is.

46. Fatigue (n.) फ़टीग-थकान

She fainted of fatigue.

49. Fault (n.) फ़ॉल्ट-1. ग़लती, भूल

It was the employer's fault that the employees were not paid in time.

2. दोष, कमी, त्रुटि

The mechanic quickly repaired the fault in the car engine.

50. General (adj.) जेनरल-1. आम, सार्वजनिक

The general elections were marred by many incidents of booth-capturing.

2. सामान्य, साधारण

As a general rule, we are at home in the

evening.

3. (n.) सेनापति, सेनानी, जनरल

My friend's uncle is a General in the army.

51. Generate (v.) जेनरेट–उत्पादन करना

News agencies generate useful information about the various events.

52. Generation (adj.) जेनरेशन–पीढ़ी, पुश्त

The young generation today is more fun-loving than their elders were in their youth.

53. Generous (adj.) जेनरस–उदार, दानशील

May we expect a generous donation from you for our charity?

Vagish was always generous in sharing his sweets.

(n.) He showed great generosity.

54. Genius (n.) जीनिअस–1. प्रतिभा, प्रवृत्ति

My son has a genius for different languages.

2. प्रतिभाशाली व्यक्ति

Kalidas was a genius, who wrote "Abhigyan Shakuntalam", one of the greatest plays of the world.

55. Lass (n.) लैस–लड़की, किशोरी

She is a very industrious young lass.

56. Last (adj.) लास्ट–1. पिछला, गत

What were you doing last night?

2. अन्त, अन्तिम, आखिरी

You are the last to speak.

3. (v.) टिकना, बने रहना

How long will the function last?

57. Latch लैच–सिटकनी, अर्गला (लगाना)

(v.) Always latch the door from inside at night.

(n.) The door could not be closed properly because of the faulty latch.

58. Late (adj. & adv.) लेट–1. देर से, देर का, विलम्बित

(adj.) Why are you so late?

2. दिवंगत

Did you know the late Mr. Kapur?

(adv.) I came late last night.

59. Harm हार्म–हानि, क्षति, हानि या चोट पहुंचाना

(n.) The crops suffered great harm due to the unseasonal rains.

(v.) The strong should not harm the weak.

(adj.) Excessive use of chemicals in agriculture is harmful.

60. Harmony (n.) हार्मनि–1. स्वरसंगति, तालमेल

Let us sing in harmony.

2. सामंजस्य, मेल, मैत्री

Two neighbouring countries can progress only if they live in harmony.

61. Harness (v.) हार्निस–1. साज़, साज़ चढ़ाना

Harness the horse to the carriage.

2. (n.) घोड़े की काठी, काम (पर)

My friend died in harness (on duty).

62. Harp (v.) हार्प–राग अलापना

Why are you harping on this topic?

63. Judicious (adj.) जूडिशस–विवेकपूर्ण

Judicious use of words will make your essay more interesting.

64. Jug (n.) जॅग–सुराही, घड़ा, जग

Please bring some cold water in a jug.

65. Juggler (n.) जॅग्लर्–बाज़ीगर

The juggler did a trick by tossing five knives together.

66. Juice (n.) जूस–रस

Would you like some orange-juice?

67. Kneel (v.) नील–घुटने टेकना

Let us kneel in prayer.

68. Manuscript (n.) मैन्सुस्क्रिप्ट-पाण्डुलिपि, हस्तलिखित

Have you sent the manuscript to the publishers?

69. Many (adj.) मे'नि-अनेक, बहुत से

I met many old friends at the party.

70. Map (n.) मैप-नक्शा, मानचित्र

I want to buy a map of India.

71. Marble (n.) मार्बल-1. संगमरमर

Are you using marble in the construction of your house?

2. गोली, कंचा

My son plays marbles with his friends every evening.

72. Satisfy (v.) सैटिस्फ़ाइ-संतुष्टि करना, संतोष देना

It is difficult to satisfy a greedy person.

(n.) Good shopkeepers aim at the satisfaction of their customers.

(adj.) Your work is not satisfactory.

73. Sauce (n.) सॉस-चटनी

Tomato sauce is eaten with bread pakoras.

74. Saucer (n.) सॉसर्-(कप के साथ की)प्लेट, तश्तरी

He put the cup on the saucer.

75. Savage (n.) सैविज-असभ्य, जंगली इंसान

Is man not still a savage?

(adj.) Everybody hates his savage behaviour.

76. Save (n.) सेव-1. बचाना, बचाकर रखना

Save something for tomorrow.

2. सुरक्षित करना, संकट से बचाना

She was saved from drowning by a life-guard.

3. नष्ट होने से बचाना

You must save time by cycling to work.

77. Neutral (adj.) न्यूट्रल-तटस्थ

I always remain neutral when two people quarrel.

78. Never (adv.) ने'वर्-कभी नहीं

I have never seen such a strange animal before.

79. New (adv.) न्यू-नया, नवीन, ताज़ा

When did you buy this new car?

I am not new to this city.

(adv.) My sister is newly married.

80. News (n.) न्यूज़-समाचार, ख़बर

You can read the news in the daily papers.

Where is today's newspaper?

81. Tea (n.) टी-चाय

Mother makes tea. She pours boiling water on tea-leaves, and mixes milk and sugar. Thus tea becomes ready.

The Darjeeling tea is famous world over.

82. Teach (v.) टीच-सिखलाना, शिक्षा देना, पढ़ाना

The teachers teach us very efficiently.

We must teach the baby to talk properly.

83 Team (n.) टीम-एक साथ काम करने वाले लोगों का दल या टोली

Ravi is a member of the cricket team in his school.

(adj.) We should do our work with a team spirit.

84. Tear टिअर्-1. फाड़ना, चीरना, फटाव

(v.) Rama has torn her frock.

(n.) Her mother will mend the tear.

2. आंसू

When we cry, tears drop from our eyes.

She was in tears to see her new doll broken.

85. Onset (n.) ऑनसेट्-(किसी अप्रिय स्थिति का) आरंभ

This seems to be the onset of typhoid.

86. Onto (prep.) ऑनटु-किसी वस्तु के ऊपर

Stick this paper onto the cardboard.

87. Onwards (adv.) ऑनवर्ड्ज़-समय विशेष के बाद

I'll go on a leave from next month onwards.

88. Open (v.) ओपन-1. खोलना, प्रकट करना

Please open the door.

2. खोलना (पुस्तक, टिन, मुंह आदि)

Please open the book (the tin/the mouth, etc.)

3. (adj.) सार्वजनिक

It was an open mango eating competition in which we contested.

4. खुला, मुक्त

You should take a walk in the open air.

5. खुला, उदार

Have an open mind when you argue with others.

89. Quill (n.) क्विल-पक्षी का पंख

In olden times, people used two write with quill.

90. Elegant (adj.) एलिगन्ट-रमणीय, सुरुचिपूर्ण

The young lady looked elegant in her new dress.

(adv.) Some people are always dressed very elegantly.

91. Elememtary (adj) एलिमेन्ट्रि-प्राथमिक, प्रारंभिक

Do you have at least elementary knowl edge of Chemistry?

92. Elephant (n.) एलिफन्ट-हाथी

My younger so had an elephant ride in Jaipur.

93. Elevator (n.) एलिवेटर-लिफ़्ट

He took the elevator to reach the third floor.

94. Wavelenght (n.) वेवलेंथ-साझी रुझान

We enjoy working together because we are on the same wavelength.

95. Waver (v.) वेवर्-डाँवाँडोल होना, अस्थिर होना

Don't waver too long about buying the almirah, otherwise someone else may buy it.

96. Wax (v. & n.) वैक्स-बढ़ना, मोम

(v.) The new moon will wax until it is full.

(n.) Wax is used for making candles.

97. Way (n.) वे-1. मार्ग, रास्ता, सड़क

(v.) The little child lost his way. He could not find his way back home.

Which is the way to the interstate bus stand?

2. दिशा, ओर, तरफ

Always look at both the ways before crossing the road.

3 विधि, तरीका, प्रकार, उपाय

This book tells you the way to use words in sentences.

4. दूरी

Will you meet me half way?

98. Declare (v.) डिकलेअर्-1. प्रकट करना, घोषित करना, बताना

Morality demands that all politicians must declare their assests.

(n.) The company's declaration of a special bonus was a pleasant surprise.

2. (v.) क्रिकेट में पारी-समप्ति की घोषणा करना

The captain declared the innings when the total score reached 450.

99. Decline (v.) डिक्लाइन-1. अस्वीकार करना

Ramesh declined Rahul's invitation to dinner, as he had to go to Kolkata.

2. (n.) क्षय, ह्रास होना

Moral values are on a decline these days.

100. Decode (v.) डिकोस-गुप्त संदेश का अर्थ निकालना

This is a secret message; we need to decode it.

SPOKEN VOCABULARY
Set - 10

1. **Decompose (v.)** डीकम्पोज़-विघटित होना
   (v.) A decomposed body was found in the forest last week.

2. **Raw (adj.)** रॉ-1. कच्चा (सामान)
   All the raw materials for building the house have been acquired.
   2. बिना पकाया हुआ
   We prefer raw vegetables.

3. **Ray (n.)** रे-1. किरण
   We should expose ourselves to the direct rays of the sun early in the morning.

4. **Razor (n.)** रेज़र्-उस्तरा
   The barber uses the razor to shave.

5. **Re (pre.)** रि-दुबारा
   1. Reappear - (परीक्षा में) दुबारा बैठना
   His brother reappeared in the B.A. examination.
   2. Recall (v.) - याद करना, स्मरण करना
   We can recall the days when we were children.
   3. Recount (v.) - दुबारा गिनना, वर्णन करना
   He recounted how he had shot the lion.
   (n.) The defeated candidate requested a recount of votes in the election.
   4 Reconstruct (v.) - दुबारा निर्माण करना
   The shop destroyed in the fire has been reconstructed
   5. Reopen (v.) - दुबारा खुलना
   Our school closes on Saturday evening and reopens on Monday morning.
   6. Rewrite (v.) - दुबारा लिखना
   Your story is badly written. Please re write it.

6. **Reach (v.)** रीच-1. पहुँचना
   We shope to reach Delhi tomorrow morning.
   2. पहुँचना
   Will you reach me that bag please?
   3. (तक) बनना
   The labourers are making a new road but it hasn't reached Shahdara yet.
   4. (n.) पहुँच, पकड़
   Dry fruits are out of reach of a common man.
   5. (v.) पहुँचना, आयु का होना
   When I reach the age of sixty, I shall reduce my working hours.

7. **Verbatim (adv.)** वर्बेटिम-शब्दश:
   She copied the article for Internet verbatim.

8. **Verdict (n.)** वर्डिक्ट-1. अभिनिर्णय, पंच फैसला
   Honour the verdict on the jury.
   2. बहुत सोच-विचार के बाद निर्णय
   What is your verdict on the quality of this cloth?

9. **Verge (n.)** वर्ज-किनारा, सिरा, छोर, सीमा
   There is a verge of bricks on each side of the road.

10. **Verify (v.)** वे'रिफ़ाइ-प्रमाणित करना, सत्य सिद्ध करना
   Your statement must be verified by a witness.

11. **Vermin (n.)** वर्मिन-पीड़क जन्तु, कीड़े-मकौड़े

Lice and fleas are considered to be vermin.

(adj.) Don't neglect the dog, otherwise it will be verminous.

12. Participate (v.) पार्टिसिपेट-भाग लेना

Will you participate in the dance competition?

13. Particle (n.) पार्टिकल-कण

Some particles of ust are sticking to your shirt.

14. Particular (adj.) पर्टिक्यलर्-1. विशिष्ट, खास, अमुक

There are many pictures in this art gallery, but I want to look at this particular one.

(adv.) We should be particularly careful on dark nights.

2. सख्त, नियमित, विशेष, सावधान

Ramesh is very particular about his food.

3. विवरण

Please give particulars of all your achievements.

15. Partition पार्टिशन-विभाजन, बंटवारा, बाँट देना

(n.) We divided our sitting room into two parts with a partition.

(v.) The two brothers partitioned their house.

16. Jumble जॅम्बल-अस्तव्यस्त कर देना, अव्यवस्था

(v.) Ramesh quickly wrote the correct sentence from the jumbled up words.

(n.) Human mind is a jumble of ideas.

17. Jump जॅम्प-कूद, छलाँग, कूदना, चौंकना

(n.) I won a prize in high jump.

(v.) Don't jump to false conclusions.

18. Junction (n.) जंक्शन-1. संगम, मिलन

Be careful while driving through a junction of the main road with a lane.

2. जंक्शन

Our train halted for half an hour at Mathura junction.

19. Jungle (n.) जंगल-जंगल, वन

My native place is a village on the edge of the jungle.

20. Accumulate (v.) ॲक्यूम्यलेट-इकट्ठा करना या होना

Dust will accumulate in the room if you do not clean it daily.

21. Accurate (adj.) ऐक्यरट-अचूक, सही, ठीक

My wrist-watch always shows the accurate time.

22. Accuse (v.) अक्यूज़्-दोष लगाना, दोषी या अपराधी ठहराना

The servant was accused of stealing a golden ring.

23. Accustom (v.) अकस्टम-अभ्यास डालना, परिचय कराना

We are not accustomed to very cold weather.

We should accustom ourselves to the idea of space travel.

24. Ache एक-पीड़ा, कष्ट,

(n.) If you have a tooth-ache, you should go to a dentist.

पीड़ा होना

(v.) My leg is aching.

25. Capital (n.) कैपिट्ल-1. राजधानी

Delhi is the capital of India.

2. पूँजी

He invested his capital in business.

3. (adj.) उत्तम, प्रमुख

Whether or not to start this venture would be a decision of capital importance.

4. (adj.) बड़ा अक्षर

Write the address in capital letters.

26. Capsicum (n.) कैप्सिकम-शिमला मिर्च

My mother prepared stuffed capsicums for lunch.

27. Capsize (v.) कैपसाइज़ नाव का पानी में पलट जाना

The sea storm capsized the boat.

28. Capsule (n.) कैप्स्यूल-पुटी, संपुटिका

The doctor prescribed B-complex capsules to my mother to overcome her weakness.

29. Unique (adj.) यूनीक-एकमात्र, अकेला, अनुपम

Qutub Minar is a unique monument.

30. Unit (n.) यूनिट

1. समूह

We work as a unit in the office.

2. (adj.) खण्ड

The book is divided into five units.

3. इकाई

Hectare is a unit of area.

31. Universe (n.) यूनिवर्स-विश्व, जगत्

The earth is only a part of the universe.

32. University (n.) यूनिवर्सटि-विश्वविद्यालय

A University should be a place of light, of liberty, and of learning.

33. Barge बार्ज

1. संकरी नौका

(n.) We saw an ancient barge in the museum.

2. ज़बरदस्ती घुसना

(v.) The thieves barged into the house at right.

34. Bark (v.) बार्क्-1. भौंकना

My dog began to bark when it saw a stranger approaching our house.

2. (n.) छाल, वल्कल

The barks of some trees have medicinal values.

35. Barn (n.) बार्न-खलियान

We have a huge barn in the village.

36. Baron (n.) बैरन-संभ्रांत व्यक्ति

His father is a printing baron.

37. Favour (v.) फ़ेवर्-1. कृपा, अनुग्रह

Will you do me a favour?

2. (v.) पसंद करना, चाहना

Between blue and red, which colour do you favour?

(adj.) Blue is my favourite colour.

38. Fear फ़िअर-डर, डरना, आशंका करना

(n.) Fear is a powerful enemy.

(v.) I fear I might miss the train.

39. Feast फ़ीस्ट-दावत, प्रीतिभोज, पर्व, दावत खाना

(n.) Ram invited all the neighbours on his daughter's birthday feast.

(v.) Our friends feasted and sang songs.

40. Feat (n.) फ़ीट-कमाल, करतब, असाधारण कार्य

Children were thrilled on seeing the feats of the acrobat.

41. Yoke (n.) योक-पराधीनता, जोतना,

They worked under the yoke of a cruel master.

(v.) Yoke your bulls to the carts.

42. Immediate (adj.) इमीजिअट-1. तात्कालिक

Your complaint to the mayor will receive immediate attention.

2. निकटतम

The police informed the immediate relations of the accident victim about his serious condition.

(adv.) This payment is to be made immediately.

43. **Immense (adj.)** इमेन्स-अत्याधिक, विशाल

The famine caused immense suffering.

(adv.) I liked this book immensely.

44. **Immerse (v.)** इमर्स-किसी वस्तु को द्रव में पूरी तरह डुबाना

The kid immersed the stick in water.

45. **Immoral (adj.)** इमॉरल-अनैतिक

It is immoral to trouble yor parents.

46. **Gentle (adj.)** जेन्टल-1. कोमल, सौम्य

Your manners should always begentle.

2. मन्द, हल्का

Let us go for a walk and enjoy the gentle breeze.

47 **Gentleman (n.)** जेन्ट्लमन-सज्जन, कुलीन/भद्र पुरुष

A gentleman speaks politely and be haves sensibly.

48. **Genuine (adj.)** जेन्युइन-असली, सच्चा

Is your overcoat made of genuine fur?

49. **Geography (n.)** जिऑग्रफि-भूगोल

Geography was my favourite subject in the school.

50. **Lately (v.)** लेट्लि-हाल में

Have you seen Mohan lately?

51. **Latest (adj.)** लेटिस्ट-नवीनतम

What is the latest news in business?

52. **Latrine (n.)** लट्रीन-पाखाना, संडास

You must clean the latrine every day.

53. **Latter (adj.)** लैट्र-बाद का, पिछला

Between Anil and Sunil, I found the latter more intelligent.

54. **Germ (n.)** जर्म-जीवाणु, रोगाणु

Cleanliness is the best protection against germs.

55. **Gesture (n.)** जेस्चर्-चेष्टा, इशारा, संकेत

If you want to be a successful public speaker, you must practise effective gestures.

59. **Get (v.)** गेट्-1. पाना, प्राप्त करना

How many marks did you get in Mathematics?

2. हो जाना

I hear you got married recently.

60. **Getaway (n.)** गेटवे-रफूचक्कर हो जाना

Our getaway on the weekend was very refreshing.

61. **Laugh (v.)** लाफ़्-हँसना, हँसी

Laughing is good for health, but we should not laugh at others.

(n.) I could hear you laughter in the other room.

We all had a good laugh when our father told us story.

62. **Launch (n.)** लॉन्च-1. लाँच, मोटर से चलने वाली किश्ती

We were taken round the harbour in a launch.

2. (v.) आरंभ कर देना

Diwali is considered auspicious to launch a new business.

63. **Laundry (n.)** लॉन्ड्रि-धोबीखाना, धुलाईघर

Send all these dirty clothes to the laundry.

64. **Lavatory (n.)** लैवट्रि-शौचघर

Where is the lavatory in this theatre?

65. **Harsh (v.)** हार्श-कठोर, निष्ठुर, कर्कश

Do not speak in a harsh voice.

(adj.) Do not treat your children harshly.

66. **Harvest (n.)** हार्विस्ट-फ़सल (काटना), परिणाम

Farmers are very busy during the time of harvest.

(adj.) Have you visited a farm at harvest

time?

67. Hassle (n.) हैसल-परेशानी

Do you have any hassle about coming to my place tomorrow?

68. Haste (n.) हेस्ट-जल्दी, जल्दबाज़ी, उतावली

Haste makes waste.

(adj.) I am sorry for my hasty decision.

69. Knife (n.) नाइफ़-चाकू, छुरी

Please sharpen the edge of this knife.

70. March मार्च-प्रयाण (करना), कूच करना

(v.) We stood by the side of the road as the soldiers marched past.

(n.) The police barricaded the road to stop the agitationist's march.

71. Mare (n.) मेअर्-घोड़ी

The mare was decorated for the wedding.

72. Margin (n.) मार्जिन-हाशिया, किनारा, गुंजाइश

Always leave a margin when you write.

73. Marine (adj.) मरीन्-समुद्री

Oil slick is a threat to marine animals.

74. Saw (n.) सॉ-आरी

The carpenter cuts the wood with his saw.

(v.) आरी से काटना

He is sawing the wood.

75. Say (v.) से-कहना

Listen to what others say and do what you ought to do.

(n.) Saying and doing are two different things.

76. Scald (v.) स्काल्ड-(गर्म पानी से) जलाना

Don't scald your tongue in other people's broth. A cat who is scalded once fears even cold water.

77. Scale (v.) स्केल-1. ऊपरी परत

Scrape the scales off the fish before cooking it.

2. परिमाण, मात्रा

At present, we grow vegetables and fruits on a small scale only.

3. पैमाना, फुटा

Have you a scale for measurements?

4. (v.) चढ़कर पार करना

You cannot scale the wall unless someone lifts you.

78. Next (adj.) ने'क्स्ट-अगला, आगामी

Next week I am going on a holiday.

79. Nibble (v.) निबल-कुतरना

A mouse has nibbled my notebook.

80. Nice (adj.) नाइस-सुंदर, मनोहर, रुचिकर

You look nice in this dress.

This restaurant serves nice food.

81. Niche (n.) नीश्-विशिष्ट स्थान

By doing selected roles, Konkona Sen has carved a niche for herself in the film industry.

82. Tease (v.) टीज़्-तंग करना, परेशान करना

Don't tease animals.

Don't take my words seriously, I was only teasing you.

83. Technical (adj.) टे'क्निकल-तकनीकी, प्राविधिक

Have you got a technical training to handle this kind to machinery?

It is a technical error. Ordinary man can't judge it.

84. Tedious (adj.) टीडिअस-नीरस, थकाने वाला, उबाले वाला

The speaker's speech became tedious after he had been talking for twenty minutes.

85. Teem (v.) टीम-भरा होना

The road was teeming with various big and small vehicles.

86. Teenage (adj.) टीनेज-किशोरावस्था का

(adj.) She is a mother of two teenage children.

(n.) Teenagers often find the advice of their parents rubbish.

87. Operation (n.) आपरेशन 1. आपरेशन, शल्य-क्रिया

The surgeon took two hours to perform the operation.

2. संचालन, क्रिया, व्यापार

The boys watched with interest the operation of the huge machine.

88. Opinion (n.) अपिन्यन-विचार, राय, मत

What are your political opinions?

Ask an expert to give his opinion on the feasibility of your plan.

87. Opponent (n.) अपोनन्ट-प्रतिपक्षी, विरोधी, प्रतिद्वंद्वी

We defeated our opponents in the cricket match.

88. Opportunity (n.) ऑप'ट्यूनटि-मौक़ा, अवसर

I would like to have an opportunity to visit Kashmir.

89. Quit (v.) क्विट-छोड़ना

"Quit the hall at once", ordered the teacher.

90. Eligible (n.) एलिजब्ल-कुछ करने या पाने का अधिकार रखने वाला

Anyone passing the SSC examination is eligible to join a college.

91. Eliminate (v.) इलिमिनेट-स्पर्धा में आगे बढ़ने से रोकना

Out of five teams, three will be eliminated and two will qualify for the finals.

92. Else एल्स्- 1. दूसरा, अन्य, और

(adj.) No one else knows what I am going to tell you.

This isn't my book, it is someone else's.

2. (adv.) अन्यथा, नहीं तो

Walk carefully or else your may slip.

You must take a taxi, how else can you catch the train?

93. Elite (n.) एलीट-संभ्रात वर्ग

They consider themselves the intellectually elite people.

94. Email (n.) ईमेल-ई-मेल

I sent him all the information by an email.

95. Embark (v.) एम्बार्क्-(जहाज़ पर) चढ़ना, चढ़ाना, प्रारंभ करना

The announcer requested the passengers travelling to Mumbai to embark on the plane.

96. Emancipate (v.) इमैन्सिपेट-अधिकार-संपन्न होना

Today's women are emancipated enough to fend for themselves.

97. We (pron.) वी-हम, हम लोग

We reside in a big bungalow.

98. Weak वीक्-दुर्बल, कमज़ोर, निर्बल (व्यक्ति)

(adj.) She is feeling weak after her illness.

(n.) Have the weak no right to live?

We all have weaknesses.

99. Wealth (n.) वे'ल्थ-सम्पत्ति, धन-संपदा

The rich man gave away all his wealth to build a hospital for the poor people.

Wealth is not his who has it, but his who enjoys it.

100. Weapon (n.) वेपन-हथियार

Swords, shields, spears and guns are weapons.

SPOKEN VOCABULARY
Set - 11

1. **Decor (n.)** डेकॉर्-आंतरिक सजावट की शैली

   The interior decor of the building was praiseworthy.

2. **Decorate (v.)** डेकरेट-सजाना, अलंकृत करना, पदक देना, सम्मानित करना

   Sita has decorated her drawing room very beautifully.

3. **Decrease (v.)** डिक्रीज़्-घटना या घटाना

   The manager will decrease your pay if you work for fewer hours this week.

4. **Decree** डिक्री-सरकारी आदेश

   (n.) He was expelled from the services on the royal decree.

   (v.) We thought we would win the competition, but fate decreed otherwise.

5. **Dedicate (v.)** डेडिकेट-समर्पित करना

   (v.) Mother Teresa dedicated her whole life to serving the poor.

   (adj.) She is completely dedicated to her career.(n.) Her dedication to work is praiseworthy.

6. **React (v.)** रिएक्ट-प्रतिक्रिया करना

   The accused reacted fiercely to the charge.

   (n.) What was the reaction of your father?

7. **Read (v.)** रीड-1. पढ़ना

   We should not read lying down on the bed.

   2. पढ़कर सुनाना

   Now please read me the story of Rama.

   The boy will read this letter to his grandmother.

   3. आशय समझना

   You cannot read my thoughts.

   4. (adj.) The Delhi Public Library has a big reading room.

   5. (n.) Hundreds of readers come there every day.

8. **Ready (adj.)** रे'डि-1. तैयार

   Please come soon. Breakfast is ready.

   Be ready to do anything for your country.

   2. उद्यत, (पहले से) तैयार

   Amitabh always has a ready answer.

   3. (adv.) शीघ्रता

   Come to me any time. I will readily help you.

9. **Real (adj.)** रिअल-असली

   (adj.) Are these pearls real?

   Yes, these are real pearls.

   (adv.) Have your really lost your book?

   (n.) In reality, no man is as powerful as he appears to be.

10. **Realise (v.)** रिअलाइज़्-एहसास होना

    It was only affer the failure that we realised our mistake.

11. **Realm (v.)** रि'अल्म-राज्य, क्षेत्र

    Ghosts exist only in the realms of fantasy.

12. **Reap (v.)** रीप-फ़सल काटना

    As you sow so shall you reap.

13. Vernacular (n.) वनैक्यूलर्-देशी भाषा, बोली

In India, we have several vernaculars.

14. Verse (n.) वर्स-कविता, पद्य

A verse is a short piece of poetry.

Can you recite a verse from Milton's poetry?

15. Version (n.) वर्शन-विवरण, वर्णन

We both saw the same accident, but Amit's version of it was different from that of mine.

16. Versus (prep.) वर्सस-विपरीत, विरुद्ध

Today's international match is Pakistan versus India.

17. Vertical (adj.) वर्टिकल-खड़ा, लंबवत्

He rode the bike in an almost vertical position.

18. Partner (n.) पार्टनर्-भागी, साझेदार, साथी

Would you like to become my partner is setting up a business?

19. Party (n.) पार्टि-1. दल, पार्टी

Which political party do you belong to?

2. गोष्ठी, प्रीतिभोज

Yesterday I was invited to a tea party.

3. समर्थक, भाग लेने वाला

My brother was never a party to the fraud.

20. Pass (v.) पास-1. उत्तीर्ण होना

Has your son passed his final examination?

2. बीतना

The days are passing very quickly.

3. निर्णय देना

The judge passed sentence.

4. हस्तान्तरित करना

Please pass the salt.

5. (से) गुजरना, पार जाना

Will you pass a bookshop on your way to office?

6 प्रवेश-पत्र

Please show you entry pass before you go in

21. Passage (n.) पैसिज-1 गलियारा

My room is at the end of the passage

2. परिच्छेद, उद्धरण

Please read out to me any passage from your article

22. Passenger (n.) पैसिन्जर्-यात्री, मुसाफ़िर

Passengers are requested not to lean out of the windows

23. Passion (n.) पैशन-भावावेश, मनोवेग, अनुराग

This short story is full of passion.

24. Knight (n.) नाइट्-घुड़सवार योद्धा

Every girl has an image of her knight in shining armour in her mind.

25. Knit (v.) निट-बुनना

Can you knit a sweater?

26. Achieve (v.) अचीव-कार्य पूर्ण करना, अन्त करना, जीतना

Congratulations on achieving success in the I.S.A examination!

27. Acknowledge (v.) अक्नॉलिज - 1. मान लेना, सत्यता स्वीकार करना

They all acknowledged that Deepak was the best player in the team.

2. रसीद लिखकर स्वीकार करना

I acknowledged the receipt of his letter.

28. Acquaintance (n.) अक्वेन्टन्स-परिचय, जान - पहचान, परिचित व्यक्ति

Harish has many acquaintances but

very few friends.

29. Acquire (v.) अक्वाइअर्-कमाना, प्राप्त करना

The businessman acquired a lot of money by hard work.

30. Across अक्रॉस-आरपार, एक ओर से दूसरी ओर

(prep.) There are many bridges across the Yamuna in Delhi.

(adv.) I came across an old school friend in the market today.

31. Captain (n.) कैप्टिन-1. कप्तान, अधिपति

Balraj is a captain in Army.

2. खिलाड़ियों की टीम का नायक

Anil was selected as the captain of the football team of his school.

32. Caption (n.) कैप्शन-अनुशीर्षक

Please write an interesting caption for this picture.

33. Captive (n.) कैप्टिव-बन्दी, कैदी

The captive was put in a dark cell.

34. Capture (v.) कैप्च (र्)-बन्दी बनाना, गिरफ़्तार करना

The thief was captured by the policeman after a chase

35. Caravan (n.) कैरवैन-कारवां, काफिला

The caravan slowly travelled across the desert.

36. Unknown (adj.) अॅन्नोन-अज्ञात, अनाम

Take delight in being unknown and unregarded.

He who can live unknown is really a gentleman.

37. Unless (conj.) अॅन्ले'स-यदि नहीं, जब तक

You must not go out unless you have your shoes on.

He cannot go home unless I pay him fare.

38. Unlike (adj.) अॅन्लाइक-(के) समान नहीं, असमान, की तरह नहीं

Your appearance is quite unlike your brother's.

39. Unlikely (adj.) अॅन्लाइकलि-आशा न होना, संभव न होना

It is unlikely that I would be preasent there on Monday.

40. Barracks (n.) बैरक्स-बैरक, वारक

Soldiers live in barracks.

41. Barrel (n.) बैरल-1. नली, नाल

The hunter pointed the barrel of his gun at the tiger.

2. पीपा

He poured the oil into the barrel.

42. Barren (adj.) बैरन-बांझ, बन्ध्या, बंजर, व्यर्थ

You cannot grow any crop in this barren land.

A barren woman cannot bear a child.

43. Barrier (n.) बैरिअर्-रोक, रोध, घेरा

The police put up a barrier to stop all cars.

44. Feather (n.) फ़ेदर्-पंख

Collecting feathers of different birds is my hobby.

45. Feature (n.) फ़ीचर्-1. चेहरा-मोहरा, नाक-नक्शा

Who is that young lady with sharp features?

2. विशेषता, विशिष्टता

Dusty winds are a feature of Delhi summers.

3. नियमित लेख

The newspapers carry features on environment regularly.

46. Federation (n.) फ़ेडरेशन-संघ

The Federation is headed by a

reputed industrialist.

47. Fee (n.) फ़ी-फ़ीस, शुल्क

Have you paid your son's school fees?

We pay fees to doctors, tutors and lawyers.

48. Yolk (n.) योक-ज़रदी, अंडे का पीला भाग

The yolk of an egg is a very useful part of it.

49. Immunity (n.) इम्यूनटि-रोग से बचाव

This vaccine offers immunity to polio.

50. Impact (n.) इम्पैक्ट-परिणाम

The direct impact of the cartridge controversy was the Revolt of 1857.

51. Impart (v.) इम्पार्ट-ज्ञान प्रदान करना

The newspapers impart information in detail.

52. Impartial (adj.) इम्पार्शल-निष्पक्ष

The judge was highly impartial and announced his decision against the rich and affluent culprits.

53. Impeccable (adj.) इम्पेकबल-त्रुटिहीन

Konkona Sen's performance in Page 3 was impeccable.

54. Get-together (n.) गेट-टुगेदर्-पार्टी

We had a family get-together on the New Year.

55. Ghost (n.) गोस्ट-भूत, प्रेतात्मा

Not all people believe in the existence of ghosts.

56. Gift (n.) गिफ़्ट-उपहार, भेंट

Nine received many gifts on her birthday.

57. Gigantic (adj.) जाइगैन्टिक-अति विशाल, विराट

While in Mumbai, we went on-board a gigantic ship.

58. Giggle गिग्ल-ही-ही करके हंसना

(v.) The girls giggled at his funny outfit.

(n.) The girls were taken by giggles at his funny outfit.

59. Ginger (n.) जिन्जर्-अदरक

I had a cup of giner tea in the morning.

60. Hat (n.) हैट-हैट, टोपी

You should wear a hat when you go out in the sun.

61. Hatch (v.) हैच-1. सेहने की क्रिया, सेहना, अण्डे से निकलना

Don't count the chickens before thy are hatched.

2. योजना या षड्यन्त्र तैयार करना

Rahul's colleagues hatched the plan to make an April Fool of him.

62. Hate (v.) हेट-वैर या द्वेष रखना, घृणा करना,

You should not hate anyone.

(n.) There should be no feeling of hatred in your heart.

63. Haughty (adj.) हॉटि-घमंडी

It is useless to argue with him; he is very haughty.

64. Juncture (n.) जंक्चर-विशिष्ट क्षण

At this juncture, our objective should be to build a good rapport with our clients.

65. Knob (n.) नॉब-गुमटा, मूठ, दस्ता

We saw decorative knobs on all the doors in the royal palace.

66. Martial (adj.) मैरिटल-विवाह-संबंधी

What is your marital status?

67. Mark (n.) मार्क-1. अंक, नंबर

How many marks did you get in Mathematics?

2. निशान, चिह्न, चिह्नित करना, लगाना

We walked straight till we came to a mark indicating right tum.

There is a dirty mark on your shirt.

(v.) Vikash and Sonia wee marked absent.

68. Market (n.) मार्किट-बाज़ार, बेचना

(n.) I have to go the market to buy some vegetables.

(v.) Our company markets electrical appliances.

69. Marry (v.) मैरि-विवाह करना/कराना

I hear Rekha married a doctor.

70. Martial (adj.) मार्शल-युद्ध-संबंधी

He is a professional in martial arts.

71. Scalp (n.) स्कैल्प-सिर की खाल

She massaged her scalp with oil.

72. Scam (n.) स्कैम-घोटाला

You should scan this page to see if there are any spelling mistakes.

73. Scanty (adj.) स्कैन्टी-कम मात्रा में, अल्प, थोड़ा

We received scanty rainfall this year.

74. Scandal (n.) स्कैन्डल-कलंक, बुराई, निंदा, लोकापवाद

A lie has no legs, but a scandal has wings.

Never listen to scandals has wings.

(adj.) There has never been a scandalous tale without some foundation.

75. Scar (n.) स्कार्-धब्बा, दाग, कलंग

God will not look you over for medals, but for scars!

76. Nickname (n.) निक्नेम-उपनाम

My son Vikram's nickname is Bittu.

77. Niece (n.) नीस-भतीजी, भानजी

My niece came to stay with us during her holidays.

78. Night (n.) नाइट-रात, रात्रि

What were you doing last night?

79. Nimble (adj.) निम्बल-फुर्तीला

A nimble boy like you should easily win the race.

80. Nip (v.) निप्-फुरती से काटना

The child nipped on the biscuit.

81. Teetotaller (n.) टीटोट्लर्-धूम्रपान और मदिरापान न करने वाला व्यक्ति

When offered a drink, he politely refused and said that he was a teetotaller.

82. Telecommunications (n.) टेलिकम्यूनिकेशन्ज़ - दूरसंचार

The government will invest more money in the industry of telecommunications.

83. Telegraph (n.) टे'लिग्राफ्-तार-यंत्र, तार-प्रेक्षण

Telegraph was one of the initial steps towards telecommunications.

84. Telepathy (n.) टे'लेपथि-अतींद्रिय बोध, दूर बोध

I was feeling that you would come today and you came. Was it a case of telepathy?

85. Oppose (v.) अपोज़्-विरोध/सामना करना

I oppose your proposal as I think it is unwise.

(n.) He went abroad in opposition to his parent's wishes.

86. Opposite (adv.) ऑपॅज़िट-1. सम्मुख, सामने

I live opposite the post office.

2. (adj.) विपरीत, उल्टा

You are an opposite of your brother in temperament.

87. Oppressive (adj.) अप्रेसिव-कष्टप्रद

The Indians opposed the oppressive British policies.

88. Opt (v.) ऑप्ट-चयन करना

Which subject will you opt for?

89. Quite (adv.) क्वाइट-अधिक नहीं, नितांत, निश्चय ही

The orange was quite nice in taste.

Are you quite certain that you will pass?

90. Embarrass (v.) इमबैरस-लज्जित होना

(v.) Tripping on the stage embarrassed me a lot.

(adj.) I was embarrassed at tripping on the stage.

91. Embassy (n.) एमबसि-दूतावास

Her father works in a Russian embassy.

92. Embellish (v.) इम्बेलिश-अलंकृत करना

The dress was embellished with stones and sequins.

93. Emblem (n.) एम्ब्लम्-प्रतीक चिह

We should respect our national emblem and flag.

94. Embrace (v.) इम्ब्रेस्-अलिंगन करना, गले लगाना, स्वीकार करना

My grandmother embraced me when I went to see her.

95. Wear वेअर्-1. पहनना, धारण करना, पहनावा, लिबास

(v.) The poor lady is wearing an old dress.

She always wears the same dress.

That beautiful girl always wears a happy smile.

(n.) In ready made clothes shop, you can find children's wear also.

2. टूट-फूट, धीरे-धीरे होने वाली क्षति

This table is showing signs of wear and tear.

96. Weary विअरि-थका-माँदा, निढाल, थकाना, उकता देना, थक जाना, ऊब जाना

(adj.) Are you not weary after the day's work?

(v.) Please don't weary me with your silly talk.

(adv.) We walked the last two kilometres wearily.

97. Weather (n.) वे'दर्-ऋतु, मौसम

A change in the weather is enough to renew the world and ourselves. When two Englishmen meet, their talk usually begins with a discussion on weather.

98. Weave वीव-बुनावट, बुनना

(n.) Do you prefer a losse weave for your sweater?

(v.) The weaver wove some fine cloth.

99. Deed (n.) डीड-काम, कार्य, दस्तावेज़

Raju has done a good deed by saving a drowning child.

Two businessmen singned a deed of partnership.

100. Deduct (v.) डिडक्ट-कुल राशि से कुछ अंश काटना

The teacher deducted his marks for bad handwriting.

SPOKEN VOCABULARY
Set - 12

1. **Deem (v.)** डीम-किसी बात को विशेष रुप में समझना

   The airplane was deemed unsuitable for flying.

2. **Deep (adj.)** डीप-1.गहरा (दूरी में, भाव में, रंग में)

   Why have you dug such a deep hole in your garden?

   Death of a dear son is a cause of deep sorrow for his parents.

   My car is deep blue in colour.

   (adj.) Have you thought deeply before deciding to resign from your present job?

3. **Deer (n.)** डिअर्-हिरन, मृग

   Let us take our children to the zoo to show them the golden deer.

4. **Nickname (n.)** निक्नेम-उपनाम

   My son Vikram's nickname is Bittu.

5. **Niece (n.)** नीस-भतीजी, भानजी

   My niece came to stay with us during her holidays.

6. **Night (n.)** नाइट-रात, रात्रि

   What were you doing last night?

7. **Nimble (adj.)** निम्बल-फुर्तीला

   A nimble boy like you should easily win the race.

8. **Nip (v.)** निप्-फुरती से काटना

   The child nipped on the biscuit.

9. **Telephone** टेलिफ़ोन-दूरसंचार (पर बात करना)

   (v.) Mother telephoned father.

   You can telephone from here.

   (n.) Never talk senselessly on telephone.

10. **Tell (v.)** टे'ल-1. बताना, कहना, प्रकट करना

    Tell me what you want.

    Kindly tell the principal that I want to see him.

    2. कल्पना करना

    It is difficult to tell the end of this struggle.

    3. आज्ञा देना

    I have told you many times that you must obey the rules of the institution.

11. **Temper (n.)** टे'म्पर्-मिजाज़, मनोदशा, तबियत, प्रकृति

    My father is in a bad temper today because he is very angry with me.

12. **Temperament (n.)** टे'म्प्रम 'न्ट्-प्रकृति, स्वभाव, मिजाज़

    Rupa has a sad temperament, she is often unhappy.

13. **Tempest (n.)** टेम्पस्ट-तूफान, झंझावात

    The tempest destroyed the ships on the seashore.

    (adj.) Our ship rolled heavily in the tempestuous sea.

14. **Optician (n.)** आपृटिशन्-आंखों की जांच करने वाला व्यक्ति

    I'll go to an optician to get my eyes tested.

15. **Optimist (n.)** ऑप्टिमिस्ट-आशावादी

    I am an optimist and always hope that things will change for the better.

16. **Option (n.)** ऑप्शन्-विकल्प

I had no option but to stay back.

17. Oral (adj.) ऑरल-मौखिक, ज़बानी

How did you fare in your oral examination?

18. Quiver (v.) क्विवर्-काँपना

The leaves of the tree quivered in the wind.

(adj.) Minakshi sang the song in a quivering voice.

19. Embroidery (n.) इम्ब्रॉइडरि-बेल-बूट काढ़ने की कला

How good is your daughter at embroidery?

20. Emerald एमरल्ड-पन्ना, पन्ने के सदृश

(n.) Emerald is a precious stone.

(adj.) Emerald green is my favourite colour.

21. Emerge (v.) इमर्ज्-(बाहर/ऊपर) निकलना, प्रकट होना

All were waiting for the doctor to emerge from the operation theatre.

22. Emergency (n.) इमर्जन्सि-मनोभाव, आवेग

The doctors are trained well to deal with the emergencies.

23. Emotion (n.) इमोशन-मनोभाव, आवेग

Even animals have emotions.

(adj.) Women are emotional by nature.

24. Emperor (n.) एम्परर्-सम्राट

Julius Caesar was a great Roman emperor.

25. Web (n.) वे'ब-जाल

Flies were caught in the spider's web.

(adj.) A duck has webbed feet.

26. Wedding (n.) वे'डिंग-विवाह, शादी

Have you got Ramesh's wedding card?

How many guests have you invited to the wedding?

27. Wedge (v. & n.) वे'ज-पच्चर, खूंटा लगाना, ढोकना, कसना या पकड़ना

(v.) Please wedge the door open.

The cutter wedged the dog.

(n.) Take out the wedge from the log.

28. Wednesday (n.) वे'न्ज़्डे-बुधवार

Wednesday is the day between Tuesday and Thursday.

29. Weed वीड-फालतू उगने वाली घास-पात (उखाड़ना)

(n.) A weed is a wild plant.

(v.) The gardener is weeding the field.

30. Defeat डिफ़ीट-हार, पराजय, हराना, विफल कर देना

(n.) Losing his very first match was an upsetting defeat for the last year's champion.

(v.) How could a good player like you be defeated so easily?

31. Default (n.) डिफ़ॉल्ट-किसी की अनुपस्थिति के कारण, न कि प्रयास से

They won the championship by default.

32. Defend (v.) डिफ़ेन्ड-1. समर्थन करना, सफ़ाई देना

Father did not defend his son's bad conduct in the school.

2. (n.) सफ़ाई, रक्षा

What do you want to say in your derfence?

33. Defect (n.) डिफ़ेक्ट-दोष

She has a slight defect in her eye.

34. Definite (adj.) डेफ़िनट-निश्चित

It is definite that she will not come.

35. Definitely (adv.) डेफ़िनटलि-निश्चित रुप से

I shall definitely call you tonight.

36. Rear (n.) रिअर्-1. पृष्ठ भाग, पिछला हिस्सा

We want to sit in the rear of the bus.

There was garden at the rear of the palace.

2. (v.) (चौपाया का) पिछले पाँवों पर खड़ा होना

When horses take fright, they rear.

3. जन्तुओं की देखभाल करना

The farmer rears milch animals.

37. Reason (n.) रीज़न-1. कारण, हेतु

Do you know the reason of her absence?

2. तर्क, दलील

He was foolish for her refused to listen to reason.

3. (v.) तर्क करना

When the teacher reasoned with the naughty pupil, he begged his pardon.

38. Rebel रे'बल-1. विद्रोह (करना), विद्रोही

(v.) Students rebel against the rules of their school.

(adj.) All the rebel candidates in the election fray were expelled by their parties.

(n.) The district is swarming with rebels.

39. Rebuke (v.) रिब्यूक-किसी अनुचित काम को करने से मना करना, भर्त्सना करना

Our father often rebuked us for not speaking the turth.

(n.) The rebuke chastened us.

40. Very वे'रि-1. बहुत, अत्यंत

(adv.) I am very fond of ice-cream.

Thank you for telling me a very interesting tale.

2. (adj.) मात्रा, केवल

The very idea of it makes me saa.

3. यही, दूसरा नहीं

He is the very person I sought to see.

41. Vessel (n.) वे'सल-1. बर्तन, पात्र

Empty vessels make much noise.

2. रुधिरवाही नलिका

Our veins are blood-vessels. They carry blood throughout the body.

42. Vest (n.) वे'स्ट-1. बनियान, अंदर पहनने का बिना बाहों का वस्त्र

It is essential to wear a vest in winters.

2. (v.) निहित होना

In India, power is vested usually in the Prime Minister and the cabinet.

43. Vested Interest (adv.) स्वार्थ

He has a vested interest in whatever he is doing for you.

44. Passive (adj.) पैसिव-निष्क्रिय

In the olden times, women played a passive role in the worldly affairs.

45. Passport (n.) पासपोर्ट-पासपोर्ट, पारपत्र

Have you obtained your passport for your proposed foreign tour?

46. Past पास्ट

1. (adj.) बीता हुआ

Our past mistakes proved to be a learning experience.

2. (prep.) बजकर (समय बताने के लिए प्रयुक्त)

I'll see you at hafl past ten.

3. (adv.) किसी वस्तु या व्यक्ति को पार करके

She walked past me without even looking at me.

4. (n.) अतीत

We often try to forget our past, but it haunts us always?

47. Paste (n.) पेस्ट-1. पेस्ट, लेई

I want to buy a tube of tooth-paste

2. (v.) चिपकाना

A notice was pasted on the wall.

48. Pasture (n.) पास्चर्-गोचर भूमि

We strolled around the green pastures.

49. Lavish लैविश-खर्चीला

(n.) They threw a lavish party at their wedding.

(v.) He lavished expensive gifts on his wife on her birthday.

50. Law (n.) लॉ-कानून, विधि

You should always abide by the law.

51. Lawn (n.) लॉन-मैदान, लॉन

My children like to play in the lawn near our house.

52. Lay (v.) ले-1. रखना, बिछाना, लेटना

I laid my book on this table last night.

2. (अण्डे) देना

Our hen has laid an egg.

53. Layer (n.) लेअर्-परत

I saw a thin layer of frost on my car.

54. Act (n.) ऐक्ट - 1. कार्य, व्यवहार

A boy-scout does an act of +kindness every day.

2. कानून

There are many acts in the Indian Penal Code.

3. नाटक का अंक

4. (v.) कार्य करना, व्यवहार करना

One should never act in haste.

55. Active (adj.) ऐक्टिव-सक्रिय

(adj.) A balanced diet makes you more active.

(adv.) He climbed up the stairs actively.

56. Activist (n.) ऐक्टिविस्ट-कार्यकर्ता

His father is a social activist.

57. Actual (adj.) ऐक्चुअल-निष्चित, यथार्थ

This is an expensive ring, but I do not know the actual price.

58. Carcass (n.) काकस-पशु का मृत शरीर

The carcass of a pig was found on the beach.

59. Card (n.) काड-कार्ड, पत्र, पत्रक, पत्रिका, सूचिका गत्ता

I am interested in playing cards.

Do you have your visiting car?

Please bring this invitation card with you.

He packed the books in a cardboard box.

Do not fail to drop me a post-card.

60. Cardamom (n.) काडमम-इलायची

The porridge became tastier with the flavour of cardamom.

61. Cardiac (adj.) काडिऐक-हृदय-संबंधी

She died of a cardiac arrest.

62. Cardigan (n.) काडिगन-बुनी हुई ऊनी जाकेट

Uma wore a matching cardigan over her sari.

63. Care केअ (र्)-सावधानी, देखभाल, परवाह करना, ध्यान रखना, पसंद करना, चाहना

(n.) Take care when you cross the road.

(v.) There was no one to care for (look after) the child after its parents died.

I don't care (it does not matter to me what you do.

64. Unmistakable (adj.) अन्मिस्टेकबल-सुस्पष्ट, जिसमें गलती नहीं

The voice I hear was unmistakable, because it could not be anyone else's but Rajendra's.

65. Unreasonable (adj.) अन्रीजनबल-अनुचित

In our shop, you will not find unreasonable rates.

66. Untidy (adj.) अॅन्टाइडि-अस्त-व्यस्त, बेढंगा

Never leave your room untidy.

(adv.) The woman is untidily dreassed.

67. Until (prep.) अॅन्टिल-जब तक नहीं

Asha will not go to bed until 9:30. P.M.

Wait her until I come to fetch you

68. Unwell (adj.) अॅन्वे 'ल-अस्वस्थ

I am feeling unwell now. Kindly allow me to leave early.

69. Base (n.) बेस- 1. तल, तह

Some dirt was sticking to the base of the glass.

2. नीच, अधम

Even a good deed done with a base motive is not appreciable

70. Basement (n.) बेसमन्ट-तहखाना

His house has a large basement.

71. Bash बैश

1 जोर से प्रहार

(v.) He bashed his car in the tree.

2 उत्सव

(n.) A huge birthday bash awaited me at home

72. Basic (adj.) बेसिक-बुनियादी

I have gathered the basic information about the place.

73. Basics (n.) बेसिक्स-सबसे साधारण और महत्त्वपूर्ण तथ्य

For mastering any subject, it is important to understand the basics first.

74. Basin (n.) बेस्न-हौज, कुंड

The doctor asked for hot water in the basin.

75. Feeble (adj.) फ़ीबल-1. कमज़ोर, अशक्त

My long illness has made me feeble.

2. मद्धिम, धुंधला

I was unable to read in the feeble candle light.

76. Feed (v.) फ़ीड-खिलाना, भोजन देना

To feed an infant with the mother's milk is good for his health.

(adj.) Where is the baby's feeding bottle?

77. Feedback (n.) फ़ीडबैक-प्रतिपुष्टि

Let me have your feedback, so that I improve the article accordingly.

78. Feel (v.) फ़ील-1. स्पर्श करना, छूना

The doctor felt the injured arm of Usha to see if there was a fracture.

2. लगना, प्रतीत होना

We all felt happy at the good news.

3. (n.) अनुभव करना, महसूस करने की शक्ति

The old woman had no feeling in her numb fingers.

79. Feign (v.) फ़ेन-स्वांग भरना

The child feigned a headache to miss the school.

80. You (pron.) यू-तुम

You shold go home now.

(poss. pron.) Is this bag yours?

(poss. adj.) Is this your book?

81. Imperative (adj.) इम्पेरटिव-आवश्यक

It is imperative that you file your tax returns by the end of this month.

82. Imperfect (adj.) इम्परफ़ेक्ट-सदोष

Everything is imperfect in the world.

83. Impertinent (adj.) इम्पर्टिनन्ट-ढीठ, गुस्ताख, अनुपयुक्त

You must talk to your son about his impertinent behaviour.

(n.) He must be punished for his im pertinence.

84. Impetus (n.) इम्पिटस-ऐसी वस्तु जो दूसरी वस्तु की क्रियाशीलता बढ़ाए

The tsunami campaign gained impetus with the association of celebrities.

85. Implement इम्प्लिमन्ट

1. (n.) औज़ार, उपकरण

Do you have some implement to open this jammed lock?

2. (n.) अमल में लाना

We implemented the plan into action immediately.

86. Giraffe (n.) जिराफ़-जिराफ़

We saw a tall giraffe in the zoo.

87. Girder (n.) गर्डर्-गर्डर, धरन, शहतीर

Can you count the girders of this bridge?

88. Girl (n.) गर्ल-लड़की, वालिका

Who is that girl in the pink saree?

These girls are very talkative.

89. Gist (n.) जिस्ट-सारांश

I did not have time to go through the whole book, so I requested him to tell me the gist of it.

90. Give (v.) गिव-देना, सौंपना, पहुँचाना

Please give me your pen.

How much milk does this cow give?

I have given up (stopped) writing.

91. Glad (adj.) ग्लैड-खुश, प्रसन्न, सुहावना

Rakhi's parents were glad to know about her selection for a good government job.

92. Haunt (v.) हॉन्ट

1. भुतहा होना

They entered the bungalow that was believed to be haunted.

2. दिमाग पर छाए रहना

What happens to us after death is a question that often haunts me.

93. Have (v.) हैव-1. पास होना, रखना

Do you have a spare pencil?

2. खाना/पीना

Will you have a cold drink?

3. (n.) धनी या निर्धन व्यक्ति

The nations of the world are divided between the haves and the have-nots.

94. Haven (n.) हेवन-1. बन्दरगाह

Despite the storm, our ship safely reached its haven.

2. आश्रय स्थान

My bedroom is my haven.

95. Havoc (n.) हैवक-बरबादी, तबाही, विध्वंस

The hilly village presented a sad picture of the havoc caused by the earthquake.

96. Hawk (n.) हॉक-बाज़

How swiftly can a hawk fly?

97. Hay (n.) हे-सूखी घास

Make haywhile the sun shines.

98. Haywire (adj.) हेवाइअर्-अव्यवस्थित हो जाना

The project started off well, but the problems between the co-workers made the whole thing go haywire.

100. Junior (adj.) जूनिअर्-छोटा

By how many years is your brother junior to you?

SPOKEN VOCABULARY
Set - 13

1. **Knock (v. & n.)** नॉक-1. खटखट, खटखटाना

(v.) Who is knocking at the door?

2. प्रहार करना, ठोंकना

The champion boxer knocked down his opponent very easily.

(n.) My sister opened the door at the first knock.

2. **Martyr (n.)** मार्टर्-शहीद, हुतात्मा

Have you visited the martyrs' memorial in Kolkata?

3. **Marvel** मार्वल-चमत्कार, आश्चर्य करना

(n.) Your house is full of marvels of technology.

(v.) We marvel at the way you help your friends.

(adj.) They had a marvellous journey through the Himalayas.

4. **Masculine (adj.)** मैस्क्यलिन्-पुरुषोचित, मरदाना

You have a deep, masculine voice.

5. **Mash (v.)** मैश-कुचलना

Mash the potatoes and add salt to it.

6. **Mask (n.)** मास्क-मुखौटा

The child frightened his friend by wearing a devil mask.

7. **Scarce (adj.)** स्केअर्स-दुर्लभ, अपर्याप्त, बहुत कम

Some animals are becoming scarce in India.

Straweberries are scarce this year.

(adv.) I had scarcely sat down when the bell rang.

8. **Scare** स्केअर्-डर, भय, आतंक, डराना, भयभीत करना

(n.) A good scare is worth more to a man than good advice.

The crows got a scare when they saw a scare-crow.

(v.) The scare-crow scares away the crows.

9. **Scarf (n.)** स्कार्फ़-स्कार्फ़

She wore a scarf to protect herself from cold.

10. **Scarlet (adj.)** स्कॉर्लट-सिंदूरी रंग

Her dress was scarlet in colour.

11. **Scatter (v.)** स्कैटर्-छितराना

The string broke and all the pearls scattered on the floor.

12. **Scenario (n.)** सनारिओ-दृश्य योजना

The worst scenario would be backing out from the competition.

13. **No** नो-नहीं, बिल्कुल नहीं

(adj.) Have you no money to lend me?

(adv.) When he asked me if I could accompany him, my answer was 'no'.

14. **Nobody (n.)** नोबडी-कोई नहीं

Nobody came here.

15. **Noble (adj.)** नोबल-अच्छा, उमदा, उच्च

It was really a noble service.

You have indeed done a noble deed.

I appreciate your noble sentiments.

16. **Nod** नॉड-1. नोबडी-कोई नहीं

(n.) Give me a nod when you need a glass of water.

(v.) If you agree with me, just nod your head.

2 ऊँघना

The old lady was nodding in her chair.

17. Template (n.) टेम्प्लेट्-नमूना

I have prepared the template for you. Now prepare all the documents in the same style.

18. Temple (n.) टेम्पल्-मंदिर

I visit the temple every morning

19. Tempo (n.) टेम्पो

1. संगीत रचना की गति

The tempo in this song keeps on changing from slow to fast

2 समान ढोने वाला तिपहिया वाहन

Load the material in a tempo

20. Temporary (adj.) टे'म्पॅररि-अस्थायी. काम चलाऊ

The church hall will be used as a temporary school until the new school is built.

This post is quite temporary.

I want to get a temporary job because I am waiting for my appointment in the university

(adv.) I have managed a room temporarily

21. Orator (n.) ऑरटर्-वक्ता

A political leader has to be a good orator.

22. Orbit ऑर्बिट-ग्रह-उपग्रह का परिक्रमण-पथ

(n.) The planets revolve around the sun in their fixed orbits.

(v.) The planets or bit the sun.

23. Quiz (n.) क्विज़्-प्रश्नोत्तरी

Let us try to answer this poetry quiz.

24. Emphasis (n.) इम्फ़सिस-विशेष महत्त्व

(n.) The teacher laid emphasis on studying in the morning, rather than staying awake all night.

(v.) The teacher emphasised on studying in the morning.

25. Employ (v.) इम्प्लॉइ-1. नौकर रखना, काम में लगाना

Ram was employed in a bank.

2. काम में लाना, प्रयोग करना

How will you employ your time during the vacation?

26. Empty एमप्टि-खाली (करना/होना)

(adj.) Give me an empty glass.

(v.) Empty this glass and clean it.

27. Enable (v.) एनेबल्-समर्थ करना, शक्ति देना

My bonus enabled me to buy a TV set.

28. Week (n.) वीक-1 सप्ताह. हफ़्ता

There are seven days in a week and fifty-two weeks in a year

2 काम के दिन

Every day of the week is week-day except Saturday and Sunday

29. Weep (v.) वीप्-रोना. आँसू बहाना

She wept bitterly when her father died.

30. Weigh (v.) वे-वजन करना. मूल्यांकन करना

How much do you weigh?

(n.) Do you know your exact weigh?

31. Weird (adj.) विअर्ड-विचित्र अलौकिक. असामान्य

In childhood, I used to hear weird sounds from the pond.

32. Welcome (n. & v.) वेल्कम-स्वागत, स्वागत करना

(n.) They gave us a warm welcome

(v.) Aunt welcomed us warmly.

Welcome everybody.

33. Weld (v.) वे'ल्ड-टॉक कर जोड़ना, आपस में मिलाना

A welder welds pieces of metal by heat and pressure.

Standing by each other in the times of need has welded our friendship.

34. Deficiency (n.) डिफिशियन्सि-कमी

(n.) Night blindness is caused by the deficiency in Vitamin A.

(adj.) Junk food is deficient in nutrients.

35. Deformity (n.) डिफ़ॉर्मिटी-विरुपता

The doctor recorded no deformity in the child.

36. Defy (v.) डिफ़ाइ-अवज्ञा करना, चुनौती देना

An obedient son does not defy his parents.

37. Defuse (v.) डिफ़्यूज-बम को निष्क्रिय करना

The bombs were defused successfully.

38. Degenerate (v.) डिजेनरेट-किसी स्थिति में गिरावट करना

Corruption has degenerated out society.

39. Degree (n.) डिग्री-1. उपाधि

Has your son taken the degree in Physics?

2. मात्रा, अंश

I agree with you to some degree (to some extent).

40. Degrade (v.) डिग्रेड-किसी की स्थिति को बिगाड़ना

(v.) Growing urbanisation degrades the natural habitats of animals.

(n.) Pollution is the major cause of environmental degradation.

41. Deity (n.) डेअटि-देवता की मूर्ति

The devotee prostrated himself before the deity.

42. Delay डिले-देर/विलंब करना या लगाना

(v.) I was delayed by the traffic jam.

(n.) Do your homework without delay.

43. Receive (v.) रिसीव-1. प्राप्त करना

We hope to receive a letter from our father.

2. स्वागत करना, (घर में आये व्यक्ति का) आदर-सत्कार करना

The lady received her guests.

44. Recent (adj.) रीसन्ट-हाल ही

Have you fully recovered from your recent illness?

(adv.) I came to know recently that she went to Shimla last month.

45. Reception (n.) रिसे'प्शन- 1 . स्वागत कक्ष

The manager is busy, please sit at the reception.

2. आदर, सत्कार, स्वागत

My aunt gave a warm reception when I went to see her.

3. स्वागत-समारोह

Most of the guests have been personally invited to the wedding re ception.

46. Recess (n.) रिसे'स-काम या पढ़ाई के बीच मध्यान्तर, अल्पकालिक छुट्टी या अवकाश

Can we go out to play during the twenty-minute recess at school?

47. Recipe (n.) रेसपि-भोजन बनाने की विधि

Mother gave us the recipe for making a masala dosa.

48. Reciprocate (v.) रे'सिप्रकेट्-भावनाओं या आचरण का परस्पर आदान-प्रदान करना

She reciprocated his smile with a frown.

49. Veteran (n.) वे'टरन-अनुभवी व्यक्ति

Our manager is a veteran at management.

50. Veterinary (n.) वे'टनरि-पशु-चिकित्सा, पशु-चिकित्सक

Our cow was ill, so we took it to the

veterinary surgeon.

51. Vex (v.) वे'क्स-चिढ़ाना, खिजाना, परेशान करना

We will vex our teacher if we keep asking him silly questions.

We should avoid vexing our mother.

52. Via (prep.) वाइआ-स होकर, के मार्ग से, मार्ग

One of the ways from Delhi to Kolkata is via Varanasi.

53. Viable (adj.) वाइअबल-व्यवहार्य

Do you think this project is commercially viable?

54. Pat (v.) पैट-थपकी देना, थपथपाना

I patted the boy on the back.

(n.) My teacher's pat on my back encouraged me to do better.

55. Patch (n.) पैच-1. थिगली, पैवन्द, फाहा

I repaired the puncture in my bicycle with a patch of rubber.

2. धब्बा, चित्ती

What are these patches on your arm?

56. Path (n.) पाथ-पाथ, रास्ता

I walked by the path across the lawn.

57. Pathetic (adj.) पथेटिक-करुणाजनक, भावपूर्ण

This story has a pathetic ending.

58. Patient (n.) पेशन्ट-1. रोगी, मरीज़

The doctor's waiting room was full of patients.

2. (adj.) धैर्यवान, सहनशील

Be patient, you will also be served food.

(adv.) My dog waited patiently for me to return.

59. Patriot (n.) पैट्रिअट-देश-भक्त

Subhash Chandra Bose was a great patriot.

60. Mason (n.) मेसन-राजमिस्त्री

We shall have to call a mason to repair this wall.

61. Mass (n.) मैस-ढेर, राशि

Look at the mass of dark clouds, it is about to rain.

62. Masses (n.) मैसज़-जनसमह, भीड़

Your speeches have the power to move the masses.

63. Massacre (n.) मैसकर्-हत्याकांड

No Indian would ever forget the Jallianwala massacre of 1919.

64. Massive (adj.) मैसिव-भारी, विशाल

What is the massive machine supposed to do?

65. Acute (adj.) एक्यूट-1. बहुत अधिक

She complained of an acute pain in her stomach last night.

2. बीमारी जो खतरनाक बन ज़ाए

He is a patient of acute bronchitis.

3. तीक्ष्ण

Animals have an acute sense of hearing.

66. Adapt (v.) अडैप्ट-अनुकूल करना

We should try to adapt ourselves to changing circumstances.

67. Add (v.) ऐड-जोड़ना, बढ़ाना

You have made a mistake in adding these figure.

(n.) जोड़

We are going to do some of the additions today.

68. Addict (n.) ऐडिक्ट-व्यसनी

(n.) I encountered a drug addict in the subway.

(adj.) He is addicted to smoking.

(n.) I have an addiction for chocolates.

69. Address (v.) अॅड्रैस - 1. पता, पत्र का सिरनामा, व्याख्या

He wrote down my address in his note book.

2. व्याख्यान देना, निवेदन करना

(v.) The headmaster addressed the students.

70. Career (n.) करियर्-किसी कार्यक्षेत्र में जीविका हेतु नौकरियां

Journalism offers good career opportunities.

71. Caress (v.) करेस-दुलारना

The mother caressed the sleeping child.

72. Caretaker (n.) केअटेकर्-रखवाला

The caretaker of the old bungalow opened the gate for us.

73. Cargo (n.) कार्गो-जहाज़ी माल

A ship can carry a lot of cargo.

74. Caricature (n.) कैरिकचुअर-व्यंग्यचित्र

She raised objection against her cari cature in the magazine.

75. Up (adv.) अॅप-1. ऊपर

Kamla and Vimla went up the hill.

It is the time to wake up.

Get up early in the morning.

Stand up when an elderly person comes to you.

Climb up the tree for plucking mangoes.

2. पूरी तरह से

I ate up all the bananas.

3. और ऊँचे

Please speak up, I cannot hear you well.

76. Uphold (v.) अॅप्होल्ड-समर्थन करना

No sensible person would uphold the idea that the dowry system is a good thing.

77. Upon (prep.) अपॉन-(के) ऊपर

Once upon a time, there was a king.

The birds are sitting upon the turret.

78. Basis बेसिस

1. विचारधारा

(n.) We improved the product on the basis of the feedback received from the customers.

2. रीति-विशेश

(n.) I play cricket on a regular basis.

79. Bask (v.) बास्क-धूप सेंकना

Basking in the winter sun is a soothing experience.

80. Basket (n.) बास्किट-टोकरी, डालिया

She put the flowers in a basket.

81. Bat (n.) बैट-1. बल्ला

Rahul was presented a cricket bat by his father on his birthday.

2. चमगादड़

Bats can fly at night.

82. Batch (n.) बैच-टोली, जत्था

A batch of doctors was sent to the area affected by the epidemic.

83. Fellow फ़ेलो

1. रत्न सदस्य

(n.) He is a fellow of the School of Planning and Architecture.

2. कोई पुरुष

(n.) Don't let the fellow enter my room.

3. सहभागी

(adj.) I share a good rapport with my fellow workers.

84. Female (adj. & n.) फ़ीमेल-मादा, स्त्री

A female peacock is not beautiful.

(n.) The female of a deer is called doe.

85. Ferninine (adj.) फे़मनिन-स्त्री-संबंधी, स्त्री-सुलभ

The boy with feminine looks was given a female role in the play.

86. Fence फे़न्स-बाड़ा; घेरा, बाड़ा लगाना

(n.) Can you jump over this fence?

(v.) He fenced his garden to protect it from animals.

87. Young (adj.) यंग-1. छोटा, कम उम्र का

A young child is called a baby.

A young tiger is called a cub. A young sheep is called a lamb. A young goat is called a kid.

2. (n.) बच्चा, बच्चे, युवा जन, लड़के, लड़कियां

The old know what they want, the young are bewildered.

88. Implicit (adj.) इम्प्लिसिट-अंतर्निहित

The issues that might affect the working of the company in future were implicit in his argument.

89. Imply (v.) इम्प्लाई-बिना कुछ कहे संकेत करना

He did not say that I was the culprit, but he implied that.

90. Impolite (adj.) इम्पोलाइट-अभद्र

Do you think it would be impolite to ask her to leave us alone for some time?

91. Import इम्पॉर्ट-आयात (करना)

(n.) How are you doing in your export-import business?

(v.) Wool is imported from Australia.

92. Glance ग्लान्स-दृष्टिपात (करना), सरसरी दृष्टि (डालना)

(n.) The doctor could see in a glance that the patient was anaemic.

(v.) She has just glanced at his letter.

93. Glare ग्लेअर्-1. कोप-दृष्टि (से देखना)

(v.) Why do you glare at me in anger?

2. (n.) चमक, चमचमाना, भड़कीला या चटकीला होना

We were almost blinded by the glare of the car's headlights

94. Glass (n.) ग्लास-1. काँच, शीशा

Is this bowl made of glass or plastic?

2. दर्पण, आरसी, गिलास

While looking into the glass, Sheeba discovered a black spot on her face.

Please give me a glass of water.

95. Glasses (n.) ग्लासिज्-चश्मा, ऐनक

I began to wear glasses af forty.

96. Gleam ग्लीम-झलक/चमक, झलकना/चमकना

(n.) A faint gleam of sunshine lit up the cloudy afternoon.

(v.) Your necklace gleams even in this faint light.

97. Glee (n.) ग्ली-उल्लास, हर्ष

Why are you laughing with such glee?

98. Layman (n.) लेमैन-अविशेषज्ञ

He is a complete layman in the field of computers.

99. Lazy (adj.) लेज़ि-आलसी, सुस्त

If you are lazy, you will never succeed in life.

100. Lead लीड-लेड 1. ले चलना, मार्गदर्शन (करना)

(v.) Where are you leading me?

2. नेतृत्व करना

The Geography teacher was to lead the students' educational trip to Goa.

3. बिताना

The old couple led a quiet life.

4. (n.) सीसा

I require some lead-pipes for a water connection

5. (adj.) सिक्के की

Please get me lead pencil.

SPOKEN VOCABULARY
Set - 14

1. **Leaf (n.)** लीफ्-1. पत्ता, पर्ण

In autumn, most trees shed their leaves.

2. पृष्ठ, पन्ना

Don't tear any leaf out of your exercise-book.

2. **Hazard** हैज़र्ड-1. जोखिम, खतरा, खतरे में डालना

(n.) The climbers faced many hazards on their way to the Everest.

2. (v.) दाँव पर रखना, कल्पना करना

Can you hazard a guess he want to see you?

(adj.) It was really a hazardous

3. **Haze (n.)** हेज़्-1. धुंध

There was a haze over the mountain this morning.

(adj.) Our plane could not take off because of the hazy weather.

2. उलझन, अनश्चिय

I had hazy idea of the weather and surroundings of the hills station before I went there.

4. **Heal (v.)** घाव का भरना

Bandage the wound; it will heal up quickly.

5. **Head (n.)** हे'ड 1. सिर, बुद्धि

My head is aching.

2. प्रधान, अध्यक्ष

Who is the head of your company/.

3. चोटी, शीर्षभाग, अग्रभाग

When he called on me, I was standing at the head of the staricase.

4. शीर्षक

What is the heading of your article?

5. (v.) की ओर बढ़ना या मोड़ना

To which direction are you heading?

6. **Jury (n.)** जूरी-निर्णायकगण

The jury was alleged to be partial

7. **Knot (n.)** नॉट-1. गाँठ, उलझन बाधना

Please untie this knot.

2. समूह, पुंज

Why have these people gathered in knots?

3. गाँठ, ग्रंथि

This piece of wood is full of knots.

8. **Master (n.)** मास्टर्-1. मालिक, अधिकारी, शिक्षक

Is your master at home?

2. (v.) वश में कर लेना, अधिकार प्राप्त करना

Have you mastered this subject?

9. **Masterpiece (n.)** मास्टर्पीस-अतिश्रेष्ठ रचना

Taj Mahal is a masterpiece of architecture.

10. **Mat (n.)** मैट-चटाई, पायदान

We should get a new mat for our room.

11. **Match (n.)** मैच-1. दियासलाई

Where is the match-box?

2. मैच, प्रतियोगिता

Will you accompany me to the cricket

match?

3. (adj.) जोड़, जोड़ीदार, मेल खाना

You are dressed in matching colours.

(v.) These colours do not match.

12. Mate (n.) मेट-1. साथी, सखा

Anil is my class-mate.

2. पति-पत्नी, जोड़

We want a mate for our parrot.

13. Scene (n.) सीन-1. (नाटक का) दृश्य

The curtain was lowered at the end of each scene.

2. आँखों के आगे का दृश्य

They were charmed by the beautiful scene.

The scenery was very beautiful.

14. Scent (n.) सेंट-सुगंधि

I like the scent of roses.

The sweet scent of lavender filled the garden.

(v.) The air was scented with honeysuckle.

15. Schedule शेड्यूल-योजना (बनाना), कार्यक्रम (बनाना)

(n.) This schedule allows you one week to finish the work.

(v.) The bus is scheduled to arrive at 8.15 A.M.

16. Scheme (n.) स्कीम-1. योजना

His scheme to fake certificates got him into trouble.

2. (v.) षड्यंत्र करना

The prime minister schemed to dethrone the king.

17. Scholar (n.) स्कॉलर्-विद्वान

He is really a scholar and knows a lot about different things.

18. Noise (n.) नॉइज़्-शोर, कोलाहल

No noise, please!

19. Nomad (n.) नोमैड-ख़ानाबदोश

The nomads were looking for a suitable place to spend the night.

20. Nominate (v.) नॉमिनेट-नियुक्त/नामज़द करना

A local leader was nominated by his partto contest the municipal elections.

21. None (prep.) नॅन-कोई (भी) नहीं

None of my friends stays in Mumbai

22. Nonsense (n.) नॉन्से'न्स-अनापशनाप, मूर्खता-भरी बातें

Don't talk nonsense!

23. Tempt (v.) टे'म्पट्-लुभाना, बहकाना, प्रेरित करना

Do not tempt the little boy to eat too many sweets.

Can I tempt you to have some more of this cake?

(n.) I can't resist the temptation of buying clothes.

(adj.) The cake is very tempting, but I cannot eat any more.

24. Tenant (n.) टे'नन्ट-किरायेदार

Every month the landloard collects the rent from his tenatns.

Our tenant is very gentle fellow.

25. Tend (v.) टे'न्ड-1. देखभाल करना, ध्यान देना, (का कारण उत्पन्न करना

Nurses tend sick people. They serve mankind.

Ranjana's accident will tend to make her more careful while crossing roads.

26. Tender (adj.) टे'न्डर्-1. कोमल, सहृदय

You have such tender skin that you get rashes after a short exposure to sun.

Mother is tender with her baby.

2. छोटी उम्र

This solid food is not suitable for the child at tender age.

3. (n.) टेंडर, ठेकेदार द्वारा प्रस्तुत होने वाले काम के लिए देय राशि का ब्यौरा (पहले से प्रस्तुत)

The council has invited tenders for the building of a hall.

4. (n.) प्रस्तुत करना

Have you tendered your resignation from the post of editor?

27. Orchard (n.) ऑरचर्ड-फलों का बाग

I have brought some apples for you from orchard.

28. Orchestra (n.) ऑकिस्ट्रा-ऑर्केस्ट्रा

The orchestra was playing Italian music.

29. Enchanting (adj.) इनचान्टिंग-मोहक

The song that she sang in the concert was really enchanting.

30. Enclose (v.) इन्क्लोज़्-1. घेरना, बाड़ा लगाना

The garden was enclosed with a fence to keep the animals away.

2. जोड़ देना, साथ रखना

She enclosed a form along with her letter.

(n.) The form was an enclosure.

31. Encounter इन्काउन्टर्

1. कठिनाई का सामना करना

(v.) Aged people often encounter dis crimination at work.

2. आकस्मिक भेंट

(v.) I encountered a saint on my flight to Bangalore.

3. मुठभेड़

(n.) The criminal was killed in a police encounter.

32. Encourage (v.) इन्करिज-हिम्मत बढ़ाना, प्रोत्साहित करना

The students cheered loudly to encourage their school hockey team which was on victory path.

(n.) The teacher's kind words gave Arun encouragement to do better in exams.

33. Welfare (n.) वे'ल्फ़ेअर्-कल्याण, खैरियत

Mother looks after the welfare of the family.

34. Well (n.) वे'ल-1. कुआँ

The well is full of water.

2. (adj.) अच्छा, स्वस्थ

I am not well.

3. (adv.) अच्छी तरह से बखूबी

He is doing very well in business. I know him very well.

4. शाबाश

Well done!

5. (adj.) सन्तोषजनक

All is well that ends well.

6. भाग्यशाली

It was well for us that we were not inside the auditorium when a fire broke out there.

7. (adv.) मशहूर

Indian cine artistes are quite well know in Russia.

35. West (n.) वे'स्ट-पश्चिमी, पश्चिम की ओर

Can the east and the west meet?

(adv.) The west wind always brings us rain.

Do you like to visit the western part of the country?

(adj.) This building faces west.

36. Wet वै'ट-1. गीला, तर, भीगा

(adj.) It is raining. It is a wet day.

2. (v.) भिगोना, गीला करना

Please wet the towel and wash the table-glass.

37. Dejected (adj.) डिजेक्टिड-हताश

He felt dejected with his marks.

38. Delegate डेलिगेट-प्रतिनिधि, दायित्व सौंपना

(n.) We must impress the foreign delegates coming next week.

(v.) Delegate your work to your juniors.

(n.) Delegation of authority is an important principle of management.

39. Deliberately (adv.) डिलिबरटलि-जान-बूझकर, सोच-समझकर

Some mischievous students deliberately make their teacher angry.

40. Delicate (adj.) डेलिकट-कोमल, सुकुमार, नाजुक (कमज़ोर)

Let us not agrue over this delicatepoint. Your son's heath is delicate, you should give him a good tonic.

41. Recite (v.) रिसाइट-ऊँचे स्वर से मौखिक रुप में दोहराना

The leader recited the poem 'Vande Mataram' from the beginning till the end.

42. Reckless (adj.) रे'कलस-अंधाधुंध, असावधानी से पूर्ण

Motorists are being fined for reckless driving.

43. Reckon (v.) रे'कन-1. हिसाब करना गिनना, सोचना

The price was reckoned high.

I reckon Premchand among our best writers.

2. भरोसा रखना, अवलम्बित होना

Can you reckon on her help?

44. Recognise (v.) रिकगनाइज़्-1. पहचानना

We can easily recognise our neighbour in this picture.

2. स्वीकार करना, मान्यता देना

Gita recognises that Rama is a better singer than she (Gita) is.

(n.) Bangladesh got recognition from India in the very beginning.

45. Recoil (v.) रिकॉइल-अप्रिय वस्तु से पीछे हटना

She recoiled disgust on seeing an open dustbin.

46. Recollect (v.) रे'कलेक्ट-बीती हुई घटना या बात याद होना

She cannot recollect when Raja came to see her last summer.

(n.) Recollection of my past fills me with many sweet memories.

47. Recommend (v.) रे'कमेंड-1. परामर्श देना

This motor-cycle is defective. I would recommend purchasing another.

2. सिफ़ारिश करना

Can you recommend her to a good watchmaker?

3. स्वीकृति होना

This book has been recommended for the tenth class by Central Board of Secondary Education.

48. Vibrate (v.) वाइब्रेट-कांपना, कंपाना

Father's voice vibrated with anger.

(n.) The vibration of the engine shook us.

49. Vicar (n.) विकर्-पादरी

The vicar lives in a church.

50. Vice (n.) वाइस-व्यसन, दुर्गुण, दोष

Gambling is a vice that leads to great unhappiness.

51. Vice (prefix.) वाइस-उप, उप-प्रधानाचार्य

Since you are the Vice-Captain, you will take the Captain's place when he is ill.

The Principal could not come, so the Vice-Principal presided over the meeting.

52. Patron (n.) पेट्रन-संरक्षक

Shah Jahan was a patron of art and architecture.

53. Pattern (n.) पैटर्न-1. नमूना, पैटर्न

Meena used a paper pattern to make her new dress.

2. आदर्श

Your behaviour should be a pattern for others.

3. (v.) ढालना

Children often pattern their personality after that of their parents.

54. Pauper (n.) पॉपर्-कंगाल

A rich man all his life, he died a pauper.

55. Pause (v.) पॉज़्-विराम, ठहर जाना

The speaker paused for a minute and took a sip of water.

(n.) After a brief pause, he spoke again.

56. Pavement (n.) पेवमन्ट-पटरी

Pedestrians should always walk on the pavement.

57. Material (n.) मटिअरिअल-1. सामान, माल

Have you got all the material for making a kite?

2. कपड़ा

Will you please show me some good quality dress material?

58. Maternal (adj.) मेटर्नल-मातृत्व-विषयक

She was taken over by maternal in stincts and refused to send her child to the hostel.

59. Matrimony (n.) मेट्रिमनि-दांपत्यावस्था

After facing a lot many problems, they finally entered the matrimony.

60. Matron (n.) मेट्रन-मेट्रन

I want to discuss an important matter with you.

2. बात, मामला

What is the matter with you?

3. (v.) महत्व देना

It matters a great deal.

61. **Mattress (n.)** मैट्रिस-गद्दा, तोशक

What is the price of this foam rubber mattress?

62. **Adept (adj.)** अडेप्ट-कुशल

He is adept at public speaking.

63. **Adequate (n.)** ऐडिक्वट-पर्याप्त, योग्य

The amount of money I have is not adequate for buying a car.

84. **Adhere (v.)** अड्हियर् - 1. मज़बूती से चिपक जाना,

Make sure the paper is adhered to the carboard properly.

2. किसी नियम का पालन करना

It is better you adhere to the company rules.

85. **Adjacent (adj.)** अडजेसन्ट-किसी के निकट

My house is adjacent to the school.

86. **Adjoin (v.)** अडजॉइन-जोड़ना, मिलाना, संयुक्त होना

The officer's residence adjoins his office.

87. **Adjoining** (adj.) एडजॉइनिंग-सटा हुआ, निकटवर्ती

Rama and Uma live in adjoining house.

88. **Carnival (n.)** कानिवल-मनोरंजन मेला

Visiting Goa at the time of carnival was an exciting experience.

89. **Carnivore (n.)** कानिवॉर्-मांसभक्षी

A lion is a carnivore.

90. **Carpenter (n.)** कापेन्टर्-बढ़ई

Some carpenters specialise in making artistic furniture.

91. **Carpet (n.)** कापिट-कालीन, ग़ालीचा, दूरी

The rich man bought an expensive carpet for his sitting room.

92. **Carriage (n.)** कैरिज-रेलगाड़ी का डिब्बा

They always travel by the first-class carriage.

93. **Upper (adj.)** ॲपर्-(दो की तुलना में) ऊपर का, वरिष्ठ

I live in the upper storey.

Parliament has two houses-the up per house and the lower house.

94. **Upright (adj.)** ॲप्राइट-1. सीधा, खड़ा

Please stand upright while I measure your height.

2. ईमानदार

We can trust Ravi, for he has always been upright in his dealings with us.

95. **Bath (n.)** बाथ-स्नान

I was taking a bath when he came to see me.

96. **Baton (n.)** बैटॉन-छड़ी

A policeman carrying a baton walked towards him.

97. **Battalion (n.)** बटैलिअन-सैनिकों की टुकड़ी

The commander called another battalion for the war.

98. **Batter (n.)** बैटर्-मारना, कूटना, चकनाचूर करना

The angry crowd battered the hooligan with fists and kicks.

2. तोपखाना

They could not bold out before the enemy's battery.

99. **Ferocious (n.)** फ़रोशस-हिंसक

Lion is ferocious animal.

100. **Ferry** फ़ेरि-तारण, नौघाट, नौका, पार उतारना

(n.) We crossed to the Swarga Ashram in a ferry.

(v.) The pilgrims were ferried across the Ganges.

SPOKEN VOCABULARY
Set - 15

1. **Fertile (adj.)** फ़र्टाइल-उपजाऊ, कल्पनाशील, उर्वर

   My farm is quite fertile.

   You have a fertile brain.

2. **Fervour (n.)** फ़र्वर्-जोश

   Diwali was celebrated with great fervour in the city.

3. **Youngster (n.)** यंगस्टर्-किशोर

   This movie will appeal more to the youngsters.

4. **Important (adj.)** इम्पॉर्टन्ट-महत्त्वपूर्ण, प्रभावित करना

   I saw many important personalities at the club meeting.

   (n.) Don't give any importance to his foolish talk.

5. **Impose (v.)** इम्पोज़्-थोपना

   Our boss never imposes himself on anyone.

6. **Impossible (adj.)** इम्पॉसिबल-असंभव

   Walking such a long distance is completely impossible for me.

7. **Impress (v.)** इम्प्रेस-1. छाप लगाना, प्रभावित करना

   I was very much impressed by the artist's personality.

   2. प्रभाव डालना

   He impressed on me the value of learning Sanskrit.

   (n.) You have created a very good impression on the boss.

8. **Glide (v.)** ग्लाइड-बहना, विसर्पण करना

   The skaters were gliding gracefully over the ice.

   (adj.) I am a member of the gliding club.

9. **Glimmer (n.)** ग्लिम (र्)-टिमटिमाना, टिमटिमाहट

   In the glimmer of the distant candle light, I could not find my shoes.

10. **Glimpse (n.)** ग्लिम्प्स-झलक, झाँकी, झाँकना

    I caught a glimpse of the thief as he ran away.

11. **Glitter** ग्लिटर्-चमक-दमक, चमकाना, जगमगाना

    (n.) The glitter of the princess's jewellery attracted everybody.

    (v.) All that glitters is not gold.

12. **Leak** लीक-चूना, टपकना

    (v.) Rainwater has leaked through the ceiling and spoilt some furniture.

    (adj.) We must repair our leaking roof before the monsoon starts.

    (n.) The leakage of toxic waster contaminates the underground water.

13. **Lean (v.)** लीन-1. झुकना, टेकना

    I was so tired that I leaned against the wall.

    2. निर्भर होना, आश्रित होना

    Try to be self-reliant, don't lean on others every time a problem arises.

    3. (adj.) दुबला-पतला, कृश, क्षीण

    You look so lean.

14. **Leap (n.)** लीप-उछाल, कुदान

    He crossed the ditch in one long leap.

(v.) How high can you leap?

15. Learn (v.) लर्न-1. सीखना, अध्ययन करना

We have to learn Chemistry from this year onward.

2. पता चलना

I learned that you are going abroad.

16. Health (n.) हे'ल्थ-स्वास्थ्य, तन्दुरुस्ती

Health is wealth.

17. Heap (v. & n.) हीप-ढेर (लगाना), संचय (करना) बरसाना

(v.) Don't heap your plate with food.

(n.) Don't jump over that heap of stones.

18. Hear (v.) हिअर्-1. सुनना, ध्यान देना

Can you hear me clearly?

2. पता चलना, जानना

I hear you have been promoted.

19. Hearsay (n.) हिअर्से-सुनी-सुनाई बातें

Don't go by hearsay, use your own judgement.

20. Heart (n.) हार्ट-1. हृदय, दिल

The doctor found nothing wrong with the patient's heart.

2. प्रकृति, स्वभाव

You have a warm heart.

3. केन्द्र, मध्यभाग

Try to go to the heart of the subject.

21. Just जॅस्ट-1. मात्र, भर, मुश्किल से

(adj.) The poor man had money just enough to buy a loaf of bread.

2. न्यायपूर्ण, वैध, उचित

The employer's decision to reward the laborious workers was just.

(n.) My father is known for his sense of justice.

3. (adj.) तनिक

Just look at the rainbow in the sky.

4. अभी, तुरंत

They are just going.

22. Know (v.) नो-1. जानना

I know the way to Surekha's house.

2. ज्ञान होना

Do you know geometry?

3. परिचित होना

I know Sudhir because he was my classmate.

23. School (n.) स्कूल-विद्यालय, शिक्षा स्थान

We learn different lessons in the school.

24: Science (n.) साइंस-विज्ञान

Science increases our power of observation.

Science without religion is lame.

(adj.) The laboratory is full of scientific instruments.

25. Scissors (n.) सिज़र्ज-कैंची

Ila cut out the picture with a pair of scissors.

These scissors are very sharp,

26. Scold स्कोल्ड-डाँटना, झिड़कना, डांट, झिड़की

(v.) I was scolded for coming home very late.

(n.) You'll get a scolding from mother for breaking the dish.

27. Noon (n.) नून-दोपहर, दिन के 12 बजे का समय

I shall return by noon.

28. Norm (n.) नॉर्म-मानदंड

India has her own cultural and

political norms.

29. Normal (adj.) नॉर्मल-साधारण, सामान्य

The normal weather in December is chilly and cold.

Today my temperature has come down to normal.

(adv.) When do you normally go to bed?

30. Nose (n.) नोज़-नाक

You have a very sharp nose.

31. Tenement (n.) टे'नमन्ट-छोटे फ्लैटों वाली बड़ी इमारत (विशेषत: शहर की गरीब बस्ती में)

Two large houses have been divided into tenements.

32. Tennis (n.) टेनिस-टेनिस नामक खेल

Two players played on a tennis court.

Tennis is very popular in European countries.

33. Tense (adj.) टे'न्स-1. तनावयुक्त

The whole audience was tense with excitement about the result of the music competition.

2. (n.) काल

There are three tenses in grammar-past tense, present tense and future tense.

34. Tent (n.) टे'न्ट-तम्बू, खेमा, शिविर

A tent is made of canvas. It is held in place by tent-pegs.

35. Ordeal (n.) ऑडील-अग्नि-परीक्षा

Working in shifts is really an ordeal.

36. End एन्ड-अन्त, समाप्ति, मिटना/मिटाना, नष्ट होना/करना

(n.) In the end, Arun agreed to accompany Suresh on his trip to Agra.

Do you like films with a sad ending?

(v.) Where does this road end?

37. Endangered (adj.) इन्डेंजर्ड-संकटग्रस्त

We must protect the endangered species.

38. Endeavour (n. & v.) इन्डेवर्-प्रयास/कोशिश (करना)

Students endeavour to score good marks.

(v.) Rahul endeavoured to win the marathon race.

39. Endure (v.) इन्ड्यूअर-1. सहना, झेलना, टिकना

Dr. B.R. Ambedkar endured many a hardship during his early education.

2. (n.) सहनशक्ति, धीरज

Gandhiji was a man of endurance.

40. Whale (n.) व्हेल-व्हेल मछली

Whale is the biggest creature in the sea.

41. Wharf (n. & v.) वॉर्फ़-घाट, जहाज़ घाट, घाट पर लगाना

A ship was unloaded at the wharf.

The captain ordered his men to wharf the ship.

42. What (pron.) वॉट-1. क्या (प्रश्नवाची)

What is the time by your watch?

What is the use of a saw?

What will be your excuse for reaching home late?

2. क्या, जो

I have finished replies to what letters were left.

3. विस्मयादिबोधक अर्थ में

What nonsese!

43. Delicious (adj.) डिलिशस-स्वादिष्ट, रुचिर

One tends to overeat if food is delicious.

44. Delight डिलाइट–आनन्द, हर्ष, आनन्दित होना

(v.) Shyam was delighted to receive the news of his son succeeding in the IAS exam.

(n.) Suresh was filled with delight to see his old friend.

45. Deliver (v.) डिलिवर्–1. पहुँचाना, सौंपना

The postman delivered a parcel to Ramesh.

2. (भाषण) देना, प्रदान करना

You delivered your speech very well.

3. जन्म देना

She delivered a healthy baby boy.

(n.) She had a normal delivery.

46. Demand (v.) डिमान्ड–1. मांग/दावा करना

Have you demanded the compensation for your losses in the flood?

2. (n.) मांग, तकाजा, जिज्ञासा

The demand for the new brand of soap is not good.

47. Reconcile (v.) रेकन्साइल–1. झगड़ा मिटाना, कलह के बाद मित्र बनना

Amitabh was glad to be reconciled to his cousin after they quarrelled.

After both the parties had apologised, the two became reconciled.

(adj.) I have learnt to reconcile with my fate.

48. Record (n.) रेकॉर्ड–1. रिकार्ड, विवरण, हिसाब, लेखा

Has she a good record?

2. कीर्तिमान, रिकार्ड

Salim has broken the record for the high jump. It is on record that I have done this work and not she, though she may claim credit for it.

3. (v.) अंकित करना, टेप करना

Father's voice has been recorded on the tape.

49. Recover (v.) रि'कवर्–1. खोई हुई वस्तु प्राप्त करना

I recovered my bag which I had lost in the market.

2. स्वास्थ्य लाभ करना

Has she recovered from the illness?

(n.) We are delighted to learn about her recovery from pneumonia.

50. Recreation (n.) रे'क्रिएशन–मन बहलाव, मनोरंजन (का साधन)

My favourite recreation is playing cards.

Gardening is a good recreation.

51. Recruit (n.) रिक्रूट–1. रंगरुट

Many recruits will join the police force.

2. (v.) भरती करना

The object is to recruit 500 policemen a month.

52. Vicinity (n.) वसिनटि–निकटता, नज़दीकी

There are beautiful gardens in the vicinity of this village.

53. Victim (n.) विक्टिम–शिकार, पीड़ित या उत्पीड़ित

There are many victims of this road accident.

Food is being collected for the victims of the floods.

54. Victory (n.) विक्टरि–विजय, सफलता, जीत

Our army won a great victory over Pakistan in the battle on the North-

Western border.

Everyone hankers after a victory.

Abha was the victor in the last race in the sports.

(adj.) She was victorious.

55. View व्यू-दृश्य, देखना, निरीक्षण करना

(n.) We had a clear view from the top of the hill. Really it was a lovely view.

(v.) We can view the inside of the castle.

56. Pavilion (n.) पविलिअन-पैविलियन

After being caught by Ricky Ponting, Sehwag went back to the pavilion.

57. Paw (n.) पॉ-पंजा, चंगुल

I gently removed the thorn from my dog's paw.

58. Pawn पॉन-मोहरा

(n.) The servant was used as a pawn by the rich industrialist in the murder case.

(v.) The servant was pawned by the rich industrialist in the murder case.

59. Pay (n.) पे-1. वेतन, तनख्वाह

Have you received this month's pay?

2. (v.) चुकाना, अदा करना, दाम चुकाना

What did you pay for this pen?

3. (मिलने) जाना

I hope to pay you a visit this week.

60. Pea (n.) पी-मटर

Pea is my favourite vegetable.

61. Peace (n.) पीस-शांति

Please don't quarrel, let us have peace.(adj.) I liked to do my writing in the peaceful atmosphere of a secluded place.

62. Notable (adj.) नोटबल-उल्लेखनीय, असाधारण

Congratulations on your notable success in the examination.

63. Note (n.) नोट-1. नोट, पत्र

Please give him this note when he comes.

2. नोट

Do you have a ten-rupee note?

3. स्वर

Can you play all the notes on this musical instrument?

4. (v.) नोट कर लेना, ध्यान देना

Please note the contents of his letter carefully.

64. Adjourn (v.) अडजर्न-स्थगित करना

The meeting was adjourned till the next day.

65. Adjust (v.) अड्जस्ट-ठीक करना, व्यवस्था करना

He adjusted the lamp so that he could read better.

66. Administer (v.) अडमिनिस्टर्-प्रबंध करना, शासन करना

The headmaster administers the school.

(n.) प्रबंध, शासन

The administration of a city is the work of its municipal corporation.

67. Admire (v.) अडमाइअर्- ठीक करना, शासन करना

(v.) All the friends of Smita admired her beautiful sari.

(adj.) प्रशंसनीय

Courage is an admirable quality.

(n.) प्रशंसा

We all felt admiration for his great strength.

68. Admit (v.) अड्मिट – 1. मान लेना, स्वीकार करना

The boy admitted that he broke the win dowpane.

2. प्रवेश देना, (अंदर) आने देना

The headmaster admitted the new boy to his school.

69. Adolescent (n.) ऐडोलसन्ट-किशोर/किशोरी

(n.) Adolescents often find the advice of their parents rubbish.

(v.) Adolescence is the age of emotional changes in the children.

70. Carrier (n.) कैरिअर्

1. सामान ढोने वाला वाहन

We need a carrier to transport our goods to the other city.

2. रोग़ संवाहक

Insects are the carriers of germs.

71. Carrot (n.) कैरट-गाजर

It is good to eat carrots in winter.

72. Carry (v.) कैरि-ढोना, वहन करना

The porter carried Ram's luggage.

The soldiers carried out (obeyed) the General's orders.

(n.) We travelled in the rear carriage of the train.

73. Cart (n.) कार्ट-छकड़ा, ठेला, गाड़ी

The farmer bought a pair of bullocks for his cart.

74. Carton (n.) कार्टन-गत्ते का डिब्बा

Arun bought a carton of ice-cream for his son's birthday party.

75. Uproar (n.) अॅपरॉर्-होहल्ला, शोरगुल, कोलाहल, हंगामा

The girls made such an uproar that the head-mistress had to come to quieten them.

76. Battle बैटल-लड़ाई, युद्ध करना

(n.) There was a fierce battle between the two armies.

(v.) Both the armies battled fiercely.

77. Be (v.) बी-होना

Don't be late for the meeting.

78. Beach (n.) बीच-समुद्र-तट, किनारा

Kerala has many lovely beaches.

79. Bead (n.) बीड़-मनका, दाना

The girl wore a string of colourful beads.

80. Beam (n.) बीम-1. किरण, किरणपुंज

The diamond sparkled in the beams of sunlight.

2. कड़ी, कांडी, दंड

The roof was supported by a thick beam in the centre.

81. Bear (n.) बेअर्-1. रीछ, भालू

There are white bears in Siberia.

2. (v.) सहन करना, बरदाश्त करना

She could not bear the pain.

3. जन्म देना, उपजाना, फलना

To bear children is a natural function of women.

82. Festival (n.) फ़ेस्टिवल-त्योहार, उत्सव

India is a land of festivals.

83. Fetch (v.) फ़ेच-लाना, ले आना

Please fetch me a glass of water.

84. Feud (n.) फ़्यूड-पुश्तैनी रंजिश

The issue of property resulted in a feud between the brothers.

85. Fever (n.) फ़ीवर्-बुखार, ज्वर

The doctor advised rest to Dinesh as

he was having high fever.

86. Few (adj.) फ्यू-1. गिने-चुने, कुछ

A few of my friends know that I can paint.

2. बहुत कम, शायद ही कोई

Few of my friends know that I can paint.

87. Imprison (v.) इम्प्रिज़न-कैद करना, बन्दी बनाना

I hear the manager of your firm has been imprisoned on charges of misappropriation of funds.

(n.) His imprisonment lasted for one year.

88. Impromptu (adj.) इम्प्रॉम्प्ट्यू-बिना तैयारी के किया गया

She won the first prize in the impromptu debate competition.

89. Improper (adj.) इम्प्रॉपर्-अनुपयुक्त

I feel it is improper to sign a new project until we compete the previous ones.

90. Improve (v.) इम्प्रॉपर्-अनुपयुक्त

You must improve your handwriting.

Is your son's health improving now?

(n.) The non-resident Indian was disappointed not to see any improvement in the condition of his native village.

91. Impulse (n.) इम्पल्स-आवेग, आवेश

On a generous impulse, Manoj gave his wrist watch to his friend.

(adv.) If you act imulsively now, you may have to regret later.

92. Globe (n.) ग्लोब-भूमण्डल, पृथ्वी, गोला

Have you travelled all over the globe?

I bought a globe to teach my son Geography.

93. Gloom (n.) ग्लूम-अन्धकार, अंधेरा, उदासी, विषाद

A lonely man's life is full of gloom.

(adj.) Why are you looking so gloomy?

94. Glory (n.) ग्लॉरि-गौरव, महिमा, प्रशंसा

Ram's topping the secondary school exam has brought glory to his school.

(adj.) Look, what a glorious sunset!

95. Glamour (n.) ग्लैमर्-लुभावनापन

(n.) She was taken by the glamour of the modelling profession.

(adj.) Journalism is a glamorous pro fession and attracts many.

97. Glossary (n.) ग्लॉसरि-शब्दावली

We must provide a glossary of foreign words at the end of this book.

98. Left ले'फ्ट-1. बायाँ

Always keep to the left.

2. (adj.) बायें, बायाँ

I have learnt to write with my left hand.

(adv.) Turn left from here.

99. Leg (n.) ले'ग 1. टाँग, पैर

You have longs legs.

2. पाया

Call a carpenter to repair the legs of this table.

100. Legal लीगल्-1. कानूनी

(adj.) I was entangled in legal matters.

2. (adv.) कानूनी रुप से

Ramesh was legally entitled to inherit his father's property.

SPOKEN VOCABULARY
Set - 16

1. Legend (n.) लेजन्ड-किंवदंती

(n.) As per the legend, Krishna killed many demons when he was just an infant.

(adj.) Lata Mangeshkar is a legend ary singer.

2. Legible (adj.) लेजिबल-सुपाठ्य

Use a legible ink to write your letter.

3. Hearty (adj.) हार्टि-भरपेट, भरपूर

We had a hearty meal before we set out.

4. Hearth (n.) हार्थ-अंगीठी, चूल्हा, भट्ठी

We sat near the hearth.

5. Heat (n.) हीट-1. गरमी, ताप

The heart of the burning fire made me sweat.

2. उत्तेजना, आवेग

Do not speak with such heat.

6. Heave (v.) हीव-1. उठाना, उछालना

I pitied the laboured when I saw him heave a very heavy load on his head.

2. भरना

The parents heaved a sigh of relieft when their abducted son returned home.

7. Jut (v.) जॅट-बाहर निकला हुआ होना

Hammer that nail jutting out from the chair.

8. Scope (n.) स्कोप

1. गुंजाइश

There is lot of scope in a career in journalism..

2. कार्य-क्षेत्र

What is the scope of work in this project?

9. Scooter (n.) स्कूटर्-स्कूटर

Do you own a scooter?

10. Scorch (v.) स्कॉर्च-झुलसाना

The iron was very hot. It scorched the cloth.

(adj.) The farmer worked under the scorching sun.

11. Score स्कॉर्-(खेल में) अंक (बनाना)

(v.) The captain scored two goals for his team.

Has Vishwa Nath scored yet?

(n.) The score at the end of the game was two hundred for five.

12. Scorn (n.) स्कॉर्न-अवज्ञा, अनादर, तिरस्कार

Silence is the most perfect expression of scorn.

(adj.) Of all griefs, the most bitter is a scornful jest.

13. Noted (adj.) नोटिड-नामी, प्रसिद्ध

My brother is noted scientist.

14. Nothing (n.) नथिंग-कुछ नहीं

I have nothing to give you.

15. Tentative (adj.) टेन्टटिव-अनिश्चित

I have decided the name of my book, though it is still tentative.

16. Tenure (n.) टेन्यर्-अवधि

She wrote many fiery articles during her tenure as a journalist in the newspaper

17. Term (n.) टर्म-अवधि, मियाद, सत्र

I was absent from college for the whole of the summer term.

18. Terms (n.) टर्म्स-शर्ते, समझौता

Find out the terms on which we can get a room for the holidays.

If you are willing to sell your house, we can settle the terms.

19. Order ऑर्डर्-1. आदेश/आज्ञा (देना)

(v.) The commander ordered the souldiers to fire.

2. मँगाना, मंगवाना

My father has ordered a new sofa set from the furniture shop.

3. (n.) क्रम, अनुक्रम

Arrange these words in an alphabetical order.

4. व्यवस्था, क्रम

Your wrist-watch does not seem to be in working order.

5. विधि और व्यवस्था

It is the duty of the police to maintain the law and order.

20. Ordinary (adj.) ऑर्डिनरि-साधारण, सामान्य, मामूली

I bought an ordinary time-piece, but it works well.

(adv.) Ordinarily, we spend our evenings in Connaught place.

21. Enemy (n.) एनमि-दुश्मन, शत्रु

Believe me, I'm your friend, not your enemy.

22. Energy (n.) एनर्जि-1. कर्मशक्ति, तेज

Doctor advised the patient to take some tonic to increase his energy.

2. ऊर्जा

Energy is essential for the working of both the human body and the machines.

23. Engage (n.) इन्गेज-1. सगाई करना, वाग्दान करना

I am very happy to hear that you are engaged?

2. काम में लगाना, नौकरी पर रखना

How do you find the new servant you have engaged?

3. व्यस्त होना

In what work are you engaged at present?

(n.) Do you have any engagement this evening?

24. Engineer (n.) एँजिनिअर्-अभियंता

I called an engineer when my com puter crashed.

25. Engrossed (adj.) इन्ग्रोस्ड-तल्लीन

When I went to her place, she was engrossed in playing games on computer.

26. Wheat (n.) वीट-गेहूं

Wheat is the major harvest of northern India.

27. Wheel वील-पहिया, चक्कर, घूमना, धुमाना

(n.) A car has four wheels. My uncle has a two-wheeler. A rickshaw has three wheels.

28. Wheeze (v.) वीज़-कष्ट से स्रांस लेना

She started wheezing while climbing the stairs.

29. When वेन-1. कब (प्रश्नवाची)

When did the train leave?

When are you going to Mumbai?

2. जब, तब, कब (जब के अर्थ में)

How can I tell when he will be able to come?

You will see me next Sunday when I shall attend a meeting of the welfare association.

Speak whenever you like.

30. Where (adv.) वेअर्-1. कहां, जहां

Where does the king live?

The king lives in a palace. That is where he lives.

Masoodpur is the village where I live.

My friends follow me wherever I go.

31. Delete (v.) डिलीट-लिखित अंश हटाना

Delete this sentence; it is not re quired.

32. Demise (n.) डिमाइज़्-मृत्यु

The sudden demise of the president shocked the whole nation.

33. Democracy (n.) डिमॉक्रसि-लोकतंत्र

India is the largest demorcracy in the world.

34. Demolish (v.) डिमॉलिश-गिरा देना, नष्ट करना

We decided to demolish the wall between our two houses.

35. Demon (n.) डीमन-राक्षस

Anger is a demon we must fight against.

36. Demonstrate (v.) डेमन्स्ट्रेट-दिखाना, सिद्ध करना, स्पष्ट करना

The housewife asked the salesman to demonstrate the right way of using the washing machine.

37. Rectify (v.) रेक्टिफ़ाइ-अशुद्ध को शुद्ध करना

How long will you take to rectify this mistake?

38. Recur (v.) रिकर्-पुनरावृत्त होना

The imagery of fire recurs throughout the novel.

39. Recycle (v.) रीसाइकल-पुनर्चक्रण

Use paper bags: they are easy to recycle.

40. Redden (v.) रे'डन-1. लाल होना

The young girl reddened when the principal shouted at her.

2. लाल करना, पकाना

The sun reddens the plums.

41. Reddish (adj.) रेडिश-कुछ-कुछ लाल

Her hair was painted in reddish colour.

42. Redeem (v.) रिडीम अधिक खराब होने से बचा लेना

She redeemed the blunder by apologising and rectifying the mistake.

43. Viewpoint (n.) व्यूपॉइन्ट-दृष्टिकोण

Consider this issue from my view point.

44. Vigil (n.) विजिल-रात्रि-जागरण

(n.) The watchman kept vigil all night.

(v.) The police was vigilant all the time and caught the thief in a few days.

45. Vigour (n.) विगर्-बल, ताकत, तंदुरुस्ती, ओज, उत्साह

We will not win many games unless we put more vigour into our play.

The vigour with which you work is amazing.

46. Vile (adj.) वाइल-दुष्ट, चरित्रहीन, बहुत अप्रिय या ख़राब

Do you think me capable of such vile conduct?

47. Villa (n.) विला-देहाती बंगला, ग्राम निवास, बगीची सेघिरा मकान

My father has a beautiful villa in a small town.

48. Peak (n.) पीक-चोटी, शिखर

The mountaineering team reached the peak after a hard struggle.

(adj.) One of my friends always wears

a peaked cap.

49. Peal (n.) पील–1. घंटानाद

As we approached the temple, we could hear the peal of the temple bells.

2. गड़गड़ाहट

There was a peal of thunder and then the rain started.

50. Peanut (n.) पीनट

1. मूंगफली

We enjoyed roasted peanuts while basking in the sun.

2. बहुत ही थोड़ी रक़म

Why are you working for peanuts when you have so much of talent?

51. Pear (n.) पेअर्–नाशपाती

The mother sliced the pears for the child.

52. Pearl (n.) पर्ल–मोती

I bought a necklace of pearls as a present for my wife.

53. Peasant (n.) पेज़न्ट–किसान

As our trains passed through the countryside, we saw peasants working in the fields.

54. Notice (n.) नोटिस–1. सूचना, नोटिस

Did you not read the notice saying that parking is not alowed here?

2. ध्यान

I smiled at Hari but he took no notice.

3. (v.) देख लेना

I noticed that you had left the door open.

(adj.) The error was not noticeable.

55. Notion (n.) नोशन–धारणा, विचार, मत

You seem to have no notion about how to tackle this job.

56. Adopt (v.) अडॉप्ट – 1. स्वीकार करना, पारित करना

The Lok Sabha adopted the annual budget for discussion.

2. अपनाना, गोद लेना

The childless couple adopted a boy.

57. Adore (v.) अडॉर्–बहुत प्यार करना, बहुत पसन्द करना

Every mother adores her child.

58. Adrift (adv.) अड्रिफ्ट –इधर-उधर बहता हुआ

The small boat was adrift on the high seas for four days.

59. Adult (n.) ऐडल्ट–वयस्क, बालिग

Adults have the right to marry as per their will.

60. Advance (v.) अड्वान्स–आगे बढ़ना, उन्नति करना

The army advanced towards the enemy's fort.

(n.) पेशगी

Ramesh requested his employer to pay him an advance of Rs. 2000.

61. Carve (v.) कार्व–काटना, तराशकर मूर्ति बनाना

The sculptor carved a beautiful statue out of the rock.

62. Case (n.) केस–1. सन्दूक, मंजूषा, पेटी

The carpenter made a book-case for me.

2. मुकदमा

Ram filed a caseagainst his employer.

63. Cash (n.) कैश–1. नक़द, रोकड़, नक़दी

(n.) It is safe to make large payments through cheque instead of cash.

(v.) I have to go to the bank to cash a cheque.

2. (n.) खजांची

He received the payment from the cashier.

64. Casserole (n.) कैसरोल–खाना गर्म रखने वाला

ढक्कनदार बर्तन

Food stored in a casserole remains warm for a long time.

65. Cast कास्ट–1. फेंकना, डालना

(v.) The fisherman cast his net into the sea.

2. भूमिका, अभिनेतावृंद

Some films flop despite their big start cast.

66. Upset अॅप्से'ट–विचलित, परेशान

(adj.) Shanta was very much upset when she heard about her husband's accident.

(v.) Never upset other people's programmes.

68. Bearer (n.) बेअरर्–धारक, वाहक

Rehman received an urgent note from the bearer sent by his father.

2. बैरा

Ramesh ordered the bearer to bring him a cup of coffee.

69. Beard (n.) बिअर्ड–दाढ़ी

Rabindranath Tagore had a flowing beard.

70. Beast (n.) बीस्ट–पशु, जानवर

Tiger is a ferocious beast.

71. Beat (v.) बीट–1. मारना, पीटना

Some cruel masters beat their servants even on minor mistakes.

2. हराना, पराजित करना

Our team was beaten in the match.

3. धड़कना

My heart was beating loudly before my result was announced.

72. Beautiful (adj.) ब्यूटिफुल–सुंदर, रमणीय खूबसूरत

Beautiful girls mostly take modelling as a areer

73. Fibre (n.) फ़ाइबर्–रेशा, तन्तु, सूत्र

Of what fibre is your shirt made?

74. Fickle (adj.) फ़िक्ल–अस्थिरमति

Don't believe him; he is very fickle-minded

75. Fiction (n.) फ़िक्शन–कथा साहित्य

I like to read fiction.

76. Fiddle (v.) फ़िडल–निरुद्देश्य किसी वस्तु के साथ खिलवाड़ करना

Why are you fiddling with my purse?

77. Fidelity (n.) फ़िडेलटि–एकनिष्ठता

He probably doubted her fidelity.

78. Fidget (v.) फ़िजिट–चंचलता दिखाना, हाथ-पैर चलाते रहना

You cannot concentrate on what you are reading if you keep fidgeting.

79. Youth (n.) यूथ–उठती जवानी, किशोरावस्था

In youth, they suffer less from their own mistakes than from older people's wisdom.

In youth, we run into difficulties; in old age, difficulties run into us.

80. Impure (adj.) इम्प्युअर्–अशुद्ध

The water in this region is highly im pure.

81. In (prep.) इन–1. भीतर, अन्दर

Please com in.

2. उपस्थित

Is the boss in?

3. में

Is your brother in the Navy?

4 (स्थिति) में

I don't want to go out in the dark.

Don't talk in such a loud voice.

82. Inane (adj.) इनेन्–निरर्थक

Let's not waste our time in this inane discussion.

83. Inaugurate (v.) इनॉग्यरेट-उद्घाटन करना

My new house will be inaugurated next week.

84. Incarnation (n.) इन्कार्नेशन-अवतार

Krishna was an incarnation of Lord Vishnu.

85. Glove (n.) ग्लव-दस्ताना

Has anybody seen my rubber glove?

86. Glow ग्लो-दीप्ति, उज्जवलता, जोश, चमकना, प्रफुल्ल होना

(n.) We can see glow coming from cinders even after the fire has been extinguished.

(adj.) The photograph of Brindavan Garden was full of glowing colours.

(v.) My mother glowed with pride when I got the first prize.

87. Glue (n.) ग्लू-1. गोंद

Do you have some glue to seal this envelope?

2. (v.) चिपकाना

The carpenter gluded the two boards together to make a longer shelf.

88. Glutton (n.) ग्लटन-पेटू, खाऊ

Don't eat like a glutton.

89. Gnaw (v.) नॉ-कुतरना. सताना

A rat seems to have gnawed a hole in this wooden box

90. Go (v.) गो-1. जाना

When do you go to the office?

2. करने का विचार करना

Are you going to write him a letter?

3. आगे बढ़ना या चलना

Go on with your work.

4. बुझना, अंत होना

Have the lights gone out?

91. Legislation (n.) ले'जिस्लेशन-विधि-निर्माण, विधान, कानून

Now that you are a lawyer, you will understand the intricacies of legislation.

92. Legitimate (adj.) लिजिटिमट-न्यायसंगत, यथार्थ

Do you have a legitimate reason for taking a leave today?

93. Leisure (n.) ले'शर्-अवकाश, फुरसत

His job left him little leisure.

94. Lemon (n.) लेमन-नींबू

The little girl loves to eat lemon pickles.

95. Lemonade (n.) लेमनेड-शिंकजी

It's so hot; have some lemonade.

96. Lend (v.) लेन्ड-उधार देना

Would you lend me ten rupees?

97. Heaven (n.) हे'वन-स्वर्ग, आकाश, परलोक

God is in the heaven.

(adj.) What a heavenly sight!

98. Heavy (adj.) हे'वि-1. भारी, वज़नदार

Can you lift a heavy load?

2. भारी, तीव्र बड़ा

We had heavy rains last night.

3 उदास. खिन्न

I bade him good-bye with a heavy heart.

99. Hedge (n.) ह'ज-बाड़ा, घेरा

You should have a hedge around your garden.

100. Heed हीड

1. सलाह पर ध्यान देना

(v.) They heeded the advice of the teacher to recheck the answers before submitting the final sheet.

2. किसी के कहे पर विशेष ध्यान देना

(n.) He did not pay any heed to his mother's advice to return home early.

SPOKEN VOCABULARY
Set - 17

1. **Heel (n.)** हील-एड़ी
I do not like shoes with high heels.

2. **Jute (n.)** जूट-जूट
He carried the onions in a jute bag.

3. **Scoundrel (n.)** स्काउन्ड्रल-बदमाश, दुष्ट
This scoundrel stole my pen.

4. **Scout (n.)** स्काउट-बालचर, स्काउट
A scout is supposed to do a good deed every day.

5. **Scowl (v.)** स्काउ-त्यौरी चढ़ाना
The old man scowled at her when she abused him.

6. **Scramble (v.)** स्क्रैम्बल-(हाथ पैर के बल) चढ़ाना
The monkey scrambled up the trees.

7. **Scrap (v.)** स्क्रैप-टुकड़ा
Throw away these scraps of paper.

8 **Notorious (adj.)** नोटॉरिअस्-बदनाम
Veerappan was notorious for smuggling sandalwood.

9. **Nourish (n.)** नॅरिश-पोषित करना
We need more fertiliser and water to nourish the plant.
(adj.) I like a simple but nourishing meal.

10. **Terminate (v.)** टर्मिनेट-समाप्त होना, समाप्त करना
The manager terminated the services of the clerk because he had disobeyed him.

11. **Terminal (adj.)** टर्मिनल-तिमाही, त्रैमासिक, आखिरी
Have you had your terminal exami nations?

12. **Terminus (n.)** टर्मिनस-रेल या बस का अंतिम स्टेशन
Wait for them at the bus terminus.
All passengers must leave the lorry at the terminus.

13. **Terrace (n.)** टे'रस-चबूतरा, छज्जा, वेदिका
Minakshi and Rachna had tea on the terrace.

14. **Terrible (adj.)** टेरबल-1. भयानक, भीषण, प्रचण्ड, तीव्र, बहुत खराब
There was a terrible storm in which many ships were wrecked.
I can't bear this terrible cold.

15. **Organise (v.)** ऑर्गनाइज़्-आयोजित/संघटित करना
Our school is going to organise a fete this winter.
(n.) May I become a member of your organisation?

16. **Oriented (adj.)** ऑरिएन्टिड-केंद्रित
Her approach is always result-oriented.

17. **Origin (n.)** ऑरिजिन-उद्‌भव, आरंभ
Has the doctor found out the origin of your illness?

18. **Enhance (v.)** इनहान्स-बेहतर बनाना
You can enchance this article by keeping the sentences short.

19. **Enjoy (v.)** इन्जॉइ-रस लेना, भोगना, आनंद प्राप्त करना
Did you enjoy your trip to Simla?
I hope you enjoyed the dinner.
You will enjoy your visit to the zoo.
(n.) Some people find enjoyment in doing their work efficiently.

20. **Enlarge (v.)** इन्लार्ज-बढ़ना, बढ़ाना, विस्तार देना
There is a plan to enlarge our school by building new rooms.
Please get this photograph enlarged.

21. **Enormous (adj.)** इनॉर्मस्-बहुत बड़ा, विशाल
Former President of India Dr. S.D. Sharma gifted his enormous

collection of books to the Bhopal library.

22. Enough इनफ़-पर्याप्त, काफ़ी

(adj.) You will find enough food in the fridege.

(adv.) Is the tea hot enough?

23. Enter (v.) एन्टर्-1. प्रवेश करना, घुसना

Ram stood in the queue to enter the theatre.

2. भाग लेना, नाम लिखना, दर्ज करना

The teacher entered the name of the new student in the attendance register.

24. Whereabouts (n.) वेअर्अबाउट्स-अता-पता

Can you give me an idea about his whereabouts?

25. Whet (v.) वे'टू-किसी वस्तु की सुंदरता और बढ़ाना

Whet the language of this article and make it more readable.

26. Whether (conj.) वे'दर्-1. (मुझे संदेह है कि) या, दो में से एक, यदि

I have not yet decided whether to go out or to stay in.

2. यदि (है कि नहीं)

The child asked the mother whether there was any more milk left.

27. Which विच-1. जो, कौन, कौनसा, जो कोई

(adj.) Try to find out which man stole my sewing machine.

Mother asked Harish which pen he had selected.

The book which I bought is on the shelf.

This is the bookshop which also sells magazines.

2. (pron.) कौन, कौन-सा

Which of these lanes shall wer prefer?

I'll solve whichever question you say.

28. Den (n.) डेन-गुफ़ा

The decoits seem to be hiding in the den.

29. Denial (n.) डिनाअल-वंचन, खंडन

(n.) How do we change his denial to affirmation?

(v.) Mother denied me permission to go out.

30. Dense (adj.) डेन्स-1. घना, सघन

In some dense forests, there is darkness even during the day time.

2. मन्द बुद्धि

I am sure he is not as dense as he looks.

31. Dent (n.) डे'न्ट-छेद, गड्ढा

When did your car get this dent?

32. Dentist (n.) डेन्टिस्ट-दन्त चिकित्सक

The dentist looks after out teeth.

33. Reflect (v.) रिफ़्ले'क्ट-1. चिन्तन करना

Reflect before you make a decision.

2. प्रतिबिंबित होना परछाई डालना.

A mirror reflects light

(n.) You can see your reflection in the mirror

34. Reform (v.) रिफ़ॉर्म-सुधार करना

The new principal has greatly reformed the administration of the school.

(n.) People are pleased with the new manager's reforms of the bonus rules.

35. Refrain (v.) रिफ़्रेन-1. न करना

We must refrain from spitting on the floor.

People must refrain from talking in the cinema hall.

2. (n.) गाने की बार-बार दोहरायी जाने वाली लाइनें

All the students should join in singing the refrain of this song.

36. Refresh (v.) रिफ़्रेश-ताज़ा करना या होना, नई शक्ति प्रदान करना (या प्राप्त होना)

Sleep refreshes us when we fell tired.

(n.) Refreshments were provided after the meeting.

(adj.) When you are tired, a cup of tea is very refreshing.

37. Refrigerator (n.) रिफ्रिजिरेटर्-वस्तुएं ठंडा करने की मशीन

The housewife took a bottle of Coca Cola out of the refrigerator.

38. Village (n.) विलिज-गांव, ग्राम

Is there a high school in your village?

Many villagers go to big cities for better livelihood.

39. Villain (n.) विलन-दुष्ट, बदमाश, खलनायक, शरारती

In many plays, the villain meets bad end.

(adj.) Rama killed Ravan for his villainous acts.

40. Vine (n.) वाइन-अंगूर की बेल

Vine is a creping plant. Grapes grow on the grape vine.

41. Pebble (n.) पेबल्-रोड़ा

Children are found of collecting coloured pebbles.

42. Peck (v.) पैक-चोंच मारना

The sparrows pecked at the grains on the floor.

43. Peculiar (adj.) पिक्यूलिअर्-विलक्षण।

Why are you behaving in such a peculiar fashion today?

44. Pedal (n.) पेडल्-पेडल

One of the pedals of my bicycle is broken.

45. Pedal (n.) पेडल्-पेडल

One of the pedals of my bicycle is broken.

46. Pedestrian (n.) पडेस्ट्रिअन-पादचारी

Pedestrians should watch out while crossing busy streets.

47. Pedlar (n.) पेड्लर्-फेरी वाला

I bought this brush from a pedlar at the door.

48. Advantage (n.) अड्वान्टिज-लाभ, फायदा

Knowledge of English is a great advantage.

49. Adventure (n.) अड्वेन्चर्-साहसिक कार्य

I like to read the stories of adventure.

50. Adverse (adj.) ऐड्वर्स - प्रतिकूल

(adj.) Deserts offer adverse living conditions.

(n.) Sweet are the uses of adversity.

51. Advertise (v.) ऐड्वर्टाइज़्-विज्ञापन देना, विख्यात कराना

This book is widely advertised.

52. Advertisement (v.) ऐड्वर्टिइज़्मेन्ट- विज्ञापन

If you want to sell your product, give its advertisements in the newspapers.

53. Advice (n.) अड्वाइस-सलाह या परामर्श

You must follow the doctor's advice to take rest for a week.

(v.) सलाह देना

He adviced me to consult a doctor.

54. Castle (n.) कासल-दुर्ग, गढ़, महल

Akbar built many castles.

55. Casual (adj.) कैशुअल-1. आकस्मिक, अनियत

His question was only a casual inquiry.

2. सादा

Raju was casually dressed.

56. Casualty (n.) कैशुअल्टि-दुर्घटना में घायल व्यक्ति

The casualties of the blast were admitted to the hospital.

57. Cat (n.) कैट-बिल्ली

My mother is very fond of cats.

58. Catalogue (n.) कैटलॉग-सूचीपत्र, सूची, तालिका

At the book fair, one can collect catalogues of many publishers.

59. Urge (n.) अर्ज-लालसा, तीव्र इच्छा, प्रेरणा

Anupam had an urge to eat ice-cream.

Subhash Chandra Bose had felt a

great urge to achieve the freedom of our country from the British.

60. Ugent (adj.) अर्जन्ट-बहुत आवश्यक

I got an urgent message from my aunt and went to see her at once.

(n.) It is a great misfortune to be of no use to anybody.

61. Because बिकॉज़-क्योंकि, इसलिए कि

I did not go to work yesterday be cause I was not well.

Because of the rain, we could not go for a walk.

62. Beckon (v.) बेकन-इशारा करना, इशारे से बुलाना

I beckoned the waiter to come to my table.

63. Become (v.) बिकम-1. हो जाना

Mr. Rao became the headmaster last year.

2. शोभा देना, जंचना

This sari becomes you.

64. Bed (n.) बेड-पलंग, शय्या

When did you go to bed last night?

65. Bee (n.) बी-मधुमक्खी, भौंरा

Bees gather nectar to produce honey.

66. Beef (n.) बीफ़-गोमांस

Hindus do not eat beef.

67. Field (n.) फ़ील्ड-1. खेत

What do you grow in your field?

2. क्षेत्र

Do you have any experience in the field of social work?

68. Fierce (adj.) फ़िअर्स् खूंखार, हिंस्त्र

I assure you my dog is not a fierce animal.

69. Fight फ़ाइट-लड़ाई (करना)

(v.) The two neighbours were fighting over a petty issue.

(n.) It was a fierce fight among street dogs.

70. Figure (n.) फ़िगर्-1. अंक, रक़म आँकड़ा

I am good at figures.

2. रुप, आकार, आकृति

In the dark, I could make out a figure moving about in the room.

(v.) कल्पना करना, हिसाब लगाना

Can you figure out how we can persuade the minister to preside over the function?

71. Incense (n.) इन्सेन्स-अगरबत्ती

I lighted the incense sticks to make the room fragrant.

72. Incentive (n.) इन्सेन्टिव-प्रोत्साहन देने वाली वस्तु

We get separate incentives for working late in the office.

73. Incessant (adj.) इन्सेसन्ट-निरंतर

The incessant rainstorm made me cancel my trip.

74. Incident (n.) इन्सिडन्ट-घटना, प्रसंग

The newspapers gave extensive coverage to the child kidnapping incident.

75. Inclined (adj.) इन्क्लाइन्ड-1. प्रवृत्त, प्रवण

I am inclined to accept your argument.

2. ढलुआ होना, ढलान होना

The roof was slightly inclined to al low the rain to run off.

(v.) He inclined the pot to drain out the water.

76. Goal गोल

1. लक्ष्य

(n.) Being a doctor is the ultimate goal of my life

2. फुटबॉल या हॉकी आदि में गोल

(n.) We won the match by two goals.

77. Goat (n.) गोट-बकरी, बकरा

Have you ever tasted goat's milk?

78. Gobble (v.) गॉबल-भकोसना

He gobble up the food served to him.

79. God (n.) गॉड-1. ईश्वर, भगवान्

Trust in God and do your duty.

2. देवता

Hindus worship many gods and goddess.

80. Goggles (n.) गॉग्ल्ज़्-धूप का चश्मा

I wore goggles to protect my eyes from pollution.

81. Length (n.) लेन्थ्-लंबाई

What is the length of this river?

82. Lenient (adj.) लीनिअन्ट-नरम, सौम्य

She is a lenient teacher and avoids punishing her students.

83. Leprosy (n.) लेप्रसि-कुष्ठ रोग

This dispensary offers free medical treatment to the leprosy patients.

84. Less (adj.) ले'स-कम

You must eat less if you want to become slim.

85. Lesson (n.) ले'सन-1. पाठ, सबक़

Have you revised all the lessons for your coming exam?

2. चेतावनी, सीख, सबक़

Let this mistake teach you a lesson.

86. Let (v.) ले'ट-1. अनुमति देना

Let me accompany you.

2. किराये पर देना, भाड़े पर उठाना

I want to let a three-room flat.

If this flat is to let, please let it to me.

3. रहने देना, दखल नहीं देना

Let him stay alone.

87. Hefty (adj.) हेफ़्टि-बड़ा या भारी

We spent a hefty amount to buy the new car.

88. Height (n.) हाइट-ऊँचाई

What is your height?

89. Heir (n.) एअर्-उत्तराधिकारी

Rahul was the only heir to his father's property.

90. Hell (n.) हे'ल-नरक

Do you believe in the existence of heaven and hell?

91. Helm (n.) हे'ल्म-1. पतवार

How can you guide a boat without a helm?

2. नियंत्रण, संचालन

Who is at the helm of affairs in your firm?

92. Helmet (n.) हेल्मेट-टोप, शिरस्त्राण

Don't fail to wear a helmet when you ride a scooter.

93. Mature (adj.) मैच्युअर्-परिपक्व

She is mature enough to solve this problem at her end.

94. Maverick (n.) मैवरिक-स्वतंत्रचेता व्यक्ति

Vijay Tendulkar was maverick in the field of Indian theatre.

95. Maxim (n.) मैक्सिम-सूत्र

Follow the maxim-boss is always right-and you will never be unhappy in your job.

96. Maximum (adj.) मैक्सिमम-अधिकतम, महत्तम

What is the maximum number of people that you invite to your parties?

97. May (v.) में-1. संभव होना, (अनुमति में) सकना

May I go home now?

I may go to Mumbai next month.

You may take these clothes to the dry cleaner.

2. (आशीर्वाद अर्थ में)

May he live long!

3. मई मास

(n.) My birthday is on the Ist of May.

98. Mayor (n.) मेअर्-महापौर

He defeated the old mayor by just a few votes.

99. Maze (n.) मेज़्-भूल-भुलैया

I am caught up in the maze of my own problems.

100. Scrape (n.) स्क्रेप-मुसीबत, उलझन

You are so mischievous that you often get into a scrape.

SPOKEN VOCABULARY
Set - 18

1. **Scratch (v.)** स्कैच-मुसीबत, उलझन

   Who scratched the paint off this almirah?

   My legs were scratched by thorns.

   (n.) Her hands were covered with scratches from the thorns.

2. **Scream** स्क्रीम-चीख (मारना)

   (n.) The girl let out a sudden scream when she was frightened.

   (v.) The child screamed loudly when she saw a dog.

3. **Screen (n.)** स्क्रीन-1. सिनेमा पट, पर्दा

   My father writes stories for the screen.

   2. (v.) चित्रपट पर दिखाना

   All the feature films are screened only after they are certified by the Censor Board.

4. **Screw (v.)** स्क्रू-1. पेंच (कसना)

   (v.) The carpenter, screwed down the lid of the box.

   (n.) I need some nails and screws to repair this table.

5. **Scribble (v.)** स्क्रिबल-घसीट में लिखना, घसीटना

   If you scribble your homework, the teacher will make you rewrite it properly.

6. **Terrify (v.)** टेरिफ़ाइ-भयभीत करना, दहलाना

   Our dog terrified the ducks when it jumped into the pond.

   I am terrified of walking home at night.

7. **Territory (n.)** टेरटरि-क्षेत्र

   There is a great deal of forest territory in India.

8. **Terror (n.)** टे'रर्-त्रास, आतंक, दहशत

   Animals have a great terror of fire.

   She has a particular terror of floods.

9. **Test** टे'स्ट-परीक्षण (करना), जांच (करना)

   (n.) Her teacher gave her a test in spelling.

   (v.) Before we buy an equipment we should always test it.

10. **Testament (n.)** टे'स्टमन्ट-विधान

    The Old and New Testaments are the two parts that make up the Bible.

11. **Testify (v.)** टे'स्टिफ़ाइ-गवाही या साक्ष्य देना, सिद्ध करना

    When we speak to the judge, we testify before him.

    (n.) What we say is our testimony.

12. **Tether (v.)** टे'दर्-खूंटे पर बाँधना

    Tether your horse to this post while you go for shopping.

13. **Original (adj.)** अरिजनल-1. मूल

    Is this picture original or is it a copy?

    2. प्रारंभिक, आद्य

    The original way of travelling was on foot, now we travel by train.

14. **Ornament (n.)** ऑर्नमन्ट -आभूषण, गहना

    It is in the nature of women to like ornaments.

15. **Entertain (v.)** एन्टटेन-1. रिझाना, मन बहलाना

    The elder brother entertained the children by telling them stories.

2. सत्कार/स्वागत करना

The host entertained the guestlavishly.

16. Enthusiasm (n.) इन्थ्यूज़िऐज़्म-उत्साह

(n.) He expressed great enthusiasm at the idea of a vacation in Ladakh.

(n.) He is a sports enthusiast.

(adj.) He is very enthusiastic about sports.

17. Entire (adj.) एनटायर्-सम्पूर्ण, समग्र

Have you brought the entire collection of your photographs?

(adv.) I entirely agree with you.

18. Envelope (n.) एन्वलोप्-लिफ़ाफा, आवरण

Put this letter in an envelope and post it.

19. Whiff (n.) विफ़्-गंध, हल्की बदबू

Did you not notice a whiff of cigar smoke as you entered the room?

20. While (n.) वाइल-1. समय, अरसा, दूर

Father will worry if you do not get home in a short while.

I shall telephone you in a little while.

2. (conj.) किन्तु, पर जबकि

Amit brought the milk, while Minakshi prepared the breakfast.

21. Whim (n.) विम्-सनक

He lives in a world of his own whims and fancies

22. Whimper (v.) विम्पर्-ठुनकना

The baby whimpered for milk.

23. Deny (v.) डिनाइ-इनकार करना, नहीं मानना

Politicians are often quick to deny statements attributed to them.

(n.) What is the departure time of your train?

24. Depart (v.) डिपार्ट्-चले जाना, प्रस्थान करना

The train departed on schedule.

(n.) What is the departure time of your train?

25. Department (n.) डिपार्टमन्ट-विभाग, क्षेत्र

For a company's success, all its de partments must work in coordination.

26. Depend (v.) डिपेन्ड-भरोसा या विश्वास करना

Villagers depend on agriculture for their livelihood.

27. Dependent (n.) डिपेन्डन्ट-आश्रित

How many dependents are there in your family?

28. Depict (v.) डिपिक्ट-चित्रांकन करना

The teacher asked us to make a chart depicting the effects of pollution.

29. Deplete (v.) डिप्लीट-किसी वस्तु की मात्र को घटाना

Harmful gases are depleting the ozonelayer.

30. Refuge (n.) रिफ़्यूज-संरक्षण प्राप्त करना

During the rain, we took refuge under a shade.

31. Refugee (n.) रेफ़्यू 'जी-शरणार्थी

Delhi was crowded with refugees following the partition of India.

32. Refuse (v.) रिफ़्यूज-1. अस्वीकार करना

I asked her for help, but she refused.

(n.) Her refusal disappointed me.

2. कूड़ा-करकट

The industrial refuse should be disposed off properly.

33. Regal (adj.) रीगल्-राजसी, शाही

He was not a king, but his robes were regal.

34. Regard (v.) रिगार्ड-1. आदर देना, सम्मान करना

(v.) I regard Pratibha as my best friend.

(n.) I have great regard for Pratibha.

2. शुभ कामनाएं

Please give my best regards to your mother.

3. (v.) ध्यान देना

Why don't you regard your parent's advice?

4. विषय (में)

As regards Sudha, I will write to you at once.

35. Regiment (n.) रेजिमन्ट-1. सैन्यदल

2. (v.) अनुशासित होना

The tourists regimented into large parties for sight seeing.

36. Region (n.) रीजन-भाग, प्रदेश

In India, there are many regions, so there are many regional languages.

37. Vinegar (n.) विनगर्-सिरका

Vinegar is used in many kinds of pickles.

38. Violent (adj.) वॉइअलन्ट-तेज़, प्रबल, हिंसक

The violent storm blew down the huts.

(adj.) Why are you knocking violently on the window?

39. Violet (adj.) वाइअलट-बैंगनी

Violet is a flower. It is pale purple in colour.

Violet is also a colour. It is like the colour of the flower of the same name.

40. Violin (n.) वाइअलिन-वायलिन

You are learning to play the violin. Can you play some tunes on it?

41. Viper (n.) वाइपर्-एक छोटा ज़हरीला साँप

Have you ever seen a viper?

42. Peek (v.) पीक्-छिपकर देखना

The beggar child peeked at the children celebrating Diwali.

43. Peel (v. & n.) पील-छीलना, छिलका

(v.) I like to help my mother to peel potatoes.

(n.) Throw the peels in the dustbin.

44. Peep (v.) पीप-झाँकना

I peeped into the room to see if there was anyone inside.

45. Peer (v.) पिअर्-ताकना

The old man peered at me through his thick spectacles.

46. Peevish (adj.) पीविश-चिड़चिड़ा

She gave him peevish glances when he came late.

47. Peg (n.) पे'ग-खूंटी, मेख

I took off my coat and hung it on a peg.

48. Orphan (n.) ऑर्फ़न-अनाथ, यतीम

This little boy is an orphan, he lost his parents in an accident.

49. Orthodox (adj.) ऑर्थडॉक्स-रुढ़िवादी

She belongs to an orthodox family.

50. Advocate ऐडवकेट-वकील, समर्थन करना

(n.) His father is an advocate in the Supreme Court.

(v.) I advocated the plan suggested by him.

51. Affair (n.) अफ़ेयर् - 1. काम, कार्य

Cooking is largely considered a woman's affair.

2. मामला; घटना

Affer the affair was over, everyone went home.

52. Affect (v.) अफ़ेक्ट-असर करना, प्रभाव डालना

His chest was affected by constant smoking.

53. Affection (n.) अफ़ेक्शन स्नेह, अनुराग

There was great affection between Ram and Laxman.

(adj.) प्यार करने वाला

My brother is a very affectionate person.

54. Affluent (adj.) ऐफ्लुअन्ट-धनवान

(adj.) She belongs to an affluent family of businessmen.

(n.) She offen boasts of her affluence.

55. Catapult (n.) कैटपल्ट-1. गुलेल, शिला प्रक्षेपक

Boys used catapults to hit the birds with stones.

2. ऊपर फेंकना

A single box-office success can catapult a new actor to fame.

56. Cataract (n.) कैटरैक्ट-1. मोतियाबिंद

He has cataract in the left eye.

2. जलप्रपात

The water fell down the hillside in a roaring cataract.

57. Catastrophe (n.) कटैस्ट्रफि-आकस्मिक महाविपत्ति

(n.) Tsunami proved to be a major catastrohe and killed many people.

(adj.) Earthquake was catastrophic to the whole city.

58. Catch (v.) कैच-1. पकड़ना

He could not catch the ball.

2. बराबर आ पहुंचना

He ran fast but I caught up with him.

3. लग जाना

The baby has caught (got) a cold.

4. (n.) अड़ानी

There is no catch on this window.

59. Category (n.) कैटगरि-संवर्ग

The garments were divided into categories as per their texture.

60. Use (n. & v.) यूज़्-प्रयोग (करना)

(n.) It is a great misfortune to be of no use to anybody.

What is the use of being a cross? It doesn't do any good.

(v.) We use our cycles to ride.

(adj.) A pin is a very useful thing.

A fountain pen is useless unless it has ink in it.

61. Beehive (n.) बीहाइव-मधुमक्खी का छत्ता

The boy threw a stone at the beehive.

62. Beer (n.) बिअर्-बियर

He ordered for a bottle of beer.

63. Beetle (n.) बीटल-भृंग

I saw many beetkes in the garden.

64. Beetroot (n.) बीट्रुट-चुकंदर

We purchased some beetroots from the market.

65. Before (Adv.) बिफ़ॉर्-1. पहले, पूर्व

Sunil reached office before time.

I have seen him before. but I cannot remember where he had lived twenty years ago.

66. Beg (v.) बेग-1. भीख मांगना

The hungry man begged for food.

2. प्रार्थना करना, विनय करना

Uma begged her husband not to consume liquor.

3. जब किसी को गलती से स्पर्श किया (ठेस लगाई) हो अथवा किसी का बोलना सुन न सके तो-

I beg your pardon.

52. Beggar (n.) बेग्र्-भिखारी

(n.) I met an old beggar at the stairs of the temple.

(n.) Beggary is a curse on humanity.

53. File फाइल-1. फाइल, संचिका, फाइल में रखना

(n.) Where is the file of our correspondence with the government?

(v.) File these paper carefully.

2. कतार, ताँता

Boys, march to you classrooms in a single file.

3. रेती

I bought a carpenter's file for some wood work in the house.

54. Fill (v.) फ़िल-भरना, भर जाना/देना, पूरा करना

Please fill this glass with cold water.

Students were filled with joy at the declaration of vacations.

55. Film (n.) फ़िल्म-1. चलचित्र, फ़िल्म

Are you fond of films?

2. फ़िल्म

Is there a film in your camera?

3. परत, तह, पटल

Don't drink this water, it has a film of oil on it.

There is a film of dust on the table.

56. Filter फ़िल्टर्-फ़िल्टर (करना), छानना

(v.) Filter this water before you drink it.

(n.) I have bought a water filter.

57. Filthy (adj.) फ़िल्थि-मैला, गन्दा, अश्लील

The house had been empty for years and was filthy inside.

58. Include (v.) इन्क्लूड-सम्मिलित करना, (में) लगा देना

The shopkeeper included all the purchases of David in a single bill.

59. Income (n.) इन्कम-आय, आमदनी

What is your monthly income?

60. Increase (v.) इन्क्रीज़्-बढ़ना, बढ़ाना, वृद्धि करना

I have increased my secretary's salary.

Don't increase the speed until the road is clear.

(n.) I am expecting an increase in my salary.

61. Incredible (adj.) इन्क्रेडिबल-अविश्वसनीय

The way he jumped from the multi-storeyed building was incredible.

62. Indebted (adj.) इन्डेटिड्-कृतज्ञ

I am greatly indebted to you for all your help.

63. Indulge (v.) इन्डल्ज्-मौज-मस्ती के लिए किसी काम में लिप्त होना

I love to indulge myself in shopping on weekends.

63. Indeed (adj.) इन्डीड-सचमुच, अवश्य ही

I am indeed very glad to see you.

64. Gold (n.) गोल्ड-सोना, धन-संपत्ति, स्वर्ण

Is your ring made of pure gold?

65. Good (adj.) गुड-1. अच्छा, उत्तम

I and Anil are good friends.

2. भला, सच्चरित्र

A good man is recognised by his behaviour.

3. टिकाऊ, टिकनेवाला

Is your car good for another two years?

4. (n.) भलाई, भलापन

Always try to do good to others.

66. Goods (n.) गुड्स-माल, सौदा, पदार्थ

What goods do you transport in your truck?

67. Goose (n.) गूस-हंस, कलहंस

Do you keep any goose in your poultry farm?

68. Gorge (v.) गोर्ज-भकोसना

The child gorged himself on the

chocolates.

69. Letter (n.) ले'टर्-1 पत्र खत

Did you receive my letter?

2. वर्ण, अक्षर

How many letters are there in the English alphabet?

70. Level ले'वल-1 तल

(n.) How many feet above the sea level is Shimla.?

2 स्तर

What is the general level of the students in your class?

3 (adj.) समतल

The surface of this table is not quite level.

4. (v.) (ताप आदि) साधना बराबर करना

He levelled his rifle and took aim

71. Lever (n.) लीवर्-हैंडिल

Would you please help me pull the lever?

72. Liability (n.) लाइअबिलटि-मुसीबत

Afte the death of her parents, she was brought up by her uncle as a liability.

73. Liable (adj.) लाइअबल-किसी समस्या से ग्रस्त होने की सभावना मे युक्त

The defaulters will be liable to be punished

74. Help हे'ल्प-1 सहायता/मदद (करना)

(n.) I got much help from my friend

2 खुराक परोसना

Would you like a second helping?

3 टालना दूर करना

I could not help laughing at the funny joke

75. Hen (n.) हे'न-मुर्गी मादा

How many hens do you have on your poultry farm?

76. Hence (adv.) हेन्स-1. इसलिए

I am late. hence I must rush

2 अब से

A week hence I shall be in shimla

77. Herald (n.) हेरल्ड-1 अग्रदूत

The death of the king was announced by the herald

2 (v.) घोषणा करना

The leader's call to the people heralded a new movement against corruption

78 Here (adv.) हिअर यहाँ इधर

Come here

79. Meagre (adj.) मीगर स्वल्प

Why did you agree to work for such a meagre amount

80. Meal (n.) मील-भोजन

What time do you have your meal

81. Mean (v.) मीन 1 अर्थ होना या रखना

Do you really mean what you say

2 अर्थ अभिप्राय

Tell me what these words mean in Sanskrit.

3. (adj.) नीच, घटिया

Never be mean-minded.

82. Meaning (n.) मीनिंग

1 अर्थ

Did you understand the meaning of this line?

2 किसी अनुभव का प्रयोजन या महत्व

Theatre gives meaning to my life

83. Means (n.) मीन्ज़्-1 सम्पत्ति, आय

You are a man of various means.

2 उपाय, साधन

By what means did he climb the wall?

84. Script (n.) स्क्रिप्ट - लिखावट, लिपि

Your script is altogether illegible

2 पटकथा

Have you reviewed the script of shekhar's play?

86. Scripture (n.) स्क्रिप्चर्-धर्मग्रंथ

The Hindu scriptures teach various ways to reach the God

87. Scrub (v.) स्क्रॅब-पानी और ब्रश से साफ़ करना

Please scrub the kitchen floor.

88. Scrutiny (n.) स्क्रूटनि-सूक्ष्म परीक्षण

(n.) Her work was under close scrutiny.

(v.) Her work was closely scrutinised.

89. Sculpture (n.) स्कल्प्चर्-मूर्तिकला

I intend to take a course in sculpture at the arts college

The exhibition was filled with find pieces of sculpture

90. Scuttle (v.) 1 दौड़ जाना, भागना

A frightened rabbit scuttled into the hole as I passed by the field.

2 डुबा देना

The enemy was trying to capture the ship, but the captain scuttled it.

91. Novel (n.) नॉवल-1 उपन्यास

Do you like to read novels?

2 (adj.) अभिनव

Your idea is indeed novel

3 (n.) नवीन वस्तु, कौतुक

Is there a shop of novelties near your house?

92. Now (adv.) नाउ-अब, इस समय, अभी

Can you come now or in the evening?

Boys, now listen to me carefully.

93. Nowhere (adv.) नोवेअर्-कहीं (भी) नहीं

I looked for you but could find nowhere

The book was nowhere to be found

94. Nucleus (n.) न्यूक्लिअस केन्द्र

Could the doctor locate the nucleus of the pain?

This is the girl that lives in Lajpat Nagar.

95. Nudge (v.) नॅज-कोहनी मारना

I shall nudge you when you nod

96. Text (n.) टे'क्स्ट-मूल पाठ, मूल विषय

The text of a book does not include the picture.

We have a separate textbook for each subject in college.

97. Textile (n.) टे'क्स्टाइल-कपड़ा, वस्त्र का उद्योग

My friend works in a textile mill.

98. Than (conj.) दैन-(की) अपेक्षा

A motorcycle can go faster than a bicycle.

99. Thank थैन्क-धन्यवाद (देना), शुक्रिया (अदा करना), कृतज्ञता (प्रकट करना)

(v.) You must thank your lucky stars that you were not in the house when the robbers attacked it

(n.) Please convey my thanks to your mother for the nice sweets she sent for me

(adj.) I am thankful to you for your timely help.

100. That (pron) दैट-वह, अर्थात्, यानी, जो

This is the dog that bit the thief. This is the cat that killed a rat

I told Ramesh I hated him, and that he should leave the room immediately.

He is a cutler, that is to say, a man who sells knives and sharp tools.

SPOKEN VOCABULARY
Set - 19

1. **Envious (adj.)** एन्विअस-ईर्ष्यालु

Neighbours were envious of Rahul's new car.

2. **Environment (n.)** इनवाइरनमेंट

1. पर्यावरण

We must protect our environment from pollution.

2. वातावरण

Our office has a good work environment.

3. **Episode (n.)** एपिसोड

1. घटना

We should forget that humiliating epi sode and move on.

2. धारावाहिक की कड़ी

I missed the last episode of that serial.

4. **Equal (adj.)** ईक्वल्-समान, बराबर

The poor can never consider themselves equal to the rich.

5. **Equip (v.)** इक्विप-सज्जित करना

Are you equipped to go on a hunting trip?

Dinesh wanted to equip his office with modern equipment.

(n.) He ordered some office equipments.

6. **Whine (n.)** वाइन-चीखना, चिल्लाना, झींखना

Never whine about your worries, but try to be more careful.

7. **Whip** विप-कोड़ा (मारना), चाबुक (मारना)

(v.) The cartman is in a hurry and whips his bull.

(n.) The tongawala has a long whip.

8. **Whirl (v.)** वर्ल-तेज़ी से घुमाना या घूमना

The strong wind whirled the dead leaves round and round in the garden.

2. (n.) हड़बड़ी, चक्कर, घुमाव

Your mind is now a whirl. Please whink about your problem colly later on.

9. **Deport (v.)** डिपॉट-तड़ीपार करना

All the illegal immigrants were immediately deported from the country.

10. **Deposit (v. & n.)** डिपॉज़िट- 1. सुरक्षित रखना, अमानत रखना

(v.) It is safe to deposit the valuables in bank locker.

2. (n.) जमा, धरोहर

Cooperative societies give loans against a compulsory deposit to their members.

11. **Depot (n.)** डे'पो-डिपो, गोदाम, भंडार

The ordnace depot supplies weapons to the armed forces.

12. **Depress (v.)** डिप्रेस-उदास करना

Poverty and human suffering depress me very much.

Wet weather always depresses me.

13. **Depression (n.)** डिप्रेशन-मंदी, उदासी

Depression causes unemployment.

Failure causes depression.

14. **Deprive (v.)** डिप्राइव-वंचित करना

Depriving the dog of food would affect its health.

15. Register रे'जिस्टर्-1. रजिस्टर्, दाखिल (करना)

(n.) The teacher checked the attendance register the thoroughly.

(v.) You have to register your case with the police.

2. (adj.) रजिस्ट्री

I sent you certificates by registered post.

16. Regressive (adj.) रिग्रेसिव-प्रतिगामी

The theme of the movie seemed to be regressive.

17. Regret रिग्रे'ट-1. खेद (होना), अफसोस (होना)

(v.) I regret being so late for the meeting.

We regret for breaking the agreement.

2. दु:ख होना

(v). I regret to tell you my mother-in-law is ill.

(n.) There was great regret in the town at the minister's death.

Yes, I failed but I have no regrets.

18. Regular (adj.) रे'ग्युलर्-नियमित

Our regular hours of work at the office are from 10 to 5:30.

Try to be regular in your office.

(adv.) These days trains run regularly.

(n.) Regularity is the key to success.

19. Regulation (n.) रेग्युलेशन-नियम या कानून

The new rules and regulations of the company were made clear to all.

20. Rehabilitate (v.) रीअबिलिटेट-पुनर्वासित करना

The government was taking measures to rehabilitate the earthquake victims.

21. Virgin (n.) वर्जिन-कुमारी, कुँवारी लड़की

Rima was married last year. Her sister Kusum still remains a virgin.

(adj.) Virgin soil of this forest is very fertile.

22. Virtue (n.) वर्चू-सदगुण, विशेषता, खूबी

No virtues of society are vices of the saint.

23. Vision (n.) विशन-1. दृष्टि, नज़र

He has to wear eye-glasses as his vision is weak.

Writing needs men of vision.

2. (adj.) अवलोकन की प्रतिभा

The India Gate is visible from the Qutub Minar.

The students have some visual aids such as maps and charts in their lessons.

24. Visionary दिव्यदर्शी

(n.) Gautam Buddha was really a visionary.

(adj.) Gautam Buddha was a visionary preacher.

25. Pen (n.) पे'न-क़लम, लेखनी

I bought a pen for my son as a birthday gift.

26. Penalty (n.) पेनल्टि-दंड, सजा, जुर्माना

In this library, you have to pay a penalty for returning the book late.

27. Penance (n.) पेनन्स-तपस्या

Ravana performed penance for serveral years and pleased Lord Shiva.

28. Pencil (n.) पेनसिल-पेंसिल

Have you sharpened your pencil?

29. Pending (adj.) पेन्डिंग-बचा हुआ

If you have leisure time, finish your pending work.

30. Penetrate (v.) पेनिट्रेट-छेदना, बेधना

The surgeon's knife penetrated deep into the patient's body.

31. Afford (v.) अफॉर्ड-(खर्च)दे सकना, समर्थ होना

The poor rickhsaw-puller could not afford to send his children to school.

32. Afraid (adj.) अफ्रेड - 1. भयभीत, डरा हुआ

Little children are afraid of dogs.

2. खेद प्रकट करने की शिष्टाचार-पद्धति

I am afraid I cannot accept your invitation.

33. After (prep.) आफ्टर्-1. बाद

The boys played cricket after the school was over.

2. पीछे

The horses galloped one after another.

34. Again (adv.) अगेन-दुबारा, फिर

Please sing that song once again.

35. Against (prep.) अगेन्स्ट - 1. विरुद्ध. खिलाफ

He fought bravely against the enemy.

2. पास के सहारे

Keep your bicycle against the wall.

36. Age (n.) एज-1. वय, उमर अवस्था

What is your age?

2. युग, काल

The period of Chandragupta Maurya is known as the Golden Age of India.

37. Penknife (n.) पेन्नाइफ़्-चाकू

I sharpened my pencil with a penknife.

38. Pension (n.) पेन्शन-पेंशन, निवृत्ति-वेतन

How much pension does your father get?

39. People (n.) पीपल्-1. लोग

The railway platform was full of people.

2. जनसाधारण

People say that we shall have a cold winter this year.

40. Peon (n.) पीअन-चपरासी

The officer asked the peon to get a glass of water.

41. Cater (v.) केट्र-आवश्कतानुसार सेवाएं प्रदान करना

We cater to the overseas markets only.

42. Caterpillar (n.) कैटपिलर्-तितली का बच्चा

A caterpillar grows into a butterfly.

43. Cattle (n.) कैटल्-ढोर, मवेषी, गाय-बैल

The cattle grazed in the shade of the tree.

44. Cause कॉज़्-कारण, हेतु कारण बनना, उत्पन्न करना

(n.) An inquiry is on to find out the cause of the rail accident.

(v.) The accident caused the traffic jam.

45. Usual (adj.) यूज़ुअल-सामान्य, पहले के समान

Uncle has gone out for his usual morning walk.

Always go to school at the usual time.

(adv.) When do you get up usually?

46. Begin (v.) बिगिन-आरंभ करना या होना

The meeting began half an hour late.

47. Behave (v.) बिहेव-व्यवहार करना, पेश आना

Every mother teaches her children to behave properly.

(n.) Everyone praised Amit's courteous behaviour.

48. Behind (adv.) बिहाइन्ड - 1. पीछे, पीछे की ओर

The ball fell behind the wall.

2. देर से

The train was running behind time.

49. Being (n.) बीइंग-प्राणी, जीव

We are all human beings.

50. Belief (n.) बिलीफ़्-विश्वास, यकीन

He is ready to sacrifice everything for the sake of his beliefs.

51. Believe (v.) बिलीव-विश्वास करना

I strongly believe in the existence of God.

52. Final (adj.) फ़ाइनल-आखिरी, अन्तिम

When is your final examination starting?

(adv.) Ram finally agreed to accompany Suresh to the trade fair.

53. Financial (adj.) फ़ाइनैन्शल-आर्थिक, वित्तीय

The government offered financial aid to the farmers whose crops were de stroyed in the floods.

54. Find (v.) फ़ाइन्ड-पाना, प्राप्त करना, पता लगाना

Have you found the purse you had lost?

On reaching home, Rahul found his friend waiting for him.

55. Fine फ़ाइन-1. उत्तम, उत्कृष्ट

(adj.) The acrobats presented a fine show.

2. महीन, सूक्ष्म, पतला

Sharpen your pencil and draw a fine line.

3. जुर्माना

Ramesh had to pay a fine of five ruppes for returning the library book late.

56. Finger (n.) फिंगर्-उँगली

This ring looks beautiful on your little finger.

57. Independent (adj.) इन्डिपेन्डन्ट-1 स्वतत्र, स्वाधीन

The property Rahul has inherited has made him independent.

2. स्वावलंबी

I like your independent attitude.

(n.) Did you attend the Independence Day celebrations?

58. Indicate (v.) इन्डिकेट-दिखाना, बताना, सूचित करना

Sushil indicated his consent to the marriage proposal brought by his auntie.

59. Indignant (adj.) इन्डिग्नन्ट-रुष्ट, क्रुद्ध

Rohit was indignant when he was blamed for a mistake made by somebody else.

60. Individual इन्डिविजुअल-व्यक्तिगत, व्यक्ति, एक-एक

(adj.) The new officer redressed the people's complaints in his individual way.

(n.) Isn't Mr. Prasad a pleasant individual?

(adv.) Five of us were called into the room individually by the principal.

61. Gorgeous (adj.) गॉर्जस-शानदार, भड़कीला, अलंकृत

Your saree is indeed gorgeous.

62. Gorilla (n.) गरिला-गोरिला

Do they have a gorilla in the Delhi Zoo?

63. Gossip (n. & v.) गॉसिप-गपशप करना, गप

(n.) Don't waste your time in gossip.

(v.) Don't gossip about others.

64. Govern (v.) गवर्न-1. शासन करना, नियंत्रित करना

Hong Kong is now governed by China.

2. प्रभावित करना

In this delicate matter, I would like to be governed by what you say

(n.) Do you think the government would be able to control prices?

65. Liberal (adj.) लिबरल-दानी, उदार

The businessman gave a liberal donation to the relief fund for earthquake victims.

66. Liberty (n.) लिबर्टि-1. अधिकार, अनुज्ञा, मुक्ति

You are now at liberty to go home

5. धृष्टता

The mischievous students had taken the liberty of making April Fool of their teacher.

67. Library (n.) लाइब्रेरी-पुस्तकालय

I got this book from the library

68. Licence (v.) लाइसन्स-अनुज्ञा प्रदान करना

I am a licensed electrician.

69. Lick (v.) लिक-चाटना

My cat licks my legs.

70. Lid (n.) लिड-ढकना

Where is the lid of the bread-box?

71. Lie (n. & v.) लाइ-1. झूठ (बोलना)

(n.) Anyone who tells a lie is a liar.

(v.) Don't lie to me.

2. (v.) लेटना, लेट जाना

Please lie on the bed.

3. पड़ा रहना

I saw all his books lying on the floor.

4. स्थित होना

In which continent does India lie?

72. Hereditary (adj.) हेरेडिट्रि-आनुवांशिक

Baldness is a hereditary disease in their family.

73. Heritage (n.) हेरिटिज-देश की चिरकालिक परंपराएं

The national flag and the emblem are the heritage of our country.

74. Hermit (n.) हर्मिट-एकान्तवासी

While passing through the forest, we came across a hermit.

75. Hero (n.) हीरो-1. वीर, नायक

Rama is the hero of the epic Ramayana.

(adj.) We should take inspiration from the heroic deeds of our freedom fighters.

76. Meanwhile (adj.) मीनवाइल-इसी बीच, इतने में

You write the letter, meanwhile I will get a stamp.

77. Measles (n.) मीजल्ज़-खसरा

The scientists have developed a vaccine for measles.

78. Measure (v.) मेशर्-1. माप का होना, मापना

Please measure the length and breadth of this sheet.

2. (n.) उपाय

New measures have been taken to prevent theft and cheating.

79. Meat (n.) मीट-मांस, गोश्त

Go to the butcher's shop and buy some meat.

80. Mechanic (n.) म'कैनिक्-मिस्त्री, मैकेनिक

Call a mechanic to repair this typewriter.

Manoj is interested in the mechanism of television.

81. Medal (n.) मे'डल-पदक

I hear your son got a gold medal for his essay.

82. Sea (n.) सी-1. समुद्र

Oil has been found under the sea.

2. समुद्र की स्थिति, लहरों की गति

There was a stormy sea running that day.

83. Seal (n.) सील-1. मुद्रा, मुहर, प्रतीक

Put the office seal on this letter.

2. सील मछली

Seals live in the sea.

(v.) पूरी तरह से बंद करना

The police sealed the room so that it could be examined later.

84. Seam सीम-सीवन, दो टुकडो को एक साथ सीना

(n.) The tailor sewed the seam carefully.

(v.) She carefully seamed the two pieces of the old cloth together.

85. Search सर्च-तलाशी (लेना), छानबीन (करना), खोज (करना)

(v.) Search others for their virtues, and youself for yur vices.

(n.) You can make a search for your

lost book.

All day long the search went on.

86. Season (n.) सीज़न-ऋतु, मौसम

There are six seasons in a year in India.

(adj.) This work is seasonal, not permanent.

87. Seasoned (adj.) सीज़न्ड्-अति अनुभवी

He is a seasoned writer and has writ ten a number of books.

88. Nuisance (n.) न्यूसन्स-उपद्रव, कण्टक

It's such a nuisance waiting for someone all alone.

89. Thatch (v.) थैच-छप्पर डालना

(adj.) The cottage had been newly thatched.

The farmer lived in a thatched hut.

90. Thaw थॉ-द्रवण, गलन, पिघलना, पिघलाना

(n.) After the thaw, the streams flow fast.

(v.) The ice on the pond will thaw when the weather gets warmer.

91. The (adj.) द, दी-वह, वही, (निश्चायक आर्टिकल)

The moon is very cool. The sun is very hot.

The man you met steals money.

The shopkeeper you know is a dishonest man.

I saw the fellow you had wanted.

The sooner you go from this sad atmosphere, the better you will feel.

I saw a cow on the road. The cow was grazing the grass.

92. Theatre (n.) थीअॅटर्-1. रंगमंच, नाचघर, नाट्यशाला

Had you gone to the theatre last night?

2. अस्पताल में चीर-फाड़ करने का स्थान

The patient was moved to the operation theatre.

93. Theft (n.) थेफ़्ट-चोरी

The police arrested a man for the theft of my bicycle.

Theft is a crime.

94. Theme (n.) थीम-सार, संक्षेप, मूल विषय

Please tell me the theme before nar rating the whole story.

95. Other (adj.& n.) अॅदर्-1. दूसरा, अतिरिक्त

This room is my office, the other one is the library.

2. अन्य, भिन्न

Some people like milk, others do not.

3. हाल में

I met Prakash the other day.

96. Out (adv.) आउट-1. बाहर

Do not go out in the rain.

2. खत्म, खाली, अलग

The lights suddenly went out.

3. रहस्य न रहना

The results of the election are out at last.

97. Era (n.) इअरा-इतिहास का कालखंड

The Qutub Minar was constructed long before the British era.

98. Eradicate (v.) इरैडिकेट-उन्मूलन करना

The new Prime Minsiter promised to eradicate unemployment completely.

99. Erase (v.) इरेज़-मिटाना

She erased the previous answer and wrote a new one.

100. Erect (adj.) इरेक्ट-1. एकदम सीधा

Stand erect!

2. (v.) खड़ा करना, निर्माण करना

How much time does it take to erect a steel mill?

SPOKEN VOCABULARY
Set - 20

1. **Err (v.)** अर्-गलती करना भूल करना/होना

   To err is human, to forgive divine

2. **Depth (n.)** डेप्थ-गहराई

   Before stepping into a lake, you must be aware of its depth.

3. **Deputy** डेप्युटि-प्रति, उप-(उपसर्ग), प्रतिनिधि

   My brother has been promoted to the post of deputy superintendent of police

4. **Derive (v.)** डिराइव-व्युत्पन्न होना, से उत्पन्न होना

   The name of this place is derived from the famous temple of Shiva

5. **Descend (v.)** डिसेन्ड-उतरना, नीचे आना

   The sick old man was unable to descend the steep staircase of his home

   2. उत्पन्न होना (का) वंशज होना

   Do you believe that man has descended from monkey?

   (n.) Is it true that Harish's neighbours are descendants of a royal family?

6. **Rehearse (v.)** रिहर्स-पूर्वाभ्यास करना

   This is the second time we are going to rehearse the play.

   (n.) It will be the finial rehearsal.

7. **Reign (v.)** रेन-शासन करना

   The English rules reigned over India for about one hundred and fifty years

   (n.) The queen introduced many reforms during her reign of forty-five years

8. **Rein (n.)** रेन-बागडोर

   When the reins were pulled tightly, the horse reared.

9. **Relent (v.)** रिलेन्ट-नरम पड़ जाना

   After denying for long, she relented and agreed to come for the excursion

10. **Reinforce (v.)** रीइन्'फ़ॉर्स-कुमुक भेजना, बढ़ाना, सुदृढ़ करना

    When China attacked our country, our army was reinforced.

    The army would be reinforced to meet enemy attacks.

11. **Reject (v.)** रिजे'क्ट-अस्वीकार करना, रद्द करना

    I was foolish to reject Indra's offer of help

    The lady rejected a cup in the crockery shop because it was cracked

12. **Visit** विज़िट-(से) मिलने जाना या आना, भेंट

    (v.) My mother has gone to visit my grandmother.

    (n.) An old friend paid a visit to my father

13. **Vital (adj.)** वाइटल-1. अनिवार्य (जीवन के लिए)

    Air is vital to us for without it we would soon die

    2. ओजस्वी, तेज़पूर्ण

    He has a vital personality

    3. बहुत आवश्यक

    Getting good marks in the examination is vital to you.

14. **Rejoice (v.)** रिजॉइस-प्रसन्न होना, आनंदित होना

    The family rejoiced when the son returned home from a foreign trip

    (n.) There was great rejoicing among the cricketers when they won the match.

15. **Relate (v.)** रिलेट-कहानी कहना, कथा सुनाना

    The hunter related some of his

adventures in the Himalaya's jungles

16. Relation (n.) रिलेशन-1. रिश्ता, नातेदारी

I have many uncles, cousins, nieces and other relations in Delhi.

2 व्यावहारिक संबंध

Relations between teachers and students in our school are very good

17. Relax (v.) रिलेक्स-1. आराम करना

After the test, we relaxed

2 ढीला करना

Relax your grip on my arm you are hurting me

18. Release (v.) रिलीज़-छोड़ना, मुक्त करना

The judge ordered the police to release the innocent boy

19 Relish रेलिश

1. (v.) किसी बात की उत्सुकता से प्रतीक्षा करना

She relished the idea of going abroad.

2. (n.) अत्यंत आनंद

The child ate the chocolate with great relish

20 Volume (n.) वॉल्यूम-1 पुस्तक ग्रंथ

This volume contains all of Sharat Chandra's writings.

2 मात्रा

The volume of sound coming from your transistor is too low.

21. Voluntary (adj.) वॉलन्टरि-स्वैच्छिक, ऐच्छिक, बिना कोई पारिश्रमिक के लिए

To members of Arya Samaj render many voluntary services.

This library has been running on voluntary contributions.

(v.) The brave women volunteered themselves to go into the burning house.

22. Perfume (n. & v.) परफ़्यूम-सुगन्ध, खुशबू

(n.) She wears a very pleasing perfume.

(v.) She perfumed her hanky before putting it in the purse.

23. Perhaps (adv.) पर्हैप्स-शायद, कदाचित्

Perhaps I will be in Mumbai next week.

24. Peril (n.) पेरिल-जोख़िम, ख़तरा

Our journey through the forest was full of peril.

25. Period (n.) पीरिअड्-1. अवधि, मुद्दत

We lived for a short period in Agra before shifting to Delhi.

2. युग, काल

The period of Chandra Gupta Maurya was the golden age of Indian history.

3. घंटा

My son has seven periods in school.

26. Perish (v.) पेरिश-नष्ट हो जाना, मर जाना

More than a hundred people perished in the cyclone.

27. Permanent (adj.) पर्मनन्ट-स्थायी

Have you been made permanent in your job?

Is this temporary arrangement or a permanent one.

28. Sector (n.) सेक्टर्-कार्यक्षेत्र

The new budget provided some relief to the service sector.

29. Secular (adj.) सेक्युलर्-धर्म-निरपेक्ष

India is a secular country.

30. Secure (adj.) सिक्युअर्-1. सुरक्षित

Baby is a secure inter fram.

2. निश्चित

Your victory is secure.

3. (v.) प्राप्त करना

My son secured sixty-six percent marks.

31. See (v.) सी-देखना

We see the moon.

A wise man sees as much as he ought to, not as much as he can.

32. Seed (n.) सीड-बीज

Most plants grow from a seed.

We put seeds in the ground.

33. Seek (v.) सीक-ढूँढ़ना

Seek and you shall fined.

34. Seem (v.) सीम-दिखाई देना

You seem to be sick. What's the matter?

35. Aged (adj.) एज्ड-बड़ी उम्र का

It is difficult to change the habits of aged people

36. Agency (n.) एजन्सि-कोई विशेष सेवा प्रदान करने वाला व्यवसाय

We contacted an advertising agency to promote our brand.

37. Agenda (n.) अजेन्डा/-कार्यसूची

Eradicating unemployment is the first thing in the government agenda.

38. Aggravate (v.) ऐग्रवेट-गंभीर बनाना, बदतर कर देना

Going out into the cold will aggravate your illness.

39. Aggregate (n.) ऐग्रिगट-कुल जोड़

In the India-Pakistan match, the aggregate score of both the teams crossed 500.

40. Causeway (n.) कॉज़वे-सेतुपथ, पक्का जलपथ,

Mumbai has many causeways.

41. Caution कॉशन-सावधानी, सचेत करना

(n.) You must take due caution while crossing a busy street.

(v.) Ram cautioned the new employee against his boss's short temper.

(adv.) The salesman cautiously opened the crockery box.

42. Cavalry (n.) कैवल्रि-रिसाला, घुड़सवार फौज

Shivaji was famous for his cavalry.

43. Cave, Cavern (n.) केव, कैवर्न्-गुफा, गुहा

The hermit lived in a cave high in the hills.

The wounded tiger hid in a cavern.

44. Caw (v.&n.) कॉ-काँव-काँव करना

I was disturbed by the cawing of a crow.

45. Cease (v.) सीस-बन्द होना या बन्द करना

(v.) The milkman has ceased supplying milk because of non-payment of previous bills.

(adv.) The rain came down ceaselessly (continuously).

46. Ceiling (n.) सीलिंग-छतगीरी, (भीतरी) छत

This room has a high ceiling.

47. Utensil (n.) यूटे'न्सिल-पात्र, बर्तन

A pan is a cooking untensil.

48. Utilise (v.) यूटिलाइज़्-उपयोग करना

We should utilise natural resources.

49. Belittle (v.) बिलिट्ल-महत्त्व घटाना

By comparing to his own achievements, the father belittled the small success of his son.

50. Bell (n.) बेल-घण्टा, घण्टी

There are many bells in the temple.

51. Bellow (v.) बेलो-गरजना, चीखना

The bull bellowed because it was tied up.

52. Belly (n.) बेलि-पेट

These days she is exercising to get her belly in shape.

53. Belong (v.) बिलॉन्ग-का होना, की संपत्ति होना, का सदस्य होना

This book belongs to me.

We belong to the same club.

(n.) He put all his belongings in the room.

54. Finish (v.) फिनिश-1. समाप्त करना, पूर्ण करना

Have you finished your homework?

2. (n.) परिष्कार, परिसज्जा

Your dining table has a nice finish.

55. Finished (adj.) फ़िनिश्ड–तैयार

Can you provide us the finished product if we provide you the raw material?

56. Fire (n.) फ़ाइअर्–1. आग, ज्वाला

Last night, a fire broke out in out colony.

2. (v.) गोली चलाना, दागना

The police fired in the air to disperse a rioting mob.

57. Firm (n.) फ़र्म–1. कंपनी, फ़र्म

I learn you have joined a big firm.

2. (adj.) दृढ़, निश्चित, अटल

It's my firm belief that God rewards hard work.

3. ठोस, पक्का, मज़बूत

I jumped from the boat on to the firm ground.

58. Induce (v.) इन्ड्यूस–प्रवृत्त करना, राज़ी करना, फुसलाना

Ram could not induce Anwar to accompany him to the cinema.

(n.) What inducement can I offer to make you keep quiet?

59. Industry (n.) इन्डस्ट्री–उद्योग, उद्योग-धंधा, परिश्रम

After agriculture, industry is the second largest employer of the workforce.

(adj.) I have purchased a shed in the industrial estate to put up a factory.

60. Industrious (adj.) इन्डस्ट्रिअस–परिश्रमी, मेहनती

To succeed in your career, you should be as industrious as an ant.

61. Infant (n.) इन्फन्ट–नवजात शिशु

The infants are fed on only milk for a few months.

62. Infect (v.) इन्फेक्ट–संदूषित करना, छत लगाना, बिगाड़ना

You were infected with typhoid by drinking polluted water.

(n.) The doctor diagnosed Sushila's fever as an infection.

63. Inferior (adj.) इनफिअरिअर्–घटिया, निकृष्ट, निचला

Suresh's performance was is no way inferior to Akram's who won the badminton championship.

64. Inflammable (adj.) इनफ्लैमबल–ज्वलनशील

He was asked not to smoke at the petrol pump, as petrol is highly inflammable.

65. Governess (n.) गवर्नस–आया

She is a governess to our kinds.

66. Gown गाउन–गाउन, चोगा

What is the price of this night-gown?

67. Grab (v.) ग्रैब–पकड लेना, हथियाना, छीनना

Anwar grabbed the pickpocket before he could escape.

68. Grace (n.) ग्रेस–1. कृपा, दया

By the grace of God, all the pilgrims were saved when their boat sank in the Ganges.

2. लालित्य, मनोहरता

There is a grace in your gait.

(adj.) It was very gracious of the film star to agree to attend the slumdwellers's function.

(v.) Many celebrities graced the inauguration of the new depart mental store.

69. Grade (n.) ग्रेड–1. श्रेणी, कोटि, वर्ग, दरजा, वेतन-क्रम

How many grades of offices do you have in your company?

These are second-grade oranges.

2. (v.) दरजा या कोटि निर्धारित करना

The Principal will grade the new pupils according to their marks.

70. Lieutenant (n.) लेफ़्टिनेंट-लेफ़्टिनेंट

He is promoted to the post of lieutenant.

71. Life (n.) लाइफ़

1. जीवन

Mother Teresa devoted all her life to serving poor.

2. ज़िंदादिली

She is full of life.

3. किसी वस्तु के बने रहने की अवधि

Mishandling reduces the life of the machine.

72. Lift (v.) लिफ़्ट-1. उठाना

How will you lift such a heavy load?

2. (n.) लिफ़्ट, उत्थापक

The lift in this building is out of order.

73. Light लाइट-1. बत्ती, दीपक

(n.) Please switch on the ligh'.

2. प्रकाश, रोशनी

In the light of the lamp, I read his letter.

3. (v.) जलाना, सुलगाना

Please light a candle.

4. (adj.) मन्द, हल्का, फीका

I like fabrics of light colours.

5. हलका

I can carry this light box.

6. हर्षित

We all felt light-hearted.

74. Lightning (n.) लाइटनिंग-बिजली, विद्युत

There was a sudden flash of lightning.

75. Hesitate (v.) हे'ज़िटेट-हिचकना, अटकना

Once you take a decision, do not hesitate to act upon it.

76. Heyday (n.) हेडे-समृद्धि-काल,

He had a number of friends in his hey days.

77. Hibernate (v.) हाइबनेट-शीत-स्वाप करना

The polar bear hibernates in the winters.

78. Hiccup (n.) हिकंप

1. हिचकी आना

She started having hiccups on eating the spicy food.

2. व्यवधान

After the initial hiccup, the work proceeded well.

79. Hide (v.) हाइड-1. छिपना, छिपाना

Where have you hidden my pen?

2. (n.) खाल, चमड़ी

The shoes made of a superior hide last longer.

80. Hierarchy (n.) हाइअरार्की-श्रेणीबद्ध संस्था

We have a definite hierarchy in our department.

81. High (adj.) हाइ-1. उत्तुंग, ऊँचा

How high is the building in which you live?

2. श्रेष्ठ, महान्, ऊँचा

I have friends in high places.

3. असंयत, प्रबल

I have nothing but high praise for you.

4. तूफ़ानी, घोर

A high wind has been blowing since morning.

82. Meddle (n.) मेडल-दखलअन्दाजी करना

We should not meddle in other people's affairs.

83. Medicine (n.) मे'ड्सन-दवा, औषध

What medicine has the doctor prescribed for your fever?

(adj.) There are a number of good medical colleges in India.

84. Mediocre (adj.) मीडिओकर्-औसत दर्जे का

We don't want mediocre performers in our team.

85. Meditate (v.) मेडिटेट-चिंतन करना

He has been meditating upon a work able solution over the past one week

86. Medium मीडियम

1. (adj.) औसत

I have medium-length hair

2. (n.) माध्यम

New channel are a faster medium than newspapers.

87. Seat सीट-आसन या कुर्सी (पर बैठना)

(n.) Let me bring you a seat

(v.) This cinema hall seats about a thousands people

Please be seated. He is just coming.

88. Secluded (adj.) सिक्लूडिड-निर्जन स्थान

We enjoyed a few quiet moments at a secluded beach.

89. Second (n.) से'कंड-मिनट का साठवाँ भाग

How many seconds are there in a minute?

(adj.) दूसरा

Monday is the second day of the week

I shall buy a second-hand typewriter

After the primary school, students go to the secondary school

90. Secret (n.) सीक्रट-1. गुप्त भेद, रहस्य

He who confides his secrets in a servant makes him his master

(adv.) गुप्त रहस्यपूर्ण

The robbers made a secret plan to rob the bank

(n.) This is a matter of utmost secrecy

(adj.) Why should we be so secretive about our plans?

91. Secretary (n.) से'क्रटरि-सचिव

We can telephone his secretary it we need to see him earlier

92. Section (n.) सेक्शन-1. भाग, अश, खंड हिस्सा

How many sections are there in this catalogue?

2. विभाग

My brother is a section-officer in the Law Ministry

93. Numb (adj.) नम-सुन्न

My foot has gone numb

94. Then (adv.) दे'न-उस समय तब

Come, let us go to him at about 9 P.M he will be at home by then

We know it is wrong then what is the alternative for it?

95. Thence (adv.) दे'न्स-उस स्थान से तत्पश्चात्

We went to Delhi and thence to Amritsar

96. Theory (n.) थिअरि-सिद्धात पत

If anybody wants to study art properly he should also learn the theory of it

Old stories had been based on the false theory that the sun is revolving and the earth is stationary

97. Therapy (n.) थरेपि बिना औषधि के रोगोपचार

(n.) Aroma therapy is said to relieve tension and stress

(adj.) Visiting that quiet and calm place was a therapeutic experience in itself

98. There (adv.) दे'अर्-1 वहाँ (उस स्थान या स्थिति में)

Please do not go there be seated

2 किसी स्थान के साथ पूरक रूप में

There are fifteen students in the class

There is no money in my purse

99. Outcome (n.) आउटकम-नतीजा

Growth in sales is the outcome of the hard work we put in.

100 Errand (n.) एरन्ड-सौपा हुआ) काम

The servant was tired of doing many errands for his master

SPOKEN VOCABULARY
Set - 21

1. **Escape (v.)** इस्केप-1. भाग निकलना, निकल भागना

   Prisoners' attempt to escape from the jail was foiled by altert guards.

   2. बचना, बच जाना

   Amit escaped narrowly when his bike skidded.

   (n.) He had a narrow escape when his bike skidded suddenly on the road.

2. **Escort (v.)** इस्कॉर्ट-(रक्षार्थ) साथ जाना

   I have to escort my daughter to school.

3. **Especially (adv.)** इस्पेशलि-खास तौर पर, असाधारण रुप से

   Uma especially prepared delicious dishes for her daughter's birthday party.

4. **Essay (n.)** एसे-निबंध, प्रयास

   My son won the first prize in the es say writing competition.

5. **Whisk** विस्क-झाड़ना, उड़ा देना, चंबर, झाडू

   (v.) The cow whisks flies with its long tail.

   (n.) While the husband ate, the wife kept the flies away with whisk.

7. **Whisker (n.)** विस्कर्-मूंछ-दाढ़ी, गलमुच्छा

   Cat's whiskers were long and white in colour.

8. **Whisky (n.)** विस्कि-ह्विस्की

   Whisky is an alcoholic drink made from grains.

9. **Whisper** विस्पर्-फुसफुसाना, फुसफुसाहट, कानाफूस (करना)

   (v.) Whisper to mother so that no one else can hear.

   (n.) In the presence of teacher, students spoke in whispers.

10. **Describe (v.)** डिस्क्राइव-वर्णन करना, बनाना

    Arun described the accident in detail.

    (n.) The woman gave the description of the man who tried to snatch her necklace.

11. **Desert (n.)** डेज़र्ट-1. रेगिस्तान, मरुभूमि

    Travelling in the desert is very difficult without having sufficient stock of water.

    2. (v.) छोड़ भागना, त्याग देना

    We should not desert our friends just when they need us.

12. **Deserve (v.)** डिज़र्व-पात्र, योग्य होना

    The school topper received the prize he deserved for his record marks.

13. **Design** डिज़ाइन

    1. आकृति, रुपरेखा

    (n.) I appreciated the design of the building.

    (v.) He designed the interiors well.

    2. योजना

    (n.) We got to know about his evil designs on time.

14. **Vitamin (n.)** विटमिन-विटामिन

    Always take a balanced food enriched with multi-vitamins.

15. **Vivacious (adj.)** विवेशस-खुशमिज़ाज

    She is known for her vivacious nature.

16. **Vivid (adj.)** विविड-चमकीला, तेज़, उज्जवल

    A vivid lightning flash lits the sky.

17. **Vocabulary (n.)** वकैब्यलरि-शब्द भण्डार, शब्दावली

We can improve our vocabulary by learning some new words everyday.

Your dictionary has a vocabulary of six thousands words.

18. Vocal (adj.) वोकल

1. कंठस्वर से संबंधित

She excels in vocal music.

2. अपने विचारों को खुलकर प्रकट करते हुए

You should be vocal about your grievances.

19. Pepper (n.) पे'पर्-काली मिर्च

The dish became tastier with a tinge of pepper.

20. Perception (n.) परसेप्शन-प्रत्यक्षण

(n.) The circumstances were same, but their preception differed.

(v.) How do you perceive this problem?

I could perceive from his appearance that he was a foreigner.

21. Perch (v. & n.) पर्च-टिकना, बैठना

(v.) The cuckoo perched on a branch high in the tree and sang melodiously.

(n.) The bird sang sweetly from its perch on the tree.

22. Perfect (adj.) परफ़ेक्ट-आदर्श, सही

Can you make a perfect copy of this design?

23. Perform (v.) परफ़ॉर्म-1. पालन करना, पूरा करना, अभिनय करना

I always perform my duties sincerely.

All the actors performed their roles remarkably in the play.

24. Aggressive (adj.) अग्रसिव-झगड़ालू

(adj.) He had never expected such an aggressive behaviour from the teacher.

(n.) Growing aggression in children is a matter of concern for the parents.

25. Agile (adj.) ऐजाइल-फुर्तीला

(adj.) A rabbit is an agile animal.

(n.) Running between the wickets requires a lot of agility from both the batsmen.

26. Agitate (v.) ऐजिटेट-आंदोलन करना

(v.) The workers agitated when forced to stay late in the office.

(adj.) The agitated students boycotted the exams.

(n.) The policy of reservation led to agitation among the doctors.

27. Ago (adv.) अगो-पहले

He left this city four years ago.

28. Agony (n.) ऐगनि-घोर व्यथा

I was in great agony when I broke my arm.

29. Celebrate (v.) सेलिब्रेट-उत्सव

We celebrate Diwali with grea

The young couple celebrated the firs birthday of their child.

30. Celebrated (Adj.) सेलिब्रेटिड-प्रख्यात, यशस्वी

Kalidas was celebrated poet.

31. Celebrity (n.) सलेब्रिटि-जाना-माना व्यक्ति

These days everyone wants to be a celebrity.

32. Cell (n.) सेल्-1. कोठरी

The prisoner was kept in a dark cell.

2. विभाग

The police department set up a separate cell to deal with car thieves.

33. Cellar (n.) सेलर-तहखाना

Residential house are usually without a cellar.

34. Beloved बिलविड - परम प्रिय, प्रेमिका

(adj.) At last, I reached my beloved grandmother's place.

(n.) He introduced her as his beloved.

35. Below (prep.) बिलो-नीचे

The boy hid the novel below the desk.

Some rich men think it is below their dignity to talk with the poor people

36. Belt (n.) बेल्ट-पेरी, कमरबंद, पट्टा

Broad belts are in fashion among the young people

37. Bench (n.) बेंच-बेंच, तख्त

Many patients sat on the bench outside the doctor's cabin

38. Bend बेन्ड-झुकाना, मोडना मोड़ घुमाव

(v.) It is not easy to bend a steel rod

(n.) His house is round the bend on the main road

39. Beneath बिनीथ-नीचे तल

(adv.) The mountaineer looked beneath from the top of the hill.

(prep.) The tired shepherd sat down to take rest beneath the tree

40. Benefit बेनिफिट-लाभ हित लाभ उठाना या पहूंचाना

(n.) His wise advice was of great benefit to me.

(v.) I benefited greatly from his advice.

41. Benevolent (adj.) बनेवलन्ट-दयालु

God is believed to be very benevolent.

42. First (adj.) फ़र्स्ट-1. पहला, प्रथम

My son came first in the competition.

2. First-aid-प्राथमिक उपचार

Always keep a first-aid box in the house.

3. (adv.) पहले

Mother asked Usha to first take dinner and then watch TV programmes.

43. Fish (n.) फ़िश-मछली

Would you like fried fish for lunch?

44. Fist (n.) फ़िस्ट-मुक्का, मुट्ठी

The children were imitating a fight sequence from the film by waving their fists in the air.

45. Fit (v.) फिट 1 ठीक आना ठीक बैठ जाना

The shirt fits me very well

2 (adj.) स्वस्थ, दुरुस्त

I was ill last month, but now I am fit

3 अनुरूप लायक योग्य

The employer asked the job applicant whether he was fit enough to hold a supervisor's post

4 (n.) दौरा

He slapped his son in a fit of anger.

46. Fix (v.) फिक्स-1 तय करना, निश्चित करना

What day shall we fix for the party?

2 लगना

Who fixed this frame on the wall?

47. Inflate (v.) इन्फ़्लेट-हवा भरकर फुलाना

I inflated the balloons and decorated the room with them.

48. Inflict (v.) इन्फ्लिक्ट-पहुंचाना, लगाना, देना

You hasty decision has inflicted a big loss on the company.

49. Influence इन्फ्लुअन्स-प्रभाव/असर (डालना)

(n.) Can you use your influence to get me pass for the fashion show?

(v.) My mother has influenced me greatly.

(adj.) Her father is a very influential person.

50. Inform (v.) इन्फ़ॉर्म-1. सूचित करना, जानकारी देना

Why did you not inform me that you were not well?

2. पुलिस को बताना

The thief was caught because some one had informed against him.

(n.) What information do you have about the flooded localities?

51. Informal (adj.) इन्फ़ॉर्मल-अनौपचारिक

This will be just an informal meeting.

52. Inherit (v.) इन्हेरिट-1. (धन-सपत्ति) उत्तराधिकार में प्राप्त करना

Do you expect to inherit a large amount of money from you rich uncle?

2. (रक्त-संबंध से) अपने पूर्वजों पर जाना

Reena has inherited her mother's good looks and gentle behaviour.

53. Gradual (adj.) ग्रैजुअल-क्रमिक

The company had a gradual and steady progress.

54. Graduate ग्रेजुएट-स्नातक

(n.) She is a graduate in literature.

(v.) She graduated from Princeton College.

55. Graffiti (n.) ग्रफ़ीटि-सार्वजनिक स्थान में दीवार पर की गई लिखावट

Graffiti destroys the beauty of monuments.

56. Graimn (n.) ग्रेन-1. अनाज, धान्य

Are you a grain-merchant?

2. कण

There is not a grain of truth in your story.

57. Like लाइक-1. पसन्द करना

(v.) Do you like my dress?

2. (conj.) समान, सदृश

I bought a pen like yours.

58. Likely (adj.) लाइक्लि-संभवत:, कदाचित्

Are you likely to go to Mumbai next week?

59. Limb (n.) लिम्ब-अंग, अवयव

I hope none of your limbs was injured in the accident.

2. शाखा

I watched the squirrel run up a limb of the tree.

60. Limit लिमिट-1. सीमा

(n.) There is a limit to the powers of the Prime Minister.

2. (adj.) सीमित करना, प्रतिबंध लगाना

One must try to limit one's own expenditure.

(adj.) I have only limited interest in classical music.

61. Highlight हाइलाइट

1. किसी चीज़ की ओर ध्यान आकृष्ट करना

(v.) The teacher highlighted the need to study well to get good marks in the exams.

2. झलकियां

I watched the highlights of the World Cup Finals on TV last night.

62. Highness (n.) हाइनस-शाही खानदान के आदर में प्रयुक्त

The minister said, "Welcome to the court, your Highness!"

63. Highway (n.) हाइवे-राजमार्ग

Drive carefully on the highway.

64. Hijack (v.) हाइजैक-विमान का अपहरण करना,

The terrorists hijacked the plane going to Afghanistan.

65. Hike (n. & v.) हाइक-1. पैदल सैर

I like to go on hikes in the county side.

2. बढ़ना

The shopkeepers have hiked the prices of everything.

66. Medley (n.) मेड्लि-गीत-मिश्रण

They danced on tthe medley of Kishore Kumar songs.

67. Meek (adj.) मीक-नम्र, विनीत

You cannot forge ahead it you are too meek.

68. Meet मीट-1. मिलाना, भेंट होना

Where shall we meet tomorrow?

2. मिलना, एकत्र हो जाना, जुड़ना

Does this lane meet the main road?

3. चुकाना

Can you meet my bill until next month?

4 (n.) सभा

Will you attend the meeting?

69. Melancholy (adj.) मेलन्कलि-उदास, दुःखी

Why are you in such a melancholy mood?

70. Melody (n.) मेलडि-1 लय, राग

I shall now sing you an Indian classical melody

2. स्वरमाधुर्य

We hear the melody of singing birds in the morning.

(adj.) You voice is so melodious.

71. Number (n.) नम्बर्-1. संख्या, अक, नंबर

Write down some numbers on this sheet of paper.

2. समूह, बहुत से

I met a number of old friends at the meeting.

(v.) Gita numbers Rita among her best friends.

3. गिनना, गिनती लगाना

Have you numbered the pages of your manuscript?

72. Therefore (adv.) दे'अर्फ़ॉर्-इसलिए, अतः, इस कारण से

We are going to the cinema in the evening, therefore we will be home late.

73. Thermometer (n.) थर्मॉमीटर्-तापमापी, थर्मामीटर

A thermometer measures temperature.

Do you know how to read a thermometer?

74. Thesaurus (n.) थिसॉरस-पर्याय-कोश

Consult a thesaurus and tell me a better word for 'big'.

75. Thesis (n.) थिसिस-शोध-प्रबंध

I did my thesis on modern Indian literature.

76. They (pron.) दे-वे, ये (लोग)

There are your notebooks They are on the table.

77. Thick (adj.) थिक-1. घना, मोटा, गाढ़ा, गहरा

It is hard to walk through the thick forest.

This board is thicker than that.

2 (n.) कठिन समय

I shall be with you through thick and thin.

3. सबसे व्यस्त, जरुरी हिस्सा

Don't disturb me, I am in the thick of a job.

What is the thickness of it?

78. Thicket (n.) थिकिट-झुरमुट, झाड़-झंखाड़

The robbers were hiding in the thicket.

79. Thief (n.) थीफ़्-1. चोर-उचक्का

People who steal things are called thieves. They are put into prison.

Did anybody see the thief leaving the house?

2. (v.) चुराना

Someone has been thieving the sweets I think.

80. Thigh (n.) थाइ-जांघ, रान, जंघा

Her thighs were swollen, the doctor prescribed an ointment.

81. Outdated (adj.) आउटडेटिड-प्रचलन से बाहर

This machine has become outdated.

82. Essential (adj.) इसे'न्शल-अत्यावश्यक, लाज़िमी, मुख्य, मूलभूत

Food, clothing and shelter are essential needs of a human being.

83. Establish (v.) एस्टैब्लिश-स्थापित करना, सिद्ध करना

How long ago was your business established?

84. Estate (n.) इस्टेट-1. जागीर, जायदाद

Rohit bought a large estate outside the town.

2. भूमि, भूभाग

Rahul has a factory in the industrial estate.

85. Estimate (n.) एस्टिमट-अनुमानित खर्च/मूल्य, अनुमान, विचार

The building contractor gave an estimate of the construction cost of Rahul's house.

86. Eternal (adj.) इटर्नल-शाश्वत

Romeo and Juliet is an eternal love story.

87. Ethics (n.) एथिक्स-उचित-अनुचित का विचार

We must not violate the code of ethics of our profession.

88. Whistle (adj.) विसल-सीटी (बजाना), चहचहाना

(n.) The guard blows a whistle.

(v.) The policeman whistled.

89. White (adj.) वाइट-सफे़द रंग सफे़द, गोरा-चिट्टा, श्वेत

The old lady's hair was completely white.

My house is being white-washed.

(v.) The new toothpowder has whitened my teeth.

90. Whither (adv.) विदर्-जहां कहीं

We may go whither we wish.

91. Who (pron.) हू-1. जो

Minakshi is the girl who sang the song.

The policeman enquired about the person whose purse was stolen.

2. कौन

Who informed Nisha we were there?

Who was the lady wearing the blue saree?

92. Whole (adj. & n.) होल-सम्पूर्ण योग, कुल, पूरासमूचा

(adj.) The whole city was filled with rats.

I have spent the whole night coughing.

I will spend the whole rainy season in Mumbai.

(n.) We must sell our plot as a whole.

Had your father not kept the whole of his money in the bank?

(adj.) We must not wholly believe what others say.

(adj.) We are selling these shoes at wholesale prices.

93. Designate (v.) डेज़िग्नेट-पद सौंपना

(v.) She was designated as the Mar keting Executive.

(n.) She hold the designation of a Marketing Executive in the company.

94. Desire (v.) डिज़ायर्-इच्छा करना, माँगना

Humans always desire to live a happy and peaceful life.

(n.) All the desires can't be fulfilled.

(adj.) An applicant for a job must have all the desirable qualifications.

95. Desk (n.) डेस्क-डेस्क, मेज़

I have to order some desks for my office.

96. Desktop (n.) डेस्क्टॉप-कम्प्यूटर स्क्रीन जिस पर संकेत अंकित होते हैं

Suddenly, all the icons vanished from my computer desktop.

97. Desolate (adj.) डेसलट- 1. सुनसान, निर्जन

Very few people prefer to live in a desolate place.

2. अकेला, उदास

Why are you felling so desolate?

98. Despair (n.) डिस्पेअर-निराशा

Never let despair overcome you.

99. Desperate (adj.) डेसपरट-निराश, उद्दण्ड

Don't get desperate; keep calm.

100. Despise (v.) डिस्पाइज़्-तिरस्कार करना

We despise Ravana because he was an evil man.

SPOKEN VOCABULARY
Set - 22

1 **Relief (n.)** रिलीफ-1 आराम (आना), राहत (पाना)

Father got relief from headache after I rubbed some balm on his forehead.

2 सहायता

The timely relief sent for the refugees saved their lives

(v.) When he took one tablet of Aspro his headache was immediately relieved

2. **Religion (n.)** रिलिजन-धर्म, सम्प्रदाय, मत

We should not discriminate on the basis of religion.

(adj.) Arvind Ghosh was religious man

3. **Reluctant (adj.)** रिलॅक्टन्ट-अनिच्छुक

Vivek is usually reluctant to take sweets.

(n.) I show reluctance to share my room with anybody

(adv.) The beggar accepted the old clothes reluctantly

4. **Rely (v.)** रिलाइ-विश्वास करना, भरोसा करना

We should always rely on our our efforts.

(adj.) Are you a reliable person?

5. **Remain (v.)** रिमेन-बने रहना, जारी रहना, बचा-खुचा रहना

The weather remained very hot on Monday

The shop will remain closed on Sunday.

(n.) After dining, the remains should be collected for the birds

Take 4 from 13, and what is the remainder?

6. **Vocation (n.)** वोकेशन-अपने लिए उपयुक्त प्रतीत होने वाला व्यवसाय

Finally, he has got into the vocation he likes.

7. **Voice (n.)** वॉइस-1 आवाज़, ध्वनि, वाणी, कंठस्वर

The poor have no voice in this world.

Lata has such a pleasant voice that everybody enjoys listening to her songs

2. वाच्य

A verb has two voices-active voice and passive voice

8. **Void (n.)** वॉइड - खालीपन

I often feel a void in my life

9. **Permit (v.)** परमिट अनुमति देना

Please permit me to go home early today

(n.) Do I have permission to use your pen?

10. **Perpetual (adj.)** पर्पेचुअल-अविरल

There was perpetual smile on her lips

11. **Perplexed (adj.)** पर्प्लेक्स्ड-हतबुद्धि

He was perplexed when fired from his job

12. **Perse (adv.)** पर से-स्वत:

The theme of the novel was interesting perse but the language was bad

13. **Persecute (v.)** पर्सिक्यूट-सताना, अत्याचार करना

Hitler persecuted Jews mercilessly during the Second World War

(n.) Religious persecution was common all over the world in the past

14. Thin (adj.) थिन-पतला, दुर्बल, कमज़ोर

If you do not eat your dinner well, you will grow thin.

You are a thin girl but she is a fat.

This needle is too thin. Please get me a thicker one.

15. Thing (n.) थिंग-वस्तु, चीज़

Please give me something to eat.

A thing of beauty is a joy for ever

16. Think (v.) थिंक-1. सोचना

Look before you leap. Think before you speak.

2. समझना

Father thinks that Rajan is a nice man.

We should never think of taking what belongs to others.

I think you should see the doctor.

(n.) All philosophers are thinkers.

17. Thirst (n.) थर्स्ट-प्यास. लालसा तीव्र इच्छा

The traveller quenched his thirst at the well

My son has a great thirst for knowledge.

18. This (pron. & ad.) दिस-यह, इस

What is this?

Would you rather have this pen or that one?

Please look at these mangoes.

Did you find this purse on the road?

I intend to go to Kolkata this month.

19. Thither (adv.) दिदर्-परला

He was running hither and thither

20. Agree (v.) अग्री-सहमत होना बात मान लेना

He did not agree to my proposal

(n.) समझौता

The partners signed an agreement before starting their business.

(adj.) प्रिय लगने वाली

Late has an agreeable (pleasant) personality.

21. Agriculture (n.) ऐग्रिकल्चर्-खेती-बाड़ी, कृषि

Most people in India depend upon agriculture for their livelihood

22. Ahead (adv.) अहेड-आगे

People go ahead; I will follow you.

23. Aid (n.) एड्-सहायता. मदद (करना)

When the tiget attacked me. the hunter came to my aid

(v.) मदद करना

I aided my mother in cooking the food

24. Cemetery (n.) सेमट्री-कब्रिस्तान

There is a cemetery just outside the village.

25. Censure (v.) सेन्शर्-अनुचित काम करने के लिए निंदा करना

The revolutionary was censured for misleading the masses.

26. Centre (n.) सेन्टर-1. केन्द्र, मध्य, मध्यबिंदू

The office of the municipal corporation is in the centre of the city.

2. संस्था

India International Centre in New Delhi is famous as a meeting place of intellectuals.

27. Century (n.) सेंचुरि-1. सदी, शताब्दी

We are living in the twenty-first century.

2. शतक

Scoring a century at the Lord's in London is a dream of every batsman.

28. Cereal (n.) सिअरिअल-अनाज, अन्न, धान्य

Rice and wheat are cereals

29. Utmost (adj.) अट्मोस्ट-चरम, अत्याधिक

Don't worry, I will go to the doctor with the utmost speed.

30. Berserk (adj.) बर्ज़क-आपे से बाहर

When the team did not win the match, the coach went berserk.

31. Berth (n.) बर्थ-1 शायिका

I reserved a berth on the night train

2 गोदी घाट

The huge ship by the berth was an oil tanker

32. Beside (prep.) बिसाइड-पास बग़ल में

He stood beside his brother

33. Besides (prep.) बिसाइड्ज़्-इसके सिवाय इसक अतिरिक्त

Besides your raincoat. you should also bring an umbrella.

34. Best (adj.) बेस्ट-मर्वात्तम

It is best to consider various aspects before starting a new venture

35. Flair (n.) फ़्लेअर्-जन्मजात कौशल

She has a flair for writing.

36. Flake फ़्लेक-पपड़ी

(n.) Huge flakes of snow covered the earth.

(v.) Plaster flaked off the wall.

37. Flag (n.) फ्लैग-झण्डा. ध्वज

The tricolour is our national flag.

38. Flame (n.) फ़्लेम-ज्वाला, लपट

Before sleeping, put out the flames in the fireplace.

39. Flap फ़्लेप-1. कपड़ा, पल्ला

(n.) He sewed a flap on his pocket.

2. फड़फड़ाना

(v.) The pigeon flapped its wings to fly.

40. Flare (n.) फ़्लेअर्-1. धधक, प्रदीप्ति

In the flare of the match, I saw the lost ring on the floor.

2. (v.) भड़कना, क्रोधित होना

You must give up your habit of flaring up without cause.

41. Flash फ्लैश-1. दमक, चौंध, दमकना

(n.) There was a sudden flash of lightning in the clouded sky.

(v.) Why are your eyes flashing with anger?

2. तीव्र गति से भागना

The cars participating in the race flashed past us.

42. Initial (adj.) इनिशल-1. आरंभिक. प्राथमिक

Once you overcome your initial shynes, you can become a good speaker

2. (n.) संक्षेप से हस्ताक्षर करना

Put your initials on the cheque at the right place.

43. Initiate (v.) इनिशिएट-आरंभ करना

After remaining silent for a long time, she finally initiated the talk.

44. Injection (n.) इन्जेक्शन-टीकाकरण

I'm taking my dog for an injection.

45. Injure (v.) इन्जर्-1. चोट या हानि पहुंचाना

I hope you were not seriously injured in yesterday's accident.

2. अपमानित

We felt injured at not receiving an invitation for Dinesh's wedding

(n.) The boy sustained many injuries when he fell down from the bicycle.

46. Ink (n.) इन्क-स्याही

There is no ink in your fountain pen.

47. Inmate (n.) इन्मेट-संवासी

When the theft was committed. all the inmates of the house were asleep.

48. Grammar (n.) ग्राम (र्)-व्याकरण

If you want to master English, you must learn its grammar thoroughly.

49. Grand (adj.) ग्रैन्ड-भव्य, वैभवशाली, उच्च, मुख्य, प्रसिद्ध

We visited many grand palaces on out trip of Europe.

50. Grandparent (n.) ग्रैनपेअरेन्ट-दादा-दादी/नाना-नानी

My grandparents live in Rajasthan.

51. Grant (n. & v.) ग्रान्ट-1. अनुदान

(n.) Does your institution receive a grant from the government?

2. (v.) मानना, स्वीकार करना

I grant that you may be right, but I am also not wrong.

The employer granted the employee's request of drawing some advance against his salary.

52. Limp लिम्प-1. लँगड़ाना, लँगड़ापन

(v.) Why are you limping?

2. (adj.) शिथिल, निर्जीव

These flowers have become limp.

53. Link (n. & v.) लिन्क-1. कड़ी

(n.) Are all the links in the chain equally strong?

2. (v.) संबंध, संबद्ध करना, जोड़ देना

Let us link hands to dance around the tree.

54. Line (n.) लाइन-1. रेखा, लकीर

Draw a straight line

2. कतार, ताँबा

Sit in a line, all of you.

3. पथ, मार्ग

By which airline did you travel?

(v.) People lined up to cast their vote.

55. Linen (n.) लिनिन-सन का बना वस्त्र, घरेलू कपड़े

Give this dirty linen to the washerman.

56. Linger (v.) लिन्गर्-ठहर जाना, ठहरना, देर लगाना

Why are you lingering here though the show is over?

57. Lining (n.) लाइनिंग-अस्तर

She tore th lining of her skirt.

58. Hilarious (adj.) हिलेरिअस-हास्यपूर्ण

That was a hilarious joke.

59. Hill (n.) हिल-पहाड़ी, टीला

Lakhs of people visit the shrine of Vaishno Devi in the hills every year.

60. Hind (adj.) हाइन्ड-पिछला

My hourse fell and injured one of its hind legs.

61. Hinder (v.) हिन्डर्-रोकना बाधा डालना

The strikers hindered the movement of the office-goers by putting roadblocks.

(n.) Don't be a hindrance in my work.

62. Hinge (n.) हिन्ज-कब्ज़ा, चूल

Oil the hinges of the door.

63. Hint (n. & v.) हिन्ट-संकेत/इशारा (करना)

(n.) The manager gave me a hint regarding my increment.

(v.) I hinted that I would attend the meeting.

64. Hip (n.) हिप-कूल्हा, नितंब

I fell down and hurt my hip.

65. Hire (n. & v.) हाइअर्-किराया, किराये पर लेना/देना

(n.) Let us take taxi on hire.

(v.) I hired a mechanic to repair my car.

66. Melt (n.) मेल्ट-गलना, गलाना, द्रवित होना

I melted the butter to make ghee out of it.

The show melted when the sun came out.

My heart melted when I saw the

beggar's plight.

67. Member (n.) मे'म्बर-सदस्य, सभासद

Will you become a member of our club?

Have you renewed you club member ship?

68. Memento (n.) ममेन्टो-स्मृति-चिह्न

The chief guest was presented a memento at the function

69. Memo (n.) ममो-ज्ञापन

He was issued a memo for arriving late in the office every day.

70. Memory (n.) मेमरि-1 स्मरण-शक्ति, याददाश्त

She has a sharp memory.

2. स्मृति, याद

I have happy memories of my first visit to America.

(v.) We must memorise our parts till the next rehearsal of the play.

71. Menace (n.) मे'नस-खतरा, जोखिम (में डालना), धमकाना

(n.) Don't drive in such a way that you become a menace to pedestrians.

(v.) It is menacing to cross a highway amid speeding trucks.

72. See-saw (n.) सी-सॉ-झूमा-झूमी खेल का लकड़ी का बना ढाँचा

Kamla and Vimla are on a see-saw.

The see-saw moves up and down.

73. Seize (v.) सीज़-घेरा डालकर पकड़ लेना

The smuggled goods were seized by the customs officers.

74. Seldom (adv.) से'ल्डम-कभी कभार, विरले ही

Breaking dogs seldom bite.

75. Selct (v.) सिले'क्ट-चुनना

I selected one banana out of three.

(n.) Were not you a member of the selection board?

The selectors of the party-candidates will meet tomorrow morning

76. Self (n.) से'ल्फ़-आत्म स्वय

The best victory is to conquer one's own self

(adj.) Self help is the best help

Self control is the best form of discipline

77. Selfish (adj.) से'ल्फ़िश-स्वार्थी

Don't be too selfish.

(n.) Selfishness is the root of all evils

78. Nurse नर्स-नर्स, परिचारिका, सेवा-शुश्रूषा करना

(n.) I learn your daughter has qualified as a nurse.

(v.) Nurse your young child and he will grow strong.

(adj.) I was admitted to a nursing home.

79. Outling (n.) आउटिंग-भ्रमण

Let's go for an outing.

80. Ethnic (adj.) एथ्निक-विशेष जाति या धर्म का प्रतिनिधि

She gave an ethnic look to her boutique.

81. Etiquette (n.) एटिकेट-शिष्टाचार

He doesn't even have the etiquette to speak to a woman.

82. Evade (v.) इवेड-कन्नी काटना

Why are you trying to evade the question?

83. Evaluate (v.) इवैल्युएट-मूल्यांकन करना

We must evaluate the market demands before launching a new product.

84. Evaporate (v.) इवैपरेट-भाप बन जाना

The water in the bowl evaporated

when kept in the sun.

85. Why (adv.) वाइ-1. क्यों, किस समय, किसलिए

Why do you think that I have no money?

Why have you come to meet me?

2. जिस कारण, जिसके लिए

This is why I informed you about the matter very early.

86 Wick (n.) विक-बत्ती, वर्तिका

Before lighting the kerosene lamp, you must see that the wick is clean.

87. Wicked (adj.) विकिड-दुष्ट, पापी, बुरा, चरित्रहीन

Man is not born wicked, he becomes so, as he becomes sick.

(n.) To see and listen to the wicked is the beginning of wickedness.

88. Dessert (n.) डिज़र्ट-खाने के बाद परोसा जाने वाला मीठा

The host served the dessert after the dinner was over.

89. Destination (n.) डेस्टिनेशन-लक्ष्य, गन्तव्य (स्थान)

Delhi is the destination of most of the trains starting from other states.

90. Destiny (n.) डेस्टनि-किस्मत

Don't curse the destiny for what happened.

91. Destroy (v.) डिस्ट्रॉड- 1. तोड़-फोड़ करना, खराब करना

The children often destroy their books by using them carelessly.

2. बिगाड़ना

Children should not do anything that would destroy their parents' confidence in them.

92. Destruction (n.) डिस्ट्रक्शन-तोड़-फोड़ विनाश

Have you seen what destruction an earthquake can cause?

93. Volatile (adj.) वॉलटाइल

1. वाष्पशील

Perfume is a volatile liquid.

2. अस्थिर

She has a volatile nature.

94. Persevere (v.) पर्सिविअर्-दृढ़ रहना

The brave always persevere in the face of struggle.

(n.) The mountaineers could conquer the high peak only through perseverence.

95. Persist (v.) पर्सिस्ट-अड़ जाना, करते रहना

Why do you persist in your unfriendly behaviour towards him?

96. Person (n.) पर्सन-व्यक्ति

When I reached the office, two persons were waiting for me.

I came in person to attend to this important matter.

(adj.) I keep my personal letters in a separate file.

97. Personality (n.) पर्सनैलिटि

1. व्यक्तित्त्व

The man in black at the party had a pleasing personality.

2. प्रसिद्ध व्यक्ति

Tagore was an unmatched personality.

98. Personnel (n.) पर्सनेल-स्टाफ़

We need some more technical personnel in the department.

99. Perspective (n.) पर्स्पेक्टिव-दृष्टिकोण

When you cannot change the situation, it is better you change your perspective.

100. Volcano (n.) वॉल्केनो-ज्वालामुखी

In Kangra, there is a volcano which disgorges fire.

SPOKEN VOCABULARY
Set - 23

1. **Volley** वॉलि-(कुछ बंदूकों की एक साथ) बौछार, वर्षा, बौछार करना

(n.) A volley of missiles was fired to hush, the enemy back

(v.) In tennis, the players volley the ball. They keep volleying before it was touched the ground.

2. **Ailment (n.)** एलमन्ट-बीमारी जो गभीर न हो

She will soon recover from her ailment.

3. **Aim (v.)** एम - 1. निशाना बांधना या लगाना

The hunter aimed his gun at the tiger.

2. (n.) लक्ष्य, उद्देश्य

My aim is to become an engineer.

4. **Air (n.)** एअर-वायु, हवा

Without air, we would not be able to live.

5. **Aisle (n.)** आइल-मध्यवीथि

It was difficult to find the way through the aisles.

6. **Alarm (n.)** अलार्म-1. भीति, भय

When the plane began to dive, the passengers were filled with alarm.

2. अलार्म, खतरे का संकेत, संकट-सूचना

The silence of the night was suddenly broken by a fire alarm.

(v.) डरा देना

You really alarmed me by screaming so loudly.

7. **Ceremony (n.)** सेरमनि-धर्मक्रिया, शिष्टाचार, तकल्लुफ़

The marriage ceremony will begin after the Pandit arrives.

8. **Certain (adj.)** सर्टन्-1. निश्चित, पक्का

Prakash is certain to pass the I.I.T. exam

2. कोई, कुछ

Certain people are very fond of bragging.

9. **Certificate (n.)** सर्टिफिकेट-प्रमाणपत्र

If you want medical leave, you must produce a doctor's certificate.

10. **Chain** चेन-जंजीर, श्रृंखला, माला, कड़ी, पर्वतमाला श्रृंखला, बांधना

(n.) Uma wore a beautiful golden chain round her neck.

The Himalayas is a chain of moutains.

(v.) We chain our door at night

11. **Chair (n.)** चेअर्-1. कुर्सी, आसन, पीठ

Please sit in this chair.

He was elected chairman (head) of the company

2. पद

(v.) The chair of Prime Minister is not a bed of roses.

12. **Bestow (v.)** बिस्टो-अर्पित करना

The title of Padma Shri is bestowed by the president.

13. **Bestseller (n.)** बेस्टसेलर्-बड़ी संख्या में बिकने वाली किताब

All her novels have turned out to be bestsellers.

14. **Bet** बेट्-शर्त

(v.) I bet you'll miss the flight.

(n.) My bet is that you'll miss the flight.

15. Better (adj.) बेट (र्)-किसी अन्य से बेहतर

His performance in the second match was better than that in the first match.

16. Betray (v.) बिट्रे-विश्वासघात करना, पकड़वा देना

Jesus Christ was betrayed by one of his disciples.

17. Between (prep.) बिट्वीन-बीच में, मध्य में

She divided the sweets between her two sons.

(adv.) Please see me between two and three o'clock.

18. Flat (n.) फ़्लैट-1. फ़्लैट, कक्ष

My flat has three room.

2. (adj.) समतल, सपाट, सीधे पीठ के बल

Lie flat on the bed to overcome tiredness.

19. Flatter (v.) फ़्लैटर्-खुशामद करना, चाटुकारी करना

Everybody is flattered by a compliment

(n.) The people who are adept at flattery are called flatterers.

20. Flavour फ़्लेवर्-सुगध

(n.) Do you have the icecream in chocolate flavour?

(v.) Sheela's birthday cake was flavoured with vanilla essence.

21. Flaw (n.) फ़्लॉ-दोष, त्रुटि

The advocates try to find a flaw in every law.

(adj.) In a TV programme, the famous beauty expert gave many tips to maintain a flawless complexion.

22. Flee (v.) फ़्ली-भागना, भाग जाना

We all fled from the house on fire.

23. Fleet (n.) फ़्लीट-वाहनों का समूह

I dream of owning a huge fleet of cars.

24. Flesh (n.) फ़्लेश-मांस, गोश्त, गूदा

You have put on flesh during your foreign trip.

25. Flexible (adj.) फ़्लेक्सिबल्-झुकने योग्य, मुड़ने योग्य

Our arms and legs are flexible.

(n.) They have flexibility.

26. Innate (adj.) इनेट-जन्मजात

She has an innate ability to dance.

27. Innocent (adj.) इनसन्ट-निरपराध, निष्पाप, बेगुनाह

You have nothing to fear if you are innocent.

(n.) Is there any doubt about their child's innocence?

28. Input (n.) इन्पुट-निवेश

Let me have your inputs to improve my performance further.

29. Inquiry (Enquiry) (v. & n.) इन्क्वाअर्-पूछना, पता लगाना

(v.) Let us inquire about the arrival time of the train.

(n.) The police conducted an inquiry into the bank robbery.

30. Insane (adj.) इन्सेन-पागल

The insane man was taken to the mental hospital.

31. Insect (n.) इन्सेक्ट-कीड़ा-मकोड़ा

The insects filled up the garden after the rain.

32. Insight (n.) इन्साइट-गहन जानकारी

The movie provides an insight into the lives of celebrities.

33. Insist (v.) इन्सिस्ट-आग्रह करना

I insisted him on going for a drive.

34. Grape (n.) ग्रेप-अंगूर, दाख

Please have some grapes.

35. Grasp ग्रास्प-1. कसकर पकड़ना, पकड़, चंगुल

(v.) Had I not grasped the bridge railing, I would have fallen into the river.

2. समझ, समझना, ज्ञान

Can you grasp what your teacher says?

(n.) The scholar had a good grasp on the Vedas.

36. Grass (n.) ग्रास-घास, तृण

Grass grows very rapidly in the rainy season.

37. Grate (v.) ग्रेट-कद्दूकस करना

Mother grated the cheese and made balls out of it.

38. Grateful (adj.) ग्रेटफुल-कृतज्ञ, एहसानमन्द

I am grateful to you for your help.

39. Lint (n.) लिन्ट-फाहा, घाव ढकने का नरम सूती कपड़ा

Get some lint to dress the wound.

40. Lip (n.) लिप्-1. होंठ, अधर

Uma applied veseline on her cracked lips.

2. किनारा, चोंच, धार

The lip of this cup is not clean.

41. Liquid (adj.) लिक्विड-द्रव, प्रवाही, तरल

The doctor has advised me to take only liquid food.

(n.) What is the golden-coloured liquid in that glass?

42. Liquor (n.) लिकर्-तेज़ शराब

That is famous liquors shop in this area.

43. Lisp (n.) लिस्प-तुतलाहट

The child has lisp in his voice.

44. Hiss (v. & n.) हिस-1. फुफकार, फुँकार

(v.) I became alert when a snake hissed.

2. फुसफुस की आवाज़ (होना)

(n.) The tyre of my cycle gave a hiss, so I knew it was punctured.

45. History (n.) हिस्टरि-इतिहास

History is an interesting subject.

(adj.) I like to read historical novel.

46. Hit (v. & n.) हिट-1. प्रहार (करना), मारना

I hit the ball straight into the net.

2. ठीक अनुमान करना, पता लगाना

Have you hit upon any solution to the Maths problem?

(n.) The boxer's powerful hit broke his opponent's jaw.

47. Hitch (n.) हिच-छोटी-मोटी समस्या

I am facing a technical hitch while working on my computer.

48. Hitherto (adv.) हिदर्टु-अब तक

Hitherto I thought he was a fool, but now I think he is a rogue.

49. Mend (v.) मे'न्ड-मरम्मत करना, ठीक कर देना

Cobbler, cobbler, mend my shoe!

We will have to mend our fence.

Mend your ways if you want to improve your financial condition.

50. Menial (adj.) मीनिअल-छोटे स्तर का

No one likes to do the menial jobs, but some people just don't have a choice.

51. Mental (adj.) मे'न्टल-1 मानसिक चिकित्सालय पागलखाना

Is there a mental-hospital in your city.

2 मनोभाव. मनोवृत्ति मन का

By mental effort, we can remember the details of past happenings

(adv.) I was mentally unprepared for such a situation.

(n.) You have an unusual mentality if you do not like any game.

52. Mention (n.) मे'न्शन-उल्लेख, जिक्र

There was mention of poor boy's bravery in the circle

(v.) You may mention my name to him.

53. Mentor (n.) मेन्टॉर्-अनुभवी परामर्शदाता

He is my mentor in singing.

54. Sell (v.) से'ल्-बेचना

What does the baker sell?

(n.) Sale of liquor is prohibited in Haryana.

55. Semester (n.) सेमिस्टर्-अध्ययन सत्र

The course is divided into four semesters.

56. Semi (pre.) सेमि-आधा, अर्ध

My brother is employed in a semi-government concern.

57. Seminar (n.) सेमिनार-संगोष्ठी

I will leave for the seminar tomorrow

58. Send (v.) से'ड-भेजना

He wants to send a parcel to his son

My mother is ill. She must be sent for the doctor.

Mr. Agarwal sends us his good wishes.

(n.) Who is the sender of this letter?

59. Nurture (v.) नर्चर्

1. देखभाल करना

She nurtures her plants as someone nurtures his children

2 विकसित करना

It is important to nurture a good work environment

60. Thorn (n.) थॉर्न-काँटा, कटक

Baby's balloon settled on a rose bush and was punctured by its thorns.

Life is full of thorns.

61. Thorough (adj.) थर-सम्यक् सम्पूर्ण

You need a thorough check-up

(adv.) Check the laggage thoroughly.

62. Thoroughfare (n.) थॅरफ़ेअर्-आम रास्ता

This is not a thorough check-up

We can pass this way. it is a thoroughfare.

63. Though (conj.) दो-यद्यपि, भले ही

The medicine will do you good though you may not like the taste of it.

She walks as though her feet hurt her.

64. Thousand (adj.) थाउज़ॅन्ड-हज़ार

Ten hundreds make a thousands.

A family man has to face a thousand and one worries in life

65. Ovation (n.) ओवेशन-अभिनंदन

She received a standing ovation for her performance

66. Eve (n.) इव किसी महत्त्वपूर्ण अवसर की पूर्व संध्या

They met on the eve of Christmas

67. Even ईवन 1. भी से भी, ज्यो, जिस समय

(adv.) Even if you have a good hand you should get your letters typed.

2. (adj.) समतल, बराबर

Your table does not have an even

surface.

68. Evening (n.) ईवनिंग-शाम, सायंकाल

By what time do you return from office in the evening?

69. Event (n.) इवेन्ट-घटना, परिणाम

Sushil's selection for the IAS was an event suitable for celebration in his family.

70. Eventually (adj.) इवेन्चुअलि-आखिरकार, अन्ततः

Eventually, Sheela realised her mistake.

71. Ever (adv.) एवर्-1. कभी, सदा

Have you ever travelled by air?

2. जब से, तब से

I have known Anil ever since we were children.

72. Wicker (n.) विकर्-लचीली टहनी, टोकरी बुनने के काम आने वाली तीली

Warn the child not to sit on a wicker.

Do you not want to buy a wicker basket?

73. Wicket (n.) विकिट-विकेट, आधा दरवाज़ा, छोटा फाटक

A wicket is one of the two sets of three stickes which are used in cricket.

(adj.) As the main gate was closed, we entered the building through the wicket door

74. Wide (adj.) वाइड-चौड़ा, विशाल

The door of the cow shed is wideopen.

(n.) The width of the door is five feet.

For years I have wandered far and wide in the deserts of life

75. Widow (n.) विडो-विधवा

A rich widow's tears dry soon

Being the widow of a traitor is dreadful.

76. Widower (n.) विडोअर्-विधुर, रडुआ

A widower cannot forget his first wife even when he gets married again.

77. Wield (v.) वील्ड-चलाना, संभालना, नियंत्रित करना

The manager wielded his power very carefully.

78. Detach (v.) डिटैच-अलग करना

He detached the hood from his coat and folded it.

79. Detail (n.) डीटेल-ब्योरा, विस्तृत वर्णन करना

Please narrate the incident in detail.

(adj.) Give me a detailed account of the incident.

80. Detain (n.) डिटेन- 1. रोकना

Rahul could not reach college in time because he was detained in the traffic jam.

2. हवालात में रखना

Many political prisoners were detained in the jails during freedom struggle.

81. Detect (v.) डिटेक्ट-पता लगाना, ढूँढ़ निकालना

The architect detected some faults in the building construction.

82. Deteriorate (v.) डिटिअरिअरेट-स्थिति को बिगाड़ना

His health has been deteriorating ever since he returned back from Jaipur

83. Determine (v.) डिटरमिन्-तय करना, निश्चय करना

My son is determined to become a writer

(n.) Strong determination is needed to succeed in life

84. Remark रिमार्क-राय (प्रकट करना) टिप्पणी (देना)

(v.) The chief guest remarked favourably about the arrangements.

(adj.) There were many remarkable books in the book exhibition.

(n.) I wish to make a few remaks about the elections.

85. Remedy (n.) रे'मडी-1. दवा

The physician suggested the patient a remedy for his fever.

2. उपाय

No remedy is left to correct this situation.

86. Remember (v.) रिमें'बर-(ज़बानी) याद करना, रटना

You should remember your lesson every day.

87. Remind (v.) रिमांइड-स्मरण कराना, याद दिलाना

Please remind me about it when you come again.

(n.) The company sent the reminders to all its members.

88. Reminisce (v.) रेमिनिस्-बीती हुई घटनाएं याद करना

(v.) She was reminiscing her days at school.

(n.) The book is a collection of reminiscences of her days at school.

89. Remit (v.) रिमिट-कर्ज़ या सजा माफ़ करना

The child requested to remit the fine charged by the teacher.

90. Perspiration (n.) पर्‌स्पिरेशन-पसीना

Beads of perspiration rolled down the labourer's face.

91. Persuade (v.) पर्‌स्वेड-समझना, राज़ी करना

My friend wanted to leave, but I persuaded him stay on.

92. Pertinent (adj.) पर्टिनन्ट-प्रासंगिक

She had raised a pertinent question in her article.

93. Perturb (v.) पर्टर्ब-चिंतित होना

We were perturbed with the non-arrival of the maid-servant.

94. Peruse (v.) परुज़-अवलोकन करना

Peruse the story well to detect the errors.

95. Pervade (v.) पर्वेड्-व्याप्त होना

God pervades everywhere.

96. Wife (n.) वाइफ़-पत्नी, जोरु, गृहिणी

Ascend a step to choose a friend, descend a step to choose a wife.

97. Wig (n.) विग-बालों की टोपी (असली या नकली बालों की बनी)

In olden days, people used to wear wigs on their heads.

98. Wiggle (n.) विगल-तेज़ी से हिलना-डुलना

The dog wiggled its tail on seeing its master.

99. Wild (adj.) वाइल्ड-1. हिंसक, हिंस्र, जंगली

Lions are wild animals.

2. तूफ़ानी, भयानक

It was a wild night, with wind and heavy rain.

3. अत्यंत मदमस्त, चूरचूर

I was wild with joy when I won the first-prize.

4. (n.) जंगल, निर्जन स्थान

I saw a hunter hunting in the wild.

100. Alas (interj.) अलैस-हाय!

We wanted to go for a walk, but alas, it rained.

SPOKEN VOCABULARY
Set - 24

1. **Album (n.)** ऐलबम-एल्बम, संग्रह पुस्तक

He has pasted the stamps of many countries in his album

2. **Alcohol (n.)** ऐल्कहॉल्-मादक पेय

Don't drive after consuming alcohol.

3. **Alert-** अलर्ट-सतर्क, चौकस

The alert engine driver averted a major accident of his train

4. **Alien -** एलिअन

(n.) The movie showed the hero fighting against a group of aliens from the other planet

5. **Alight (v.)** अलाइट-1. उतरना

The driver opened the door and his master alighted from the car

2. (adj.) प्रज्जवलित

He struck the match and it was alighted.

6. **Alike** अलाइक-सदृश, समान

(adv.) The twin brother look alike

(adj.) The mother and the daughter are alike in their looks

7. **Chalk (n.)** चॉक-खडिया

The teacher wrote on the blackboard with a piece of chalk

8. **Challenge** चैलिंज-चुनौती ललकार आपत्ति, ललकारना

(n.) He looked upon the difficult task as a challenge to his capability.

(v.) Mike Tyson challenged Evander Holyfield for a world heavyweight boxing match

9. **Chamber (n.)** चेम्बर्-1. कमरा, कक्ष

After the verdict was given, the judge retired to his chamber.

2. वाणिज्य मंडल

The Maratha Chamber of Commerce has its headquarters in Pune

10. **Chameleon (n.)** कमीलिअन-गिरगिट

I saw a chameleon in the garden

11. **Champion (n.)** चैम्पिअन्-1. विजेता सर्वश्रेष्ठ

He was declared the champion bats man of the year

2 समर्थक, हिमायती

Gandhiji was a champion of the downtrodden.

12. **Beverage (n.)** बेवरिज-पेय

We need to decide upon the food and beverage for the party.

13. **Beware (v.)** बिवेअर्-सतर्क, सावधान रहना या होना

Beware of pick-pockets

14. **Bewilder (v.)** बिविल्डर्-उलझन या अचरज में डालना

He was bewildered to see the sudden change in her mood

15. **Bewitch (v.)** बिविच-लुभाना

The beautiful interiors of the building bewitched us.

16. **Beyond (prep.)** बियॉन्ड-परे, पार

There was a temple beyond the mountains

17. **Bias** बाइअस-पक्षपात

(n.) A bias against aged workers is visible in most of the companies

(v.) His opinion about the best cricket

player was biased towards Yuvraj Singh.

18. Flicker (v.) फ़्लिकर्-1. टिमटिमाना, झिलमिलाना

The candle flame flickers in the wind.

(adj.) Reading in the flickering flame of the candle is not good for one's eyes.

2. (n.) किरण

The marooned flood victims had flicker of hope that they would be rescued.

19. Flimsy (adj.) फ़्लिम्ज़ि-अविश्वसनीय

Stop making such flimsy excuses.

20. Fling (v.) फ़्लिंग-फेंकना, पटकना

Both the wrestlers were trying to fling each other on the ground.

Don't fling baseless charges at me

21. Flip (v.) फ़्लिप-झटके से पलटना

She flipped through the pages of the book of find the 10-rupee note inside it

22. Flip (v.) फ़्लिप-झटके से पलटना

She flipped through the pages of the book to find the 10-rupee not inside it.

23. Float (v.) फ़्लोट-पानी के तल तक टिकना

I float for a while before I begin to swim.

People swim. wood floats, but a stone sinks.

24. Flock (n.) फ़्लॉक-1. झुण्ड, समूह. दल

Look at that flock of birds in the sky.

2. (v.) जमा या एकत्र दल

At the fair, the children flocked around the toy shops.

25. Inspect (v.) इन्स्पेक्ट-जांच करना

The police inspected the house to get some clues

26. Inspire (v.) इन्स्पाइअर्-प्रेरित करना

He claims to be inspired by Sachin Tendulkar.

27. Install (v.) इन्स्टॉल-लगाना, रखना, स्थापित करना

What will it cost me to install an air-conditioner in my bedroom?

(n.) The installation of the air-conditioner took the whole day

28. Instalment (n.) इन्स्टॉलमन्ट-किस्त

Arun bought the new car on instalments.

29. Instance (n.) इन्स्टन्स-उदाहरण, मिसाल

Maharana Pratap was an instance for man of great courage and self-respect.

30. Instant (n.) इन्स्टन्ट-1 क्षण

The instant I opened the window. I saw you coming slowly.

2 (adj.) तुरंत

That tablet gave Sheela instant relief from headache.

(adv.) In yesterday's accident, two men died instantly

31. Instead (adv.) इन्स्टेड-किसी वस्तु या व्यक्ति के स्थान पर

Why do you take coffee all the time? Have some milk instead.

32. Instinct (n.) इन्स्टिंक्ट-स्वाभाविक वृत्ति

Just go by your instinct. everything will be fine

33. Grave (adj.) ग्रेव 1 गंभीर

Why ate you looking grave?

There was some grave news in the letter that mother had written to Ram

2. महत्वपूर्ण. घोर संगीन

Akbar made a grave mistake by not attempting all the questions of his

Mathspaper.

3. (n.) क़ब्र, समाधि

The devotees visited the grave of the famous Fakeer.

A graveyard near our house has been turned into a park.

34. Gravel (n.) ग्रैवल-कंकड़, बजरी

Where can I get some gravel for my garden?

35. Gravy (n.) ग्रेवि-मांस-सार, तरी

Gravy plays an important role in making a dish delicious.

36. Graze (v.) ग्रेज़्-चरना, चराना, खरोचना

The cows were grazing in the field.

We might graze our arm against the wall if we run too close to it.

37. Grease ग्रीज़्-चरबी, ग्रीस, चिकनाई, चिकनाई लगाना

(v.) It is necessary to grease all parts of machine for its smooth functioning.

(n.) Amitabh rubbed some grease on his shoes to make the leather softer.

38. List (n.) लिस्ट-सूची, तालिका

Please prepare a list of all the participants in the debate.

39. Listen (v.) लिसन-सुनना, ध्यान देना

Students were listening attentively to the teacher's talk.

Please listen to me.

40. Literally (adv.) लिटरलि-किसी बात पर बल देने के लिए प्रयुक्त

They were literally on roads after their father's accident.

41. Literate (adj.) लिटरट-पढ़ने-लिखने में सक्षम

My maid-servant is a literate and can also read a newspaper.

42. Literature (n.) लिट्रचर्-साहित्य

Have you read modern English

43. Litter लिटर्-कूड़ा-कचरा (बिखराना)

(n.) Dump the litter in the dustbin

(v.) His room was littered with old newspapers and magazines.

44. Little (adj.) लिटल-1. छोटा, लघु

I saw a little boy playing with marbles.

2. किंचित्

I feel a little unwell today.

3. थोड़ा, कुछ ही

I have little time to waste.

44. Hive (n.) हाइव-शहद की मक्खियों का छत्ता

Take care, there is a hive on a tree in our garden.

45. Hoard (n. & v.) हॉर्ड-(अप) संचय करना

(n.) A beehive is a hoard of honey.

Hoarders of essential commodities should be punished.

(v.) The miser hoards a lot of money.

46. Hoarding (n.) हॉर्डिंग-सड़कों आदि पर लगे विज्ञापन हेतु बड़े-बड़े बोर्ड

I saw a huge hoarding on the roadside.

47. Hoarse (adj.) हॉर्स-कर्कश, फटा

My voice became hoarse due to cold.

48. Hobby (n.) हॉबि-शौक

Coin collection is my favourite hobby.

49. Hockey (n.) हॉकि-हाकी

Do you play hockey or cricket?

50. Hoist (v.) हॉइस्ट-फहराना, उठाना, ऊपर उठाना

The Prime Minister hoists the National Flag at Red Fort on every Independence Day.

My mother hoisted the baby upon her shoulder to show it a dancing monkey.

51. Hold (v.) होल्ड–1. पकड़, पकड़ना

Hold my hand.

2. धारण करना, (में) स्थान होना

How much milk does this bottle hold?

3. अधिकार होना, पास रखना

Does he hold a Ph.D?

4. समझना, मानना

I hold that honest men should contest the election.

5. करना, आयोजन करना

When are you going to hold the cub meeting?

6. नियंत्रित करना

Hold your breath and jump into the water.

7. अधिकार बनाए रखना, अपने नियंत्रण में बनाए रखना

The army was ordered to hold the fort against my attack.

52. Menu (n.) मे'न्यू–व्यंजन–सूजी, भोजन

Waiter, please bring the menu.

53. Merchant (n.) मॅर्चन्ट–व्यापारी, दुकानदार

My uncle is a wholesale grain merchant.

59. Mercy (n.) मर्सि–दया, करुणा

Oh God, have mercy on us!

60. Mere (adj.) मिअर्–निरा, मात्र

You are still a mere kid.

61. Merely (adj.) मिअर्लि–केवल, मात्र, सिर्फ़

I merely want to give her a little advice.

62. Merge (v.) मर्ज–विलीन हो जाना

The large waves in the sea merged into each other.

63. Merit (n.) मेरिट–खूबी

The admission in this course will be strictly on merit basis.

64. Mermaid (n.) मर्मेड–जलपरी

The child bought the book The Little Mermaid.

65. Merry (adj.) मे'रि–1. आनन्दित, प्रमुदित

Wish you a merry Christmas!

2. प्रसन्नचित, ज़िन्दालि

The merry laughter of children cheers up all.

66. Mess (n.) मे'स–1. गड़बड़ी, बखेड़ा, गंदगी

You will have to clear up this mess before you leave from here.

2. मेस, भोजनालय

Do you take your food from a mess?

67. Senior सीनिअर्–बड़ा, बड़ा (अधिकारी)

(adj.) Vagish is the senior of the two brothers.

(n.) We must consult our seniors.

68. Sensation (n.) सेन्सेशन–संवेदन

(n.) The news created a lot of sensation among the masses.

(adj.) The news channels feature only sensational stories these days.

69. Sense (n.) से'स–इंद्रिय, होश

We have five senses, a sense of smell, a sense of touch, a sense of hearing, a sense of seeing and a sense of taste.

No man in his senses behaves in a silly manner.

70. Sensible (adj.) सेन्सिबल–समझदार, तार्किक

No sensible person would disagree with you.

71. Sentence (n.) सेन्टे'न्स–1. वाक्य

The best sentence is the shortest one.

(v.) दण्ड देना/दंड

The thief was sentenced to one month's imprisonment.

(n.) The murdere was given the death sentence

72. Sentiment (n.) से 'न्टिम 'न्ट-मनोभाव, भाव

What were her sentiments about you?

(adj.) His approach towards this problem is sentimental.

73. Separate सेपरेट-1. अकेले

(adj.) They came into the room separately.

(v.) पृथक करना

Separate the good mangoes from the bad ones.

(adj.) पृथक

I cut the apple into two separate parts.

74. Septic (adj.) से 'प्टिक-विषाक्त

The wound turned septic.

75. Sequel (n.) सीक्वल-उत्तर कथा

The director is planning to make a sequel to the movie

76. Sequence (n.) सीक्वन्स्-क्रम

The editor ensures that the scenes of the movie are in correct sequence

77. Nut (n.) नॅट-1 गरी

Can you break this nut with your teeth?

2 ढिबरी

Bring some nuts and screws for repairing this door

78. Thrash (v.) थ्रैश-पीटना मारना

The mother will thrash the child if she catches him stealing the coins.

79. Thread थ्रे 'ड-धागा (डालना)

(v.) I will thread the needle

(n.) Have you a reel of black thread?

80. Threat थ्रे 'ट-धमकी (देना)

(v.) The teacher threatened to punish the whole class if there was any more noise

(n.) The gardener's threat to thrash the boys who steal the mangoes has frightened them away

81. Three (adj.) थ्री-तीन

Three little pigs had a race. The black pig came bird.

Three is an odd figure.

82. Thresh (v.) थ्रेश्-अनाज को गाहना

After harvesting, the crops were threshed to get the grains.

83. Threshold (n.) थ्रे 'शोल्ड-दहलीज़

As soon as we crossed the threshold of uncle's house, his dog barked loudly.

84. Thrift (n.) थ्रिफ्ट-मितव्ययिता, कमखर्ची

By continuous thrift, Vagish saved enough money to buy a bike.

(adj.) Mother taught us all to be thrifty.

85. Thrill थ्रिल-रोमांचित करना, पुलकित करना, रोमांच, पुलक

(n.) I can't forget the thrill of winning my first prize.

(adj.) It was a thrilling moment when the mother found her lost baby

(v.) The news that she had won a prize thrilled her parents

86. Thrive (v.) थ्राइव-फलना-फूलना

We thrive on fresh air and wholesome food.

87. Throat (n.) थ्रोट-गला, कंठ

The throat the front part of the neck

Wear a scarf lest you should get a sore throat

88. Throb (v.) थ्रॉब-धड़कना

If you run very fast, you heart will throb loudly.

89. Oven (n.) अॅवन-चूल्हा, तंदूर

My wife has bought an electric oven.

90. Every (adj.) एव्रि-प्रत्येक, हर एक, हर कोई

Students have to get up early everyday.

Have you arranged everything properly?

91. Evidence (n.) एविडन्स-सबूत, प्रमाण, गवाही, साक्ष्य

You cannot accuse your servant of theft without evidence.

Gopal's injured eye was an evidenece that he had a fight.

92. Evil ईव्ल-बुरा, अशुभ, बुराइयां

(adj.) You will not escape the consequences of yourt evil acts.

(n.) Try to recognise evil and improve yourself.

93. Exact (adj.) इग्ज़ैक्ट-सही, सुनिश्चित

Ram didn't know the exact location of his father's office.

(adv.) I left my office exactly at five o'clock.

94. Exaggerate (v.) इग्ज़ैजरेट-बढ़ा-चढ़ा कर कहना

He exaggerated his performance by comparing himself to Sachin Tendulkar.

95. Examine (v.) इग्ज़ैमिन-परीक्षा लेना, परखना, जाचना

The police examined the accident site

(n.) परीक्षा

After examination, results are eagerly awaited.

96. Example (n.) इग्ज़ाम्पल-1. उदाहरण दृष्टांत

Refer to the example if you cannot understand this question.

2. नमूना, आदर्श

Your conduct should be an example to the others.

97. Exceed (v.) इक्सीड-से अधिक होना, से आगे बढ़ जाना

Never exceed the permissible speed limit when you drive.

98. Will, Would (v.) विल-1. भविष्य सूचक, वुड-विल का भूतकालिक रुप

You will send me a letter, won't you?

She will not attend the marriage, will she?

I shall ask you the question you would not want to answer.

My friend told me that he would not reach in time.

2. (n.) संकल्प, अभिप्राय

You have no will of your own.

Great men have the will to succeed

3. उत्तम पुरुष की भविष्यत्काल की क्रिया, जिसमें 'अवश्य' का बोध होता है

Don't worry, I will reach there whatever happens.

4. (v.) अंतिम इच्छा के रुप में वसीयतनामा (लिखना)

Shanker had willed all his property to his only daughter.

(n.) Character is a perfectly educated will.

99. Willow (n.) विलो-एक वृक्ष जिसकी लकड़ी से बैट बनाए जाते हैं

Willow is mostly used for making cricket bats.

100. Wilt (v.) विल्ट-(पौधे का) मुरझाना, कुम्हलाना, सूख जाना

The scorching sun made the flowers in our garden wilt.

SPOKEN VOCABULARY
Set - 25

1. **Wily (adj.)** वाइलि- धूर्त चालाक

   Beware of her, she is cunning and wily

   He is a wily fellow never trust him

2. **Win (v. & n.)** विन-जीत (लेना) विजय (पाना) विजय

   (v.) Who will win the race?

   (n.) Our team has had three wins and two losses in this year's cricket tour naments.

3. **Wince (v.)** विन्स-दर्द से मुंह पर शिकन आ जाना

   I winced in pain when he held my hand tightly.

4. **Wind (v.)** वाइंड-1. टेढ़े-मेढ़े चलना

   The streams wind their way through the wood.

   I saw a winding track. It wound through the wood.

   2. लपेटना

   Wind the wire round this stick.

5. **Wind (n.)** विंड-पवन, हवा

   There was a strong wind yesterday and the leaves were blown off the trees.

   (adj.) It was a windly night. We could not sleep well.

6. **Window (n.)** विंडो-खिड़की, झरोखा

   The windows were open when it rained. The window-panes were smashed by the storm.

7. **Detest (v.)** डिटेस्ट-घृणा करना

   I detest boastful talk.

8. **Devastate** डेवस्टेट

   1. सर्वनाश करना

   (v.) The nuclear bomb devastated Hiroshima completely

   (n.) The city faced a total devastation because of the earthquake

   2. (adj.) अतिस्तब्ध

   He was devastated when he failed in exams.

9. **Develop (v.)** डिवेलप-1. बढ़ना, बढ़ाना

   Your son has developed into healthy young man.

   2. विकसित होना/करना

   Amit has developed a liking for coffee.

   3. फोटो को साफ करने के लिए कैमरा फ़िल्म को रासायनिक पदार्थों में डालना

   Rakesh didn't develop the film properly, so the photographs were spoilt.

   (n.) All of us should contribute for the development of our country.

10. **Device (n.)** डिवाइस-उपाय, साधन

    The scientist praised his students for the scientific devices made by them.

11. **Devil (n.)** डेव्ल-शैतान

    The child is a naughty little devil.

12. **Devoid (adj.)** डिवॉइड-विहीन

    She was devoid of words and did not know what to say.

13. **Devote (v.)** डिवोट- 1. दे देना, अर्पित करना

    During examination, sincere students devote more time to their studies.

    2. भक्ति, श्रद्धा करना

    The servant was devoted to his kind

master.

(n.) The followers of the saint held him in great devotion.

14. Remnant (n.) रे'म्नन्ट-बचा हुआ अंश

The remnants of the dinner will be fed to the dogs.

15. Remorse (n.) रिमॉर्स-पछतावा

The criminal expressed his remorse for his crimes.

16. Remote (adj.) रिमोट-बहुत पहले

Many Buddhist monuments were built in the remote past.

17. Remove (v.) रिमूव-1. उतारना, पृथक् करना

Please remove your shoes when you enter the temple.

2. हटाना

Will you remove the stain from my shirt?

18. Render (v.) रे'न्डर-देना, अर्पित करना

Doctors rendered their services free of charge at the charitable health check-up camp.

We hope to render certain services to your company.

19. Renew (v.) रिन्यू-(कोई काम) दुबारा करना, नया करना

We should renew our library mem bership for one more year.

We must renew the decorations of our shop.

(n.) The renewal of their contract gave them much satisfaction.

20. Vomit (v.) वॉमिट-उल्टी करना, वमन करना

She was seriously ill and began to vomit.

The chimney of the mill vomits black smoke.

21. Voracious (adj.) वरेशस-प्रचुर मात्रा में नई जानकारी प्राप्त करने का इच्छुक

He is a voracious reader and always carries a book with himself.

22. Renounce (v.) रिनरउन्स-त्याग देना

We renounced out plan to go on a vacation.

23. Renovate (v.) रिनवेट्-मरम्मत करना

I am getting my house renovated.

24. Pessimit (n.) पेसिमिस्ट-निराशावादी

Never be a pessimit always be an optimist

25. Pest (n.) प'स्ट्

1. कीट, पशु, पक्षी आदि

The farmer sprayed the pesticides to kill the pests.

2. चिढ़ पैदा करने वाला व्यक्ति

Her son is quite a pest.

25. Pester (v.) पे'स्टर्-परेशान करना

My child pestered me with questions.

Pet (n.) पे'ट-पालतू-पशु

We have two pets, a dog and a cat.

26. Petal (n.) पे'टल-पंखुड़ी

In the flower show, I saw roses with big petals.

27. Petition (n.) पटिशन-आवेदन, अर्ज़ी

The people of the locality sent a petition to the mayor asking for adequate supply of drinking water.

28. Petrified (adj.) पेट्रिफ़ाइड्-अत्यधिक भयभीत

We were petrified to encounter armed men in the house.

29. Petrol (n.) पेट्रोल-पेट्रोल

Do you have enough petrol in your car for a long trip?

30. Petty (adj.) पे'टि-क्षुद्र, तुच्छ

Why are you quarrelling over such a

petty thing?

31. Phantom (n.) फैन्टम-काल्पनिक भूत-प्रेत

I don't believe in the existence of phatoms.

32. Phase (n.) फेज़्-किसी वस्तु के विकास की अवस्था या चरण

Their relationship was going through a bad phase.

33. Bid (v.) बिड-बोली लगाना

Our company is also bidding for the land to be auctioned.

34. Big (adj.) बिग-बड़ा, लंबा-चौड़ा

They bought a big cake for their son's birthday.

35. Bill (n.) बिल-1. बिल

The shopkeeper gave me the bill and I paid the money.

2. चोंच

A stock has a long bill.

36. Billion (number) बिलियन-एक अरब

Hinduism has about one billion followers all over the world.

37. Billow (n.) बिलो-बड़ी लहर, लहराना

As the force of the tempest grew, the ocean became a mass of roaring billows.

38. Bin (n.) बिन-खत्ती, कूड़ा आदि डालने का स्थान

I threw the scraps of paper into the dust bin.

39. Bind (v.) बाइन्ड-बांधना

After the thief was caught, the policemen bound him with a rope.

40. Binoculars (n.) बाइनॉक्युलज़्-दूरबीन

The sailor looked through his binoculars to find the seashore.

41. Biography (n.) बाइऑग्रफि-जीवनी

I enjoyed reading the biography of Kishore Kumar.

42. Bird (n.) बर्ड-पक्षी, चिड़िया

Birds lay eggs in the nests.

43. Birth (n.) बर्थ-जन्म

Mrs. Kapur gave birth to a son this morning.

44. Bit (n.) बिट-टुकड़ा, अंश

The glass was broken into many bits.

45. Flood (n.) फ़्लड-1. बाढ़, ज्वार, मूसलाधार वर्षा

I could not go to Patna last year be cause of the floods there.

2. प्रचुरता, आधिक्य, अधिक

On becoming an IAS officer, Sheela received a flood of greeting cards.

(v.) The rain water flooded our street.

46. Floor (n.) फ़्लॉर-1. फ़र्श, जमीन

Don't throw the waste paper on the floor.

2. मंजिल, तल्ला

How many floors does your school building have?

47. Flop फ़्लॉप-असफल पुस्तक या फ़िल्म

(n.) The film was big flop.

(v.) The film flopped badly.

48. Flour (n.) फ़्लाउअर्-आटा, पिसान

Give me some flour to make bread.

49. Flourish (v.) फ़्लरिश-1. उन्नति करना, फलना-फूलना

I hear your business is flourishing.

2. घुमाना, हिलाना

Don't flourish your pen in my face.

50. Flow फ़्लो-प्रवाह, धारा, गति बहना

(n.) The flow of the river is swift in the hilly areas.

(v.) The river flows into the sea.

51. Flower (n.) फ़्लाउअ(र्)-फूल, पुष्प

For whom are you making a garland

of flowers?

52. Fluctuate (v.) फ़्लक्चुएट-उतार-चढ़ाव होना

The prices of shares keep on fluctuating.

53. Alive (adj.) अलाइव-ज़िन्दा, जीवित

Some people were still alive under the debris of a collapsed building

54. All ऑल-सब कुछ, सभी

(n.) Very few people come forward to sacrific their all for the country.

(adj.) I have read all the books on this subject

55. Allege (v.) अलेज्-बिना प्रमाण के आरोप लगाना

(v.) The lady alleged that he had attacked her

(n.) The lady put the allegation of an attack on him

(adv.) The lady was allegedly attacked by him

56. Allergy (n.) ऐलर्जि- एलर्जी

(n.) I have an allergy to pollen grains.

(adj.) I am allergic to pollen grains.

57. Alliance (n.) अलाइअन्स-मैत्री, सबंध

The two groups formed an alliance to oppose he government.

58. Allot (v.) अलॉट-अंश देना

We entered the room allotted to us

59. Allow (v.) अलाउ-अनुमति देना, होने देना

Please allow me to help you

60. Allowance (n.) अलाउअन्स- भत्ता

I give my son a monthly allowance for sundry expenses

61. All-round (adj.) ऑल-राउण्ड-अनेक कार्यों मे सक्षम

Virat Kholi is an all-round cricket player

62. All-time (adj.) ऑल-टाइम-सदैव का

This is my all-time favourite movie

63. Institute (n.) इन्स्टिट्यूट-1 संस्थान, पीठ

My son is a student at the Indian Institute of Technology.

2 (v.) प्रारंभ करना, स्थापित करना

An inquiry was instituted to investigate the corruption charges against the minister.

64. Instruct (v.) इन्स्ट्रक्ट-1. शिक्षा देना सिखलाना

The handicraft master instructed the girls in weaving.

2. (v.) आदेश, सूचना देना

Please instruct Vikas Verma to come to my office at 11 o'clock.

(n.) I gave my servant the necessary instructions for the party.

Who is the physical instructor at your school?

65. Instrument (n.) इन्स्ट्रुमन्ट-उपकरण, यन्त्र

Which musical instruments do you play?

66. Insult इन्सल्ट-अपमान, अनादर (करना)

(n.) Unable to bear the insult by his master, the servant at last left the job

(adj.) I felt insulted when he did not return my greetings

(v) The miser insulted his poor, needy friend.

67. Insurance (n.) इल्शॉरंस-बीमा

So you have a medical insurance?

68. Intellect (n.) इन्टलेक्ट-बुद्धि, प्रतिभा

Rabindra Nath Tagore was a person of great intellect.

Intellectuals think differently from the ordinary people.

(adj.) I feel happy in the company of

intellectual people.

69. Intelligence (n.) इन्टेलिजन्स-1. बुद्धि, समझ

You are a man of great intelligence.

2. समाचार, खबर

I run a journal devoted to economic intelligence.

3. सूचना

The police passed on the intelligence about the terrorist's movements to the army.

70. Intense (adj.) इन्टेन्स-तीव्र, प्रचण्ड, उत्तेजित, भावप्रवण

There was intense cold in Shimla.

(adv.) Rahul's grandmother dislikes non-veg food intensely

71. Intention (n.) इन्टेन्शन-इरादा, मंशा, अभिप्राय

I have no intention of going to cinema today.

72. Chance (n.) चान्स-1. अवसर, मौका

In the quiz contest, Arun was given three chances to give the right answer.

2. संयोग, दैवयोग

We met at a common friend's place by chance.

(v.) If you chance to meet Vishal, please tell him I am waiting for him here.

73. Change (v.) चेंज-1. बदल जाना या बदल देना

The boss changed his travelling plan at the last moment.

2. रेज़गारी, खुदरा

Do you have some change?

3. कपड़े बदलना

The guest wished to have a wash and a change.

74. Channel (n.) चैनल-नहर, जलमार्ग, मार्ग, माध्यम

The English Channel separates England from the the continent of Europe.

75. Chant चान्ट-धार्मिक गीत

(n.) A holy chant was echoing the temple.

(v.) The priests were chanting hymns in the temple

76. Chaos (n.) केऑस-अव्यवस्था

Heavy rains caused a chaos on the roads

77. Chapter (n.) चैप्टर्-अध्याय

The textbooks have many chapters.

78. Character (n.) कैरक्टर्-1 गुण, स्वभाव, चरित्र

Good character is a man's most precious possession.

2 पात्र

How many characters are there in this play?

79. Characteristic कैरक्टरिस्टिक-1. विशिष्ट लक्षण

(n.) A round dome is a major characteristic of Muslim architecture.

2. विशिष्टतासूचक

(adj.) She laughed her characteristic sarcastic laugh.

80. Charcoal (n.) चार्कोल-काठ कोयला

Charcoal is commonly used as a fuel in India.

81. Vote वोट-मत (देना), वोट (देना), चुनाव (करना)

(n.) Vote is the most important instrument of democracy

(v.) The panchayat member did not vote for the corrupt president.

82. Live (v.) लिव-1. रहना, निवास करना

Where do you live?

2. जीना, जीवित होना

Is your grandfather still living?

3 (n.) आजीविका

How do you earn your living?

83. Liver (n.) लिवर्-जिगर, यकृत

My doctor is treating me for liver trouble.

84. Load (n.) लोड-1. भार, बोझ

Can you carry this heavy load?

2. (v.) लादना

Have they loaded all our household items in the truck?

3. भरना

Have you loaded your gun?

85. Loaf (n.) लोफ़्-1. डबल रोटी

Go to the bakery and buy a loaf of bread.

2. (v.) आवारगर्दी में समय खराब करना

You do nothing but loaf in the streets.

86. Loan (n.) लोन-उधार, कर्ज़

Have you repaid the bank loan?

87. Loathe (v.) लोद-घृणा/नफरत करना

I loathe the very sight of him

88. Hole (n.) होल-छेद, कोटर

The burglars entered the house by making a hole in the rear wall

89. Holiday (n.) हॉलिडे-छुट्टी, अवकाश

Where are you going to spend your holidays?

90. Hollow (adj.) हॉलो-खोखला, पोला

Unlike a cricket ball, a football is hollow

Some pillars, when tapped, make a hollow sound.

91. Holy (adj.) होलि-पवित्र, पावन

I took my grandmother on a pilgrim age to holy places.

92. Homage (n.) होमिज-श्रद्धांजलि

The ministers gathered to pay homage to the dead Prime Minister.

93. Home (n.) होम-1. घर, (स्व) गृह, निवास, परिवार

Home is the best place to rest after a hard day's work.

2. आश्रम, केन्द्र

Have you seen the freedom fighters's home in Delhi?

(adj.) One who has no home is homeless.

94. Homesick (adj.) होमसिक-गृहासक्त

I always feel homesick whenever I go back to the hostel.

95. Honest (adj.) ऑनिस्ट्-सच्चा, सत्यवादी, ईमानदार

Our servant is very honest

What is your honest opinion on the corruption in our society?

(n.) Honesty is the best policy.

96. Honey (n.) हनि-शहद, मधु

Please give me a jar of honey.

97. Honk (v.) हौंक-कार का हॉर्न बजाना

The car honked loudly.

98. Message (n.) मे'सिज-संदेश

Please give him this message.

99. Messiah (n.) मसाइआ-मसीहा

He really proved to be a messiah for us in the middle of that chaos.

100. Metal (n.) मे'टल-धातु

Of what metal are these articles made?

SPOKEN VOCABULARY
Set - 26

1. **Method (n.)** मे'थड-ढग, तारीका रीति

By what method will you solve this sum?

2. **Mew (v.)** म्यू-म्याँव (करना)

I hear a cat mewing outside the door.

3. **Microphone (n.)** माइक्रोफोन-माइक. ध्वनिग्राहक

We could not hear your speech, as the microphone was not working properly.

4. **Microscope (n.)** माइक्रोस्कोप-सूक्ष्मदर्शी, खुर्दबीन

I could inspect the tiny insect only through a microscope.

5. **Midday (n.)** मिड्डे-मध्याह्न

I'll finish this work by midday

6. **Middle** मिडल-1. मध्य, दरमियानी बीच में

(n.) Don't disturb me in the middle of my work.

There was a pillar in the middle of the room.

2. (adj.) अधेड़

Who is that middle-aged gentleman?

7. **Sergeant (n.)** सार्जन्ट-सार्जेन्ट

My uncle was sergeant in the army.

8. **Serial (adj.)** सिरीअल-क्रमिक, क्रम संख्या

What is your serial number?

9. **Series (n.)** सिरीज़-माला, श्रृंखला, सिलसिला

My favourite publisher is coming up with a new series of romantic novels.

10. **Serious (adj.)** सीरिअस-1. गंभीर

One must be serious about one's career.

(adv.) My father is seriously ill.

2. महत्वपूर्ण

This is a serious issue and requires immediate action.

11. **Sermon (n.)** सर्मन-प्रवचन

A religious sermon changed his life completely.

12. **Serve (v.)** सर्व-1. सेवा करना सहायता करना

We should serve our nation selflessly.

My uncle served the country as a soldier for fifteen years.

2 परोसना

The dinner was served to each and every member of the family.

13. **Session (n.)** से'शन-अधिवेशन, बैठक, सत्र

The court is in session.

In the next session, we shall do an advance course.

14. **Set (n.)** से'ट-1. (रेडियो) सेट आदि

Have you purchased a radio set?

2. (v.) अस्त (होना)

The sun has set.

3. व्यवस्थित करना

The manager set the clerks to work and went to see the owner.

15. **Wine (n.)** वाइन-अंगूरी शराब, मदिरा

French wines are supposed to be very good.

16. **Wing (n.)** विंग-1. पंख, डैना

A bird has two wings. It flies with its wings.

An aeroplane has wings.

2. खंड, भाग

Students from the primary wing will be taken for a picnic.

3. (v.) उड़ना

The summer was over and the swallows were winging their ways away.

17. Wink विंक-झपकाना, पलक मारना, बहुत थोड़ा समय, झपकी

(v.) There is a time to wink as well as to see.

(n.) You have not slept a wink all day.

18. Winter (n.) विंटर्-शीत ऋतु, जाड़ा

Winter is a cold season. It is the coldest season in the western countries.

19. Wipe (v.) वाइप-पोंछना

Wipe the crockery w he tea cloth.

The table is wet, please wipe its top.

20. Wire (n. & v.) वाइअर्-तार, तार देना

Please don't forget to send me a wire.

Wire me to inform about the time of your arrival.

21. Wise (adj.) वाइज-बुद्धिमान, समझदार

We must listen to her advice, for she is a wise lady.

It was wise of the mother to keep her child indoors while he had a cold.

22. Throne (n.) थ्रोन-राजसिंहासन, राजगद्दी

The English are loyal to the throne.

(v.) The young queen was dethroned by rioters.

23. Throng (v.) थ्राँग-भीड़ लगाना, भीड़ से भर जाना

People thronged the roads.

24. Throttle (v.) थ्रॉटल-गला घुटना, घोटना

The tight collar of my overcoat is throttling me.

25. Through (prep.) थ्रू-(के) आर-पार, (के) पार, (के) दौरान

The sun shines through the day and moon shines through the night.

The accident happened through my own carelessness.

26. Throw (v.) थ्रो-फेंकना, गिराना

The horse threw its rider off.

Throw me the ball, I will kick it.

This information may throw light upon the mystery of the rich man's death.

27. Thrust (v.) थ्रॅस्ट-पेलना, ढकेलना

Hari thrust his hand into his pocket to find out how many coins were there.

28. Thumb (n.) थॅम-अंगूठा

We have two thumbs. The thumbs is the thickest of our fingers.

Illiterate persons put their thumb impressions as signature.

29. Thump (v.) थम्प-ज़ोर-ज़ोर से धड़कना

My heart was thumping with fear.

30. Thunder (n.) थन्डर्-1. गर्जन, बादलों की गरज

The lightning flashed and the thunder roared.

2. (v.) गड़गड़ाने की आवाज़ करना

This engine came thundering along the rails.

3. क्रोध में भरकर बोलना, गरजना

The manager thundered--- "Get out of here at once."

31. Thursday (n.) थर्सडे-बृहस्पतिवार

Thursday comes after Wednesday.

32. Thus (adv.) दॅस-इसलिए

We knew that he was dishonest, thus we did not believe him.

33. Phenomenal (adj.) फ़नॉमिनल्-उल्लेखनीय

She played a phenomenal role in taking the company to new heights.

34. Phenomenon (n.) फ़नॉमिनन्-प्राकृतिक या सामाजिक घटना

The arrival of monsoons is a natural phenomenon.

35. Philosophy (n.) फ़'लॉसफि-तत्त्वज्ञान, दर्शन (शास्त्र)

I was a student of philosophy in college.

Dr Radhakrishanan was a noted philosopher.

36. Phobia (n.) फ़ोबिआ-किसी वस्तु के प्रति अत्यधिक भय या घृणा

She has phobia for heights.

37. Phone (n.) फोन-फोन

Can I use your phone?

38. Photograph (n.) फोटोग्राफ़-फोटो

I took many photographs during my trip to Kashmir.

39. Phrase (n.) फ्रेज़-वाक्यांश

He is fond of using idiomatic phrases in his speeches.

40. Physical (adj.) फिजिकल-शारीरिक

A physical fitness certificate was re quired for the job.

41. Physician (n.) फ़िज़िशन-वैद्य, डॉक्टर

Is there a physician nearby?

42. Pick (v.) पिक-1. उठाना

Please pick up those pieces of paper.

2. चुनना

Please pick a good book for me.

43. Pickle (n.) पिकल्-अचार

Indian pickles have become popular abroad.

44. Picture (n.) पिक्चर्-चित्र, तस्वीर

His drawing room is decorated with beautiful pictures.

45. Picturesque (adj.) पिक्चरेस्क-आकर्षक

Kashmir had picturesque mountains.

46. Excel (v.) इक्सेल-से बढ़कर, होना, से उत्कृष्ट होना

In her dancing, Usha excelled all the other performers.

(adj.) The magazine cover had an excellent picture.

47. Except (prep.) इक्सेप्ट-1. को छोड़कर, के सिवाय

2. (n.) अपवाद

Exceptions are always there.

48. Excess (n.) इक्सेस-अतिक्रमण, असंयम, अतिरेक

Excess of flowery phrases lessens the impact of a serious article.

(adj.) He died of excessive drinking.

49. Exchange (n. & v.) इक्सचेन्ज-1. विनिमय करमान, आदान-प्रदान करना बदले में

(n.) I can give you my pen in exchange of your book.

(v.) The shopkeeper refused to exchange the shirt for any other item.

2. मिलान-केंद्र

Where is the telephone exchange?

50. Excite (v.) इक्साइट-भड़काना, उकसाना, उत्तेजित करना

The union leader's speech excited the workers.

(adj.) Students were excited about their educational tour to Goa.

(n.) What is all this excitement about?

51. Exclaim (v.) इक्स्क्लेम-चिल्ला उठना, चिल्लाना

Ravi exclaimed in surprise when he saw his long lost friend.

52. Exclude (v.) इक्सक्लूड-छोड़ देना

She was excluded from the volleyball team.

53. Excursion (n.) इक्स्कर्शन-सैर, भ्रमण

I took my family on an excursion to Suraj Kund.

54. Nutrition (n.) न्यूट्रिशन-पोषाहार

(n.) You should take care of your nutrition well.

(adj.) Milk has high nutritional value

(adj.) We should have nutritious food.

55. Devour (v.) डिवाउअर-निगल जाना, खा जाना, उड़ाना

Don't devour your food, chew it properly.

56. Devout (adj.) डिवाउट-श्रद्धालु, धर्मपरायण

My grandmother is a devout lady

57. Dew (n.) ड्यू-ओस

There were tiny drops of dew on the leaves in the morning.

58. Diabetes (n.) डाइअबिटीज़-मधुमेह

My grandfather was frobidden sweets as he was suffering from diabetes.

59. Diagnose (n.) डाइअग्नोज़-रोग की पहचान करना

He was diagnosed for typhoid.

60. Diagram (n.) डाइअग्रैम-रेखाचित्र

The child drew a diagram of water cycle.

61. Dial (n.) डायल- 1. डायल, घड़ी का सीधा रुख जिस पर घड़ी के घंटे, मिनट आदि के निशान लगे होते हैं।

The watch-maker changed the old dial of Uma's watch with a fancy one.

2. (v.) नंबर मिलाना, मापना

I dialled your number, but it was engaged

62. Dialect (n.) डाइअलेक्ट-बोली, उपभाषा

My wife understands our servant's dialect.

63. Dialogue (n.) डाइअलॉग

1. संवाद

She forgot her dialogue son the stage.

2. वार्तालाप

A dialogue between the board of directors would solve this problem.

64. Diamond (n.) डाइअमन्ड्-हीरा

The diamond ring looked very pretty on the bride's finger.

65. Diary (n.) डाइअरि-डायरी, दैनिकी

Ever since my school days, I am fond of writing a dairy.

66. Dice डाइस

1 पासा

(n.) I threw the dice and moved my piece five spaces ahead.

2. छोटे टुकड़ों में काटना

(v.) Dice the potatoes in small pieces.

67. Renown (n.) रिनाउन-1. प्रसिद्धि

He is a doctor of renown.

2. (adj.) Renowned - सुप्रसिद्ध

Ashoka was renowned king if India.

68. Rent (n.) रे'नन्ट-1. किराया

How much rent do you pay for your shop?

2. (v.) किराये पर देना

Will you rent this house?

3. किराये पर लेना

I rented this house two years ago.

69. Repair रिपेअर्-1. मरम्मत (करना)

(n.) The house is under repair.

Your watch is beyond repairs, you must buy a new one.

2. (v.) सुधारना, ठीक करना

The cobbler will repair our shoes.

Has your TV been repaired?

70. Repay (v.) रिपे-(राशि या कोई अन्य वस्तु) चुकाना

Have you enough money to repay

your debts?

We can never repay or mother for her kindness and effection.

71. Repeat (v.) रिपीट-1. दुबारा कहना

Her mother was almost deaf so I had to repeat my question.

2. दोहराना

Can you repeat what you said?

(adj.) I mad repeated attempts to see you.

(adv.) I have told you repeatedly not to be talkative.

72. Repel (v.) रिपेल-1. भार भगाना, पीछे धकेलना

The enemy's attack was repelled.

2. बुरा लगना

The way he ate with dirty hands and licked his finger repelled everybody.

73. Repent (v.) रिपे'न्ट-पछताना

If we repent, father will forgive us.

(n.) Is your repentance sincere?

74. Great (adj.) ग्रेट-1. महान्

For inspiration, we should read biographies of great men.

2. सुंदर

You look great in these clothes.

3. बड़ा, विशाल

Mumbai is the greatest city I have ever visited.

4. महत्वूपर्ण, खास

Are you and Prakash great friends?

75. Greedy (adj.) ग्रीडि-लोभी, लालची

We all are greedy for fortune's favours.

The greedy dogs gobbled up their food quickly.

(adv.) Don't swallow your food greedily.

76. Green (adj.) ग्रीन-1. हरा, हरित, हरा-भरा

The green saree in the showcase was very expensive.

2. स्वागत करना

The principal's speech was greeted with a loud applause by the students.

77. Grey (adj.) ग्रे-सलेटी, धुंधला

Your hair has started turning grey.

78. Grief (n.) ग्रीफ़्-दु:ख, व्यथा, शोक

On the death of Anuj's father, his neighbour came to console him in his hour of grief.

79. Grim (adj.) ग्रिम-1. भयंकर, कराल, डरावना

Why are you looking so grim?

2. दृढ़, कड़ा

If you want to succeed against heavy odds, you must have grim determination.

80. Grin गिन-दाँत निकालना, मुस्कराना, खीस, मुस्कराहट

(n.) He has a happy grin on his face.

(v.) She didn't answer me but only grinned.

81. Over ओवर्-1. ऊपर, पार

(prep.) The boys climed over the fence.

2. ऊपर, पर (अधिकार में)

I always sleep with the blanket over my face

Who is over in your department?

3. (adj.) खत्म, समाप्त

When will the show be over?

4. फिर

Please go through the sum over and over again

5. अधिक, अतिरिक्त

Over five hundred people attended the function.

82. Fluent (adj.) फ़्लूअंट-धाराप्रवाह, प्रवाही

Sohan is fluent in French.

(adv.) Gurmeet can speak four lan guages fluently.

83. Fluid (n.) फ्लूइड-1. तरल पदार्थ

What is this golden-coloured fluid in the bottle?

2. (adj.) अस्थिर, आसानी से बदला जा सकने वाला

The picnic programme is still fluid.

84. Flute (n.) फ्लूट-बांसुरी

Krishna enchanted everyone by his flute.

85. Flutter (v.) फ़्लटर्-फड़फड़ाना, मंडराना

I watched a sparrow fluttering its wings.

86. Fly (v.) फ़्लाइ-1. उड़ना, उड़ाना

At what speed does a jet plane fly?

2. भाग जाना

It is very late, I must fly home.

3. (n.) मक्खी, मक्षिका

Don't let flies sit on your food.

87. Foam (n.) फ़ोम-झाग, फेन

Does this soap give a lot of foam?

88. Focus (v.) फ़ोकस-ध्यान लगाना

Focus on the work you are doing and you will always succeed.

89. Fodder (n.) फ़ॉडर-चारा

His father asked him to cut fodder for the cattle.

90. Foe. फ़ो-दुश्मन, शत्रु

You should be able to distinguish between friends and foes.

91. Fog (n.) फ़ॉग-कोहरा, धुंधलका

Ships cannot sail safely in the fog.

(adj.) Don't drive in the foggy weather.

92. Bitter (adj.) बिटर्-1. स्वाद में कड़वा, कटु

This medicine is very bitter.

2. दुःखी, संतप्त

The servant was bitter about the rude behaviour of his cruel master.

93. Black (adj.) ब्लैक-काला

Please give me a bottle of black ink.

94. Blade (n.) ब्लेड-1. धार

This knife has a sharp blade.

2. पत्ती

Not even a blade of grass grows in this field.

95. Blame ब्लेम-निन्दा (करना), दोष (देना या करना)

(v.) The bus driver was blamed for the accident.

(n.) Everybody put the blame on him.

96. Blank (adj.) ब्लैंक-कोरा, खाली

She took out a blank sheet of paper to write.

97. Blanket (n.) ब्लैंकिट-कम्बल, आवरण

As winter is nearing, I must buy a blanket.

98. Blare (v.) ब्लेअर्-गरजना, चिल्लाना, चिल्लाहट

During the traffic jam, the car horns blared full blast.

99. Blast (n.) ब्लास्ट-1. धमाका, विस्फोट

The blast of the motorist's horn startled the pedestrian.

The blat of the explosion shook the whole building.

2. झोंका, झकोरा

As Arun opened the door, he was thrown back by a blast of wind.

(v.) धमाके से फटना

A bomb blasted in the market this morning.

100. Blaze (n.) ब्लेज़्-चमक, ठाट-बाट, ज्वाला

The decorated hall was a blaze of light.

(v.) The bonfire blazed brightly in the

SPOKEN VOCABULARY
Set - 27

1. **Blazer (n.)** ब्लेज़र्-रंगीन जाकेट

   All the members of the cricket team wore blazers.

2. **Allure** अलुअर्-प्रलोभन, आकर्षण

   (n.) The allure of working in a foreign country can never fade.

   (v.) Big cities always allure people of small towns.

3. **Ally (n.)** ऐलाइ-सखा, सहायक, मित्र

   England and America were allies in the second world war.

4. **Almighty (n.)** ऑलमाइटि-सर्वशक्तिमान

   Have faith in Almighty and do your best.

5. **Almost (adv.)** ऑल्मोस्ट-लगभग, करीब-करीब

   The little boy walked almost four miles treach home.

6. **Alms (n.)** आम्ज्-भीख भिक्षा

   The rich lady distributed alms among the beggars.

7. **Alone** अलोन-अकेला, एकाकी, सिर्फ, केवल

   (adv.) She was afraid to go out alone in the dark.

   (adj.) The general alone could give the order to attack.

8. **Along (prep.)** अलॉन्ग-साथ-साथ, समानान्तर

   He followed the path along the river.

9. **Aloud (adv.)** अलाउड-ज़ोर से, ऊंचे स्वर में

   He spoke aloud so that I could hear him.

10. **Already (adv.)** ऑलरेडि-पहले ही, पहले से ही

    Our guests have already arrived.

11. **Also** ऑलूसो-भी, साथ ही

    (adv.) When Anil came, Anita also came.

    (conj.) She not only plays piano, but also writes songs.

12. **Intern (n.)** इंटर्न-इंटर्न

    She worked in the hospital as an intern for six months.

13. **Interest (n.)** इन्ट्रस्ट-1. रुचि, रस

    Most Indians take a keen interest in the game of cricket.

    2. ब्याज, सूद

    At what interest did the bank give you the loan?

    (v.) I am not interested in gossip.

14. **Interfere (v.)** इन्टरफ़िअर्-दखल देना, बाधा डालना

    I could have finished my homework by now if you had not interfered.

    (n.) Nobody likes interference in personal affairs.

15. **Interior (adj.)** इन्टिअरिअर्-भीतरी, आंतरिक

    I live in the interior of the town.

16. **Internal (adj.)** इन्टर्नल-अन्दरुनी, आन्तरिक

    Have you completed the internal audit of your firm?

17. **Interpret (v.)** इन्टर्प्रिट-समझना, अर्थ लगाना, दुभाषिया का काम करना

    Can you interpret Russian into Hindi?

18. **Interrupt (v.)** इन्टरप्ट-बीच में बोलना या रोकना

    Amit's illness interrupted his studies.

19. **Intervene (v.)** इन्टरवीन-टोकना

    She intervened and suggested an easy solution to the problem.

20. **Charge** चार्ज-1. आरोप

    The police arrested the servant on a charge of theft.

2. भाड़ा, शुल्क

What will be your charge for repairing my watch.

3. (v.) निगरानी, देखरेख, उत्तरदायित्व

I would like to see an honest person in charge of the office.

4. हमला करना

The soldiers charged the enemy.

21. Chariot (n.) चैरिअट

The king stopped his chariot outside the castle.

22. Charisma (n.) करिज़्मा-आकर्षण

We were instantly charmed by her charisma.

23. Charity (n.) चैरिटि-सद्भाव, उदारता, परोपकार

The rich man gave away his wealth in charity.

(adj.) Homeopathy dispensaries are mostly charitable (free).

Ram has a charitable (kind) disposition.

24. Charm (n.) चार्म-1. तावीज़

Arun wears a charm round his wrist.

2. आकर्षण, सौजन्य

Rekha is a lady with great charm.

3. प्रसन्न करना

Rakhi will charm you with her sunny smile.

25. Chart चार्ट-1. रेखाचित्र

(n.) We prepared a chart on environmental problems.

2. किसी घटना के विकास का विस्तारपूर्वक वर्णन

(v.) The book charts the growth and development of India cinema over the years.

26. Voucher (n.) वाउचर्-खर्च का पर्चा, वाउचर

Have you signed your slary voucher?

Am I not entitled to a gift voucher?

27. Lobby (n.) लॉबि-लॉबी, प्रतीक्षा कक्ष

Does this door open into the lobby?

28. Local (adj.) लोकल-1. स्थानीय, मुकामी

Where is the local bus stop?

2. थोड़ी सी जगह पर

The injury was local and was cured in two or three days.

(adv.) Is this electric kettle locally made?

29. Lock लॉक-ताला (लगाना)

(v.) Do not forget to lock the safe.

(n.) I bought a new lock for my cupboard.

30. Locate (v.) लॉकेट-स्थापित, ठिकाने का पता लगाना

(v.) Have you been able to locate the lost book?

(adj.) Where is your house located?

31. Locomotive (n.) लोकमोटिव-इंजन

Does our country export locomotive?

32. Lodge (v. & n.) लॉज-1. रहना, ठहरना

I am lodging with my aunt these days.

2. (n.) झोंपड़ी, रहने की जगह, छोटा घर

When I go for hunting, I stay in a lodge in the forest.

33. Lofty (adj.) लॉफ़्टि-1. ऊँचा, उत्तुंग

Our old mansion has a lofty ceiling.

2. उच्च, उत्कृष्ट

I appreciate your lofty ideals.

34. Log (n.) लॉग-लट्ठा, कुन्दा

Put a log in the fire.

35. Honorary (adj.) ऑनररि-अवैतनिक

He is the honorary president of this organisation.

36. Honour (n. & v.) ऑनर्-1. प्रतिष्ठा, इज्जत, ईमानदारी, सम्मान (करना),

बात रखना

It was a great honour for a boy from the far-off hills to be rewareded for his bravery in Delhi.

Will you give me your word of honour?

2. उपाधि

My friend's name has figured in this year's Republic Day Honours List.

(v.) Honour your word.

37. Hood (n.) हुड-1. टोप, शिरोवेष्टन

I want to buy a raincoat with a hood.

2. टप, बरसाती

These days you hardly see a car with a folding hood.

38. Hoof (n.) हुफ़-खुर, टाप

As the horseman approached, I could hear its hoof-beats.

39. Hook (n. & n.) हुक-काँटा, खूंटी, कंटिया से बाँध ना / पकड़ना

(v) The fisherman sat all day on the river bank but hooked only three fish.

(n.) Have you fixed a hook in the bathroom for hanging a towel?

40. Hooligan (n.) हूलिगन-उपद्रवी

Th boys were behaving like hooligans on the Holi festival.

41. Hoop (n.) हूप-धातु या प्लास्टिक का बड़ा छल्ला

Hang the towel in the metal hoop.

42. Might (n.) माइट-1. शक्ति, सामर्थ्य

I tried with all my might to move the heavy load.

2. May का भूतकाल

He might have returned home.

43. Migrate (v.) माइग्रेट-प्रवास करना

Both his sons have migrated to the foreign country in search of better opportunities.

44. Mild (adj.) माइल्ड-1. कोमल, सौम्य, नरम

You always speak in a mild manner.

2. सुहावना

The weather is mild today.

3. हल्का

It was the first offence of that woman, so she was given a mild sentence.

45. Mile (n.) माइल-मील

I walk a couple of miles every morning.

46. Military (adj. & n.) मिलट्रि-सैनिक, फ़ौजी, सेना, फ़ौज

(adj.) Do you get military training in your school?

(n.) Strict discipline is followed in the military.

47. Milk (n.) मिल्क-दूध, दुग्ध

I take a glass of milk every morning.

48. Mill (n.) मिल-चक्की, कारखाना, मिल

How many textile mills are there in your city?

49. Millennium (n.) मिलेनिअम-सहस्त्राब्दी

Amitabh Bachchan was awarded with the title of the star of the millennium.

50. Million (adj.) मिल्यन-दास लाख, दशलक्ष

The tennis champion earned milions of dollars.

I learn your guest is a millionaire.

51. Settle (v.) से'टल-1. फैसला करना

The two parties settled in West Punjab.

2. बस जाना

Our forefathers had settled in West Punjab.

(n.) We came to a settlement with one another.

Our forefathers were among the first settlers in Fiji.

52. Seven (adj.) से'वन-सात

There are seven days in a week.

53. Several (adj.) से'व्रल-कुछेक, कई, अनेक

I requested you several times but you did not care.

The workers had put forth several demands but none of them was fulfilled.

54. Severe (adj.) सिविअर्-सख्त, कड़ा, कठोर, तीव्र, कठिन

The burn caused me severe pain.

My father is just recovering from a severe illness.

55. Sew (v.) सो-सीना

Mother can sew expertly.

She sews bottuns on Gita's coat.

Rajni is sewing a dress for her doll.

56. Sex (n.) से'क्स-यौन, लिंग

Every citizen of India enjoys equal rights

irrespective of his/her sex.

Modern movies are full of sex and violence.

57. Shabby (adj.) शैबि-1. फटा-पुराना, जीर्ण-शीर्ण

My skirt is shabby. I want to buy a new one.

2. दुर्व्यवहार

Vivek's treatment of his friends is very shabby.

58. Shade (n.) शेड-1. छाया

The cow is lying in the shade of a tree.

2. थोड़ा अंतर, रंग के प्रकार

There were many shades of opinion among the friends.

Give me a lighter shade of blue.

59. Wish (adj.) विश्-इच्छा, कामना (करना), इच्छा (करना) चाहना

(v.) I wish I were a king!

(n.) If a man could have half the wishes, he would doubles his troubles.

If wishes were horses, beggars might ride.

60. Wistful (adj.) विस्टफुल-उदासी भरा

The writer gave a wistful singh on getting the rejection letter.

61. Wit (n.) विट्-बुद्धि, समझ, हाज़िर जवाबी

Wit without employment is a disease.

(adj.) My uncle is a very witty person.

62. Witch (n.) विच-डाइन, जादूगरनी

In fairy tales, witches have very important roles.

63. With (prep.) विद-के साथ, के पास, सहित

Bring your brother with you.

With the arrival of the President, the Republic Day function started.

We saw a policeman with a rod in his hand.

Never find faults with others.

64. Withdraw (v.) विदड्रॉ-बैंक के खाते से पैसे निकालना

Withdraw a sum of Rs. 5000 from the bank next week.

65. Wither (v.) विदर्-पौधों का मुरझा जाना

The leaves withered away in autumn.

66. Thwart (v.) थ्वॉट-कोई बात न होने देना

The work pressure at office thwarted my vacation plans.

67. Tick (v.) टिक-निशान लगाना

The manager ticked the names of the employees who had been late in the morning.

68. Ticket (v.) टिकिट-टिकट

Always buy a ticket when you travel by bus or train.

69. Tickle (n.) टिकल्-गुदगुदाना

Baby laughs when mother tickles his toes.

70. Tide (n.) टाइड-ज्वार-भाटा, लहर

At low tide, the sea falls and goes far out.

Time and tide wait for none.

71. Tidy टाइडि-साफ़-सुथरा (रखना), सुव्यवस्थित

(adj.) Asha always keeps her room tidy.

(v.) She is tidying her room.

72. Piece (n.) पीस-टुकड़ा, अंश

I tore the letter into small pieces.

73. Pierce (n.) पिअर्स-छेदना, भेदना

These days many girls have their noses pierced so that they may were nose-rings.

74. Piggy bank (n.) पिगी बैंक-बच्चों की ग़ोलक

The child dropped the one-rupee coin the piggy bank.

75. Pigheaded (adj.) पिग-हेडिड-अड़ियल

The child was pigheaded enough not to acknowledge his mistake.

76. Pile (n. & v.) पाइल-ढेर, राशि, ढेर लगाना

(n.) Please give this pile of dirty clothes to the washerman.

(v.) She piled up all her clothes on the bed before packing them.

77. Pilgrim (n.) पिल्ग्रिम-तीर्थ-यात्री

During my trip to Amarnath, I saw many pilgrims making the journey to the holy cave barefoot.

78. Pill (n.) पिल-गोली

Nowadays there is a pill for almos every ailment.

80. Pillar (n.) पिलर्-खम्भा

The pillars of the old palace were painted in gold.

81. Excuse (v.) इक्स्क्यूज़्-1. माफ़ करना

Please excuse me for being late.

2. छुटकारा देना, से मुक्त करना

You will have to excuse me from coming to the meeting, as I am not well.

3. (n.) बहाना

What is your excuse for being late?

82. Execute (v.) एक्सिक्यूट-1. पूरा करना, पालन करना, निष्पन्न करना

At the public rally, the VIP security plan was executed efficiently.

2. फाँसी देना

The murderer was executed early this morning.

83. Exercise एक्सर्साइज़्-1. व्यायाम, कसरत करना

(n.) You must take exercisse to keep fit.

(v.) We can exercise our brain as well as the body.

2. अभ्यास

Most students could not do the exercise given by the geometry teacher.

84. Exert (v.) इग्ज़ट-प्रसास करना

You will have to exert yourself to pass the tough examination with good marks.

85. Exhaust इग्ज़ॉस्ट-1. पूरी तरह समाप्त होना, करना

(v.) The explorers had exhausted their food-supply before the rescue party arrived.

2. (adj.) पूरी तरह से थक जाना

After a hard day's work, it's natural to

feel exhausted.

86. Exhibit इग्ज़िबिट-1. प्रदर्शित करना, प्रदर्शित वस्तु

(v.) At which art gallery are you going to exhibit your paintings?

(n.) Among exhibits at the show was a rare antique piece.

2. प्रदर्शनी

Have you visited the exhibition of handloom fabrics?

87. Exist (v.) इग्ज़िस्ट-होना, अस्तित्व रखना

Man cannot exist without air and water.

(n.) Tell me, which is the largest animal in existence?

88. Dictate (v.) डिक्टेट-1. लिखाना, लिखवाना

The teacher dictated a poem, and the students wrote it down.

2. हुक्म चलाना, आदेश देना

You cannot befriend people if you dictate to them.

(n.) Take this dictation and type it fast.

89. Dictionary (n.) डिक्शनरि-शब्दकोश

We should refer to a dictionary if we do not know the meaning of a word.

90. Die (v.) डाइ-मरना मर जाना, बुझ जाना

Last evening, a man died in a car accident.

91. Diet (n.) डाइअट- 1. आहार, भोजन, पथ्य

Wheat is the staple diet of North Indians.

2. स्वास्थ्य सुधारने के लिए विशिष्ट पदार्थ विशिष्ट मात्रा में रखना

Rekha was dieting to get slim.

92. Difference (n.) डिफ़रन्स-भेद, फ़रक

There should be no difference between what you say and what you mean.

93. Difficult (adj.) डिफ़िकल्ट-कठिन, मुश्किल

Many consider Maths a difficult subject.

(n.) Life these days is full of difficulties.

94. Dig (v.) डिग-खोदना, खोज निकालना

Why are you digging a hole in your own garden?

95. Digest (v.) डाइजेस्ट- 1. पचाना, हज़म करना

I cannot digest spicy food.

2. (n.) सार/संक्षेप

Please prepare a digest of this article.

96. Dignity (n.) डिग्निटि-प्रतिष्ठा, महिमा, गौरव, शान, आनबान

We should accept the dignity of labour.

Always receive your guests with dignity.

(adj.) Be dignified in your behaviour always.

97. Digress (v.) डाइग्रेस-मुख्य विषय से हटना

Let's not digress from the main point of the discussion.

98. Replace (v.) रिप्लेस-1. बदलना, बदलकर देना

These cells are defective, kindly replace them.

2. लौटाना, (पहले वाली जगह पर) लाना या रखना

We can take the magazine down from the shelf, but after reading we must replace it.

3. (की जगह पर) लेना

Hamid is unwell, so he has been re placed with Majid in the team.

99. Replenish (v.) रिप्लेनिश-पुनर्भरण करना

The only way to replenish the shortage of greenery is by plantation of trees.

100. Replete (adj.) रिप्लीट-परिपूर्ण

The book is replete with pictures.

SPOKEN VOCABULARY
Set - 28

This book seems to be a replica of a famous novel.

2. **Grind (v.)** ग्राइन्ड-पीसना, रगड़ना

The miller grinds the corn into flour.

We grind a knife to sharpen it.

3. **Grip** ग्रिप-1. पकड़, दिलचस्प होना

(n.) The thief could not free himself from the firm grip of Ram's hand.

(adj.) The film we saw today had a gripping plot.

2. (v.) पकड़, कसकर पकड़ना

Grip the bag firmly, lest it should fall.

4. **Groan** ग्रोन-कराहना

(n.) The sick man's groans moved my heart.

(v.) I groaned in pain when I fell down the staircase.

5. **Grocer (n.)** ग्रोसर-पंसारी

Some grocers keep their profits to the bare minimum.

6. **Groom (n.)** ग्रूम-1. दुल्हा, वर

You are dressed up like a groom.

2. साईस

Have you engaged a groom to look after your horse?

3. (v.) सिखाना, सँवारना

It is easy to groom an in experienced worker.

7. **Groove (n.)** ग्रूव-खाँचा, नाली

The door of my wardrobe slides into a groove.

8. **Grope (v.)** ग्रोप-टटोलना, ढूंढना

9. **Gross (adj.)** ग्रोस-घोर, भारी, मोटा

The minister's act of giving undue favours was a gross misuse of his authority.

10. **Ground (n.)** ग्राउण्ड-1. भूमि, ज़मीन, मैदान

Our school has a large cricket ground.

My house stands on a flat ground.

2. आधार, कारण, मूल

The judge was not convinced by the grounds given by the lawyer for his client's bail.

3. (v.) पिसा हुआ, पीसा (Grind का भूतकाल)

She ground spices.

(adj.) Fresh ground coffee beans smell very pleasant

11. **Overwhelming (adj.)** ओवर्वेल्मिंग-तीव्र

I felt an overwhelming need for solitude.

12. **Alter (v.)** ऑल्टर्-बदल देना, हेरफेर करना

The tailor altered David's old coat to fit him.

13. **Alternate (adj.)** ऑल्टर्नेट-एक छोड़कर एक

We have our classes on alternate days.

14. **Alternative** ऑल्टर्नेट-विकल्प

(n.) Is there any alternative to this plan?

(adj.) These days, people have little faith on alternative medicine.

15. **Although** (conj.) ऑलूदो-हालांकि, यद्यपि

He ran fast although his leg was injured.

16. Altogether (adv.) ऑलटुगेद्र–पूर्ण रुप से, पूर्णतया

Altogether, at home and in the bank, I have five thousand rupees.

17. Always (adv.) ऑल्वेज–हमेशा, सर्वदा

He is always busy.

18. A.M. ए.एम–दोपहर के बारह बजने से पहले

My office starts at 10.00 A.M.

19. Amateur (n.) ऐमटर्–नौसिखिया, अव्यवसायी

The amateur althetes surprisingly put up a good show in comparison to the professional ones.

20. Amaze (v.) अमेज़्–चकित या विस्मित करना

The child wrestler's great strength amazed everybody.

21. Ambassador (n.) ऐम्बैसडर्–राजदूत

Ambassadors' role is quite significant in projecting their country's good im age to the outside world.

22. Ambience (n.) ऐम्बिअन्स–माहौल

Dim lights and soft music were providing a romantic ambience.

23. Foil (n.) फ़ॉइल–वर्क

Mother wrapped the chapattis in aluminium foil.

24. Fold फ़ोल्ड–लपेटना, तह, परत

(v.) Fold this letter and put it in an envelope.

(n.) The invitation card had three folds.

25. Folk (n.) फ़ोक–लोक, जनता, जनसाधारण

The country folk were very kind to me.

26. Follow (v.) फ़ॉलो–1. पीछे–पीछे चलना

Follow me into my room.

2. समझना

Do you follow your professor's lectures?

27. Folly (n.) फ़ॉलि–मूर्खता, बेवकूफी

It was a folly on Ashok[s part to turn down a nice job offer.

28. Fond (adj.) फ़ॉन्ड–शौकीन, प्रिय

My little son is fond of pastries.

29. Interview (n.) इन्टर्व्यू–1. साक्षात्कार

Have you received a call for interview?

2. मुलाकात, भेंट

(n.) The paper carried a report on the Prime Minister's interview given to the BBC.

(v.) The veteran journalist interviewed many celebrities during his long career.

30. Intimate (adj.) इन्टिमट–1. घनिष्ठ, जिगरी

Are you and Sunil intimate friends?

2. (v.) सूचना देना, संकेत करना

Will you intimate me the time of your arrival?

31. Intimidate (v.) इन्टिमिडेट्–डराना या धमकाना

I was intimidated by the unknown person following me.

32. Intricate (adj.) इन्ट्रिकट–डराना या धमकाना

Extracting silk from a silkworm is an intricate process.

33. Bleach (v.) ब्लीच–रंगहीन करना, साफ़ करना

Ladies with a dark complexion often bleach their skin to look fair.

34. Bleak (adj.) ब्लीक–उजाड़, ठंडा, रुखा, कठोर

A bleak wind blew over the mountain top.

Geeta's bleak face indicated that something was wrong with her.

35. Bleary (adj.) ब्लियरि-थकी हुई लाल आंखों वाली

He looked bleary-eyed with her.

36. Bleat (v.) ब्लीट-मिमियाना

The sheep bleated in the field.

37. Bleed (v.) ब्लीड-रक्त निकलना या निकालना

His wound was bleeding.

38. Blemish ब्लेमिष-धब्बा

(n.) The pimple left a blemish on her face.

(v.) The politician's corrupt behaviour blemished the image of the party.

39. Blend ब्लेन्ड-मिश्रण, मिलाना मिश्रण करना मिल जाना

(n.) In the evening the sky appeared a beautiful blend of colours

(v.) The painter blended the colours before starting to paint

40. Bless (v.) ब्लेस-आशीर्वाद देना

The temple priest blessed the devotees.

(n.) The painter blended the colours before starting to paint.

41. Blind (adj.) ब्लाइण्ड-1. अंधा, नेत्रहीन, विवेकशून्य

She felt pity for the blind beggar.

(n.) परदा

She pulled down the blinds to avoid the light.

42. Charter (n.) चार्टर्-घोषणापत्र, अधिकारपत्र

The textile workers presented a charter of demands to the goverment.

2. (v.) किराए पर लेना

The millionaire chartered a plane for his business tours.

43. Chase (v. & n.) चेस-पीछा करना, पीछे पड़ना

(v.) The policeman chased the thief.

(n.) The policeman gave the thief a good chase.

44. Chat (v.) चैट-गपशप करना

The two friends sat chatting for a long time.

(n.) The chat of two old friends was quite long.

45. Chatter (v. & n.) चैटर्-चहक/बकबक करना

The talkative took us to the venue within an hour

46. Chauffeur (n.) शोफर्-कार का वतन भोगी ड्रावर

The chauffeur took us to the venus within an hour

47 Vow (n.) वाउ व्रत मन्नत, मनोती, प्रतिज्ञा, वायदा

A newly married man and woman take vows to love and cherish each other.

48. Logic (n.) लॉजिक-तर्क

(n.) There was no logic in his answer.

(adj.) His answer was completely logical.

49. Logo (n.) लोगो-लोगो

We should change the logo of our company and make it catchier.

50. Loiter (v.) लॉइटर्-मटरगश्ती करना

He spends all this day loitering around the college campus.

51. Lonely (adj.) लोन्लि-अकेला और उदास

• I felt so lonely after her departure.

52. Loner (n.) लोनर्-एकांतप्रिय

He is an eccentric loner and never meets anyone.

53. Long (adj.) लॉन्ग-1. लम्बा

Draw a line four inches long.

2. (adv.) देर तक

How long will you be away?

3. दीर्घकालीन

I have not seen you for a long time.

(v.) तरसना, लालायित होना

I have to go on a long holiday.

54. Look लुक-1. दृष्टि (डालना), देखना

(v.) Look at this picture.

2. खोजना

Are you looking for someone?

3. प्रतीत होना, लगना

Sushila looked charming at the party.

(n.) There was a look of surprise on his face.

55. Loom (n.) लूम-1. करघा

(n.) Is this hand-loom cloth?

2. (v.) अस्पष्ट या धुँधला दिखाई देना

As we sat on the seashore, a ship loomed into sight.

56. Hop (n. & n.) हॉप-1. कूदना, उछलना, उड़ान

(n.) The child was curiously watching the sparrows hopping from one branch to the other.

(v.) We flew from London to U.S.A. in one hop.

57. Hope (n.) होप-1. आशा (करना)

(v.) Hope for the best and he prepared for the worst.

2. उम्मीद (करना), भरोसा (रखना)

I hope you will be able to come to my home this evening.

(n.) Hope never dies in human heart.

(adj.) Your handwriting is hopeless.

58. Horde (n.) हॉर्ड-भीड़

A horde of people arrived at the election booth.

59. Horizon (n.) हॉरिअज़न-क्षितिज, दिगन्त, सीमा

As we sat on the seashore, we saw a ship on the horizon.

(adj.) Draw a horizontal (as against vetical) line.

60. Mince (v.) मिन्स-क़ीमा करना, काटकर टुकड़े-टुकड़े करना

I want to buy half a kilogram of minced meat.

61. Mind (n.) माइन्ड-1. मन, चित्त

Is your mind in your job?

2. इरादा, विचार

I thought I would return the same day but now I have changed my mind.

3. (v.) (पर) ध्यान देना, चिंता करना, बुरा मानना

Don't mind what he says. Never mind.

4. देखरेख करना

Who minds your child when you are away?

5. आपत्ति करना, आपत्ति होना

Would you mind if I smoke?

62. Mine माइन-1. मेरा

(pron.) That book is your] this one is mine.

2. (n.) खान, खदान

During our tour to Bihar, we visited a coal mine.

63. Mingle (v.) मिन्गल-मिलाना, मिलना-जुलना

Some policemen in plain clothes mingled with the crowd.

I like to mingle with all sorts of people.

64. Miniature (n.) मिनएचर्-लघुरुप

She made a miniature of Hawa Mahal.

65. Minimum (adj.) मिनिमम-कम से कम, अल्पतम

The trade union demanded an

increase in the minimum wages.

Who promises to give the maximum value at the minimum price?

66. Minister (n.) मिनिस्टर्-मंत्री

A close friend of mine has now become a minister in the cabinet.

67. Minor (adj.) माइनर्-मंत्री

Don't bother me about such minor matters.

2. (n.) नाबालिग्, अल्पवयस्क, अवयस्क

My son can't vote, as he is still a minor.

68. Shadow (n.) शैडो-1. छाया

Shadows grow longer towards evening.

2. (v.) पीछा करना

The fugitives were shadowed by the police.

69. Shake (v.) शेक-हिलाना, झिंझोड़ना, झकझोरना

If you don't wake up, I shall shake you up.

The earthquake has shaken the foundations of the house.

70. Shallow (adj.) शैलो-उथला

This pond is too shallow to swim in.

We can't swim in shallow water.

71. Sham (n.) शैम-झूठा, असत्य

His illness is merely a sham, he is quite well.

(v.) She was not hurt, she was only shamming.

72. Shame (n.) शेम-लज्जा, शर्म, हया

Shame is worse than death.

73. Shampoo शैम्पू-शैम्पू करना, (बाल) साफ़ करना

(v.) You must shampoo your hair, it is very dirty.

(n.) I shall buy a shampoo.

74. Shape शेप-रुप, आकृति, आकृति देना

(n.) What is the shape of his radio set?

(v.) I am shaping clay into a ball.

75. Shark (n.) शार्क-शार्क मछली

Have you ever seen a shark?

76. Within विदिन

1. (prep.) समयावधि की सीमा के अंदर

He was back within an hour.

2. (adv.) व्यक्ति या वस्तु के भीतर

All the blessings were coming from deep within her.

77. Without (n.) विदाउट-बिना

Had you not gone out without your shoes?

78. Witness विट्नस-गवाह, गवाही भरना, देखना

(n.) She is the only witness who has seen the accident.

(v.) I have really witnessed many odd things in my life.

79. Wizard (n.) विज़र्ड-जादूगर, प्रतिभाशाली, विशेषज्ञ

Do you still believe in witches and wizards?

I have a great regard for Kalidasa, he was a wizard indeed.

80. Woe (n.) वो-शोक, बिषाद, उदासीन, संकट

The villagers told many tales of woe that befell them when the river flooded their houses.

81. Wolf वुल्फ-भेड़िया, गटकना, भकोसना

(n.) One day, a wolf attacked me in the wood.

Ravi behaves like a friend but he is really a wolf in sheep's clothing.

(v.) The hungry beggar greedily wolfed down the food.

82. Tie (v.) टाइ–1. बाँधना

Mother, please tie my shoelaces

Do you know how to tie a knot?

2 (n.) टाई, गले में बाँधने का कपड़ का टुकड़ा

Father wears a tie round his neck

83. Tiger (n.) टाइगर्–बाघ व्याघ्र

Tiger is a wild animal

84. Tight (adj.) टाइट–तंग वायु/जल–गर्भा

My new shoes are too tight

Food should be kept in air-tight tins

(v.) Tighten your belt and wear your coat

85. Tile टाइल–खपड़ा टाइल बिछाना

(n.) The bathroom tiles are of golden colour

(v.) The masons were tiling the kitchen

86. Pillow (n.) पिला तकिया

I cannot sleep without a pillow

87. Pilot (n. & v.) पाइलट– चालक पायलट जहाज चलाना

(n.) My son is a pilot in the Indian Airlines

(v.) He piloted the ship very carefully through the storm

88. Pimple (n.) पिंपल–मुहांसा

She fumed over the pimple she got on her face

89. PIN (n.) पिन्–पिन नंबर

Specify the PIN code on the letter.

90. Pin (n. & v.) पिन–पिन (लगाना)

(v.) Pease pin these sheets of paper together.

(n.) I need a safety pin.

91. Pinch (v.) पिंच 1 चिकोटी काटना

I cried out in pain when he pinched my arm

2 (n.) चुटकी भर

Please put a pinch of salt in this curry.

92. Pine (v.) पाइन–लालायित होना, मुरझाना

She pined for the return of her missing son

93. Pink (adj.) पिंक–गुलाबी

Jaipur is called the Pink City.

94. Pinpoint (v.) पिन्पॉइन्ट–किसी बात का सही–सही निरुपण करना

Can you pinpoint the main reason behind the argument?

95. Exit एग्जिट–बाहर जाने का रास्ता, बाहर जाना

(n.) As fire broke out in the cinema hall, we all rushed towards the exit.

(v.) We exited through the back door when the fire broke out.

96. Expand (v.) इक्स्पैंड–फैलाना, बढ़ाना, विस्तार करना

Ravi is planning to expand his business.

97. Expect (v.) इक्स्पेक्ट–राह देखना, आशा/अपेक्षा करना

I did not expect you to return so soon.

98. Expel (v.) इक्स्पेल–निकाल देना, निष्कासित करना

The principal expelled the misbehaving students from the school.

99. Expend (v.) इक्स्पेन्ड–खर्च करना, व्यय करना

Some youth expend most of their money and energy on entertainment

(adj.) Your suit looks quite expensive (costly).

100. Dilemma (n.) डाइलेमा–दुविधा

I was in a dilemma for a week as to which company to join.

SPOKEN VOCABULARY
Set - 29

1. **Diligent (adj.)** डिलिजन्ट-परिश्रमी

   (adj.) She is a diligent student and always stands first in the class.

   (n.) He was appreciated for his diligence at work.

   (Adv.) She works diligently in the office.

2. **Dilute (v.)** डाइलूट-किसी द्रव में पानी या अन्य कोई द्रव मिलाना

   He diluted the wine with a little water.

3. **Dim (adj.)** डिम-धुंधला, मंद फीका

   It was difficult to find our way in the dim light.

4. **Dimension (n.)** डाइमेन्शन

   1. लंबाई, चौड़ाई, ऊंचाई का माप

   Have you taken the dimensions of the room?

   2. आयाम

   The victim's mother's statement has given a new dimension to the case.

5. **Diminish (v.)** डिमिनिश-महत्व घटाना

   The rain diminished all the enthusiasm of the fortcoming watch.

6. **Dimple (n.)** डिम्पल-मुस्कराते समय गाल में पड़ने वाला गड्ढा

   When she smiles, dimples from in her cheeks.

7. **Reply** रिप्लाइ-मौखिक या लिखकर उत्तर (देना)

   (v.) The judge asked repeatedly, but the thief did not reply.

8. **Report** रिपॉर्ट-1. विवरण (देना)

   (v.) The occurence was reported in the Hindustan Times.

   (n.) Have you got the police for trespassing.

   3. (बहुधा अपने से वरिष्ठ अधिकारी को) मिलकर सूचित करना

   I have been ordered to report for duty.

9. **Repose (n.)** रिपोज़-विश्राम, नींद

   After a day's repose, I shall try to join my night duty.

10. **Represent (v.)** रेप्रिज़ेन्ट-प्रतिनिधित्व करना

    Leander Paes represented India in Atlanta Olympics and won a bronze medal in tennis.

11. **Repress (v.)** रिप्रेस-दमन करना

    (v.) She somehow repressed her de sire to go on a holiday.

    (adj.) Her anger repressed for several days suddenly burst out at a minor mistake.

    (adj.) The British had formed a repressive government in India.

12. **Reprimand (v.)** रे'प्रिमान्ड-फटकारना

    The police reprimanded the people for spreading false rumours.

13. **Group (n. & v.)** ग्रुप-समूह, गण, एकत्र करना या होना

    (n.) A group of people was waiting to see the minister.

    (v.) The students grouped together to move the heavy table.

14. **Grove (n.)** ग्रोव-उपवन, बाग

    Children like to play hide-and-seek in the grove.

15. **Grow (v.)** ग्रो-1. विकास पाना, बढ़ना

    Your son has grown up into a fine young man.

    2. उगना, उगाना

    What flowers do you grow in your garden?

    3. होना

    The nights grow colder in winter.

(n.) The massive growth in Rehman's business has been very surprising.

16. Growl ग्राउल-गुर्राना, गरजना, गुर्राहट

(n.) The growl of thunder could be heard at a distance.

(v.) The dog always growls at the cat.

17. Grudge ग्रज-1. अनिच्छा से देना

(v.) The master grudged every rupee that he gave to the lazy servant as wages.

2. (n.) दुर्भाव, मनमुटाव, ईर्ष्या करना

I hope you don't hold any grudge against me.

18. Gruff (adj.) ग्रफ़्-रुखा

Why has your voice become so gruff?

19. Grumble (v.) ग्रम्बल-शिकायत करना, बुड़बुड़ाना

Some people are always grumbling.

20. Owe (v.) ओ-1. देनदार होना

When can you repay the money you owe me?

2. आभारी होना

I owe my present position in life to the guidance of my father.

21. Intrigue इन्ट्रीग-रुचि या उत्सुकता जगाना

(n.) The movie was full of thrill and intrigue.

(v.) He was quite intrigued by the news.

22. Blink (v.) ब्लिंक-पलक मारना, आंखें झपकाना

The strong light made him blink.

23. Blister (n.) ब्लिस्टर्-छाला, फ़फ़ोला

The intense heat caused blisters on the baby's tender skin.

(v.) The boiling water fell on Amit's hand and blistered it.

24. Bloated (adj.) ब्लोटिड्-फूला हुआ

He felt bloated after the heavy lunch.

25. Block (n.) ब्लॉक-1. खंड, कुन्दा, शिलाखण्ड,

This house was built with the blocks of cement.

2. एक बड़ी इमारत का हिस्सा

I have rented a three-room block.

3. (v.) रोक देना, बाधा डालना

The demonstrators blocked the road.

26. Blonde (n.) ब्लॉन्ड-जिसके बाल हल्के रंग के हों, शुभ्रकेशी

It is rare to come across a blonde in India.

27. Blood (n.) ब्लड्-रक्त, लहू, खून

It is a misconception that healthy persons become weak after donating blood.

28. Bloom ब्लूम्-फूल, बहार, फूलना, खिलना

(v.) Many flowers bloom in my garden.

(n.) The blooms of this plant wilt in the evening.

29. Blossom ब्लॉसम-कली, फूल खिलना

(n.) I saw a new blossom in the rose plant.

(v.) The rose plant is blossoming.

30. Food (n.) फूड-अन्न, आहार, भोजन, खाना

Have you taken your food?

31. Fool फूल-1. मूर्ख, मूढ़

(n.) Don't be a fool.

2. (v.) मूर्ख बनाना, धोखा देना

Don't fool me.

32. Foot (n.) फुट-1. पैर, पाँव

I hurt my left foot yesterday.

2. अधोभाग, मात्रा, पैताना

Come up; don't stand at the foot of the staircase.

3. फुट (माप)

How many inches are there in a foot?

34. Forbid (v.) फ़ॉबिड्-मना करना, निषेध करना

I forbid you to go out in the rain.

35. Force (n.) फ़ॉर्स-1. जोर, ताक़त

Don't bang the door with geat force.

2. सेना

Would you like to join the Air Force?

3. (v.) विवश करना, मजबूर करना

Sustained questioning forced the

robber to disclose his accomplices' names.

36. Forecast फॉर्कास्ट-पूर्वानुमान

(n.) As per the weather forecast, it might rain today.

(n.) Astrologer forecast huge success in his career

37. Forehead (n.) फॉर्हेड-माथा

She fell from the stairs and injured

38. Massage मसाज-मालिश

(n.) An oil massage will relax your tired body

(v.) Massage your hair well.

39. Amble (v.) ऐमब्ल-टहलना, रहवाल चलना.

The weary traveller ambled alone the street.

40. Ambulance (n.) ऐम्ब्युलन्स-अस्पताल-गाड़ी

The wounded man was taken to the hospital in an ambulance.

41. Amend (v.) अमेन्ड-संशोधित करना

(v.) Our constitution has been amended many times.

(n.) Certain clauses in this agreement need amendment.

42. Amenity (n.) एमिनटि-सुविधाएं

Big cities offer good civic amenities.

43. Amiable (adj.) एमिअबल-मिलनसार

My mother is an amiable lady.

44. Introduce (v.) इन्ट्रोड्यूस-परिचय करना, आरंभ करना, चलाना

Let me introduce you to my friend Prakash.

(n.) A brief introduction of the author should be included in the book.

45. Introvert (n.) इन्ट्रवर्ट-अंतर्मुखी

He is an introvert and prefers to stay at home on weekends.

46. Intrude (v.) इन्टूड-घुसपैठ करना

(v.) The media apologised for intruding the actor's privacy.

(n.) The intruders were sent to the jail immediately.

(n.) The Prime Minister said that intrusion would not be tolerated.

47. Intuition (n.) इन्ट्युइशन-अंतः प्रज्ञा

I'm having a strong intuition that we will win this match.

48. Invade (v.) इन्वेड-आक्रमण करना

The Mughals invaded the Rajput kingdoms.

49. Cheap (adj.) चीप-1 सस्ता

Nothing is cheap these days.

2 अनुदार, तुच्छ

Amit played a cheap trick on me.

3. हल्के दर्जे की

His taste in clothes in rather cheap.

50. Cheat (v.) चीट-धोखा देना, बेईमानी करना

A dishonest shopkeeper cheats his customers.

(n.) धोखेबाज़

Beware! He is a cheat.

51. Check (v.) चेक-1. जाँच-पड़ताल, परीक्षण करना

Have you checked the air pressure in your car tyres?

2. रोकना

The policemen at the gate of the Parliament House checked people from going in.

3. (n.) चारखाना

Shaloo wore a shirt with checks.

52. Cheek चीक-1. गाल

(n.) The teacher slapped him on his cheek.

2. आदरहीनता

(n.) She's got a cheek, coming late to the office every day!

(adj.) She is a cheeky little girl.

53. Cheer चिअर्-1. खुशी, प्रसन्नता, प्रसन्न करना

(n.) Cheers for the holiday.

(v.) My visit cheered the sick man.

(adj,) He has a cheerful temperament.

2. जयध्वनि करना, ताली बजाना

The school boys cheered when their team won the hocky match.

54. Vowel (n.) वाउअल-स्वर

The English language has five vowels - a, e, i, o, u.

55. Loop (n.) लूप-फंदा, छल्ला

She made a loop in a rope.

56. Loose (adj.) लूज़-1. ढीला, शिथिल

This knot is very loose, please make it tight.

2. अलग

One of my teeth is getting loose

57. Loot लूट-लूट

(v.) The robbers looted all the money from the house.

(n.) What was the extent of their loot?

58. Lose (v.) लूज़-1 खोना, खो देना

Do not lose this pen

2 हार जाना

Did you lose the match?

3. नही (देख, सुन, समझ, पकड़) पाना

If you do not hurry, you will lose the train (the picture/lecture/debate etc).

4. भटक जाना

Have you lost your way?

59. Horn (n.) हॉर्न-1 भोंपू, तुरही

Don't blow your unnecessarily when you drive.

2. सींग, श्रृंग

The farmer painted his bullock's horns.

60. Horoscope (n.) हॉरस्कोप-जन्मकुंडली

Their marriage was cancelled as the horoscopes did not match.

61. Horrid (n.) हॉरिड-भयंकर, जघन्य, बुरा

If you behave in such a horrid manner, no one will befriend you.

62. Horror (n.) हॉरर्-घृणा, संभास, वीभत्सता

I stared in horror as the two cars collided

(adj.) I could not bear to look at the horrible accident sight.

63. Horse (n.) हॉर्स-घोड़ा

Do you know horse-riding?

64. Hose (n.) होज़्-होज़, रबर का पाइप, मोज़ा

I require a long hose to water my garden.

65. Hospital (n.) हॉस्पिटल-अस्पताल, चिकित्सालय

We took the injured man to the hospital

66. Minus माइनस-1 ऋण, ऋणात्मक

(n.) Arithmetic begins with plus and minus.

2 (prep.) सिवाय, बिना

Why have you come minus your cap?

As I arrived at my office I found that I was minus my golden chain

67. Minute मिनिट/माइन्यूट-1 मिनट क्षण मेमा नाट

(n.) I can do this job in ten minutes

(adj.) सूक्ष्म अति लघु

I did not notice the minute specks of dirt on my specs.

(adv.) The advocate studied the case minutely.

68. Miracle (n.) मिरकल-चमत्कार, करामात

As a miracle, most of the passengers were saved when their bus fell into a gorge.

(adj.) Yesterday I was involved in an accident but had a miraculous excape.

69. Mirage (n.) मिराज-मृग-मरीचिका

Don't pursue the dream of making a place in film industry; it's just a mirage.

70. Sharp (adj.) शार्प-1. तेज, तीक्ष्ण

Is your knife sharp?

I heard a sharp cry of pain.

2. तीव्र, (गति में), तेज़

His memory is very sharp.

(v.) Sharpen your pencil with a sharpener.

71. Shatter (v.) शैटर्-टूट कर टुकड़े-टुकड़े होना

The looking glass fell to the ground and was shattered.

72. Shave (v.) शेव-चेहरे की हज़ामत करना, शेव करना

I shave myself every morning.

73. Shawl (n.) शॉल-गर्म कपड़े की शाल, दुशाला

Put on your shawl before you go out.

74. She शी-वह (स्त्रीलिंग)

(pron.) She is a lovely woman.

(adj.) I have two he-goats and four she-goats.

75. Sheaf (n.) शीफ़-गट्ठा, गट्ठर

What does this sheaf contain?

76. Sheath (n.) शीथ-म्यान, आवरण

He put his sword in its sheath.

77. Shed (v.) शे'ड-झड़ना, गिरना

In autumn, the trees shead their leaves.

The young girl shed tears when her mother went out.

78. Sheen (n.) शीन्-चमक

In summers, the skin loses its sheen.

79. Sheep (n.) शीप-भेड़ (भेड़ें)

A sheep is an animal that has a coat of wool.

A man who looks after sheep is called a shepherd.

80. Sheepish (adj.) शीपिश-शर्म-संकोच भरा

She looked sheepish when caught copying in exams.

81. Sheer (adj.) शिअर्-एकदम ढालू, खड़ा

Over the edge of the cliff was a sheer drop.

82. Sheet (n.) शीट-पन्ने

How many sheets of paper do you need?

93. Woman (n.) वुमन-महिला, नारी, औरत

Baby is little girl. When she grows up she, will be a woman.

94. Wonder वंड्र्-आश्चर्य करना, अचरज, अचम्भा, विस्मय

(v.) I wonder where Sarla has gone.

How I wonder what you are!

(n.) As knowledge increases, wonder deepens.

95. Wood (n.) वुड-1. जंगल, वन

There are many trees in the wood.

2. लकड़ी, जलाने की लकड़ी

We get wood from trees. This table is made of wood.

(adj.) Wooden furniture is long lasting.

96. Till (prep.) टिल-1. (उस समय) तक

The farmer works from morning till evening.

Do not put off till tomorrow what you can do today.

2. (v.) (ज़मीन) जोतना, हल चलाना

The cultivators till the soil.

3. (n.) दराज़, पैसा रखने की जगह

While the cashier was out someone robbed the till.

97. Timber (n.) टिम्बर-इमारती लकड़ी

A huge forest of timber has been de stroyed by fire.

98. Time (n.) टाइम-1. समय

What is the time now?

We want to reach the office in time.

2. सैकड़ों मिनटों, घण्टों, दिनों, महीनों या वर्षों का बीतना

Time seemed to stand still.

3. बार, दफ़ा, मर्तबा

It is useless to repeat, I heard you the first time itself.

Cowards die many times before their death.

99. Timid (adj.) टिमिड-भीरु, डरपोक, संकोची

The child is still a little timid when he meets the puppy.

Squirrels are timid creatures.

100. Tin (n.) टिन-कनस्तर, डिब्बा, टीन

We need two tins of vegetable oils.

SPOKEN VOCABULARY
Set - 30

1. **Tinge (v. & n.)** टिंज-(का) पुट (देना), रंगत (चढ़ाना)

   (v.) The rays of the setting sun tinge the clouds pink.

   (n.) There is no tinge of regret in his voice.

2. **Tinkle (v.)** टिंकल-टनटनाना

   The bells on the pony's harness tinkle as it trots along.

3. **Pioneer (n.)** पाइअनिअर्-अगुआ, अग्रसर

   The Americans have been pioneers in space travel.

4. **Pious (adj.)** पाइअस-धर्मपरायण

   My grandmother is a very pious lady.

5. **Pipe (n.)** पाइप-1. नल, नली

   Even in olden days, water was carried through undergound pipes.

   2. चिलम

   Do you smoke a pipe?

6. **Piracy (n.)** पाइरसि-पुस्तकों, वीडियो टेप आदि की अवैध नकल, समुद्री डकैती

   Video piracy is a glaring problem these days.

7. **Pit (n.)** पिट-गड्ढा

   I fell into a pit on a dark night and injured my leg.

8. **Pitch (n.)** पिच

   1. खेल-पट्टी

   The rains dempened the cricket pitch.

   2. स्वर की ऊंचाई का स्तर

   The children were shouting at a high pitch.

9. **Pitcher (n.)** पिचर्-सुराही

   Do you have some water in that pitcher?

10. **Pity (n.)** पिटि-करुणा, दया

    My wife felt pity for the beggar.

11. **Placard (n.)** प्लैकार्ड-सूचना पत्रक

    "We want justice" read the placard in the woman's hand.

12. **Place (v.)** प्लेस-1. रख देना

    Place the box in this corner.

    2. (n.) स्थान, जगह

    Is there any quiet place where can talk?

13. **Plagiarism (n.)** प्लेजरिज़्म-साहित्यिक चोरी करना

    The author was alleged of plagiarism.

14. **Plague (n.)** प्लेग्-प्लेग्

    Many people in Surat died of plague.

15. **Experience (n.)** इक्स्पीरिअन्स-1. अनुभव, तजुरबा

    Do you have any experience of office work?

    Tell me about your experiences abroad.

    2. (v.) अनुभव करना, झेलना

    The mountaineers experienced many difficulties on their way to the Everest.

16. **Experiment (n. & v.)** इक्स्पेरिमन्ट-प्रयोग, परीक्षण करना

    (n.) Ram was very happy with the outcome of his experiment in Physics.

    (v.) Scientists experimented with a model of the space shuttle to test its power supply system.

17. **Expert (adj.)** एक्स्पर्ट-विशेषज्ञ, निपुण

    The automobile mechanic was an expert at repairing all kinds of motor engines.

18. **Expire (v.)** इक्सपाइर्-1. श्वास छोड़ना, मरना

When did the old man expire?

2 अन्त होना समाप्त होना

Our holidays expire next week.

19. Explain (v.) इक्सप्लेन-स्पष्ट करना, समझाना

Please explain to me the working of this machine.

20. Explode (v.) इक्सप्लोड-विस्फोट होना/करना, फूट पड़ना

The boiler will explode unless you let some steam out of it.

(n.) We were all alarmed by the loud explosion in our neighbourhood.

21. Exploit (v.) इक्स्प्लॉइट-शोषण करना

The child labourer was exploited by being made to work the whole day for a small amount..

22. Din (n.) डिन-शोरगुल, हल्ला

Sanjay made a great din with his drum.

23. Dinner (n.) डिनर्-रात का मुख्य भोजन, दावत

Avoid taking dinner very late in the night.

24. Dip (v.) डिप-झुकाना, डुबोना

Don't dip your finger in the curry.

25. Direct (v.) डाइरेक्ट- 1. मार्ग दिखाना, पथ-प्रदर्शन करना, भेजना

Ram directed Arun to the nearest STD booth for making an urgent call.

2. निर्देशन करना, संचालन करना

Gulzar directed the award-winning film'Maachis'.

3. सीधा

Which is the direct route to your house?

(n.) Which direction should I take to reach Janpath?

26. Directly (adv.) डाइरेक्ट्लि-सीधे, तुरन्त

The speeding truck rammed directly into the stationary car.

27. Directory (n.) डाइरेक्टरि-निर्देशिका

The telephone directory is updated every year.

28. Dirty (adj.) डर्टि-गन्दा, मैला, नीच, कुत्सित

Please wash your dirty hands before sitting down to eat.

29. Disabled डिसेब्ल्ड-अपंग

(n.) The college has a separate section for the disabled.

(v.) The accident disabled his arm.

30. Disadvantage (n.) डिसॅएडवान्टिज-असुविधा, हानि, घाटा

In the job market, being less educated is considered a major disadvantage.

31. Disagree (v.) डिसग्री-सहमत न होना

I searched for him, but he disappeared in the crowd.

32. Reproduce (v.) रिप्रॉड्यूस-चित्रण करना, प्रतिलिपि तैयार करना

The artist reporduced the scene in an oil painting.

(n.) It was really a good reproduction.

33. Reptile (n.) रेप्टाइल-रेंगने वाला जन्तु

A snake is a reptile.

34. Reputation (n.) रेप्युटेशन-प्रतिष्ठा, ख्याति, मान

Your father lived up to his reputation.

Netaji Subhash was a man of blameless reputation.

If you do anything wrong, your reputation will suffer.

35. Request (v.) रिक्वे'स्ट-प्रार्थना करना

You are requested not to talk loudly.

(n.) The candidate made a request to the voters to vote for him. Luckily, the request was granted.

36. Require (v.) रिक्वाइअर्-ज़रुरत होना

The hungry man requires food.

I require you to be here now.

(n.) Can you meet all my requirements?

37. Rescue रेस्क्यू-रक्षा (करना)

(n.) My friend always comes to my rescue when I need him.

(v.) The youngman dived into the river to rescue the drowning boy.

38. Research (n.) रिसर्च-खोज

The scientists conducted many researches.

(adj.) She has been deputed as research adviser.

39. Resemble (v.) रिज़े'मबल-शक्ल मिलना, आकृति का मेल होना

You resemble your father closely.

(n.) There was a family resemblance between all the sisters.

40. Grunt ग्रन्ट-घुरघुराना, घुरघुराहट

(v.) Pigs grunt as they search for food.

(n.) He only gave a grunt of approval when I asked him if he liked my painting.

41. Guarantee गैरन्टी-गारंटी, जिम्मा लेना

(n.) My car has the guarantee for replacement if any fault was found in its functioning.

42. Group (n. & v.) ग्रुप-समूह, गण, एकत्र करना या होना

(n.) A group of people was waiting to see the minister.

(v.) The students grouped together to move the heavy table.

43. Grove (n.) ग्रोव-उपवन, बाग

Children like to play hide-and-seek in the grove.

44. Grow (v.) ग्रो-1. विकास पाना, बढ़ना

Your son has grown up into a fine young man.

2. उगना, उगाना

What flowers do you grow in your garden?

3. होना

The nights grow colder in winter.

(n.) The massive growth in Rehman's business has been very surprising.

45. Amid (prep.) अमिड-में, बीच में

In India, we often see honesty amid poverty.

46. Amiss (adv.) अमिस-बुरा, बुरा मानना

I did not mean to hurt his feeling, but he took it amiss.

(adj.) गलत

There is nothing amiss in the plan.

47. Among (st) (prep) अमंग-में, में से, बीच में मिलकर

She distributed the sweet among her children.

48. Amount (n.) अमाउंट- 1. रकम, धनराशि It is risky to carry a large amount in cash.

2. मात्र, परिणाम

What is the amount of flour needed to prepare a small cake?

49. Ample (adj.) ऐमूपल-पर्याप्त, प्रचुर

The little boy has an ample stock of story books.

50. Amuse (v.) अम्यूज़्-मन बहलाना, मनोरंजन करना

The clown in the circus amused the children with his antics.

51. Analyse (v.) ऐनलाइज़्-विश्लेषण करना

(v.) Let us analyse the situation well and come up with an appropriate solution.

(n.) The situation needs an in-depth analysis.

52. Invalid (adj.) इन्वैलिड-अमान्य, रद्द, रोगी, असमर्थ

Without your signature, this cheque is invalid.

(n.) His father has been an invalid for the last five years.

53. Invaluable (adj.) इन्वैल्युअबल-अनमोल

The advice that you gave me was invaluable.

54. Invariably (adv.) इन्वेअरिअब्लि-सदा, निरपवाद रुप से

I invariably go for a stroll after dinner.

55. Invent (v.) इन्वेन्ट-आविष्कार करना, गढ़ना, कल्पना करना

The gramophone was invented by Edison.

Don't invent an excuse for your deliberate absence from the Maths class

(n.) The telephone is a useful invention.

56. Blot (n.) ब्लॉट-धब्बा, दाग, कलंक

There was a large blot of ink on the clean sheet of paper.

Ram's miscondcut is a blot on the fair name of his family.

(v.) Ram's behaviour has blotted the good image of his parents.

57. Blotch (n.) ब्लॉच-कच्चा दाग

Sweat left blotches on his shirt.

58. Blouse (n.) ब्लाउज़्-कुरता, कुरंती, चोली

She stitched a matching blouse for her new sari.

59. Blow (n.) ब्लो-1. प्रहार, घूँसा, चोट

They had a fight and exchanged blows.

2. (v.) बहना, फूँकना

Cool air was blowing gently.

Please blow out (extinguish) the candle.

Terrorists blew up (destroyed) the bridge with dynamite.

60. Blue (adj.) ब्लू-नीला, आसमानी

Blue is my favourite colour.

61.Blunder (n.) ब्लन्डर्-भारी भूल

Your refusal to go with him was a blunder for yourself.

(v.) You have blundered by agreeing to lend him the money.

62. Blunt (adj.) ब्लन्ट-1. कुंद, भोथरा

This knife is of no use, its edge is blunt.

2. स्पष्ट, रुखा

Your blunt storm blurred my vision.

63. Blur (v.) ब्लर्-धुंधला करना

The dust storm blurred my vision.

64. Foreign (adj.) फ़ॉरिन-विदेशी, परराष्ट्रीय

Do you know any foreign language?

(n.) Would you like to meet a foreigner?

65. Forest (n.) फ़ॉरिस्ट-वन, जंगल

My native place is a village on the edge of the forest.

66. Forever (adv.) फ़रेवर्-सदा के लिए

I feel like leaving this place forever.

67. Forge (v.) फ़ॉर्ज-जालसाज़ी करना

He forged his father's signature on the report card.

68. Forget (v.) फ़गेट-भूल जाना, भुला देना, बिसारना

I forgot your telephone number.

69. Forgive (v.) फ़गिव-माफ़ करना, क्षमा करना

Please fill up this admission form.

2. रुप, आकृति

A cloud in the sky had taken the form of an elephant.

3. (v.) संगठित करना

We have formed a literary association.

70. Formal (adj.) फ़ॉमल-औपचारिक, बाहरी, यथानियम

Some clubs allow entry to their members only in the fromal dress.

71. Cheese (n.) चीज़-पनीर

Rahul ordered for a plate of cheese pakoras.

72. Chemist (n.) केमिस्ट-औषधविक्रेता

At the chemist's shop, we can buy medicines.

73. Cheque (n.) चेक-चेक, हुण्डी, धनादेश

It's safe to make paymetns by cheque.

74. Chess (n.) चेस-शतरंज

The game of chess originated in India.

75. Chest (n.) चेस्ट-1. छाती, सीना

A wrestler has a broad chest.

2. तिजोरी, संदूक

The jeweller locked his valuables in a strong chest.

76. Chew (v.) चू-चबाना, मनन करना

Young children should be taught to chew their food well.

Stop chewing over the past.

77. Chick(en) (n.) चिक् चिकिन-1. चूजा, चिंगना

He bought a dozen chicks for his poultry farm.

2. पकी हुई मुरगी

(n.) I had chicken for lunch.

73. Voyage (n.) वॉइएज-यात्रा (करना)

We were seasick on the voyage around the world.

(v.) I have an ambition to voyage around the world.

74. Lost (adj.) लॉस्ट-चकराया हुआ

He looks quite lost these days.

75. Lot लॉट

1. (n.) ढेर

The whole lot of garments was rejected.

2. (adv.) बहुत अधिक

She danced a lot at the party.

3. (det.) ढेर सारा

There are a lot of mistakes in your drawing.

76. Lotion (n.) लोशन-लोशन

Please give me some lotion for the boils on my skin.

77. Lottery (n.) लॉटरि-लॉटरी

Buying and selling of lottery tickets is banned in Delhi.

78. Loud (adj.) लाउड-1. ऊँचा, तीव्र

Do not speak in a loud voice.

2. चटकीला

I do not like loud colours.

79. Hospitable (adj.) हास्पीटेबल-मेहमाननवाज़

She is a hospitable lady and treats all her guests very well.

80. Host (n.) होस्ट-1. मेज़बान, मेहमानदार

Our host at yesterday's party was very hospitable.

2. झुंड, जमघट, भीड़, सेना

A host of fan had besieged the film star.

81. Hostel (n.) होस्टल-धामावास, सराय

My son lives in the college hostel.

82. Hostile (adj.)होस्टाइल-विरोधी, प्रतिकूल

Why are you lives in the college hostel.

83. Hot (adj.) हॉट-1. गरम, उष्ण

Give me a hot cup of tea.

It is a hot day today.

2. चरपरा, तिक्त, तेज

I do not like to eat hot things like pepper.

84. Hotel (n.) होटे'ल-होटल

At which hotel do you stay when you visit Mumbai?

85. Mirror (n.) मिरर्-आईना, शीशा

Who broke the mirror?

86. Mirth (n.) मर्थ-मनोरंजन

There was an atmosphere of mirth in the house.

87. Misapprehension (n.) मिसऐप्रिहेन्शन -गलतफ़हमी

He had the misapprehension that the house belonged to Mrs. Reynolds.

88. Miscellaneous (adj.) मिसलेनिअस-विधि

The box was full of miscellaneous sports instruments.

89. Mischief (n.) मिस्चिफ़-1. शरारती, नटखट

My youngest son is always up to some mischief.

(adj.) A mishievous boy drew a cartoon on the blackboard.

2. (n.) हानि

You are too late, the mischief is done.

90. Miser (n.) माइज़र्-कंजूस, कृपण

Some rich people behave like misers.

(adj.) I do not like people with miserly habits

91. Shelf (n.) शे'ल्फ़्-अलमारी का एक खाना, ताक

The baby's toys are on the shelf

Our shelves are full of books

92. Shelter शे'ल्टर्-शरण (लेना), आश्रय

(v.) The children sheltered under a tree until it stopped raining

(n.) We took shelter in a house until the strom was over

93. Shepherd (n.) शे'पर्ड-गड़रिया

The shepherd secured his sheep from the wolf

94. Shield शील्ड-1. बचाना

How can I tell a lie to shield you from punishment?

2. (n.) ढाल, कवच

The soldier came out armed with a sword and a shield.

95. Shift शिफ़्ट

1. (n.) पाली

One week he works the day shift and the next week the night shift.

2. (v.) उठाना, खिसकाना, हटाना

Who has shifted my chair?

Shiftless (adj.) 3. उत्साहहीन

My servant is a shiftless person. He does not work willingly.

Shifty (adj.) 4. चालबाज़

Beware of him. He is a shifty fellow.

He can't be trusted.

96. Wool (n.) वूल-ऊन

My mother bought some wool to knit a sweater for me.

Bring a ball of wool from the almirah.

(adj.) Have you got a wollen jersey?

97. Word (n.) वर्ड-1. प्रतिज्ञा, वचन, आश्वासन

Give me your word that you will pay me a visit next Sunday.

2. संकेत, संदेश

Send me a word when you hear from Rachna

3 शब्द

He who does not know the force of words can't know a man

This is the word for word message he gave me

4 (v.) शब्दों में कहना

How shall I word this story?

98. Work वर्क-काम (करना)

(v.) Everybody is working. Daddy works in the office. Mother works in the kitchen Brother works in the garden

(n.) I have some urgent work to do in the office.

An ounce of work is worth many pounds of words.

Work is worhip.

99. World (n.) वर्ल्ड-संसार, दुनिया, जगत्

The world is the place we live in.

The world is nothing but an endless seesaw.

The world is a net: the more we stir in it, the more we are entangled.

100. Tint टिंट-हल्का रंग (रंगना), आभा, रंगत, झलक

(v.) You can tint the sky in your picture with some light blue paint.

(n.) There were tints of yellow and gold in the morning sky.

SPOKEN VOCABULARY
Set - 31

1. **Tiny (adj.)** टाइनि–बहुत छोटा, नन्हा

   A tiny lamp was burning near the shrine.

   The tiny boy won the race

   The midge is a tiny insect.

   A fly is very small. It is tiny.

2. **Tip (v.)** टिप–1. झुकाना, तिरछा करना, उलटाना

   I tipped my glass over by mistake

   2. नोक, नुकीला सिरा

   She touched the cat with the tip of her cane.

3. **Tiptoe (n.)** टिप्टो–1. पंजा (पंजों के बल)

   The thief entered the room on tiptoes and stole the money

4. **Tire (v.)** टाइर्–थकना, थकाना

   The long journey boy bus has tired me.

   Climbing up that steep hill will tire you.

5. **Tissue (n.)** टिस्यू–टिश्यू–1. ऊतक

   The body is held together by muscular tissues.

   2. ढेर, लड़ी

   You answered with a tissue of lies.

6. **Titbits (n.)** टिट्बिट्स–चटपटी ओर मज़ेदार खबर

   We always find him ready with jokes and funny titbits.

7. **Title (n.)** टाइटल–1. पुस्तक का नाम

   What is the title of your novel?

   2. उपाधि, व्यक्ति के पद व्यवसाय ओहदा प्रकट करने का विशेष नाम

   Some Indians were honoured with the title 'Sir' for their services to the British during the latter's rule in India.

8. **Plain (n.)** प्लेन–1. मैदान

   A fierce battle was fought on this plain once upon a time.

   2. (adj.) सरस, सुस्पष्ट

   My instructions to you were quite plain.

   3. सादा

   My wife likes to wear a plain white dress

   4 असुन्दर, कुरुप

   Our neighbour's wife is rather plain-looking.

9. **Plait (n.)** प्लैट–बालों की चोटी

   She always ties her hair in two plaits.

10. **Plan (n.)** प्लान–1. योजना

    What are your plans for the summer holidays?

    2. नक्शा

    Have you submitted the plan of your proposed house to the municipality?

    3. (v.) योजना बनाना, इरादा करना

    When are you planning to get married?

11. **Plane (n.)** प्लेन–1. विमान

    I went to Mumbai by plane.

    2. रन्दा

    A carpenter cannot work without a plane.

12. **Planet** प्लैनिट–ग्रह

    The earth is one of the planets in the solar system.

13. Explore (v.) इक्स्प्लॉर्-खोज करना, छान-बीन करना

As soon as we arrived at the beach, we began to explore it.

14. Export इक्स्पॉर्ट-निर्यात, निर्यात करना

(n.) Are you in the export business?

(v.) We export mangoes to the Western countries.

15. Disappoint (v.) डिस्अपॉइन्ट-निराश करना, आशा पर पानी फेरना

Suresh was disappointed when he was not selected in the school cricket team.

(adj.) Your work is disappointing.

think you could do better.

(n.) The goalkeeper was filled with disappointment when he could not save the goal.

16. Disapprove (v.) डिसअप्रूव-नापसंद करना

I strongly disapproved of giving alms to beggars.

17. Disaster (n.) डिज़ास्टर्-दुर्घटना, घोर विपत्ति या संकट

Sixty persons were killed in the train disaster.

18. Disbelief (n.) डिसबिलीफ़्-शंका

She shook her head in disbelief.

19. Dishcarge (v.) डिस्चार्ज- 1. हटा देना, बरखास्त करना

The clerk was discharged from his job when he was caught taking bribe.

2. (अस्पताल, जेल या सेना से) छुट्टी देना, रिहा करना, मुक्त करना

After recovery, Asha's mother was discharged from the hospital.

3. निबाहना, अपना काम ठीक-ठाक करना

A sincere worker discharges his duty diligently.

20. Disciple (n.) डिसाइपल-चेला

Ananda was the most loved disciple of Gautam Buddha.

21. Discipline (n.) डिसिप्लिन-अनुशासन

Don't you agree that self-discipline is the best form of discipline?

22. Discolour (v.) डिस्कलर-बदरंग हो जाना

The season of autumn discoloured the leaves.

23. Discord (n.) डिस्कॉड-झगड़ा

A discord took place between them.

24. Discourage (v.) डिस्करिज-निरुत्साहित करना

Her mother discouraged her from going for a movie.

25. Resent (v.) रिज़ेन्ट-क्रुद्ध होना, नाराज़ होना

She resented his rude remarks about her character.

Though her brother treated her badly, Pramila didn't feel any resentment.

26. Reserve (v.) रिज़र्व-1. बचाकर रखना

I always reserve some money for the weekend.

(n.) You should spend some money and keep the rest in reserve.

(v.) The best fruits are reserved for the loving child.

26. Reside (v.) रिज़ाइड-रहना, वास करना

We reside in New Delhi

(n.) They are residents of Rohtak.

Where is your residence?

27. Residual (adj.) रेज़िडुअल-अवशेष

(adj.) The residual waste products were disposed off immediately.

(n.) The residue left after the distillation of the petroleum is used to make paraffin wax.

28. Resign (v.) रिज़ाइन-त्यागपत्र देना

The Prime Minister asked the minister facing corruption charges to resign from the cabinet.

(n.) The minister's resignation was forwarded to the President for acceptance.

29. Resist (v.) रिज़िस्ट-प्रतिरोध करना, सामना करना

The Indian army is able to resist all aggressions by the enemy.

(n.) Despite the thief's resistance, the police arrested him.

30. Resolute (adj.) रेज़लूट्-दृढ़ संकल्प, करना

Explorers have to be resolute in the face of difficulties.

31. Growl ग्राउल-गुर्राना, गरजना, गुर्राहट

(n.) The growl of thunder could be heard at a distance.

(v.) The dog always growls at the cat.

32. Grudge ग्रज-1. अनिच्छा से देना

(v.) The master grudged every rupee that he gave to the lazy servant as wages.

2. (n.) दुर्भाव, मनमुटाव, ईर्ष्या करना

I hope you don't hold any grudge against me.

33. Gruff (adj.) ग्रफ़-रुखा

Why has your voice become so gruff?

34. Chickenpox (n.) चिकिनपॉक्स-छोटी चेचक

The child was suffering from chickenpox.

35. Chief चीफ़-मुख्य, प्रमुख

(n.) The Army head is called the Chief of staff.

(adj.) Rarely, one rises from a cleak's post to become the chief executive.

(adv.) मुख्यत:

We eat chiefly rice and wheat.

36. Child (n.) चाइल्ड-1. बच्चा, बालक

Mr. and Mrs. Sen brought their child with them to the party.

2. बचपन

Where did you spend your childhood?

37. Chill (n.) चिल-1. सरदी

Infants quickly catch a chill.

2. (Adj.) ठण्डा

A chilly wind was blowing.

38. Chime (n.) चाइम-घण्टानाद

The chime of the church bell could be heard from a distance.

(v.) The wall clock chimes every hour.

39. Chimney (n.) चिम्नि-चिमनी, धुआँरा, धुआँदान

The chimney smoke pollutes the atmosphere.

39. Chimpanzee (n.) चिम्पैन्ज़ी-वनमानुष

Human beings evolved from the chim panzees.

40. Chin (n.) चिन-ठोढ़ी

He nicked his chin while shaving.

41. China (n.) चाइना-चीनी मिट्टी (के बरतन)

I went to the crockery store to buy china.

42. Chip (n.) चिप-1. चिप्पड़, टुकड़ा

Chips of wood catch fire quickly.

(adj.) This tea cup is old and chipped.

43. Vulgar (adj.) वॅल्गर्-असभ्य, अशिष्ट

Don't induge in vulgar talk.

44. Blurt (v.) ब्लर्ट-बिना सोच-समझे अचानक बोलना

She suddenly blurted out the secret she did not want to reveal.

45. Blush (v.) ब्लष-शरमाना, लज्जित होना

She blushed at the sight of her lover.

46. Boar (n.) बॉर्-जंगली सूअर

The hunter killed a wild boar.

47. Board (n.) बॉर्ड्-1. तख्ता, फलक

That wooden house has walls made of boards.

2. (v.) चढ़ना, सवार होना

The train started only a couple of minutes after he boarded it.

3. नियमित भुगतान पर खरीदा भोजन

What does your hotel charge for bed and board?

48. Boast बोस्ट-डींग, शेखी मारना

(v.) One should never boast of one's accomplishment.

(n.) His boast that he could fight with a lion impressed nobody.

49. Boat (n.) बोट-नाव, किश्ती

He went to England by boat.

50. Body बॉडि-शरीर, बदन, व्यक्ति

The police found the dead body of a man in the lake.

Somebody (some person) informed the police about the road acc'dent.

51. Former (adj.) फ़ॉर्मर्-भूतपूर्व, पुराना, पहला

My former tenant was a lawyer.

52. Formula (n.) फ़ॉम्यूला-नुस्खा, नियम, सूत्र

Do you know the chemical formula of water?

53. Forsake (v.) फ़ॅसेक-छोड़ देना, त्याग देना

I cannot forsake my old friends.

54. Fort (n.) फ़ॉर्ट-किला, गढ़

On their trip to Rajasthan, students saw many historical forts.

55. Forth (adv.) फ़ॉर्थ-सामने

The workers brought forth the problems they were facing at work.

56. Fortnight (n.) फ़ॉटनाइट-पखवाड़ा, पक्ष

The bank manager was on leave for a fortnight.

57. Fortune (n.) फ़ॉर्चून-1. भाग्य, किस्मत

Do you believe in fortune-telling?

2. सम्पत्ति, ऐश्वर्य, धन

Satpal made a fortune in the export trade.

58. Anarchy (n.) ऐनकि-अराजकता

The death of the Chief Minister led to anarchy in the city.

59. Ancestor (n.) ऐन्सेस्टर्-पूर्वज, पुरखा

According to Drawin, monkeys were the ancestors of human beings.

60. Anchor (n.) ऐन्कर्-लंगर

A large ship was at anchor in the harbour.

(v.) लंगर डालना

The ship was anchored when it arrived at the port.

61. Ancient (adj.) एन्शन्ट्-प्राचीन, पुरातन, पुराना

(adj.) Ancient India was a land of glory.

62. Angel (n.) एन्जल-देवदूत, फरिश्ता

It is said that when a saint dies angels come to take his soul to heaven.

63. Anger (n.) ऐन्गर्-गुस्सा क्रोध

Good people do not get filled with anger for others's lapses.

(adj.) क्रोधित

My brother will be angry with me if I lose his pen.

64. Angle (n.) ऐन्गल-कोण

A triangle has three angles

65. Anguish (n.) ऐंग्विश-वेदना

Three consective defeats caused anguish to the captain.

66. Animal (n.) ऐनिमल-जानवर, पशु

The zoo in New Delhi has some rare wild animals.

67. Invest (v.) इन्वेस्ट

1. धन का निवेश करना

I invested some money in shares.

2. समय या शक्ति लगाना

Are you ready to invest another year in your struggle?

68. Investigate (v.) इन्वेस्टिगेट-अनुसंधान करना, जाँच पड़ताल करना

The police investigated the cause of the fire accident.

(n.) The investigation into the case is in progress.

69. Lounge (n.) लाउन्ज-बैठक खाना, विश्राम-कक्ष

We sat in the lounge of the hotel.

70. Lousy (adj.) लाउज़ि-बहुत बुरा

It was a lousy dinner.

71. Hound (n.) हाउन्ड-(शिकारी) कुत्ता

Is your dog a hound?

72. Hour (n.) आउर्-घंटा

I shall be back in couple of hours.

73. House (n.) हाउस-1. घर, मकान

Won't you come to my house?

2. सदन

Our Parliament has two houses.

3. सामान रखने की जगह

Put these bags of grain in your store house.

74. Hovel (n.) हॉवल-झोंपड़ी

I was shocked to see the stinking hovel in which the poor man lived.

75. Misery (n.) मिज़रि-दुर्दशा, विपत्ति, दु:ख

I have seen people live in great misery because of poverty.

(adj.) Why do you look so miserable?

76. Misfit (n.) मिस्‌फ़िट-अनुपयुक्त व्यक्ति

Being the youngest one, she often felt she was a misfit in the organisation.

77. Mishap (n.) मिस्‌हैप्-मामूली दुर्घटना

She passed off falling from stairs as a small mishap.

78. Mislead (v.) मिस्‌लीड्-भ्रमित करना

(v.) The advertisements of fairness creams mislead the masses

(adj.) The advertisements of fairness creams are misleading.

79. Miss (v.) मिस-1. चूकना, न मिलना

If you do not hurry, you will miss the train.

2. अभाव का अनुभव करना

We shall all miss you when you go away.

3. न कर, सुन या देख पाना

I learnt she was at the party but I missed her.

4. अभाव मालूम हो जाना, गुम होना

One of my books is missing.

5. (n.) कुमारी

What is your name, miss?

80. Missile (n.) मिसाइल-मिसाइल

The nuclear missile destoyed the whole city.

81. Mission (n.) मिशन-1. दूतावास

Are you wiking with the poor Indian mission is the USA?

2. दूतकार्य, शिष्टमंडल

I was sent on a mission to Sri Lanka.

3. जीवन-लक्ष्य

Spreading education among the poor is the mission of my life.

82. Missionary (n.) मिशनरि-धर्म-प्रचारक

The school was established by some Christian missionaries.

83. Shimmer (v.) शिमर्-झिलमिलाना

The waves in the river were shimmering in sunlight.

84. Shine (v.) शाइन-1. चमकना

Make hay while the sun shines.

2. चमकाना

Have you shined your shoes today?

85. Ship (n.) शिप-जहाज़, पोत

A ship is a large vessel for carriage of passengers and goods by sea.

Battle-ships are used in war.

86. Shirk (v.) शार्क-(काम से) जी चुराना

Lazy men shirk work.

My brother does not shirk any job.

87. Shirt (n.) शर्ट-कमीज़

I bought three readymade shirts.

88. Shiver शिवर्-(सर्दी, भय या उत्तेजना से) काँपना, सिहरना, ठिठुरना

(v.) He is shivering with cold.

(n.) A shiver ran through him when someone touched him in the dark.

89. Shock (n.) शॉक-धक्का

The news of my friend's death was a great shock for me

(v.) I was shocked when my best friend cheated me.

90. Worm (n.) वर्म-कीड़ा, केंचुआ

A worm is a small creature that lives in the ground. It creeps like a snake.

Don't be a book-worm.

91. Worry वॅरि-चिंता (करना), फिक्र (करना)

(v.) Mother worries about Raju's cought.

(n.) It is a worry for her.

My life is full of worries.

92. Worship वर्शिप-पूजा (करना), आराधना (करना)

(n.) Do your duty and act according to the rules of reason. this is true worship.

(v.) For your happiness worship God.

93. Titter (v.) टिटर्-गुपचुप, मूर्खतापूर्वक हंसना

Why are you tittering without any reason?

94. To (prep.) टु-1. को, की ओर

The old lady is going to the market.

It is five minutes to four.

2. के लिए, अथवा संयुक्त क्रिया के प्रयोग में

The old man is going to buy meat.

Do you want to finish your job today?

95. Toast टोस्ट-1. डबल रोटी का सेंका हुआ टुकड़ा

(v.) Mother toasts bread for the family's breakfast.

(n.) Would you like toast and coffee for breakfast?

2. (v.) किसी व्यक्ति के स्वास्थ्य एवं शुभकामना के लिए कहे गए शब्दों के बाद मद्यपान करना

Let us toast the newly weds

96. Tobacco (n.) टबैको-तम्बाकू

Chewing or smoking tobacco is injurious to health.

97. Today टुडे-आज, आजकल

(n.) Today is this day. Yesterday was the day before today.

Today is a holiday.

(adv.) He is leaving today.

98. Toe (n.) टो-पैर की अँगुली

We have five toes on each foot.

99. Toffee टॉफि-टाफी, चीनी और क्रीम-चाकलेट के द्वारा बनाई गई मिठाई

The children like toffee very much

100. Plank (n.) प्लैंक-तख्ता, पटरा

The villager built his house with wooden planks

SPOKEN VOCABULARY
Set - 33

1. **Plant (v. & n.)** प्लान्ट-1. पौधा (लगाना). वनस्पति

(v.) Which flower trees have you planted in your garden?

2. (n.) This is an evergreen plant.

3. During our trip to Darjeeling, we visited a tea plantation.

2. **Plaster** प्लास्टर्

1 (n.) पलस्तर

The plaster of the wall was chipped

2 (v) टूटी हड्डी पर पलस्तर चढ़ाना

The doctor plastered his broken leg.

3. **Plastic (n.)** प्लास्टिक-प्लास्टिक

Many house hold articles are made of plastic.

4. **Plate (n.)** प्लेट-1. थाली, रकाबी

He brought some sweets in a plate.

2. (v.) मुलम्मा चढ़ाना

My wrist-watch is gold-plated.

5. **Platform (n.)** प्लैटफ़ॉर्म-प्लैटफ़ार्म

Please give me a platfrom ticket.

6. **Discover (v.)** डिस्कॅवर्-पता लगाना. खोज निकालना

Columbus discovered America

(n.) It was a great discovery.

7. **Discriminate (v.)** डिस्क्रिमिनेट-भेदभाव करना

In some Indian states, girls are still discriminated against boys.

8. **Discuss (v.)** डिस्कस्-विचार-विमर्श/वादविवाद करना

The Lok Sabha discussed the bud get proposals.

(n.) A serious discussion on any subject helps us to reach a conclusion.

9. **Disease (n.)** डिज़ीज़्-रोग. बीमारी

Sometimes several tests are conducted to diagnose a patient's disease.

10. **Disgrace (v.)** डिस्ग्रेस-कलंकित करना

A society is disgraced by the criminal acts of its members.

11. **Disguise (n.)** डिस्गाइज़्-छद्मवेश (धारण करना). बहाना. छल-कपट

Sometimes adversity turns out to be a blessing in disguise.

(v.) Pushpa tried to smile but she could not disguise her anger.

12. **Disgusting (adj.)** डिसगस्टिंग-घृणाजनक, अरुचिकर

Rahul's rude manners were disgusting.

13. **Dish (n.)** डिश- 1. थाली, रकाबी

Usha wants to buy some dishes.

2. पकवान, भोजन

For her guests, Sita prepared so many dishes in a very short time.

14. **Expose (v.)** इक्स्पोज़्-खोलकर रखना. उधेड़ना

The inquiry committee exposed all dubious deals of the corrupt minister.

15. **Exposure (n.)** इक्सपोश(र)-प्रदर्शन

Too much of media exposure succeeded in drawing the audience to the movie theatres

16. **Grumble (v.)** ग्रम्बल-शिकायत करना. बुड़बुड़ाना

Some people are always grumbling.

17. **Grunt** ग्रन्ट-घुरघुराना, घुरघुराहट

(v.) Pigs grunt as they search for food.

(n.) He only gave a grunt of approval

when I asked him if he liked my painting.

18. Resolve (v.) रिज़ॉल्व–1. संकल्प, अटल

We should resolve not to tell a lie.

2. प्रस्ताव पास करना

It is resolved to re-elect the president.

(n.) It's my resolve not to tell a lie.

19. Resort रिज़ॉर्ट–शरण (लेना)

(n.) As a last resort, I'll have to borrow some money.

(v.) He resorted to smuggling because he was not satisfied with his honest earnings.

20. Resource (n.) रिसॉर्स–साधन, उपाय

I used all my resources to set up this new business.

(adj.) He is very resourceful person, and can make good use of everything he has.

21. Respect रिस्पेक्ट–1. सम्मान (करना)

(v.) We should respect our elders and never be rude to them.

(adj.) He is very resourceful person, and can make good use of everything he has.

2. (कुछ) हद तक, (कुछ) अंश तक

I may agree with her in some respects, but on the whole I think she is not right.

22. Respond (v.) रिसपॉन्ड–उत्तर देना, प्रतिक्रिया दिखाना

The enquiry-clerk responded quickly to my questions.

(n.) The patient's response to the medicine is quite good.

23. Bog (n.) बॉग–दलदल

The wild buffalo got stuck in the bog.

24. Bogus (adj.) बोगस–जाली

These papers are not original, but bogus.

25. Boil (v.) बॉइल–1. उबलना, जोश में आना

She boiled the milk.

2. (n.) फोड़ा, व्रण

He has a big boil on his arm.

26. Bold (adj.) बोल्ड–निडर, निर्भीक

The bold man refused to tell a lie to save himself.

(adv.) The young man boldly faced the angry bull.

27. Bolster (v.) बोल्स्टर्–सहारा देना संभालना

His sweet smile bolstered his sagging spirits.

28. Bolt (v.$n.) बोल्ट–1. चटखनी (लगाना)

(v.) Did you bolt the door?

(n.) After closing the door, he slipped the bolt in the place.

2. छलाँग मारकर भागना

The horse bolted down the lane.

29. Fortunate (adj.) फार्चनट–भाग्यशाली

I was fortunate enough to pass the pre-medical exam.

30. Forward फ़ॉर्वर्ड–1. आगे, अगला, प्रगतिशील

(adv.) Please move forward.

2. (v.) भेज देना, आगे बढ़ाना

Have you forwarded my application?

31. Foul (adj.) फ़ाउल–मैला, गन्दा, घृणित, बीभत्स

Foul smell emanated from the man hole.

32. Found (v.) फ़ाउन्ड–1. पाया, प्राप्त किया (Find का भूतकाल)

Have you found the book you had lost?

2. स्थापित करना, नींव डालना

Have founded your school?

(n.) The fondation stone of Lok Nayak

Setu in Delhi was laid by the then Prime Minister Chandra Shekhar.

33. Fountain (n.) फ़ाउन्टिन्-झरना, फौआरा

In Delhi, many gardens have musical fountains.

34. Fowl (n.) फ़ाउल-मुर्गा, मुर्गी

I want to buy some fowl for my poul try farm.

35. Fox (n.) फ़ॉक्स-लोमड़ी

Some persons are as cunning as a fox.

36. Ankle (n.) ऐन्कल-टखना, गुल्फ

I sprained my ankle this morning.

37. Annihilate (v.) अनाइअलेट-नष्ट करना

(v.) The fireannihilated the whole forest.

(n.) The sages guided the parth from annihilation to resurrection.

38. Annotate (v.) ऐनटेट-टिप्पणियां देना

(v.) The translator annotated the poem to make it easy to understand.

(n.) Annotations to the regional words are provided at the end of the book.

39. Announce (v.) अनाउन्स-बतलाना, सूचित/घोषित करना

The Principal announced that the school would be closed for winter vacation.

(n.) उद्घोषक

The announcer reaed out the news on the radio.

(n.) घोषणा

The chief guest made an announcement of the name of the prize winners.

40. Annoy (v.) अनॉइ-चिढ़ाना, परेषान करना

(v.) The student's carelessness annoyed the teacher.

(adj.) It is annoying to miss a bus when you are ina hurry.

(n.) A loud radio is often an annoyance.

41. Annual (adj.) ऐनयुअल -1. वार्षिक, सलाना

The annual gathering of our club will be hel next month.

2. (n.) (पत्रिका का) वार्षिक विषेषांक

Generally, the annual of a monthly magazine is bigger than its regular issue.

42. Invite (v.) इन्वाइट-निमंत्रण देना, बुलाना

Have you invited Ramesh to the party?

(n.) Thank you for the invitation.

43. Inviting (adj.) इन्वाइटिंग-आकर्षक, मोहक

The pool looked so inviting that we went for a swim.

44. Chirp (v.) चर्प्-चीं-चीं करना

Sparrows chirp together at the time of sunrise.

45. Chisel (n.) चिज़ल-छेनी

The sculptor worked on the block of stone with a chisel.

46. Chit (n.) चिट-परची

I left the note for him on a chit.

47. Chivalry (n.) शिव्लरि-स्त्रियों के प्रति पुरुषों का नम्र आचरण

The days of chivalry are now gone.

48. Chocolate (n.) चॉकलेट-चॉकलेट

The child cried for a chocolate.

49. Choice (n.) चॉइस-चुनने का अधिकार

I had no choice but to shift to Mumbai

50. Choir (v.) क्वाइयर्-गायक-मंडली

She was a part of musical choir in the church.

51. Choke (v.) चोक-1. दम घुटना, गला घोंटना

In the Bhopal gas leakage tragedy,

hundreds of people were choked to death.

2. बंद करना या होना

The sewer gets choked with dirt.

52. Choose (v.) चूज़-चुनना, पसंद करना

Usha chose a black sari.

53. Love (v. & n.) लव-1. प्रेम/प्यार (करना)

2. (में) रुचि होना

I love music.

3. चाहना, अच्छा समझना

Do you love me, master?

(n.) Love is immortal.

54. Low (adj.) लो-1. अल्प

I got this shirt at a very low price.

2. निम्न, धीमा

Please speak in a low voice.

3. निचला, नीचा

Do not build your house on a low ground.

(adv.) He bent low to speak to the sick old man.

55. Hover (v.) हॉवर्-1. मँडराना

Excited children looked up as the helicopter hovered over house.

2 भागे-पीछे फिरना

My children hovered around me in the expectation that I would tell them a story.

56. How (adj.) हाउ-कैसे, किस तरह, क्यों

How did you break this dish?

How is your father today?

57. Howl हाउल-चीखना, चीख

(v.) The win howled, so I could not hear the knock at the door.

(n.) At night, we heard the howl of the jackal.

58. Hub (n.) हॅब-1. पहिए या कार के बीच का हिस्सा

I have bought decorative hub-cups for my car.

2. केन्द्र

Mumbai is the hub of film industry.

59. Hubbub (n.) हबब-कोलाहल

There was a real hubbub in the Parliament.

60. Hue (n.) हयू-किसी रंग की विशेष छटा

The sky was painted with bright hues.

61. Hug (n.) हग-आलिंगन, लिपटना

(n.) The mother gave the child a lovinghug.

(v.) My grandmother hugged me fondly when I called on her.

62. Huge (adj.) ह्यूज-विशाल

Have you even seen such a huge cake?

63. Mist (n.) मिस्ट-कुहरा

I did not go for my morning walk because of the mist.

64. Mistake मिस्टेक-1. भूल/ग़लती (करना)

(n.) You have made a mistake in this sentence.

I took your book by mistake.

2. (v.)दूसरा समझना

I mistook you for your younger brother.

65. Misunderstand (v.) मिसअन्डरटेंड-किसी व्यक्ति या वस्तु को समझने में गलती करना

I completely misunderstood what he said.

66. Misuse मिस्यूज़-दुरुपयोग करना

(n.) It was a clear case of misuse of power.

(v.) He was accused of misusing the

funds of the company.

67. Shoe (n.) शू-जूता

I want to buy a new pair of shoes.

68. Shoot शूट-1. गोली (दागना)

(v.) The farmer shoots the fox that kills his chickens.

(n.) How many shots did you hear?

2. पौधे की आँख जहां से नई शाखाएं निकलती हैं/नई कोपलें

We saw a lot of new shoots on the plant.

69. Shop (n.) शॉप-दुकान, हाट

Shops were closed on Sunday.

70. Shore (n.) शॉर्-किनारा, तट

We can find many shells on the sea-shore

The children walked along the shore picking up pebbles

71. Short (adj.) शॉर्ट-छोटा, अल्प, थोड़ा

Short prayers reach heaven.

(v.) Wherever you can shorten a sentence, do so.

72. Shortlist (v.) शॉर्टलिस्ट-संक्षिप्त सूची में नाम रखना

Five candidates were shortlisted for the interview.

73. Shoulder (n.) शोल्ड्र-कंधा

The labourer carried the luggage on his shoulders

(v.) I can happily shoulder all the responsibilities.

74. Worth (adj. & n.) बर्थ-(के) योग्य, (के) लायक

(adj.) This book is worth five hundred rupees.

Your work is worthy of reward.

(n.) The worth of this gem is unknown.

75. Wound वून्ड-घाव (लगाना), घायल (करना)

(v.) Uncle Sharma was wounded in the war.

(n.) His wounds were not serious.

76. Wrapper (n.) रैपर्-किसी चीज़ पर लपेटा गया कागज़

The child ate the candy and threw away the wrapper.

77. Together (adv.) टुगेद्र-1. मिलकर, आपस में

My brother and I had gone for a walk together.

2. सभी (वस्तुओं) के साथ

We gathered together our belongings and left.

78. Toil (v.) टॉइल-कठिन परिश्रम करना

The farm-workers toil until late in the evening.

79. Toilet (n.) टॉइलट-स्नान, कपड़े पहनने और बाल काढ़ने आदि की जगह, शौचालय

Every day Shanta spends minimum twenty minutes in her toilet.

80. Token (n.) टोकन-चिन्ह्, प्रतीक, संकेत

The enemy waved a white flag as a token of surrender.

81. Tolerate (v.) टॉलरेट-सहन करना, समझौता करना,

We have to tolerate in others what we permit in ourselves!

We tolerated each other for thirty years.

82. Toll (v.) टोल-1. घंटा बजाना

The bell ringers will toll the bell during the funeral service.

2. (n.) मार्गशुल्क, राहदारी, महसूल

In some countries, people pay a toll to use the motorways.

83. Play (v. & n.) प्ले-1.खेल (खेलना)

(v.) What games do you like to play?

2. बजाना

Can you play the piano?

3. (n.) नाटक, तमाशा

I have acted in many plays.

84. Plea (n.) प्ली-दलील, तर्क, प्रार्थना

I urged him not to be so thoughtless but he ignored my pleas.

85. Please प्लीज़-1. कृपया

Please take a seat.

2. (v.) अच्छा लगना, खुश करना

I shall be pleased to help you.

The new servant's hardworking nature pleased the master.

3. (adj.) रमणीय

She has pleasing features.

86. Pledge (n.) प्लेज़-प्रतिज्ञा (करना), वचन (देना)

(n.) It's my pledge to help you whenever you need me.

(v.) Our government has pledged to eradicate poverty from the country.

87. Plenty (n.) प्लेन्टि-1. यथेष्टता

We have plenty of time to catch the train.

2. (adj.) बहुत मात्रा में, अधिक

Apples are plentiful in Kashmir.

88. Pliers (n.) प्लाइअर्ज़-प्लास

The electrician pulled the cables by pliers.

89. Plight (n.) प्लाइट-दुर्दशा

The chief minister was moved by the plight of the blast victims.

90. Express इक्स्प्रेस-1. व्यक्त करना, प्रकट करना

(v.) If you want to become a good speaker, you must learn to express yourself effectively.

2. (adj.) जल्द, आशुगामी, जल्द पहुंचाने वाला

Is this an express train?

91. Disheartening (adj.) डिसहार्टनिंग-निराशाजनक

It was disheartening to know that India lost the match against Kenya.

92. Dishonest (adj.) डिसऑनिस्ट-बेईमान

The dishonest servant was fired from the job.

93. Dislike (v.) डिस्लाइक-नापसंद करना

I dislike reaching late to the office.

94. islocate (v.) डिस्लोकेट-हड्डी का अपने स्थान से हट जाना

The accident dislocated his arm.

95. Dismal (adj.) डिज़्मल-दु:खद, उदास, निराशाजनक

The cancer patient's face was very dismal.

96. Dismay डिसमे-घबराहट, व्याकुलता, हिम्मत तोड़ना

(n.) Amitabh was filled with dismay when he found he had to go alone in the dark.

(v.) Passengers were dismayed when they missed the train by just five minutes.

97. Dismiss (v.) डिस्मिस-निकाल देना, दूर करना

The master dismissed his dishonest servant.

98. Disorder (n.) डिसॉर्डर-अव्यवस्था

The political state of the country is in a complete disorder.

99. Dispatch डिस्पैच-भेजना, शीघ्रता से सम्पन्न करना, समाचार, संवाद

(v.) Please dispatch this message im mediately.

(n.) The reporter sent a quick dispatch on train accident to his newspaper office.

100. Responsible (adj.) रिस्पॉन्सिबल्-उत्तरदायी

We are not responsible for the losses you suffer.

Who is responsible for breaking the looking glass?

SPOKEN VOCABULARY
Set - 34

1. **Rest** रे'स्ट-विश्राम (करना)

(n.) Please take rest for a while.

(v.) They rested under a big tree.

2. **Restaurant (n.)** रेस्ट्रॉन्ट्-खाने का होटल

Let us go to a good restaurant for lunch.

3. **Restore (v.)** रिस्टॉर्-1. लौटाना

The police restored all the stolen articles to its owner.

2. नया बनाना

The old picture was cleaned and restored.

3. फिर से संभाल कर रखना

We must restore the books to the shelf after reading them.

4. **Restrain (v.)** रिस्ट्रेन-रोकना, नियंत्रण (में रखना)

Restrain you dog from attacking people.

(n.) Saints keep their passions under restraint.

5. **Restrict (v.)** रिस्ट्रिक्ट-सीमित करना

Restrict youself to two cups of tea a day.

(n.) There are no restrictions on walking here.

6. **Result (n.)** रिज़ॅल्ट-परिणाम

The result of the hockey match was a draw.

(v.) The accident resulted in a fracture in Abdulla's leg.

7. **Resume (v.)** रिज़्यूम-आरंभ करना, दुबारा आरंभ करना

After some rest, we must resume work.

8. **Guarantee** गैरन्टी-गारंटी, जिम्मा लेना

(v.) My car has the guarantee for replacement if any fault was found in its functioning.

9. **Guard** गार्ड-1. रक्षा/रक्षण (करना)

(v.) You should use sunglasses to guard your eyes.

(n.) We put the wire guard in front of the fire to keep the children from getting burnt.

2. गार्ड

As soon as we boarded the train, the guard blew his whistle.

10. **Hullabaloo (n.)** हलाबलू-शोरगुल

The teacher shouted to calm the hullabaloo in the classroom.

11. **Hum (v.)** हम-1. गुनगुनाना

I hummed a tune while taking a bath.

2. गुँजन

The hum of the bees indicated the presence of a hive up in the tree.

12. **Bomb** बॉम-बम, बम बरसाना

(n.) A bomb exploded and killed two persons on the spot.

(v.) The air force planes bombed the enemy's camps.

13. **Bone (n.)** बोन-हड्डी, अस्थि

The broken bones of his leg took a long time wirtten by famous writers.

14. **Involve (v.)** इन्वॉल्व-उलझना, संबंधित होना, सहभागी होना

Never get involved in a pointless

argument.

(n.) Without teacher's involvement, the students could not solve the complex Maths problem.

15. Chop (v.) चॉप-काटना, चीरना

The woodcutter chopped down the tree with an axe.

16. Chore (n.) चॉर-अरुचिकर परंतु अनिवार्य काम

I always get bored of the household chores.

19. Choreograph (v.) कॉरिअग्राफ्-नृत्य-रचना का संयोजन करना

(v.) Vaibhavi Merchant choregraphed the song.

(n.) Choregraphy of Farah Khan is praiseworthy.

(n.) Saroj Khan is a veteran choreographer.

20. Chorus (n.) कोरस-1. गायक-वृन्द, वृन्दगान

Some plays end with a chorus.

The agitators were shouting slogan in a chorus.

2. (v.) एक साथ चिल्लाना

"We want to play cricket." the children chorused

21. Chubby (adj.) चबि-गोल-मटोल

I was very chubby in childhood.

22. Chuckle (v.) चकल्-धीरे-धीरे हँसना

The old man chuckled at his own joke.

23. Chunk (n.) चंक-किसी वस्तु का बड़ा टुकड़ा

He took a large chunk of meat.

24. Church (n.) चर्च-गिरजाघर

The church was decorated beautifully on Christmas.

25. Churn (v.) चर्न-उग्रता से हिलाना

The cyclone churned the sea completely.

26. Cinder(s) (n.) सिन्डर्ज़्-अंगारा

She tried to light a fire with the cinders.

27. Loyal (adj.) लॉइअल-ईमानदार, वफ़ादार

Our servent is very loyal.

28. Human (adj.) ह्यूमन-मानस, मानवीय, मानवोचित

We are all human beings.

Don't behave in such an in human manner.

29. Humble (adj.) हम्बल-1. दीन-हीन, साधारण

K.R Narayanan rose from the humble beginnings to become the President of India.

2. विनीत, नम्र

Rakhi is very humble. in spite of being rich.

30. Mite (n.) माइट-कुटकी

She sprayed the insecticide to kill the mites.

31. Mitigate (v.) मिटिगेट-किसी बुरे प्रभाव को कम कर देना

Plantion of trees mitigated the effects of soil erosion.

32. Mix (v.) मिक्स-1. मिश्रण करना, मिलाना

Sita mixed some water in orange squash to make a cold drink

2. मिलना-जुलना

You are good at mixing with people

3. (adj.) उलझन में

You are all mixed up.

(n.) Water is a mixture of hydrogen and oxygen.

33. Moan मोन-कराह, कराहना

(v.) Are you in pain? You were moaning in your sleep.

(n.) The wounded man's moans could be heard all night.

34. Shout (n.) शाउट-1. चिल्लाना

Am I deaf? Why are you shouting at

me?

Your shouts could be heard from outside.

35. Show (v.) शो-1. दिखाना

Show me the man who did this.

2. बताना, समझाना

Please show me how to do this job.

Would you show me the way to the bus-stop?

3. ज्ञात होना, सिद्ध होना

Her face showed how happy she was.

4. (n.) प्रदर्शन

Are you going to the film-show?

36. Showdown (n.) शोडाउन-झगड़ा

There was a huge showdown in the Parliament.

37. Shower (n.) शॉउअर्-बौछार, बारिश

Rakhi and Rina have been caught in a shower in rain.

38. Shred (n.) श्रे'ड-1. चीथड़ा

In the scuffle, his shirt was torn to shreds.

2. लेश मात्र

There was not a shred of truth in his report.

39. Wrap (n.) रैप-लपेटना, कम्बल, चादर (ओढ़ना)

(v.) Please wrap this book by paper.

40. Wrath (n.) रॉथ-क्रोध

I could not control my wrath at his foolish action.

41. Tomato (n.) टमाटो-टमाटर

Can you tell what ciolour a tomato is?

Tomato is a vegetable.

42. Tomb (n.) टूम्-क़ब्र, समाधि, मक़बरा

Muslims bury a dead body in the ground and build a tomb over it.

43. Tomorrow (n.) टुमॉरो-आने वाला कल (का दिन)

Tomorrow is the day after today. If this is Monday, tomorrow will be Tuesday.

Do not put off till tomorrow what you can do today.

44. Tone (n.) टोन-स्वर, शब्द ध्वनि

The piano has an excellent tone.

I knew by the angry tone of Vatsya's voice that he was annoyed.

45. Tongue (n.) टंग-1. ज़बान, जीभ

We taste with our tongue. We also speak with it.

Nature has given us two ears and one tongue, remember this.

To speak kindly does not hurt the tongue.

Be slow of tongue and quick of eye.

2. भाषा

What is your mother-tongue?

46. Plot (n.) प्लॉट-1. भूखण्ड

I have recently bought a plot of land.

2. कथानक

This story has an interesting plot.

3. (v.) षड्यन्त्र करना

The army general plotted to overthrow the government.

47. Plough (n. & v.) प्लाउ-हल (चलाना)

(n.) Our farmers should use mechanised ploughs.

(v.) The farmer ploughed his field before sowing the seeds.

48. Pluck (v.) प्लॅक-1. तोड़ना, बीनना

Do not pluck flowers.

2. (n.) हिम्मत, साहस

The little boy was full of pluck.

49. Plug प्लग

1. (n.) बिजली का प्लग

Get a new plug for the television cable.

2. (v.) किसी वस्तु से छेद को भरना

She plugged her ears on listening to the minister's speech.

50. Expression (n.) एक्सप्रेशन–रुख, मुद्रा

Why do you have such a sad expression on your face?

51. Dispensary (n.) डिस्पेंसरी–औषधालय

The wounded man was taken to the dispensary.

52. Dispense (v.) डिस्पेन्स– 1. अलग करना, दूर करना

One should dispense with the services of an inefficient secretary quickly.

2. दवा तैयार करना, देना

Does that chemist dispense good medicines?

53. Display डिस्प्ले– 1. दिखाना, सजाना

(v.) New sarees are displayed in the shop window.

2. (n.) प्रर्दशन

Both girls and boys participated in the acrobatic display.

54. Dispose (v.) ड्सिपोज़– 1. बेचना

I have disposed my old car.

2. निपटाना, प्रबंध करना

I have disposed of my work and now I and free.

55. Disposition (n.) डिस्पज़िशन–प्रवृत्ति, मनोवृत्ति, व्यवस्था

Sheela has a very kind disposition.

56. Dispute डिस्प्यूट– 1. विवाद, कलह, झगड़ा

(n.) It is best to avoid taking your familial disputes to a court of law.

2. (v.) प्रर्दशन

Both girls and boys participated in the acrobatic display.

57. Dispose (v.) ड्सिपोज़– 1. बेचना

I have disposed of my work and now I am free.

58. Disposition (n.) डिस्पज़िशन–प्रवृत्ति, मनोवृत्ति, व्यवस्था

Sheela has a very kind disposition.

59. Retail (n.) रीटेल–परचून, खुदरा

Usually the shopkeeper buy goods in large quantities and sell in retail to make profit.

60. Retain (n.) रिटेन–रख लेना, रोक लेना

Yo must retain this pen until you know who owns it.

61. Retire (v.) रिटाइअर–1. सो जाना

You must retire early tonight.

2. सेवा–निवृत्त होना

My father retired at the age of sixty-two.

(n.) He is now living in retirement.

63. Retort (v.) रिटॉर्ट–(गुस्से से) रुखा उत्तर देना

The clerk retorted with anger when he was questioned by the manager.

64. Retreat (v.) रिट्रीट–शत्रु के सामने होने पर पीछे लौटना

The general commanded his troops to retreat.

(n.) Their retreat was carried out very quietly.

65. Retrospect (n.) रेट्रोस्पेक्ट–पुरानी बातों पर विचार

In restrospect, I laugh at how foolish I had been.

66. Retrieve (v.) रिट्रीव–संचित सूचना को प्राप्त करना

How can we retrieve the lost data from the computer?

67. Return (v.) रिटर्न–1. लौटना

You must return the pen she lent you.

2. वापस आना, लौटना

We returned to Mumbai by the

Frontier Mail.

3. लोकसभा आदि में चुना जाना

Mr. A.B. Vajpayee was returned by a good majority to the parilament.

68. Guess गे'स-अनुमान (करना), अन्दाज़ा (लगाना)

(n.) What is your guess about the winne of the India-Pakistan match?

(v.) Can you guess how many times I tried to contact you on the phone?

69. Guest (n.) गे'स्ट-मेहमान, अतिथि

We usually have guests in winters.

70. Mob (n.) मॉब-1. उत्तेजित भीड़, जनसाधारण

From my window, I saw the police firing in the air to disperse the riotous mob.

2. (v.) मिलकर घेर, लेना, तंग करना

As we stood outside the theatre, we saw the popular film star being mobbed by his fans.

71. Mobile (adj.) मोबाइल-चलना, गतिशील

We have a mobile post office in our city.

72. Mock (v.) मॉक-1. उपहास करना, हँसी उड़ाना

If I fail, my friends would mock at me.

2. (adj.) नकली, दिखावटी

Have you ever participated in a mock Parilament?

73. Model (adj.) मॉडल-1. नमूना

I bought a model aeroplane for my son.

Please show me the model of the proposed hospital building.

2. आदर्श

Your son is a model student.

3. (n.) मॉडल

I learn your daughter is working as a model.

4. (v.) (किसी व्यक्ति का) अनुकरण करना

She is modelling herself on her aunt.

74. Book (n.) बुक-1. पुस्तक, ग्रंथ

This is an interesting book.

2. (v.) टिकट लेना

I have booked a ticket for the evening show.

Have you booked your ticket for Mumbai?

75. Boom (n.) बूम-गरम बाज़ारी

Last month, there was a major boom in the stock market.

76. Boon (n.) बून-वरदान

Working with like-minded and experienced people proved to be a boon.

77. Boot (n.) बूट-1. जूता, बूट

Soldiers wear heavy boots.

2. डिक्की, सामानदानी

He put the bag in the boot of his car.

78. Booth (n.) बूथ-प्रकोष्ठ

Voters crowded the voting booth.

79. Booty (n.) बूटि-लूट का माल

The robbers shared the booty among themselves.

80. Antibiotic (n.) ऐन्टिबाइऑटिक-औषधि

An antibiotic might cure your headache.

81. Antique (adj.) ऐन्टीक-प्राचीन होने के कारण असाधारण और मूल्यवान

My mother is fond of collecting antiquepieces of art.

82. Antisocial (adj.) ऐन्टिसोशल-असामाजिक

Dealing with antisocial elements is really a headache for the government.

83. Antithesis (n.) ऐन्टिथीसिस-विपरीत

The aged wrestler now looks an antithesis of what he was earlier.

84. Anvil (n.) ऐन्विल-अरहन, सन्दान, निहाई

The blacksmith was shaping a hot piece of iron on his avail.

85. Anxious (adj.) ऐन्क्शस- 1. व्याकुल

He was anxious to see her.

2. चिंतित, चिंताग्रस्त

Students were anxious about their examination result

(n.) चिंता

The boby's mother was full of anxiety about her infant's health

86. Any (adj.) एनी-1. कोई, कुछ

Have you any stamps?

2. कोई भी

You can buy pastries from any bakery.

87. Involved (adj.) इन्वॉल्व्ड-दुर्भेद्य, जटिल

The message I received was so involved that I could not understand it.

88. Fraternity (n.) फ्रटनटि-एक ही वर्ग के नोगों की बीच परस्पर बंधुता

He is a known person in the architectural fraternity

89. Fraud (n.) फ्रॉड-धोखा, कपट

An enquiry exposed the fraud played by the former bankmanager.

90. Freak फ्रीक-1. कट्टर

(n.) She is a real fitness freak.

2. कठोर प्रतिक्रिया व्यक्त करना

(v.) The mother freaked on seeing her child in dirty clothes

91. Free फ्री-1. स्वतन्त्र (करना)

(v.) She opened the cage and freed the little bird.

(adj.) On what date did India become free?

2. खाली, सावकाश

Are you free this evening?

3. मुफ्त, निःशुल्क

I got a toothbrush free with a jar of face-cream

92. Freeze (v.) फ्रीज़-जमकर बर्फ़ बनाना, जमना अकड़ना, स्तंभित करना

Dal Lake freezes in the winter

93. Frequent (adj.) फ्रीक्वन्ट-बारंबार होने वाला लगातार

I have made frequent trips to Mumbai

94. Cinema (n.) सिनेमा

1. सिनेमा घर

Let's which a movie in a cinema hall.

2. फ़िल्म उद्योग

India cinema has progressed a lot in the past few years.

95. Cinnamon (n.) सिनमन-दालचीनी

Rice tasted better with the aroma of cinnamon.

96. Circle सर्कल-वृत्त, चक्कर, चक्र, चक्कर लगाना, घेर लेना

(n.) The geometry teacher taught the students to draw a circle.

(v.) The dancers circled the tree as they danced.

97. Circular सर्क्युलर्-1. गोल, वर्तुल

(adj.) The parliament House is a circular building.

2. (n.) परिपत्र

The company sent a circular to all its clients about its new product.

98. Circuit (n.) सर्किट-विद्युत धारा का परिपथ सर्किट

The factory caught fire because of the short circuit.

99. Circumstances (n.) सरकम्स्टान्सस्-घटना, बात परिस्थिति

A man's courage and tolerance are put to test in adverse circumstances

100. Circulate (v.) सर्क्युलेट-प्रचारित करना

(v.) The pamphlets were circulated to all the houses in the area.

(n.) The Times of India claims to have the largest circulation.

SPOKEN VOCABULARY
Set - 35

1. **Circus (n.)** सर्कस-सर्कस
Children laughed at the clown in the circus.

2. **Cite (v.)** साइट-उदाहरण की सहायता से किसी बात का उल्लेख करना
Can you cite an example to prove your point?

3. **City (n.)** सिटि-नगर, शहर
Tokyo is the biggest city in the world.

4. **Lubricate** लूब्रिकेट-तेल देना, चिकना करना
(v.) You must lubricate the engine of your car regularly.
(n.) This machine needs lubrication.

5. **Lucid (adj.)** लूसिड-सरल और सुबोध
The books is written in a lucid style.

6. **Humility (n.)** ह्यूमिलिटि-विनय, दीनता
Your greatness lies in your humility.

7. **Humour (n.)** ह्यूमर्-1. मज़ाक, विनोद
You have a good sense of humour.
2. मिज़ाज़, मनोदशा
Why are you in such a bad humour?
Ramesh was in good humour because he had won a lottery prize.

8. **Shrewd (adj.)** श्रूड-चुस्त-चालाक, तीक्ष्ण बुद्धि
A shrewd businessman would never say such a thing.

9. **Shriek (v.)** श्रीक-चीखना
The kids shrieked with joy.

10. **Shrill (adj.)** श्रिल-तेज़ और अप्रिय आवाज़
She has a shrill voice

11. **Shrine (n.)** श्राइन-समाधि
Many foreigners visit the shrine of Swami Vivekanada

12. **Shrink (v.)** श्रिंक-सिकुड़ना, संकोच करना
Your sweater may shrink if you wash it.
Some persons shrink from meeting a stranger.

13. **Shroud** श्राउड-कफ़न
(n.) The dead body was wrapped in a shroud.
(v.) Silence was shrouding the atmosphere.

14. **Shrub (n.)** श्रब-झाड़ी
The rose shrub in the garden looks beautiful.

15. **Shrug** श्रग-कंधा उचकाना
(v.) The shopkeeper simply shrugged when I told him that his prices were very high.
(n.) Mother answered with a shrug

16. **Wreath (n.)** रीथ-माला, हार, गजरा
The people showed respect to their dead leader

17. **Wrath (n.)** रॉथ-क्रोध
I could not control my wrath at his foolish action.

18. **Tonic (n.)** टॉनिक-स्फूर्तिदायक पदार्थ
Mother's milk is a tonic for infants

19. **Tonight (n.)** टुनाइट-आज की रात
Tonight is the night of today.

20. **Tonsil (n.)** टॉन्सिल-गले के दोनों ओर की गिल्टिया को ज़बान की जड़ के दोनों ओर होती हैं
If we open our mouth wide in front of a mirror, we shall be able to see our tonsils

21. **Too (adv.)** टू-भी, अत्याधिक, ज्यादा, (आवश्यकता से अधिक)

You can see a star. Can you see a fairy too?

The patient is too weak to walk.

Never be too clever.

Your shoes are too big for you.

22. Tool (n.) टूल-औज़ार, हथियार

Hammer is a tool. Plumbers and carpenters have tools.

23. Tooth (n.) टूथ-दाँत, दाँता

Go to the dentist if you have a tooth-ache.

We chew with our teeth.

My comb has lost three of its teeth.

24. Top (n.) टॉप-1. लट्टू

Can you spin the top round and round?

2. (adj.) सर्वोच्च

Please give top priority to this work.

(n.) The staff was corrupt from top to bottom.

25. Topic (n.) टॉपिक-विषय, प्रसंग, प्रकरण

Fashion, films and politics are the topics on which people generally talk.

What are the topics of today's discussion?

26. Plum (n.) प्लॅम्-आलूबुंखारा

The child liked to eat fresh plums.

Children like to eat fresh plums.

27. Plumage (n.) प्लूमिज-पक्षियों के पर

The pigeon had a thick plumage.

28. Plumber (n.) प्लमर्-नलसाज़, नल का मिस्त्री

I called the plumber to repair our wash-basin.

29. Plume (adj.) प्लूम-पर, पंख

The peacock has beautiful plumes.

30. Plump (adj.) प्लम्प-गोल-मटोल

She is rather plump, isn't she?

31. Plunder (v. & n.) प्लन्डर्-लूटना, लूट

(v.) The decoits plundered the rich man's mansion.

(n.) They loaded the plunder in a truck and drove away.

32. Plunge (n. & v.) प्लॅन्ज्-गोता/डुबकी (लगाना)

(v.) I plunged into the water to save the drowning child.

(n.) A careless plunge into the water can be harmful.

33. Ply (v.) प्लाइ-सड़कों पर सेवा उपलब्ध कराना

The man was plying rickshaw on the road.

34. Extend (v.) इक्स्टेन्ड-फैलना, बढ़ाना, देना

You will have to extend your boundary wall to protect your garden.

Rahul thanked his friend for the warm hospitality extended to him.

35. Dispute डिस्प्यूट- 1. विवाद, कलह, झगड़ा

(n.) It is best to avoid taking your familial disputes to a court of law.

2. (v.) खंडन करना, प्रतिवाद करना

The minister's statement on the improved law and order situation was disputed by the opposition members.

36. Disrupt (v.) डिस्रप्ट-पिघ्न डालना

Rain disrupted the match telecast.

37. Dissatisfaction (n.) डिस्सैटिस्फैक्शन-असंतोष

(n.) The students expressed their dissatisfaction at the exam results.

(v.) The students were dissatisfied with the results.

38. Dissolve (v.) डिज़ॉल्व- 1. घुलना, घोलना

A small piece of ice soon dissolves in water.

Sugar does not dissolve quickly in the chilled water.

2. समाप्त करना, विसर्जित करना

When was the last Lok Sabha dissolved?

39. Distance (n.) डिस्टन्स-दूरी, फ़ासला

What is the distance between your school and your home?

(adj.) Don't you like to read books on distant places?

40. Reveal (v.) रिवील-गुप्त बात प्रकट करना (या होना)

I promised Amitabh that I would never reveal his secrets.

The truth was revealed at last.

41. Revenge (n.) रिवेन्ज-बदला, प्रतिरोध

He swore to take a revenge on his enemies.

Revenge is not a remedy to establish peace on earth.

42. Reunion (n.) रीयूनिअन्-पुनर्मिलन पार्टी

All the old students were invited for the college reunion.

43. Revenue (n.) रेवन्यू-राजस्व

Income tax is one of the major sources of revenue for the government.

44. Reverberate (v.) रिवर्बरेट-ध्वनि का गूंजना

After the performance, the auditorium reverberated with the sound of claps.

45. Revere (v.) रिविअर्-आदर करना

Gulzar is revered as one of the greatest lyricists in the industry.

46. Guide गाइड-1. मार्गदर्शक, गाइड, नेता

(n.) We should engage a guide when we go to Ajanta caves.

2. संदर्शिका, गाइड

You should learn from your textbook, not from a guide.

3. (v.) मार्ग दिखाना

Can you guide me to the post office?

47. Guilty (adj.) गिल्टि-दोषी

The judge found the accused guilty of the crime.

(n.) Your guilt is not proved.

48. Shudder (v.) शॅडर्-कांप उठना, थरथराना, रोंगटे खड़े होना

The terrible thought made her shudder.

(n.) A shudder passed through me when I looked at the dead body.

49. Shuffle (v.) शफ़ल-ताश के पत्ते फेंटना

She shuffled the cards well.

50. Shun (v.) शॅन-(से)दूर रहना, (से) बचना, टालना

We should shun cheats.

51. Shunt (v.) शॅन्ट-छकड़े आदि को बगल की पटरी या रेल पर लाना

Our carriage was shunted aside until the Toofan Express had passed.

52. Shut (v.) शॅट-बंद करना, मीचना, बंद होना (काम समाप्त होना)

Shut all the doors and windows.

Shut your eyes.

Shut up! Keep quiet.

The concern was shut down because it was running in loss.

If you come to the hotel late, you will be shut out.

53. Shy (adj.) शाइ-1. संकोची, शर्मीला

Don't feel shy before the interview-board.

(adv.) Why do you answer shyly when you are asked a question?

2. (v.) जी चुराना

He always shies away from work.

54. Sibling (n.) सिबलिंग-सगे भाई-बहन

How many siblings do you have?

55. Sick (adj.) सिक-अस्वस्थ, बीमार, रोग-ग्रस्त

It is very difficult for a sick man to move briskly.

56. Side (n.) साइड-1. किनारे

Sonia was riding by the side of the road.

2. एक तरफ़

When you prepare a manuscript, don't write on both sides of the paper.

3. पास

You must stand by my side.

4. दिशा

People gathered from all sides of the area.

5. पक्ष

Is she on your side or Amitabh's?

57. Sieve (n.) सीव-छानना (गाहना)

These seeds will grow better if the soil is sieved before they are sown.

58. Border (n.) बॉर्डर्-1. सीमा

The border between the two countries is heavily guarded.

2. किनारा

She wore a yellow sari with a black border.

59. Bore (v.) बॉर्-1. छेद करना, खोदना

It is necessary to bore deep holes in the earth to find petroleum.

2. (n.) कानखाऊ, उबाने वाला

Everybody avoids a bore.

3. छेद, नली

He drilled a deep bore in the ground.

60. Borrow (v.) बॉरो-उधार लेना

May I borrow your pen for a few minutes?

61. Boss बॉस-मालिक

(n.) Her boss was irritated when she could not complete the project on time.

(v.) No one likes to be bossed around.

(adj.) Stop behaving so bossy.

62. Both (adj.) बोथ-दोनों

Both my brothers are elder than me.

I put both the apples on the table.

(prep.) Both of us are going.

63. Fresh (adj.) फ्रेश-1. ताजा, नवीन

Seeing fresh flowers in the morning is quite refreshing.

2. चुस्त, फुर्तीला

I feel fresh after I have a cup of tea.

64. Fret (v.) फ्रेट-चिढ़ाना, कुढ़ना

Why do you fret so much about domestic difficulties.

65. Friend (n.) फ्रेन्ड-मित्र, दोस्त

I have a large circle of friends.

66. Fright (n.) फ्राइट-भीति, आतंक

I had a fright when the dog rushed at me.

67. Fringe (n.) फ्रिन्ज-किनारा

There was a hunting lodge on the fringe of the forest.

68. Apart (adv.) अपार्ट-1. अलावा

Apart form movies, Ramesh was also fond of good food.

2. पृथक्, अलग

The child tore the book apart.

69. Apartment (n.) अपार्टमन्ट-कमरा, फ्लैट

Apartments on the main road are very costly.

70. Ape (n.) एप - 1. वानर, बंदर

I saw an ape in the zoo.

2. (v.) नकल करना

We should not ape the western manners.

71. Apologise (v.) अपॉलजाइज़्-क्षमा मांगना, खेद प्रकट करना

(v.) The minister apologised for arrivinglate.

Rakesh sent an apology for not being able to attend my sister's wedding.

72. Apostle (n.) अपॉसल-भयभीत करना

Gandhiji is known as an apostle of

non-violence.

73. Appal (v.) अपॉल-भयभीत करना

(v.) The news of a likely bomb blast appallend the whole city.

(adj.) The news of the bomb blast was appalling.

(adj.) The city was appalled at the news of a likely bomb blast.

74. Apparent (adj.) अपैरन्ट-प्रकट, स्पष्ट, प्रत्यक्ष

It was apparent from Arun's face that he didn't like Amit's rude manners.

(adv.) The traveller was apparently lost, for he was not sure which way to proceed.

75. Iron (n.) आइरन्-1. लोहा

Is this hammer made of iron?

2. (v.) इस्तरी करना

Will you please iron my shirt?

76. Civil (adj.) सिविल-सभ्य नागरिक, असैनिक, सरकारी नौकरी

(adj.) Under civil rule, the Army has no role in the government functioning. Subhash Chandra Bose was selected for the civil services (government service except service in the armed forces.

(n.) सभ्यता

In ancient times, many civilisations prospered on the river banks.

77. Civilian (n.) सिविल्यन-असैनिक, असैनिक पदाधिकारी

Rehman has retired from the Army, now he is a civilian.

78. Citizen (n.) सिटिज़न-नागरिक

We are responsible citizens of the country.

79. Civilisation (n.) सिविलाइज़ेशन-सभ्यता

Cleopatra was a powerful empress of the Roman civilisation.

80. Civilised (adj.) सिविलाइज़्ड-नम्र और विवेकपूर्ण

His behaviour was highly civilised and sophisticated.

81. Claim (v. & n.) क्लेम-दावा, अधिकार, दावा करना

(v.) Daughters can also claim a share in their father's property.

(n.) A son's claim to his father's property is universally accepted.

82. Luck (n.) लक-भाग्य, सौभाग्य

Good luck for your exams.

(adj.) You are lucky to win such a nice prize.

83. Hump (n.) हम्प-कूबड़

The child asked. "How did the camel get that hump?"

84. Hunger हन्गर्-1. भूख, क्षुधा, भूखा होना

(n.) Hunger for food can easily be satisfied but not hunger for wealth.

(adj.) Are you hungry now?

2. (v.) लालसा करना

Why do you hungers so much for fame?

85. Money (n.) मनी-रुपया-पैसा

Can you lend me some money?

86. Monitor (n.) मॉनिटर्-छात्रनायक, कक्षानायक, प्रबोधक

My son has been made the monitor of his class.

87. Monk (n.) मॉङ्क-संन्यासी

The monks helped the wounded man they found.

80. Monopoly (n.) मनॉपलि-नीरसता

The company has a monopoly in garment making.

81. Wreath (n.) रीथ-माला, हार, गजरा

The people showed respect to their dead leader with the wreaths of flowers.

82. Wreck रें'क-1. बरबाद, जहाज, नष्ट-भ्रष्ट पोत

(n.) Nothing could be saved from the wreck.

2. (n.) बरबाद होना, नष्ट-भ्रष्ट होना

The bogey ran off the rail-track and was wrecked.

83. Topple (v.) टॉपल-गिर पड़ना

The big pile of books toppled over.

The pile of bricks came toppling down.

84. Torch (n.) टॉर्च-मशाल, टार्च (सेलों वाली)

My friend gave me a torch to see my way in the night.

85. Torment टॉर्मे न्ट-यातना (देना), यंत्रणा (दंना)

(v.) Sudha was tormented by a toothache.

(n.) The prisoner could not bear the torment ın the cell and died.

86. Tornado (n.) टॉनेडो-चक्रवात

The tornado ıs Orissa uprooted a number of trees.

87. Torpedo (v.) टॉर्पीडो-प्रक्षेपास्त्र माना, (जलयान को) बरबाद कर देना

Thıs ship sank within a few minutes of being torpedoed.

88. Torrent (n.) टॉरन्ट-प्रचण्ड धारा वाली नदी, बौछार

After the heavy rain, the stream became a torrent.

It rained in torrents.

89. Tortoise (n.) टॉर्टस-कछुआ, कूर्म

Some tortoises live on land and the others in sea.

90. Torture (v. & n.) टॉर्चर्-यातना (देना), यंत्रणा (देना), उत्पीड़न (देना)

The police tortured the thief to make him tell about the things stolen by him.

(n.) Political prisoners were put to torture.

91. Pneumonia (n.) न्यूमोनिआ-निमोनिया

The child was suffering from pneumonia.

92. Poach (v.) पोच-गैर-कानूनी ढंग से पशुओं का शिकार करना

Poaching is banned by the governments of most of the countries.

93. Pocket (n. & v.) पॉकिट-जेब, जेब में रखना

(n.) My pockets are always full of odds and ends.

(v.) He pocketed the note after reading it.

94. Poetry पोअट्रि-कविता

She has been writing poetry since she was a child.

95. Poignant (adj.) पॉइन्यन्ट्-मार्मिक

It was a poignant tale of an orphaned girl.

96. Point (n.) पॉइंट-1. दिखलाना

Can you point out the man who spoke to you?

2. (n.) नोक

He pricked me with the point of his pencil.

3. विषय

There are several points in your article which I wish to discuss with you.

97. Poise (n.) पॉइज़्-आत्मविश्वासपूर्ण आचरण

She delivered her speech with poise and confidence.

98. Exterior (n.) इक्स्टिअरिअर्-बाहरी हिस्सा

The exterior of the building was decorated with wooden carvings.

99. Distinct (adj.) डिस्टिन्क्ट-भिन्न, अलग, सुस्पष्ट

I can easily read Minakshi's handwriting because it is so distinct.

Write your name distinctly.

100. Distinction (n.) डिस्टिन्क्श्न्- 1. श्रेष्ठता, प्रतिष्ठा

Suresh's son passed the examination with distinction.

2. भिन्नता, भेदभाव

Is there any distinction between nylon and cotton?

SPOKEN VOCABULARY
Set - 36

1. **Distinguish (v.)** डिस्टिन्ग्विश- 1. पहचानना

I could not distinguish the approaching truck in the fog.

2. प्रसिद्ध होना, ख्याति पाना

He distinguished himself as a doctor.

(adj.) He became a distinguished doctor.

2. **Distress (n.)** डिस्ट्रेस-दु:ख, कष्ट, संकट

The poor old man was in great distress.

(v.) The bad news distressed us.

3. **Distribute (v.)** डिस्ट्रिब्यूट-बाँटना, वितरण करना

Rahul distributed sweets on the birth of his daughter.

4. **District (n.)** डिस्ट्रिक्ट-जिला

The case was passed on to the High Court from the District Court.

5. **Disturb (v.)** डिस्टर्ब-शांति भंग करना, बाधा डालना

Do not disturb the people who are reading in the library.

(n.) Raju was feeling disturbance in his studies due to a marriage reception in the neighbourhood.

6. **Reverse** रिवर्स-विपरीत

(n.) What is there at the reverse of the painting?

(v.) Writing is reversed in the mirror.

(adj.) The new policy had the reverse effect of what was expected.

7. **Revert (v.)** रिवर्ट-वापस आना

We reverted back to the old rules.

8. **Review** रिव्यू

1. समालोचना

(n.) The movie got good reviews in newspapers.

(v.) The movie was favourably reviewed in the newspapers.

2. सर्वेक्षण

(n.) The company decided to hold an annual review of the progress.

(v.) The company reviewed the progress over the past one year.

9. **Revise (v.)** रिवाइज़-दोहराना, फिर से पढ़ना

We can improve our composition if we revise it.

Your eassay needs revision.

10. **Guise (n.)** गाइज़-वेश

He was a policeman under the guise of a bus passenger.

11. **Wrench** रे'न्च-दु:ख, मानसिक पीड़ा, मरोड़ना, कसने का यंत्र

(n.) I felt a wrench when my younger brother left home.

Use your wrench and tighten the screws of my bike.

(v.) Wrench the screw of your pressure cooker with this small instrument.

12. **Wrestle (v.)** रे'सल-कुश्ती (लड़ना), मल्लयुद्ध (करना)

The poor wretch looked so distressed that I felt sorry for him.

The man who stole the money from the poor window was a wicked wretch.

13. **Bother (v.)** बॉदर-तंग करना, परेशान करना-होना

Please do not bother me when I am working.

Please do not bother to come personally.

14. **Bottle (n.)** बॉट्ल-बोतल, शीशी

He poured the milk from the bottle into the pot.

15. Bottom (v.) बॉटम-तल, तह

The ship sank to the bottom of the sea.

16. Bough (n.) बाउ-शाखा, डाल

The bough of the tree was laden with fruits.

17. Boulder (n.) बोल्डर्-शिलाखंड, गोल पत्थर

The seashore was strewn with boulders.

18. Bounce (v.) बाउन्स-1. उछल कर वापस आना

The ball bounced back after hitting the wall.

2. (चेक) वापस आना

The cheque bounced as there was not enough money in the account.

19. Bound (v.) बाउन्ड-1. कूदना, छलाँग मारना

The dog bounded after the rabbit.

2. सीमा, हद

This area is out of bounds for civilians.

(adj.) अवश्य ही

He is bound to win the race.

20. Frivolous (adj.) फ़्रिवलस-अगंभीर

Let's not get into a frivolous conversation now.

21. Front फ़्रन्ट-अग्रिम, अग्र भाग

(adj.) Please open the front door.

(n.) The front of my house faces a park.

22. Frontier (n.) फ़्रन्टिअर्-सरहद, सीमा

Our frontier with Pakistan has been fenced in Punjab.

23. Frost (n.) फ़्रॉस्ट-बर्फ़ की पतली परत

The front on the windscreen made'it difficult to drive the car.

24. Froth (n.) फ़्रॉथ-झाग

The child licked at the froth on the shake.

25. Frown (v. & n.) फ़्राउन-भौंहे चढ़ाना, तेवर, अप्रसन्नता प्रकट करना

Why are you frowning at me?

We could tell by her frown that she was angry.

26. Appear (v.) अपिअर्-1. दिखाई देना, प्रकट होना

The passengers were happy to see the long delayed train appear on the platform.

2. लगना, प्रतीत होना

It appears that he wants to avoid me.

3. (परीक्षा में) बैठना

Geeta has appeared for I.A.S. examination this year.

29. Appetite (n.) ऐपिटाइट-भूख, क्षुधा

During illness, patients often lost their appetite.

30. Applaud (v.) अप्लॉड-वाह-वाह करना, तालियां बजाना

The entire gathering applauded the little boy's fine acting.

(n.) Our principal was greeted with applause when he rose to speak at the annual function.

31. Appliance (n.) अप्लाइअन्स-उपकरण, यंत्र

The modern housewife has many domestic appliances at her disposal.

32. Apply (v.) अप्लाइ-1. आवेदन करना, दरख्वास्त देना

Shikha and Juhi applied for a job in the same firm.

2. लगाना

It will take a week to apply paint to our house.

3. लागू होना या करना

Laws of the land apply to everyone.

(n.) अर्जी

Rama's job application was rejected.

33. Appoint (v) अपॉइन्ट-1. नियुक्त करना, नौकरी पर रखना

My brother has been appointed as the manager in a good company.

2. (n.) नियोजित भेंट

Today my father has got an appointment with the dentist.

34. Irregular (adj.) इरेग्यलर्-1. बेकायदा, अवैध

I must point out that the procedure you have followed is very irregular.

2. अनियमित

Why is your son so irregular in attending school?

35. Clan (v.) क्लैन-वंश

Chanakya vowed to destroy the Whole Nand clan.

36. Clap (v.) क्लैप-ताली बजाना

Everyone clapped when the political leader rose to speak.

37. Clarification (n.) क्लैरफ़िकेशन-स्पष्टीकरण

(n.) I don't want any clarification for the mistakes you committed.

(v.) Le me clarify my point.

38. Clarity (n.) क्लैरटि-स्पष्टता

Your eassay lacks clarity of thought.

39. Clash (n.) क्लैश-1. भिड़न्त, संघर्ष, टकराव

Some people were injured during the clash between the two groups.

2. शोर

With a clash of cymbals, the band began to play.

3. (v.) झगड़ा करना

The two groups clashed and many people were injured.

40. Clasp (v.) क्लास्प - 1. पकड़ना, जकड़ना गले लगाना

He clasped my hand warmly.

2. (n.) बकलस, बकसुआ

She bought a beautiful golden clasp.

41. Class (n.) क्लास-1. वर्ग, श्रेणी, कक्षा

Under 10+2 system, the students study in school up to 12th class.

Rail journey in the first class is quite comfortable.

2. प्रकार, किस्म

Cats and tigers belong to the same class of animals.

42. Lucrative (adj.) लूक्रटिव-लाभप्रद

He got a lucrative offer from the rival company.

43. Hunt (v.) हन्ट-1. शिकार करना

How many tigers have you hunted?

2. खोज करना

I hunted everywhere but could not find my book.

(n.) Everyone joined in the hunt for the lost bag.

44. Hurdle (n.) हर्डल-बाधा

These are just temporary hurdles.

45. Monotony (n.) मनॉटनि-एकाधिकार

(n.) The atmosphere in a call centre is shrouded with monotony.

(adj.) Working in cali centres often tends to become monotonous.

46. Monsoon (n.) मॉन्सन्-वर्षा-ऋतु

Now that the monsoon is near, we must repair our leaking roof.

47. Monster (n.) मॉन्स्टर-शैतान

These kids are little monsters.

48. Month (n.) मन्थ-महीना, मास

I have not come to you for a month.

(adj.) Is this a monthly magazine?

49. Monument (n.) मॉन्युमन्ट-स्मारक, कीर्ति, स्तम्भ

Have you seen all the old monuments in Delhi?

50. Mood (n.) मूड-मनोदशा, चित्तवृत्ति

The boss seems to be in a happy mood today.

I want to speak to him when he is in a better mood.

51. Toss टॉस–सिक्का या गेंद उछालना, सिक्का उछालने की क्रिया

(v.) Toss the ball over the wall.

The ball was tossed from one player to another.

(n.) In cricket much depends on which team wins the toss.

52. Total (adj.) टोटल–पूर्ण, सम्पूर्ण, सारा, समूचा

The ship struck the rock and became a total wreck.

(v.) जोड़ करना

Now you total up the bills and I shall check them.

53. Totter (v.) टॉटर्–लड़खड़ाना, डगमगाना

Young children totter about when they first try to walk.

The old man tottered along and nearly fell once or twice.

54. Touch टॅच–1. स्पर्श (करना)

(n.) The nurse had a gentle touch.

(v.) I can barely touch the ceiling.

2. मर्महित करना, द्रवित करना/होना

We were touched by her kindness.

3. सम्पर्क में आना

Are you in touch with Mr. Sanjay Pandit?

55. Tough (adj.) टफ़्–1. ठोस, कड़ा

Meat that is tough, is difficult to cut and eat.

2. कठिन

To succeed both in education and sports is really a tough job.

56. Tour (n.) टुअर्–दौरा, यात्रा, पर्यटन

We made a tour of the city.

Many tourists visit the Taj Mahal every day.

(v.) We are touring the Himalayas this summer.

57. Poison (n.) पॉइज़न–विष, ज़हर

Potassium cyanide is a deadly poison.

(adj.) Not all snakes are posionous.

(v.) ज़हर देना

Socrates was poisoned to death.

58. Poke (v.) पोक्–खरोंचना, कुरेदना

The little girl poked a stick into the hole in the garden.

59. Pole (n.) पोल–बल्ला, डंडा

There is a telephone pole just opposite our house.

2. ध्रुव

The explorers went up to the North Pole.

60. Police (n.) पोलिस्–पुलिस

Where is the nearest police station?

61. Policy (n.) पोलिस्–नीति

It is my policy to pay all my bills without delay.

62. Polish (n. & v.) पॉलिश–1. पालिश (करना)

(n.) I want some polish for my car.

(v.) He polished his shoes before wearing them.

2. (adj.) परिष्कृत

He is polished gentleman.

63. Polite (adj.) पलाइट–शिष्ट, भद्र

He is always polite in his behaviour.

(n.) Politeness costs nothing.

64. Political (adj.) पलिटिकल–राजनीतिक

I have participated in political activities since my school days.

65. Poll (n.) पोल्–मतदान

We might have a mid-term poll very soon.

66. Pomegranate (n.) पॉमिग्रैनिट्–अनार

There was a pomegranate tree in the village.

67. Extra (adj.) एक्सट्रा–अधिक, अतिरिक्त

Do you have an extra pencil?

68. Ditch (n.) डिच-नाली, खाई

The street leading to your house is full of ditches.

69. Dive (v.) डाइव-गोता लगाना, डुबकी मारना

Can you dive into the swimming pool?

70. Divert (v.) डाइवर्ट- 1. दूसरे मार्ग पर ले जाना, मोड़ना

2. ध्यान हटा देना

Don't let your attention get diverted while studying

71. Diverse (adj.) डाइवर्स-विविध

India is the land of diverse cultures.

72. Divide (v.) डिवाइड-बाँटना, विभाजित करना

Let us divide this amount equally between us.

73. Division (n.) डिविश्न्- 1. विभाग, वर्ग

How many divisions does your company have?

2. विभाज़न, भाग

Is your child good at division?

74. Divine (adj.) डिवाइन-दिव्य, दैवी

Don't you agree that there is something divine about Nature's beauty?

75. Dizzy (adj.) डिज़ि-चक्कर से आक्रान्त, व्याकुल, भौचक्का

After riding the merry-go-round, I felt dizzy.

76. Revive (v.) रिवाइस-1. पुनर्जीवित होना

The plant revive after I watered it.

77. Revolt रिवोल्ट-विद्रोह (करना)

(v.) The peasants revolted against their landlords.

(n.) The peasants's revolt was badly crushed.

78. Revolve (v.) रिवॉल्व-घूमना, (चारों ओर) चक्कर लगाना

The moon revolves round the earth, and earth revolves round the sun.

79. Reward रिवॉर्ड-इनाम (देना), पुरस्कार (देना)

(n.) The conductor of the D.T.C bus, who found the gentleman's purse, was rewarded for his bravery.

80. Rhyme (n.) राइम-तुकान्त गीत या कविता

The children recited nursery rhymes.

81. Rhythm (n.) रिद्म-लय, ताल, सामंजस्य

The audience started to clap in rhythm with the music.

82. Rib (n.) रिब्-पसली

Eve was said to be born from Adam's rib.

83. Ribbon (n.) रिबन-पट्टी

The hair of the girl was tied with a ribbon.

84. Rice (n.) राइस-चावल

In Bengal, people mostly take rice.

85. Rich (adj.) रिच-1. संपन्न, धनी

Hard work made him a rich man.

2. भारी, गरिष्ठ

I cannot digest rich food. It makes me feel ill.

86. Rid (v.) रिड-मुक्त करना

Get rid of this old cycle.

87. Riddle (n.) रिडल-पहेली

Can you guess the answer to this riddle?

88. Ride (v.) राइड-चढ़ाना, सवारी करना

Can you ride a motorcycle?

(n.) We had a pleasant ride.

Both the donkey and the rider fell into the stream.

89. Gulf (n.) गल्फ़-खाड़ी, खाई, अन्तर

He left India when he got a lucrative job in Persian Gulf country.

90. Gullible (adj.) गलब्ल-भोला-भाला

Eve was gullible enough to believe the words of Satan.

91. Tournament (n.) टॉर्नमन्ट-खेल-प्रतियोगिता

What was the result of India-

Australia cricket tournament?

92. Tout (v.) टाउट्-ज़ोर-शोर से प्रचार करना

The product was touted as the best among its rivals.

93. Tow (v.) टो-खींचना, घसीटना

The lorry towed the battered car to the garage.

The damaged ship was towed back to the port.

94. Towards (prep.) टुवॉर्डज-की ओर, के प्रति, के लिए

Vagish walked towards the car.

The millionaire behaves generously towards all poor people.

95. Towel (n.) टाउअल-तौलिया

We wipe our wet hands on the towel.

Have you a bath-towel in your bathroom?

86. Tower (v. & n.) टाउअर्-ऊँचा उठना, मीनार, लाट, बुर्ज

The tall fir trees tower over the small house.

We can hear the bells ringing in the clock-tower.

87. Town (n.) टाउन-क़स्बा, छोटा शहर

A town is a small city.

There are streets and shops in a town.

She would rather live in a village than in a town.

88. Toxic (adj.) टॉक्सिक-ज़हरीला

Vehicles release toxic gases in the air.

89. Toy (n.) टॉय-1. खिलौना

Children play with their toys.

2. (v.) खेलना, खिलवाड़ करना

All the time she talked, she was toying with her purse.

90. Boundary (n.) बाउन्डरि-सीमा, मर्यादा

The river is the boundary between the two countries.

91. Bouquet (n.) बुके-गुलदस्ता, गुच्छा

He presented her with a lovely bouquet.

92. Bow (n.) बो-1. धनुष, चाप

Arjun attached an arrow to his bow.

2. सरकफन्दा

She tied the ribbob into a bow.

(v.) बाउ-3. झुक जाना, नमस्कार करना

He bowed respectfully to the old man.

(n.) The servant welcomed his master with a bow.

93. Bowl (v.) बोल् - 1. गेंद चलाना, आउट करना

The batsman was bowled out.

2. (n.) कटोरा

She poured some milk in a bowl for her cat.

94. Box (n.) बॉक्स-1. संदूक, बक्सा, डिब्बा

Tinku put his toys in a box.

2. मुक्केबाजी, मुष्टि युद्ध करना

(v.) He boxed his opponent.

95. Boy (n.) बॉय-लड़का, बालक

How many boys are there in your class?

96. Boycott (v.) बॉइकॉट-बहिष्कार करना

Opposition boycotted the proposal of the ruling party.

97. Fruit (n.) फ्रूट-1.फल

Which is your favourite fruit?

2. परिणाम, नतीजा

Good score is the fruit of regular study.

98. Frustrate (v.) फ्रस्ट्रेट-खीझना

She got frustrated when he arrived late.

99. Fry (v.) फ्राइ-तलना, भूनना

I am frying fish.

100. Fuel (n.) फ्यूअल-ईधन, जलावन

We use petroleum gas for fuel.

SPOKEN VOCABULARY
Set - 37

1. **Fugitive (n.)** फ़्यूजटिव-फ़रारी, भगोड़ा

   The newspapers published the picture of the fugitive prisoner.

2. **Fulfil (v.)** फुल्फ़िल-पूरा करना, पालन करना

   I shall do my best to fulfil your expectations.

3. **Appreciate (v.)** अप्रीशिएट-रसास्वादन करना, गुण पहचानना

   He appreciates classical music.

   (n.) सराहना, प्रशंसा

   The audience showed their appreciation for the singer by clapping.

4. **Apprehend (v.)** ऐप्रिहेन्ड-गिफ़्तार करना

   The servant was apprehended for the theft in the house.

5. **Apprentice (n.)** अप्रेन्टिस-प्रतिक्षार्थी

   He is working as an apprentice with a carpenter.

6. **Approach (v.)** अप्रोच-पास जाना, पहुंचना

   The thief approached the locker silently.

7. **Appropritate (adj.)** अप्रोप्रिअट-1. उचित, समुचित, उपयुक्त

   The guest of honour made a brief speech appropriate to the occasion.

   2. (v.)किसी खास काम के लिए अलग रखना

   My mother appropriated some money to buy our school uniform.

   3. बिना अनुमति के रुपया अपने लिए प्रयोग करना

   The union leader was accused of appropriating the employees' welfate found for his personal gains.

8. **Approve (v.)** अप्रूव - मंजूर करना, पसंद करना, अच्छा समझना

   No one can approve of such misbehaviour.

   (n.) स्वीकृति

   His proposal could not get anybody's approval.

9. **Irritate (v.)** इरिटेट-1. चिढ़ाना, उत्तेजित करना, गुस्सा दिलाना

   Don't irritate the teacher with your funny questions.

   2. दाह या जलन उत्पन्न करना

   My new shoes irritate my toes.

10. **Classic (adj.)** क्लासिक-कालजयी

    Mrs. Dalloway is a classic novel.

11. **Classify (v.)** क्लासिफ़ाइ-वर्गीकृत करना

    (v.) The books were classified into various subjects.

    (n.) The classification of books makes it easier for the reader to browse through.

12. **Clatter (n. & v.)** क्लैटर्-खड़खड़ाहट (होना)

    The plate fell down from Usha's hand with a clatter.

    (v.) Open doors and windows clattered in the storm.

13. **Clause (n.)** क्लॉज़्-कानूनी दस्तावेज़ का खंड

    She raised an objection against the clause of three-year bond.

14. **Claw (n.)** क्लॉ-पंजा, चंगुल

    The eagle flew away with the serpent in its claws.

15. **Luggage (n.)** लॅगिज-सामान, असबाब

Keep an eye on the luggate during the journey.

16. **Hurl (v.)** हर्ल-फेंकना, फेंककर मारना, लगाना

Don't hurly your books around carelessly.

Don't hurl baseless charges at me.

17. **Moon (n.)** मून-चन्द्रमा, शशि

Look at the full moon!

18. **Mop (n.)** मॉप-झाड़न

Ask the maid-servant to clean the floor with a mop.

(v.) She was mopping the floor.

19. **Moral (adj.)** मॉरल-1. नैतिक, सदाचारी

We should try to lead a moral life.

2. (n.) शिक्षा, सीख

What is the moral of this story?

20. **More** मोर्-अधिक, ज्यादा

(adj.) Put more milk in this cup.

I have more encils than pens.

(adv.) You must walk more briskly.

21. **Morning (n.)** मॉर्निन्ग-प्रभात, सवेरा

At what time do you get up in the morning.

21. **Morsel (n.)** मॉर्सल-ग्रास, कौर

(adj.) All men are mortal.

No mortal can expect to live longer than a hundred years.

22. **Sift (v.)** सिफ़्ट-छानना, छानबीन करना

We must sift the flour before baking.

The magistrate tried to sift the truth from the murderer's story.

23. **Sigh (v.)** साइ-आह (भरना), ठंडी साँस (लेना)

It is better not to sigh for days that are gone.

She heaved a sigh of relief when the loan was paid back.

24. **Sight (n.)** साइट-नज़र, दृष्टि, नज़ारा, दर्शनीय स्थान

Her uncle lost his sight in an accident.

We went for sight-seeing.

25. **Sign (v.)** साइन-1. हस्ताक्षर करना

Never forget to sign a letter before you post it.

2. (n.) चिन्ह्

There was no sign of life in the patient.

26. **Signal** सिग्नल-संकेत (करना), सिग्नल (देना)

(n.) A red signal is a signal of danger.

The bell gives the signal for a new period.

(v.) The referee signalled the players to begin.

The driver of the bus signals when he wants to stop it.

27. **Signature (n.)** सिग्न'चर्-हस्ताक्षर

Please put your signature on the cheque.

Is this your usual signature?

28. **Signify (v.)** सिग्निफाइ-सूचित करना, अभिप्राय प्रकट करना

We put up our hands to signify that we agreed with the speaker.

(n.) We must understand the significanceat the Prime Minister's speech.

29. **Silence (n.)** साइलन्स-शान्ति, मौन

Silence is wisdom, when speech is folly.

Silence is a friend that will never betray.

(adj.) Silent men are deep and dangerous.

30. Wretch (adj.) रेंच-अभागा, कमबख्त, नीच

The poor wretch looked so distreesed that I felt story sorry for him.

The man who stole the money from the poor widow was a wicked wretch.

31. Trace (v.) ट्रेस-1. खोजना, निकालना

The police are trying to trace the man who stole the van.

2. अनुरेखित करना, खींचना

You can trace a map from your atlas.

3. (n.) थोड़ी मात्रा, अल्प मात्रा

The soup has trace of onion in it.

32. Track (v.) ट्रैक-1. खोजना, पीछा करना

Hunters track elephants by their footprints.

2. पगडंडी, कच्चा रास्ता

There was only a rough track across the ground.

33. Tractor (v.) ट्रैक्टर्-इंजिन द्वारा परिचालित हल, ट्रेक्टर

Tractors are used by farmers for pulling the plough.

34. Trade (n.) ट्रेड-1. व्यवसाय, लेनदेन

Speculation is the romance of trade.

2. (v.) व्यापार करना

We trade in second-hand cars.

35. Tradition (n.) ट्रेडिशन-परम्परा

Everywhere the basis of principles is tradition.

36. Traffic (n.) यातायात, सड़क पर चलने वाले लोगों का आना

A big city like Delhi faces many traffic problems.

37. Tragedy (n.) ट्रैजडि-त्रासदी, दुखांत घटना, दारुण विपत्ति

Life is a tragedy - we are its spectators.

You cannot forget your personal tragedy.

38. Trail (n.) ट्रेल-पुछल्ला

The aeroplane left a long trail of white smoke behind it.

39. Train (n.) ट्रेन-1. रेलगाड़ी, गाड़ी

Some trains carry people. They are called passenger-trains. Some trains carry goods.

They are called goods-trains.

2. (v.) सिखाना, प्रशिक्षण देना

The mother trained Nina well in house hold work.

(adj.) Is she a trained teacher?

(n.) I am under training.

40. Pomp (n.) पॉम्प-तड़क-भड़क

The festival was celebrated with pomp and enthusiasm.

41. Pond (n.) पॉन्ड-तालाब, सरोवर

There is a small pond outside our village where we go for a swim.

42. Ponder (v.) पॉन्डर्-चिन्तन करना

Please ponder on all aspects of the situation before taking a decision.

43. Pool पुल-तालाब

I go to the swimming pool every evening.

44. Poor (adj.) पॉर्-1. दरिद्र, निर्धन

India is a poor country

2. बेचारा, अभागा

The poor dog had injured its paw.

3. घटिया, निकृष्ट

This cloth is of poor quality.

45. Popular (adj.) पॉप्यलर्-लोकप्रिय

My son is popular among his school-mates.

46. Population (n.) पॉप्युलेशन-जनसंख्या, आबादी

What is the population of your city?

47. Extraordinary (adj.) इक्स्ट्रॉडिनरि-विलक्षण, असामान्य

Child artist's performance in the play was extraordinary.

48. Do (v.) डू- 1. पूरा/सम्पन्न करना

Do you homework before going to play.

2. करना

What are you doing this evening?

3. लाभ पहुँचाना

This medicine will do you good.

49. Docile (adj.) डोसाइल-शांत और विनीत

She is very docile; I don't think she'll raise any objection against the plan.

50. Doctor (n.) डॉक्टर- 1. डॉक्टर, चिकित्सक

The doctor advised Shankar to take rest for a week.

2. आचार्य

Doctor Ram Lal Verma completed his Ph. D. at the young age of twenty-six

51. Document (n.) डॉक्युमंट-दस्तावेज़

Send this document by courier.

52. Documentary (n.) डॉक्युमेंट्रि-वृत्तचित्र

Shah Rukh Khan first starred in a documentary named Anne.

53. Ridiculous (adj.) रिडिकुलस-बेतुका, हास्यास्पद

You look ridiculous in this long gown. Your fringed hair makes you look ridiculous.

54. Rifle राइफ़ल-1. बन्दूक

(n.) I went out armed with a rifle.

2. (v.) लूटने की दृष्टि से उथल-पुथल करना

The whole house has been rifled.

55. Rift (n.) रिफ़्ट-दरार

The difference of opinion created a rift between them.

56. Right (adj.) राइट-1. उचित

It was not right of you to help my opponent.

2. दायाँ (हाथ या ओर)

We write with our right hand. Is it not the right way to write?

3. ठीक

Is your watch right?

4. (n.) अधिकार

You have no right to shout at me.

5. (adv.) पूरी तरह से

Somebody has rightly remarked that truth always wins.

57. Rigid (adj.) रिजिड्-सख्त

He is a rigid old man, and does not welcome changes.

58. Gulp (n.) गल्प-निगल जाना, गटगट निगलना, हाँफना

Don't gulp down hot tea in a haste.

59. Gum (n.) गम-1. गोंद

I want to buy a bottle of gum.

2. मसूड़ा

Strong teeth require strong gums.

60. Porch (n.) पॉर्च-द्वारमंडप

I halted the car in the porch of the house.

61. Pore (n.) पॉर्-छिद्र

Regular bathing keeps the pores of our skin clean.

62. Porridge (n.)पॉरिज-दलिया

I had some porridge in breakfast.

63. Port (n.) पोर्टर-बन्दरगाह

Cochin is one of finest ports in India.

64. Porter (n.) पॉर्टर-कुली

The porter put my luggage in the train.

65. Portofolio (n.) पॉर्टफ़ोलिओ-छायाचित्र, आरेख, कागज़ात आदि का संग्रह

She had an impressive portfolio.

66. Portion (n.) पॉर्शन-भाग, हिस्सा

We have so far completed only a small portion of our course.

67. Portrait (n.) पोट्रेट-चित्र, प्रतिकृति

He asked a well-known artist to paint a portrait of his father.

68. Brace ब्रेस-1. दांतों में पहनी जाने वाली धातु की तार

(n.) The use of braces shaped his teeth.

2. किसी परिस्थिति के लिए तैयार होना

(v.) Brace youself for a termination.

69. Bracelet (n.) ब्रेस्लट-कंगन,कंकण

Anil presented a bracelet to Neera on her birthday.

70. Bracket (n.) ब्रैकिट-1. कोष्ठक चिह

The meanings to the foreign words are given in the brackets.

2. वर्ग

Editors too come in the bracket of journalists.

3. (v.) एक ही वर्ग में रखना

A number of problems are bracketed together with working in night shifts.

71. Brag (v.) ब्रैग-डींग हांकना

Stop bragging about your high contacts.

72. Braid (n.) ब्रेड-वेणी, चोटी

She coiled her hair into a braid.

73. Brain (n.) ब्रेन-दिमाग, भेजा, बुद्धि

Arun used his brains to solve a complex Maths problem.

74. Brainchild (n.) ब्रेनचाइल्ड-आविष्कार, विचार

This book is a brainchild of a famous painter

75. Brainstorm ब्रेनस्टॉर्म-विचार करने के क्रिया

(n.) We had a brainstorm for so long but could not find a solution to the problem.

(v.) We brainstormed a lot, but could not find a solution.

76. Brainwash (v.) ब्रेनवॉष-मत-आरोपण करना

His friends brainwashed him into taking Science instead of Commerce.

77. Brake (n.) ब्रेक-1. ब्रेक, रोक लगाना

He applied the brake to stop the car when he saw a pit in the middle of the road.

2. रेलगाड़ी में सामान रखने का डब्बा

I put all my luggage in the brake van.

78. Full (adj.) फुल-पूर्ण, पूरा, भरा, पूरी तरह से, सीधे

My room is full of books.

Put a full stop at the end of each sentence.

The water tank is full.

(adv.) Only an honest person can look you full in the face.

79. Fumble (v.) फ़म्बल-टटोलना

She fumbled with the letter to find the name of sender.

80. Fumes (n.) फ़्यूम्ज़-धुआं या बदबूदार गैस

The diesel fumes made it difficult to breathe.

81. Approximate (adj.) अप्रॉक्सिमट-लगभग, करीब

What is the approximate number of students in your school?

(adv.) The distance between Delhi and Agra is approximately a hundred and twenty miles.

82. Apt (Adj.) ऐप्ट-योग्य, संगत, संभावना या प्रवृत्ति होना

The accomplished speaker made an

apt speech.

I am apt to doze if I sit in an easy chair.

83. Aptitude (n.) ऐप्टिट्यूड्-विशेष रुझान

She has an aptitude for literature.

84. Arbitrary (adj.) आबिट्रिरि-मनमाना और अनुचित

Their decision of shifting to Dwarka turned out to be arbitrary.

85. Arch (n.) आर्च्-तोरण

Many arches were erected on the roads to welcome the visiting leader.

86. Architect (n.) आकिटेक्ट-वास्तुकार, शिल्पकार, निर्माता

Your beautiful house is obviously designed by an able architect.

87. Ardent (adj.) आउन्ट-प्रशंसा की भावना से परिपूर्ण

The ardent kids admirers of Harry Potter.

88. Area (n.) एरिआ-इलाका, क्षेत्र

The Chambal ravines are known as an area of dacoits.

89. Isolated (adj.) आइसलेटिड-अलग-थलग

(adj.) The child suffereing from chickenpox was kept in an isolated room.

(v.) The child suffering from chichenpox was isolated from other children.

90. Clay (n.) क्ले-चिकनी मिट्ठी

Crockery is made of clay.

91. Clean क्लीन-1. सफ़ाई, साफ़

(v.) Did you clean your teeth today?

Sheela cleaned out the cupboard.

(Adj.) We should wear clean clothes.

2. शुद्ध

People with clean reputation get respect from all.

92. Clear (adj.) क्लिअर्-1. स्वच्छ, निर्मल

The sky was clear and cloudless.

2. स्पष्ट, साफ़.

What you say is not quite clear to me.

3. (v.) सुव्यवस्थित करना, सुलझाना

I was busy clearing up my old papers.

93. Clench (v.) क्लेन्च-भींचना

He clenched his fists in anger.

94. Clerk (n.) क्लार्क-क्लर्क, मुन्शी

It is not easy to get even a clerk's job.

95. Clever (adj.) क्लेवर्-1. चतुर, बुद्धिमान, धूर्त

Clever students generally score good marks.

2. प्रवीण, निपुण

Reena is clever at embroidery.

96. Cliche (n.) क्लीशे-घिसी-पिटी उक्ति

You must avoid cliches in your writings.

97. Click क्लिक

1. 'खटाक' की आवाज़ करना

(v.) She clicked her fingers to call the driver.

2. माउस से क्लिक करना

(v.) Click on Start button.

3. माउस का बटन दबाने की क्रिया

(n.) Sending e-mails is just a matter of a click.

98. Hurricane (n.) हरिकेन-आंधी-तूफ़ान

The hurricane broke many trees in the village.

99. Mortgage (n.) मॉर्गिज्-गिरवी रखना

They mortgaged their house to send their son abroad.

100. Mosque (n.) मॉस्क्-मस्जिद

The mosque was beautifully decorated on Eid.

SPOKEN VOCABULARY
Set - 38

1. **Mosquito (n.)** मस्कीटो-मच्छर

   Mosquitoes breed in the stagnant water.

2. **Moss (n.)** मॉस-काई

   Don't swim in that lake, it is full of moss.

3. **Most (adjj. & adv.)** मोस्ट-1. सबसे अधिक, अत्याधिक

   (adv.) Which book do you find the most interesting.

   (adj.) अधिकांश, ज्यादातर

   Most of my friends are science students.

4. **Silk (n.)** सिल्क-रेशम

   My shirt is made of silk.

   (adj.) I usually wear silken clothes.

5. **Silly (adj.)** सिलि-भोंडा, निरर्थक

   We must not say silly things.

   The clown does silly things to make us laugh.

6. **Silver (n.)** सिल्वर्-चाँदी, रजत

   Some coins are made of silver.

   His wife has a silver ring.

7. **Similar (adj.)** सिमिलर्-समान

   My pen is similar to yours.

   (n.) There is a great similarity between you and me.

8. **Simmer (v.)** सिमर्-धीमी आँच पर पकना

   Let the gravy simmer for a while.

9. **Simple (adj.)** सिम्पल-सादा, साधारण

   A simple life has its own reward.

   The greatest truths are the simplest, and so are the greatest men.

10. **Simultaneous (adj.)** साइमल्टेनिअस -सहकालिक

    Several simultaneous blasts took place in the city.

11. **Sin (n.)** सिन-पाप

    The recognition of sin is the beginning of happiness.

12. **Since (adv.)** सिन्स-तब से अब तक

    She came to Delhi two years ago and ever since she has been living here.

13. **Sincere (adj.)** सिन्सिअर्-ईमानदार

    Ramesh is a sincere man.

14. **Sing (v.)** सिंग-गाना

    I shall sing you a song.

    (n.) We gave the poor singer some money.

15. **Singe (v.)** सिन्ज्-हल्का-सा झुलसना

    I singed my eyebrows while bending over the flame.

16. **Wriggle (v.)** रिगल-कुलबुलाना, तड़पना

    I watched the worn wriggling across the path.

17. **Traitor (n.)** ट्रेटर्-विश्वासघाती, देशद्रोही

    The rogue was condemned to death as a traitor.

18. **Tram (n.)** ट्रैम-ट्राम, बिजली से पटरी पर चलने वाली गाड़ी

    Trams in Delhi have been replaced by buses.

19. **Tramp (n.)** ट्रैम्प-1. पद यात्रा, आवारा

    We went for a tramp across the

woods.

No one will trust a tramp like you.

2. (v.) मारा-मारा फिरना, धब-धब करते चलना

Don't tramp about the garden.

20. Trample (v.) ट्रैम्पल-रौंदना

The kids trampled the grass.

21. Trance (n.) ट्रान्स-सुषुप्ति की अवस्था

She was walking on the road in a state of trance.

22. Tranquil (adj.) ट्रैन्क्विल-शांत

My mind was tranquil and at peace.

23. Transact (v.) ट्रैन्ज़ैक्ट-पूरा करना, सम्पादित करना

When my father transacted all his business, he left Bhagalpur.

(n.) He made many transactions.

24. Transfer (v.) ट्रैन्स्फ़र-तबादला करना, दूसरी जगह ले जाना

The luggage was transfeered from the station to the ship. She transferred the almirah from one room to another.

25. Transform (v.) ट्रैन्स्फ़ार्म-एक रुप से दूसरे रुपाकार में बदलना

The witch transformed the goat into a princess.

26. Transfusion (n.) ट्रैनफ़्यूज़न-किसी व्यक्ति को रोग के कारण दूषित रक्त के स्थान पर नया रक्त चढ़ाना, रक्तदान (करना)

Many patients have been saved because of blood transfusion.

27. Pose पोज़

1. (v.) परेशानी उत्पन्न करना

Pollution poses a major threat to the environment.

2. (n.) फोटो खिंचवाने के लिए खड़े होने या बैठने की मुद्रा

She got her photograph clicked in Madhubala pose.

28. Posh (adj.) पॉश-समाज के उच्च वर्ग का प्रतिनिधिक

They live in a posh colony.

29. Position (n.) पज़िशन-1. स्थिति

Who has moved my writing table from its original position?

2. पद

My brother has got a position as a lecturer.

3. अवस्था

You should stand in an upright position.

4. परिस्थिति

In my present position, I cannot help you.

30. Positive (adj.) पॉज़िटिव-निश्चित

Are you positive that she loves you?

31. Possess (v.) पज़ेस-मालिक होना

Do you possess a TV set?

(n.) I put all my possessions in the room.

32. Possible (adj.) पॉसिबल-संभव

Is it possible to leave for Mumbai immediately?

If possible, come back before the nightfall.

(adj.) I may possibly meet you in Kolkata.

33. Post (n. & v.) पोस्ट-1. डाक (से भेजना)

(n.) Send this letter by post.

(v.) Please post this letter.

2. (n.) पद, नौकरी

I am trying for a post in this office.

3. खम्भा

The fence was made of wooden posts.

34. Extravagant (adj.) इक्स्ट्रैवगन्ट-खर्चीला

She is very extravagant and often buys things she does not require.

35. Dodge (v.) डॉज-हट जाना, वार बचाना

Ramu fell down while trying to dodge the cyclist.

36. Dog (n.) डॉग-कुत्ता

Do you like a dog as a pet?

37. Doll (n.) डॉल-गुड़िया

Rahul bought a doll for his little daughter.

38. Dome (n.) डोम-गुम्बद

The dome of Golden Temple is plated with gold.

39. Domestic (adj.) डमेस्टिक-घरेलू, पारिवारिक

Modern men do not hesitate in helping their wives in the domestic work.

40. Dominate (v.) डॉमिनेट-आधिपत्य जमाना

The Indian cricket team dominated the 20-20 World Cup.

41. Donate (v.) डोनेट-दान करना

He donated blood on his 18th birthday.

42. Donkey (n.) डॉङ्कि-गधा

The washerman's donkey carried the clothes to the river.

43. Door (n.) डोर-दरवाज़ा, द्वार

It's safe to keep the main door closed.

Salesmen go door to door to sell their products.

44. Rigorous (adj.) रिगरस-परिशुद्ध

The performance did not meet the regorous standards.

45. Rim (n.) रिम्-किसी गोलाकार वस्तु के किनारे

The rim of her spectacles was golden in colour.

46. Ring (n.) रिंग-1. अंगूठी

The bride wears three rings on her fingers.

2. (v.) बजाना

The peon will ring the bell.

47. Rinse (v.) रिन्स-साफ़ करना, धोना

Mother rinses wollen sweaters in warm water.

48. Riot राइअट-दंगा, कोलाहल, हंगामा (हंगामा)

(n.) The rebels who took part in the riot broke many articles in the shop.

(v.) There was a big rip in my dress.

49. Ripe (adj.) राइप-1. परिपक्व, पका हुआ

We should eat fruit when it is ripe.

2. परिपक्व (अवस्था)

I have reached the ripe age of seventy-two.

50. Ripple (n.) रिपल्-छोटी-सी लहर

The air was creating small ripples in the pond.

51. Rise (v.) राइज़्-1. उठाना, उदय होना

The sun rises in the morning and sets in the evening.

We can see the sun rising in the morning.

2. विद्रोह करना, (विरुद्ध) उठ खड़े होना

Some day, the exploited peole will rise against the cruel ruler.

3. (n.) बढ़ोत्तरी, वृद्धि

There has been a rise in the prices of some essential commodities.

52. Gun (b. & v.) गन-बन्दूक (चलाना)

(n.) Who discovered the gun-powder?

The new recruits in the army were taught the use of guns.

(v.) The hunter gunned down a wolf.

53. Extreme (adj.) इक्स्ट्स्ट्रीम 1. अत्यधिक, नितान्त

Martyrs showed extreme courage by sacrificing their life for the country's freedom.

2. सिरे का, दूरतम, अंत का

I live at the extreme end of this street.

(adv.) I am extremely grateful to you for your assistance.

54. Bramble (n.) ब्रैम्ब्ल-कांटेदार झाड़ी

This area is full of brambles.

55. Branch (n.) ब्रांच-डाल, डाल, शाखा

The nimble boy climbed a high brach of the tree.

The big banks have branches in all major cities and towns.

56. Brand ब्रैंड-1. छाप, दाग

(n.) Which brand of toothpaste do you use?

2. (adj.) नवीनतम, एकदम नया

Today he came to office in a brand new car.

57. Brass (n.) ब्रास-पीतल

Indian housewives use utensils of brass.

58. Brave (adj.) ब्रेव-साहसी, बहादुर

The brave man fought with the tiger without a weapon.

59. Brawl (n.) ब्रॉल-झड़प

Children had a brawl while playing.

60. Fun (n.) फ़न-मजाक, आमोद-प्रमोद

We had a great fun at the party.

61. Function फँक्शन

1. जलसा

(n.) Our school organised a big function at the Founder's Day.

2 काम करना

(v.) How does this machine function?

63. Fund (n.) फ़न्ड-निधि, कोष

We have started a fund for the school building.

64. Argue (v.) आग्यू-वाद-विवाद करना, तर्क से सिद्ध करना, आपत्ति करना

The critics argued a lot about the good and bad points of the celebrated painting.

(n.) तर्क

Today, the argument that all politicians are after power seems true.

65. Arise (v.) अराइज़्-1. उठना, उठ खड़ा होना

Arise, awake, and stop not till the goal is reached.

2. उत्पन्न होना

Because of the limited seats, a quarrel arose among the passengers.

66. Aristocrat (n.) ऐरिस्टक्रैट-उच्चतम सामाजिक वर्ग

His forefathers belonged to the class of aristocratsin pre-independence India.

67. Arm (n.) आर्म्-बांह, बाहु, भुजा

I have hurt my arm.

68. Armed (adj.) आम्ड्-सशस्त्र

Four armed men broke into the house and committed the robbery.

69. Issue (v.) इशू-1. जारी करना, प्रकाशित करना, देना

I have issued instruction to the staff about the Annual Day Function.

2. (n.) सन्तान

Is she without an issue?

3. वाद विषय

What is the main issue in your discussion?

70. Client (n.) क्लाइअन्ट-सेवार्थी

The clients were impressed by the quality of work.

71. Cliff (n.) क्लिफ़-खड़ी चट्टान

As the ship approached the shore of England, we could see the white cliffs of Dover.

72. Climate (n.) क्लाइमट-1. जलवायु, आबोहवा

In summer, Delhi's climate is extremely hot.

2. वातावरण

How is the political climate in the capital these days?

73. Climb (v.) क्लाइम्-चढ़ना, आरोहण करना

You require special training to climb a mountain.

The old man climbed the staircase with great difficulty.

(n.) Climb to success is hard.

74. Cling (v.) क्लिंग-चिपकाना, लिपटना

Small children cling to their mother while sleeping

75. Clip (n.) क्लिप-1. क्लिप, चुटकी, पंजा

The loose sheets are put together with a paper clip.

2. (v.) कतरना, काटना

Little boys like to clip pictures out of newspapers.

76. Lullaby (n.) लॅलबाइ-लोरी

I sang a lullaby to put my child to sleep.

77. Hurry हॅरि-उतावली, जल्दी, उत्सुकता, जल्दी करना, कराना

(n.) You are always in a hurry.

(v.) As it was about to rain, the office-goers hurried to their homes.

78. Moth (n.) मॉथ-कपड़ों में लगने वाला कीड़ा

These naphthalene balls will protect your clothes from moths.

79. Mother (n.) मदर्-माता

The mother picked up the child in her arms.

74. Mother-tongue (n.) मदर-ढंग-मातृभाषा

What is your mother-tongue?

75. Motif (n.) मोटिफ़-किसी वस्तु का चित्र

Each chapter in the book started with a motif related to Lord Krishna.

76. Motion (n.) मोशन 1. गति, चाल

You must not open the door of the compartment while the train is in motion.

2. प्रस्ताव

Was your motion carried in the meeting?

77. Singe (v.) सिन्ज्-हल्का-सा झुलसना

I singed my eyebrows while bending over the flame.

78. Single (adj.) सिंगल-1. अविवाहित

Are you still single?

2. एकमात्र

The bush has a single flower.

(adv.) Do you sell these packets singly?

79. Singular (n.) सिगुलर्-एकवचन

Do you know the singular of 'children'?

(adj.) Rita's rescuing of the young child from drowing was a deed of singular bravery.

80. Sinister (adj.) सिनिस्टर्-अमंगलसूचक

He looks sinister to me.

81. Sink (v.) सिंक-1. डूबना

The ship sank in the storm.

A stone cannot float on the water It sinks.

2. डुबाना

Our warship sank one of the enemy's ships.

3. (आवाज़) खो जाना

Your voice sank amidst the loud noise and we could hardly hear you.

82. Sip सिप्–छोटा घूंट, छोटा-सा घूंट (भरना)

(n.) You must take small sips.

(v.) I sipped my coffee slowly because it was very hot.

83. Sir (n.) सर्–1. उपाधि

Sir Francis Drake was a great English seaman.

2. श्रीमान

Follow me, sir.

84. Siren (n.) साइरन–(संकट के साथ) चेतावनी के रुप में

The ship's siren sounded when the f g came down.

85. Sister (n.) सिस्टर्–1. सगी बहन

My sister works in Ahmedabad.

2. अस्पताल की नर्स

This sister nursed the patient in the hospital.

86. Wring (v.) रिंग–1. मरोड़ना, निचोड़ना, एंठना

Wring the wet shirt to get the water out of it.

2. यत्नपूर्वक निकालना

At last, the policemen wrung the truth from the thief.

87. Transgress (v.) ट्रैन्स्ग्रे'स–उल्लंघन करना, अतिक्रमण करना

We must remember the promise not to transgress again.

88. Translate (v.) ट्रा'न्सलेट–अनुवाद करना

The New Testament was translated from Greek into English.

What has been translated is a translation.

(n.) The art of translation requires a good knowledge of many languages.

89. Transmit (v.) ट्रैंज़्मिट–भेजना, संप्रेषित करना, स्थानांतरित करना

Trams in Delhi have been replaced by buses.

90. Tramp (n.) ट्रैम्प–1. पद यात्रा, आवारा

We went for a tramp across the woods.

No one will trust a tramp like you.

2. (v.) मारा-मारा फिरना, धब-धब करते चलना

Don't tramp about the garden.

91. Poster (n.) पोस्टर–इश्तिहार, विज्ञापन

During election time, posters appear everywhere.

92. Posterity (n.) पॉस्टेरटि–भावी पीढ़ियां

We must make some investments for the good of our posterity.

93. Posthumous (adj.) पॉस्ट्युमस्–मरणोपरांत

The general received the posthumous medal for bravery.

94. Postpone (v.) पोस्पोन–स्थगित करना, आगे बढ़ाना

Our examinations have been postponed.

95. Posture (n.) पॉस्चर्–बैठने, खड़े होने, चलने की मुद्रा

Always maintaining a good posture ensures good health.

96. Pot (n.) पॉट–पात्र, बर्तन

My wife uses stainless steel pots for cooking.

97. Potential पटेन्शल

1. (adj.) संभाव्य

A good salesman must know tricks of attracting the potential buyers.

2. (n.) व्यक्ति या वस्तु में विद्यमान गुण

She has a great potential as a dancer.

98. Pouch (n.) पाउच्–कुछ मादा पशुओं में बच्चा रखने की थैली

A baby kangaroo remains in its mother's pouch for some time.

99. Pounce (v.) पाउन्स्–झपट्टा मारना

The cat pounced on the pigeon.

100. Poultry (n.) पोल्ट्रि–मुर्गा, मुर्गी

I get fresh eggs every day from my friend's poultry farm.

SPOKEN VOCABULARY
Set - 39

1. **Dormitory (n.)** डॉमिट्रि-शयनशाला, शयनागार

   The school had a big dormitory for its resident students.

2. **Dose (n.)** डोज़-डोस, खुराक, मात्रा

   The doctor asked the patient to take a dose of the medicine every four hours.

3. **Dot (n.)** डॉट-बिंदु (लगाना)

   (n.) The teacher asked the children to circle the red dot.

   (v.) You should dot the i's and cross dot.

4. **Dote (v.)** डोट-किसी को बहुत प्यार देना

   She dotes on her only child.

5. **Risk** रिस्क-जोखिम (उठाना), दाँव पर लगाना

   (n.) You are taking a risk of displeasing your boss if you just stay away from work.

   (v.) Vinayak risked his life to save a child from drowning.

6. **Ritual (n.)** रिचुअल्-कर्मकांड

   His last rituals were performed in Haridwar.

7. **Rival (n.)** राइवल-प्रतिद्वन्द्वी

   Rita and Gita were rival candidates for the post of receptionist.

   There has been a long rivalry between the two companies.

8. **Gurgle (v.)** गर्गल-गड़गड़ की ध्वनि निकालना

   The sea was gurgling loudly.

9. **Double** डब्ल-दुगुना (करना/होना)

   (adj.) In the absence of his colleague, Ram had to do double work in the office.

   (v.) Why have the vegetable prices doubled in such a short time?

10. **Doubt** डाउट-संशय, संदेह करना, अविश्वास करना

    (n.) This is without a doubt your handwriting.

    (v.) I doubt whether you are telling me the truth.

11. **Dough (n.)** डो- 1. गुंधा आटा

    If you knead the dough well, the bread would be soft.

    2. धन

    I am not a rich man, I do not have a lot of dough.

12. **Breach (n.)** ब्रीच-1. नियम-भंग

    The Company fired him on the grounds of breach of confidence.

    2. दरार

    Hunger for power created a breach between the politician brothers.

    3. (v.) कानून अथवा समझौते का उल्लंघन

    I do not intend to breach the contract in the middle.

13. **Bread (n.)** ब्रेड-रोटी, जीविका

    I eat bread and butter for breakfast.

    Labourers toil whole day to earn their bread.

14. **Breadth (n.)** ब्रेड्थ-चौड़ाई

Area is defined as length into breadth.

15. Break (v.) ब्रेक-तोड़ना, टूटना

The boy broke the window-pane with a stone.

Fire broke out (suddenly started) in the kitchen of the house.

The thieves broke into (forcibly entered) the house at night.

Arun's car broke down (stopped working) when he was about to reach his office.

(n.) पढ़ाई या काम के बीच में मध्यांतर

School children came out to play during the break.

16. Breakfast (n.) ब्रेकफ़ास्ट-कलेवा

According to some dieticians, break fast is the most important meal of the day.

17. Fundamental फ़न्डमेंटल

1. मौलिक

(adj.) Right to speech is our fundamental right.

2. मूल सिद्धांत

(n.) Understand the fundamentals before starting the venture.

18. Armour (n.) आर्मर्-कवच

(n.) The shell of a tortoise protects it like the armour protects a warrior.

19. Arms (n.) आर्म्ज़्-हथियार, शस्त्रास्त्र

There seems to be a race to possess more arms among the countries of the world.

20. Army (n.) आर्मी-1. फौज

The India Army fights bravely at the times of wars.

2. दल, भीड़

There was a huge army of ants in the garden.

21. Aroma (n.) अरोमा-सुगंध

An aroma of various delicacies was surrounding the kitchen.

22. Itch (n. & v.) इच-1. खुजली, खाज (होना)

He scratched himself continuously unable to bear the itch on his back.

2. बेचैन होना

I am itching to go on a hill station.

23. Cloak (n.) क्लोक्-लबादा

The judge wore a long black cloak.

24. Clock (n.) क्लॉक-घड़ी

Some wall clocks chime every hour.

25. Clog (v.) क्लॉग-बाधा डालना, अवरुद्ध या बन्द हो जाना

The sewer was clogged with dirt.

26. Close क्लोज़्-बन्द करना

(v.) Please close the door.

2. (adj.) निकट, पास

The children sat close together.

3. (adj.) सूक्ष्म

The audience paid close attention to the sermons of the Saint.

27. Clot क्लॉट

1. खून का थक्का

(n.) A blood clot formed inside his brain.

2. खून का थक्का जमना

(v.) The blood inside his brain began to clot.

28. Cloth (n.) क्लॉथ-कपड़ा, वस्त्र

Nowadays shirts are made of synthetic cloth.

29. Clothes (n.) क्लोद्ज़-पोशाक, पहनावा

Youngsters like fashionable clothes.

30. Cloudy (adj.) क्लाउडी-बादलों से भरा, धुँधला जाना

On a cloudy day, we cannot see the sun.

31. Clown (n.) क्लाउन-विदूषक, मसखरा

The children laughed at the circus clown's antics.

32. Club (n.) क्लब-1. क्लब

Club is a place for recreation.

2. भारी डण्डा, लाठी, बल्ला

When the tiger attacked the farmer, he defended himself with his club.

33. Clue (n.) क्लू-संकेत, इशारा, सूत्र

The detectives looked for clues that could lead them to the murderer.

34. Clumsy (adj.) क्लम्ज़ि-बेडोल, बेढ़ंगा

Radha is so clumsy that she is always breaking something or the other.

35. Cluster (n. & v.) क्लस्टर्-गुच्छा, झुण्ड, समूह, जमा होना या करना

(n.) The rabbit ran to the cluster of bushes to hide from the hound.

(v.) The children clustered round the ice cream vendor.

36. Clutch (v.) क्लच-जकड़ना/पकड़ना

The frightened child clutched his mother's hand.

37. Clutter क्लटर्

1. बेढ़ंगेपन से बिखरी वस्तुएं

(n.) There was a lot of clutter on the table.

2. बेढ़ंगेपन से वस्तुएं फैलना

(v.) She cluttered the table with cosmetics.

(adj.) Her desk is always cluttered.

38. Luminous (adj.) लूमिनस-प्रकाशमान

My wrist-watch has luminous hands.

39. Hurt (v.) हर्ट-1. चोट, हानि (पहुंचाना)

Ram was mildly hurt in the bus accident.

2. दु:ख देना

I felt hurt at his unkind remarks.

Please try not to hurt anybody.

40. Husband (n.) हज़्बन्ड-पति, भर्ता

Now, husbands mostly don't feel shy in doing household chores with their wives.

41. Motive (n.) मोटिव-मकसद, प्रयोजन

What was your motive in telling me a lie?

42. Motto (n.) मॉटो-ध्येय वाक्य

The motto of my life is - Never despair!

43. Mould मोल्ड-1. गढ़ना, साँचे में ढालना

(v.) If you want to become a sculptor, you must first learn how to mould clay.

2. (n.) साँचा, ढाँचा

Get me the star-shaped mould; I'll prepare cookies.

3. फफूंदी

Don't eat that bread, it is full of mould.

44. Mound (v.) माउन्ड-टीला

My children like to climb a mound near our house.

45. Wrinkle रिंकल-झुर्री (पड़ना)

(n.) The old man was worn and wearied.
His face was full of wrinkles.
The baby wrinkled its face and began to cry.

46. Sit (v.) सिट-1. बैठना

Please sit down for a while.

2. अंडे देना

The hen has been sitting for five days.

47. Site (n.) साइट-(मौके की) जगह

This is a good site for the shop.

48. Situation (n.) सिचुएशन-1. स्थिति

The situation is now under control.

2. नौकरी, काम

Uncle obtained a situation as a clerk.

49. Size (n.) साइज़-आकार, नाप

What is the size of your shirt?

50. Sizzle (v.) सिज़ल-सुरसुराना

Sausages were sizzling in the frying pan.

51. Skate (n.) स्केट-1. बर्फ पर फिसलने में सहायता करने के लिए पहिये लगी चम्पल

Have you got a new pair of skates?
Skating is a good fun.
Have your ever gone for skating?

52. Skeleton (n.) स्केलिट्न्-1. हड्डियों का ढाँचा

Have you ever seen the skeleton of an animal in the museum?

2. प्रारंभिक ढाँचा

I'll prepare a skeleton for the next year's programmes.

53. Sketch (n.) स्केच-हाथ से बनी अपूर्ण कलाकृति

The artist drew a pencil sketch.

54. Ski (v.) स्की-बर्फ़ पर फिसलने के लिए लकड़ी का पतला लम्बा और तिरछा पटड़ा बाँधकर चलना

Is the snow firm enough for us to ski?
One who skies is a skier.

55. Skid (v.) स्किड-फिसलन नियंत्रण से बाहर होना

The motorcyle skidded on the wet road.

56. Skill (n.) स्किल-दक्षता, कौशल, कारीगरी

The mechanic maintained his skill in repairing sewing machines.
(adj.) He was a skilled workman.

57. Skim (v.) स्किम-ऊपर आये झाग या गंदगी को धीरे से हटाना

Mother skimmed the milk before drinking it.

2. ऊपरी सतह या हवा में हल्के से तैरना

Seagulls skim the water in search of fish.

58. Skin (n.) स्किन-खाल, छाल, आवरण

Our body is covered with skin.
Peel off the skin before you eat the orange.

59. Skip (v.) स्किप-कूद जाना, (बीच में) छोड़ जाना

These two pages are too difficult.
You can skip them.

60. Skirmish (n.) स्कर्मिश-झड़प

One of our soldiers was lost in a skirmish with the enemy.

61. Skirt (n.) स्कर्ट-घाघरा, स्त्रियों का लहंगा

The poor woman's skirt was covered with dust.

62. Trample (v.) ट्रैम्पल-रौदना

The kids trampled the grass.

63. Trance (n.) ट्रान्स-सुषुप्ति की अवस्था

She was walking on the road in a state of trance.

64. Tranquil (adj.) ट्रैन्क्विल-शांत

My mind was tranquil and at peace.

65. Transact (v.) ट्रैन्ज़ैक्ट-पूरा करना, सम्पादित करना

When my father transacted all his business, he left Bhagalpur.

(n.) He made many transactions.

66. Transfer (v.) ट्रैन्स्फ़र-तबादला करना, दूसरी जगह ले जाना

The luggage was transferred from the station to the ship.

She transferred the almirah from one room to another.

67. Transform (v.) ट्रैन्स्फ़ार्म-एक रुप से दूसरे रुपाकार में बदलना

The witch transformed the goat into a princess.

68. Pound (v.) पाउन्ड्-दिल का ऊंची आवाज़ में धड़कना

My heart was pounding with fear.

69. Pour (v.) पॉर्-उड़ेलना

Please pour some hot water in this glass.

70. Poverty (n.) पॉवर्टि-निर्धनता, गरीबी

Many people live in poverty.

71. Powder (n.) पाउडर-पाउडर, चूर्ण

Please give me a pack of face powder

72. Power (n.) पाउअर्- 1.बल, अधिकार

The police have the power to arrest people.

2. शक्ति

I shall do everything in my power to help you.

(adj.) My uncle is a powerful man.

73. Practice (n.) प्रैक्टिस-आदत

It is a dangerous practice to get off a moving bus.

74. Practise (v.) प्रैक्टिस-आदत डालना, अभ्यास करना

I have to practise my part in the play.

75. Praise (n. & v.) प्रेज़्-प्रशंसा (करना)

(n.) He is unaffected by praise or blame.

(v.) My son's teacher praised him for his good marks.

76. Pray (v.) प्रे-प्रार्थना करना

We pray to God to help us.

(n.) People from all communities used to attend Gandhiji's samadhi for prayer meetings on October 2.

77. Preach (v.) प्रीच-प्रवचन या उपदेश देना

Gandhiji preached truth fulness and continence.

78. Extrovert (n.) एक्स्ट्रवर्ट-बहिर्मुखी

He is an extrovert, while his brother is completely opposite.

79. Dove (n.) डव-सफ़ेद कबूतर, पंडुक

The dove is considered a symbol of peace.

80. Down (adj.) डाउन-नीचे, नीचे की ओर

Please sit down here.

Are prices really coming down?

Write down your name and address.

Our air-conditioner has broken down (it does not work).

81. Download (v.) डाउनलोड-कम्प्यूटर से फाइल उतारना

I downloaded a few pictures from the Internet.

82. Downmarket (adj.) डाउनमार्किट-घटिया

Arriving late in formal meetings is s downmarket.

83. Down-to-earth (adj.) डाउन-टू-अर्थ-यथार्थवादी

Despite being very rich and affluent, she is very down-to-earth.

84. Dowry (n.) डाउरी-दहेज

Dowry is a blot on humanity.

85. Doze (v.) डोज़-झपकी लेना, ऊँघना

I like to doze for some time after a heavy lunch.

86. River (n.) रिवर-नदी, नद, दरिया

Ganga and Yamuna are holy rivers.

We can see boats sailing on the river.

87. Road (n.) रोड-सड़क, मार्ग

Rama is driving a car long the road.

Many people like to go by road.

Is this the road to India Gate?

88. Roam (v.) रॉम-घूमना, भटकना

The tiger sprang up towards me with a roar.

2. (v.) ध्वनि करना, शोर मचाना

The listener roared with laughter at my story.

89. Roast (v.) रोस्ट-भूनना

The cook roasted the chicken.

90. Rob (v.) रॉब-1. लूटना

The pickpockets robbed the passengers and disappeared quickly.

(n.) Three armed robbers were arrested by the police immediately after the robbery.

91. Gust (n.) गस्ट-झोंका, झकोरा

A sudden gust of wind blew away my cap.

92. Wrist (n.) रिस्ट-कलाई, मणिबंध

My wrist is itching; please, rub some balm.

Have you got your wrist-watch back?

93. Funeral (n.) फ़्यूनरल-मृतक-क्रिया, दफ़न, अन्त्येष्टि

Did you attend the old man's funeral?

94. Funnel (n.) फ़नल-कीप, चिमनी

Use a funnel to fill kerosene in bottle.

We could see the funnel of the approaching ship.

95. Breakthrough (n.) ब्रेकथ्रू-कोई महत्वपूर्ण खोज

Introduction of colour was a major breakthrough in cinema.

96. Breath (v.) ब्रेथ-साँस, दम, श्वास

The swimmer took a deep breath and plunged into the water.

97. Breathe (v.) ब्रेथ-साँस, लेना, जीना

He was finding it difficult to breathe

98. Breed (n.) ब्रीड- 1 नस्ल

Dobberman is a breed of dogs.

2. (v.) जनना, जन्म देना, पैदा करना

Mosquitoes breed and multiply very fast.

3. (n.) शिष्टाचार, सौजन्य

He is a man of noble breeding

99. Breeze (n.) ब्रीज़-हल्की हवा

He sat in the garden to enjoy the cool breeze.

100. Brevity (n.) ब्रेवटि-संक्षिप्तता और सटीकता

Brevity is the soul of wit.

SPOKEN VOCABULARY
Set - 40

1. **Bribe (n. & v.)** ब्राइब-घूस रिश्वत देना

   (n.) Never give or take a bribe.

   The clerk was arrested on a charge of bribery.

   (v.) He bribed the clerk to get his work done.

2. **Husk (n.)** हस्क-धान

   The grandmother separated husk from the rice grains.

3. **Skull (n.)** स्कॅल-खोपड़ी

   The motor-cyclist fractured his skull in the accident.

4. **Sky (n.)** स्काइ-आकाश, आसमान

   Birds fly in the sky and chirp cheerfully.

5. **Slack (adv.)** स्लैक-ढीला, मंदा

   Business is slack this month.

6. **Slam (v.)** स्लैंग-गंवारन बोली, अपभाषा

   'Shut up' is the slang for 'be quiet'

7. **Slap (v.)** स्लैप-थप्पड़ मारना

   Was it not wrong of you to slap the baby?

8. **Slash** स्लैश-चीरा

   (n.) The razor left a slashon his cheek.

   (v.) He slashed his cheek while shaving.

9. **Slate** स्लेट-पत्थर का समतल भाग, पटिया, स्लेट-पत्थर लगाना

   (n.) Children used to do their sums on the slates.

   (v.) The roof of the old house has just been slated.

10. **Slaughter** स्लॉटर्-हत्या (करना)

    (n.) There was a great slaughter in the battle.

    (v.) Animals are slaughtered for food.

11. **Slave (n.)** स्लेव-दास, गुलाम

    In the 19th century, there were slaves in America.

    Abraham Lincoln considered slavery illegal.

12. **Slay (v.)** स्ले-जान से मारना

    Hunters slay many animals while hunting.

    Has the butcher slain two cocks?

13. **Sleek (adj.)** स्लीक-चिकना और आकर्षक

    The ipod was very sleek.

14. **Sleep** स्लीप-नींद (लेना), निद्रा, सुस्ती

    (n.) Seven to eight hours sleep is essential for human beings.

    (v.) The baby is sleeping in cradle.

15. **Around (adv.)** अराउन्ड-चारों ओर

    People gathered around the famous film star.

16. **Arouse (v.)** अराउज़्-जगाना, सचेत करना

    She aroused her sleeping son.

17. **Arrange (v.)** अरेंज-1. सजाना, संजोना, व्यवस्थित करना

    She arranged the furniture in her sitting room.

    2. निश्चित करना

    Rupa arranged to meet Shikha.

    3. (n.) प्रबंध, संयोजन

    It's a beautiful flower arrangement.

18. **Arrest** अरेस्ट-गिरफ्तार करना रोकना

    The policemen arrested the thief.

    (n.) गिरफ्तारी

    The arrest of the notorious smuggler caused a great sensation.

19. **Arrive (v.)** अराइव-पहुंचना, आना

The Rajdhani Express arrives in the morning.

(n.) आगमन

Delay in the arrival of the train is not unusual

20. Arrogant (n.) ऐरगन्ट-घमंडी

Being the only son of a rich industrialist, he is very arrogant.

21. Dozen (n.) डज़न-दर्जन

I bought a dozen of bananas.

22. Draft ड्राफ्ट-मसौदा/पाण्डुलेख (बनाना)

(v.) The workers leader drafted the memorandum of demands to present to the management.

(n.) Several amendments were made in the rough draft of the project.

23. Drag (v.) ड्रैग-घसीटना

If this load is too heavy for you to lift, you will have to drag it.

24. Dragon (n.) ड्रैगन-ड्रैगन

The child made a picture of a dragon breathing fire.

25. Drain ड्रेन-नाली, मोरी, (जल) निकालना

(n.) All the drains in the colony were overflowing following a heavy downpour.

(v.) As I cleaned the outlet, the water drained out.

26. Transfusion (n.) ट्रैन्सफ्यूज़न-किसी व्यक्ति को रोग के कारण दूषित रक्त के स्थान पर नया रक्त चढ़ाना, रक्तदान (करना)

Many patients have been saved because of blood transfusion.

27. Transgress (v.) ट्रैन्ग्रे'स-उल्लंघन करना, अतिक्रमण करना

We must remember the promise not to transgress again.

28. Translate (v.) ट्रा'न्सलेट-अनुवाद करना

The New Testament was translated from Greek into English.

What has been translated is a translation.

(n.) The art of translation requires a good knowledge of many languages.

29. Robe (n.) रोब-लाबादा

The girl was dressed in an attractive robe.

30. Roboat (n.) रोबॉट-यंत्र-मानव

It seems in future, all the work would be done by the robots.

31. Robust (adj.) रोबस्ट-तगडा और स्वस्थ

Despite being old, he is quite robust and healthy.

32. Rock (n.) रॉक्-1. चट्टान

There are many big rocks in the sea.

2. (v.) हिलाना, झुलाना

She rocked her baby and dang a lullaby to put him to sleep.

33. Lump (n.) लॅम्प-1. ढेला, पिण्ड, डला

I put lumps of earth into the flower pot.

2. सूजन

What is this lump on your arm?

34. Mount (v.) आउन्ट-1. चढ़ना, सवारी करना

Can you mount a horse?

2. फ्रेम चढ़ाना

Please mount my photograhs with silver frames.

3. राशि या आकार बढ़ना या बढ़ाना

Don't you think that your debts are mounting up?

35. Coach (n.) कोच-कोच, सवारी, डिब्बा

The Rajdhani Express has air-conditioned coaches only

36. Coal (n.) कोल-कोयला

Most industries in India run on coal energy.

37. Coalition (n.) कोअलिशन-गठबंधन सरकार

A coalition government always faces problems.

38. Coars (adj.) कॉर्स–1. मोटा

The poor woman wore a sari of coarse cloth.

39. Coast (n.) कोस्ट–तट, समुद्रतट

We could see the coast from the deck of the ship.

40. Coat (n.) कोट–1. कोट, कुरता, अंगरखा

The poor man had no coat to wear.

2. तह, परत, लेप

This door needs a fresh coat of paint.

3. लेपना, परत चढ़ाना

She coated the dough with fine flour before rolling it.

41. Coax (v.) कोक्स–फुसलाकर राज़ी करना

Don't coax him to cook today.

42. Cobbler (n.) कॉब्लर्–मोची

The cobbler repairs and polishes the shoes.

43. Cobweb (n.) कॉबवेब–तन्तुजाल, मकड़ी का जाला

The unused room was dusty and full of cobwebs.

44. Precaution (n.) प्रिकॉशन–बहुमूल्य

I took the precaution of locking my house before going out.

45. Precede (v.) प्रिसीड–पहले आना या घटित होना

Please follow me, I shall precede you.

46. Precious (adj.) प्रेशस–बहुमूल्य

A very precious painting has been stolen from the museum.

47. Precise (adj.) प्रीसाइस्–यथार्थ, सही

If you follow my precise directions, you can easily find my house.

48. Predecessor (n.) प्रीडिसेसर्–पूर्वाधिकारी

We did not like our present manager's predecessor very much.

49. Preen (v.) प्रीन–स्वयं को संवारने में समय व्यतीत करना

She spent an hour preening herself in front of the mirror.

50. Gutter (n.) गटर्–नाली, परनाला, मोरी

Yesterday's heavy rain caused the gutters in our street to overflow.

51. Transmit (v.) ट्रैंज़्मिट–भेजना, संप्रेषित करना, स्थानांतरित करना

That message was transmitted by telephone.

Usually messages are transmitted by radio.

52. Transparent (adj.) ट्रैंसपेअरन्ट–पारदर्शी

Clear water is transparent.

Glass is transparent.

53. Transport ट्रान्सपोर्ट–ढोना, एक जगह से दूसरी जगह से जाना

(v.) Many ships are required to transport food across the oceans.

(n.) The ships are used for transport.

54. Trap (n.) ट्रैप–1. पिंजरा, चूहेदानी

Have you set a trap to catch the mice?

2. जाल

The army fell into a trap, as they found themselves between the sea and the enemy.

55. Trauma (n.) ट्रॉमा–आघात

Manto's story Toba Tek Singh deals with the trauma of partition.

56. Fur (n.) फ़र्–लोभ, समूर

I bought a fur coat during my visit to Kashmir.

57. Furious (adj.) फ़्युअरिअस–भीषण, अति क्रुद्ध, उग्र

The manager became furious at the blunder of the clerk who sent an important letter at the wrong address.

58. Furnace (n.) फ़र्निस–भट्टी

During a visit to the steel plant, the students were shown a huge furnace.

59. Brick (n.) ब्रिक–ईट

Houses are built with bricks.

60. Bride (n.) ब्राइड-दुलहन, नववधु

The bride wore a gorgeous sari

61. Bridge (n. & v.) ब्रिज-पुल बाँधना/दूरी (मिटाना)

(n.) There are many bridges across the Yamuna in Delhi.

(v.) It is difficult to bridge the gap between the rich and the poor.

62. Bridegroom (n.) ब्राइडग्रूम-वर

The bridegroom was dressed in a sherwani at the wedding.

63. Bridle (n.& v.) ब्राइड्ल्-लगाम (लगाना)

(n.) You cannot control a horse with out a bridle.

(v.) He bridled his horse and started on his journey.

64. Hustle (v.) हसल-धकेलना

People were hustling each other at the railway platform.

65. Sleeper (n.) स्लीपर्-1. सोने वाला

Some people are light sleepers, others are heavy sleepers.

2. रेलगाड़ी में सोने के लिए सीट

I reserved a sleeper on the train to Mumbai.

66. Sleeve (n.) स्लीव-बाजू के भाग को ढकने वाला कपड़ा, आस्तीन

I tore the sleeve of my shirt.

67. Slender (adj.) स्लेन्डर-लम्बी और पतली

Sony has beautiful hands with long slender fingers.

68. Slice स्लाइस-फाँक

(n.) Can I have a slice of bread?

(v.) She sliced the apple.

69. Slide (v.) स्लाइड-सुगमता से सरकना

The window slides up and down very easily.

The children love to slide on ice.

2. (n.) शीशे की पट्टी

Children prepared slides for their experiments in the science class.

70. Slight (adj.) स्लाइट-थोड़ा, मामूली

I am not in the slightest hurry.

(adv.) Are you not slightly better today than yesterday?

71. Slim स्लिम-पतला (होने का प्रयत्न करना)

(v.) Some people slim down by avoiding heavy meals.

2. क्षीण

She has slim hopes of getting what she wants.

72. Slime (n.) स्लाइम्-कीचड़

(n.) Slime deposited on the walls in the rainy season.

(adj.) The pond was very slimy.

73. Lunatic (n. & adj.) लूनटिक-पागल, बावला

(n.) A great loss in busines turned the businessman into a lunatic.

(adj.) We have a lunatic asylum in this town.

74. Arrow (n.) ऐरो-1. तीर

The hunter shot an arrow at the deer.

2. संकेत

Follow the arrows to reach the venue.

75. Art (n.) आर्ट-कला, कौशल, निपुणता

Painting is a fine art.

76. Artful (adj.) आर्टफुल-चालाक

She escaped the teacher's anger through her artful behaviour.

77. Artist (n.) आर्टिस्ट-कलाकार

The articles in India Today give a good coverage of current topics.

2. सामान, पदार्थ

She put all the articles in her shopping bag.

78. Artificial (adj.) आर्टिफिशल-नकली, कृत्रिम

Nowdays we can buy sweaters made of artificial wool.

79. Drama (n.) ड्रामा-नाटक

The child artist's performance in the drama was appreciated by all.

80. Drape (v.) ड्रेप-लपेटना

Before leaving for vacations, they draped the furniture in plastic covers.

81. Draw (v.) ड्रॉ- 1. चित्र बनाना, अंकित करना

Can you draw good pictures?

2. खींचना, घसीटना

Two horses were drawing the carriage.

3. (पास या दूर) जाना

The spectators cheered loudly as the marathon winner drew closer to the finishing line.

4. लॉटरी

Winners of the lucky draw looked very happy.

82. Drawback (n.) ड्रॉबैक-त्रुटि

A non-dancing partner proved to be a drawback for her in the dance competition.

83. Drawer (n.) ड्रॉअर्-दराज़

In which drawer have you put my pen?

84. Dread ड्रे'ड- 1. डरना, भयभीत होना, भय

(v.) A burnt child dreads the fire.

2. (adj.) डरावना

Have you read the newspaper report of the dreadful accident?

85. Dream ड्रीम-सपना, स्वप्न

(n.) Do you sleep soundly or do you have dreams?

(v.) I always dream about being rich.

86. Travel ट्रैवल-यात्रा (करना), भ्रमण (करना)

(v.) We have been travelling for over a month now.

(n.) Air travel is quick but expensive.

87. Traverse (n.) ट्रैवर्स-आरपार जाना

It took us ten days to traverse the desert.

88. Tray (n.) ट्रे-ट्रे, रकाबी

The mother brought tea in a tray.

89. Treacherous (adj.) ट्रेचरस-विश्वासघाती, बेईमान, अविश्वसनीय (नमक हराम)

The treacherous scientist sold some of his country's secrets to the enemy.

(n.) We didn't think you could be guilty of such treachery.

90. Rocket (n.) रॉकिट-राकेट

Rockets are also used as signals of distress.

91. Rod (n.) रॉड-छड़

Carry the fishing rod with you.

92. Rogue (n.) रोग-गुण्डा, दुष्ट

Beware of him, he is a rogue.

93. Role (n.) रोल

1. भूमिका

What will be my role in this campaign?

2. नाटक या फ़िल्म में निभाया गया पात्र

She played the role of a widowed mother in the play.

94. Mountain (n.) माउन्टिन-पर्वत, पहाड़

Next summer, I shall go trekking in the mountains.

(adj.) Nepal is a mountainous country.

95. Mourn (v.) मॉर्न-शोक करना/मनाना

We all mourned the death of your kind neighbour.

96. Mouse (n.) माउस-चुहिया

I want to buy a mouse-trap.

97. Moustache (n.) मस्टाश-मूंछ

He had long and bushy moustache like that of Veerappan.

98. Cock (n.) कॉक-मुर्गा

The cock crows at the daybreak.

99. Cockroach (n.) कॉक्रोच-तिलचट्टा, चपड़ा

Lizards eat the cockroaches.

100. Coconut (n.) कोकनट-नारियल

The coconut is considered a sacred fruit in India.

SPOKEN VOCABULARY
Set - 41

1. **Code (n.)** कोड-1. संहिता, नियमावली

There is a code of conduct for Government servants.

2. कूट, संकेत-पद्धति

The spy sent his secret message in code.

2. **Coffin (n.)** कॉफ़िन-शवपेटी

The departed leader's coffin was ready for its last journey.

3. **Coil (v. & n.)** कॉइल-गेंडुरी, कुण्डल बनाना, लपेटना

The fan motor has a coil of wire.

(v.) Nisha got her hair coiled from a beauty parlour.

4. **Coin (n.)** कॉइन-सिक्का, मुद्रा

Coins last longer than paper currency.

5. **Coincidence (n.)** कोइन्सिडन्स-संयोग

I met him in the market by a sheer coincidence.

6. **Cold (adj.** कोल्ड-1. ठण्डा, शीतल

I like cold coffee.

2. तटस्थ, उदासीन, भावशून्य

Ram was upset by Gita's cold behaviour.

3. ठण्डक, सर्दी

Anil got wet in the rain and caught a cold.

7. **Collaborate (v.)** कलैबरेट-सहयोग देना

(v.) She collaborated with a colleague to complete the project.

(n.) She has written this book in collaboration with a friend.

8. **Collapse (v.)** कलैप्स-1. ढह जाना, बैठ जाना

The old house collapsed in the storm.

2. जवाब दे देना, समाप्त हो जाना

In spite of expert medical treatment, the old man collapsed in a matter of hours.

9. **Collar (n.)** कॉलर्-कालर, गरदनी, पट्टा

Shirts with short collars are no more in fashion.

10. **Predicament (n.)** प्रिडिकमन्ट-अप्रिय स्थिति

The predicament of the parents at the loss of their son was unimaginable.

11. **Predict (v.)** प्रिडिक्ट-भविष्यवाणी करना

An astrologer has predicted that I shall settle abroad.

12. **Preface (n.)** भूमिका, प्राक्कथन

I requested the minister to write a preface for my book.

13. **Prejudice (n.)** प्रेजुडिस-प्रबल नापसंदगी या अविश्वास

He seems to have a prejudice against me.

(v.) पूर्वाग्रहित करना, पूर्वाग्रह रखना

The newspaper gossip prejudiced her against him.

14. **Preliminary (adj.)** प्रिलिमिनरि-प्राथमिक

The finalists will be selected after the preliminary round.

15. **Write (v.)** राइट-लिखना, लेखन कार्य करना

I can read the words you write.

I haven't written a letter since long.

(n.) लिखाई

Your writing is not clear.

R.K. Narayan is a famous writer.

16. **Sling (n.)** स्लिग-1. ज़ख़मी हाथ, कलाई को सहारा देने के लिए प्रयुक्त पट्टी, गल पट्टी

His fractured arm was put in a sling.

2. फेंकना

Tell the children not to sling stones

at the puppy.

17. Slip (n.) स्लिप-1. गलती

You have made a slip in the bill.

2. (v.) गिरना (फिसलकर)

The looking-glass slipped through my fingers and was broken.

(adj.) The heavy rain has made the ground slippery.

18. Slipper (n.) स्लिपर-1. पहनने का खुला जूता, जिसकी एड़ियां पतली होती हैं

Mother will buy a pair of slippers for me today.

19. Slit स्लिट-चीरना, चीर

(v.) I received an envelope and slit it open with a knife.

(n.) The boys watched the football match through a slit in the fence.

20. Slogan (n.) स्लोगन-प्रचार वाक्य

She won the first prize in the slogan writing contest.

21. Slope (n.) स्लोप-ढाल, उतराई

It is very difficult to walk up the slope of the hill.

22. Slow (adj.) स्लो-1. धीमा

The clock is slow. It is showing incorrect time.

My work is making slow progress.

2. मोटी बुद्धि का, भौंदू

She is very slow to understand anything.

3. (v.) धीरे चलना (या चलाना)

Slow down before reaching the stop signal.

(adv.) He walked slowly.

23. Furnish (v.) फ़र्निश-प्रस्तुत करना, (ला) देना, सजाना

I would like to furnish my flat.

24. Brief (adj.) ब्रीफ-संक्षिप्त

He gave me a brief account of the accident.

25. Brigade (n.) ब्रिगेड-ब्रिगेड, वाहिनी

The fire brigade was called to put out the fire in the cinema hall.

26. Bright (adj.) ब्राइट-चमकीला, चटकीला, तेज़, होनहार

A bright light was shining in the room.

Children like toys of bright colours.

He is one of the brighttoys in the class

27. Brilliant (adj.) ब्रिलिअन्ट्-चमकीला, प्रकाशमान, होशियार

We should wear goggles to protect our eyes from the brilliant sunlight.

Neeraj is a brilliant student.

28. Brim (n.) ब्रिम-1. किनारा, मुंह

The glass was full to the brim with tea.

2. टोपी का निचला भाग

29. Bring (v.) ब्रिंग-किनारा

Please bring me a glass of water.

30. Brink (n.) ब्रिंक-लाना

The mountaineer went to the brink of the cliff and looked down.

31. Brisk (adj.) ब्रिस्क-तेज़, फुर्तीला

Property business is brisk these days.

32. Slum (n.) स्लम-झुग्गी-झौंपड़ी

There are slums close to that colony.

33. Slumber (n.) स्लॅम्बर्-गहरी नींद सोना

The family was in a deep slumber when the thieves came.

34. Sly (adj.) स्लाइ-कपटपूर्ण, बेईमान, अविश्वसनीय

The shopkeeper is sly. He speaks politely but sells inferior things.

35. Small (adj.) स्मॉल-1. थोड़ा, लघु, अल्प, कम

Small courtesies matter a lot in life.

2. साधारण

Don't worry. It is a small quarel, it will be over soon.

36. Smart (adj.) स्मार्ट-1. चुस्त, चालाक, बुद्धिमान

Do you want a smart worker for your office?

Really you are very smart.

2. देखने में साफ़-सुथरा

The soldiers were praised for their smart appearance

[illegible]

The thick smoke from the bonfire made my eyes smart.

37. Smash (v.) स्मैश-चूर-चू[illegible] हो जाता

The furniture smashed [illegible]to pieces.

38. Smear (v.) स्मिअर-गन्दा करना, [illegible] करना

Please don't smear the [illegible] with your di[illegible]y hands.

39. Smell (v.) स्मे[illegible]ल-1. सूँघना, गंध देना

We smell with our nose.

Roses smell sweet.

(n.) All are attracted by the sweet smell of flowers.

40. Roll (v.) रोल-1. लुढ़कना, ढुलकना

The baby is about to roll down the bed.

(n.) नामों की सूची

I will call the roll now.

3. गड़गड़ाहट, गर्जन

Suddenly, the sky became dark and they heard a roll of thunder.

41. Romance (n.) रोमांस-साहस और प्रेम की कहानी

Modern young girls mostly read nothing but books of romance.

42. Roof (n.) रुफ़-छत (का ऊपरी भाग)

The roof was made of stones and bricks.

43. Hut (n.) हॅट-झोंपड़ी, कुटिया

Our servant lives in a hut near our house.

44. Ascend असेन्ड-चढ़ना, आरोहण करना

The old man ascended the steep staircase with great difficulty.

45. Ascertain (v.) ऐसटेन-पता लगाना

We need to ascertain the practicality of this plan.

46. Ascetic (n.) असेटिक-संन्यासी

The ascetic did penance for severa years.

47. Ash (n.) ऐश-राख, भस्म

A major fire reduced the house to ashes.

48. Ash[illegible]d (adj.) अशेम्ड-लज्जित

Are you not ashamed of being seen in the company of such vagabonds?

49. Ashore (adv.) अशोर्-तट पर, जमीन पर

When the ship anchored at the harbour, the sailors came ashore.

50. Drench (v.) ड्रे'न्च-सराबोर कर देना

I was drenched in the rain while coming to see you.

51. Dress (n.) ड्रे'स- 1. पोशाक, कपड़े

I'm not very particular about my dress.

2 (v.) मरहम्-पट्टी करना

Do you know how to dress a wound?

52. Drift (v.) ड्रिफ्ट- 1. बह जाना, बेमतलब घूमना-फिरना

Clouds were drifting in the wind.

2. च्युति, पदच्युत होना

Never drift from the path of righeousness.

(n.) It is easy to swim with the drift of the stream.

53. Drill ड्रिल-कवायद, व्यायाम, कवायद/व्यायाम करना

(n.) In our school, we have drill every day.

(v.) बरमा (चलाना), छेद करना

Can you drill hole in a very thick wall?

84. Tread (v.) ट्रे'ड-पैर रखना, कुचलना

Don't tread on the carpet with your muddy boots.

Don't tread on the cat's tail.

The mob passing through these fields have trodden down the plants.

85. Treadle (n.) ट्रे'डल-पांवों से चलाई जाने वाली (सिलाई मशीन)

Have you bought a treadle sewing machine from the agency?

86. Treason (n.) ट्रीज़न-देशद्रोह, राजद्रोह

Treason is one of the most serious crimes.

87. Treasure (v.) ट्रेशर्-संजोय रखना, बहुत संभालकर रखना

I treasure my gold watch.

(n.) Many treasures of gold and silver have been found in old castles.

88. Treat ट्रीट-1. इलाज करना

(v.) Doctors treat their patients.

2. (n.) आनन्ददायक वस्तु

It was a treat to hear such good singing.

3. (v.) व्यवहार करना, बर्ताव करना

Old age needs to be treated gently in words as well as in deeds.

89. Lunch लॅन्च-मध्याह्न-भोजन

(n.) Have you had your lunch?

(v.) I'll lunch today with my brother-in-law.

90. Mouth (n.) माउथ-1. मुंह, मुख

Always keep your mouth clean.

2. मुहाना

We went on a trip in a launch up to the mouth of the river.

91. Move (v.) मूव-1. हटाना, हिलाना

Who has moved my cot?

2. आना-जाना, चलना-फिरना

From my seat, I watched the guests moving about the hall.

3. घर या जगह बदलना

We moved from Mumbai to Delhi many years ago.

4. प्रभावित करना, प्रेरित करना

We were moved to tears by his sad story.

92. Collect (v.) कलेक्ट-जमा करना या होना, संग्रह करना

Children love to collect coloured pebbles on the seashore.

93. College (n.) कॉलिज-कालेज, महाविद्यालय

Students face tough competition for getting admission in reputed colleges of Delhi.

94. Collide (v.) कलाइड-1. टकराना, टक्कर लगना

When a taxi collided with a bus, all the traffic came to halt on the busy road.

2. टक्कर

The taxi was smashed in the collision.

95. Colloquial (adj.) कलोक्विअल-बोलचाल की अनौपचारिक भाषा

Avoid colloquial words in your eassays.

96. Colony (n.) कॉलनि-बस्ती, उपनिवेश .

Deep in the woods, the traveller came across a colony of tribal people.

97. Colour (v.) कलर्-वर्ण, रंग

White colour is a combination of seven colours.

98. Column (v.) कॉलम-1. स्तम्भ, खम्भा

The old palace had huge columns.

2. कालम, स्तम्भ

3. दस्ता, सैन्य दल

99. Comb कोम-1. कंघी करना

(v.) The mother combed her daughter's hair.

2. छान डालना

The police combed the town for the thief.

(n.) I want to buy a new comb.

100. Combat कॉम्बैट-लड़ाई

(n.) A combat took place between the police and the protestors.

(v.) Government is taking measures to combat poverty.

SPOKEN VOCABULARY
Set - 42

1. **Combine (v.)** कम्बाइन-मिलाना, जोड़ना, व्यापार - संघ

   The two companies combined to form one big corporation.

2. **Come (v.)** कम्-आना, पहुंचना

3. **Premier (adj.)** प्रमिअर्-सर्वोत्तम

   It is a premier hotel in the city.

4. **Premiere (n.)** प्रेमिअर्-नाटक या फ़िल्म का पहला सार्वजनिक प्रदर्शन

   The actress was hounded by media at the premiere.

5. **Premises (n.)** प्रेमिसिज़्-भवन, परिसर

   No one is allowed on these premises after 7 P.M.

6. **Prepare (v.)** प्रिपेअर्-1. बनाना

   What sweet dish have you prepared today?

   2. तैयार होना

   He is not prepared to help me.

   (n.) Have you made the preparations for the journey?

7. **Prescribe (v.)** प्रिस्क्राइब-नुसख़ा लिखना

   The doctor prescribed an effective medicine.

   (n.) नुसख़ा

   I have lost the prescriptions some where.

8. **Prestige (n.)** प्रेस्टीज-आदर-सम्मान

   (n.) The school has maintained its prestige over the years.

   (adj.) This is the most presented a trophy to the school.

   2. (n.) उपहार, भेंट

   I received many presents on my birthday.

   3. (adj.) उपस्थित

   Were you present when the fire broke out?

   4. वर्तमान कालिक

   Our present teacher is very good.

9. **Preserve (v.)** प्रिज़र्व-1. बचाना, सुरक्षित रखना

   Preserve this document carefully.

   (n.) परिरक्षण

   Food preservation is a growing industry.

10. **Preside (v.)** प्रिसाइड-संचालन करना, सभापति होना

    Who is going to preside over our meeting?

    Ram came to see me as I was ill.

11. **Gymnasium (n.)** जिम्नेज़ियम्-व्यायामशाला

    Does your school have agymnasium?

    My son is good at gymnastics.

12. **Room (n.)** रुम-1. स्थान, जगह

    Is there room for me in the compartment?

    2. कमरा

    There is enough space in the room.

    3. अवसर, मौका

    There is room for improvement in this situation.

13. **Root (n.)** रुट-1. जड़ (वृक्ष या पौधों की)

    The roots keep the plant steady, and help it to grow.

2. मूल

The family doctor is trying to get to the root of my mother's illness.

14. Rope (n.) रोप-1. रस्सा

The cows were tied with strong ropes.

2. (v.) रस्से से बाँधना

The traveller roped his horse to the tree and lay down to take rest.

15. Rosary (n.) रोज़रि-सुमिरनी

The old woman was carrying a string of rosary beads in her hands.

16. Further (adj.) फ़र्दर्-1. और दूर

The soldiers were too tired to move further.

2. (adj.) और, अधिक, इससे अधिक

I have nothing further to say.

17. Bristle (adj.) ब्रिस्ल-आसानी से टूटने वाला

My toothbrush is made of plastic bristles.

18. Brittle (adj.) ब्रिट्ल-आसानी से टूटने वाला

Glass is a brittle substance.

19. Broad (adj.) ब्रॉड-चौड़ा, व्यापक, विस्तृत

In Old Delhi, it is rare to find a broad avenue.

20. Broadcast (n.) ब्रॉडकास्ट-प्रसारण, रेडियो प्रोग्राम

I heard the news in the morning broadcast.

(v.) AIR broadcasts a running commentary of the Republic Day Parade.

21. Broadly (adv.) ब्रॉडलि-मोटे तौर पर

I will explain you the situation broadly.

22. Broad-minded (adj.) ब्रॉड-माइन्डिड-खुले विचारों वाला

Today parents do not mind their daughters travelling alone; they have become broad-minded.

23. Brochure (n.) ब्रोशर्-विवरणिका

Get me the brochures of the companies.

24. Broker (n.) ब्रोकर्-दलाल

I called the broker to know about some good investment plans.

25. Hymn (n.) हिम-भजन, स्त्रोत

Can you recite Sanskrit hymns correctly?

26. Smile (n. & v.) स्माइल-मुस्कराहट, मुस्कराना

(n.) Smile is the language of love.

(v.) A face that does not carry a smile is never pretty.

27. Smith (n.) स्मिथ-धातुकार, वह व्यक्ति जो किसी धातु में काम करता हो

In our villages, there are many artisans such as blacksmith, tinsmith, goldsmith etc.

The blacksmith works with iron, he makes horse shoes.

28. Smoke (n. & v.) स्मोक-धुआँ, धूम्रपान करना

(n.) Where there is smoke, there is fire.

(v.) Smoking is prohibited. Please don't smoke here.

29. Smooth (adj.) स्मूद-कोमल, मृदु, सरल, अर्थात् अच्छा

Smooth words make smooth ways.

30. Smother (n.) स्मॅदर्-(से) भर देना, भरा होना, लिप्त होना

The player returned home from the playground smothered in mud.

31. Smoulder (v.) स्मोल्डर्-धीरे-धीरे जलना, सुलगना

The fire has not gone out. It is smouldering.

32. Smudge (v.) स्मॅज्-फ़ैल जाना

Water smudged the kohl of her eyes.

33. Smuggle (v.) स्मॅगल-एक देश से दूसरे देश में चोरी-छिपे बिना कर दिए वस्तुएं लाना (तस्करी करना)

In olden days, smugglers brought wines.

Nowadays some people smuggle watches and jewellery.

34. Hygiene (n.) हाइजीन-साफ़-सफ़ाई

She is very concerned about her personal hygiene.

35. Aside (adv.) असाइड-एक ओर, अलग

He took me aside to tell something confidential

36. Ask (v.) आस्क्-1. पूछना, कहना

"How are you?" he asked me.

2. मांगना, कहना

The beggar asked him for money.

Please ask Anil to see me this evening.

37. Asleep (adv.) अस्लीप-सोता हुआ

The tired man fell asleep immediately.

38. Aspect (n.) ऐस्पेक्ट-पहलू, पक्ष

You should consider all the aspects of the matter before taking a decision.

39. Assault (v.) असॉल्ट-1. हमला करना, प्रहार करना

He was arrested for assaulting his neighbour.

2. (n.) चढ़ाई

The mountaineers launched an assault on the high peak.

40. Assemble (v.) असेम्बल-एकत्र होना या करना, जुटना, जोड़ना

The headmaster asked the students to assemble in the courtyard of the school.

(n.) सभा

The assembly passed the resolution unanimously.

41. Assert (v.) असर्ट-दावा करना, बलपूर्वक कहना

He kept asserting that he was not wrong.

42. Assess (v.) असेस-आंकना

(v.) The causes of failure of this strategy must be assessed soon.

(n.) It is important to make an assessment of the expenditure involved.

43. Drink ड्रिन्क- 1. पीना, पेय, शर्बत

(v.) Drink your tea before it gets cold.

2. मदिरापान

Wayward youths are prone to start drinking.

(n.) He asked for a drink, but I refused.

44. Drip (v.) ड्रिप-टपकना

The tap in my bathroom has been dripping since yesterday.

45. Drive (v.) ड्राइव- 1. चलाना, हाँकना

Can you drive a car?

2. (n.) (गाड़ी में) सैर

Let us go for a drive round the lake.

3. जोश, कर्मशक्ति

A man with a strong drive is bound to succeed in his career.

46. Droop (v.) ड्रूप- 1. झुकना, कुम्हलाना

The flowers in the garden were drooping due to intense heat.

2. निराश या उदास हो जाना

Don't let your spirits droop.

47. Drop (n.) ड्रॉप- 1. बूँद

Sometimes even a drop of medicine does a lot of good to the patient.

2. (v.) छोड़ देना या घट जाना

Be careful, don't drop that glass.

48. Drought (n.) ड्राउट-सूखा, अनावृष्टि

The crops were spoilt by the drought

49. Tree (n.) ट्री-वृक्ष, पेड़

There are many trees in the wood.

A saw can fell a tree that took a hundred years to grow.

50. Trek ट्रेक-पर्वतों की लंबी कठोर पैदल यात्रा

(n.) They finally reached the top after a three-day trek across the mountains.

(v.) Let's go trekking this summer.

51. Tremble (v.) ट्रेम्बल-कांपना

We tremble when we are excited or full of fear.

52. Tremendous (adj.) ट्रमन्डस-ज़बरदस्त भयानक

There was a tremendous explosion and the house crumbled to the ground.

53. Tremor (n.) ट्रेमर्-कपन

Cold weather made a tremor run through her limbs

54. Trench (n.) ट्रैन्च-खाई

Trenches have been dug across the town to drain off the water.

55. Trend (n.) ट्रेन्ड-नया फ़ैशन

(n.) It is usually the movie stars who set the trends in fashion.

(adj.) She loves to wear trendy clothes.

56. Trespass (v.) ट्रेस्पस-अतिक्रमण करना, बिना आज्ञा प्रवेश करना

They were caught trespassing on government property.

57. Trial (n.) ट्राइअल-परीक्षण, जांच, परख

The latest car model is having its trial this week.

Truth fears no trial.

58. Lung (n.) लॅन्ग-फेफड़ा, फुफ्फुस

Too much smoking would damage your lungs.

59. Movie (n.) मूवी-फ़िल्म

The scene of the mother rushing to the hospitals with her ill child was very moving.

60. Moving (adj.) मूविंग-ह्रदयस्पर्शी

The scene of the mother rushing to the hospitals with her ill child was very moving

61. Mow (v.) मा-काटना कतरकर हल्का करना

Has the gardener mowed the lawn?

62. Much (pron.) मॅच-बहुत प्राय:

How much did you pay for this pen?

(adj.) Is there much water in the jug?

(adv.) Thank you very much

63. Comfort कम्फर्ट-आराम चैन सान्त्वना. दिलासा देना

(v.) Rich men live in great comfort

(adj.) Five-star hotels are very comfortable.

(v.) I comforted the weeping child.

64. Command कमान्ड-आदेश, हुक्म, आज्ञा देना

(n.) The General gave the command to march.

A captain is in command of a company of soldiers.

(v.) The king commanded his army to attack.

65. Commence (v.) कमेन्स-प्रारंभ करना या होना

When does the show commence?

66. Commendable (adj.) कमेन्डबल-प्रशंसनीय

She has really done a commendable job.

67. Comment कॉमेन्ट-टिप्पणी

(n.) She ignored the comment he made about her dress.

(v.) He commented on her dress.

68. Commit (v.) कमिट-करना, कर डालना

A committed many thefts before being caught.

69. Committee (n.) कमिटि-कमेटी, समिति

A committee was set up to go into the affairs of the company.

70. Commodity (n.) कमॉडटि-व्यापार की वस्तु

Gold is a precious commodity.

71. Common (adj.) कॉमन-1. सामान्य, आम

The crow is a common bird in India,

2. साधारण

A common man can't afford to buy a car.

3. सामान्य बुद्धि, सहज बुद्धि

Fools have no common sense.

72. Press (n.) प्रेस-1. मुद्रणालय, छापाखाना

In what press was this book printed?

2. समाचार-पत्र, अख़बार

I often write letters to the press.

3. (v.) दबाव डालना

Please do not press me to eat more.

4. दबाना

I pressed the button of the door bell.

73. Presume (v.) प्रिज़्यूम-अटकलें लगाना

Don't presume this consent to work with us.

74. Pretext (n.) प्रीटेक्स्ट-बहाना

She left the job on the pretext of getting married.

75. Pretend (v.) प्रिटेन्ड-ढोंग रचना

He likes to pretend that he is a rich man.

76. Priest (n.) प्रीस्ट-पादरी

The temple priest bathed deities in the morning.

77. Mud (n.) मॅड-कीचड़

Take care Rakesh, lest you would fall in the mud.

Don't bring your muddy shoes into the room.

78. Muddle मॅडल-गड़बड़ी, अव्यवस्था, अस्तव्यस्त कर देना

(n.) Everything in the house was in a muddle.

(v.) If you mind is muddled, you cannot think clearly.

79. Mug (n.) मॅग-प्याला

I like to drink coffee from a mug.

80. Multiply (v.) मल्टिप्लाइ-1. गुणा करना

If we multiply 4 by 6, the result is 24.

2. बढ़ना, बढ़ाना

(n.) Have you learnt multiplication?

81. Fury (n.) फ़्युअरि-प्रकोप, आवेश

Avoid the fury of the storm by remaining indoors.

82. Brooch (n.) ब्रोच-जड़ाऊ पिन

She pinned a diamond brooch on her blouse.

83. Brood (v.) ब्रूड-1. चिंता करना, विचार करना

Why are you brooding over the past?

2. (n.) बच्चे, संतान

The mother goose waddled across the street with her brood.

84. Brook (n.) ब्रुक-1. नाला, छोटी नदी

Some rivers are fed by many brooks.

2. (v.) सहना, बरदाश्त करना

He brooks no interference in his work.

85. Broom (n.) ब्रूम-झाड़ू, कूँचा

The minicipal sweepers were given new brooms.

86. Brother (n.) ब्रदर्-भाई, बन्धु

How many brothers do you have?

87. Rose (n.) रोज़-1. गुलाब

My garden is full of a large variety of roses.

(adj.) The young girl had rosy cheeks.

88. Rotate (v.) रोटेट्-धुरी पर घूमना

Apart from revolving around the sun, the planets also rotate on their own axis.

89. Rotten (adj.) रॉटन-सड़ा-गला

The basket is full of rotten mangoes.

Most of the walnuts in the box were rotten.

90. Rough (adj.) रॅफ़्-1. सस्ता, खुरदरा

I need some rough cloth.

2. कठोर, कर्कष

Don't be rough with women and babies.

Father was angry and spoke in a rough voice.

3. जल्दी-जल्दी तैयार किया हुआ, कच्चा, कच्चे रंग से तैयार किया हुआ

This is a rough drawing.

4. (adv.) लगभग

There were roughly thirty persons in the gathering.

5. बुरे ढंग से, दुर्व्यवहारपूर्वक

The policeman roughly pushed the prisoner into the cell.

91. Hype हाइप-बढ़ा-चढ़ाकर वर्णन करना

(v.) The media hyped the movie greatly.

(n.) Despite the media hype, the movie was a big flop.

92. Snack (n.) स्नैक-अल्पाहार

We ordered tea and snacks.

93. Snake (n.) स्नेक-साँप

All snakes are not poisonous.

Snakes are worshipped in India on Nagpanchami.

94. Snap (v.) स्नैप-1. दाँत गड़ाना

Do not tease the dog. It may snap at your hand.

2. जल्दी से फ़ोटो खींचना

He snapped you as you were coming round the corner.

95. Snarl (v.) स्नार्ल-1. दाँत दिखाकर गुर्राना

Her dog snarls at the visitors.

2. रुखे और कठोर स्वर में कहना

The angry mother snarled, "Why didn't you straight come home from your school?"

96. Snatch (v.) स्नैच-1. छीनना, झपटना

The thief snatched the girl's chain and ran away.

2. भकोसना, जल्दी-जल्दी खाना

I want only five minutes to snatch some food.

97. Sneak (v.) स्नीक-आँख़ बचाकर निकलना

I saw the thief sneak down the stairs and out of the shop.

98. Sneer (v.) स्निअर्-खिल्ली उड़ाना, उपहास करना

He is only a beginner at tennis, so we should not sneer at him for missing easy shots.

99. Sneeze (v.) स्नीज़-छींकना

You are catching a cold. You have sneezed many times today.

(n.) Mostly sneezing is a sign of cold.

100. Snide (adj.) स्नाइड-व्यंग्यात्मक

He made a snide remark on her performance.

SPOKEN VOCABULARY
Set - 43

1. **Sniff (v. & n.)** स्निफ्-(नाक) सुड़कना सूँ-सूँ करना

   Please don't sniff use your handkerchief

2. **Snob (n.)** स्नॉब्-घमंडी

   She is a big snob

3. **Snooze** स्नूज-झपकी

   (n.) The labourers had a snooze after lunch

   (v.) The labourers snoozed after lunch.

4. **Snore (v. & n.)** स्नॉर्-खर्राट (भरना)

   (n.) I was distrubed the whole night by my brother's snores

   (v.) Your snoring was intolerable.

5. **Assign (v.)** असाइन-कार्यभार सौपना

   I was assigned the job of collecting funds

6. **Assist (v.)** अंसिस्ट सहायता करना सहयोग देना

   He assisted the blind man to cross the street

   (adj.) सहायक

   There are half a dozen assistant editors on the staff on that newspaper.

   (n.) सहायता

   Can I be of any assistance to you?

7. **Association (n.)** असोसिएशन-1. संस्था, सभा, समाज

   They have formed an assoication called Friends of Freedom.

   2. संबंध, साहचर्य

   He warned his son against association with bad boys.

8. **Assume (v.)** अस्यूम - 1. मान लेना, कल्पना करना

   Why do you assume that you are never wrong?

   2. ग्रहण करना, धारण करना

   The price assumed sovereign power on the death of the king.

9. **Assure (v.)** अशॉर्-आष्वासन देना, विश्वास दिलाना, मंदेह दूर करना

   He assured me of his full co-operation.

   (n.) आश्वासन

   I give you my assurance that you will come to no harm.

10. **Drown (n.)** ड्राउन-डूब मरना, डुबाकर मारना

    Thirty persons were drowned in the boat tragedy.

    (adj.) Do you know how to rescue a drowning person?

11. **Drowsy (adj.)** ड्राउज़ि-निद्रालु

    After staying awake for the whole night, I was feeling drowsy in the morning.

12. **Drug (n.)** ड्रग

    1. दवा

    Penicillin is a wonder drug.

    2. नशीली दवा

    Taking drugs is injurious to health.

13. **Drum (n.)** ड्रम-ढोल, मृदंग

    I want to buy a toy drum for my child.

14. **Dry** ड्राइ- 1. सूखा, सुखाना

    (adj.) Are your hands dry or wet?

    (v.) I dried my clothes in the wind.

    2. नीरस, शुष्क

    You cannot make friends if you have a dry manner.

15. **Triangle (n.)** ट्राइऐन्गल-त्रिकोण, त्रिभुज

    Can you draw a triangle?

16. **Tribe (n.)** ट्राइब-जन-जाति

    There are many tribes in India.

17. **Tribunal (n.)** ट्राइब्यूनल-विशेष अदालत, न्यायालय

    The Supreme Court is the highest tri

bunal in India.

18. Tributary (n.) ट्रिब्यट्रि-सहायक नदी

Yamuna is a tributary of Ganga

19. Tribute (n.) ट्रिब्यूट-प्रशंसा, आभार

The newly elected member of Parliament paid tribute to the voters who had voted for him in the elections

20. Trick ट्रिक-युक्ति दाँव-पेंच

(n.) Every profession has its tricks

(v.) We are bitter against those who trick us.

21. Trickle (v.) ट्रिकल-बूंद-बूंद टपकना

A tear trickled down her cheeks

22. Tricycle (n.) ट्राइसाइकल-तीन पहियो वाली साइकिल

A tricycle runs on three wheels

23. Trifle (n.) ट्राइफ़ल-छोटी-सी बात तुच्छ बात छोटा मसला

Mother told Raju not to cry over trifles.

Those who apply themselves too much to trifles usually become incapable of achieving great things.

Trifles make perfection and perfection is not trifle

24. Trigger (n.) ट्रिगर्-बदूक का घाड़ा (जिसे दबाने से राइफल, गन या पिस्तौल से गोली छूटती है)

The gunners pressed the triggers and the guns went off.

25. Lush (adj.) लॅश-हरा-भरा

The bungalow was surrounded by lush green farms.

26. Multitude (n.) मल्टिट्यूड-भीड़, जनसाधारण

I was impressed by the multitude of people at yesterday's public meeting.

27. Mumble (v.) मम्बल-गुनगुनाना, फुसफुसाना

The child was mumbling in the sleep.

28. Munch (v.) मॅन्च-आवाज़ करते हुए खाना

We watched the movie munching on popcorn.

29. Mundane (adj.) मन्डेन्-मामूली

Stop musing over these mundane issues.

30. Municipal (adj.) म्यूनिसिपल-नगर, नगरपालिका -सबधी

Are you a candidate for the coming municipal elections?

31. Community (n.) कम्यूनटि-समाज समूह सम्प्रदाय

There is a large community of shoemakers in this locality

The Parsi community is mainly concentrated in Mumbai

32. Commute (v.) कम्यूट दैनिक यात्रा करना

(n.) I commute from my home to office by bus

(n) The strike of buses created a problem for the commuters

33. Companion (n.) कम्पैनिअन-1 साथी सखा सहचर

Without a companion. one feels lonely on a long rail journey.

2. (adj.) संबद्ध. साथ का

This is a companion volume to the previous publication.

34. Company (n.) कम्पनि-1. कम्पनी, समवाय

At last the company started making profits.

2 दल

A Captain commands a company of soldiers.

3. संगति, मित्र, साथी

A man is known by the company he keeps.

35. Compare (v.) कम्पेअर्-तुलना करना, मिलाना, बराबर समझना या होना

One must compare the price and performance of different brands before buying a washing machine.

(n.) There is no comparison between the lifestyles or rich and poor.

(adj.) Of all the problems in the question paper, the last one was comparatively easy.

36. Pretty (adj.) प्रिटि-रमणीय, सुंदर

She is a pretty girl.

39. Prevail (v.) प्रिवेल-1. सफल होना

After a hard struggle, we prevailed

over the opposite team.

2. राज़ी करना

Can I prevail on you to have dinner with us?

40. Prevent (v.) प्रिवेन्ट-रोकना

I tried to prevent the boys from quar relling.

41. Previous (adj.) प्रिविअस-पिछला, पहले का

Have you read the previous page?

42. Prey (v.) प्रे-1.शिकार करना, लूटना

Leopards prey on deer.

2. (n.) शिकार

This forest is full o birds of prey.

43. Price (n.) भाव, दाम

What is the price of this TV set?

2. मूल्य

This ancient work of art is priceless.

44. Prick (v.) प्रिक-छेदना, चुभाना

A thorn pricked my foot.

45. Pride (n.) प्राइड-अभिमान, अहंकार

I take pride in my son's academic record.

46. Prince (n.) प्रिन्स-राजकुमार

The prince punished the culprit.

47. Luxury (n.) लॅक्शरि-ऐयाशी, विलसिता

I cannot afford to live in luxury.

(adj.) Everybody wants to lead a luxurious life.

48. Fuse फ्यूज़-पसीज, बत्ती, फ्यूज़

I want a fuse for my electric connection.

49. Brow (n.) ब्राउ-भौंह, भ्रू

He has thick eye-brows.

50. Brown (adj.) ब्राउन-भूरा

Brown is my favourite colour.

51. Browse (v.) ब्राउज़

1. घूमना, समय बिताना

I browsed in the bookshop for half an hour.

2. सरसरी नज़र डालना

I browsed the Internet for information on latest cars.

52. Bruise (v. & n.) ब्रूज़-चोट, चोट पहुंचाना

(v.) I bruised my leg when I fell down.

(n.) My bruise is not healing.

53. Brush ब्रश-कूँची, बुरुष, छू जाना, माँजना, चमकाना

(n.) I have lost my tooth-brush.

(v.) We should brush our teeth regularly.

54. Brute (n.) ब्रूट-पशु

The big brute rushed towards us.

(adj.) He is notorious for his brutal behaviour.

55. Round (n.) राउण्ड

1. घटनाओं का दौर

The company is considering a fresh round of interviews from next week.

2. फेरा

The director is on his daily round.

3. प्रतियोगिता का एक चक्र या दौर

Australia has qualified for the next round.

4. प्रशंसा-प्रक्रिया

He was welcomed with a huge round of applause.

5. समाप्त करना

(v.) He rounded his speech with a quotation.

6. चक्कर लगाना

(v.) His car was rounding the whole city.

7. गोलकार

(adj.) The table was round in shape.

8. किसी वस्तु के चारों ओर

(adv.) The dog went round and round the car.

56. Route (n.) रुट-मार्ग, रास्ता

We must take the shortest route from here to Ambala.

57. Routine (n.) रुटीन-दिनचर्या, दैनिक कार्य

Whenever visitors call on me all of a sudden, it affects my daily routine.

58. Rove (v.) रोव-घूमना, भटकना

You spent all day roving through the jungle.

59. Row (n.) रो-1. पंक्ति, कतार

The people were standing in a row near the ratio shop.

2. (v.) चप्पू चलाना, नाव चलाना

The boatmen row their boats.They make the boats travel through the water.

60. Hypnotise (v.) हिप्नटाइज़-सम्मोहित करना

The magician hypnotised the small girl.

61. Snow (n. & v.) स्नो-हिम, बर्फ़ (पड़ना)

(n.) The snow was falling from the sky.

(v.) It started snowing in the hills.

62. Snub (v.) स्नॅबू-रुखा बरताव करना

She snubbed him badly for entering the room without asking for permission.

63. Soak (v.) सोक-1. भीगना

You have been out in the rain and are soaked.

2. भिगोना

Soak the raisins in water for two hours.

64. Soap सोप-साबुन (लगाना)

(n.) Which soap do you use?

(v.) He soaped himself well to clean the dirt.

65. Soar (v.) सॉर्-ऊँचा चढ़ना, बढ़ना

Don't soar too high to fall, but stop to rise.

Last year, the prices of foodgrains soared up very high.

66. Sob (v. & n.) सॉब-सिसकना, सिसकी

(v.) The baby was sobbing.

(n.) Her sobs could be heard clearly from outside.

67. Sober (adj.) सोब्र्-1 तर्कपूर्ण, शांत-गंभीर

Pay heed to your teacher's sober advice.

2. नशा त्यागने वाला

He is now sober.

68. Society (n.) ससाइअटि-1. समाज, सोसाइटी

Society doesn't love it critics.

2. दूसरों के साथ मित्रता

We like the society of interesting people.

69. Sock (n.) सॉक-जुर्राब, मोज़ा

I bought a pair of socks.

I need a clean pair of socks todays.

70. Soda (n. & adj.) सोडा-खारा पानी, क्षार, सज्जी

Soda bicarbonate is used in baking.

In small towns, people enjoy soda-water.

71. Sofa (n.) सोफ़ा-सोफा, बैठने का आरामदेह आसन

Father bought a new sofa-set from the market.

72. Soft (adj.) सॉफ़्ट-कोमल, नरम, मुलायम

Wool is soft to touch.

Your mother is soft-hearted.

73. Soggy (adj.) सॉगि-बहुत गीला और नरम

The sandwiches became soggy when left in open.

74. Soil (v. & n.) सॉइल-1. मैला करना, कूड़ा-कर्कट

(v.) She will soil her dress if she sits on the muddy grass.

2. (n.) मिट्टी

This soil is very fertile.

75. Astonish (v.) अस्टॉनिश-चकित होना या करना, अचंभे में पड़ना या डालना

I was astonished to hear him say such a foolish thing.

76. Astrology (n.) एस्ट्रोलॉजि-ज्योतिष

Not everyone believes in astrology

77. Astronomy (n.) एस्ट्रॉनमि-खगोलविज्ञान

India is making huge progess in the field of astronomy.

78. Athlete (n.) ऐथ्लीट-कसरती, व्यायामी

The college selected five athletes to participate in the race competition.

79. Atlas (n.) ऐट्लस-एटलस, भू-चित्रावली

You cannot learn Geogrphy without an atlas.

80. Atmosphere (n.) ऐट्मस्फ़िअर्-वासुमण्डल, वातावरण

Pollution of the atmosphere becomes a serious problem in industrialised countries.

81. Atrocity (n.) एट्रॉसटि-अत्याचार

The institute committed atrocity on the poor students by abolishing the scholarship

82. Dub (v.) डब एक भाषा की फिल्म का दूसरी भाषा मे अनुवाद

The movie Taare Zameen Par has been dubbed in other languages as well

83. Due ड्यू- 1 देय. दातव्य

(adj) Ram paid his insurance premium even before it became due.

2 अपेक्षित

The train is due in half an hour.

3. (adj.) के कारण, फलस्वरुप

I met with an accident due to my careless driving.

(n.) Give the devil his due.

84. Dull (adj.) डल- 1. मन्दबुद्धि

Your son will pass, he is not dull.

2. नीरस, उबानेवाला

A dull book mars the reputation of its author.

3. मेघाच्छादित, धुँधला

Today is a cloudy and dull day.

85. Trim (v.) ट्रिम-1. काटना-छांटना, कतरना, सुव्यवस्थित करना

I must trim the hedge because it looks so untidy.

86. Trinket (n.) ट्रिंकिट-सस्ता गहना

I shopped for trinkets in the Tibetan market.

87. Trio (adj.) ट्रीओ-तिकड़ी, तीन व्यक्तियों का समूह

These comedians are a comical trio.

88. Trip ट्रिप

1. यात्रा, भ्रमण

(n.) Uncle and aunt have gone for a trip to the sea.

2. लड़खड़ाना, गिरना

(v.) Tommy tripped over a loose stone.

89. Tripod (n.) ट्रिपॉड, ट्राइपॉड-तिपाई, तीन पांवों वाला स्टूल (कैमरा सेट करने का)

The photographer set up a tripod for taking some snapshots.

90. Triumph (n.) ट्राइअंफ़-विजय, जीत, सफलता

We were given a day's holiday to celebrate our triumph in the football cup.

91. Murder मर्डर्-खून, हत्या (करना)

(v.) The young girl was murdered at midnight.

(n.) Has the police caught the murdere?

Who was accused of the murderer?

92. Compass (n.) कम्पस्-1. कम्पास, दिक्सूचक

A ship cannot be kept on its course without a compass.

2. परकार

The geometry teacher asked the students to buy a compass box.

93. Compassion (n.) कम्पैशन-सहानुभूति

He has no compassion for the poor.

94. Compatible (adj.) कम्पैटब्ल-अनुकूल

They were not compatible with the fast lifestyle abroad.

95. Compel (v.) कम्पेल-लाचार/मजबूर करना, बाध्य करना

It's not good to compel a person to do something against his wish.

96. Compensate (v.) कॉम्पेन्सेट्-क्षतिपूर्ति करना

(v.) I had to compensate for the damage I caused to their car.

(n.) She did not ask for any compensation after she divorced her husband.

97. Primary (adj.) प्राइमरी-1. प्राथमिक

I have admitted my son to a primary school.

2. मूल, मूलभूत

My primary intention in coming here was to meet you.

98. Principal (n.) प्रिन्सिपल-1. सिद्धांत

He is a man of noble principles.

2. आधारभूत तत्त्व

Have you understood the principle of the law of Physics?

99. Print (n. & v.) प्रिन्ट-छापना, छाप/मुहर

(n.) My book is at present under print.

(v.) We print books of high standard.

100. Prior (adj.) प्राइअर्-पूर्व, पूर्ववर्ती

We met him prior to his trip aboard.

SPOKEN VOCABULARY
Set - 44

1. **Hypocrisy (n.)** हि'पॉक्रसि-पाखंड

The politicians emphasies on using Indian goods, while they themselves travel in foreign cars. This is the height of hypocrisy!

2. **Fuss (n.)** फ़स-बतंगड़, शोर शराबा

Don't make a fuss if there is no milk.

Don't be so fussy about your clothes.

3. **Bubble (n. & v.)** बबल-बुलबुला, बुदबुदाना, चहकाना

(n.) Children are fond of blowing soap bubbles.

Bubbles rose on the boiling water.

(v.) The bride bubbled with happiness on the wedding day.

4. **Bucket (n.)** बकिट-बाल्टी, डोल

Please bring me a bucket of hot water.

5. **Buckle (n.)** बकूल-बकुसआ, बकलस, बकसुए से बन्द करना, कसना

(n.) He bought a fashionable new buckle for his belt.

(v.) He buckled his shoes and left for work.

6. **Bud (n.)** बड-कली, मुकुल

These buds will bloom by tomorrow morning.

7. **Budge (v.)** बज-सरकना

She budged a little and slept again.

8. **Solace (n.)** सांत्वना

After travelling to so many places, I found solace in my own home.

9. **Solar (adj.)** सोलर्-सौर, सूर्य-संबंधी

The earth is a part of the solar system. It revolves round the sun.

10. **Soldier (n.)** सोल्ज्र्-सैनिक

Soldiers fight and kings become heroes.

There are many soldiers in an army.

11. **Sole (adj.)** सोल-1. अकेला, एकमात्र

She was the sole child of her parents.

2. (n.) पैर का तलुआ, जूते का तल्ला

Please show me a shoe with a rubber sole.

12. **Solemn (adj.)** सॉलम-गंभीर

The manager had a solemn manner when he addressed the staff.

13. **Solid (adj.)** सॉलिड-ठोस, सख्त

The patient cannot take solid food. He can only take tea or milk.

14. **Solidarity (n.)** सॉलिडैरटि-एकजुटता

They expressed their solidarity with her opinion.

15. **Solitary (adj.)** सॉलिटरि-एकांत, निर्जन

Few people like to live in solitary places.

16. **Solution (n.)** सल्यूशन, सलूशन-1. समाधान, समस्या का हल

Provide me a solution to this problem.

2. घोल

The solution of these two chemicals can be explosive.

17. Solve (v.) सॉल्व-समाधान करना, हल करना

Let me help you solve that crossword puzzle.

Solve your problems youself.

18. Attach (v.) अटैच-1. लगाना, जोड़ना

Babu attached a nice new chain to his puppy's collar.

2. अनुरक्त होना, आसक्त होना

Babu is very attached to his auntie.

19. Attack (v.) अटैक- 1. हमला (करना), आक्रमण (करना)

The tiger attacked the deer.

2. आक्षेप करना

The newspapers attacked the new policy of the government.

(n.) हमला

Attack is the best form of defence.

3. दौरा

He is recovering from an attack of 'flu'.

20. Attain (v.) अटेन-कुछ करने या पाने में सफल होना

I attained success after strong efforts.

21. Attempt अटेम्प्ट्-प्रयत्न (करना), हाथ में लेना

(n.) Deepak passed the tough examination at the first attempt.

(v.) Dilip attempted to climb the tall tree, but it was too steep.

27. Attend (v.) अटेन्ड-1. उपस्थित या हाज़िर होना

Do you attend school regularly?

2. ध्यान देना

Please attend to what I say.

3. सेवा करना, परिचर्या करना

This nurse has to attend to many patients.

(n.) उपस्थिति

Your teacher must certify your attendance.

28. Dumb (adj.) डम-गूँगा, मूक

There is a school for the deaf and dumb near my house.

29. Dump डंप

1. (n.) कूड़ा डालने का स्थान

Throw this letter in the waste paper dump.

2. (v.) अवांछित वस्तु को फेंकना

She dumped the rubbish in the dustbin.

30. Dummy (adj.) डमि-1. नकली, दिखावटी

I want to buy a dummy gun for my young son.

2. (n.) कठपुतली

This dummy of the dancer looks real.

31. During (prep.) ड्युअरिंग-के समय में

You can always find me in my office during the working hours.

32. Trivial (adj.) ट्रिविअल-तुच्छ, नगण्य, छोटी-सी

I made only a trivial motoring offence.

33. Trolley (n.) ट्रॉलि-एक छोटी छकड़ा गाड़ी या ठेला जिसे हाथों से धकेला जाता है।

In the hospital, tea is served from a trolley.

34. Troop (n.) टूप-1. दल, टोली, मंडली

A troop of school children marched along the pavement.

2. सैन्यदल, सेना

The troop galloped into battle.

35. Rowdy (adj.) राउडि-उपद्रवी

They are a group of rowdy teenagers.

36. Royal (adj.) रॉइअल-शाही

He belongs to the royal family of Rajasthan.

37. **Murmur** मर्मर्-मरमराना, सरसराना, मरमराहट

(n.) When I entered the room, the murmur of conversation stopped.

(v.) She murmured but no one heard what she said.

38. **Muscle (n.)** मंसल-पेशी, बाहुबल

We should work manually to strengthen our muscles.

(adj.) I have muscular pain in the left arm.

39. **Competent (adj.)** कॉम्पिटन्ट-सक्षम

She is one of the most competent workers of her company.

40. **Competition (n.)** कॉम्पटिशन-प्रतियोगिता, होड़

Ramesh won the first prize in the painting competition.

41. **Compile (v.)** कम्पाइल-सूचना का संग्रह कर उसे संयोजित करना

He compiled a book of short stories written by some great Indian writers.

42. **Complacent (adj.)** कम्प्लेसन्ट-अपनी उन्नति से अति-संतुष्ट

(adj.) He was complacent that he would win the elections; defeat came as a blow to him.

(n.) We lost that match because of complacency.

43. **Complain (v.)** कम्प्लेन्-शिकायत करना, दुखड़ा रोना

The guests in the hotel complained about the bad food.

(n.) He lodged a complaint with the police about the theft in his house.

44. **Complement** कॉम्प्लिमन्ट-संपूरक

(n.) This scarf is a perfect complement to that dress.

(v.) This scarf complements that dress very well.

45. **Complete** कम्प्लीट-1. पूर्ण/पूरा करना

(adj.) My work here is not yet complete.

(v.) Complete your homework before you go to play.

2. (adj.) पूर्णतया, संपूर्ण रुप से

The building was completely destroyed in the fire.

46. **Complex** कॉम्प्लेक्स

1. पेचीदा

(adj.) This is a complex problem, but we need to find a solution to it.

2. भवनों की संयुक्त श्रेणी

(n.) I shall see you in the shopping complex.

3. हीन भावना

(n.) She has developed a complex about her looks.

47. **Complexion (n.)** कम्प्लेक्शन-चेहरे की त्वचा कर रंग

She has a dusky complexion, but still look good.

48. **Complicated (adj.** कॉम्प्लिकेटड-1. जटिल, पेचीदा

The Maths problem was too complicated to solve without the teacher's help.

Watch has a complicated machinery.

49. **Prison (n.)** प्रिज़न-कैदखाना

The thief was sent to the prison.

50. **Private (adj.)** प्राइवट-1. निजी

I work in a private concern.

2. (adv.) एकान्तिक

May I speak to you privately?

51. Privilege (n.) प्रिवलिज-सौभाग्य, विशेषाधिकार

It would be a privilege for us to have you with us for dinner.

52. Prize (n.) प्राइज़्-पुरस्कार, इनाम

Who won the first prize in the music contest?

53. Probable (adj.) प्रॉबबल-संभावित

It is probable that most of these boys will pass.

54. Probation (n.) प्रबेशन - परिवीक्षा-काल

He is on probation for six months.

55. Probe (v.) प्रोब-गुप्त बातें मालूम करने के लिए सवाल पूछना

The press was probing into the personal life of the actor.

56. Problem (n.) प्रॉब्लम-समस्या

We must learn to live with our problems.

57. Proceed (v.) प्रसीड-1. आगे बढ़ाना

After a short rest, we preoceeded on our way.

2. करने लगना

After taking a cup of tea, mother proceeded to cook the dinner.

3. (n.) कार्यवाही

Have you read the account of the court proceedings in the murder case?

58. Futile (adj.) फ़्यूटाइल-व्यर्थ

They made a futile attempt to make her join a medical college.

59. Budget बजट-आय-व्यय पत्र

(n.) We might go over-buget in this project.

(v.) The government budgeted a huge amount for an amusement park.

60. Buffalo (n.) बफलो-भैंस

In India, we normally drink the milk of buffalo.

61. Buffet बुफ़े-1. खाने का ऐसा प्रबंध जहां मेहमान स्वयं भोजन परोसते हैं

(n.) We will follow buffet system in the party.

2. बफ़िट्-धकेलना

(v.) The car was buffeted by the truck.

62. Bug (n.) बग-खटमल, कीड़ा

I could not sleep last night because of bugs.

63. Bugle (n.) ब्यूगल-बिगुल

At the call of the bugle, the soldiers hurried out of their barracks.

64. Royalty (n.) रॉइअल्टि-रॉयल्टी

The author was offered a royalty for his work.

65. Rub (v.) रॅब-लगड़ना

Don't rub harder, your shoes are already shining.

(n.) Please give me a rubber to rub pencil- marks.

66. Sombre (adj.) सॉम्बर्-अंधकारपूर्ण औविषादयुक्त

The graveyard was shrouded with a sombre darkness.

67. Some (pron. & adj.) सॅम-कुछ (लोग या वस्तु आदि)

Some are born great, som achieve greatness.

Some men are wise and some are otherwise.

Sometimes a half is better than the whole.

Do you want something to drink?

68. Son (n.) सॅन-पुत्र, संतान

We all are the sons and daughters of Mother India.

69. Song (n.) सॉन्ग्-गीत

Which is your favourite song in the Album?

70. Soon (adv.) सून-शीघ्र ही, जल्दी, तुरंत

Don't worry, we shall soon be back.

Sooner or late, the strong need the help of the weak.

71. Soot (n.) सूट-कालिख, काजल

Clouds of soot rose from the chimney.

72. Soothe (v.) सूद-सांत्वना देना, ढाढ़स बंधाना

The boy was very excited but his sister soothed him and made him calm.

73. Sophisticated (adj.) सफ़िस्टिकेटिड-अनुभवी और सयाना

She is a smart and sophisticated lady.

74. Sore (adj.) सॉर-1. दुखता हुआ

My eyes are sore from reading too much.

2. (n.) दुखते घाव, ज़ख्म

My sores have healed.

75. Sorrow (n.) सॉरो-दु:ख, व्यथा

Sorrow will pay no debts.

Sorrows are our best educators.

76. Sorry (adj.) सॉरि-1. खेदपूर्ण (खेद प्रकट करना)

I am sorry I shall not be able to come.

2. (किसी भी बीमारी आदि पर दु:ख प्रकट करना) दु:खपूर्ण, दु:खी

I am sorry to know that your mother is ill.

77. Attendant (n.) अटेन्डन्ट-नौकर, परिचारक

The attendant in the cinema hall showed me my seat.

78. Attention (n.) अटेन्शन-1. ध्यान, अवधान

The huge gathering listened to the leader's speech with great attention.

2. सीधा, निश्चत मुद्रा

The soldiers stood in attention.

(adv.) ध्यान से

I listened attentively to what he had to say.

79. Attest (v.) अटेस्ट-सत्यापित करना

The copies of the documents read to be attested for admission.

80. Attire (n.) अटाइअर्-पोशाक

She looked beautiful in the bridalattire.

81. Attitude (n.) ऐटिट्यूड-रवैया, व्यवहार

The attitude of the society towards working women has changed a lot.

82. Duplicate ड्युप्लिकेट-प्रतिरुप

(n.) This key is a duplicate of the original one.

(adj.) Do you have a duplicate key of the car?

(v.) It is unethical to duplicate the original album.

83. Trophy (n.) ट्रोफि-विजय स्मारक, विजय स्मृति के रुप में दी गई वस्तु

Vagish won a trophy in swimming.

84. Trot ट्रॉट-दुलकी चाल चलना, उछल-उछल कर चलना

(n.) This horse always keeps up a steady trot.

(v.) The child trotted along besides his father.

85. Trouble (v.) ट्रॅबल-1. तंग करना, कष्ट देना

Don't trouble your teacher by asking silly questions.

I am sorry to trouble you.

2. कठिनाई

The trouble with opportunity is that it always comes in the disguise of hard work.

86. Trough (n.) ट्रॉफ़-नाँद, जानवरों को चारा आदि देने का खुला पात्र

The farmer poured the horses' food into the trough.

87. Museum (n.) म्युज़ीअम-संग्रहालय, अजायबघर

Have you seen the Salar Jang museum of Hyderabad?

88. Music (n.) म्यूज़िक-संगीत

I love music very much but I am not skilled in it.

(adj.) Which musical instrument do you play?

89. Compliment कॉम्प्लिमन्ट-सकारात्मक टिप्पणी

(n.) I paid her a compliment for organising the party so well.

(v.) I complimented her for organising the party so well.

90. Component (n.) काम्पोनन्ट-अवयव

The components of this machine have rusted.

91. Composed (adj.) कम्पोज़्ड-शांत

He looked composed at the funeral of his son.

92. Composition (n.) कॉम्प 'ज़िशन्-1. रचना, सर्जन

Arun's eassay on Gandhiji was a fine piece of composition

2. संयोजन, संघटन, बनावट

The balanced composition of the new Cabinet was praised by the media

93. Compound काम्पाउंड

1. (n.) दीवार से घिरा गया भूक्षेत्र जिस पर भवन बने हों

Her dead body was found in the compound of the building.

2. (v.) स्थिति को बिगाड़ना

The bad performance of the team along with the recent controversy compunded the problem further.

94. Comprehend (v.) कॉम्प्रिहेन्ड-समझना

(v.) I could not comprehend what he wanted to say.

(adj.) Illustrations and diagrams make the book more comprehensible.

(n.) Her excuses for arriving late every day are beyond my comprehension.

95. Comprehensive (adj.) कॉम्प्रहेन्सिव-विस्तृत

This dictionary is quite comprehensive.

96. Comprise (v.) कम्प्राइज़्-अंशो से युक्त होना

Our family comprises four members in all.

97. Compromise कॉम्प्रमाइज़्-समझौता

(n.) Both the parties made a compromise to bring the situation under control.

(v.) With no other option left, we compromised with the situation

98. Compulsory (adj.) कम्पल्सरि-अनिवार्य

It is compulsory to wear a helmet while riding a bike

99. Comrade (n.) कॉमरेड-सखा, सहचर, साथी

He has been my comrade for many years

100. Conceal (v.) कन्सील-छिपाना, गुप्त रखना

The stolen necklece was concelaled in the cupboard

SPOKEN VOCABULARY
Set - 45

1. **Concentrate (v.)** कॉन्सन्ट्रेट-ध्यान लगाना

   (v.) You need to concentrate on your studies to pass the exams.

   (n.) I lost my concentration and hit my bike against a car.

2. **Process** प्रोसेस

   (n.) 1. क्रियाओं की श्रृंखला

   Though a failure, the project proved to be a learning process for us.

   2. (adj.) संसाधित पदार्थ

   It is better to avoid processed food to stay healthy.

3. **Profess (v.)** प्रॉफ़ेस-मनोभाव व्यक्त करना

   She professed her resentment for the new budget scheme.

4. **Profession (n.)** प्रफ़ेशन-1. व्यवसाय, पेशा

   I am a lawyer by profession.

   2. घोषणा

   It is foolish to believe his for professions.

5. **Durable (adj.)** ड्यूअरबल-टिकाऊ

   This seems to be a durable plastic.

6. **Duration (n.)** ड्यूरेशन-अवधि

   The duration of the movie was more than 3 hours.

7. **Trousers (n.)** ट्राउज़र्ज-पाजामा, पतलून

   Do you want to make a new pair of trousers?

8. **Trout (n.)** ट्राउट-एक छोटी मछली (जो नदी में मिलती है)

   Have you ever seen a trout in the river?

9. **Truant (adj. & n.)** ट्रूअंट-नामा करने वाला, कामचोर

   They are a bunch of truant school boys.

   (n.) Don't be truant.

10. **Truck (n.)** ट्रक-1. ट्रक

    Our transport company owned about fifty trucks.

    2. दो पहियों की गाड़ी, जिसे रेलवे कुली हाथों से पकड़कर, रेलवे प्लेटफार्म पर, उसके ऊपर सामान रखकर ढोते हैं।

    The railway porter piled our luggage on his truck.

11. **Build (v.)** बिल्ड-बनाना, निर्माण करना

    When are you going to build your own house?

12. **Bulb (n.)** बल्ब-बल्ब, लट्टू, कंद

    There was just one electric bulb in the big room.

13. **Bulge** बल्ज-उभार, उभरना, फूलना

    (n.) The thick wallet in his pocket made a bulge in his coat.

    (v.) His eyes bulged out as he tried to lift the heavy box,

14. **Bulk (n.)** बल्क-भारी मात्रा

    We ordered the raw material in bulk.

15. **Bull (n.)** बुल-सांड, वृषभ नर

    An angry bull is a fearsome animal.

16. **Bullet (n.)** बुलिट-गोली

    A revolver contains six bullets.

17. **Rubbish (n.)** रॅबिश-1. कूड़ा-करकट

We must throw our rubbish in the dustbin.

2. ऊल-जलूल, निरर्थक

She is talking rubbish. Really she knows nothing about it.

18. Rude रुड-कठोर, अनपढ़, असभ्य

Amita is a polite girl. She is not rude.

It is ruide to speak with your mouth full.

Such rudeness can't be excused.

19. Ruffian (n.) रॅफ़ियन-गुंडा, बदमाश

The landlord was attacked by a gang of ruffians.

20. Attract (v.) अट्रैक्ट-आकर्षित करना, मोहित करना

Nature attracts one and all.

(adj.) आकर्षक

She has attractive features.

(n.) आकर्षण

Movies have great attraction for the youth today

21. Attribute (v.) अट्रिब्यूट-श्रेय देना

He attributed his success to hard work.

22. Aunction ऑक्शन-नीलामी

(n.) To auction of the land is scheduled to take place next week.

(v.) The land was auctioned last week.

23. Audience (n.) ऑडिअन्स-श्रोतागण, दर्षकगण, सभा

A good speaker always attracts a large audience.

24. Muslin (n.) मॅज़लिन-मलमल

Is your frock made of muslin?

25. Must मॅस्ट-अवश्य, आवश्यक, वस्तु

(v.) It is very late, I must go home now.

(n.) This book is a must for every student of history.

26. Sort (n.) सॉर्ट-1. किस्म, प्रकार

What sort of sweets do you like most?

2. (v.) चुनना

Sort out these letters quickly.

27. Soul (n.) सोल-1. आत्मा

I must put my heart and soul into my studies.

2. (कोई) व्यक्ति

There is not even a single soul in the house.

28. Sound (n.) साउंड-1. ध्वनि, आवाज़

Listen! What sounds can you hear?

Did you hear the sound of a shot?

2. (v.) आवाज़ निकालना, सुनाई देना

How does it sound?

3. (adj.) स्वस्थ; प्रसन्न

She has reached safe and sound.

A sound body has a sound mind.

29. Soup (n.) सूप-शोरबा, रसा

You must start your lunch with a bowl of chicken soup.

30. Sour (adj.) साउअर्-खट्टा, अम्ल, कटु

Lemons taste sour. Grapes are sweet.

(adv.) The manager replied very sourly because he was unhappy.

31. Source (n.) सोर्स-1. स्त्रोत, उद्गम

The source of the Ganges is a spring in the Himalayas.

2. मूल कारण, आधार

His friendship is a source of great pleasure to us.

32. South (n.) साउथ-दक्षिण दिशा

The south is on our right at sunrise.

(adj.) Chennai is the southern part of India.

33. Concept (n.) कॉन्सेप्ट-मूल सिद्धांत

Unless your concepts are clear, you won't understand trigonometry.

34. Concern (v.) कन्सर्न-1. संबंध रखना

This order concerns all government employees.

(prep.) Books concerning crime detection are very popular among the people.

2. (adj.) चिंतित

Amit is concerned about his health.

35. Concession (n.) कन्सेशन-छूट

The poor students were granted half fee concession by the school.

36. Conclude (v.) कन्क्लूड-1. समाप्त करना या होना, खत्म करना, निष्कर्ष निकालना

The leader concluded his speech with an appeal for unity.

2. (n.) निष्कर्ष

On the basis of the evidence, the judge came to the conclusion that the accused was not guilty.

37. Concrete (n.) कॉन्क्रीट-1. कंकरीट

Lot of concrete is required to build a durable house.

2. (adj.) मूर्त, ठोस, निश्चित

The employees gave some concrete proposals to the management to reduce the company losses.

38. Condemn (v.) कन्डेम-निंदा करना

Arya Samaj condemned idol worhip.

39. Condense (v.) कन्डेन्स-गाढ़ा करना, संक्षिप्त करना

The long report of our school function was condensed into one paragraph by the newspapers.

40. Condition (n.) कन्डिशन-1. दशा, स्थिति, अवस्था

This house is not in a good condition.

2. शर्त

What is your condition for joining us?

3. परिस्थिति

Under the stormy conditions, it is better to stay indoors.

41. Proficient (adj.) प्रफिशन्ट-दक्ष

He is proficient in both English and Hindi.

42. Profit (n. & v.) प्रॉफिट-लाभ (कमाना), नफ़ा

(n.) He sold his goods at a big profit.

(v.) He profited by the sale of his car.

43. Programme (n.) प्रोग्रैम-1. प्रगति, उन्नति

Have you chalked out your programme for the vacation ?

44. Progress (n.) प्रोग्रेस्-1. प्रगति, उन्नति

My teacher was pleased with my progress.

2. (v.) आगे बढ़ना

How far have your progressed with the book you are writing.

45. Condolence (n.) कन्डोलंस-शोक की अभिव्यक्ति

I offered my condolences to the father of my dead friend.

46. Conduct (n.) कन्डक्ट-1. आचरण, व्यवहार या बरताव

A new recuit's conduct is always

under watch.

2. (v.) मार्ग दिखाना

The doorkeeper conducted me to my seat in the cinema hall.

3. संचालन करना

He presided over the conference and conducted it ably.

47. Conference (n.) कॉन्फ्रस-सम्मेलन

A conference of religious leaders was held to discuss communal harmony.

48. Confess (v.) कन्फ़ेस-मानना, कबूल करना, स्वीकार करना

The boy confessed that he broke the window pane.

(n.) The thief made a full confession of his crimes before the judge.

49. Bulletin (n.) बुलेटिन-प्रसारित समाचार

I'll watch the news bulletin at 8.

50. Bullock (n.) बुलक-बैल

The farmer yoked the bullocks to the plough.

51. Bully (n. & v.) बुलि-दबंग, धौंसिया, धमकाना, सताना

(n.) Everyone dislikes a bully.

(v.) The robber bullied the bus passengers to surrender their valuables.

52. Bump (n.) बम्प-1. गूमड़ा. गुमटा

There appeared a bump on Amit's head where the ball hit him.

2. (v.) धक्का. टक्कर. टक्कर खाना

While walking hurriedly, Arun bumped into a stranger.

53. Rug (n.) रॅग-कम्बल, क़ालीन, गलीचा

Our cat likes to sit on the rug.

We have a rug in the car.

The lady purchased a fine rug.

54. Ruin रुइन-नाश (होना), धराशायी (होना)

(n.) We visited the ruin of an old palace.

(v.) A severe earthquake totally ruined the big city.

55. Aunt (n.) आन्ट-चाची, मौसी, बुआ

She has gone to stay with her aunt for a week.

56. Auspicious (adj.) ऑसपिशस्-सौभाग्यशाली

Her birth was considered auspicious in the family.

57. Authentic (adj.) ऑथेन्टिक-असली

This is an authentic MF Hussain painting.

58. Author (n.) ऑथर्-लेखक ग्रन्थकार

A best-seller book makes its author famous.

59. Dusk (n.) डस्क-झुटपुटा, अँधेरा

I must return home before dusk.

60. Dusky (adj.) डस्की-सांवला

She has a dusky complexion, but looks beautiful.

61. Sovereign (adj.) सॉव्रिन-प्रभुसत्ता सम्पन्न

A sovereign nation is a nation which has freedom and power to rule itself.

India which was once ruled by British is now a sovereign state.

62. Sow (v.) सो-बोना, रोपना

Sow good work and you will reap sat is faction.

The farmers sowed the seeds after

they had ploughed the fields.

63. Spa (n.) स्पा-हैल्थ स्पा

I will go to a health spa this weekend.

64. Space (n.) स्पेस-दूरी, अंतरिक्ष, आकाश

Leave proper space between words.

Man can travel into Space in a space ship.

65. Spacious (adj.) स्पेशस-लम्बा-चौड़ा, विस्तृत

Our library hall is quite spacious.

66. Span (n.) स्पैन-चौड़ाई

The railway bridge across the canal has a span of fifty yards.

67. Spank (v.) स्पैन्क-1. (थप्पड़ की) मार, पिटाई (करना)

The boy who teases cats and puppies deserves a good spanking.

2. थप्पड़ बरसाना

The teacher spanked the students who had disobeyed him.

68. Spanner (n.) स्पैनर्-पेंच कसने का औज़ार, रेंच

The electrician tightened the nuts with a spanner.

69. Spare (v.) स्पेअर्-1 दे सकना

I can spare a little money, if you want.

2 (adj.) अतिरिक्त, फालतू

Come and stay with us, we have a spare room.

70. Mute (adj.) म्यूट-मूक

(adj.) He is mute by birth

(adj.) She replied with a nasty smile. it was a muted reaction

71. Trudge (v.) ट्रंज-पैदल (पैर घसीटकर) चलना थकने के कारण

We had to trudge more than 9 kilometres through a dust-storm.

72. True (adj.) ट्रू-सच, असली, सच्चा

Say what is true.

(n.) If you tell the truth, you don't have to remember anything.

Truth wins in the end.

73. Trumpet (n.) ट्रम्पिट-1. तुरही, भोंपू

My uncle plays the trumpet in a military band.

2. (v.) घोषित करना, प्रचारित करना

Netaji Subhash's praise was trumpeted throughout India.

74. Prohibit (v.) प्रहिबिट-मना करना

Smoking is prohibited in the cinema hall.

75. Project (n.) प्रोजेक्ट-1. परियोजना

Have you prepared a project report for the industry you want to set up?

2. (v.) प्रभाव डालना

This company is trying to project a new image in the market.

76. Prolific (adj.) प्रलिफ़िक-बहुकृतिक

Gulzar is a prolific writer.

77. Prolong (v.) प्रलॉन्ग-लम्बा करना, बढ़ाना

I would not like to prolong my stay in Kolkata.

78. Bun (n.) बन-मीठी रोटी, जूड़ा

I went to the bakary to buy a bun

She coiled her hair into a bun.

79. Bunch (n.) बन्च-गुच्छा, पुँज

She put the bunch of fresh flowers in a flower-vase.

80. Bundle (n). बन्ड्ल-पोटली, गठरी

He gave the bundle of soiled clothes to the washerman.

81. Bungalow (n.) बनालो-बंगला

There was beautiful bungalow on the top of the hill.

82. Burden बर्डन-भार, बोझ, लादना, बोझ डालना

(n.) The old man was carrying a heavy burden on his frail shoulders.

(v.) Do not burden youself with unnecessary work.

83. Spark (n.) स्पार्क-चिंगारी, स्फुलिंग

Sparks flew from the fire.

84. Sparkle (v.) स्पार्कल-चमकना, झिलमिलाना

Diamonds sparkle, and so do stars in the sky.

85. Sparrow (n.) स्पैरो-चिड़िया, गौरैया

A sparrow built a nest in the tree.

86. Sparse (adj.) स्पार्स-छिटपुट

The population in Ladakh is quite sparse.

87. Speak (v.) स्पीक-बोलना, कहना

Speak well of your friend, of your enemy say nothing.

(n.) His speech was impressive.

The speaker remained undisturbed even when the audience started hooting.

88. Spear (n.) स्पिअर्-बरछा, भाला

Caveman used spear to hunt.

89. Special (adj.) स्पेशल-विशेष, विशिष्ट

This is my father's special pen. No one else may write with it.

90. Specific (adj.) स्पे'सिफ़िक-विशेष

What was the specific reason behind the fight?

91. Specimen (n.) स्पे'सिमन-नमूना, बानगी

Please give us some specimens of your new publications.

92. Speck (n.) स्पे'क्-दाग़, धब्बा

Now the ship was a mere speck on the horizon.

93. Spectacle (s) स्पे'क्टेकल (ज़्)

1. समारोह

Our annual procession was a very fine spectacle.

2. चश्मा

Please lend me your spectacles.

94. Spectator (n.) स्पे'क्टेटर्-दर्शक

Many spectators stood round the field to watch the hockey match.

95. Speculate (v.) स्पेक्युलेट-अटकल लगाना

Scientists speculated about the possibility of life on Mars.

96. Speech (n.) स्पीच-वाणी, कथन, उक्ति, भाषा

Speech is the gift of all, but thought of few.

Speech is silver, silence is golden.

97. Speed स्पीड-तेज़ी से चलना, गति, रफ़्तार, चाल

(v.) If we speed up our work, we shall be able of finish it before Sunday.

(n.) Your speed of working is not satisfactory.

98. pell (v.) स्पे'ल-1. हिज्जे करना

Can you spell my name?

2. (n.) जादू

The fairy cast a spell on the little boy and turned him into a young ox.

99. Spelling (n.) स्पेलिंग-वर्तनी

He is very bad at spellings.

100. Authority (n.) ऑथॉरटि-अधिकार, सत्ता, सत्ताधारी

In any company, the authority to sign cheques is normally given to trustworthy persons.

SPOKEN VOCABULARY
Set - 46

1. Automatic (adj.) ऑटोमैटिक-स्वचालित

Automatic machines saves us a lot of manual labour.

2. Trunk (n.) ट्रैंक-1. सूँड

An elephant has a trunk. It is his long nose.

2. वृक्ष का तना

The stem of a tree is called a tree trunk.

3. लोहे का बक्सा

We put our clothes in a trunk.

3. Trust ट्रॅस्ट-विश्वास करना, भरोसा रखना, विश्वास, आस्था

(v.) Love all but trust a few.

A wise man does not trust anything blindly.

(n.) Have trust in God.

4. Try (v.) ट्राइ-1. प्रयत्न करना, कोशिश करना

Time is short, but I shall try to catch the bus.

2. सिले हुए कपड़े को पहनकर नाप देखना

You had better try on the coat before you buy it.

3. (n.) प्रयत्न, प्रयास, कोशिश

Come on, it is worth a try.

5. Tub (n.) टब-पानी जमा करने का टब, बाल्टी, नाँद

Mother stored water in a tub.

Father bought a bath tub for daily use.

6. Dust (n.) डस्ट-धूल, गर्द

Wipe the dust off your desk daily.

7. Dusty (adj.) डस्टि-धूल से भरा

I cannot work in such a dusty room.

8. Rule (n.) रुल-1. नियम

You will be disqualified for disobeying the roles of the club.

2. (v.) शासन करना

Aurangzeb, the mightly Mughal emperor, ruled India for many years.

9. Mutiny (n.) म्यटनि-ग़दर

The Revolt of 1857 was dismissed by the British as a sepoy mutiny.

10. Mutter (v.) मॅटर्-बुदबुदाना, फुसफुसाना

What are you muttering under your breath?

11. Confide (v.) कन्फ़ाइड-किसी को गोपनीय बात बताना

I confided my feelings to my best friend.

12. Confidence (n.) कॉन्फ़िडन्स-भरोसा, विश्वास

The confidence on a friend is tested in a crisis.

(adj.) Ram was very confident of scoring good marks in the annual exams.

13. Confine (v.) 1. कन्फ़ाइन-सीमित करना या रखना बंद करना

A fracture in the leg kept Ram confined to his home for a month.

2. (n.) कैद

The murderer was kept in a solitary confinement.

14. Confirm (v.) कन्फ़र्म-सुदृढ़ करना

(v.) The India-Pakistan cricket tournament has been confirmed.

(n.) You need to send me a confirmation before coming for the meeting.

15. Conflict (n.) कॉन्फ़्लिक्ट-1. संघर्ष, युद्ध

Pakistan and India have witnessed three conflicts.

2. (adj.) परस्पर-विरोधी

Newspapers published conflicting (contradictory) reports about the plane hijack.

(v.) Sometimes, young generation's ideas conflict with those of their parents.

16. Confuse (v.) कन्फ्यूज़्-1. चकरा देना, उलझाना

The lawyer's question confused the witness.

2. एक को दूसरा समझना

Between the twins, it is usual to confuse one with the other.

17. Confusion (n.) कन्फ्यूशन-गड़बड़, घपला, उलझन

A great confusion ensued on the overcrowded platfrom with the arrival of train.

18. Congested (adj.) कन्जेस्टिड-भीड़-भाड़ वाला

The roads in Old Delhi are very congested.

19. Prominent (adj.) प्रॉमिनन्ट-प्रमुख, मुख्य

I saw many prominent people at the glittering function.

20. Promise (n.) प्रॉमिस-1. वादा (करना), वचन (देना)

You should always keep your promise.

2. विश्वास/आशा (दिलाना)

She shows promise as a singer.

(v.) My mother promised to buy me a watch on my birthday.

21. Promote (v.) प्रमोट-1. चढ़ाना

My son has been promoted to the higher class.

2. (n.) तरक्की

My brother has been given a promotion to the rank of captain.

22. Prompt (adj.) प्रॉम्प्ट-तत्पर, उद्यत

You must take prompt action to remedy this situation.

23. Available (adj.) अवेलबल-उपलब्ध, प्राप्त

For some days cooking oil was not available in the market.

24. Avalanche (n.) ऐवलांश-हिमधाव, हिमस्खलन

Mountaineers must always guard themselves against avalanches.

25. Burglar (n.) बर्गलर्-चोर, सेंधमार

The burglar broke open the safe but was caught before he could escape with the valuables.

26. Burn बर्न-जलने का घाव, जलना, जलाना

(n.) Apply a soothing ointment on the burn.

(v.) The fire burned brightly.

She burnt all the letters her lover had written to her.

27. Spend (v.) स्पेन्ड-1. बिताना, गुजारना

I ave spent the whole week in my re search.

2. खर्च करना

How much money did you spend on your new TV set?

My brother is a spendthrift. He spent all the money he had.

28. Sphere (n.) स्फ़िअर्-1. कार्य-क्षेत्र

(n.) This work is beyond my sphere of specialisation.

2. गेंद के आकार का

(adj.) Most of the clestial bodies are spherical in shape.

29. Spice (n.) स्पाइस

1. मसाला

Addition of spices made the food tastier.

2. दिलचस्पी

Media added spice to the whole incident.

30. Spider (n.) स्पाइडर्-मकड़ी, आठ टांगों वाला जीव, जो कीड़े-मकोड़े खाकर जीता है।

Spiders spin webs in which they catch insects.

31. **Spill (v.)** स्पिल-छलकाना, छलकना

You will spill the milk if you do not hold the jug straight.

The milk was spilt due to my carelessness.

32. **Spin** स्पिन-बुनना, कातना, चक्रण, घुमाव

(v.) In the village, the old lady was spining wool.

(n.) I have been in a spin since I came to this place.

33. **Spire (n.)** स्पाइअर्-मीनार

The spire of Salisbury Cathedral is one of the highest in the world.

34. **Spirit (n.)** स्पिरिट

1. उत्साह

Roma was a girl of spirit. She knew what she wanted to do and no one could stop her from doing that.

2. आत्मा

Some people believe that the spirits of the dead exist in the world.

35. **Spit (v.)** स्पिट-1. थूकना

Don't spit on the floor. Spitting is prohibited here.

2. (n.) मांस पकाने की लोहे की सींख

The chicken was roasted on the spit.

36. **Spite (n.)** स्पाइट-हानि पहुँचाने की इच्छा

Don't tear his exercise-book out of spite.

(adj.) No one likes spitefull people.

(v.) Never spite others.

37. **Splatter (v.)** स्प्लैटर्-छलकना

She splattered water all over the room.

38. **Duty (n.)** ड्यूटि-1. कर्त्तव्य, फ़र्ज

Do your duty and have faith in God.

2. काम, कार्य

Shyam is always late for his duty.

39. **Mutton (n.)** मॅटन-भेंड़ का मांस

Mutual understanding is necessary to keep a relationship alive.

40. **Mutual (adj.)** म्यूचुअल-आपसी

Mutual understanding is necessary to keep a relationship alive.

41. **Congratulate (v.)** कन्ग्रैचुलेट्-बधाई देना

Prakash congratulated Prabhat on his outstanding success in the examination.

(n.) Dinesh received a telegram of congratulations on his wedding day.

42. **Connect (v.)** कनेक्ट-जोड़ना, मिलाना, संबद्ध करना

He is well connected in Delhi's political circle.

This lane connects two busy streets.

43. **Conquer (v.)** कॉन्कर्-जीतना, हराना, अधीन करना

Hitler conquered a large part of Europe.

Tenzing conquered Mount Everest.

44. **Conscience (n.)** कॉन्शन्स-सद्विवेक, आत्मा

Even a criminal's conscience warns him against committing crimes.

45. **Conscious (n)** कॉन्शस-1. सचेतन

The fatally injured accident victim was conscious enough to give his address to the policeman.

2. से अभिज्ञ

Are you conscious of the serious consequences of you bad deeds?

46. **Consecutive (adj.)** कन्सेक्यटिव-क्रमिक

She was absent for three consecutive days.

47. **Consent (v.)** कन्सेन्ट-1. राज़ी होना, स्वीकृति देना

She consented to her daughter's marriage with a man of different caste.

2. (n.) स्वीकृति

Students were asked to have their parent's consent for a tour to Agra.

48. **Consequence (n.)** कॉन्सिक्वॅन्स-परिणाम,

नतीजा, महत्त्व

Often, thoughtless acts lead to serious consequences.

(Conj.) I missed the bus and consequently (as a result) was late for office.

49. Tube (n.) ट्यूब-नली, नलिका, ट्यूब

The inner part of a bicycle tyre contains a rubber tube.

The water runs along a tube into the boiler

50. Tuberculosis (n.) ट्यूबर्क्युलोसिस-तपेदिक, यक्ष्मा

Tuberculosis is a very dangerous disease.

51. Prone (adj.) प्रोन-किसी रोग या दुर्घटना की संभावना से ग्रस्त

Diabetic patients are prone to many other diseases.

52. Pronounce (v.) प्र'नाउन्स्-1. उच्चारित करना, सुनाना, बनाना

Some words are very difficult to pronounce.

2. (n.) उचित उच्चारण

You must improve your pronunciation.

53. Splendid (adj.) स्प्ले'न्डिड-भव्य, शानदार, गौरवपूर्ण, उत्कृष्ट

The prince lived in a splendid palace.

(adv.) Lila sang splendidly at the concert.

(n.) The rich man lived in great splendour in his newly built palace.

54. Splinter स्प्लिन्टर-छोटा-सा टुकड़ा, टुकड़े-टुकड़े होना

(n.) The soldier was severely wounded by a shell splinter.

(v.) The wooden cup crashed to the floor and splintered.

55. Split (v.) स्प्लिट-आपस में बाँटना

The friends split the bill and paid Rs. 50 each.

Differences of opinion split the association.

56. Spoil (v.) स्पॉइल-बिगाड़ना, सिर चढ़ाना

Don't spoil my time with your foolish talk.

(adj.) A spoilt child never cares for his parents.

57. Spoke (n.) स्पोक-धुरी से लेकर रिम से बीच लगी हुई तार

The hub of a wheel is connected with spokes to the rim.

58. Sponge (n.) स्पन्ज-स्पंज

Have you a sponge to clean the slate?

Wash the scooter with a sponge and clean water.

59. Spontaneous (adj.) स्पॉन्टेनिअस-अनायास

His comic acts evoke a spontaneous laughter.

60. Spooky (adj.) स्पूकि-डरावना

Going inside the deserted bungalow was a spooky experience.

61. Spoon (n.) स्पून-चम्मच

Stir the gravy with a wooden spoon.

62. Dwarf (n.) ड्वार्फ़-बौना

He is a dwarf by birth.

63. Tuck (n.) टक-1. तह, परत, चुन्नट, मोड़ना

I shall put a tuck in your dress as it is too long for you.

2. (v.) तह लगाना

I tucked the napkin under mu chin.

64. Tuesday (n.) ट्यूज़डे-मंगलवार

If this is Sunday, the day after tomorrow will be Tuesday.

65. Muzzle (v.) मज़ल-1. मुँह पर जाली लगाना

You should muzzle your ferocious dog.

2. दबा देना, नियंत्रण करना

How can democracy survive when the Press is muzzled?

3. नालमुख

Be careful while cleaning the muzzle of the gun.

66. Conservation (n.) कॉन्ज़्वेशन-संरक्षण

We must take steps towards environmental conservation.

67. Consider (v.) कन्सिडर्-1. सोचना, विचार करना

Please consider this matter carefully.

2. मानना, समझना

I do not consider it an important matter.

68. Considerable (adj.) कन्सिडरेबल-बहुत, काफ़ी

Dhanaraj has a considerable amount of money in the bank.

69. Consist (v.) कन्सिस्ट-में होना, (से,का) बना होना

Our colony's welfare committee consists of five members and a chairman.

70. Console (v.) कन्सोल-सांत्वना देना

She was hard to console when she came to know about her failure.

71. Conspire (v.) कन्स्पाइअर्-षड्यंत्र रचना

(v.) The commander was held responsible for conspiring against his own country.

(n.) The commander was held responsible for hatching a conspiracy.

72. Constable (n.) कन्स्टबल्-सिपाही

The traffic police constable signalled the speeding car to stop.

73. Constant (adj.) कॉन्स्टन्ट-1. नियत, स्थिर, एक समान

I drive my car at a constant seed.

2. (adv.) बराबर, निरन्तर

She is constantly reading novels.

74. Constitution (n.) कॉन्स्टिट्यूशन्-1. विधान, नियम-संग्रह

Students of law have to study the Indian Constitution.

2. शरीर गठन

Meena has a delicate constitution.

75. Constraint (n.) कन्स्ट्रेन्ट-अवरोधकारी तत्व

(n.) We left that project because of financial constraints.

(v.) Lack of funds constrained the expansion of our business.

76. Burrow बरो-बिल, बिल खोदना

(n.) The rabbit jumped into its burrow when it saw a dog.

(v.) The rabbit burrowed a deep hole under a tree.

77. Burst (v.) बर्स्ट-फटना, फूटना, फट पड़ना

The tyre of the car burst with a bang.

They burst out laughing at the funny story.

78. Rumour (n.) र्यूमर्-अफ़वाह, उड़ती खबर

People started stocking foodrains following rumours of food shortage.

79. Avenue (n.) ऐवन्यू-मार्ग, रास्ता, वृक्षवीथि

New Delhi is full of tree-lined avenues.

80. Average (n.) ऐवरिज-औसत, साधारण, सामान्यस्तर

(adj.) What is the average attendance in your class?

(n.) Your marks are below average.

81. Proof (n.) प्रूफ-सबूत

(n.) What is the proof that he committed the theft.?

82. Propaganda (n.) प्रॉपगैन्डा-मतप्रचार

Despite the whole propaganda, the movie was a big flop.

83. Proper (adj.) प्रॉपर्-1. ठीक, सही

Put all these books in the proper place.

2. (adv.) उचित

You are not dressed properly.

84. Tuft (n.) टॅफ़्ट-गुच्छा, झाड़ी का एक हिस्सा

There was sand and few tufts of coarse grass

85. Tug (n. & v.) टॅग-एक छोटा जहाज़ जो बड़े जहाजो को बन्दरगाह की ओर खींचकर ले आता है एक छोटा शक्तिशाली जहाज जोर से खींचना

(n.) A tug is a little ship It helps to pull a big ship into dock

(v) We shall tug the boat out of the water on the river bank

86. Tuition (n.) ट्यूइशन-ट्यूशन

He takes private tuitions at home

87. Tulip (n.) ट्यूलिप-कप के आकार का एक बसती फूल जो कई रंगों का होता है

A tulip is a spring flower. We can grow tulips in many different colours

88. Tumble (v.) टॅम्बल्-गिर पड़ना, धड़ाम से गिरना, ढहना

Ila fell dwon and broke her leg and Uma came tumbling after

89. Tumbler (n.) टॅम्बलर्-कांच का गिलास

The child broke the glass tumbler

[illegible] (v.) बरि-दफनाना गाड़ना

[illegible] slims and Christians bury their

91. Bu[illegible]

[illegible] es to school by bus

92. Sport (n.) [illegible]ट-मनोरंजन, मनबहलाव

Wrestling in one of the international sports

93. Spot (n.) स्पॉट-स्थान जगह धब्बा दाग़

Please find a quiet spot where we can discuss the matter

My clothes are spotless.

94. Spout (n.) स्पाउट-1. टोंटी

Our teapot lost its spout

2 (v.) जोड़ से निकलना

Tea spouted from the broken teapot.

95. Sprain स्प्रेन-मोच (आना)

(n.) It was a bad sprain.

(v.) She fell and sprained her toe.

96. Spray स्प्रे-छिड़कना, फुहारना, फुहार, छिड़काव

(v.) He sprayed fresh paint on his motorcycle.

97. Spread स्प्रे'ड-फैलाना, फैलाव, प्रसारण

(v.) Please spread a cloth on the table.

The parrot spread its wings and flew away.

(n.) Doctors try to prevent the spread of contagious diseases.

98. Spring स्प्रिंग

1. (n.) वसंत ऋतु

In spring, flowers begin to grow.

2. स्प्रिंग-पुर्जा, छल्ला

The spring of your watch is broken so it stopped.

3. (v.) उछालना

The little lambs spring about in the field.

99. Sprinkle (v.) स्प्रिंकल-(कम मात्रा में) छिड़कना, बुरकना

Please sprinkle some salt on the salad.

100. Sprint स्प्रिंट-थोड़ी-सी तेज दौड़, थोड़ी दूरी तक तेज़ दौड़ना

(n.) We cheered when our friend won the sprint.

(v.) Sprint along the road and catch the train.

SPOKEN VOCABULARY
Set - 47

1. **Bush (n.)** बुश-झाड़ी, झाड़

   There are no big trees here. only bushes

2. **Business (n.)** बिज़नेस-व्यापार, व्यवसाय, कारोबार

   Ram joined his father's business after completing his education.

3. **Property (n.)** प्रॉपर्टि - जायदाद

   He owns residential property in Goa.

4. **Proportion (n.)** प्रपॉर्शन- अनुपात

   What is the proportion of boys and girls in your class?

5. **Construct (v.)** कन्स्ट्रक्ट-बनाना, निर्माण करना

   The company has constructed flats for its employees

6. **Consult (v.)** कन्सल्ट-परामर्श लेना या करना

   The rich lady consulted many specialists about her illness.

7. **Consume (v.)** कन्'स्यूम्-कुछ खाना या पीना

   He consumed several cups of tea.

8. **Contact** कॉन्टैक्ट-संपर्क

   (n.) I don't have his contact details.

   (v.) You can contact me at this number.

9. **Contagious (adj.)** कन्टेजस- संसर्गज

   Tuberculosis is contagious disease.

10. **Contain (v.)** कन्टेन-रखना, बराबर होना

    Textbooks contain many chapters

11. **Contemplate (v.)** कॉन्टम्प्लेट-विचार करना

    I am contemplating taking a long leave.

12. **Contempt (n.)** कन्टेम्प्ट-घृणा

    I was filled with contempt for the family who killed their daughter-in-law.

13. **Contend (v.)** कन्टेन्ड

    1. समस्या का सामना करना

       I have my own problems to contend with.

    2. मुकाबला करना

       Several companies were contending for the tender.

    3. दावा करना

       The servant contended that he did not commit the theft.

14. **Content (adj.)** कान्टेन्ट-संतुष्ट, राज़ी

    The distinguished guest was content with the arrangements made for him.

15. **Mystery (n.)** मिस्टरि-रहस्य, भेद

    The detective novel ended with the solving of the murder mystery.

16. **Dwell (v.)** ड्वेल-निवास करना, रहना, बसना

    Don't dwell on your troubles.

17. **Sprout** स्प्राउट-अंकुरित अनाज

    (n.) I had sprouts in the breakfast.

    (v.) The seeds sprouted at the appropriate time.

18. **Spur** स्पर-प्रेरणा, उकताहट, उसी क्षण

    (n.) The performer thought of a wonderful trick at the spur of the moment.

    (v.) Hunger spurred the poor man to

seek work.

19. Spurt (v.) स्पर्ट-निकल पड़ना

Water spurted out of the broken pipe.

20. Spy (n.) स्पाइ-गुप्तचर

Isn't it a dangerous thing to be a spy?

21. Squabble स्क्वॉबल-टंटा (मचाना), तू-तू मै-मैं (करना)

(n.) We never like squabble about petty things.

(v.) Never squabble with your relations.

22. Squadron (n.) स्क्वॉड्रन-सैनिक टुकड़ी

The commander ordered his squadron to attack.

23. Squall (v. & n.) स्क्वॉल-चीख मारना, तूफ़ान

(v.) Don't squall, I shall not hurt you.

(n.) The boat was overturned in a squall.

24. Squander (v.) स्क्वॉनडर-पैसा बरबाद करना

She squandered a lot of money on shopping.

25. Square (n.) स्क्वेअर्-1. चतुर्भुज, चतुष्कोण

A square has four equal sides.

2. (adj.) अच्छा

We give every customer a square deal.

3. पूर्ण, संतोषजनक

I could not have a square meal for a week.

4. (v.) चतुष्कोण बनाना

Square the corners of this wood.

26. Squash (v.) स्क्वॉश-कुचलकर भुरता बनाना

She squashed the boiled tomatoes to make the soup.

27. Squat (v.) स्क्वॉट-उकड़् बैठना

Monkeys were squatting on the tree.

28. Avoid (v.) अवॉइड-1. टालना, दूर रहना

He tries to avoid me because he owes me some money.

2. बचना, बचकर रहना

You should try to avoid catching a cold.

29. Await (v.) अवेट-राह देखना, प्रतीक्षा करना

The whole assemble awaited the chief guest's arrival.

30. Dwindle (v.) ड्विन्ड्ल-घटना, कम होना

The food stock has been dwindling alarmingly over the past two years.

31. Bustle बसल-हलचल

(n.) There was a lot of bustle in the market.

(v.) The market was bustling with people.

32. Tumult (n.) ट्यूमॅल्ट-हंगामा, गुलगपाड़ा, शोर-गुल

I tried to make my voice heard above the tumult, but in vain.

33. Tune ट्यून-धुन, राग, लय, स्वर निकालना, सुर मिलाना

(n.) Can you play a tune on the piano?

(v.) I tune my violin before playing it.

34. Propose (v.) प्रपोज़्-1. इरादा/विचार करना

I propose to go abroad in the near future.

2. विवाह का प्रस्ताव करना

I hear Madhav has proposed to Meena.

35. Proprietor (n.) प्रोप्राइअटर्-मालिक

The proprietor of the hotel received me at the door.

36. Prospect (n.) प्रॉस्पेक्ट-1. संभावना

Do you have good prospects in this concern?

2. प्रत्याशा

I look forward to the prospect of seeing you.

37. Run (v.) रॅन–1. भागना

The policeman is running after the theif.

2. उम्मीदवार के रुप में (लोकसभा आदि के लिए)

He is running for parilament.

3. बहना

The Ganges runs through a thick valley.

4. संचालन करना

Who is running the business?

38. Contents (v.) कन्टेन्ट्स–विषयसूची

It is better to go through the contents of the book before buying it.

39. Contest (n.) कॉन्टेस्ट–प्रतियोगिता, विवाद

Rajendra bagged the first prize in the essay contest.

40. Continent (n.) कॉन्टिनन्ट–महाद्वीप, महादेश

India is in the continent of Asia.

41. Continue (v.) कन्टिन्यू–जारी रखना, आगे बढ़ाना

Many TV serials are continued even after a century of their episodes.

42. Contract (n.) कॉन्ट्रैक्ट–1. ठेका, इकरारनामा

The two friends entered into a contract to set up a company.

2. (n.) ठेकेदार

Some firms prefer to give their various jobs to contractors.

3. (v.) सिकुड़ना

Metals contract as they grow colder.

43. Contradict (v.) कॉन्ट्रडिक्ट–खण्डन करना, विरोधी होना

The minister contradicted the statement attributed to him by the press.

44. Contrary (adj.) कॉन्ट्ररी–विपरीत, प्रतिकूल

What Ram had done was contrary to the rules of his company.

Contrary to my expectations, Ramesh declined my invitation.

45. Contribute (v.) कॉन्ट्रिब्यूट–1. चन्दा देना, अंशदान करना

People contribute generously to the flood relief fund.

2. सहयोग या लेख देना

I contribute articles to many journals.

46. Prospect (n.) प्रॉस्पेक्ट–1. संभावना

Do you have good prospects in this concern?

2. प्रत्याशा

I look forward to the prospect of seeing you.

47. Awake अवेक–जाग्रत, जागरुक, सतर्क, जगाना, जाग जाना

(adj.) Yesterday I was awake till midnight.

48. Award अवॉर्ड–पुरस्कार इनाम (देना)

(v.) Rekha was awarded a stereo tape recorder for winning the first prize in music competition.

(n.) Our company has won an award for export promotion.

49. Squeak (n.) स्क्वीक–चूँ-चूँ, चीं-चीं (की आवाज)

I heard a faint squeak from the

bedroom

(v.) The old stool squeaked as Ram climbed on it.

50. Squeal (v.) स्क्वील-चिल्लाना, किलकारी मारना

The children squealed with joy when the dancing monkey entered the stage.

(n.) The children's squeals could be heard from a long distance.

51. Squeeze (v.) स्क्वीज़-1. निचोड़ना

Squeeze two lemons together in the glass.

2. दबाना

Don't squeeze my hand.

52. Squint स्क्विन्ट-भेंगापन, अधखुली आंखों से देखना

(n.) He has a squint in her eye.

(v.) We squinted in the bright sunlight.

53. Squirrel (n.) स्क्विरल-गिलहरी

A squirrel lives in a tree. It has a long bushy tail.

54. Stab (v. & n.) स्टैब-छुरा घोंपना, प्रहार

(v.) A robber stabbed him in the neck.

(n.) There were two stab wounds on the body.

55. Stable (n. v. & adj.) स्टेबल-1. घुड़साल, अस्तबल

(n.) Jesus was born in a stable.

2. अस्तबल में रखना

(v.) Can we stable our horses in this shed?

3. अचल, स्थिर, टिकाऊ

(adj.) Was the provincial government not stable?

56. Stack स्टैक-ढेरी

(n.) Get the red book from the stack

(v.) Stack the books well on her shelf

57. Stadium (n.) स्टेडिअम-मैदान, स्टेडियम

We saw the hockey match in the National Stadium.

58. Staff (n. & v.) स्टॉफ़-1. कर्मचारीगण, कर्मचारीगण रखना

(n.) Have you not recently joined the staff of this office?

(v.) Our office is staffed by seven employees.

2. छड़ी

The old man walked with the help of a long wooden staff.

59. Stag (n.) स्टैग-हिरण, मृग

The stag was caught by its horns in a thorny bush.

60. Stage (n.) स्टेज-1. मंच, मंजिल, पड़ाव

Would you like to go on the stage?

Her cancer is on the final stage.

2. (v.) अभिनीत होना

The play had been staged.

61. Busy (adj.) बिज़ी-व्यस्त

Are you busy this evening?

62. Tunnel (n.) टॅनल-सुरंग

Trains sometimes run through the tunnels.

63. Turban (n.) टर्बन-पगड़ी, पाग

In India, some people wear turbans on their heads.

64. Control कन्ट्रोल-नियंत्रण रखना, वश में रखना

(n.) The car suddenly got out of control

The police brought the law and order situation in the riot-torn city under control.

(v.) The jockey controlled the untamed horse skilfully.

65. Convenient (adj.) कन्वीनिअन्ट-सुविधाजनक, आरामदेह

When will it be convenient to you to come to my place?

66. Conventional (adj.) कन्वेन्शनल-रुढ़िगत

I never liked the conventional 9 to 5 job.

67. Conversation (n.) कॉन्वर्सेशन-वार्तालाप, बातचीत

Geeta had a long conversation with her friend on the phone.

68. Turbulent (adj.) टर्ब्यलंट-उपद्रवी, उग्र

Nothing could control the turbulent mob.

69. Turkey (n.) टर्कि-अमरीकी चिड़िया

A turkey is a big bird. The Americans like to eat it.

70. Protect (v.) प्रटेक्ट-रक्षा करना, बचाना

I wear a hat to protect myself from the sun.

71. Protest प्रोटेस्ट-विरोध (करना)

(n.) The union organised a protest against low wages.

(v.) The employees protested against the policy of the management

72. Dye डाइ-रंग, वर्ण, रंगना, रंग जाना

(v.) Can you dye this saree deep blue?

(n.) What is the price of this hair-dye?

73. Butcher (n.) बुचर्-कसाई

I went to the butcher's shop to buy some meat.

74. Butter (n.) बटर्-मक्खन

We always have bread and butter for breakfast.

75. Protrude (v.) प्रोटूड-सतह से बाहर निकलना

The branches from the old wall of cave.

76. Dynamic (adj.) डाइनैमिक-गतिशील

It is time to bring some dynamic changes in our work culture.

77. Stagger (v.) स्टैग्र्-विचलित करना/होना, लड़खड़ाना

I staggered to know that he had died in the accident.

He staggered as he got up suddenly

78. Stagnant (adj.) स्टैग्नन्ट-ठहरा हुआ पानी

(adj.) Stagnant water is a cause of various diseases.

(v.) Water stagnated on the road in the rainy season.

79. Stain (n. & v.) स्टेन-1. धब्बा या निशान (बनाना)

(n.) The ink fell and left a stain on the table.

2. रंग लगाना, धब्बा डालना

Her fingers were stained with blue ink.

80. Stair (n.) स्टे'अर्-सीढ़ी, सोपान, जीना

Is there a toilet at the top of the stairs?

All the stairs together are called a stair-case

81. Stake स्टेक-दाँव

(n.) If we lose this contract, we will lose our credibility. Stakes are very high.

(v.) Why are you staking your future by getting involved in this issue?

82. Stale (adj.) स्टेल-1 बासी

The meal is stale. It is not fit to be eaten.

We can throw our stale bread to the birds

2. पुराना

This joke is stale. There is nothing new or fresh about it.

83. Stalk (n.) स्टॉक-1. डंठल

This rose has a long stalk.

2. (v.) छिपकर पीछा करना

Our party stalked the tiger in the jungle.

84. Stall (n.) स्टॉल-1. छोटी दुकान, स्टॉल

Delhi station has many bookstalls.

2. (v.) अचानक रुक जाना

The engine of my car stalled, so I had to push the car to the side of the road.

85. Stamina (n.) स्टैमिना-दम-खम

He can play cricket all day. He has a lot of stamina.

86. Stammer (v.) स्टैमर्-अटक-अटक कर बोलना तुतलाना, हकलाना

When a man stammers, the listeners laugh.

(n.) He speaks with a slight stammer.

87. Convert कन्वर्ट

1. परिवर्तित करना

(v.) Her very presence converted a dull party into a lively one.

2. धर्मांतरित व्यक्ति

(n.) After reading so many books on sikhism, I almost feel like a covert now.

88. Convey (v.) कन्वे-1. बतलाना, सूचित करना

Did you convey my message to Ram?

2. (n.) वाहन

I go to office in my own conveyance.

89. Convict कन्विक्ट-अपराधी

(n.) The convict was arrested soon.

(v.) He was convict was arrested soon.

90. Conviction (n.) कन्विक्शन-पक्का विश्वास

It was with great conviction that I contacted him.

91. Convince (v.) कन्विन्स-मनवाना, स्वीकार कराना

The judge was convinced of the guilt of the accused.

92. Cook कुक-पकाना, भोजन बनाना, बावरची

(v.) Sita's mother cooks very tasty food.

(n.) She is an excellent cook.

93. Cool (adj.) कूल-1. शीतल, ठण्डा

The weather became quite cool after rain.

2. शांत, धीर

Arun's behaviour is always cool and composed.

94. Cooperate (v.) कोऑपरेट-सहयोग देना, मिलकर काम करना

All the villagers cooperated in building the village school.

95. Coordinate (v.) कोऑर्डिनेट-तालमेल बनाना

I'll have to coordinate with her to get this project completed.

96. Cope (v.) कोप-कठिन स्थिति से सफलतापूर्वक निपटना

It's difficult to cope with the ever-changing technology.

97. Copy कॉपि-नकल, प्रतिकृति, नकल/अनुकरण करना

(n.) Usha asked for a copy of Sita's picture in the bridal make-up.

(v.) I copied down some booksellers phone numbers from the directory.

98. Cord (n.) कॉर्ड्-रस्सी, डोरी, डट्टा

He tied his bedding with a cord.

99. Aware (adj.) अवेअर्-अवगत, जानकार

Satish was not aware that his siser would also company him to London.

100. Turmoil (n.) टर्मॉइल-खलबली

The state was in turmoil after the sudden death of the Chief Minister.

SPOKEN VOCABULARY
Set - 48

1. **Turn (n.)** टर्न-1. बारी

   Gopal is having a ride on a horse. It will be my turn after him.

   It is my turn to bat.

   Ram's turn was next.

   2. (v.) घूमना, पलटना

   The horse will turn around when it comes to the fence.

   3. उलटना

   Shyama likes turning over the pages in her story book.

   4. (v.) भलाई का बदला भलाई

   One good turn deserves another.

5. **Away (adv.)** अवे-बाहर, दूर, अलग

   How long will he be away?

   The child threw away the broken toy.

6. **Turnip (n.)** टर्निप-शलजम

   A turnip is a vegetable. Mother cooks turnips for dinner.

7. **Tusk (n.)** टस्क-हाथी दाँत, हाथी के बाहर निकले हुए दो दाँत

   lovry is obtained from the tusks of elephants.

8. **Tussle (n.)** टॅसल-हाथापाई

   The child got into a tussle with his sister for a chocolate.

9. **Rural (adj.)** रुरल-ग्रामीण

   Most of our relatives live in the rural areas.

10. **Butterfly (n.)** बटर्फ्लाइ-तितली

    Butterflies are beautiful to look at.

11. **Proud (adj.)** प्राउण्ड-1. अभिमानी, घमंडी, गौरवान्वित

    Every mother is pround of her children.

    2. गौरवपूर्ण

    Abhinav Bindra's winning of Olympic gold medal was a proud moment for the whole nation.

12. **Core (n.)** कोर्-बीकोष, सारभाग, अभ्यन्तर

    One must first understand the core of a problem to solve it properly.

13. **Cork (n.)** कॉर्क्-काग, कॉर्क्, डट्टा

    He closed the bottle with a cork.

14. **Corn (n.)** कॉर्न्-अनाज, धान्य

    The farmers were busy harvesting the corn.

15. **Corner (n.)** कॉर्नर्-कोना, कोण, नाका, घेरना, घेर लेना

    The chemist's shop at the street corner had the entrance from two sides.

    (v.) The cat cornered the mouse and killed it.

16. **Corpse (n.)** कॉर्प्स-शव, लाश

    The police took away the unclaimed corpse lying on the roadside.

17. **Correct** करेक्ट-ठीक (सही करना)

    (v.) Please correct all these mistakes.

    (adj.) Only Ramesh gave the correct answer.

18. **Correspondence (n.)** कॉरसपॉन्डन्स-पत्रव्यवहार

    Correspondence plays a significant role in business dealings.

19. **Corridor (n.)** कॉरिडोर्-गलियारा

The building had a long corridorleading to the servants quarter in the backyard.

20. Corrupt करप्ट-भ्रष्ट

(adj.) A few corrupt officers have spoiled the reputation of the whole police department.

(v.) There are few who are not corrupted by money and power

(n.) Corruption has spread like a disease in India.

21. Cost कॉस्ट-दाम लगना, खर्च होना कीमती, कीमत

(v.) How much does this book cost?

(adj.) A necklace of diamonds is very costly (expensive)

(n) For job interview, you must reach in time at all costs (in spite of difficulties)

22. Costume (n.) कॉस्ट्यूम-पोशाक

This costume suits your role well.

23. Cosy (adj.) कोज़ि-आरामदेह

Homeless people dreamed of a cosy home.

24. Cot (n.) कॉट-खाट, चारपाई

The child was sleeping on the cot.

25. Cottage (n.) कॉटिज-झोपड़ी, कुटीर

The poor family lived in a cottage outside the town.

26. Cotton (n.) कॉटन-कपास, रुई, सूती कपड़ा

Cotton clothes are the best in a hot country like India.

27. Cough कॉफ़-खांसी, खांसना

(n.) He was suffering from cold and cough.

(v.) The patients coughed constantly.

28. Council (n.) काउन्सल-परिषद् समिति

Our association has General Council and an Executive Committee.

29. Stamp (n.) स्टैम्प-1. डाक टिकट, मोहर

Some children like to collect postage stamps

2 मुहर

Have you brought a rubber-stamp and an ink pad?

3. (v.) सिद्ध करना

This action stamps him as rogue.

30. Stand (v. & n.) स्टैन्ड-1. खड़ा होना, बस या गाड़ी रुकने की जगह

Can you stand on your head?

(v.) Everyone stood up when the President came in.

(n.) Where is the cycle-stand? I want to stand my bike.

3. (v.) सहना

I cannot stand all this noise.

31. Standard (n.) स्टैन्डर्ड-स्तर, कोटि, मानदंड

His work does not reach the required standard.

32. Standstill (n.) स्टैन्ड्स्टिल-ठहराव

The economy of the country came to a standstill after the war.

33. Stanza (n.) स्टैन्ज़ा-छंद

Do you remember the second stanza of the song?

34. Star (n.) स्टार्-सितारा, तारा

Stars twinkle at night.

(adj.) The sky was starry, and there was no moon.

35. Starch सटार्च-मांड, कलफ़ देना

(n.) Starch is an important part of our diet.

(v.) Starch the, collar of this shirt. That will keep its shape better

36. Stare (v.) स्टेअर्-आँखे फाड़कर देखना, टकटकी

लगाकर देखना

I stared with surprise at the strange snake.

Don't stare at the girl or she will think you are rude.

(n.) It was difficult to face his angry stare.

37. Stark (adj.) स्टार्क-कठोर और अनिवार्य

The book explores the stark realities of life.

38. Start स्टार्ट-आरंभ (करना)

(v.) We must start our work today.

(n.) Remember to take your before making a start in the morning.

39. Startle (v.) स्टार्टल-आश्चर्य और भय से पूर्ण होना

We were startled when a thief ran out of the door.

40. Starve (v.) स्टार्व-भूखों मरना,

It is a sin to waste food when a large number of people are starving in our country.

(n.) Many died of starvation during the floods last year.

41. State (n.) स्टेट-1. राज्य, सरकार

India is divided into many states.

2. (v.) प्रकट करना

It is started that all people involved in the accident are safe

(n.) The prisoner's statement was found to be a false one

3 (n) दशा

The house was in a poor state.

42. Station (n.) स्टेशन-1. कार्यालय. स्थान. जगह. ठिकाना

All workers should remain at their stations for the next twenty-four hours.

2. (v.) ठहराव, तैनात करना

The soldiers were stationed to Solan.

43. Count (n.) काउन्ट-1. गिनना, गणना करना

The little child was taught to count.

The teacher counted the students before distributing the papers.

2. अनगिनत

The Independence Day function was attended by countless people.

3. अभियोग का विषय, आरोप

On what count was he charged?

44. Counter (n.) काउन्टर्-काउन्टर, पटल

People queued up before the cashier's counter.

45. Country (n.) कन्ट्रि-1. देश, प्रदेश, इलाका

India is a very big country.

2. देहात

Agriculture is the main occupation of the people in the country side.

46. Couple (n.) कपल-1. वर-वधु, दम्पत्ति

The old man blessed the newly married couple.

2. जोड़ा, युगल

Please give me a couple of oranges

47. Coupon (n.) कूपॉन-कूपन

The boys sold coupons for the school fete.

48. Courage (n.) करिंज्-साहस हिम्मत

The soldier was awarded a medal for his extraordinary courage.

49. Courier (n.) कुरिअर्-कूरिअर

I'll send you the documents by courier.

50. Course (n.) कॉर्स-1. प्रसंग (में), मध्य (में)

In the course of his lecture, the saint talked about the evils of drinking.

2. पथ, मार्ग

The river changed its course during the flood.

3. पाठ्यक्रम, विषय

Have you completed your course for the examination?

(adv.) Of course (certainly) I shall come.

51. Court (n.) कोर्ट-1. अदालत, न्यायालय

The culprit was produced in a court of law.

2. राजदरबार, राजसभा

The noblemen took their appointed places in the royal court.

3. (v.) चाहना, पीछे लगना, प्रेम जताना

The satyagrahis courted arrest.

52. Rush (v.) रॅश-1. दौड़ना, भागना

The building caught fire and the people rushed out of it.

2. जल्दी करना

You are very late. You should rush to the office.

After the accident, the injured were rushed to the hospital.

3. (v.) भीड़

There was a great rush at the main gate of the cinema hall.

53. Buttermilk (n.) बटरमिल्क-छाछ

Buttermilk is a protein-rich drink.

54. Prove (v.) प्रूव-प्रमाणित/सिद्ध करना

Can you prove your charge of theft against this man?

(n.) सुबूत, प्रमाण

Do you have any proof?

55. Stationary (adj.) स्टेशनरि-स्थिर, अचल

The sun is stationary.

58. Stationery (n.) स्टेशनरि-लेखन सामग्री

Our address must be printed on all our stationery.

60. Stationer (n.) स्टेशनर्-लेखन-सामग्री-विक्रेता

My uncle is a well-know stationer.

61. Statuary (n.) स्टैचूअरि-बुतों का संग्रह

The statuary in this museum is remarkable.

62. Statue (n.) स्टैचू-बुत

The statue of Mahatma Gandhi, the Father of Nation, stands in the middle of the municipal park.

63. Stature (n.) स्टैचर्-कद, लंबाई

Men are generally of larger stature than women.

64. Status (n.) स्टेटस

1. वैधानिक स्थिति

Please mention your marital status here.

2. प्रतिष्ठा

The job offered him good status apart from a good salary.

65. Staunch (adj.) स्टॉन्च-कट्टर

He is a staunch follower of Buddhism.

66. Stay स्टे-ठहरना, रुकना, ठहराव, निवास

(v.) The train does not stay for long at the tation.

(n.) I had a pleasant stay in Ooty last summer.

67. Steady (adj.) स्टेडि-लगातार, एक समान

Slow and steady wins the race. (adv.) I work steadily all day.

68. Steal (v.) स्टील-भाप, वाष्प

Our maid-servant stole some money from my mother's purse.

69. Steam (n.) स्टीम-भाप, वाष्प

Some engines are driven by steam.

(v.) I like to watch the trains steam

out of the station.

70. Steel (n.) स्टील–दूसरी धातुएं मिलाकर सख्त बनायी गयी धातु

The cap of my fountain pen is made of the best steel.

71. Steep स्टीप

(adj.) 1. खड़ी (चट्टान, ढलान)

The hill is very steep. It is almost straight up.

2. (v.) भिगोना

My wife lets the clothes steep all night before she washes them.

72. Provide (v.) प्रवाइड–1. देना, प्रबंध करना

We provided the poor family with a shelter.

2. प्रबंध करना

Wise people provide for their old age.

3. (n.) खाने-पीने की चीजें

Go to the market and buy some provisions.

73. Buy (v.) बाइ–खरीदना, मोल लेना

Generally, housewives buy the vegetables.

74. Rust रॅस्ट–जंग

(n.) There were patches of rust on the motorbike.

(v.) The motorbike had rusted.

75. Courtesy (n.) कर्टसि–1. शिष्टाचार, सौजन्य

Courtesy costs nothing.

2. (adj.) शिष्ट

Some people are very courteous.

76. Courtyard (n.) कॉर्टयार्ड–बरामदा

The children were playing in the courtyard.

77. Cousin (n.) कज़न्–चचेरा, फुफेरा, ममेरा, मौसेरा भाई या बहन

I visited my cousin in Mumbai last week.

78. Cover कवर्–1. ढ़कना, बिछाना, पहना देना

(v.) The mother covered her sleeping child with a blanket.

2. (n.) आवरण, आच्छादन

The thief approached the house under the cover of darkness.

79. Cow (n.) काउ–गाय

Cow's milk is good for babies.

80. Coward (n.) काउअड्–कायर, डरपोक

A coward cannot be a soldier.

81. Crack (n.) क्रैक–1. दरक, दरार

Many cracks appeared in the building following the earthquake.

2. कड़क, चटाका

The crack of a gun startled everybody in the market.

3. प्रारंभ (दिन का)

A walk is good at the crack of dawn.

4. (adj.) चटका हुआ, फूटना, फोड़ना

The cracked cup should be dis carded.

5. (v.) चटकना

The egg cracked and the chick came out.

82. Awful (adj.) ऑफुल – 1. डरावला, भयंकर

It was an awful sight to see the dead man laying in the middle of the road.

2. (adv.) बहुत अधिक

I am awfully sorry to have kept you waiting so long.

83. Tutor (n.) ट्यूटर्–शिक्षक

Rabindra Nath was not willing to go to school, so he had to have a private tutor.

84. Provoke (v.) प्रवोक-उकसाना, उत्तेजित करना

Do not provoke me with nasty remarks.

85. Buzz (n. & v.) बज़्-गुंजन, भिनभिनाना, गुजारना

(n.) In the summer, the garden is full of the buzz of insects.

(v.) This bee is constantly buzzing and disturbing me.

86. Awkward (adj.) ऑकवर्ड-असुविधाजनक

I feel awkward while facing a large audience

(adv.) She got up awkwardly when caught cheating.

87. Tweed (n.) ट्वीड-खुरदरी सतह वाला गरम कपड़ा, ट्वीड, ऊनी कपड़ा

Do you like to wear a tweed jacket?

88. Twelve (adj.) ट्वेल्व-बारह

The child can count up to twelve.

Three is one twelfth of thirty-six

The school education is over after twelfth standard.

89. Twenty (adv.) टुवेंटी-बीस

Two tens make twenty.

90. Cradle (n.) क्रेडल-1. पालना

She put her baby in the cradle.

2. उद्गम

India is the cradle of ancient civilisations.

91. Craft (n.) क्राफ़्ट-1. कारीगरी, शिल्प, कौशल

Wood carving is a craft of skill

2. जलयान, वायुयान

The aircraft took off on schedule

92. Crafty (adj.) क्राफ़्टि-धूर्त, चालाक, चालबाज़

Never trust a crafty person.

93. Cram क्रैम

1 ठूंसना

(v.) She crammed all her cosmetics in a small bag.

(adj.) The bus was crammed with passengers.

2. रटना

(v.) I crammed the whole essay for the exams.

94. Cramp (n.) क्रेम्प-मांसपेशी में ऐंठन

I had terrible cramps in my stomach last night.

95. Cramped (adj.) क्रैम्प्ड-ठसाठस भरा होना

The room was too cramped to accommodate more people.

96. Crash (n.) क्रैश-1. धमाका, धड़ाका

The building came down with a crash.

2. (v.) टक्कर खाना

The motor-car crashed against a wall.

3. (adj.) त्वरित, जल्द

She joined a crash cooking course.

97. Crane क्रेन

1 भारी वजन उठाने वाली मशीन

(n.) The car was picked up by a crane

2 सारस

(n.) I saw two cranes near the lake

3 गरदन बाहर निकालना

(v.) She craned her neck out of the window to see what was happening outside.

98. Crawl (v.) क्रॉल-रेंगना

The little baby crawls on its hands and feet.

99. Crazy (adj.) क्रेजि-पागल सनकी

The shock of her son's death drove the old mother crazy

100. Cream (n.) क्रीम-मलाई क्रीम

I like coffee with cream

SPOKEN VOCABULARY
Set - 49

1. **Crave (v.)** क्रेव-लालायित होना

   I was craving for a chocolate since morning.

2. **Crease** क्रीज़-सिलवट

   (n.) The sari was full of creases.

   (v.) She creased the paper in the middle.

3. **Create (v.)** क्रिएट-1. उत्पन्न करना बनाना

   God created the world.

   2. (n.) जीव

   We all are God's creatures.

4. **Credit (n.)** क्रेडिट-1. गौरव

   He passed the examination with credit.

   2. उधार, ऋण

   Some shopkeepers give no credit.

   3 विश्वास

   Nobody placed credit in Rahul's story.

   (v.) Only the brave are credited with success.

5. **Rustic (adj.)** रस्टिक-सीधा-सादा

   There is a rustic charm in his mannerisms

6. **Steer (v.)** स्टीअर्-परिचालन करना चलना

   The seamen steered east in the hope of finding land.

   (adj.) Please tighten the steering-wheel of the car.

7. **Stem (n.)** स्टे'म-1. तना

   This tree has a very big stem.

   2. (v.) रोकना

   We should try to stem the flood by putting down sandbags.

8. **Step (n.)** स्टे'प-1. कदम, पग

   The baby moved towards the mother with small steps.

   The discovery of radium was a great step forward in the science of healing.

   2. (v.) कदम रखना

   We should step out together.

   3. (adj.) सौतेला (सौतेली)

   Life is Renu's step-mother. Renu is a step-daughter of Lila.

9. **Stereo (n.)** स्टेरिओ-स्टीरियो सिस्टम

   The stereo in my car is not working properly.

10. **Stereotype** स्टेरिअटाइप्-घिसा-पिटा रुप

    (n.) The women have broken the stereotype of being the housewives.

    (v.) Serials stereotype the relationship between a mother-in-law and a daughter-in-law

11. **Stern (adj.)** स्टर्न-सख्त कठोर अनुशासनप्रिय

    The Principal of our college was very stern.

    Solidiers follow stern discipline.

    The captain sternly ordered the soldiers to fight the enemy.

12. **Stew (v.)** स्ट्यू-1. कुकर जैसे किसी बन्द बर्तन में कोई वस्तु उबालना

    I'll stew some vegetables for dinner.

    2. (n.) उबला हुआ मांस

I have some stew for dinner.

13. Steward (n.) स्ट्यूअर्ड-प्रबंधक, कारिन्दा

After the death of her father, Alka made her uncle the steward of her property.

14. Stick (v.) स्टिक-1. लगाना

Did you stick the stamp to the envelop?

2. (n.) छड़ी

My old grandfather uses a walking-stick.

15. Stiff (adj.) स्टिफ़-कठोर, कड़ा, सख़्त, कठिन

You have a stiff manner. You are not a good friend.

It was very stiff to climb to the top of the hill.

16. Twice (adv.) ट्वाइस-दो बार

Brush your teeth twice a day.

17. Twig (n.) ट्विग-टहनी, शाखा

The birds were sitting on the twigs while singing.

18. Axe (n.) ऐक्स-कुल्हाड़ी, कुठार

The wood-cutter felled the tree with his axe.

19. Prudent (adj.) प्रूडन्ट-विवेकपूर्ण

Prudent use of electricity would contribute in conservation of power.

20. Creep (v.) क्रीप-रेंगना, सरकना, खिसकना

The thief crept into the house without making a sound.

21. Creeper (n.) क्रीपर्-लता, वल्लरी

The wall of the garden was covered with creepers.

22. Cremate (v.) क्रमेट-अंतिम संस्कार करना

My grandfather always wanted his dead body to be cremated in Haridwar.

23. Crescent (n.) क्रेसन्ट-बालचन्द्र, अर्धचंद्र, अर्ध चन्द्राकार

The crescent of the new moon could be seen in the clear sky.

24. Crest (n.) क्रेस्ट-शिखा, चोटी, शीर्ष

During the storm, the ship was [illegible]wn up on the crest of a huge wave.

Some leaders win the elections on the crest of their wave of popularity.

25. Crew (n.) क्रू-कर्मीदल, मल्लाहों का जत्था

The plane has a crew of six.

26. Cricket (n.) क्रिकेट-1. क्रिकेट, गेंद-बल्ला

Indians love to watch cricket.

2. झींगुर

I saw crickets flying about in the garden.

27. Crime (n.) क्राइम-अपराध

It is a crime to steal.

The crimina[illegible] sent to jail.

28. Crimson क्रि[illegible]रे [illegible] का

At su[illegible]ud[illegible]est become [illegible] in [illegible]

29. Crippled (n.) क्रिपूल्ड-अपंग, [illegible]ाग, बिगाड़ना, अपंग करना

The crippled hobbled down the street.

(v.) The spinner's absence crippled the team's bowling.

30. Stifle (v.) स्टाइफ़ल-दम घोंटना

I was almost stifled by the stale air in the room.

31. Stigma (n.) स्टिगमा-कलंक

There is still a social stigma attached to single women.

32. Stile (n.) स्टाइल-सीढ़ी, ज़ीना

Help the old man over the stile.

33. **Still (adv.)** स्टिल-1. अब भी

Vagish is still sitting. He has not moved up till now.

2. (adj.) स्थिर

Still waters run deep.

34. **Stimulate (v.)** स्टिमुलेट-प्रेरित करना, प्रेरणा देना

Jai Prakash Narayan's kind words stimulated the decoits and smugglers to give up their bad ways of living.

5. **Sting (n. & v.)** स्टिंग-डंक (मारना)

(n.) A wasp can hurt us with its sting.

(v.) A bee stung me in my face.

36. **Stink (v.)** स्टिंक-बदबू मारना

His clothes were stinking.

37. **Stipend (n.)** स्टाइपेन्ड-वृत्ति

He was getting a stipend of Rs. 2000 while working as an intern.

38. **Stir (v.)** स्टर्-हिलना-डुबना

Nobody stirred when a dacoit came into the house.

Stir the solution.

39. **Stitch (n. & v.)** स्टिच-सीना, टाँकना

(n.) A stitch in time saves nine.

(v.) The tailor stitches the shirt.

40. **Stock** स्टॉक-संचय (करना), संग्रह (करना)

(n.) We are sorry we have no grain in our stock.

(v.) Do you stock toothpaste and toothbrushes?

41. **Stomach (n.)** स्टॅमक-आमाशय, उदर, पेट, जठर

If we eat food so quickly, we shall get stomach-ache.

The patient had a weak stomach and could not digest solid food.

42. **Stone (v. & n.)** स्टोन-पत्थर (मारना)

(v.) The rioters stoned the speaker in the public meeting.

(n.) There was a heap of stones on the ground.

43. **Stool (n.)** स्टूल-1. बिना पीठ की कुर्सी, स्टूल

She sat on the four-legged stool.

2. शौच

The doctor examined the report of the urine and stool of the patient.

43. **Stop (v.)** स्टॉप-1. किसी क्रिया, गाड़ी आदि को रोकना

We stopped the car at the signal.

Usually we stop our work at 5:30 P.M.

Please stop talking now.

2. (n.) गाड़ी आदि के रुकने की जगह

Where is the bus-stop?

44. **Store (n.)** स्टॉर-1. संग्रह, भंडार, संचय

We have a lot of goods in store for the bad weather.

Have you a good store of hay for your cow?

2. घर के सामान की जगह

We put our broken pieces of furniture in our store.

3. (v.) संग्रह करना

Never store more than you need.

45. **By (prep.)** बाइ-पास, समीप, से द्वारा

I saw a couple walking by the river.

A policemen was standing by the police jeep.

The letter was delivered by hand (not by post.)

He has learnt the poem by heart.

(He can recite it without looking at the book.)

46. **Storey (n.)** स्टॉरि-तल्ला, मंजिल

We lived in a three-storeyed house.

In large cities, some buildings have more than twenty storeys.

47. Stork (n.) स्टॉर्क-सारस

A stork is a large bird that usually lives near pools.

48. Storm (n.) स्टॉर्म-1. आँधी

The storm raged all day.

2. (v.) हमला करना

The army was ordered to storm the town at midnight.

49. Story (n.) स्टॉरि-कथा, कहानी

The old man told us the story of his journeys.

Would you tell me the story of your life?

50. Stout (adj.) स्टाउट-पुष्ट शरीर, किन्तु मोटा-थुलथुला नहीं

Vivek looks stout but he lacks stamina.

Hanuman has a stout body.

51. Straight (adv.) स्ट्रेट-1. सीधा

This road goes straight to Rohtak.

2. (v.) सीधा करना

Straighten this bent wire and then use it.

3. (adj.) सीधा-सच्चा, बिना मोड़े-तोड़े, सरल

I want a straight answer from you.

Tell us the story in straight-forward way.

52. Strain स्ट्रेन-पूरी शक्ति लगाकर (सुनना, देखना आदि), दबाव, तनाव

(v.) They strained their ears to hear what the speaker was saying.

(n.) In the fast like of metropolitan cities, people work under great strain.

53. Straits (n.) स्ट्रेट्स-तंगी, संकट, दुर्गति

We were in dire straits when we lost all our money.

54. Strange (adj.) स्ट्रेंज-1. आश्चर्य (की बात)

It is strange that he is not here. He always comes at this time.

2. अपरिचित

The new boy is still strange to the school.

This handwriting is strange to me. I don't know who has written this.

55. Strangle (v.) स्ट्रैंगल-गला घोंट कर मारना

The victim was strangled to death.

56. Strap (v.) स्टैप-फ़ीता बाँधना

Strap the two packets together.

I want to carry them in one hand.

57. Strategy (n.) स्ट्रैटजी-रणनीति

What will be our new marketing strat egy?

58. Straw (n.) स्ट्रॉ-1. तिनका, पुलाल

Straw is used for making mats.

2. ठंडा पीने का पाइप

Bring me a straw to drink Coca Cola.

59. Strawberry (n.) स्ट्रॉबरि-स्ट्रॉबेरी

Do you like strawberries?

60. Stray (adj.) स्ट्रे-1. आवारा, भटका हुआ

Stray animals are causing serious traffic problems these days.

2. (v.) भटकना

We strayed from the road and lost our way.

61. Streak (n.) स्ट्रीक-1. किरण

A streak of lightning flashed in the dark sky.

2. (v.) तेज़ी से चलना

The racing cars were streaking on the

track.

62. Bygone (adj.) बाइगॉन-बीता हुआ

Taj Mahal evokes the memories of a bygone era.

63. Twilight (n.) ट्वाइलाइट-सान्ध्य प्रकाश, झुटपुटा, सूर्यास्त से पहले का समय

We must go for a walk in the twilight.

64. Twin (adj.) ट्विन-जुड़वा (बच्चा)

Lava and Kusha were twins.

65. Twinkle (v.) ट्विंकल-टिमटिमाना, चमकना

The stars twinkle in the sky.

In the dark, we could see the stars twinkling.

Your eyes twinkled with mischief

66. Crisis (n.) क्राइसिस-कठिनाई की घडी

She always supports me in the times of a crisis

67. Crisp (adj.) क्रिस्प

1. कुरकुरा

We enjoyed the crisp potato chips with tea.

2. स्पष्ट और रुखा

She gave a crisp reply to my question.

68. Criterion (n.) क्राइटिअरिअन-मापदंड

Score obtained in the entrance test is the sole criterion to get an admission in this course.

69. Critic (n.) क्रिटिक-आलोचक, समालोचक, समीक्षक

The art critic of the newspaper praised the exhibition of paintings.

The government's new education policy came in for a lot of criticism.

70. Critical (adj.) क्रिटिक्ल-1. आलोचनात्मक, छिद्रान्वेषी

Father was critical of his son's rude manners.

2. संकटपूर्ण, नाजुक

The wounded man was taken to the hospital in a critical condition.

71. Criticise (v.) क्रिटिसाइज़-आलोचना करना

The players were criticised for poor performance.

72. Croak (v.) क्रोक-टर्र-टर्र करना

Frogs are croaking in the pond.

73. Crocodile (n.) क्रॉकडाइल-मगर

There is a very big crocodile in the zoo.

74. Crook (n.) क्रुक-धोखेबाज़

Crooks are quick to cheat the innocent.

75. Crooked (adj.) क्रूकिड-1. टेढ़ा

The boy drew a crooked line on his state.

2. कुटिन, धूर्त

It is not good to keep company with crooked people.

76. Crop क्रॉप

1. फ़सल

(n.) Rain destroyed the whole crop of wheat.

2. काटकर छोटा करना

(v.) He cropped his hair very short.

3. अप्रत्याशित रुप से प्रकट हो जाना

(v.) A fight cropped up between the two neighbours.

77. Cross (n.) क्रॉस-1. क्रूस, सूली

Jesus Christ died on the cross.

2. (v.) पार करना

We must use subways to cross the busy roads.

3. काटना, काटा लगाना

The teacher crossed out the wrongly spelt words.

4. (adj.) अप्रसन्न, क्रुद्ध

Why do you look so cross?

78. Crouch क्राउच-उकड़ूँ बैठना

The cat crouched on the ground before jumping on the mouse.

79. Twirl (v.) ट्वर्ल-घुमाना, फिराना

He twirled the pen in his hand.

80. Crow (n.) क्रो-1.कौआ

The crow is a bird commonly found in India.

2. (v.) बाँग देना

Cock crows early in the morning.

81. Crowd क्राउड-भीड़, जनसमूह, ठसाठस भर देना

(n.) A large crowd gathered at the airport to greet the leader.

(adj.) In Delhi, the buses are mostly crowded.

(v.) The journalists crowded around the chief minister.

82. Crown क्राउन-1. मुकुट, मुकुट पहनाना, राज्याभिषेक करना

(n.) The king wore a glittering crown.

(v.) He was crowned as the king.

2. (n.) शीर्ष (के बाल)

82. Stride (v.) स्ट्राइड-1. लंबे-लंबे डग भरना

He strode out of the room.

2. (n.) लंबे कदम

Vamana took three long strides and measured the underworld, the earth and the sky.

83. Strife (n.) स्ट्राइफ़-विवाद, झगड़ा

The strife between the two parties ended after the election.

84. Strike (v.) स्ट्राइक-1. बजाना

When the clock struck five, the office was closed.

2. टकराना

The ship struck a large rock.

3. मारना

The naughty boy struck the donkey with a stick.

4. (n.) हड़ताल

The mill workers are on strike these days.

85. String (n.) स्ट्रिंग-1. धागा

I need a string to make a garland of flowers.

2. वस्तुओं या व्यक्तियों की पंक्ति

A string of people waited in front of the ration shop.

86. Strip (v.) स्ट्रिप-1. लूटना

The bungalow was stripped of everything of value by the robbers.

2. कपड़े उतारना, नंगा होना

The men stripped of their clothes and dived into the river.

87. Twist (v.) ट्विस्ट-बटना, बल देना, मोड़ना, ऐंठना

Rope is made by twisting lengths of cord together.

Mary twisted her ankle when she fell.

Twist those strings together to make a strong rope.

88. Cub (n.) कब-शावक

The lioness in the zoo gave birth to two cubs.

89. Culprit (n.) कल्प्रिट-दोषी, अपराधी

The culprit was sent to the jail.

90. Strive (v.) स्ट्राइव-यत्न करना

I strove hard to reach the peak of the mountain.

91. Stroke (n.) स्ट्रोक-1. प्रहार, आघात, (क्रिकेट या गोल्फ़ में) मार

The cat killed a number of mice in a single stroke.

The batsman made a good stroke at the ball.

2 (v.) सहलाना

She stroked her pet dog affectionately as it sat in her lap.

92. Stroll (v. & n.) स्ट्रोल-चहल कदमी (करना)

(v.) We were strolling in the garden when you saw us.

(n.) We went out for a stroll in the garden.

93. Strong (adj.) स्ट्राँग-1. बलिष्ठ, हष्ट-पुष्ट, ताक़तवर

The king sent a strong army to fight against the enemy.

Rakesh is very strong. He can carry a heavy load.

2. प्रचंड

On stormy days, strong winds blow.

3. पुख्ता, पक्का

This fence is strong enough to keep out the animals.

4. पदार्थ की अधिक मात्रा में तैयार हुई (चाय आदि)

Don't you like strong tea?

(n.) He has the strength of a bull.

94. Structure (n.) स्ट्रॅक्चर्-1. ढाँचा, भवन आदि

This structure cost me five lakhs nine thousands rupees.

2. बनावट

This cinema has weak structure.

95. Struggle (v. & n.) स्ट्रॅगल-संघर्ष (करना)

(v.) The people struggled to get out of the burning house.

(n.) You will be able to beat off your attackers after a hand-to-hand struggle.

96. Stubble (n.) स्टॅबल-दाढ़ी के छोटे कड़े बाल

He looks good with a one-day stubble.

97. Stubborn (adj.) स्टॅबर्न-अड़ियल, जिद्दी, हठीला, अटल

I see that you are too stubborn to change you mind.

(adv.) He refused to move from that place stubbornly.

98. Study (v. & n.) स्टॅडि-1. अध्ययन (करना)

(v.) We studied the case very care fully and made a report.

(n.) Your study of fish has enabled you to know much about their hab its.

2. अध्ययन कक्ष

Late Prime Minister Nehru's study had bookcases on every wall.

99. Stuff (n.) स्टॅफ़-1. तरल या ठोस द्रव्य, विभिन्न वस्तुएँ, रद्दी माल

You have a lot of stuff in your house that must be thrown away.

What sort of stuff do you put in the cushions?

2. (v.) (रद्दी माल) ठूंसना

She stuffed her doll with rags.

(adj.) In museum, we can see stuffed animals which almost look alive.

100. Twitter (v.) ट्विटर्-चहचहाना, चहकना

The birds twitter cheerfully in the trees.

SPOKEN VOCABULARY
Set - 50

1. **Sustain (v.)** सस्टेन-भरण-पोषण करना, गुजारा करना, बने रहना

During the famine, many people did not have enough food to sustain themselves.

During their long march, the men were sustained by tinned food.

2. **Swallow (n.)** स्वॉलो-1. अबाबील नामक पक्षी

Many swallows gather and twitter in the sky at sunset.

2. (v.) निगलना

you must chew your food thoroughly before you swallow it.

3. **Swamp (v.)** स्वॉम्प-1. समा लेना, जल से भर देना

They were afraid that the huge waves would swamp their boat.

2. (n.) दलदल

There are many large swamps in Myanmar.

4. **Swan (n.)** स्वॉन-राजहंस

Swan is very beautiful water bird.

5. **Swarm** स्वॉर्म-भीड़, झुंड (में आना)

(v.) After the show, the spectators swarmed on the road.

(n.) A swarm of honeybees attacked him when he distrubed the honeycomb.

6. **Curtain (n.)** कर्ट्न्-परदा, आवरण

Curtains help in keeping out the summer heat.

7. **Sway (v.)** स्वे-1. झूलना, डोलना

The branches of the trees sway in the wind.

2. शासन

(n.) India was under the sway of British for over a hundred years.

8. **Swear (v.)** स्वे'अर्

1. शपथ लेना, कसम खाना

We swear we shall serve our nation.

You must swear that you will speak only the truth.

2. गुस्से में बोलना

The thief swore when he bumped his head against a pole in the dark.

9. **Sweat** स्वेट्-पसीना (आना)

(v.) You are sweating. You must change your shirt.

(n.) His brow is wet with honest sweat.

10. **Curve (n.)** कर्व्-घुमाव, मोड़, वक्र रेखा

Rahul's home is round the curve.

11. **Sweep (v.)** स्वीप-झाड़ू लगाना, बुहारना

The servant sweeps the room clean.

(adj.) He uses a sweeping brush.

2. जल्दी से घेर कर सब कुछ नष्ट करना

The flood swept away the whole colonies on the baks of the river.

12. **Sweet (adj.)** स्वीट-1. मीठा, मधुर, सुरीला

Rose has a sweet smell.

Her voice was very sweet.

2 .(n.) मिठाई

Eating too many sweets is not good for health.

13. **Swell (v.)** स्वे'ल-1. सूजना, फूलना

A bee has stung her hand. It is swelling up.

If we soak rice in water for half an hour it swells.

2. (n.) सूजन

You had a swelling in your neck.

14. Swelter (v.) स्वे 'ल्टर्-पसीने से तर-बतर होना

With no shelter from the sun, we lay sweltering on the sand.

15. Swerve (v.) स्वर्व-घूम जाना

The ball swerved just as the batsman prepared to hit it.

16. Swift (adj.) स्विफ्ट-शीघ्रगामी, फुर्तीला

Are you a very swift runner?

(adv.) Seeing the policemen, the thief swiftly ran round the corner.

17. Cushion (n.) कुशन-गद्दा, तोशक

I bought cushions for my sofa set.

18. Swim (v.) स्विम-तैरना, तैरकर पार करना

Can you swim?

(n.) I want to go for a swim.

I am a good swimmer. I used to go to the swimming-pool regularly.

19. Swine (n.) स्वाइन-सुअर

Swine ate dirty things.

19. Cultivate (v.) कल्टिवेट-1. खेती करना, जोतना

The farmer cultivates his land.

2. परिचय बढ़ाना

Some people cultivate the influential people to get things done through them.

20. Stumble (v.) स्टम्बल-1. लड़खड़ाना

The old beggar stumbled while crossing the road.

2. संयोग से पता लगना

At last, we stumbled on the explanation.

21. Stump (n.) स्टम्प-1. तना

We sat on a tree-stump to rest.

2. किसी वस्तु का टुकड़ा

I took the stump of pencil and wrote down her address.

22. Stun (v.) स्टन-स्तब्ध करना

The old man was stunned when he learnt that his only son had died.

23. Stunt (n.) स्टन्ट

1. ख़तरनाक करतब

The actor performs all his stunts himself.

2. इश्तहारबाज़ी

The whole affair was merely a publicity stunt.

3. विकसित होने से रोक देना

(v.) Irregular rains stunted the growth of plants.

24. Stupid (adj.) स्ट्युपिड-मूर्ख

Only a stupid person walks in the middle of a road.

(n.) I am ashamed of my stupidity.

(adv.) The servant behaved very stupidly in front of the guests.

25. Sturdy (adj.) स्टर्डि-तगड़ा, मज़बूत

Don't worry, you are quite sturdy and will soon recover from measles.

26. Style (n.) स्टाइल-शैली, ढंग, रीति, तरीका

I did not like your style of dress.

(adj.) Vagish has bought a stylish pair of shoes.

27. Suave (adj.) स्वाव-आत्मविश्वासी और शिष्ट

Her performance was suave as always.

28. Subdue (v.) सबड्यू-1. हराना, विजय प्राप्त करना

We shall fight our enemies until we subdue them.

2. शांत करना

The baby's cries gradualy subdued.

29. Two (adj.) टू-दो

One plus one make two.

There are two words for everything.

We select either according to the relevance.

30. Culture (n.) कल्चर-संस्कृति

Our scriptures reflect the richness of the Indian culture.

31. Subject (n.) सब्जे'क्ट-1. विषय

We have to learn eleven subjects simultaneously.

2. प्रजा

The king must be kind to his subjects.

3. (v.) (का) विषय बनाना

The poor girl is subjected to her step-mother.

32. Sublime (adj.) सब्लाइम-महान्, भव्य, उत्कृष्ट, शानदार

Wordsworth felt the sublime presence of God in Nature.

The bravery of the Rani of Jhansi was sublime.

33. Submarine (n.) सब्मरीन-1. पनडुब्बी, अन्तः सागरीय, समुद्र के भीतर के

The submarine surfaced after an hour.

Sea-anemones are submarine creatures.

34. Submerge (v.) सब्मर्ज-1. डुबकी लगाना

The submarine submerged after it left the port.

35. Submit (v.) सब्मिट-1. समर्पण करना

The general agreed to submit to the enemy.

2. प्रस्तुत करना

I shall submit my plan for a new hospital to the council.

36. Subordinate सबॉर्डिनेट

1. गौण समझना

(adj.) In many places in India, women are still considered subordinate to me.

(v.) The quality was subordinated to quantity.

2. अधीनस्थ व्यक्ति

(n.) You should treat your subordinates well to gain respect from them.

37. Subscribe (v.) सब्सक्राइब-1. चंदा देना

Did you subscribe to the Lions Club?

(n.) Have you paid your half-yearly subscription?

2. (v.) सहमत होना

I don't subscribe to your view.

38. Subsequent (adj.) सॅब्सिक्वन्ट-उतरावर्ती, बाद का

His first and all the subsequent visit were kept secret.

(adv.) Subsequently, all the Indians settled in Ghana came back to India.

39. Tycoon (n.) टाइकून्-उद्योगपति

He is a powerful business tycoon.

40. Cunning (adj.) कनिंग-चालक, धूर्त

The fox is a cunning animal.

41. Substance सब्स्टन्स-पदार्थ, वस्तु, द्रव्य

Is not chalk a white substance?

Wood is a substance, and so is sand and so is sugar.

42. Substitute सब्स्टिट्यूट-स्थानापन्न, की जगह पर (निश्चित करना)

(n.) Soniya cannot play the violin today, so Sony will be her substitute.

(v.) Sony has been substituted for Soniya.

(n.) This substitution will serve the purpose.

43. Suburb (adj. & n.) सॅबर्ब-उपनगर (का)

(adj.) Every day I go to my shop by the suburban railway.

(n.) We live in the suburbs of Delhi.

44. Subway (n.) सब्वे-भूमिगत पैदल पारपथ

Let us go by the subway; there is a lot of traffic on the road.

45. Succeed (v.) सक्सीड-1. सफल होना

If we do not succeed in the first

attempt, we must try again.

(n.) We wished him success in his new profession.

I passed my examination with great success.

2. (v.) का स्थान लेना

Mr. Prakash was succeeded as director by Mr. Mahajan.

The prince succeeded his father to the throne.

(n.) He was his father's successor.

(adj.) His son has become a successful doctor.

46. Succumb (v.) सकम्-हार मान लेना

He succumbed to a heart failure.

47. Such (adj.) सॅच-इस तरह का, ऐसा

Such behaviour will be disliked by everybody.

Beware of flatterers, such men are dangerous.

I had never seen such a large non-key.

We were in such a hurry that we forgot our suitcase.

48. Suck (v.) सॅक-1. पीना

The children were sucking the cold drinks througn straws.

2. चूसना

Don't suck your thumb

49. Sudden (adj.) सॅडन-आकस्मिक

We heard a sudden cry but cold not [illegible] anything in the [illegible]

(adv.) [illegible] suddenly a [illegible] a young wo[illegible] fell forwa[illegible]

50. Cup (n.) कप- प्याला, कटोरा

Can I have a cup of tea?

51. Type टाइप-प्रकार, किस्म, मुद्रण या टंकण का अक्षर, टाइपकरना

(n.) We find several types of vegetables.

Different kinds of types are often used for one printed page.

(v.) Please ask the typist to type carefully.

52. Cure क्युअर-दवा, उपाय करना, दूर करना

(n.) There is no cure for the common cold.

(v.) The doctor cured the poor fee of charge.

53. Sue (v.) सू-मुक़दमा दायर करना

The actress sued the journalists for libel.

54. Suffer (v.) सॅफ़र्-पीड़ा या कष्ट सहना

My father often suffered toothaches.

(n.) The kind man was moved by the suffering of the poor old woman.

55. Suffice (v.) सफ़ाइस-पर्याप्त या यथेष्ट होना

One week sufficed for him to recover from his illness.

(adj.) Don't worry, I have sufficient money for shopping.

56. Suffocate (v.) सॅफ़केट-दम घुटना

I felt suffocated working in that organisation.

57. Sugar (n.) शुगर-चीनी, खांड, शक्कर

Sugar is made from a plant called sugar-cane.

58. Suggest (v.) सजे'स्ट-सुझाव देना प्रस्ताव करना

The doctor suggested that she should [illegible] week

(n.) He made this suggestion after a [illegible]

59. Suicide (n.) [illegible] आत्मघात

Why did the old lady commit suicide?

60. Suit (n.) सूट 1. पोशाक, वेश

The tailor made a nice suit for me.

2. (v.) अनुकूल होना

Tea does not suit me. I take milk.

Will it suit you if we start at 7 o'clock?

(adj.) I think it will be suitable.

(adv.) We must come to office suitably dressed.

61. Sulk (v.) सॅल्क-रुठना, नाराज़ या अप्रसन्न होना

Never sit and sulk in a corner.

62. Sullen (adj.) सॅलन-उदास एवं आनंद रहित

The atmosphere was sullen in the evening.

63. Sum (n.) सॅम- 1. गणित का प्रश्न या सवाल

Yesterday she got all the three sums correct.

2. (v.) सार प्रस्तुत करना

We can sum up all we have discussed.

64. Curious (adj.) क्यूअरिअस्-1. जिज्ञासु, कुतूहली

65. Typhoid (n.) टाइफ़ॉइड-आन्त्र-ज्वर

Typhoid is often caused by eating and drinking impure food or drink.

Father was curious to see his little daughter's dance performance at the school function.

2. विलक्षण, विचित्र

The archaeologists found some curious marks on the excavated articles.

66. Curl कर्ल-1. मोड़ना, मुड़ना

(v.) The cat curled up on the chair.

(n.) Sally's head is full of lovely curls.

2. घुँघराले बाल

Sally has curly hair.

67. Summary (n.) सॅमरि-सार-संक्षेप

I don't have time to read the whole novel; just tell me its summary.

68. Summer (n.) सॅमर्-ग्रीष्म

We enjoyed the summer vacation very much.

69. Summit (n.) समिट-1. चोटी, शिखर, चरम बिन्दु

It is very hard to climb the summit of Mount Everest.

2. संसार के चोटी के नेताओं के बीच वार्तालाप

At the summit meeting, the world leaders discussed ways to control nuclear arms.

70. Summons (n.) सॅमन-1. (सॅमॅन्स-तलबनामा) कचहरी का सम्मन आदेश

Have you received summons to attend the court day after tomorrow?

2. (v.) बुला भेजना

The General summoned his officers to discuss plans for the battle.

71. Sun (n.) सॅन-सूर्य

The sun shines during the day. The moon shines at night.

In summer, people do not sit in the sun.

Oh, it is a very beautiful sun-lit room!

(adv.) We started on a sunny day.

2. प्रसन्नचित

His sunny nature warms every heart.

72. Sunday (n.) सॅन्डे-रविवार

Sunday is the first day in a week.

Sunday is the weekly holiday in many countries.

73. Superfluous (adj.) सूपरफ्लूअस-फ़ालतू, अतिरिक्त

Delete the superfluous words from your article.

74. Superintendent (n.) सुपरिटेन्डन्ट-अधीक्षक, निरीक्षक

The superintendent of police in our zone is a very intelligent person.

75. Superior सुपिरियर-वरिष्ठ, अपने से ऊँचा अधिकारी

(adj.) An editor is superior to a proofreader in the press.

Uncle has got a superior postition in his office.

(n.) Be respectful to your superiors.

76. Supernatural (adj.) सूपर्नैचरल-अलौकिक

लोकौत्तर

Stories about ghosts describe supernatural events.

77. Superstition (n.) सूपर्‌स्टिशन-अन्धविश्वास

There is a superstition which makes some people afraid of walking under a ladder.

78. Supervise (v.) सूपर्‌वाइज़्-निरीक्षण करना, देखरेख करना

Our mother supervises her domestic work every day.

The Principal asked the teacher to supervise the examiness.

(n.) All the teachers are busy in supervision during the exams.

79. Supper (n.) सॅपर्-रात का भोजन

Supper is the last meal of a day.

Have you had your supper or not?

80. Supply (v. & n.) सप्लाइ-(खाद्य सामग्री) पहुँचाना, मुहैया करना, भंडार

(v.) The milkman supplies us milk.

Some shopkeepers supply all we want.

(n.) We have enough supply of provisions for his month.

81. Current (n.) करन्ट-1. धारा, प्रवाह

The river flows with a swift current.

2. बिजली का प्रवाह

Turn off the current before you change the bulb.

3. (n.) चालू, प्रचलित

Youngsters are quick to follow the current trends in dressing.

82. Tyrant (n.) टाइरन्ट-तानाशाह, निरंकुश शासक

The Roman Emperor Nero was a tyrant. The Romans suffered under his tyranny.

83. Support-सपॉर्ट 1. सहायता (पहुँचाना), मदद करना

(v.) The kind rich man supported many poor students.

2. समर्थन देना

Without the support of all its partners, the coalition government cannot function.

(n.) I couldn't have been successful without your support.

84. Suppose (v.) सपोज़्-समझना, विचार होना, (की) अपेक्षा रखना. कल्पना करना

She is supposed to be at home by 8 o'clock in the evening.

I do not suppose we shall see each other again.

The work was over earlier than we had supposed.

(conj.) Supposing it rains, what shall we do?

85. Suppress (v.) सप्रेस-दबाना, दमन करना, रोकना

The soldier suppressed his fear and went on fighting.

(n.) The people rose against the suppression of the tyrant ruler.

86. Supreme (adj.) सुप्रीम-सर्वोच्च, वरिष्ठ, उच्चतम

King Mahendra was the supreme ruler of Nepal.

Have you ever seen the Supreme Court of India?

The army remained supreme in the country after the war.

87. Sure (adj.) शॉर्-आश्वस्त, विश्वस्त, निश्चित

I am sure we have enough money for shopping.

Are you sure of coming tomorrow?

She is sure that she will be successful in the test.

88. Surface (v. & n.) सर्फ़िस-सतह (पर आना)

(v.) The submarine surfaced after an hour.

(n.) The surface of the teapot has been

scratched.

89. Surgeon (n.) सर्जन-शल्य चिकित्सक, सर्जन, चीरफाड़ करने वाला डॉक्टर

The surgeon performed the difficult operation skillfully.

90. Curry (n.) करि-कढ़ी, सालन

He is very fond of chicken curry.

91. Surname (n.) सर्नेम-उपनाम

My name is Jai Gopal Pipasu. Pipasu is my surname.

92. Surpass (v.) सर्पास-(से) बढ़कर होना, मात कर देना

Asha has surpassed Usha in English, but Usha is better in Sanskrit. Your performance in the drama surpassed everybody else's.

Rakesh was intelligent, but my brother soon surpassed him.

93. Surplus (n.) सर्प्लस-बढ़ती, बचा हुआ (फालतू)

The farmers use as much grain as they need and sell the surplus to other villagers.

India grows more tea than she needs for herself so she sells this surplus to foreign countries.

94. Surprise सरप्राइज़-अचरज में डालना आश्चर्य चकित (होना)

(v.) She will be surprised to see me.

(v.) The enemy was so powerful that they made us surrender the fort.

95. Surround (v.) सराउन्ड-1 घेरना, बाड़ा लगाना

The bungalow is surrounded by gardens.

2. (n.) वातावरण

The surroundings of the bungalow are very beautiful.

96. Survey सर्वे-सर्वेक्षण (करना), (भूमि की) नाप जोख (करना)

(v.) Before we buy a plot, we ask a surveyor to survey the land.

(n.) The Principal gave us a survey of the year's work.

97. Survive (v.) सर्वाइव-1. जीवित रहना, मरने से बच जाना

Only one hundred people in the village survived the epidemic.

The father is survived by two daughters and a son.

2. (n.) जीवित व्यक्ति

This woman was one of the survivors of the disaster.

98. Curse कर्स्-शाप, दुर्वचन शाप देना कोसना

(v.) My ill-natured neighbour is always cursing the world

(n.) Poverty is a curse.

99. Suspect (v.) सस्पेक्ट-संदेह करना, अविश्वास करना

She suspects her husband to be a spy.

(n.) She has suspicion that he willl kill her.

(adj.) She is very suspicious about him.

(adv.) She is acting suspiciously.

100. Suspend (v.) सस्पेन्ड-1. स्थगित करना

The chairman suddenly fell ill during the meeting and we had to suspend it until the next week.

2. लटकाना

Can you suspend the electric lamp from the middle of the ceilling?

3. निलंबित करना

After the inquiry, the general manager was suspended.

SPOKEN VOCABULARY
Set - 51

1. Swing स्विंग-1. झूला (झूलना)

(n.) Let the children play on the swing.

(v.) The strong wind made the washing on the line swing about.

2. झुलाना

We swing our arms when we walk.

2. Custody (n.) कस्टडि-अभिरक्षा

The custody of the child was granted to the mother.

3. Swirl (v.) स्वर्ल-चक्कर खाते हुए घूमना

The leaves swirled in the wind.

4. Switch (v. & n.) स्विच-बटन (दबाना), फेरना, घुमाना

(v.) Switch on the light for it is getting dark.I switched the conversation to another less painful subject.

(n.) Where is the switch-board in your house?

5. Swoop (v.) स्वूप-झपट्टा मारना

We saw an owl swoop on a mouse and kill it.

6. Custom (n.) कस्टम-रिवाज़, प्रथा

Some Indian customs are quite old.

7. Sword (n.) सॉर्ड-तलवार

The soldier drew his sword and rushed to the enemy.

Swords are not used in battle these days.

8. Symbol (n.) सिम्बल-प्रतीक, चिन्ह

Re. is the symbol for rupee.

A white flag is the symbol of surrender.

9. Sympathy (n.) सिम्पथि-सहानुभूति, हमदर्दी

I have no sympathy with students who waste their time.

(v.) We must sympathise with the poor and the needy.

(adj.) We must feel sympathetic to wards invalids.

10. Customs (n.) कस्टम-सीमा-शुल्क विभाग

Dinesh is an officer in the customs.

11. Symptom (n.) सिम्पटम-रोग का लक्षण

A gumboil is a symptom of decaying teeth.

12. Syndicate (n.) सिंडिकेट-व्यवसाय-संघ

Are you a member of New Era Writers' syndicate?

13. Customer (n.) कस्टमर्-ग्राहक

A good shopkeeper tries to please his customers.

14. Cut (v.) कट-काटना, कतरना

Uma cut her finger while slicing the apple.

2. (n.) काट, कटाव

The doctor cleaned the cut on Uma's finger with an antiseptic lotion.

3. टुकड़ा

Please give me a cut of the meat.

15. Syndicate (n.) सिंडिकेट-व्यवसाय-संघ

Are you a member of New Era Writers' syndicate?

16. Axle (n.) एक्सल-कीली, धुरी

He met with an accident when the axle of his car suddenly broke down.

17. Utter अॅटर्

1. (v.) कुछ कहना

She uttered a few words in foreign language.

2. (adj.) निरा-एकदम

He is an utter coward.

18. By-product (n.) बाइप्रॉडक्ट-उपोत्पाद

Pollution is a by-product of growing number of vehicles in the city.

19. Future फ़्यूचर्-भावी, आगामी, भविष्यत्काल

(n.) In future, never hesitate to call me when you need help.

If you work hard, your future will be bright.

(adj.) What are your future plans?

20. Item (n.) आइटम-1. वस्तु, बात

Please make a list of all the items that we have to buy.

3. समाचार

Did you read this item about a parrot that talks in English?

21. Yummy (adj.) यमी-ज़ायकेदार

The food at the party was yummy.

22. Cycle साइकल-साइकिल (चलाना), चक्र कालचक्र

(n.) Cycle of seasons is an important phenomenon of Nature.

(v.) He cycles to office every day.

23. Cylinder (n.) सिलिंडर्-सिलिंडर

The house caught fire when the gas cylinder burst.

24. Cynic (n.) सिनिक्-दोषदर्शी

(n.) Stay away from him; he is a cynic.

(adj.) Don't be discouraged with his cynical remarks

25. Vulture (n.) वॅल्चर्-गीध, गिद्ध, लोभी व्यक्ति

Vultures feed on the dead bodies of animals.

26. Lyrics (n.) लिरिक्स-किसी गीत के बोल

I liked the lyrics of that song.

27. Hysterical (adj.) हिस्टेरिकल-उन्मादग्रस्त

She was hysterical to know that her long lost son was found.

28. Juvenile (adj.) जूवनाइल-तरुण, किशोर

You are now too old for such juvenile behavior.

29. Knuckle (n.) नक्ल्-उंगली का गांठ जहां वह हथेली से जुड़ती है

I knocked at the door with my kunckles.

30. Mystical (adj.) मिस्टिकल-अद्भुत

She has a pair of mystical eyes.

31. Myth मिथ

1. काल्पनिक विचार

(n.) Some consider the story of Lord Rama a myth, while some find it genuine.

2. पौराणिक कथाएं

(n.) The Hindu mythology talks about numerous gods and goddesses.

(adj.) She loves to hear mythological stories from her grandmother.

32. Synonym (n.) सीनॉनिम-पर्यायवाची

Can you suggest a few synonyms for the word 'promise'?

33. Synopsis (n.) सिनॉप्सिस्-सारांश

Send me a synopsis of the novel before sending the whole manuscript.

34. Syrup (n.) सिरप-शर्बत, शीरा

Would you prepare come sugar syrup?

35. System (n.) सिस्टम-1. प्रणाली, पद्धति

It is difficult to do a job well unless you have some system.

2. वस्तुओं या भागों का साथ जुड़ा हुआ समूह या परिवार

Have you got any knowledge about the solar system?

36. Wrong रॉन्ग-गलत, अनुचित, खराबी

(adj.) It is wrong to tell a lie.

What is wrong with this radio-set?

It is wrong to steal.

(n.) The remedy for wrongs is to forget them.

(adv.) The remedy for wrongs is to interpreted.

37. Tyre (n.) टाइअर्-रबर के टायर

My car has four tyres.

Tyres are usually made of rubber.

38. Psychology (n.) साइकॉलजि-व्यक्ति या वर्ग के मानसिक लक्षण

She understands the psychology of children very well.

39. X-ray (n.) एक्स-रे-एक्सरे

X-ray was very important discovery in the field of medicine.

{X is a letter in English. We don't use if often at the beginning of a word.We use X in words like ox, axe, fox, example etc.}

40. Quote (n.) क्वोट-1. उद्धृत करना

The people often quote Shakespear.

2. मूल्य बताना

Ask Mr. Gopal to quote a price for his TV set.

41. Eye (n.) आइ-1. आँख, नयन

Shooters' eyes are quite sharp.

2. नाका

Please put this thread through the eye of the needle.

42. Zoom (v.) ज़ूम

1. तेज़ी से गुज़रना

The aeroplane zoomed into the air.

2. समीपी चित्र दिखाना

Zoom in the picture; I can't see it.

43. Nylon (n.) नाइलॉन्-नाइलोन

Socks made of nylon last longer.

44. Dynasty (n.) डिनस्टि-राजवंश

The Mughal Dynasty ended with Bahadur Shah Zafar deported to Rangoon.

45. Ruthless (adj.) रुथलेस-निर्गम

Aurangzeb was a ruthless king.

46. Gypsy (n.) जिप्सि-बंजारा

The gypsy claimed to foretell the future correctly.

47. Ox (n.) ऑक्स-बैल

The armer ploughed the land with the help of an ox.

◆◆◆